4-26

THE LIBRARY

COLBY JUNIOR COLLEGE

MASTERS OF THE ORCHESTRA

MASTERS
of the
ORCHESTRA

FROM BACH TO PROKOFIEFF

*by Louis Biancolli
and Herbert F. Peyser*

WITH CONTRIBUTIONS BY ROBERT BAGAR
AND PITTS SANBORN
INTRODUCTION BY DIMITRI MITROPOULOS

G. P. PUTNAM'S SONS   NEW YORK

This book is respectfully dedicated to all those who love music and cherish its preservation and growth in this country.

ACKNOWLEDGMENTS

Acknowledgments are due to the following publishers for permission to quote excerpts from copyrighted works:

To the Boston *Herald* for permission to reprint two articles on Brahms by Philip Hale.

To Henry Holt & Co., publishers of *Handel* by Romain Rolland.

To Alfred A. Knopf, Inc., publishers of *Sergei Prokofiev: His Musical Life* by Israel V. Nestyev, translated by Rose Prokofieva.

To Little, Brown & Co. and the Atlantic Monthly Press, publishers of *Old Friends and New Music* by Nicolas Nabokov.

To W. W. Norton & Co., Inc., publishers of *A Creative Life in Music* by Karl Geiringer.

To Simon and Schuster, Inc., publishers of *Victor Book of Operas,* edited by Louis Biancolli and Robert Bagar. Copyright, 1953, by Simon and Schuster, Inc.

Contents

Introduction

BY DIMITRI MITROPOULOS

*I*N THIS GALLERY of composers are fourteen masters without whose music the symphonic repertory would lose both its foundation and most of its superstructure. These are the composers chosen by the radio division of the New York Philharmonic-Symphony Society for treatment in special booklets distributed among its fifteen thousand subscribers of the air. The list, ending with the late Serge Prokofieff, stops short of living composers. Each of these fourteen is what has come to be known as a "classic," though the term may seem a little daring when used in connection with such recent masters as Richard Strauss and Prokofieff. Yet both in a sense became classics in their lifetime—classics because a tidy number of their works had established themselves in the perennial repertory of the world's major orchestras. Such, indeed, was the basis of the decision made by the Society for its series of monographs. These were the fourteen composers whose symphonies and concertos and overtures and concert suites appeared most frequently in the process of rotation during many symphonic seasons, and with particular thought to the listening multitudes of the air. Most of the inclusions are so obvious no seasoned concertgoer would today seriously question their place in a limited gallery of this kind. The Bachs and Handels and Mozarts and Beethovens have come to constitute the hierarchy of concert music. Succeeding generations have seen a few other names become permanent fixtures of the repertory. It is certain that a large percentage of today's listeners, both of the concert hall and of the air, would feel defrauded if many weeks went by without at least one work by each of these composers appearing in their symphonic experience. Even Prokofieff, the last on our list, has become the intimate symphonic friend of millions. How different the hostile response of his early years!

To a large extent a conductor is governed by the needs and tastes of his audience. These needs and tastes grow and change with the years. There is some fickleness in the musical predilections of the public as there is in the other arts; but there is a solid core of imaginative health and steadiness too. This makes for fidelity to the enduring aspects of a cherished source of beauty and gratification like music. In the long run the public, inevitably and emphatically, "knows what it likes." This does not mean that a little help from those providing it with "what it likes" is out of order.

The conductor and his orchestra have a three-fold obligation: the first, perhaps, is to those who have paid to be entertained; the second is to the deserving composer, whether he is completely accepted or far from being accepted. The third duty is to themselves. That is, a conductor and an orchestra cannot remain forever rooted in the time-honored terrain of tradition. Such complaisance could only lead to professional and artistic sterility, and symphonic music as a living art would lose its continuity. To that extent the conductor must help to mold public taste in less facile directions, sometimes in directions sharply at variance with the main trends of musical history. Many of the composers now secure in their symphonic niches were bitterly maligned rebels in their day. For them the achievement of recognition in their lifetime was a hopeless uphill climb, ending in bleak resignation or utter frustration. With too many of them the world took adequate cognizance of their genius only long after they were dead.

A conductor still has problems as regards a few of the names in our gallery of fourteen masters. There are aspects of Schumann that still require special attention, for example; some of his music is too little known and in some cases scarcely known at all. There are unique problems of presentation of this music. Berlioz represents a still more stimulating challenge to a symphonic conductor. Not too long ago it would have taken a very daring prophet to predict that this once grossly neglected French master would become one of the most frequently performed composers of the repertory. Yet, an enormous quantity of Berlioz's music is still either unfamiliar to American audiences or very infrequently played. Much of this music is of a very special character; it cannot be forced at random upon an unprepared concertgoing public. There are, too, considerations of spacing out this music in the course of a symphonic season, both in relation to other composers and to other programs. It is the thought of the belated recognition of so many of our "classics" that often prompts a conductor to lend a more sympathetic ear to the claims of contemporary composers, however inaccessible their experiments in new idiom may appear to be at first hearing. One is encouraged to believe that today's public in America is more readily responsive to such claims than yesterday's.

When is a "classic" a "classic"? The question occurs to me as I read through these essays. They supply many answers, among them a very simple and impressive one: when the public has finally taken the creative artist to its collective bosom and begins to manifest an interest in the personal and historical circumstances of his career. There is the music, novel at first, and perhaps a little disturbing in its unorthodoxy. After a slow period of assimilation, perhaps a year, perhaps a decade, sometimes a composer's lifetime, the music is wholly enfolded in the artistic consciousness of the public. There is then the beginning of an inquisitive search for the man behind the music. There are essays, program notes, memoirs, and full-length biographies. In the mind of the music-lover each of the symphonies and concertos becomes interwoven with facts and anecdotes about the composer, culled from various sources. After having been a mere name on a concert program, the composer has become now a full-fleged human being, the domestic and social realities of whose life are of vital interest to all in the community of listeners and musicians. The music and the man have become an inseparable team, each augmenting and enriching the other. It is a human and illuminating curiosity, this search for the man in the artist. Often the personal disclosure will light up a musical passage otherwise shrouded in mystery. Just as often the music will yield that final revelation of self that no verbal confession could hope to parallel. In many instances this provides room for endless speculation—another fascinating aspect of this most elusive and universal of the arts, to the perfection of which, as Walter Pater so shrewdly remarked, all other arts aspire.

These fourteen essays ably represent attempts to co-ordinate the life and music of each composer into a single narrative. Their aim is to instill into the reader the enthusiasm of these distinguished critics for the composers and their music and to lead to more extensive reading and listening. This twofold purpose, I believe, is admirably sustained throughout the volume. The reader will find himself generously served on both counts.

Preface

BY LOUIS BIANCOLLI

THE FOURTEEN ESSAYS included in this volume were originally written for the radio subscribers of the New York Philharmonic-Symphony Society. They were assigned as special booklets to be mailed to the subscribers as a reading supplement to the program notes of the Sunday afternoon broadcast. Several of these essays were subsequently revised. All four of the authors were at one time or another program annotators of the Philharmonic-Symphony. The late Pitts Sanborn was succeeded by the team of Louis Biancolli and Robert Bagar, who resigned, after nine years' service as annotators, to be in turn succeeded by Herbert F. Peyser. It was left to each annotator to handle the particular assignment as he saw fit. The one implied condition was that sufficient space be allotted to both the composer as man and the composer as musician. Though the essays vary from composer to composer, it will be seen that this condition has been observed. There is the life, and there is the music to back it up, or perhaps the other way around. As I have said, in introducing one of my contributions, "in the story of Tschaikowsky, life and art weave into one closely knit fabric." In greater or lesser degree, this is applicable to all the lives brought together in this Philharmonic gallery.

A few of these essays were printed as a series of small, separate volumes by Grosset and Dunlap some years ago. For that project Mr. Peyser expanded the original booklet on Beethoven written by Pitts Sanborn, appending, for one thing, a survey of Beethoven's chamber music, a field in which he was an eager and lifelong specialist. Mr. Peyser also amplified his monograph on Mozart for that series. Both essays appear in this volume in the expanded versions. The initials "P.H." will be found under material at the beginning and end of Sanborn's essay on Brahms. These sections were written by Philip Hale. Sanborn had intended to use them as a biographical supplement to his analysis of Brahms's major orchestral works. Space prohibited at that time, and I feel I have carried out his wishes in thus enlarging his brochure for this volume. Sanborn was an inveterate reader of the Boston critic and program annotator, and a worshipful disciple as well. I feel certain he would have been happy to find his own contribution at long last bracketed with Hale's.

One last word about the idea of this book and the man whose name appears with mine as co-author. Mr. Peyser was already critically ill when I approached him with the plan of this book. The conception was wholly mine. I assured him that he would be relieved of any work of building the material into a book. That would be my responsibility and my pleasure. Since Mr. Peyser's contribution represented almost two thirds of the actual writing, that more than sufficed as collaboration. Mr. Peyser asked only one condition of my taking on the job of editing alone—that should cutting be needed in any of his essays, I would consult him. I naturally agreed. Shortly after that Mr. Peyser suffered another attack and, after a short period in the hospital, died. I believe I have carried out my pledge to him. No cuts have been made in his material; the utmost vigilance has been exercised over each of his essays; and what editing they required consisted of fitting them into the pattern of this book, along with mine and those of Robert Bagar and Pitts Sanborn.

He was an incredibly fine scholar, my late collaborator. Thoroughness itself in his pursuit of fact, he rarely accepted anything at second hand. In this pursuit he was fortified by a huge library of books and scores and by a polyglot facility in French, German, Italian and English. If he was a fanatic in anything, it was in this severe adherence to fact. There was small room for idle speculation and fanciful hypothesis in the intellectual world of Herbert F. Peyser. A rigorous standard also governed his work as music critic. There he was almost pitiless in his stress on the absolute necessity of carrying out a composer's intentions to the letter. He could not abide slovenly work in any form, nor was he tolerant to any degree of the cavalier habits of "modernizing" or otherwise transforming the musical classics.

He was an idealist in music, but a practical and levelheaded realist too. Those who admiringly called him "the American Ernest Newman" would have been even closer to the truth had Mr. Peyser, like his esteemed British colleague, put his vast store of knowledge and unique literary gifts into the more permanent form of books.

It was partly with the idea of having some of Mr. Peyser's lengthier writings between the covers of a book that I conceived the present volume. Except for those small reprints of Grosset and Dunlap, Mr. Peyser's name, to the best of my knowledge, had never appeared on the title page of a book. This, then, in a sense, is a memorial volume to a distinguished American critic and musicologist. I can think of no better tribute than that contained in a letter from Ernest Newman to the editor of *Musical America,* which Mr. Peyser had served so brilliantly for many years:

"I was grieved to read this morning of the death of Herbert Peyser. What an immense amount of stimulating and useful work he did for the better understanding and appreciation of music! Though he and I did not meet in the flesh we kept in touch with each other by correspondence, and he showed me many kindnesses. I mourn the passing of yet another of the gallant Old Guard."

Herbert F. Peyser died of a cerebral hemorrhage in Memorial Hospital in New York City on October 19, 1953. He was sixty-seven years of age.

MASTERS OF THE ORCHESTRA

Johann Sebastian Bach

BORN: EISENACH, MAR. 21, 1685. DIED: LEIPZIG, JULY 28, 1750.

Music owes almost as much to Bach as Christianity does to its founder.—SCHUMANN.

COMPARED WITH THE unimaginable richness of his inner life as the overpowering volume and splendor of his works reveal it, Bach's day-to-day existence seems almost pedestrian. It had none of the drama and spectacular conflicts that marked the careers of men like Mozart, Beethoven, and Wagner. His travels, far less extensive than those of his great contemporary, Handel, were confined to areas of a few hundred miles at most in central and northern Germany and were undertaken chiefly for sober professional purposes. The present essay, which advances no claim whatever to any new or original slant, aims to do no more than furnish for those who read and run a meager background of a few isolated high spots in Bach's outward life and a momentary side glance at a tiny handful of his supreme creations. Its object will have been more than accomplished if in any manner it stimulates a radio listener to deepen his acquaintance with Bach's immeasurable art.

In families of unusual longevity and fruitfulness, observed Goethe, Nature has a way of bringing forth in her own good time one figure who unites all the greatest and most distinctive qualities of his various forebears. The poet of *Faust* alluded to this mystic process of genealogy with reference to Voltaire. Actually, he might with quite as much reason have been speaking of Bach. For Bach combined and brought into sharpest focus the musical talents and predilections of almost

I

three antecedent generations, as well as their physical and moral sturdiness, their spirituality, their robust clannishness. Yet the miracle of Johann Sebastian Bach transcends even this amazing fusion of ancestral traits. It is hardly excessive to look upon him as the consummation and fulfillment of all the musical trends that went before him and, in a manner of speaking, the origin of all those that came after.

There is probably nothing in the history of music to compare with Bach's ancestry from the standpoint of fertility, complexity, and endurance. There can be no question of tracing here its multiple ramifications and cross currents. Enough that we obtain our earliest glimpse of Sebastian's great-great-great-grandfather as far back as the latter part of the sixteenth century. The direct line of the great composer did not die out till 1845. Seven generations thus stretch between the extremes of this genealogical phenomenon. The Thuringian countryside around Arnstadt, Erfurt, Wechmar, Eisenach, and other communities of the region cradled the different branches of the family. Two traits, at least, all of them had in common—their love of music and their attachment to one another. Some became organists, some cantors, some town musicians, and their devotion to their craft was so proverbial that, for years after, all musicians in the town of Erfurt came to be known as "the Bachs" even if totally unrelated. The real Bachs felt each other's company so indispensable that, if the members of the family could obviously not all live in the same place, they made it a point to hold periodic reunions. After prayers and hymns they spent the day in feasting and jolly recreation. One of their favorite amusements was to extemporize choruses out of popular songs and these lusty medleys (or, as they called them, "quodlibets") they would bellow for hours on end with great good humor, while the listeners laughed till their sides ached.

Son of a Court Musician

Johann Sebastian Bach was born in Eisenach on March 21, 1685, according to the Old Style reckoning, which is ten days behind the Gregorian calendar. His father, Johann Ambrosius Bach, had married an Elisabeth Lämmerhirt nearly twenty years earlier in Erfurt, where he was town player. Probably he became Court musician to Duke Johann Georg, at Eisenach, whither he had removed. His plea to return to Erfurt was disallowed by his noble employer and so it came that Johann Sebastian saw the light in Eisenach. Not, however, in the rambling house on the Frauenplan as traditionally supposed. Comparatively recent investigation has shown that the actual birthplace is a short distance away, in a street named after Martin Luther. A rather unromantic looking dwelling, it was occupied till just before the Second World War by a barber.

There is a certain symbolic propriety that Bach should have been born in Eisenach rather than in the more prosaic Erfurt. Eisenach had powerful religious and romantic associations. Luther had been entertained by Frau von Cotta in one of its gabled houses while the Reformer was still a boy. High above the city towered the Wartburg, where Luther translated the Bible, threw his inkwell at the Devil, and composed some of his sturdiest chorales. Up there, too, had dwelt the saintly Elisabeth, while in its halls knightly Minnesingers had competed in tourneys of song. In the remoter distances rose the fabled Hörselberg, where according to legend Dame Venus held her unholy court and ensnared the souls of unwary men. Just what impression these things made on the child Bach we cannot say. At any rate he could not remain untouched by the currents of music. The boy had a pretty treble voice and at the local school he sang in the so-called Currende choir, making a few pennies now and then on feasts and holidays, at weddings and at funerals, in company with his schoolmates. He may even have sat in the organ loft of St. George's Church, pulling out the heavy stops for his uncle, Johann Christoph Bach, who had been the organist there for many years.

Nevertheless, we have no elaborate record of Johann Sebastian's boyhood. His father, indeed, taught him the rudiments of violin and viola, and Terry credits the youngster with "patient concentration" in the pursuit of these instrumental studies. We do know that he became before long an uncommonly proficient violinist but took particular delight in playing viola when he participated in ensemble work. Like Mozart in after years, the youthful Bach loved to find himself "in the middle of the harmony."

EARLY YEARS AT SCHOOL

At the Eisenach "Gymnasium" he learned reading and writing, catechism, Biblical history, and the Psalms. And when only a little over eight he was fairly immersed in Latin conjugations and declen-

3

sions. In Eisenach was laid the foundation of that learning which distinguished his whole life, though he never enjoyed the advantage of a college education such as he afterwards gave his famous sons. Yet his school attendance at this early stage showed a good deal of irregularity, due, perhaps, to illness or bereavement. He was only nine when he lost his mother. In a short time his father married again but his death terminated that union scarcely four months later.

The Eisenach household having broken up, Johann Sebastian was sent in 1695 to the home of his married brother, Johann Christoph, who lived at Ohrdruf, some thirty miles away. A pupil of the great Johann Pachelbel, the Ohrdruf Bach functioned as organist at the Church of St. Michael's. Johann Christoph, an accomplished musician, lost no time in giving his young brother his first lessons on the clavier. Presumably he supplemented them with instruction on the organ. In any case the boy seems to have had access to a large quantity of good music. He was an extraordinarily capable student with a voracious appetite for musical learning and no sooner had he mastered one difficult task than he plagued his brother for another more difficult still.

At this period occurred that celebrated incident for which Johann Christoph has been very harshly judged by posterity. A collection of clavier pieces by masters like Froberger, Kerll, Pachelbel, Böhm and Buxtehude, lay in a bookcase with a latticed front. Johann Sebastian's pleas to study them met with a stern refusal. So the youngster resorted to stratagem. By thrusting his hands through the lattice and rolling up the music he managed to extract it when his brother's back was turned. Not being allowed a candle he copied out the various works by moonlight, a job which occupied him for six months and probably laid the foundation for those eye troubles which toward the last were to rob him of his sight. Nor did he enjoy the fruit of his labors. Johann Christoph found the copy and promptly confiscated it. Before blaming him, as is usually done, it may be well to reflect that Bach's brother was not necessarily moved by an impulse of cruelty but more probably felt the need of curbing somewhat an audacious and immature young genius, who threatened to get out of hand.

During the five years he spent in Ohrdruf Bach attended the town school which enjoyed an unusually high reputation throughout Thuringia. His studies, naturally, ranged much further afield than at Eisenach and his scholastic progress appears to have been rapid. His high, clear voice and instinctive musicianship not only assured him a place (and rather substantial rewards) in the chorus of the institution but in proper season gained him the friendly interest of Elias Herder, a young musician summoned to replace Johann Arnold, a highly unpopular teacher who had been dismissed as a "pest of the school, a scandal of the church and a cancer of the community." Through the good offices of Herder young Bach found an opportunity to join the select choir (*Mettenchor*) of St. Michael's Church in Lüneburg, more than two hundred miles to the north.

STUDENT AT LÜNEBURG

The time was ripe, at all events, for Johann Sebastian to leave Ohrdruf. His brother's family was increasing apace and the organist's quarters had been growing uncomfortably cramped. Furthermore, Bach was now fifteen, an age at which boys were expected to start earning their living. So the chance to remove to Lüneburg proved a stroke of luck.

But there were more fascinating advantages to it than even the possibilities of bed and board. Easily accessible were several sources of musical and cultural inspiration. In Lüneburg itself the Church of St. John had as its organist none less than Georg Böhm, one of the outstanding personalities in German music of the era preceding the full unfolding of Bach's grandeur. Thirty miles off lay Hamburg, which harbored the venerable master of the organ, Adam Reinken; and the operatic life of that city had burst into bloom under the leadership of Reinhard Keiser. Up in the direction of the Danish frontier the town of Lübeck sheltered still another giant, the organist Dietrich Buxtehude. Sixty miles in an easterly direction lay Celle, whose Duke, Georg Wilhelm, had married a beautiful and spirited French Huguenot, Eleanore Desmier d'Olbreuse, and turned his court into a miniature Versailles, where French musicians in particular were royally welcomed. Naturally, a little opera house formed part of this island of Gallic charm, elegance and culture, enlivened by a continual succession of ballets, operas, and other musical diversions. Whether Bach obtained admission to the auditorium or whether he was smuggled into the orchestra pit by some friendly player we do not know. But of one thing we are certain: his love for the music of the French masters and his intimate acquaintance with it was in large degree the result of what he heard and learned at the gracious ducal court of Celle.

Bach spent almost three years in Lüneburg, where St. Michael's Church and its conventual buildings were his home. He continued his studies at the *Partikular Schule* of the church, sang with the *Mettenchor* and was a member of the *Chorus Symphoniacus,* of which the choir formed the nucleus. He developed, gradually, into a capable organist and came under the healthy influence of Georg Böhm at the Church of St. John, whose impress can be detected in some of Bach's early organ works. Böhm was a pupil of Adam Reinken and undoubtedly urged the young man to hear the aged master, though one can readily imagine that Bach would sooner or later have sought out Reinken of his own volition. The summer vacation of 1701 found him traveling afoot to Hamburg. The patriarch had been organist of St. Catherine's Church half his life and though now nearly eighty continued to be famous for his virtuosity and his extraordinary skill in improvisation. Nor was it his executive powers alone which captured his young listener. Reinken's compositions fascinated him and their influence is perceptible in certain of Bach's clavier pieces twenty years later.

This first trip to Hamburg was by no means Bach's last. And thereby hangs a tale—a fish story, if you will, but nevertheless true and related a number of times by Bach himself. Tired and hungry on his long jaunt back to Lüneburg, the boy sat down for a moment's rest outside the kitchen of an inn whose open windows exhaled tempting savors. Suddenly there fell at his feet the heads of two herrings, a fish prized as a great delicacy in his native Thuringia. Eagerly picking them up he found inside of each a Danish ducat obviously put there by some kindly soul who had caught sight of the famished young wanderer. Whether or not Bach ate the heads, he suddenly found himself with money enough for an ample dinner and sufficient also to defray the expenses of another visit to Hamburg.

Organist at Arnstadt

It may be taken for granted that Bach planned an eventual journey to Lübeck to hear the mighty Buxtehude. In any case this trip was deferred. Hard as he had studied at Lüneburg and greatly as his

6

musical powers had grown, it was becoming clear that he must put his talents to practical use. He had been earning a living of a sort with his singing and likewise as a violin and viola player. But his voice had changed and was no longer of great use as a source of revenue. His powers as an organist, on the other hand, were expanding prodigiously, a fact which had become known not only in Lüneburg but far away in his native Thuringia. He began to long for an organ post of his own and the steady income it would assure.

Late in 1702 the news spread that a new organ was being completed at the Church of St. Boniface in Arnstadt, one of the ancestral seats of the Bach family and rich in its traditions. Doubtless Arnstadt had its eyes on the promising disciple of Böhm and Reinken, young as he was. Bach, too, felt it wise to watch the situation at close range. So he returned to Thuringia. The new instrument of St. Boniface was not ready nor was it completed till the summer of 1703. Sangerhausen offered a possibility, but that was thwarted by the machinations of high-placed people with influence.

Yet by Easter Bach found himself enrolled in the service of Duke Johann Ernst, brother of the reigning Duke Wilhelm Ernst of Weimar. His stay in Weimar on this occasion was brief though it seems to have earned him some honors, including the useful if misleading title of "Princely Saxon Court Organist." But scarcely three months later he was back in Arnstadt, where the St. Boniface organ was ready for its test. That Bach should have been entrusted with so responsible a task indicates how high must have been his reputation already. He examined the instrument, reported favorably on it and, to demonstrate his satisfaction, played an inaugural recital which impressed the Consistory to such a degree that on August 9 he was officially appointed organist.

It was not long before he was at odds with the authorities. He had, in addition to his organ playing, the disagreeable job of training the choristers, a shiftless, good-for-nothing rabble from the local school who, as the city council complained, "behave in a scandalous manner, resort to places of ill repute and do other things we shrink from naming." Bach, for his part, had already developed that obstinate, uncompromising nature that grew more violent the older he became and brought him into no end of difficulties throughout his life. When his mind was fixed on achieving a certain end nothing would swerve him from it. He could be as hardheaded and intransigent a fighter for what he considered his rights and as ruthless in combating opposition as were Beethoven and Wagner in later generations.

His extraordinary talents did not prevent him from attracting a number of enemies which progressively increased. One of the most bitter of these was a bassoonist named Geyersbach whom Bach on more than one occasion had to reproach for his musical incompetence. Matters came to a head when the organist, escorting a lady home one night, was set upon by the ruffian accompanied by a brawling rout of students who attempted to cane him. As tough a fighter as the best of them, Bach took to his sword when Geyersbach shouted, "Hundsfott" ("Cowardly rascal"), and with a roar of "Zippelfagottist" laid about him so furiously that the "nanny-goat bassoonist" escaped man-handling only by the prompt help of his cronies. The incident caused considerable agitation among the townsfolk.

Scarcely had it subsided than Bach upset the Consistory by requesting a month's leave to make that pilgrimage to Buxtehude in Lübeck which he had been unable to carry out at Lüneburg not long before. He secured as a substitute in his absence a cousin, Johann Ernst, whose efficiency he guaranteed. Grudgingly the authorities complied, unwilling to risk an issue with so valuable, if so testy, a servant. While Bach did not make the whole journey of three hundred miles on foot he undoubtedly walked a fair part of the way. He timed his trip to arrive in Lübeck for Buxtehude's famous *Abendmusiken*, at the Marienkirche, which had been celebrated for a generation and which were continued under the veteran's successors until the nineteenth century. These evening musicales, in which instrumentalists as well as choristers participated, were carried out on a scale larger than anything to which the young organist had been accustomed. One thing this Lübeck visit did was to give Bach a heightened idea of music in its relation to public worship, an idea he strove to carry out for the rest of his life, but realized only fully when he was at the height of his tremendous powers in Leipzig.

Inspiration from the Master, Buxtehude

One may be sure that the immense inspiration he received from Buxtehude was as potent and influenced the current of his genius as fully as had Böhm and Reinken a little earlier. That he exhibited his own powers on the Lübeck organ and profited by the example and suggestions of Buxtehude is clear. Forgetting the flight of time and his obligations in Arnstadt, Bach let the winter months slip by. It is even possible that he weighed the question of stepping into the shoes of the seventy-year-old master. But there was a condition attached to that which made him hesitate as it had Handel and Mattheson before him. Whoever wanted Buxtehude's job had to take Buxtehude's daughter into the bargain. The lady, it appears, was not especially well favored and she was all of twenty-eight—scarcely the most alluring prospect to a young man only twenty, and one which involved the further possibility of having to house the father-in-law for as long as the Lord might choose to spare him!

The year of 1706 had dawned before Bach turned reluctantly toward Arnstadt once more. He took occasion to make a few side trips on the way, stopping over at Hamburg and Lüneburg to greet old associates and friends. By the end of January he was back in the organ loft of St. Boniface. His return was not exactly a love feast. The congregation and Consistory were looking for a capable, mild-mannered organist, not a disquieting virtuoso. But in a relatively short period Bach had become just that. He was plainly above the musical heads of the townsfolk. There were murmurings of discontent which were duly brought to his attention. He paid not the slightest heed, till finally the Consistory proceeded to lay down the law. The authorities had quite a number of bones to pick with their refractory young genius. They had given him a leave of one month, not of four. He answered that he imagined his substitute was competent to fill his shoes for the extra time. Far from being placated, the worthy elders then reproached him for accompanying the church hymns with all sorts of brilliant and audacious improvisations, full of unexpected harmonies and variations which left the congregation groping blindly for the melody. When people had remonstrated that his preludes, interludes and postludes were too long, he had gone to the other extreme and made them too short. And there was worse to come: when he was practicing at St. Boniface, people had been scandalized to overhear the voice of a "strange maiden," singing to his accompaniment! Such things could not be tolerated any more than an organist whose relations with his choir were so bad that he refused to rehearse it. So he could take his choice—either do what the Consistory required or else . . .

Bach did neither one thing nor the other but lived for a while in an uneasy state of compromise. He was not in the least minded to renounce the company of the "strange maiden"—probably the same one he was seeing home the night Geyersbach and his rowdies attacked him. She was none other than his cousin, Maria Barbara, and daughter of Bach's uncle Michael from nearby Gehren. It was not long before he proposed to the musically talented girl and was accepted—the first case of intermarriage between two of the Bach stock. In the fullness of time she became the mother of two of Bach's most gifted sons.

We have not alluded so far to the compositions which had their origin during Bach's Arnstadt sojourn nor are they, obviously, among his most memorable. One, however, occupies a place of its own among his clavier works. It is the famous *Capriccio on the Departure of a Beloved Brother,* a piece of program music clearly based on the example of the *Bible Sonatas* of Johann Kuhnau. The occasion of the *Capriccio* was the forthcoming journey of Bach's brother, Johann Jakob, to take service with Charles XII of Sweden, then campaigning in Poland. The work, in four movements, is of a pricelessly humorous character. The first part represents the traveler's friends, a nervous company apparently, who try to dissuade him from an adventure which they regard as full of hazards. In the second movement one person after another points out the assorted dangers he anticipates and does so in a fugue of delightfully comic effect. This is followed by a slow movement, *Adagissimo,* built over a pathetic ground bass, in which sobbing chromatic phrases lament the inability of the friends to change the wanderer's mind. As they groan and wail Bach drowns out their noisy sorrows in a lively fugue on the postilion's horn; and the "beloved brother" is off on what promises to be a wholly pleasant and profitable journey.

Bach's Arnstadt days were drawing to a close. This is not to intimate that when he left it or any other town in which he had filled positions he never returned to them. Throughout his life he traveled repeatedly over familiar ground, either to participate in family meetings, to inspect organs, give recitals or engage in other social or professional activities. To be sure these wanderings were limited to a few hundred miles in Central and Northern Germany. But such as they were he took them often and gladly, either alone or with members of his family.

Year at Mühlhausen

At Mühlhausen, in Thuringia, the death of Johann Georg Ahle, in December 1706, left a void in the organ loft of the Church of St. Blasius. It was not long before Bach was asked on what terms he would take over the post of his renowned predecessor. He asked a larger sum than the salary paid to Ahle but substantially the same as he had been earning at Arnstadt; also, a quantity of firewood "to be delivered at his door," some corn, and a conveyance to move his household goods. By June 1707, the appointment was his, the town obviously so eager to secure him that it wasted no time in negotiations. Conceivably the Arnstadt Consistory was not dissatisfied to be so conveniently rid of an irascible and troublemaking hothead.

Mühlhausen had an impressive background of musical traditions but Bach entertained nobler aims for the Church of St. Blasius than the more easy-going ideals of Ahle. For this purpose he went to a not inconsiderable private expense to improve the organ and enlarge the musical library of Mühlhausen's churches. The town council seconded his efforts in many ways even if some people resented the independence and progressive though disturbing projects of a young man of twenty-two. At this period he inherited a respectable sum of money from a maternal uncle in Erfurt, and the chances are that the magnificent cantata numbered 106 and entitled *God's Time Is the Best,* was composed for the funeral of this Tobias Lämmerhirt, which Bach dutifully attended. Soon afterwards he retraced his steps to Arnstadt and there, on October 17, 1707, in the neighboring village of Dornheim he married Maria Barbara. Their honeymoon was devoted to visiting different members of the Bach family scattered through the neighboring countryside.

The good will of the community made it possible for Bach to demand repairs and improvements on the organ of St. Blasius. Moreover, he was called upon to compose a work for a highly important Mühlhausen civic function, the annual election of the town councilors. It was for this event that he wrote a grandiose *Ratswahl Kantate,* whose music exhibits the influence of Buxtehude heightened by his own incomparable genius. In a burst of generosity the city fathers voted to publish the work. It was the only one of Bach's cantatas printed in his lifetime. Otherwise, there is no record that, aside from the cantata *God Is My King,* a single such work of his was given in the Mühlhausen churches, though from the creative standpoint he can scarcely have been idle.

Despite the high esteem Bach enjoyed in Mühlhausen he remained there only a year. The municipal heads and the authorities of the Church of St. Blasius regretted his going but were unable to prevent it. He conceded frankly that he wanted to improve his material position. Yet, a deeper reason lay at the back of his departure. It was at the bottom the by-product of a religious question. For some time a reaction had been developing against certain dogmatic formularies in the Lutheran body. The dissidents, known as Pietists, gradually came to sword's points with the orthodox sect, and Mühlhausen, especially, became a hotbed of Pietism, whose adherents strongly opposed use of music in public worship. This, of course, flew violently in the face of Bach's ideal, which was the betterment of music in the church and its heightened employment to sacred ends. It became solely a question of time when such a situation would render his position at St. Blasius untenable. The Consistory was so well disposed to Bach that it promptly agreed to a variety of modifications in the organ which he had recommended. Before these were carried out he had given notice of his departure and his employers realized they could do nothing about it. He promised, however, to come over to Mühlhausen from nearby Weimar in order to see how the alterations were being executed.

WEIMAR

Weimar, to which he now removed, became Bach's home for the next ten years, and here were created some of his mightiest works, particularly those for organ. The town was, even at that period, a cultural center. Its Duke, Wilhelm Ernst of Sachsen-Weimar, a pious, serious-minded ruler, engaged Bach not only as organist, but also as *Kammermusikus,* i.e., as a member of his household orchestra. A close friendship also developed between Bach and the young but short-lived Johann Ernst, son of Bach's earlier Weimar patron. Exceedingly musical, the youth was a talented violinist, took lessons from the *Kammermusikus,* and composed several works of conspicuous merit, three of which Bach later transcribed for clavier and which, for a long time, passed for violin concertos by Vivaldi. The acquaintances and close friendships Bach formed at the Weimar court were numerous and valuable, with musicians, writers and educators prominent among them. The ducal "Kapelle" varied in size and constitution according to circumstances. Sometimes, when opera was performed, it included singers. The instrumentalists proper seem to have numbered eleven. The conductor was one Johann Samuel Drese; the concertmaster, from 1714 on, Bach.

One of the concertmaster's duties was to provide cantatas for a variety of occasions and, beginning in 1714, he wrote a number of them. His choir consisted of twelve singers. Wilhelm Ernst had from the first been impressed by Bach's powers as an organist. The musician's diverse labors were gratifyingly recompensed and in nine years he had doubled his income. At its smallest it was twice as large as at Mühlhausen. It is claimed that never in his life did Bach have at his disposal an organ truly worthy of his powers and even at Weimar the instrument was inferior to that in Mühlhausen. Nevertheless, the organ works he composed at Weimar exceeded anything he had ever done before in sumptuousness of inspiration, imaginative grandeur, and technical exaction.

One hears comparatively little of Maria Barbara. Bach's wife appears, however, to have been a fitting helpmeet to her busy husband, handling his household and his numerous pupils with tact and discretion and bearing him children with regularity. Some of these died early, others lived till a ripe age. In 1710 was born his oldest son, Wilhelm Friedemann, a genius in his own right and ever his father's favorite, but all his life wayward and something of a black sheep. At this stage one might as well mention two other musically outstanding sons of Bach among the twenty children he was to beget. The more prominent of these was Carl Philipp Emanuel, who served Frederick the Great and whose reputation as a pianist and composer was such that, whenever in the latter part of the eighteenth century, it was a question of Bach, people usually meant Philipp Emanuel.

Another, Johann Christian (Bach's son by his second wife), lived and died in London, composed operas, and became an intimate of the youthful Mozart.

During the years of his Weimar residence Bach made three journeys which are conspicuous among the brief ones that punctuated his life. One was to Cassel toward the end of 1714, presumably to examine a new organ. Possibly, too, he accompanied his ducal master on a ceremonial visit. Like Weimar, Cassel had a reputation for culture and evidently the Duke would have been pleased to exhibit the prowess of his own court organist. A reference to Bach's incredible virtuosity on this visit has come down to us. "His feet, flying over the pedals as though they were winged," wrote an observer, "made the notes reverberate like thunder in a storm till the prince, confounded with admiration, pulled a ring from his finger and presented it to the player. Now bethink you, if Bach's skillful feet deserved such bounty what gift must the prince have offered to reward his hands as well?" Other stories of his miraculous playing had long circulated throughout the country. People said it was a habit of his to climb into the organ loft of an inconspicuous rural church and so astound people with his improvisations that the cry would go up: "That must be Bach or the Devil!" The tale, one can depend on it, is a myth.

Another trip was to Halle, birthplace of Handel. True, he did not go there in search of his greatest contemporary (though he made several sincere yet ineffectual attempts to meet him) but to examine a new organ. His playing created so profound an impression that the Collegium Musikum made an earnest effort to secure him for Halle. Bach was flattered but, because of his Weimar connections, unable to accept. The Halle council, believing he was seeking higher pay, was irritated. Nevertheless, a little later it summoned Bach in company with Johann Kuhnau and Christian Friedrich Rolle to inspect the organ of the Church of Our Lady. The officials omitted nothing that might please their distinguished guests. A staff of servants and coachmen was placed at their service, a reception was held at which the chief musical personages of the town were summoned to meet them and, after the organ had been examined in great detail, the visitors were entertained at a banquet whose culinary abundance and gastronomic quality may be judged from the following bill of fare which has come down to us:

1 piece of Boeuf à la mode	*1 boiled pumpkin*
Pike with anchovy butter	*Fritters*
sauce	*Candied lemon peel*
1 smoked ham	*Preserved cherries*
1 dish of peas	*Warm asparagus salad*
1 dish of potatoes	*Lettuce salad*
2 dishes of spinach with	*Radishes*
sausages	*Fresh butter*
1 quarter of roast mutton	*Roast veal*

As Bach returned safely to Weimar, it may be assumed he declined a few of the courses! He was even paid a fee for the little outing. It came to $4.50.

The third trip carried him to Dresden. There, under the rule of Augustus II, musical life flourished. In 1717 a season of Italian opera was in full blast. It was not opera, however, which fascinated Bach. He looked upon it with gentle condescension and, even in later years, was in the habit of chaffing his son, Friedemann, with the question: "Well, shall we go over to Dresden and listen to the pretty little tunes?" What did attract Bach was the presence at the Saxon court of the celebrated French clavecinist and organist, Louis Marchand. Bach had studied his compositions closely and admired them. A gifted but intolerably arrogant person, Marchand had fallen into disgrace in Versailles and found it prudent to emigrate. An official of Augustus II conceived the idea of summoning Bach from Weimar and arranging on the spot a musical contest between the two. Such is, at least, the traditional story. Whatever the exact truth may have been, Bach arrived on the scene of the proposed contest at the specified hour but Marchand, afraid of a rival whose prowess he well knew, left Dresden secretly and let the match go by default. Bach thereupon performed alone, stirring his hearers to unlimited admiration. Marchand returned to France where he lived, apparently none the worse for his ignominious failure, till 1732.

Things, however, were shaping for a change in the life of Bach. In 1716 the conductor of the ducal orchestra, Johann Samuel Drese, died. For two years Bach had filled the post of concertmaster and seems to have felt that he was next in line for the conductorship. It went, on the contrary, to Drese's son, a man of mediocre attainments. Bach was

15

hurt and further embittered by the fact that no more cantatas of his composition were being ordered, and his notorious temper speedily got the better of him. He had made the acquaintance of Prince Leopold of Anhalt-Cöthen, whose sister had married a younger member of Weimar's ducal family. Intensely musical, that sovereign in the summer of 1717 had asked Bach to become his Kapellmeister. Bach shortly afterwards sent an application for his release to Wilhelm Ernst, apparently mincing no words. The Duke flew into a rage. We read in the diary of one of the court secretaries: "On November 6, 1717, Bach, till now Concertmaster and Court Organist, was put under arrest in the justice room for obstinately demanding his instant dismissal." The infuriated genius remained a jailbird only till December 2. His detention appears to have been profitably employed for it enabled him to begin work on his *Orgelbüchlein*. About a week later he left Weimar for Cöthen, eighty miles to the northeast, with his wife and four children.

KAPELLMEISTER WITH PRINCE LEOPOLD

At Cöthen he began a new life. For one thing, he no longer filled the post of organist. The court of Prince Leopold was of the Calvinistic faith. Church services, being of a particularly austere nature, required no organ playing of a virtuoso type or the production of sacred cantatas, such as Bach had hitherto been turning out in quantity. Yet Leopold was an ardent music lover, whose tastes ran to instrumental composition. He maintained an orchestra of eighteen of which Bach now became Kapellmeister. Such cantatas as he wrote in Cöthen were secular ones, chiefly in honor of his employer. For the most part his creative energies were now concentrated on concertos, suites, sonatas, and clavier works including some of his very greatest.

Instrumental music before Bach's day had scarcely achieved what might be called an independent life. In the creations of his Cöthen period we discover, in effect, the most vigorous roots of our symphonic literature—especially in the four suites (or "overtures," as Bach called them) and the six "Brandenburg" Concertos! Scholars have been unable to decide definitely whether the former were composed in Cöthen or in Leipzig. At all events they were performed before the Duke and also before the Telemann Musical Society in Leipzig, of which the composer was subsequently director. The third suite, in D, is the one comprising the exalted and incomparable *Air*, which achieved, long afterwards, a popularity of its own in the transcription of it for the G string by the violinist August Wilhemj. Yet every movement of each suite constitutes a priceless jewel of instrumental music.

The Brandenburg Concertos are in a somewhat different case. They were composed for Christian Ludwig, Margrave of Brandenburg and a son of the Great Elector, whom Bach appears to have met on a journey with Prince Leopold. Christian Ludwig had a hobby of collecting concertos by various composers and he commissioned Bach to write him "some pieces." In an elaborate preface couched in extraordinary French and dated "Cöthen, March 24, 1721," the composer begged his noble patron to accept these products of his "slight talents" and to "overlook their imperfections." Whether the private orchestra of the Margrave played the works or not we cannot say. Neither do we know if Bach's gift was even acknowledged. After Christian Ludwig died, the catalogue of his richly stocked library had no mention of Bach's half dozen "trifles." The precious masterpieces turned up in a mass of scores offered for sale in job lots!

It is practically certain, however, that the Brandenburg Concertos were performed by the princely Kapelle at Cöthen in Bach's presence, for the composer had been wise enough to make copies of his scores. They are not concertos in the modern sense of the term, but continuations and developments of those "concerti grossi" of masters like Torelli, Vivaldi, and Corelli. In various permutations and combinations they contrast groups of solo instruments (the "concertino") with the background of the "tutti." The "concerti grossi" of Handel furnish examples of the same principle of balance and diversity. The fact that none of the Brandenburg Concertos is in a minor key and that somber moods are rare, points to the probability that they were written for entertainment purposes.

Their variety is astonishing, with no two quite alike. The first, in F major, is the only one which calls for horns; and for the performance of this concerto two horn players were specially engaged at Cöthen. The second, likewise in F, requires a trumpet—the solitary appearance in the entire set of this instrument. To choose between the Brandenburg Concertos, to determine their relative musical worth is impossible. Yet in some respects the sixth, in B flat, if perhaps the least frequently played, is the most unusual. No violins are used in its scoring. The employment of two violas, two violas da gamba, and cello gives the work a peculiar dark string color wholly its own.

Let us mention here the wondrous concerto for two violins, another sublime inspiration of Bach's Cöthen days. It is probable that it was played by the concertmaster, Josephus Spiess, and the excellent violinist, Johann Rose (who also played the oboe and taught fencing to the court pages!), with the composer conducting the orchestral accompaniment.

And Prince Leopold, himself, who not only enjoyed music but played it well, doubtless took part in the sonatas for clavier and viola da gamba. He could not do without his musicians apparently and when, in 1718, he went to take the "cure" at Carlsbad, he had a sextet from his Kapelle accompany him. Bach was one of the retinue. The following year the Kapellmeister made a pilgrimage to nearby Halle in an effort to meet Handel, who had come to the Continent to engage singers for his operatic ventures in London. But neither at this time nor on a subsequent occasion when he tried to make the acquaintance of his great contemporary was he successful. Handel had already returned to England, seemingly far less eager to meet Bach than Bach was to meet him.

In May 1720, Prince Leopold again went to take the Carlsbad waters and once more Bach was in his train. The visit was somewhat longer this time and it ended grievously for the composer. When he set out he left his wife in the best of health and spirits. When he came back he found her dead and buried. With Maria Barbara gone, there was, apparently, no one to look after Catherine Dorothea, Wilhelm Friedemann, Philipp Emanuel and Johann Gottfried Bernhard, the eldest not more than ten. The blow seems to have struck Bach the more heavily because, engaged in worldly music-making as he now was, he lacked the spiritual consolation of churchly activities and the communion with his inner self which he enjoyed in the organ loft.

An opportunity for a trip to Hamburg was provided by the sudden death of the organist at St. Jacob's Church of that city. Along with a number of other noted players Bach was invited to pass on the qualifications of new candidates for the post. This gave him a chance to renew old ties and stimulate new interests. Adam Reinken was still alive and in his presence, as well as before a number of municipal authorities, Bach improvised astounding variations on the chorale "By the Waters of Babylon," one of Reinken's specialties, till the veteran conceded in amazement to his younger colleague: "I thought this art was dead, but I see it still lives in you."

The Hamburg journey was but an interlude, however inspiring. There was no possibility of an organ position in that town. And another problem was now occupying him—the question of his children's education. Friedemann had received his first clavier lessons from his father shortly before Maria Barbara's death. The world has been the gainer through this instruction administered to the youngster by such a formidable teacher. With his own hands Bach wrote out a *Clavier-Büchlein für Wilhelm Friedemann Bach.* On the first page are set down the various clefs. More important for posterity is a transliteration of the ornaments, or "Manieren," showing precisely how they are to be executed. Then follow exercises in fingering, hand positions, and much else. The little book is a valuable illustration of Bach's own methods of discipline and pedagogy.

Nor are these the only things for which generations of pianists have to thank the Bach of the Cöthen period. It was for teaching purposes that he composed masterpieces like the Two- and the Three-Part Inventions. To furnish practical illustration of the advantages of the system of equal temperament he advocated for tuning, he composed, while still in Leopold's service, the first book of the *Well-Tempered Clavier,* that miraculous series of twenty-four preludes and fugues in all major and minor keys, which is the Bible of pianists to this day. The second book was written in Leipzig many years later.

It was not long before Bach realized that if his children were to be brought up in the traditions of rectitude he had himself inherited, they could not remain without a mother's care, the more so as his many occupations left him little leisure to oversee a company of lively youngsters. And so on December 3, 1721, Bach took to himself a second wife, Anna Magdalena Wilcken, the daughter of a court trumpeter of Weissenfels. A gentle, lovable soul, musical, devoted to her great husband and the mother of a fresh host of children, she was as ideal a helpmeet for Bach as her predecessor had been.

A week after his Kapellmeister's marriage, Prince Leopold took a wife in his turn. But the lady, the prince's cousin, quickly troubled the musical atmosphere of the Cöthen court. Her tastes were for masquerades, dances, fireworks, illuminations and other forms of tinseled show, not for concerts of orchestral and chamber music. Bach called her an "amusa"—a person of no culture. Her installation at Cöthen was the prelude to Bach's departure. As so often happened in his career, however, a more or less inopportune incident created a situation from which he might profit.

LEIPZIG AND THE ST. JOHN PASSION

This particular incident was the death, half a year after Bach's second marriage, of Johann Kuhnau who, for more than twenty years, had held the Cantorship of St. Thomas's School in Leipzig. Whether or not the post seemed to Bach himself as desirable as a Kapellmeistership, the sudden vacancy attracted a flock of candidates, some of them men of distinction. Most preferable in the eyes of the Leipzig civic council was George Philipp Telemann who in Bach's day ranked higher in the esteem of many musicians than Bach himself. Another was Christoph Graupner of Darmstadt. We need not pursue in detail the complicated negotiations and the extensive intrigue the choice of Kuhnau's successor involved. Telemann was offered the job and things progressed so far that the authorities debated whether the address welcoming him should be in Latin or in German. But Telemann, who already held a lucrative position in Hamburg, determined to find out which town would offer him the better inducement. Hamburg increased his already considerable stipend, so in Hamburg he remained. Graupner, on the other hand, would have come gladly. But his Darmstadt masters declined to release him.

Before the final decision was made, Bach made it his business to be on hand at Leipzig. When it became clear to Graupner that he was out of the running he heartily recommended Bach. The latter was requested, in order to prove his fitness for the post he sought, to conduct in the Church of St. Thomas on Good Friday, 1723, a work of his own composition, appropriate to the day. That work was the *Passion According to St. John* which, though it may have been written hurriedly, is a creation of such transcendent grandeur that only the later *Passion According to St. Matthew* can be said to excel it in lyric splendor and sublimity.

As soon as Graupner's decision was known, Bach asked Prince Leopold for his official leave. The letter of dismissal was couched in most friendly and flattering terms. At Leipzig Bach executed a document binding himself to discharge all the duties of the Cantorship, undertaking to teach a variety of subjects and even to give private lessons in singing without extra pay. The only thing he balked at was taking charge of Latin classes. For this chore he agreed to provide a substitute at his own expense. Then he took leave of Prince Leopold, with whom he remained on terms of the closest friendship till the prince's death five years later. On May 5, 1723 he received from the burgomaster of Leipzig the ceremonious notification of his unanimous appointment. On May 30 he conducted at the Church of St. Nicholas (which he served alternately with the Church of St. Thomas) the cantata *The Hungry Shall Be Fed*. Therewith he inaugurated his office.

Bach's Greater Work

Bach settled in Leipzig at the age of thirty-eight. He remained there the rest of his life. True, he came and went, and he made journeys of one sort or another, but they were never far distant or protracted. In Leipzig he created his grandest, his most colossal, and also his profoundest and subtlest works. His duties were incredibly numerous and often heart-breakingly heavy. He was responsible, it has been said, "to all and to none." Again and again he had the rector of the St. Thomas School, the city council, the church Consistory, and yet others about his ears. He had to look after the musical services in four churches, two of them the most important in the town. Under exasperating conditions he had to teach turbulent and ruffianly pupils. He had to combat official ill will and intrigue. For the performances he was obliged to conduct he had vocal and instrumental forces that strike us as laughably inadequate and were in numberless cases grossly unskilled. The demands on his physical and spiritual strength must have been appalling. Yet Bach appears to have had the resources and the resistance of a giant. We know that over and over again his temper, his obstinate nature and inborn pugnacity were tried to the uttermost. But in the face of all irritations he was earning enough, his home life was comfortable, he met and entertained artists, he had the satisfaction of knowing that his sons could enjoy the educational advantages of Leipzig, and he gradually gathered about him a company of greatly gifted young students and devoted disciples.

In the course of years he shifted some of his most unsympathetic duties to other shoulders. How he could otherwise have written the gigantic amount of music he did is an unanswerable question. For consider: he came to Leipzig the composer of about thirty church cantatas. When he died in 1750 he had produced there two hundred and sixty-five more. Of this staggering total (two hundred and ninety-five) two hundred and two have come down to us. As if this were not enough (these cantatas, incidentally, were week-to-week obligations), his years at Leipzig account for many secular cantatas, six motets, five masses (including the titanic one in B minor), the Passions according to St. John and St. Matthew (not to mention lost ones), the *Christmas Oratorio,* the resplendent *Magnificat,* the *Easter* and *Ascension* oratorios, besides clavier works like the *Italian Concerto,* the *Goldberg Variations,* the second book of the *Well-Tempered Clavier,* and an incredible mass of other things.

The rector of St. Thomas's School during Bach's first years in Leipzig was Johann Heinrich Ernesti, with whom Bach's relations were cordial enough, though the rector was a slipshod disciplinarian. Matters remained pleasant enough under Johann Gesner, but presently the latter left St. Thomas to assume a more profitable post at Göttingen. His successor, Johann August Ernesti, quickly proceeded to stroke Bach's fur the wrong way by declaring that altogether too much attention was given to the study of music. "So you want to be a pot-house fiddler," he used to say to youths he found practicing the violin. It was only a question of time when the surly new rector and the combustible Bach would come into collision.

What has been called the "battle of the Prefects" was long drawn out and bitter. The details need not detain us. Trouble was intensified by the appointment to a responsible position of a person named Krause, whom Bach had angrily described as "ein liederlicher Hund" ("a dissolute dog"). Things went from bad to worse. Bach accused the rector of usurping his functions. He wrote long, circumstantial letters setting forth his case to "their Magnificences," the Burgomaster, the civic council, and other outstanding authorities. "Their Magnificences" replied with legalistic hair-splittings and things grew so violent that Bach in one case undertook to drive Krause from the choir loft. The lengthy series of undignified squabbles was finally brought to an end by Augustus the Strong, King of Poland, Saxony, "etc., etc., etc." (to use Bach's own designation). We are not certain that the composer obtained the satisfaction he demanded, but everyone seems to have tired of the interminable quarrel and was relieved to see it peter out.

Meanwhile, Bach had other worries and vexations. One of his sons, Gottfried Bernhard, proved as unstable as did Wilhelm Friedemann in a later day, but died before his financial misdeeds had ended in his open disgrace. Then the composer was made the target of attacks by a certain minor musician, one Scheibe, who criticized his works for what he called their "complexity and overelaboration." Bach immortalized the fellow by satirizing him in the secular cantata, *Phoebus and Pan,* where Scheibe appears as the ignoramus Midas, adorned with a pair of ass's ears!

In 1736 Augustus the Strong conferred upon Bach the title of Court Composer. The patent of Bach's dignity was committed to the Russian envoy in Dresden, Carl Freiherr von Keyserling. He was a sufferer from chronic insomnia and it is to this circumstance that we owe one of Bach's supreme works for the clavier—the so-called *Goldberg Variations.* To ease the torment of sleepless nights the Count had in his service a gifted clavecinist, Johann Gottlieb Goldberg, a pupil of Bach's. While Bach was in the midst of his troubles with Ernesti, Keyserling commissioned him to write Goldberg "something soothing" to divert his wakefulness. Bach took a Sarabande melody he had copied into his wife's *Notenbuch* and used it as the basis of thirty variations. So delighted was Keyserling that he never wearied of listening to Goldberg playing them and actually referred to them as "my Variations." The Count, paradoxically enough, now had every reason to remain awake and enjoy the never-ending ingenuity and luxuriant fancy of these variations and the lively *Quodlibet* toward the close, which recalls those boisterous medleys the Bach family of old used to improvise at its reunions. It is pleasant to record that Keyserling paid Bach liberally for "his" *Variations.*

St. Matthew Passion and B minor Mass

On Good Friday, 1729, came the turn of St. Thomas's Church to produce the music appropriate to the day. The result of this official duty was the *Passion According to St. Matthew,* for which Christian Friedrich Henrici, who wrote under the name of "Picander" and provided Bach with innumerable "librettos" for all purposes, compiled the text. The composer himself chose and distributed the chorales which punctuate the score. Bach was still at work on it when his former patron, Prince Leopold of Cöthen, died. Rather than prepare a special memorial piece he asked Picander to adapt appropriate words to parts of the music in the *St. Matthew* and he performed them in Cöthen at his friend's obsequies.

It is hard for us to believe that the *St. Matthew Passion* did not receive on that far-off April 15, 1729, the tribute of wondering amazement which in the fullness of our hearts we bring it today. Yet we are told that the Leipzig worshipers considered its overwhelming dramatic pages "theatrical." "God help us," exclaimed a scandalized old dame, " 'tis surely an opera-comedy!" We know that, judged by our standards, the first performance of the work must have been inefficient. Whether it was much better done at its repetition in 1736 may be doubted. Be this as it may, the *St. Matthew Passion* passed into oblivion for nearly a hundred years. The glory of its rediscovery and its reawakening an exact century after its birth belongs to Felix Mendelssohn who, with its resuscitation at the Singakademie in Berlin, performed a service that would have shed immortal luster upon his name had he never done anything else.

The *St. Matthew Passion,* which is Bach at his most tender, intimate, lacerating and compassionate, stands, like the *B minor Mass,* Beethoven's Ninth Symphony and Wagner's *Tristan,* as one of the epochal feats of music, a lonely and incomparable achievement of the human spirit. Bach is believed to have written a Passion according to St. Mark, but not a trace of it survives. Another, according to St. Luke, is extant but most certainly spurious. It is hard to believe he could ever have surpassed the lyric glory of the *St. Matthew.* For generations after its re-emergence musicians paid it everything from lip-service to ecstatic tribute. A complete, full-length performance of it was, however, a rarity and not even Mendelssohn had the courage to attempt it. In our own time we have finally come to the ways of wisdom, recognizing that the *St. Matthew Passion* can produce its proper effect only when heard in its entirety, with never a bar or a phrase omitted. Those who have heard it thus are unlikely ever again to listen willingly to a cut version.

If anything can be said to rival the grandeur of the *St. Matthew Passion* it is the *Mass in B minor,* the triumphal hymn of the church militant. This utterance of subduing and inscrutable majesty, which transcends the world to bestride the universe, was completed in 1733 and offered to Augustus the Strong as "an insignificant example of my skill in Musique"! Augustus the Strong, being occupied at the moment with problems of state, did not deign to notice Bach's "insignificant" gesture. The composer never heard a performance of this gigantic creation, which soars to heights beyond human gaze and, in its proportions and technical details, is too vast to serve ordinary liturgical purposes. Yet here, as so often elsewhere, Bach followed the example of his age and employed several numbers from this Mass—with greater or lesser alteration—elsewhere. Even the triumphant *Osanna*, which expert criticism has pronounced a polonaise (apparently a subtle compliment paid to Augustus as King of Poland), and the ineffably touching *Agnus Dei* may be encountered again in several of Bach's cantatas.

VISIT TO FREDERICK THE GREAT AND LATER WORKS

Early in 1741 Bach's son Philipp Emanuel had become clavecinist to the new sovereign of Prussia, Frederick the Great. Moved, it appears, by a paternal wish to see the young man comfortably settled, the father made a trip to Berlin in the summer of that year. Details of the journey are few and it was cut short by news that Anna Magdalena, in Leipzig, was seriously ill.

Bach's famous visit to Berlin and Potsdam did not take place, however, till fully six years later. One of its chief objects was to make the acquaintance of his daughter-in-law, whom Philipp Emanuel had married in 1744, and of his first grandchild. But the visit had more spectacular consequences. Frederick the Great had learned about Bach from his court pianist. Whether or not the great Cantor went to the palace of Sans-Souci in Potsdam at the king's special command, he arrived there at a psychological moment on May 7, 1747, just as Frederick was about to begin one of his regular evening concerts at which, surrounded by his picked musicians, he loved to exhibit his own considerable virtuosity on the flute.

"Gentlemen, old Bach is here!" the monarch exclaimed and, calling off the concert, received his guest with cordiality. He immediately had Bach examine the new Silbermann claviers with hammer action newly installed in the palace and invited him to show his skill. After putting each of the instruments to a test, Bach amazed Frederick and his court by improvising a superb six-part fugue on a subject submitted him by the king himself. The next evening he transported his hosts once more with a recital on the organ of the Church of the Holy Ghost in Potsdam and a little later, in Berlin, examined the new opera house, detecting acoustical effects which the architect himself seems not to have suspected.

Back in Leipzig Bach resolved to break a rule against dedicating scores to noble patrons he had made after the shabby treatment accorded him in the case of the Brandenburg Concertos and the *B minor Mass*. But he would have been less than human if he had not thought that a gracious gesture on his part might perchance further his son's interests at court; and besides, he was genuinely pleased with the fine theme Frederick had given him to develop. So, alleging that his Potsdam improvisation had failed to do the royal theme justice, he dispatched to the monarch with a suitable dedication a series of elaborate contrapuntal developments of the theme, diplomatically incorporating in the set a sonata for flute, violin and clavier. This princely gift is the work known as the *Musical Offering,* whose beauty and ingenuity have come to be properly valued only in recent years.

Theoretical problems of music now interested Bach more and more and in 1747 he was elected to the so-called Society for the Promotion of Musical Science, founded by Lorenz Christoph Mizler. Men as illustrious as Telemann, Handel and Graun were already members and after a brief period of hesitation Bach joined it, too, presenting the Society in return for his diploma with a formidable sample of his technical skill in the shape of a lordly set of canonic variations for organ on the Christmas hymn *Vom Himmel hoch, da komm ich her.*

In 1749 he was occupied with a work in some ways his profoundest and most enigmatic, which virtually till our own time has been misconstrued even by serious musicians as a dry and abstract experiment in polyphony of no independent musical value. It is that stupendous succession of fugues and canons (or "counterpoints," as the composer himself called them) under the collective title *The Art of Fugue.* On a subject not unlike the theme given him by Frederick the Great, Bach has heaped one polyphonic marvel upon another in a manner to exploit to the limits of technique and imagination every possible device of fugal and canonic development. He was not spared to complete it but dropped his pen at a passage in the final counterpoint when the notes "B-A-C-H" (in German B flat, A, C, B natural) were woven into the contrapuntal texture. What adds to the furthur riddle of the work is the fact that the composer did not indicate for what instrument or group of instruments he intended it. In our day it has been scored by turns for a full orchestra, a chamber orchestra, a string quartet, two pianos, and the organ. It is difficult to believe that Bach did not intend this colossal conception to be performed and that he projected it merely as a theoretical problem or an exercise in what is called "eye music." It stands in relation to Bach's other works somewhat as the mystical last quartets of Beethoven do to his more popular creations. It was published posthumously and reissued by Philipp Emanuel Bach in 1752. Yet four years later not more than thirty copies had been sold and Philipp Emanuel, in disgust, sold the plates for old metal.

DEATH

Bach's eyesight had long been failing. The strain to which he had mercilessly subjected it all his life, copying music as well as engraving elaborate compositions of his own, was now telling on it. By the end of 1749 his vision was in such a state that an English eye specialist, John Taylor, who later treated Handel but at this time chanced to be touring the continent, was summoned and operated on Bach about the beginning of 1750. It was of little avail. Prolonged confinement in a dark room, medicines and dressings told on the master's ordinarily robust constitution. When his condition permitted and his sight temporarily improved he recklessly returned to his creative labors and also prepared for the engravers a set of eighteen choral-preludes for organ. But the end was at hand. Calling to his side his son-in-law, Johann Christoph Altnikol, Bach dictated to him the variation on the chorale *When We Are in Our Deepest Need,* prophetically bidding him alter the title to *With This Before Thy Throne I Come.* On July 18 he suffered an apoplectic stroke and lay for ten days in a desperate state. At nine in the evening on July 28, 1750, he passed from a world that could barely discern the shadow of his greatness.

It is excessive, perhaps, to maintain that for over three quarters of a century after his death Bach went into total eclipse. But he was disregarded if not forgotten. A handful of musicians, indeed, remembered him, among them some of his talented pupils. From time to time a few scattered works of his gained a limited circulation and came into worthy hands. Thus, in the seventeen-eighties several became known in Vienna, and at the Baron Van Swieten's Mozart had occasion to acquaint himself with a few specimens, which powerfully stimulated his genius. Afterwards, in Leipzig, being shown the parts of one of the motets, he exclaimed after closely studying them: "Here, at last, is something from which one can learn!" Beethoven, too, knew the *Well-Tempered Clavier* and even went so far as to ask someone to procure him the *Crucifixus* from the *B minor Mass*. His exclamation is well known: "Not Bach (brook) but Ocean should be his name!"

Yet, in the latter part of the eighteenth century it was chiefly Philipp Emanuel, not his father, to whom one referred when the mighty name was invoked. For the sons of Bach, not the mighty parent, embodied "the spirit of the time." Even prior to his death Johann Sebastian had passed for outmoded and rather hopelessly "old hat." Philipp Emanuel went so far as to call his father "a big wig stuffed with learning"; and such was the opinion shared by many of the young bloods in Leipzig and elsewhere. In a way this was not surprising. Bach represented a type of music whose complex profundities were giving place to homophony, entertainment and the graceful superficialities of the so-called "gallant style." The new age was concerned with the problems of the sonata and the opera. Even if Bach's scores—most of them unpublished—had been accessible, it is questionable whether the epoch we call "classical" would have been able to see him in a just perspective.

In due course the wheel was to turn full-circle and surely none would have been more amazed than Philipp Emanuel, Wilhelm Friedemann, and Johann Christian could they have known that one day their own works would be looked upon as museum pieces, while the creations of the "learned old perruque" had become the fountain of musical youth, the perpetual source of strength and of illimitable, self-renewing wonder. With Mendelssohn's revival of the *St. Matthew Passion* in 1829 there began that resurrection which went on increasingly through the nineteenth century, headed by the redemptive labors of the *Bach-Gesellschaft,* and which continues to gain momentum right through our own day. Boundless as the universe, timeless as eternity, modern as tomorrow, Bach remains from decade to decade what Richard Wagner once called him—"the most stupendous miracle in all music."

H. F. P.

George Frideric Handel

BORN: HALLE, FEB. 23, 1685. DIED: LONDON, APR. 14, 1759.

I should be sorry, my lord, if I have only succeeded in entertaining them; I wished to make them better.—HANDEL *to* Lord Kinnoul, *after the first London performance of* The Messiah, *Covent Garden, Mar. 23, 1743.*

HANDEL'S LONG CAREER resembles a gigantic tapestry, so bewilderingly crowded with detail, so filled with turmoil and vicissitude, with vast achievements, extremes of good and ill fortune, and unending comings and goings, that any attempt to force even part of it into a brief essay is as hopeless as it is presumptuous. Handel is far more difficult to reduce to such dimensions than his greatest contemporary, Bach, whose worldly experiences were infinitely less diverse and colorful, for all the sublimity, mystical quality and epochal influence of his myriad creations. The supreme master of florid pomp, Handel bulked much larger in the perspective of his own day than did, in his, the composer of the *Passion According to St. Matthew.* In spite of an everlasting monument like *Messiah,* the most popular choral masterpiece ever written, we may, however, ask ourselves if the body of Handel's music is as widely known and as intimately studied as it deserves to be. How many today can boast of a real acquaintance with Handel's operas (there are more than forty of them alone) apart from a few airs sung in concert; how many can truly claim to know by experience any of the great oratorios apart from *Messiah* and, possibly, *Judas Maccabaeus* and *Israel in Egypt?* Yet outside of such monumental works, Handel was time and again a composer of exquisitely delicate colorations, and sensuous style, not to say a largely unsuspected master of many subtle

30

intricacies of rhythm. The present essay, wholly without originality or novelty of approach, may, perchance, induce the casual reader to renew his interest in Handel's prodigious treasury, so much of it neglected, not to say actually undiscovered by multitudes of music lovers.

* * *

Some wit, comparing Bach and Handel, remarked that both masters were "born in the same year and killed by the same doctor." Born in the same year they unquestionably were, Handel almost an exact month before his great contemporary. Halle, where Handel first saw the light, is a comparatively short distance from Eisenach, where Bach was cradled. It lies not far from the eastern boundary of that Saxon-Thuringian country which harbored some of the imposing musical figures of Germany during the seventeenth century. Such names as those of the famous "three S's"—Schein, Scheidt and Schütz—of Kuhnau, Krieger, Melchior Franck, Ahle, Rosenmüller, echo powerfully through the history of that period.

George Frideric Handel was born on Monday, February 23, 1685. That the name has been variously spelled need not trouble us; strict consistency in such matters lay as lightly on folks of this epoch as it did in the age of Mozart. However, it may be pointed out that in this instance "Frideric" is retained in place of "Frederick" because Handel himself repeatedly used this form and because the British authorities thus inscribed him when he became a British citizen.

The Handel family came from Silesia, where Valentine Handel, the composer's grandfather, had been a coppersmith in Breslau. George Handel, the father, had been "barber-surgeon," attached to the service of Saxon and Swedish armies, then to that of Duke Augustus of Saxony. For a time he prospered and in 1665 he bought himself "Am Schlamm," at Halle-an-der-Saale, a palatial house, which in the course of years barely escaped total destruction by fire. In any case, Father Handel was to know the ups and downs of fortune; and the vicissitudes he endured did not sweeten an always morose and surly character. He has been described as "a strong man, a man of vast principles, bigoted, intensely disagreeable, a man with a rather withered heart." A portrait of him gave Romain Rolland "the impression of one who has never smiled." He was twice married, the first time to the widow of a barber, a woman ten years his senior, the second to Dorothea Taust, a pastor's daughter, thirty years his junior. By the first he had six children, by the second four, of whom George Frideric was the second.

Father Handel was sixty-three when his great son came into the world. The future composer of *Messiah* was born, not in the elaborate edifice which carries his bust and is inscribed with the titles of his oratorios, but in the house adjoining it which stands on a street corner and whose official address is Nicolai Strasse 5. Yet even this statement must be qualified. For this presumable "birthplace" was not built till 1800 and, according to the researches of Newman Flower, stands on the *site* of the house in which Handel was born. As for the town of Halle, it had definitely passed after the death of the Duke Augustus of Saxony, to Brandenburg; so that, strictly speaking, Handel was born a Prussian. But, as Rolland has noted, "the childhood of Handel was influenced by two intellectual forces: the Saxon and the Prussian. Of the two the more aristocratic, and also most powerful was the Saxon." At all events, after the Thirty Years' War the city of Halle, during the Middle Ages a center of culture and gaiety, had fallen into a drab provincialism.

Apparently the child's musical susceptibilities developed early and rather like Mozart's, even if unlike the latter, he had not the benefit of a friendly and understanding father. Who has not seen at some time or other the picture immortalizing the precocity of "the Infant Handel"? The story goes that the indulgent mother had smuggled a clavichord into the garret. In the dead of night the child crept to the attic till the father, aroused by faint tinklings, came with a lantern to investigate. Whether or not the clavichord was confiscated, the result of the parental raid was a stern prohibition of all sorts of music-making. Some of us may be reminded by this apparent heartlessness of a rather similar punishment visited on the youthful Bach, when his elder brother deprived him of music he had painfully copied out by moonlight for his own use.

The elder Handel's motive was, according to his own lights, perhaps quite as defensible. He had no wish to see a son of his degraded to the rank of a lackey or some form of vagabond, than which a musician at that time hardly seemed any better. The barber-surgeon fully shared the prejudice of the average "strong man" against the artist. Rolland describes the bourgeois middle class German attitude of the seventeenth century toward music: "It was for them a mere art of amusement, and not a serious profession. Many of the masters of that time, Schütz, Kuhnau, Rosenmüller, were lawyers or theologians, before they devoted themselves to music." And old George Handel is supposed to have threatened: "If that boy ever shows any further inclination towards music or noises disguised as such, I will kill it!" There was, indeed, one way in which the boy could with a certain impunity satisfy his craving for music—in church, by listening to the organ and the singing of the choir. Such enjoyment supplanted to some extent the games and childish pleasures of ordinary boys. He was, it appears, a somewhat lonely child, who made few friends and whose "playground" was a dismal courtyard opposite his home.

The father settled on the law as a fine, honest and lucrative profession for his son. Jurisprudence was to rescue Handel from the snares of music, just as in time it was to be the "salvation" of Schumann, as school mastering was by paternal decree to be the destiny of Schubert, and medicine that of Berlioz. Here, too, it was quite as ineffectual! All the same, the youth was not to escape his share of legal study; and by the time he reached sixteen he entered the University of Halle as "studiosus juris."

About eight years earlier, however, fate in the paradoxical shape of Father Handel himself took a hand in George Frideric's future. He had his son accompany him on a journey to nearby Weissenfels, the residence of the Duke of Saxony. That personage asked the lad to play something on the chapel organ and was so stirred by what he heard that he counseled the obdurate father not to thwart the child's ambition. From an ordinary person the hard-boiled parent would have taken such advice in very bad part; coming from the mouth of a prince it acquired the force of a command. So he decided to allow his son to study music with the unspoken reservation, however, that he must belong first and foremost to the law. Actually, these musical studies might be said to have begun in Weissenfels, for here young Handel had a chance to hear some of the works of the Nürnberg master, Johann Krieger; and in this same town, a mere stone's throw from Halle, he had his first taste of opera, which was to thrust deep roots into his soul.

The boy was now entrusted to the care of Friedrich Wilhelm

Zachow, from Leipzig, who at an early age had become organist of the Halle Liebfrauenkirche. Zachow appears to have been an uncommonly gifted teacher and Handel's devotion to him never wavered. As we read Romain Rolland's words we are strangely reminded of the ideals and methods of Theodor Weinlig, Wagner's unique master of composition: "Zachow's first efforts were devoted to giving the pupil a strong foundation in harmony. Then he turned his thoughts towards the inventive side of the art; he showed him how to give his musical ideas the most perfect form, and he refined his taste. He possessed a remarkable library of Italian and German music, and he explained to Handel the various methods of writing and composing adopted by different nationalities, whilst pointing out the good qualities and the faults of each composer and in order that his education might be at the same time theoretical and practical, he frequently gave him exercises to work in such and such a style. . . . Thus the little Handel had, thanks to his master, a living summary of the musical resources of Germany, old and new; and under his direction he absorbed all the secrets of the great contrapuntal architects of the past, together with the clear expressive and melodic beauty of the Italian-German schools of Hanover and Hamburg."

Around 1696 George Frideric is supposed to have gone to Berlin, though about this and possibly a subsequent trip a short time afterwards the chronicles give no clear account. Father Handel was seriously ill and, as it is unlikely that the eleven-year-old student went to the Court of the Elector of Brandenburg alone, the assumption is that he made the journey in Zachow's company. Be this as it may, the artistic enthusiasm of the Electress, Sophia Charlotte, stimulated musical activities at the electoral court and attracted thither outstanding Italian composers, instrumentalists and singers. And it may well have been here that the youth was first brought into contact with the music of the South. He played on the clavecin before a princely audience and stirred it to such enthusiasm that the Elector wished to take him into service or at least finance a trip to Italy, to complete his studies. But if we are to believe Mainwaring, Father Handel did not wish his son "tied too soon to a prince." Furthermore, the old man's health failed so alarmingly that he knew his days were numbered and wished to see the boy once more before he died.

Hardly was George Frideric back in Halle when the barber-surgeon went to his account. The youth wrote a memorial poem which was published in a pamphlet and proved to be the first time his name ever appeared in print. After settling her husband's affairs Dorothea Handel went about carrying out his wishes regarding her son's legal studies. In a spirit of duty he continued them a while; but soon after his completion of his college classes and his entrance for the Faculty of Law at the Halle University, music gained the upper hand completely. He was religious without sentimentality but as little as the youthful Bach did he have any sympathy with Pietism (of which the Faculty of Theology was a hot-bed at the time) and was violently opposed to the Pietist antagonism to music. And when the post of organist at the Cathedral "by the Moritzburg" fell vacant by reason of the dissolute habits of a roystering individual named Leporin, Handel was made his successor, though the church was Calvinist and the young new-comer a staunch Lutheran.

There was now an end to all thoughts of jurisprudence. Music claimed him solely. Handel was only seventeen but seems already to have exercised a strong musical authority in Halle. He assembled a capital choir and orchestra from among his most gifted pupils and let them be heard on Sundays in various churches of the town. Like Bach and other masters of that astonishing period, he composed an incredible number of cantatas, motets, psalms, chorales and devotional miscellany, which had to be new every week. It must not be imagined that he allowed them to wilt or evaporate. Handel's mind was a store-house, whence nothing ever escaped but was always stocked away and held in reserve for future use.

In the summer of 1703 he left his native city; not, indeed, forever, but only for occasional visits to relatives and friends, when professional business allowed him time. From Halle he turned his steps toward Hamburg, which had suffered little from the wars of the seventeenth century, and grown rich, gay and artistic because of enviable business prosperity. Commercial benefits were, of course, reflected in a musical expansion which raised the Hanseatic port above the level even of Berlin and made it the operatic city of the North. In Hamburg, notes Rolland, "they spoke all languages and especially the French tongue; it was in continual relationship with both England and Italy, and particularly with Venice, which constituted for it a model for emulation. It was by way of Hamburg that the English ideas were circulated in Germany. . . . In the time of Handel, Hamburg shared with Leipzig the intellectual prestige of Germany. There was no other place in Germany where music was held in such high esteem. The artists there hobnobbed with the rich merchants."

The Hamburg opera catered to various factions which did not invariably see eye to eye. One of these factions consisted of persons who sought in operatic entertainment out and out amusement; the other, of individuals with a religious bent, who regarded the average fantastic and extravagant opera as an invention of hell—*opera diabolica*. When Handel arrived the lyric theater was making history guided by the composer, Reinhard Keiser. Under Keiser's management Hamburg became a home of opera in the German tradition. Some of these "German" operas were coarse and in atrocious taste. Hugo Leichtentritt tells, for instance, of a work called "Störtebeker und Gödge Michaelis" (music by Keiser), a story about piracy on the high seas, with executions and massacres, in which bladders filled with sow blood and concealed beneath the costumes of the actors would be perforated in such a manner that the appalled spectators were spattered with a gory shower, often resulting in a stampede.

Keiser, though a person of unstable character and extreme presumptuousness, had indisputable genius. He was not yet thirty when Handel came to Hamburg and under him that city experienced its golden age of opera. To be sure, the weakest feature of the Hamburg Opera was the singing. For a long time the institution had no *professional* singers. The rôles were taken by students, shoemakers, tailors, fruiterers "and girls of little talent and less virtue," while ordinarily artisans "found it more convenient to take female parts." A gifted Kapellmeister named Cousser, who had been a pupil of Lully in Paris, introduced important reforms and when Handel arrived in 1703, the moment was, in truth, a psychological one. "He was rich in power and strong in will," wrote the twenty-two-year-old Johann Mattheson, the first acquaintance he was to make in Hamburg. Rolland pictures Handel as having "an ample forehead, a vigorous mouth, a full chin and a head covered with a biretta" (rather after the manner of Wagner, of whom throughout his life Handel reminds one in some amazing traits of character and genius).

Under Keiser the adventurous newcomer soon found employment as a second violin in the opera orchestra. His particular intimate was

Mattheson, a musician of many gifts and uncommon versatility, who united in himself literary talents, a critical flair and a highly volatile temperament. It was he who helped Handel find pupils and who guided him into the town's important musical circles. So that before long Handel had access to the organ lofts of Hamburg's churches and opportunities to compose works for ecclesiastical purposes. Mattheson, incidentally, was a linguist and spoke perfect English; and it was through him that Handel was to enter for the first time into negotiations with what was to become his second country.

It was not very long, however, before the temperaments and idiosyncrasies of the two brought them into collision. Mattheson criticized the music of his friend, perhaps not entirely without reason, complained that Handel was not the most perfect of melodists and that he often wrote at too great length. If these opinions may have nettled the younger man they were not wholly lost on him, as time was to show. In the early months of their friendship Handel and Mattheson went to Lübeck to listen to the playing of the renowned Danish organist, Dietrich Buxtehude, whose celebrated *Abendmusiken* at the Marienkirche were likewise a magnet which drew Bach away from his duties in Arnstadt. The young men were deeply stirred by the music of the venerable master and Handel stored away in his incredibly retentive memory ideas which were to fertilize his imagination in later years. The two youths actually competed for the post of organist and might, like Bach, have won it but for the provision that whoever succeeded a retiring organist in Lübeck had to marry the daughter—or widow —of his predecessor. In this case the daughter seems to have been more than usually undesirable and, like their famous contemporary, the ' excursionists from Hamburg turned their backs on Lübeck.

Presently the friendship was imperiled once more, this time with what might have been disastrous results. In October, 1704, an opera, *Cleopatra*, which Mattheson had composed to a text by a certain Friederick Feustkling, was produced with the composer in the part of Mark Antony and Handel at the harpsichord. The piece won a success, but on a later occasion Mattheson (Antony being "dead") hastened into the orchestra and tried to push Handel from the instrument. A quarrel flared up immediately, which seems to have broken up the performance and have lasted half an hour. In the end the throng repaired to the Gänsemarkt, outside the theater, the pair drew swords and set upon one another. Almost at once the combat came to an end, Mattheson's blade splintering against a metal button on Handel's coat. "The duel might have ended very badly for us both, if by God's mercy my sword had not broken," the young firebrand was to write later. The reconciliation was not immediate but when it did come about the two dined together, then betook themselves to the theater to a rehearsal of Handel's first opera, *Almira.* The representation, on January 8, 1705, was an instant triumph for its composer. The Hamburgers were completely captivated by the freshness and manifest genius which the score exhibited. Mattheson had sung the tenor part but does not seem to have been overjoyed by his friend's spectacular success.

Handel was spurred by his fortunate operatic debut to embark on a second work. The fact that *Almira* had been sung partly in Italian, partly in German, did not keep it from obtaining twenty performances at the outset. Handel made the mistake of interrupting its run because he believed that in his next opera, *Nero, or Love Obtained Through Blood and Murder,* he had written something better. Mattheson sang the part of Nero; but the opera died after only three hearings. To aggravate matters the Keiser regime, now largely discredited, gave promise of putting an end to the Hamburg Opera; and Handel began to see himself enmeshed in the catastrophe of the wreck, a victim of elaborate jealousies and intrigues.

*　　*　　*

In 1704 he had made the acquaintance of an Italian prince, Giovanni Gaston del Medici, an adventurer and a notorious profligate, whose father was Grand Duke of Tuscany. He was astonished that Handel seemed so little interested in Italian music, including some specimens he set before him. Handel insisted that "angels would be necessary to sing them if such stuff were to sound even agreeable." At this time his ambition was to create a German style, independent of foreign influences. And for Keiser's successor, Saurbrey, Handel turned out a new opera, *Florindo und Daphne,* which, like Wagner's *Rienzi,* proved to be so long that the composer caused it to be given in two parts, "for fear," he admitted, "that the music might tire the hearers." Then, without taking leave of Mattheson or any of his friends, he accepted the prince's invitation and went to Italy.

More or less mystery surrounds Handel's arrival in Italy, though the time was not exactly propitious, what with the War of the Spanish Succession in full blast and funds in the wanderer's pocket fairly low. But the composer did not tarry in Florence, his first stop, for long and early in 1707 went to Rome. From the operatic standpoint the Eternal City had nothing to interest him. Pope Innocent III ten years previously deciding that the opera house was immoral, had closed it; then when things promised to improve a bit for musicians a devastating earthquake renewed the religious qualms of the people, so that during the whole of Handel's Italian sojourn, Rome had not a single performance of opera. However, there was abundant church and chamber music, which spurred him to emulation. To the Easter festivities of April, 1707, he contributed a *Dixit Dominus* and a few months later he wrote a *Laudate Pueri* and other Latin Psalms. But more important for his future were the excellent connections he made. Letters of recommendation from the Medici prince opened the Roman salons to him; and in such aristocratic circles his virtuosity on the keyboard seems to have gained him more fame than even his compositions. "The famous Saxon" ("Il Sassone famoso"), as Handel was called among the Romans even as early as the summer of 1707, was the wonder of musical soirées. And he was making inestimable artistic friendships. When we note that among those with whom he was brought into contact at one time or another in Rome were the Scarlattis, father and son; Arcangelo Corelli, Bernardo Pasquini, Benedetto Marcello—to mention only a few —we can judge to what grandly fertilizing inspirations Handel was exposed. We must mention in passing Cardinals Panfili and Ottoboni, as well as the Marquis Ruspoli, who yielded to nobody in his enthusiasm for Handel's gifts. All these men belonged to a coterie called the "Arcadians," which united "the nobility and the artists in a spiritual fraternity, not only the most illustrious artists and aristocrats of Italy, but further included four Popes and members of foreign royalty."

The "Arcadians" held weekly meetings at the palace of Cardinal Ottoboni, where poetic and musical improvisations were given. It was for the concerts in the Ottoboni home that Handel composed his two Roman oratorios, *The Resurrection* and *The Triumph of Time and Truth,* which approximate operas and the second of which was to undergo several transformations during his career. In the Ottoboni palace later took place that celebrated contest between Handel and the incomparable Domenico Scarlatti, which was adjudged a draw.

The heart-warming friendship between the two masters was to endure for years. It is by no means out of the question that in the un-operatic atmosphere of Rome Handel, nevertheless, began to compose the first of his Italian operas, *Roderigo,* which was heard for the first time only when he returned to Florence in the autumn of 1707.

* * *

Handel was not to leave Italy till some time during the late spring of 1710, yet there are many blanks in his Italian travels, which it is impossible to fill out. He worked as industriously as ever—composed, played, absorbed myriad impressions. In Florence *Roderigo* had a success which it was claimed by some had been achieved partly through the favor of the Grand Duke and the love of a prima donna, Vittoria Tarquini. Possibly it was furthered by the latter but certainly not caused by it. Handel's life is conspicuously free from conventional "love interest"; and perhaps the most celebrated story of his dealings with women is the one which tells of his raging threat to throw the soprano, Francesca Cuzzoni, out of a window if she did not sing exactly as he wanted what he had written for her. Certainly the middle-aged Tarquini never attracted him physically.

Encouraged by his Florentine luck Handel was moved to try his fortunes in Venice, where opera houses had sprung up everywhere and at one time numbered fifteen. Seven were playing on one and the same evening during Carnival time and there were musical diversions or solemnities of one sort or another in churches and in those women's conservatories called "hospitals." Venice was then the musical capital of Italy, somewhat as Milan was to become at a later date. Handel does not appear to have contributed to the operatic life of the city at this time but his chance was to come before long. Yet he did make one encounter in Venice which was to have consequences—he met Ernest Augustus, Prince of Hanover, and the Duke of Manchester, English Ambassador Extraordinary. He went back to Rome (where an unsuccessful attempt was made to convert him to Catholicism); yet he loved the city and regretfully tore himself away from it to make a jaunt to Naples, which contributed importantly to his artistic sensibilities. As he had done elsewhere in Italy he haunted the picture galleries and nourished his enthusiasm for paintings. He assimilated the Spanish and French musical styles which "fought for honors in this city"; saw much of Alessandro Scarlatti, interested himself in the folk music of the place, noted down the melodies of the Calabrian Pifferari, met the Venetian Cardinal Grimani, composed for the Neapolitan "Arcadians" the *serenata, Acis and Galatea.* Grimani, whose family owned the theater of San Giovanni Crisostomo in Venice, supplied him with the libretto of an opera, *Agrippina,* which Handel probably began to compose on the spot. Its performance in Venice was as good as assured and from Naples he returned to Rome, making another useful friend in the Bishop Agostino Steffani, who was charged with secret missions by different German princes and held at the same time the post of Kapellmeister at the Court of Hanover.

Agrippina was produced in Venice, 1709-10. Its reception exceeded anything the composer had known till then. The chronicles tell of cries of "Viva il caro Sassone," also of "extravagances impossible to record." Obviously his travels in the peninsula had superbly enriched his creative powers and the Venetians found the new work "the most melodious of Handel's Italian operas." Nor was its popularity confined to Venice. He seems to have had some idea of going to Paris, became familiar with the French language, used it in his correspondence and Romain Rolland describes his style as "always very correct and having the fine courtesy of the Court of Louis XIV."

But Handel did not go to France. Instead, he returned to Germany and went to Hanover. Prince Ernest had, in Venice, been completely captivated by *Agrippina* and repeated an invitation he had made once before. The worthy Steffani invited the "dear Saxon" to succeed him as Kapellmeister at the Hanoverian Court. Wisely, "the dear Saxon" accepted. How differently things might have turned out had he not been in Venice at just that providential moment! So Handel, as Chrysander said, "walked in the steps of Steffani; but his feet were larger."

His stay in Hanover in 1710 was brief. Hardly had he prepared to take up his duties than proposals were made to him from England. He asked leave of absence and received it; accepted an invitation from the Elector Johann Wilhelm to visit his court at Düsseldorf; and then, by way of Holland, traveled to London, which he reached late in 1710, unable to speak a word of English. Before he had gone back to the Hanoverian Court he had written an opera, produced it amid prodigious enthusiasm and taken the first steps toward becoming a sovereign British institution.

* * *

He could not have timed his coming better. Purcell's death sixteen years earlier had given what was something like a death blow to English music; and what now passed for native compositions amounted to pitiable odds and ends. Rolland ridicules the claim of some unthinking people that Handel "killed English music since there was nothing left to kill." A renewal of the Puritanical opposition which poisoned the English stage contributed to the confusion and discouragement of British artists, and the worst of such attacks as the notorious Jeremy Collier had made on the "profaneness and immorality" of the theater lay in the fact that, as such things often do, they expressed the deep feelings of the nation. In consequence of a universal hypocrisy foreign elements came to fill the vacuum created. Some bad Italian librettos were set to wretched music and served up with momentary success. Other "entertainments" of the sort mingled Italian and English words and were duly satirized by the jealous and priggish Joseph Addison, nettled by the failure of his own piece, *Rosamund,* to which one Thomas Clayton had composed atrocious music.

Handel came into contact with one Aaron Hill, who managed the Queen's Theatre in the Haymarket, and received from him an opera text, *Rinaldo,* which an Italian, Giacomo Rossi, had adapted from Tasso's *Jerusalem Delivered.* The new arrival rose magnificently to his opportunity. The music was completed in just two weeks and performed on February 24, 1711. And luck aided Handel by supplying him with some extraordinary singers, all of them new to England— Giuseppe Boschi, a young and astounding bass, and the sensational castrato, Nicolini, who took London by storm. The tale of *Rinaldo* was that of the Venetian *Agrippina* all over again! In one evening the British capital was subjugated, for all the bile and venom Addison and Steele could discharge into the columns of *The Spectator* and *The Tatler.* The melodies of the opera spread like wildfire and seem to have appealed to the lower classes as well as to the aristocracy. To this day some of them have preserved their vitality. The noble air, "Lascia ch'io pianga," in sarabande rhythm, is a fairly familiar item on recital programs; and the Crusaders' March, a fine, swinging tune, was adapted to the words "Let us take the road" by Dr. Pepusch when he assembled out of countless folksongs and dances John Gay's deathless

Beggar's Opera—in 1728 a thorn in Handel's side but still, after more than two centuries, a classic with an iron constitution.

*   *   *

Roughly speaking, Handel composed forty-four operas from *Almira,* in 1705, at Hamburg to *Deidamia,* 1741, in London. It is obviously impossible to consider even a small fraction of them here and we shall have to content ourselves with little more than the names and dates of only a few. All the same, it may be well to pause here momentarily to ask ourselves what, in the first place, a Handel opera really is like. For unless we are specialists, not to say antiquarians, we have little means of definitely knowing. The lyric drama of that period cannot be judged by the works of the nineteenth and twentieth centuries nor by the handful of masterpieces of Gluck and Mozart. Its problems, its musical and dramatic aspects are basically different. A movement, which had its rise in Germany after the First World War and which continued on and off for several years (even spreading intermittently to other countries, including the United States) demonstrated that these baroque entertainments are essentially museum pieces, prizable as certain of their elements may be. To us, who have been nurtured on the theater works of Mozart, of the composers of the school of dramatic and pictorial "grand opera," of the opera buffa and the opéra comique, the *drame lyrique* of Gounod and Bizet, the works of Verdi, the music dramas of Wagner and his assorted successors of various nationalities—to us the operatic specimens of Handel seem infinitely alien and remote in their premises and calculated stylizations. The nearest we can approach them today is through such surviving examples of the old *opera seria* as Mozart's *Idomeneo* or Gluck's *Alceste.* And even those do not supply genuine parallels.

To the average person reared on the lyric drama as known to two or three generations preceding ours, the long-established description of a Handelian opera as a "concert in costume" may suffice at a pinch. But in a larger sense it begs the question, for Handel's forty odd operas are both more than this and less. We should find their librettos so cut to a pattern that the most old-fashioned "books" of the nineteenth century would strike us, by comparison, as dramatically bold, even involved. Handelian operas have no trace of psychological subtlety or elementary "conflict." What theatrical "action" there is passes before

43

us with something like lightning speed. Incidents which need to be communicated to the spectator are, in the main, recounted in recitative. What we understand as "incident" is subordinate to phases of emotional expression; and in ensemble pieces joy, rage, sadness, a broad scale of elemental feelings are recognizably embodied in musical moods and tempos unmistakable in their lyrical or dramatic communications of "affetti" ("emotions"). There is little, if indeed any, of what a later esthetic was to call "the art of transition" and it was nothing unusual for a fiery or combative *presto* to precede (or follow) a tender *largo* or *andante,* and other formalistic clichés. The accompaniment, the orchestra, indeed the "action" and the stage picture are not much more than incidental backgrounds and frames.

The true center of gravity of a Handel opera lies in the performance of the singers and their command of declamation, florid utterance, sustained song and artifices at that epoch accepted as supremely expressive. Only in grasping these facts can we put ourselves in the frame of mind needed to understand the essential principles of these baroque masterpieces and to appreciate what—apart from their sheer melodic beauties—lifts them to a higher level than curios lacking any further validity, difficult as it may be for many of us to force our imagination and our feelings into such a mold.

*   *   *

Having conquered England at a blow and become the idol not only of high society but of the common people as well, Handel recalled in the spring of 1711 that he was still Kapellmeister of Hanover. In London he had made enemies as well as friends and one of the most implacable of his foes was the great but churlish Addison. His admirers, on the other hand, included a child named Mary Granville, later Mrs. Delany, one of his staunchest friends; the Duke of Burlington, through whom he had entrée to Burlington House; and the famous eccentric, Thomas Britton, a coal dealer by day but who, on certain evenings, sponsored memorable concerts in a specially outfitted loft above his coal shop, which drew prominent London musicians and cultured aristocrats to the Clerkenwell "garret," where Handel frequently appeared as harpsichord and even organ virtuoso.

Back in Hanover June, 1711, he renewed his contacts with Bishop Steffani, composed organ concertos and other chamber music, as well as a quantity of songs to German texts by the Hamburg Senator, Brockes. He would have liked to produce *Rinaldo* but the Hanover Opera was closed. Yet London had entered his blood and nothing would content him but his speedy return, the more so because his English admirers demanded him. He obtained leave "on condition that he return to Hanover after a reasonable time"; and by November, 1712, he arrived in England to supervise preparations for a pastoral, *Il Pastor Fido,* a work hastily thrown together and variously improved more than twenty years later. This time Handel did not repeat his *Rinaldo* sensation and the piece had only half a dozen hearings. To make matters worse, a certain MacSwiney, who succeeded Aaron Hill at the Queen's Theatre, absconded, leaving nothing but unpaid bills and enraged singers. At this stage there enters the picture a Swiss adventurer, by name Heidegger, a man of unbelievable conceit and homeliness, who was, however, to play an important rôle in Handel's future. To recoup the failure of *Il Pastor Fido* the composer turned out in less than three weeks a "tragic opera" in five acts, *Teseo,* with a libretto by Nicolo Francesco Haym, and dedicated tactfully to the Earl of Burlington. *Teseo* came near duplicating the fortunes of *Rinaldo;* and if, as Rolland says, it was "full of haste," it was also "full of genius." If anything could have intrenched the composer still more firmly in London it was this opera. He went for a while to live at Burlington House at the Duke's invitation; met Pope, Gay, Arbuthnot, struck up friendships with this and that musician at the Queen's Arms Tavern in St. Paul's Churchyard and was never so happy as when he sat with some musical crony, a mug of beer at hand and a harpsichord nearby. The first work he composed in the ideal peace of Burlington House was a Birthday Ode for Queen Anne, whom he had met on his first London visit. The Ode was produced at St. James's on February 6, 1713, and was the first English he had set to music. All his life Handel's English remained bad, sometimes even grotesque, and the incorrect accenting in his compositions repeatedly betrays his deficiencies in our tongue. Of such faults the Birthday Ode has its full share, in spite of which the Queen was so delighted with the work that she settled on the composer an annual pension of two hundred pounds. He found it politic to write music for patriotic purposes, and instantly complied with the sovereign's command to supply a *Te Deum* and a *Jubilate* to celebrate the Peace of Utrecht, both compositions given at a solemn service at St. Paul's before the assembled Members of Parliament.

*   *   *

Queen Anne died on August 1, 1714, and for a time the skies over Handel threatened to cloud; for on the very day of her passing the Elector of Hanover was proclaimed by the Secret Council King of England. He arrived in London on September 20 and was crowned George I at Westminster a month later. Here was a pretty kettle of fish! His former master to whose service he had most certainly not returned "in a reasonable time" suddenly seated on the English throne —and not even a new *Te Deum* prepared against his coming to the land which Handel now regarded as home!

Handelian luck got him out of what might have been a serious predicament. He must have trusted to his destiny in the first place to help him out of an obviously awkward situation and, being tactful, he made no open move to aggravate it. George I was and remained intensely German, brought to England with him "a compact body of Germans"—chamberlains, secretaries, even his pair of elderly mistresses, the Baroness Kielmansegge and Madame Schulenburg; and all manner of comforts and consolations he could not find in his new island kingdom. He made no effort to shed his German love of music, wherefore as Rolland points out, "he could not punish Handel without punishing himself." And after he heard Handel's fascinating new opera, *Amadigi,* in May, 1715, he lost all idea (if, indeed, he ever harbored any) of disciplining his former servant. He appointed Handel music master to the little princesses and when, in 1716, the monarch had to go to Hanover the composer accompanied him on the trip, took occasion to study musical developments in Germany and even wrote a Passion on a text by Heinrich Brockes.

Here is the point to consider for a moment the tale of the *Water Music,* one of the most venerable Handelian anecdotes. The story runs somewhat as follows: Lord Burlington and Baron Kielmansegge, the Master of the King's Horse, in order to reconcile sovereign and musician, in 1715 persuaded the latter to write a set of light pieces to be played on a boat close to the royal barge at a water party on the Thames. The King liked the music sufficiently to inquire who composed it and, being told, summoned Handel, promised to let bygones be bygones and received him back into favor. Unfortunately for romance, later documents have shown that the *Water Music* was not played till 1717 and then under wholly different conditions. But the legend has become so ingrained in British musical tradition that, as Newman Flower wrote, "it is precisely what ought to have happened." At all events, the *Water Music* is an adorable suite, definitely English in character—like much else in Handel's music—and to this day an ornament of concert programs in one or another arrangement.

King George, far from remembering past annoyances, saw to it that Handel's yearly pension from Queen Anne should be increased to six hundred pounds, so that even without further earnings his financial state was tolerably secure. His good fortunes were enhanced by the musical enthusiasms of the King, who could not hear enough of *Rinaldo* and *Amadigi* (to the spectacular features of which live birds, which sometimes misbehaved, and a fountain of real water, heightened the attractions of sumptuous settings). He went to them, often incognito, several times a week sharing his private box with his bevy of lady friends, new and old; or he would vary his visits to the opera with attendance at plays or concerts, so that his chances to admire the works of Handel, in one form or another, were rarely lacking. Many found that the monarch's habit of parading his amours before London audiences added to the piquancy of a Handelian score!

By the side of the famed artificial soprano, Nicolini, sang the brilliant Anastasia Robinson, who had been a soprano but whose voice, after a siege of illness, suddenly dropped to contralto. Mrs. Robinson was particularly noted for the fact that her morals were at all times spotless. Mrs. Delany was to describe her as "of middling stature, not handsome but of a pleasing modest countenance, with large blue eyes. . . . Her manner and address were very engaging, and her behavior on all occasions that of a gentlewoman." When her husband, Lord Peterborough, died, she burned the diaries he had kept, wherein he had noted his various infidelities and other secrets not meant for the scrutiny of his wife.

Handel's star was steadily rising and his fame was not to be transcended till a number of years later and then only by virtue of his own genius and after many fluctuations of fortune. But when the King returned to London from his trip to Germany opera fell upon bad days. Musical and theatrical life flourished, indeed, yet suddenly farces and other diversions, imported from France, captured the mood of the town and delighted the monarch and his ladies. Now nobody felt like putting up money on opera, since inexpensive vulgarity was a safer bet. At just about this period Handel and James Brydges, Duke of Chandos, former Paymaster-General of the Army during the Marlborough wars, were brought into contact. The erstwhile Earl of Carnarvon had accumulated his wealth by heaven knows what sharp practices, and inherited an estate at Cannons, near Edgware, where he had erected a luxurious palace, including a chapel, a theater, and other musical appurtenances inseparable from such an establishment. The Prince of Wales was a frequent visitor at Cannons, braving even the swarming footpads of Edgware Road. The Duke of Chandos seems to have been in a position to buy anything which struck his fancy and there is a story that on one occasion, he or his son (the accounts differ) coming across a man unmercifully thrashing his well-favored wife, rescued the lady by buying her on the spot. He, therefore, had no particular trouble securing Handel as master of his music in place of his former employee, the German Dr. Pepusch. Some ten years later Dr. Pepusch had his revenge by compiling the score of the *Beggar's Opera* which was to become such a grievous obstacle in Handel's path.

But until 1720 Handel was in the service of the Duke of Chandos, even if he spent much of his time in London, busily attending to the musical instruction of the daughters of Caroline, Princess of Wales, and writing numerous "Lessons" and clavier suites for his royal pupils. Which brings us to another celebrated Handelian fiction, *The Harmonious Blacksmith*. The legend is quite as diversified and even more far-fetched than the one about the *Water Music*. For well over a century the world has been fed the story of the blacksmith and his forge near Whitchurch, close to Edgware. In the house of this blacksmith Handel is supposed to have taken refuge from a thunderstorm, the blacksmith meantime continuing his hammering. When the storm was over the composer went forth and, still haunted by the rhythm of the pounding, set down the melody and then proceeded to write variations on it. This "Air and Variations" form part of Handel's Fifth Suite of clavecin pieces, but it was not till 1820 that some imaginative publisher, taking his cue from an apprentice who continually whistled Handel's tune, invented the fanciful title; and not till 1835 that the London *Times* published an anonymous letter retailing the legend of the black-

48

smith and his forge. We have no place here to recount the complex ramifications of the amiable myth which culminated in the auctioning off of an old anvil—supposedly the very one which the composer heard struck! But the publisher had the last word and to the end of time the Fifth Suite will assuredly remain *The Harmonious Blacksmith.*

Far more important in the development of Handel's style are the *Chandos Anthems* (or Psalms), composed during the years from 1717 to 1720 while the master, at Cannons, was steadily rising. They fill three volumes of the Complete Handel edition and "stand in relationship to Handel's oratorios in the same position as his Italian cantatas stand to his operas. In these religious cantatas, written for the Duke's chapel, Handel gives the first place to the chorus. . . . There is already in them the spirit and the style of *Israel in Egypt,* the great monumental lines, the popular feeling. It was only a step from this to the colossal Biblical dramas." (Rolland) And Handel took this first step with *Esther,* called in its first form *Haman and Mordecai, a masque.* It was staged on August 29, 1720. Almost simultaneously he wrote the exquisite pastoral tragedy, *Acis and Galatea,* a Sicilian legend he had already treated during his Neapolitan days but which, in its later shape took on an unsurpassable element of classical finish.

* * *

Yet there were breakers ahead! Whether or not he could discern them from afar it is probably unlikely that the prospect of conflict would have troubled overmuch a nature as powerful and combative as Handel's. Indeed, difficulties were what this prodigious vitality and ever renewing creative inspiration best throve upon. As so often happens in lands where opera is fundamentally an exotic, people again wanted opera. It was a logical time to end the Cannons interlude. The psychology of the moment, to which Handel was sensitive, came just when company-promoting took on almost the aspect of a hobby. There was money a-plenty and the South Sea Bubble, which was indeed swelling, had not yet burst. So Lord Burlington and other peers raised capital for a new season of Italian opera, appointed Handel director-in-chief, made the ugly but efficient Heidegger stage manager, rounded up librettists and sent Handel to the Continent to engage singers for what was to be known as "The Royal Academy of Music"—an English duplication of the official name of the Paris Opéra. And the *Weekly*

Journal soon announced that "Mr. Handel, a famous Master of Musick, is gone beyond the sea, by order of His Majesty, to collect a company of the choicest singers for the Opera in the Haymarket."

"Mr. Handel" visited Hanover, Düsseldorf, Dresden and Halle, where he went to his birthplace "Am Schlamm," saw his old mother, who was going blind, and her aging spinster sister. And at this point occurred one of the most poignant incidents of musical history—that meeting of Handel and Bach, thwarted by an inscrutable destiny. Bach learned that his contemporary was in Halle, went there on foot from Cöthen to seek him out and—missed him by a day! Even Bach's subsequent dispatch of his son, Wilhelm Friedemann, to invite Handel to visit him misfired and the two were destined forever to remain personal strangers.

Handel secured some extraordinary singers in Dresden, where the Italian opera was blooming. In addition to Boschi, the bass, who had sung in *Rinaldo,* he bagged the great Signora Durastanti and the castrato Senesino, who until the subsequent coming of the mighty Farinelli, was perhaps the artificial soprano whom London most worshiped at a time when castrati were completely the rage. Senesino played incredible havoc with the hearts of deluded women. Handel, in addition to the countless duties of a music-director had also operas to compose, and in due season he was somehow turning out three a year. Nicola Francesco Haym supplied him with a libretto adapted from Tacitus, *Radamisto,* and this work, produced on April 27, 1720, was a triumph such as even Handel had never experienced. It ran till the season ended late in June; "crowds flocked to *Radamisto* like a modern mob to a notorious prize-fight." (Newman Flower)

The first season of the Royal Academy finished in a flourish, aided by the circumstance that the metropolis was in the throes of an orgy of financial speculation. We can read of incredible schemes and "bubbles" with the help of which money was to be lured from private pocket-books. Newman Flower tells of "one for trading in hair, another for the universal supply of funerals in Great Britain, one for a wheel of perpetual motion, one 'for carrying on an undertaking of great advantage, but nobody to know what it is.'" Still another project contemplated "breeding silkworms in Chelsea Park." By the time things were ready for the opening of the Academy's second season Lord Burlington imported from Rome the composer Giovanni Battista Bononcini, possibly not dreaming that he was introducing a dangerous rival to Handel. In his little way Bononcini had talent and charm, as well as a conceit out of all proportion to his pleasant gifts. An opera of his was produced at the Academy with Senesino in the cast and enjoyed a good run, while a composite work, called *Muzio Scevola,* with one act by Handel, another by Bononcini and a third by a mediocrity, Filippo Mattei, followed. The results of the increasingly complicated situation were to precipitate a contest that split London's high society into factions. The cynical John Byrom compressed it into an epigram, part of which has entered the English language:

> *Some say, compared to Bononcini,*
> *That Mynherr Handel's but a ninny;*
> *Others aver that he to Handel*
> *Is scarcely fit to hold a candle.*
> *Strange all this difference should be*
> *'Twixt Tweedledum and Tweedledee.*

Be all of which as it may, Handel presently had the mortification of seeing his own new *Floridante* fail while Bononcini's pretty *Griselda* packed the theater like nothing since *Radamisto!*

But Handel resembled the mythical Antaeus, who whenever he fell renewed his own powers by contact with Mother Earth. Before long he was turning out masterpieces in bewildering continuity. In 1723 he composed the superb *Ottone,* in 1724 *Tamerlano* and *Giulio Cesare* and the following season the sumptuous *Rodelinda;* in 1726 *Scipione,* and *Alessandro,* in 1727 *Admeto* and *Riccardo I,* in 1728 *Siroe* and *Tolomeo.* This period, incidentally, brings us to those excesses of singer worship and rivalry which stirred the public to white heat and turned the opera house into something between a wild prize fight and a three ring circus. Then, in 1722-23, the species *prima donna* suddenly invaded the scene, in the person of Francesca Cuzzoni, who was squat and ungainly, but had an astounding voice and an art of song that made high society overlook her bad temper and her worse style in dress. Handel had occasion to experience her tantrums at the rehearsals of *Ottone,* when she refused to sing an aria as the composer wanted it; whereupon he had recourse to real "Taming of the Shrew" tactics, seized her bodily and threatened to throw her out of the window, at the same time shouting to her in French: "Oh, Madame, I know full well that you are a real she-devil; but I intend to teach you that I am Beelzebub, the Chief of Devils!" Whereupon the humbled Cuzzoni sang her "Falsa imagine" exactly as Handel wanted. Possibly the incident did not end Handel's difficulties with her but in her relations with him she became more tractable and if she could not subdue the insensitive master she did subdue her audiences. "Damme, she has a nest of nightingales in her belly!" yelled one of the gallery gods on a certain occasion and the plebeian indelicacy seems to have won the approval of the boxes. Soon Anastasia Robinson, revolted by the turmoil over Cuzzoni, retired from stage life and married the Earl of Peterborough.

Cuzzoni, however, was only one obstacle of her kind. Soon afterwards the management, on the lookout for another sensation, secured the soprano's most hated Continental rival, Faustina Bordoni, who was to become the wife of the composer Hasse. Handel brought the pair on the stage together in his opera *Alessandro*. Lady Pembroke was "protectress" of Cuzzoni, Lady Burlington of Faustina. Finally, in May, 1727, things culminated when the two jealous creatures came to blows during a performance of Bononcini's *Astyanax,* tore each other's hair and pummeled one another in full view of the spectators, who took sides and shrieked with delight as the coiffures of the combatants were ruined and faces scratched. The "fighting cats," as the pair were called, later were made the subject of Colley Cibber's farce, *The Rival Queens.*

In time Cuzzoni despite her lack of taste in dressing was to set fashions; and a brown and silver attire in which she appeared in *Rodelinda* so captivated the ladies that, with modish variations, it was to be the rage for years. The various castrati (notably the great Senesino) were in many ways as capricious and difficult to manage as the prima donnas. Senesino, having irritated the Earl of Peterborough by reason of some reflection on Anastasia Robinson, was flogged by her husband. The scandal enchanted the drawing rooms and Society was even more delighted when the singer, appearing in *Giulio Cesare,* was frightened out of his wits and burst into tears because a piece of scenery fell at his feet at the very moment when, as Julius Caesar, he had to sing words to the effect that "Caesar knows no fear!"

In time came the greatest castrato of them all, the incredible Farinelli, who earned so much in London that when he retired to Italy he built himself a palace there which he sarcastically named "English Folly." People used to shout at the Opera that there was only "One God and one Farinelli!" And describing a London birthday party where this divinity was among the guests, the Duchess of Portland wrote: "There were about forty gentlemen that had an entertainment, and Farinelli wore a magnificent suit of clothes, and charmed the company with his voice as Orpheus did (and so kept them from drinking)." On the other hand when this god was once so imprudent as to walk uninvited into a party at the Duke of Modena's in St. James's Street, the infuriated host showed him the door with the words: "Get out, fellow! None but gentlemen come here!"

All these scandals, spectacular squabbles and silly exhibitions did not, in the long run, enhance the credit of the Academy. Handel, who had been naturalized on February 13, 1726 and at the same time been appointed Composer to the Court and to the Chapel Royal, was together with the rest of London, shocked in the early summer of 1727, to learn of the death of George I on a trip to Germany. On October 11 of the same year George II was crowned and, though less favorably disposed to the composer than his father, continued the pensions Handel held from the late sovereign and from Queen Anne and contributed to them another large sum for music lessons to the young princesses. Handel, for his part, wrote for the new King four Coronation Anthems which added to his glory. The Academy, after losing an appalling amount of money, presently received its death blow in the production at the theater in Lincoln's Inn Fields of *The Beggar's Opera*, by the clever satirist, John Gay, with music compiled by Dr. Pepusch, Handel's predecessor in the employ of the Duke of Chandos. This "ballad opera," that "made Gay rich and Rich, the manager, gay," which still leads a lusty existence, and has been at various times a landmark in English and American theatrical history, proved an earthy and bawdy entertainment, against the barbed shafts of whose ridicule the artifices of Italian opera could not prevail for long.

Yet Handel remained incorrigible. Once again he entered into partnership with Heidegger, planned another opera season, secured Senesino again and went abroad to engage other singers. On that occasion he traveled again to Italy, went to Hamburg and made a last visit to his aged mother in Halle. She was now paralyzed, and shortly afterwards she died. The new London opera season got off to a bad start, one failure succeeding another. Politics aggravated the situation, the more so as George II and the Prince of Wales were at odds and the supporters of the latter determined to set up a rival opera company to ruin Handel.

But the story of Handel's pertinacious efforts to float new operatic enterprises for almost another ten years is too long, involved and too honeycombed with intrigue, contending influences and low tactics of one sort or another to be examined here. The composer's Hanoverian origin stirred many parties against him. Moreover, he was a self-willed, imperious person, who, like Richard Wagner more than a century later, had the gift of stimulating antagonism. He was, wrote W. McNaught, "a pervading presence, a busybody forever intruding upon public affairs. He had taken to ordering the amusements of the town in his own interests; and he belonged to the wrong party." One almost fancies oneself confronted with a chapter from the life of the creator of *Die Meistersinger!*

Yet what a treasury of glorious music Handel was pouring out with incalculable lavishness during these agitated years! Let us mention in passing a few of the new operas as they came and went: *Ezio, Orlando, Il Pastor Fido, Ariodante, Alcina, Arminio, Berenice, Faramondo, Serse.* The last-named calls for a word by itself. *Xerxes* has nothing to do with the Persian ruler of antiquity. It is a comic opera, Handel's first and only one, which stands up extraordinarily well under modern stylized conditions of revival, apart from which it contains possibly one of the most universally beloved melodies that Handel ever wrote. This melody, heard at the very opening of the piece, appears in the score as a *larghetto* to the words "Ombra mai fu," a song of gratitude to a plane tree for its beneficent shade. But for generations it has been slowed from the pace originally prescribed to a solemn, swelling hymn known to uncounted millions as Handel's *Largo.* And far more know it as a churchly canticle than its lightly moving operatic context. Almost every one of this mass of operas, furthermore, is charged with grand arias of all the emotional varieties common to its epoch—gems enshrined in practically every one of the great anthologies of eighteenth-century song.

It was not till 1741 that Handel concluded his period of operatic creativity with *Deidamia,* written to a libretto by Paolo Rolli. London's taste for opera had, during more than a decade, shown continued fluctuation. But in 1731 a new situation brought about an event that was to provoke a development of capital importance for Handel's future. The children of the Chapel Royal presented in a private performance his masque, *Esther,* on the composer's birthday. The success of the performance was such that it resulted in others, one of which was given without Handel's consent by one of his rivals. The master was equal to the occasion. He added some numbers to the score and gave half a dozen representations at the King's Theatre; but as a Biblical subject could not be acted on the stage, the masque was given in concert form in the presence of the royal family and of High Society. The Handelian oratorio had more or less come into being!

*　　*　　*

In the summer of 1733 Handel went to Oxford. The University authorities had offered him a degree of Doctor of Music. Oxford is said to have known little of his music at that time. Yet his arrival there might, according to Newman Flower, "have been the triumphant entry of a king. The town was overcrowded; even accommodations at the hostels ran out and people slept in the streets." The composer brought with him a new oratorio, *Athalia,* composed to a text which Samuel Humphreys had adapted from Racine. Hugo Leichtentritt claims that the rector, Dr. Holmes, aimed to bring about a rapprochement between the Hanoverians and the Jacobites. A whole week of Handelian works was offered, with hearings of *Esther, Deborah, Athalia,* the Utrecht *Te Deum, Acis and Galatea* and other creations. In the end the master did *not* receive the honorary degree. Some have believed that he turned it down when he was told it would cost one hundred pounds. Like Haydn half a century after, he found the academic honors of Oxford expensive; and later a story gained currency that Handel had shouted in his particular brand of English: "Vat de dyfil I trow away my money for what de Blockhead wish; I no vant!"

Had it been practical he might have brought a whole opera production to Oxford. In place of such a luxury he compromised on oratorios, the more so because the dividing line between such entertainment and the opera of the period was not so sharply drawn as it was eventually to become. The chief differences between the two forms lay in the preponderance of choruses, such as, in opera, were regarded as hardly more than side issues.

Meanwhile, he seemed unable to resist the lure of the theater. Again and again he returned to Italian opera. He continued his earlier partnership with Heidegger; he made trips to Italy and elsewhere and secured new singers (the castrato, Carestini, the prima donna, Strada). His enemies increased in number and power and resorted to the basest tactics imaginable to discredit and injure him. The so-called Opera of the Nobility opened at a playhouse in Lincoln's Inn Fields, lured his singers away from him by fair means or foul, and by securing the great Farinelli obtained a trump card. Handel (who in time parted company with Heidegger) would burn his fingers the moment his fortunes seemed on the upgrade. Even the weather was against him, what with the Thames freezing over in one of the years that he obstinately returned to opera, and cutting down his audiences. He lost money ruinously, he went into bankruptcy, he wore himself out to such a degree that he had a mental and physical breakdown and had to go to the Continent, to Aix-la-Chapelle, for a cure. His amazing resilience of spirit and body helped him back to health and actually encouraged him to make another attempt at an operatic season with his egregious associate, Heidegger, at the King's Theatre early in 1738, for which he composed his comedy, *Serse*.

A few months earlier his royal friend, Queen Caroline, had died and Handel gave voice to his genuine grief in the great Funeral Anthem, *The Ways of Zion Do Mourn*. And despite his misfortunes he busied himself with a charitable enterprise, the promotion of a Society for the Support of Decayed Musicians, which enlisted his active sympathies for the rest of his life. Not even benefactions of this sort could mollify the legions of his implacable enemies. His aristocratic foes, to hasten his complete downfall, actually hired hoodlums to tear down his posters and precipitate noisy disturbances whenever they thought trouble-making could in some way or other harm him. Yet a few friends stood unshakably by his side, none more faithfully than the loyal Mrs. Delany.

Just when his creditors had seized him and threatened him with imprisonment, the news of his tribulations gave rise to a popular movement of sympathy. In 1735 he had delighted the English public by his *Alexander's Feast,* composed on Dryden's "Ode to St. Cecilia," produced triumphantly at the Covent Garden Theatre. It had been written in twenty days. As the years passed, Handel's composing activity seemed incredibly accelerated. In the freezing winter of 1739 he wrote, "to keep himself warm" (as Rolland says) the "little" Cecilia cantata in a week, the version of Milton's poem (under the title "L'Allegro, Il Penseroso ed Il Moderato") in just under a fortnight, and the glorious *Concerti Grossi, Opus 6,* in a month distracted by his last operatic cares! Incidentally, Handel had received about this time a testimonial of public admiration in the form of a marble statue by the sculptor, Roubiliac, which a manager of musical entertainments named Tyers had caused to be erected in Vauxhall Gardens, a meeting place of London Society, where Handel's works made up the best liked musical features.

Still, by the spring of 1741, Handel in a moment of profoundest disheartenment prepared to throw up the sponge and leave for good and all his home for the past thirty years. At long last he was fed up on the struggle and announced one last concert for April 8, 1741. And then, when the darkness before dawn seemed blackest, he sat down to create his masterpiece, the most universally beloved choral work ever composed!

That summer Charles Jennens gave Handel a compilation of Scriptural texts which he called "Messiah." Jennens was a literary amateur, born at Gopsall Hall, Leicestershire and educated at Balliol College, Oxford. Rich and bizarre, he was vastly conceited and especially proud of the manner in which he had assembled the various Biblical texts used in this case. Handel had been associated with him before —in the oratorio, *Saul* (1739), and in *L'Allegro ed Il Penseroso* a year later, as a supplement to which he had added some poor verses of his own to the lines of Milton and called the product *Il Moderato.* Robert Manson Myers thinks it "extraordinary that Handel turned to this eccentric millionaire for his libretto of *Messiah.*" Jennens was of another mind and even later wrote to an acquaintance: "I shall show you a collection I gave Handel, called 'Messiah' which I value highly; he has made a fine entertainment of it, though not near so good as he might and ought to have done. . . . There are some passages far unworthy of Handel, but even more unworthy of 'Messiah' "; and deploring Handel's "maggots" he added that he had "with greatest difficulty made him correct some of the grossest faults in the composition." Doubtless Handel, had he so chosen, could have picked his texts himself; he compiled the book of *Israel in Egypt* unaided in

1738 and when, a good deal earlier, the Bishop of London wanted to help him with the words for the "Coronation Anthems" he retorted: "I have read my Bible very well, and I shall choose for myself!" Mr. Myers, in his encyclopedic study of *Messiah* feels certain that Handel must have controlled the choice of passages selected.

Like Bach, Hadyn, Mozart, Schubert and other supreme musicians, Handel could create with a rapidity which ignominiously shames composers of our supposedly "speedy" age. Even bearing that fact in mind, the composition of *Messiah* between Saturday, August 22, 1741, and Monday, September 14, following remains one of the miracles of music. Shut up in a little room on the first floor of his home on Lower Brook Street, Hanover Square, none can say exactly what went on. Handel is supposed to have uttered afterwards the words of St. Paul: "Whether I was in my body or out of my body as I wrote it I know not." Nobody seems to have dared intrude upon this mystic concentration. Food was left near him but usually found untouched when the servant came to remove it. He sat at his desk like a stone figure and stared into space. Sometimes his man stood in awe to see his master's tears drop on the music paper and mingle with the ink. "When he was composing 'He was despised' a visitor is reported to have found the trembling composer sobbing with intense emotion." And after the *Hallelujah Chorus* he uttered those historic words: "I did think I did see all Heaven before me, and the great God Himself!" The autograph score, with its blots, its angry erasures and general untidiness, offers fierce evidence of his tumultuous feelings and flaming ecstasies. Possibly between April and late August of 1741 he was shut up in his four walls planning the work, for we have no clear idea just what he did during this period. Sketches and fragments do not clear up what mystery there may be, for the composer destroyed all but some fugitive scraps.

Handel appears to have "been reluctant to submit such music to the capricious taste of aristocratic London." So when William Cavendish, Lord Lieutenant of Ireland, invited him to visit Dublin and permit the public of "that generous and polite Nation" to hear his oratorios Handel assented at once, the more so because it was a question of assisting three benevolent institutions of Ireland (one of them the Charitable Musical Society for the Relief of Imprisoned Debtors). With his usual impulsiveness he even agreed to present "some special oratorio" solely for the benefit of the unfortunates jailed for debt. And he was happy to shake the dust of London from his feet for a while. Before starting on his Irish journey, incidentally, he composed in a fortnight part of another oratorio, *Samson,* based on Milton's "Samson Agonistes" and containing that noble air of lament, "Total Eclipse," which was to affect him so poignantly some years later. For his Dublin productions he had two exceptional women singers—Susannah Maria Cibber (also an illustrious tragic actress) and Signora Avolio, a highly trained Italian. The chorus was recruited from Dublin's St. Patrick's Cathedral and Christchurch.

Messiah did not receive its first hearing till April 13, 1742. Reports emanating from the last rehearsals greatly whetted public appetite and on the morning of April 13 *Faulkner's Journal* ran the following: "This day will be performed Mr. Handell's new Grand Sacred Oratorio, called the Messiah. The doors will be opened at Eleven, and the performance begin at Twelve. The Stewards of the Charitable Musical Society request the favor of the ladies not to come with hoops this day to the Musick Hall in Fishamble Street. The Gentlemen are desired to come without their swords." Mr. Myers relates that "Handel's 'polite' audience comprised Bishops, Deans, Heads of the Colledge, the most eminent People in the Law, as well as the Flower of Ladyes of Distinction and other People of the greatest quality." The audience was transported. In some ways the heroine of the occasion was Mrs. Cibber, who sang the air "He was despised" with such tenderness and pathos that the Reverend Patrick Delany, who had harbored a bitter prejudice against actresses and singers so far forgot himself that he rose and solemnly exclaimed: "Woman, for this be all thy sins forgiven thee!"

It was late in August, 1742, before Handel returned to London. The hostility of the English aristocracy was still strong and continued for some years, although the forceful voice of Alexander Pope had been raised in his favor, little as that poet is said to have known about music. But Pope's acknowledged belief in Handel's "talent" did something toward disarming the composer's enemies. However, he was in no hurry to let London hear *Messiah* in spite of all the great things spoken and written about it. Not till February, 1743, did Handel plunge once more into the eddies of music-making in the metropolis—not, indeed, with operatic schemes as of old but with a plan for a series of subscription concerts at Covent Garden, offering *Samson* as the first attraction.

He took his time before bringing forward *Messiah*. Even before he could advertise it his hypocritical foes in fashionable circles began a campaign against the "profanation" and the "pious" raised loud cries; clergymen in particular were scandalized "at the sacrilege of converting the Life and Passion of Christ into a theatrical entertainment." Even the idea of printing the word *Messiah* on a program led Handel to the expedient of announcing his great work simply as "A Sacred Oratorio." At that, the embattled clerics tried to enjoin the performance "on the ground that Covent Garden Theatre was a place of worldly amusement and that in any case public entertainments during Lent were sacrilegious." However, the "Sacred Oratorio" was at last given its first London hearing on March 23, 1743. The composer conducted, Signora Avolio, Mrs. Cibber, John Beard and Thomas Lowe were the chief soloists. And here let us cite once more Robert Manson Myers' superb study of the masterpiece:

"As the glorious strains of the 'Hallelujah Chorus' burst upon the awed assemblage, thick-witted George II found himself so deeply affected by Handel's music (or so eager to shift his position) that he started to his feet with all the spontaneous verve a sixty-year-old gout-ridden monarch could muster. Instantly his phlegmatic courtiers also rose, and since no Englishman may remain seated while his King is standing, the audience at once followed suit, thus inaugurating a custom which persists to the present day. Actually the King's gesture was more a tribute to Handel's impressive music than an instance of exceptional religious devotion. . . .

"It is a curious indication of public taste that this casual Eighteenth Century 'fashion' has remained for two centuries an inviolable tradition both in England and in America. Even today thousands who can scarcely distinguish F sharp from middle C punctiliously observe a custom established by a stupid Hanoverian king and his worldly court two hundred years ago."

Thanks to bigotry and organized religiosity, however, *Messiah* had only three performances in 1743, none in 1744, two in 1745 and none whatever till four years later. Newman Flower recounts that the master, being complimented on the work by a titled hearer, replied: "My lord, I should be sorry if I only entertained people; I wished to make them better." Yet as late as 1756 a Miss Catherine Talbot, one of Handel's most devoted admirers, could say that "the playhouse is an unfit place for such a solemn performance." However, in the words of Robert Manson Myers, "England's early rejection of *Messiah* may be ascribed as much to personal resentment as to shallow musical taste. . . . Handel flaunted his independence and moved with resolute determination, snapping his fingers· in the face of princely patrons and daring to defy the bluest blood in England. What was to be done with this insufferable German upstart, this mere musician, who despite persistent opposition succeeded in discharging his debts to the uttermost farthing? Chosen leaders of British 'quality' resolved to crush Handel at once. They devised a systematic campaign to boycott his oratorios, and no scheme proved too petty for the gratification of their spite."

* * *

Vain resolve! For Handel, crushed, had a most persistent habit of rising again. If political cabals brought him low, the tides of national politics brought him to the top once more. *Messiah,* to be sure, was not to become an unshakable British (shall we not rather say Anglo-Saxon) monument till after the composer's death; yet Handel was able to make the most, creatively, of the great national emergencies of his last decade. In 1743, as Composer of Music to the Chapel Royal, he wrote a *Te Deum* and an anthem to celebrate the victory of Dettingen, music that conquered the popular heart. To this period belongs the charming secular oratorio, *Semele* (source of the beloved airs "Where'er you walk" and "O Sleep, why dost thou leave me?"), at the first production of which Mrs. Delany found it significant that "there was no disturbance in the playhouse." But the old habit of launching operatic or concert enterprises was upon him once more and again threatened to consume his credit and his substance. Bankruptcy threatened. Other oratorios, *Hercules, Belshazzar,* grand masterpieces both of them, were given in 1745 to dwindling audiences. Handel's health was imperiled. Then came 1745, the Jacobite rising and the landing in Scotland of the Pretender, Charles Edward. There was consternation which culminated in the march of the Highlander army on London. Loyally, the composer identified himself with the national cause; to celebrate the early defeats of the Jacobites he wrote the *Occasional Oratorio,* a call to Englishmen to resist the invader. But this occupies a less considerable niche in history than *Judas Maccabaeus,* next to *Messiah* perhaps the most popular of Handel's oratorios, unless we choose to set above it the earlier *Israel in Egypt*— to Robert Schumann "the model of a choral work."

Judas Maccabaeus, the text of which a certain divine, Thomas Morell, had based on the Old Testament, was set by Handel between July 9 and August 11, 1746, was produced by Handel at Covent Garden, April 1, 1747. The composer was extraordinarily attuned to the emotional mood of the moment. People saw in the heroic Judas an embodiment of the victorious Duke of Cumberland, who had ferociously scattered the hosts of the Pretender. And the Jews of London, proud of the glorification of their warrior hero of old, rallied to Handel's support and packed the theater in such numbers that the composer suddenly found himself with a wholly new public at his feet, which to some degree replaced for a time to come the aristocratic patrons he had lost.

In the martial, heroic score of *Judas Maccabaeus* Handel had incorporated some music he had originally designed for other works. "See the conquering hero comes," probably the best known chorus in the oratorio, had originally been a part of *Joshua,* and was not heard in *Judas Maccabaeus* till a year after its first production. Even the chorus "Zion now her head shall raise," was a later addition and had not been composed till after Handel had lost his sight.

This is the place to comment briefly on Handel's "borrowings" about which so much ado has been made that one writer went so far as to allude to him as "the grand old thief." It is altogether too easy to lay a disproportionate stress on the practice involved, the more so as it was a fairly legitimate custom in the eighteenth century. Besides Handel, masters like Bach, Haydn, Gluck, Mozart and even Beethoven, had a way, more or less frequently, of taking their own where they found it. Often, indeed, they found it in their own earlier creations. In any case no moral or ethical question was involved, for the good reason that the *treatment* of a theme or a melody according to the esthetic of that period, mattered far more than the phrase in question. Handel, when told of some passage from another composer found in his music had a way of retorting: "The pig did not know what to do with such a theme." Then, too, he adapted to broader purposes music he had conceived earlier in other connections. *Messiah,* for instance, offers many cases in point. The chorus "His yoke is easy, His burthen is light" was adapted for better or worse from an Italian duet composed originally to the words "Quel fior che all' alba ride"; the great "For unto us a Child is born," was a madrigal denouncing "Blind Love and Cruel Beauty" thus: "No, di voi non vo' fidarmi," while "All we like sheep have gone astray" was at first the Italian duet "So per prova i vostri inganni." The great ensemble, "And with His Stripes," employs the same fugal subject which Bach put to use in the A minor fugue of the *Well Tempered Clavier* and is also found in the Kyrie of Mozart's *Requiem.* But themes of this type were "in the air" in that period and fairly recognized as general property. It would be preposterous to labor too much the points involved—the more so as every now and then the practice is "avenged" (if we like!) by some awkwardness of accent or clumsiness of declamation which results by forcing the older phrase into a newer textual association. Such things are very different from the barefaced claim Bononcini once made to having composed a certain work which, as it transpired, had been written by a minor musician living in Vienna. Then too, in the phrase of W. McNaught, "Handel did not borrow the thoughts of others; he rescued them." And it must never be forgotten that men like Bach and Handel faced deadlines unthinkable to any musician of today!

Following *Judas Maccabaeus* Handel's fortunes rose once more and after his conflicts with ill-will and intrigue he was the incontestable victor. The consequence, far from rest and relaxation, was another stream of great works not all of them, unfortunately, having become as familiar to posterity as they undoubtedly deserve to be. Oratorios like *Alexander Balus, Susanna, Joshua, Solomon* and *Jephtha,* treasurable as they are, are known to few, probably because they are eclipsed by the gigantic shadows cast by *Messiah, Judas Maccabaeus* or *Israel in Egypt.* In 1749 he had written *Theodora,* which failed. Its ill luck does not seem to have moved him to more than a kind of "wise-crack" to the effect that "the Jews would not come to it because the story was Christian and the ladies because it was virtuous." In the same year he composed a scene from Tobias Smollett's *Alceste,* parts of which he later used in his *Choice of Hercules.*

For the signing of the Peace of Aix-la-Chapelle in 1748, the King demanded a showy festival, little as there was to celebrate in the termination of a war both unpopular and remote. Handel was commissioned to compose music for an ostentatious show to culminate in a grand display of fireworks in Green Park, where a vast and grotesque wooden building, surmounted by unsightly allegorical figures, had been set up. Twelve thousand people foregathered for a rehearsal of Handel's music, in Vauxhall Gardens, and traffic as a result, was desperately tangled. At the actual celebration everything went awry, the fireworks fizzled and to provide a humiliating climax the edifice in Green Park caught fire. Newman Flower tells in a colorful account of the event that Handel had "a magnificent band worthy of the occasion . . . forty trumpets, twenty horns, sixteen hautboys, sixteen bassoons, eight pair of kettledrums; for the first time he introduced that forgotten instrument, the serpent, into his score, but took it out again. . . . He had for that night as fine a band as he ever conducted."

Handel's contribution, indeed, was the one indisputable success of the occasion. He gave the bright and sonorous *Fireworks Music* (a kind of companion piece to the *Water Music*) the month after the Green Park fiasco for the Foundling Hospital, or "The Hospital for the Maintenance and Education of Exposed and Deserted Young Children." The concert brought Handel the governorship of the institution.

The Foundling Asylum was a pride and pleasure to Handel in his declining years. He presented it with a new organ, opened it himself with a performance of *Messiah* on May 1, 1750, when countless persons of distinction had to be turned away since the Asylum chapel accommodated only 1,000. From that time on the master saw to it that the oratorio was sung there every year and that the proceeds, always considerable, were donated to the Hospital. Not to be behind his great associate, the artist, Hogarth, who subsequently shared with Handel the governorship, donated a portrait he had painted to the Hospital, raffled it off and gave the proceeds to the Asylum.

The composer went one last time to Halle and arrived in Germany, Rolland points out, just at the time his greatest contemporary, Bach, died in Leipzig. His own health was deteriorating, though his mind remained clear and his brain active. To be sure his sight had begun to trouble him. Yet when Thomas Morell, in January, 1751, gave him a libretto, *Jephtha,* he set to work composing it at once. He who had turned out the sublimities of *Messiah* in four weeks and the martial grandeurs of *Judas Maccabaeus* in even less had, however, to break off for ten days after the opening *Largo* of the chorus "How dark, O Lord, are Thy ways." And he painfully set down on the manuscript: "I reached here on Wednesday, February 13, had to discontinue on account of the sight of my left eye." On his sixty-sixth birthday he wrote, "Feel a little better. Resumed work," and set the words "Grief follows joy as night the day." Then he stopped for four months and did not complete the whole score till the end of August, 1751. The last four numbers had taken him more time than he usually spent on an entire oratorio. By that time he had gone completely blind.

Two years later he regained control of himself and played the organ at twelve oratorio productions he gave annually in Lent. He was, even, with the assistance of his pupil and secretary, John Christopher Smith, son of an old Halle school friend, to compose some more music and to remodel his old Italian oratorio, *The Triumph of Time and Truth.* He had submitted to the care of a notorious quack, the "opthalmiater" Chevalier John Taylor, who then enjoyed an extensive vogue among distinguished patients and who boasted that he had seen, on his travels, "a vast variety of singular animals, such as dromedaries, camels, etc., and particularly at Leipsick, where a celebrated master of musick [Bach] already arrived to his 88th year [*sic!*] received his sight by my hands." In any case, the different physicians hid nothing from their patient. His case was hopeless, he was afflicted with "gutta serena." With his sight his best source of inspiration was gone.

"This man," said Roman Rolland, "who was neither an intellectual nor a mystic, one who loved above all things light and nature, beautiful pictures and the spectacular view of things, who lived more through his eyes than most of the German musicians, was engulfed in deepest night. From 1752 to 1759, he was overtaken by the semiconsciousness which precedes death." He had made his will in 1750 and at different times in the next nine years he added codicils to it. On April 6, 1759, he played the organ a last time at a *Messiah* performance, broke down in the middle of a number, recovered and improvised, it was said, with his old-time magnificence. Then he was brought home and they put him to bed.

Handel expressed a desire to be buried in Westminster Abbey; and he said: "I want to die on Good Friday in the hope of rejoining the good God, my sweet Lord and Saviour, on the day of His Resurrection." On Saturday, April 14, 1759, the *Whitehall Evening Post*, announced: "This morning, a little before eight o'clock, died the deservedly celebrated George Frederick Handell Esq. And a week later: "Last night about eight o'clock, the remains of the late great Mr. Handel were deposited at the foot of the Duke of Argyll's Monument in Westminster Abbey; and though he had mentioned being privately interr'd, yet from the Respect due to so celebrated a Man, the Bishop, Prebends, and the whole Choir attended to pay the last Honours due to his Memory; the Bishop himself performed the Service. A Monument is also to be erected for him, which there is no doubt but his Works will even outlive. There was almost the greatest Concourse of People of all Ranks ever seen upon such, or indeed upon any other occasion." Nevertheless, others have testified that Handel was not "burried midst a great concourse of people." Ironically enough, the music performed at his obsequies was "Dr. Croft's Funeral Anthem."

In the Poets' Corner a rather mediocre monument, by L. F. Roubiliac, was later unveiled to his memory "under the patronage and in the presence of His Most Gracious Majesty, George III." But the lordly George Frideric Handel might have been prouder of the monument the dying Beethoven reared to his greatness when, pointing to Arnold's Handelian edition by his bed, he exclaimed: "There lies the Truth!"

H. F. P.

Joseph Haydn

BORN: ROHRAU, LOWER AUSTRIA, MAR. 31, 1732.
DIED: VIENNA, MAY 31, 1809.

*I know that God has bestowed a talent upon me, and I thank Him for it. I think I have done my duty and been of use in my generation by my works. Let others do the same.—*HAYDN.

IN THIS SKETCHY and unpretentious essay the reader must not expect to find any thoroughgoing or penetrating discussion of Haydn's works or, for that matter, more than a hasty and superficial account of his career. Haydn wrote an appalling quantity of music, some of which has to this day not been finally catalogued. In a monograph of this brief and unoriginal sort the reader will look in vain for anything more than the titles of a handful of compositions. About the vast number of symphonies, the magnificent string quartets, the clavier works, the songs there can here be no question. Nor can one do more than allude to a few of the stage pieces, for these operas, composed for the most part for the festivities arranged by the Eszterházy princes, do not pretend to fill a rôle in the history of the lyric drama comparable to those of Mozart or even to the *intermezzi* and the *buffas* of the eighteenth-century Italians or the *Singspiele* of Dittorsdorf and Hiller. Neither is there room to consider the technical advancements achieved by Haydn in the sonata or symphonic form. Yet, even a rapid glance through the following pages will, none the less, make it clear that Haydn, barring a few hardships in his youth, lived an extraordinarily fortunate life and had abundant reason for the optimism which marked every step of his progress. Not

67

even Mendelssohn was so unendingly lucky, whether in his spiritual constitution or in his year by year experiences. That Haydn was a master by the grace of Heaven and a servant only by the artificial conventions of a temporary social order, must become clear to anyone who follows his amazing development in the biography of Pohl and Botstiber, or the briefer but no less deeply perceptive accounts of a scholar like Dr. Karl Geiringer, on whose writings and analyses the present little account is chiefly based.

*   *   *

When Mendelssohn first heard Haydn's "Grand Organ Mass" he found it "scandalously merry." Now, this work, composed at Eszterháza in 1766, was by no means a mature effort and it might have been reasonable to ascribe its exuberance to the high spirits of a young man of uncommonly slow artistic development. But the fact is that, virtually to the end of his days, Haydn did not outgrow a joyfulness rooted in an unfaltering optimism of soul. This is not to say that his creative inspiration and originality did not enormously deepen and ramify and, particularly in his later years, foreshadow in startling fashion some of the most influential romantic devices of the nineteenth century. Yet his heart preserved unchanged that serene geniality of his youth. As much as anything else his churchly compositions disclose this trait, and even his later masses are distinguished by a good deal of that "merriment" which shocked Mendelssohn and not a few others.

"I don't know how to do it otherwise," he once told his friend, the poet Carpani, when the question of his treatment of the mass came up. "I have to give what is in me! When I think of God, my heart is so full of joy that the notes fly from me as from a spindle. And as God has given me a joyful heart He will surely pardon me if I serve Him cheerfully!" With these words he set about revising that selfsame "scandalously merry" Mass of 1766, making it even more "scandalous" by the addition of some cheery wind instrument parts. Having finished a work and signed it, he would almost unfailingly add a pious inscription, such as "Soli Deo Gloria," "Laus Deo" or "In Nomine Domini."

One of the outstanding authorities on Haydn today, Dr. Karl Geiringer, alludes to the "deep religious sense, stubborn tenacity of purpose and a passionate desire to rise in the world" as qualities which could be found in all Haydn's ancestors, "combined with a great pride in good craftsmanship, a warm love of the soil and a healthy streak of sensuality." Certainly, his boyhood was not calculated to make of him an incorrigible optimist had not this quality been bred in his bones. Rohrau, the little town in which he was born, is an unattractive place in a flat and marshy country, where the frequently overflowing Leitha River forms a border between Austria and Hungary. The houses are low, built of clay and roofed with thatch, which often catches fire in the hot, dry summers. Dr. Geiringer tells that Haydn's house was burned in 1813, 1833 and 1899, but always restored so carefully that few but specialists could tell the difference. The place was probably no worse than other neighboring cottages and farms; yet we are told that Beethoven, in his last illness, being shown a picture of it, exclaimed: "To think that such a great man should have been born in so poor a home!" while some years later, Liszt, on catching sight of it, burst into tears.

Haydn's father, Mathias Haydn, was born in the nearby town of Hainburg; his antecedents were hard-working, honest men, farmers, vinegrowers, millers, wheelwrights. Of musicians or artists there was not one among them. Mathias was a wheelwright and wagon-builder, like his forebears. When he finished his apprenticeship he set out on a trip, after the tradition of a journeyman, and went, we are told, as far as Frankfurt-on-the-Main. On his wanderings he bought himself a harp. Someone taught him to play it (he could not read a note of music) sufficiently to accompany himself in his favorite folk-tunes, which he sang "in a pleasant tenor voice." In 1727 he settled in Rohrau, though he remained a member of the Hainburg guild of wheelwrights. It is possible that he chose the unattractive market town in place of the more imposing and picturesque Hainburg because Maria Koller lived in Rohrau. Maria was a cook in the employ of the Counts of Harrach, the lords of Rohrau. She appears to have been a clever culinary artist. (Dr. Geiringer says she "had to handle such delicacies as turtles and crayfish and had an abundance of material at her disposal." We are told for example, that something like 8000 eggs, 200 capons and 300 chickens were delivered annually to the castle by the inhabitants of Rohrau as part of their duties to their patron.) At any rate, in 1728, she married the wagonmaker, Mathias

Haydn, and brought her husband a dowry of one hundred and twenty florins and an "honest outfit." The couple was by no means what could be called "poor" (in spite of Beethoven's pathetic exclamation and Liszt's tears!), but Maria Haydn saw to it that ends met, as they had to, considering there were twelve children (of whom half died in infancy). Moreover she was a model housewife and had inherited a deeply religious strain. It was her fondest wish to see her great son become a Catholic priest rather than prefer "the irresponsible life of a musician." She, alas, did not live to witness his first artistic successes. As for Mathias, who was very adequately paid for doing all sorts of odd jobs for the Counts of Harrach, his wife had the satisfaction of seeing him succeed her father in the judicial office of "Marktrichter." He was "responsible for the good conduct of the population, kept a sharp look-out for adultery and gambling; saw that people went to church and did not break the Sunday rest . . . while every Sunday morning at six he had to report to the steward of Count Harrach." (Geiringer) He had a wine cellar, farmland and cattle. He and his wife were of Austro-German origin, not Hungarians or Croats.

Franz Joseph Haydn (his family called their children by their second names—hence the famous brother, Johann Michael, has come down into history as Michael Haydn) was born on March 31, 1732, the second child of the Haydn couple. In only one respect did he show himself different from his paternal and maternal ancestors. At an astonishingly early age "Sepperl" (Austrian diminutive for Joseph) manifested musical talent. This talent took the form of a gift for singing, a lovely voice and an amazingly correct intonation, not to mention a sense of rhythm which disclosed itself in various ways. If he had no skill in playing any kind of instrument (though he greatly wished to imitate his father's performances on the harp) he would find himself a couple of sticks and by means of these try to "play" the violin, as he had seen the Rohrau schoolmaster do. The wonder of the neighbors became aroused, and the more "Sepperl" gave signs of other than simply manual abilities the more ardently his mother prayed that heaven might make him a teacher or, better still, a priest. For the last, the boy actually displayed a predisposition. The child had a streak of piety in him which remained with the man to the end.

*   *   *

One day a cousin of Mathias, a certain Johann Mathias Franck, came over from Hainburg. Franck seemed a person sent by Providence to further Maria Haydn's wishes. He was a school official, as well as precentor of the Church of St. Philip and St. James. At once he noticed "Sepperl's" musical inclinations and told the parents they would be wise to allow him to take the boy to Hainburg, where he could be more thoroughly schooled than in Rohrau. Naturally, he was ready to supply the youngster's bed and board (for which, he assumed, his cousin Mathias would be willing to pay). The good Maria hesitated. "Sepperl" was not yet six and though he would not be far away she felt uncertain how soon or how often she might see her boy. And what of those holy orders? Franck brushed the objections aside; the boy should have care and understanding, not to forget an education unobtainable in a village. Moreover, if "Sepperl" were eventually to take holy orders his musical training would be most helpful.

The die was cast! The barely six-year-old lad left his father's roof, never to return, save for a most brief and infrequent visit. "Sepperl's" mother was right. To all intents, the boy had left his family forever. Yet throughout his life Haydn harbored the tenderest feelings for his mother and never reproached her for permitting him to leave her. "She had always given the most tender care to his welfare," he told his intimates when he was an old man. And Karl Geiringer, in his beautiful Haydn biography, recounts how, in 1795, "when the then world-famous composer visited Rohrau to see the monument erected in his honor by Count Harrach, he knelt down and kissed the threshold of the humble cottage he had shared with his parents for less than six years."

Impressions crowded on "Sepperl" in Hainburg. He had numerous opportunities to assist Franck in his miscellaneous and seemingly unending tasks in the school house, on the organ bench, in conducting the singers and instrumentalists at church services. One of the duties of Franck (and to some extent, no doubt, of the boy Haydn) was to keep the church register, look after the church clock and ring the bells for services "and for special occasions, such as thunderstorms." In an autobiographical sketch which Haydn wrote in 1778 he said, among other things: "Our Almighty Father had endowed me with so much facility in music that even in my sixth year I stood up like a man and sang Masses in the church choir and I could play a little on the clavier and violin." And his biographer, Georg August Griesinger, tells that Haydn studied "the kettledrum as well as other instruments."

"Sepperl" was kept at work without respite, but he apparently throve on all this learning, all this musical practice and all the household chores which Franck's wife heaped upon him. Juliana Franck was not at all like his mother. If she expected the boy to help in the household she did not worry about his increasing untidiness. "I could not help perceiving," said Haydn in his old age when he talked of his Hainburg experiences, "that I was gradually getting very dirty, and though I thought rather highly of my little person, I was not always able to avoid stains on my clothes—of which I was dreadfully ashamed; in fact I was a regular little ragamuffin!" Like Schubert at the "Konvict" he was grossly "undernourished." He wore a wig "for cleanliness' sake." Yet his education, both musical and otherwise, was greatly furthered by his sojourn in Hainburg. Even if he was hungry and dirty, nothing embittered him. And in after years he said of Franck: "I shall be grateful to that man as long as I live, for keeping me so hard at work." And he had a picture of his early master wherever he lived, besides remembering Franck's daughter in his will.

* * *

Now, however, occurred another of those strokes of good fortune which punctuated Haydn's life from his cradle to his grave. Just as Franck turned up in Rohrau to take him to Hainburg, so now there appeared in Hainburg a young man from Vienna who set "Sepperl's" feet squarely on his further path. Karl Georg Reutter, composer and choirmaster at St. Stephen's in the capital, was on a trip looking for good choristers. At Hainburg, Reutter stayed at the home of the pastor, Anton Palmb, who immediately called his guest's attention to a boy from Rohrau who had "a weak but sweet voice." Haydn's friend, the Italian Carpani, has left us the story of the meeting in some detail: "Reutter gave him a tune to sing at sight. The precision, the purity of tone, the spirit with which the boy executed it surprised him; but he was especially charmed with the beauty of the young voice. He remarked that the lad did not trill, and smilingly asked him the reason. The boy replied promptly: 'How can you expect me to trill when my cousin does not know how to himself?' 'I will teach you,' said Reutter; 'mark me, I will trill'; and taking the boy between his knees, he showed him how he should produce the notes in rapid succession, control his breath, and agitate the palate. The boy immediately made a good try. Reutter, enchanted with the success of his pupil, took a plate of fine cherries and emptied them into the boy's pocket. His delight may be readily conceived. Haydn often mentioned this anecdote to me and added, laughing, that whenever he happened to trill he still thought he saw those beautiful cherries." Reutter offered to take "Sepperl" to Vienna to be a choirboy at St. Stephen's as well as to give him a much more thorough musical education than he had received so far. The matter having been put up to his father and mother, they agreed instantly and with delight, the more so as Reutter promised "to look after their boy." It was agreed that the lad should start for Vienna when he was eight. His new master gave him some exercises in scale-singing and sight-reading to work at in the meanwhile and, while waiting for the great day to arrive, the youngster diligently worked by himself to develop his voice.

Installed at the Cantor's house, next to St. Stephen's, in Vienna, "Sepperl's" illusions presently suffered a chill. Reutter suddenly turned into a hard taskmaster and an unsympathetic disciplinarian. He was responsible for the education, feeding and clothing of his choirboys, but the meals were wholly insufficient, indeed skimpier than what he had in Hainburg. A. C. Dies writes: "Joseph's stomach had to get accustomed to continuous fasting. He tried to make up for it with the musical 'academies' (concerts given by the choir in the houses of the Viennese nobility), where refreshments were offered to the choristers. As soon as Joseph made this discovery, so important for his stomach, he was seized with an incredible love for 'academies.' He endeavored to sing as beautifully as possible so as to be known and invited as a skilled performer, and thus find occasions to appease his ravenous hunger." Moreover Joseph's musical education was rather one-sided and apart from singing and a little violin and clavier playing, Reutter did not bother about his young charge's training in musical theory. Dr. Geiringer relates that when, on one occasion, Reutter found Joseph working on a twelve-part "Salve Regina" he asked with a sneer: "Oh, you silly child, aren't two parts enough for you?" But that was about as much as the instruction amounted to. Reutter was actually a composer of no inconsiderable distinction, whose teaching could have been of great help to the aspiring youngster. But in after years Haydn said that he had only two lessons from this master. All the same, he had priceless chances to hear much of the best contemporary sacred music. To Johann Friedrich Rochlitz he once confided: "Proper teachers I have never had. I always started right away with the practical side, first in singing and playing instruments, later in composition. I listened more than I studied but I heard the finest music in all forms that was to be heard in my time, and of this there was much in Vienna. Oh, so much! I listened attentively and tried to turn to good account what most impressed me. Thus little by little my knowledge and my ability were developed."

The boys from St. Stephen's sometimes had a chance to perform at the Empress Maria Theresa's newly built palace of Schönbrunn. When the choir was on one occasion commanded to sing there Joseph, in a burst of boyish exuberance, climbed some scaffolding and appeared suddenly before the Empress's window. Unawed by the imperial threats the boy repeated the exploit a little later until Maria Theresa ordered the choirmaster to give this "fair-haired blockhead" a proper thrashing. However, being extremely musical herself, and a singer of uncommon merits in the bargain, the Empress could appreciate Joseph's execution of various church solos. And he was happier than ever when Michael Haydn joined the St. Stephen's choir and added his exceptionally beautiful soprano voice, of three octaves' range, to the ensemble. Joseph was given the duty of instructing his younger brother in a number of matters. Before long Michael's talents were such as to make him outshine Joseph's. The latter does not appear to have openly displayed any feelings of jealousy. Yet it might be inquiring too closely to ask if the older boy was wholly pleased when his solos were taken away from him and given to his brother, whose singing so delighted the Emperor and Empress that they once accorded him a special audience, congratulated him and gave him a substantial money present. The good Michael promptly sent half of the money to his father, who had lately lost a cow, and gave the rest to Reutter to save for him. Reutter took such care of it that poor Michael never saw a penny of it!

*　　*　　*

Suddenly Joseph's luck seemed to turn against him. His voice cracked. Maria Theresa began to complain, about 1745, that the boy was "crowing like a cock." Joseph was keenly distressed, a fact which was not lost on Reutter. He summoned Joseph and intimated that there was a means of doing something about it. *Castrati* had well-paid positions in the imperial chapel. Joseph seems to have been wise enough to notify his father. Mathias Haydn went post-haste to Vienna and the scheme was dropped. Reutter now waited for his next chance to be rid of a useless chorister. He soon found it, for some imp of mischief provoked Joseph to cut off the pigtail of another boy. "You will be caned on the hand," shouted Reutter to the seventeen-year-old Joseph; "of course, you will be expelled after you have been caned," he went on. And on a chilly November morning in 1749, Haydn found himself on the street, penniless, with exactly three torn shirts and a threadbare coat! If he still remembered his mother's wish that he should take holy orders he might presently have had a roof over his head. But he had a deep assurance that his destiny lay elsewhere; neither did he appeal to his father for help, because he knew the little household at Rohrau was at the moment passing through a financially difficult time.

As he wandered irresolutely, uncertain where he could spend the night and where his next meal would come from, he met a certain Joseph Michael Spangler, a singer from St. Michael's Church, near the Hofburg. Haydn knew Spangler very slightly but he poured his tale of woe into sympathetic ears. Spangler was himself all but a pauper. He lived in a garret with his wife and a nine-months-old baby. Nevertheless he instantly begged his distressed young friend to follow him home. Joseph might sleep in the garret, which was a trifle better than the cold street. Food Spangler could not guarantee, since he and his little family had themselves barely enough to subsist upon.

Little by little Haydn set about making connections. He played the violin at dances, he found a few pupils (at absurdly low rates, it is true), he arranged for sundry instruments some trifling compositions by musically illiterate amateurs; or he participated in street serenades, which were vastly popular in Vienna. Such "Nachtmusiken" were more elaborate affairs than the love songs with guitar accompaniment customary in Italy. Here trios, quartets and even ensembles of wind-instruments performed compositions of some length and diversity. Crowds gathered, windows were filled with listeners and the players earned money and applause. Haydn not only played in these street performances, he wrote pieces for use at them. The folk music of Vienna served him well for this purpose, as did the melodies from those border regions where he was born and which were tinged with foreign strains and even exotic influences. In some incredible way he made enough for several months to keep body and soul together. Then a new problem developed. The Spanglers expected a new baby and now the wretched garret was definitely too small to house Haydn any longer. The young musician got around his difficulties temporarily by joining a party of pilgrims traveling to the wonder-working shrine of the Virgin at Mariazell, in one of the loveliest recesses of the Austrian Alps. His voice having returned to him, Haydn made an effort to secure a position in the Mariazell church and appealed to the choir-master. That worthy was not impressed by the newcomer's appearance and suspected a swindler masquerading as an itinerant musician. Thereupon, the story goes, Haydn resorted to a bold stratagem. He returned to the church, made his way to the choir, suddenly snatched a piece of music from an astonished singer and sang it so beautifully that, as Geiringer relates, "all the choir held their breath to listen." As a result Haydn was invited to stay a week as the choirmaster's guest and actually earned a sum of money from the delighted musicians of Mariazell. And luck, as he found, begets luck. For soon afterwards, a certain Viennese tradesman, Anton Buchholz, resolved to help the young man carry on his studies and loaned him "unconditionally" a sum of money which may well have seemed extraordinary at this stage.

Haydn came back from his pilgrimage to Mariazell rich enough to look for a garret of his own. He found one, partitioned off from a larger room, on the sixth floor of the old Michaelerhaus, adjoining St. Michael's Church, at the south end of the Kohlmarkt. Both house and church are still standing, looking to all intents as they did in 1750. Haydn had plenty of neighbors in his attic. Among them were a cook, a journeyman, a printer, a footman, and a man who tended the fires in the house of some rich man. Haydn had six hard flights to climb, besides which there was no window, no stove, no conveniences of any sort. If he wanted to wash in the morning he had to get water from a nearby spring and by the time he brought it up, it had often turned to ice. But he had a slight degree of privacy, enough quiet to study and even to play on a ratty old clavier which, somehow or other, he had managed to drag upstairs. He got hold of a number of theoretical books—Johann Joseph Fux's "Gradus ad Parnassum," Mattheson's "Vollkommener Capellmeister," Kellner's "Unterricht im Generalbass" —and figuratively devoured them. And on his clavier he played the first six piano sonatas of Philipp Emanuel Bach. "Innumerable times," he afterwards related, "I played them for my own delight, especially when I felt oppressed and discouraged by worries; and always I left the instrument gay and in high spirits."

At that time, however, he established two important ties. One was the famous harlequin, Kurz-Bernardon, who enjoyed an immense popular vogue by his clever clowning and who managed the Kärntnertor Theatre. Kurz-Bernardon had an unusually beautiful wife, whose blandishments justified numerous serenades. On one occasion, when Haydn performed in one of these, the comedian, struck by the music he heard, appeared at his door to ask who had composed it. "I did," answered Joseph; whereupon the actor bade him "Come upstairs!" Not only was he rewarded with an introduction to the lady but, according to Carpani, Joseph left with an opera libretto in his pocket and a commission to compose it at once. The opera was called *Der krumme Teufel* ("The Limping Devil"). Haydn wrote the music in a couple of days, but as some nobleman imagined the piece a lampoon on himself, the work was forbidden before it was ever presented. One effect in the score the composer admitted had given him more trouble than "writing a fugue with a double subject." This was a musical description of a storm at sea which the play called for. Now, neither Haydn nor Kurz-Bernardon had ever seen the sea, let alone a storm on it! Carpani's tale is most amusing: "How can a man describe what he knows nothing about? Bernardon, all agitation, paced up and down, while the composer was seated at the harpsichord. 'Imagine,' said the actor, 'a mountain rising and then a valley sinking, and then another mountain and another valley . . .' This fine description was of no avail and in vain did the comedian add thunder and lightning. At last, young Haydn, out of patience, extended his hands to the two ends of the harpsichord and bringing them in a *glissando* rapidly together, he exclaimed: 'The devil take the tempest!' 'That's it, that's it,' cried the harlequin, springing upon his neck and almost stifling him."

The second acquaintance proved vastly more influential than Kurz-Bernardon. In the same house—though considerably farther downstairs—lived the great Pietro Metastasio, author of innumerable opera librettos and poet laureate to the Habsburgs. Metastasio, who may have heard Haydn's improvisings from afar, was apparently struck by them. He was interested in the musical training of a friend and suggested the young pianist up in the garret as a suitable teacher. Haydn was not paid for his teaching in cash, but he enjoyed free board and a cultured atmosphere. He became acquainted with Metastasio, whose courtliness and sensibility could hardly have failed to exercise a most advantageous effect upon a youth so predisposed to benefit by genteel contacts. Moreover, Haydn was equally fortunate in meeting his pupil's singing master, the great voice teacher and famous composer, Niccolo Porpora, who spent some years in Vienna. Haydn acted as accompanist in these lessons and soon begged to be taken into Porpora's employ as pianist and pupil in singing and composition, in exchange offering to do the now old and testy Italian every kind of menial service. Surely it was worth an occasional cuff and kick, he figured, even seasoned with a few "blockheads," if the great Porpora would take the trouble to correct his musical exercises, give him an insight into the deep secrets of singing and show him how best to write for the voice. So he cheerfully brushed the old gentleman's clothes, cleaned his shoes and saw that his wig was on straight. For three months Haydn served his peppery master. And in that time the young man made inestimable progress of all sorts—one of which was to acquire a fluent command of Italian.

*　　*　　*

Joseph, for all his ambition and diligence, may yet have tasted a drop of bitterness when he reflected how his brother, Michael, seemed still to outstrip him; and when their mother died in 1754 she must have gone to her grave persuaded that the truer musician of the Haydn family was Michael who, at seventeen, was writing masses of exceptional quality. Joseph was, indeed, gradually gaining admission into noble circles. The Countess Thun, for one, was so pleased by some of his sonatas that she asked to make his acquaintance. Then, when he confronted her face to face, she decided that this homely and badly-dressed individual, could hardly be anything but an impostor. Little by little the unfavorable impression wore off and in due course the

distinguished and extremely musical lady was taking clavier and sing-
ing lessons from the man she had mistaken for a hopeless booby.
Through her family Haydn met the very musical Karl Joseph von
Fürnberg, who had a steward, a pastor and still another friend, all
very proficient players. And it was for Fürnberg and his intimates that
Haydn wrote his first string quartets. He was as industrious as ever.
Carpani said: "At daybreak he took the part of the first violin at the
Church of the Fathers of the Order of Mercy; thence he repaired to
the chapel of Count Haugwitz, where he played the organ; at a later
hour he sang the tenor part at St. Stephen's; and lastly, having been
on foot all day, he passed a part of the night at the harpsichord." Then,
in 1759, Fürnberg brought him to the attention of the Bohemian Count
Ferdinand Maximilian von Morzin, who promptly engaged him as
music director and *Kammerkompositor*. Socially, financially and otherwise Haydn had made a great step up the ladder, from which he was
destined never again to descend.

One of Haydn's duties at Count Morzin's was to accompany the
Countess Morzin when she chose to sing, which was frequently. Once,
according to Griesinger, the lady was trying over some songs with
Haydn when her scarf became loose, exposing her bosom. Instantly,
Haydn stopped playing. The lady, irritated, asked the reason. "But your
Highness, who would not lose his head over this?" he replied. This
was only one of the occasions he began to develop an eye for feminine
beauty. He was now maturing, physically, and his fortunes were improving. This conjunction of circumstances made him conclude that
the time was ripe for him to marry. It turned out to be one of the
most unfortunate inspirations of his life. Not that Haydn would have
failed to make a good husband, but for the reason that it was his fate
to pick the worst possible wife.

He gave lessons to the two daughters of a Viennese hairdresser
named Keller. It was not long before the composer fell in love with
the younger girl, whose name was Therese. But Therese was afflicted
with something of a religious mania and, about 1760, she entered a
convent, as Sister Josepha. The hairdresser, though a religious man,
wanted to keep the promising young musician in the family, and before long he prevailed upon him to consider his other daughter. The
latter, Maria Anna Aloysia Apollonia, offered the vilest imaginable
combination of qualities. She was hopelessly unmusical, poisonously

jealous, bigoted, ill-favored, slatternly, a bad housekeeper and, as such women frequently are, outrageously extravagant.

Haydn got nothing he had bargained for—neither affection, home comforts nor children. So little regard did Maria Anna Aloysia have for her husband's musical eminence that she cheerfully used his manuscripts for curl papers or else to line pie plates and cake pans. Furthermore, said Haydn, "my wife was unable to bear children and for this reason I was less indifferent to the attractions of other women" (Griesinger). Some have claimed that this Xantippe actually loved her husband, on the grounds that she obstinately refused to give up a certain picture of him. Dr. Geiringer says the composer was so little deluded by this seeming show of affection, that he insisted his wife prized the portrait so highly only because a lover of hers had painted it.

At Maria Anna's invitation the house was overrun with numberless priests, who were liberally entertained at the Haydn residence and given orders for innumerable masses, which were straightway charged to the composer's account. She could never forget that her husband had originally preferred her younger sister and she was violently jealous of the attraction he never failed to exercise on fascinating women. In his fluent Italian Haydn once remarked to the French violinist, Baillot, as he pointed out his wife's picture: "E la mia moglie; m'ha ben fatta arrabiare!" ("That is my wife; she has often infuriated me!") To an Italian singer, who held a firm place in his heart, Haydn spoke many years later of "my wife, that infernal beast," who had plagued him with such malicious letters that he had to threaten he would never return to her. Geiringer believes that Haydn "must have felt a diabolical pleasure when he came across the following Lessing poem for which he composed a canon:

> *If in the whole wide world*
> *But one mean wife there is,*
> *How sad that each of us*
> *Should think this one is his!*

Maria Anna Aloysia was further annoyed that her husband should have spent so much on various poor relations; in return, she gave considerable sums to the church. When in 1800 she died while taking a cure at Baden, Haydn seems to have received the news with complete indifference.

*   *   *

Haydn composed his first symphony for the household orchestra of Count Morzin. As a kind fate would have it one of the guests who listened to the work was Prince Paul Anton Eszterházy, of the powerful and enormously wealthy Hungarian family. He was charmed by the symphony and reflected what a priceless acquisition this young composer would be for his court at Eisenstadt. Here was a man reared in the grand tradition of the Eszterházys, always noted for their encouragement of music and other arts. Prince Paul, a talented composer in his own right, collected numberless pictorial masterworks, kept a small but trained orchestra and for years had employed a now aging conductor, Gregorius Joseph Werner.

It was only a short time after Paul Eszterházy had visited the Morzins that the last-named noble found himself in monetary straits. Among the first luxuries sacrificed were the expensive orchestra and its conductor. But instantly Haydn found a safer haven. Prince Eszterházy, remembering the composer and conductor of the enchanting symphony, acted at the first news of the Morzin débacle to secure him for himself. Haydn, offered the post of assistant conductor, accepted with delight.

*   *   *

On May 1, 1761, Haydn received a contract, of great length and elaborate detail, which is too extensive to reproduce in all its particulars. Here, however, are a few of its specifications:

"Joseph Heyden shall be considered and treated as a member of the household. Therefore his Serene Highness is graciously pleased to place confidence in his conducting himself as becomes an honorable officer of a princely house. He must be temperate, not showing himself overbearing toward his musicians, but mild and lenient, straightforward and composed. It is especially to be observed that when the orchestra shall be summoned to perform before company, the Vice-Capellmeister and all the musicians shall appear in uniform, and the said Joseph Heyden shall take care that he and all the members of his orchestra follow the instructions given and appear in white stockings, white linen, powdered and with either a queue or a tiewig . . .

"The said Vice-Capellmeister shall be under obligation to compose such music as his Serene Highness may command, and neither to communicate such compositions to any other person, nor to allow them to be copied, but he shall retain them for the absolute use of his Highness, and not compose for any other person without the knowledge and permission of his Highness . . .

"The said Joseph Heyden shall appear daily in the antechamber before and after midday, and inquire whether his Highness is pleased to order a performance of the orchestra . . . The said Vice-Capellmeister shall take careful charge of all music and musical instruments, and be responsible for any injury that may occur to them from carelessness or neglect. . . . The said Joseph Heyden shall be obliged to instruct the female vocalists, in order that they may not forget in the country what they have been taught with much trouble and expense in Vienna; and since the Vice-Capellmeister is proficient on various instruments he shall take care himself to practice on all that he is acquainted with. . . . A yearly salary of 400 florins to be received in quarterly payments is hereby bestowed by his Serene Highness upon the said Vice-Capellmeister. In addition, the said Joseph Heyden shall board at the officers' table, or receive half a gulden per day in lieu thereof.

"His Serene Highness undertakes to keep Joseph Heyden in his service for at least three years; and should he be satisfied with him, he may look forward to being appointed Capellmeister. . . ."

*　　*　　*

Eisenstadt was to be Haydn's home for the next thirty years and, in the service of the Eszterházys he was to do much—though by no means all—of his greater work. The palace of Eszterháza was a modest place when the composer first joined the Eszterházy staff compared with the gorgeous domain it became not very long afterwards. Haydn was, if you will, a servant. He wrote music to order and went, properly attired, at certain times of day, to receive the prince's directions. Dr. Geiringer says: "To await the commands of so exalted a personage as Prince Eszterházy . . . was not humiliating for a man who had only recently risen from the depths of poverty." Even the fact of having to wear livery did not irk him. We are told that old Mathias Haydn (who died in 1765) still lived "to experience the joy of seeing his son in the princely blue uniform braided with gold."

Prince Paul Eszterházy was gathered to his fathers in 1762. Haydn became the servitor of an Eszterházy who artistically was greatly the superior of Paul Anton. This one was Prince Nicholas, surnamed "the

Magnificent," because of his love of splendor and the wealth which enabled him to indulge his most luxurious tastes. He now undertook to erect a palace which rivaled Versailles and which, in fact, was a glorified imitation of the French model. Eszterháza became a vast dream palace compared to the one where Haydn had first assumed his new post. It is impossible to give here even the faintest idea of the splendor and sumptuousness of this "Hungarian Versailles." An opera house and a theater for puppet shows formed part of this superlative show place; and concert rooms suited whatever kind of musical performances might be commanded by the prince. When distinguished guests arrived the brilliancy of the festivities arranged for their enjoyment knew no limits. The Empress Maria Theresa visited the Eszterházy estate in 1773 and a special booklet published in Vienna gives an account of the festivities on that occasion, which reads like something out of the Arabian Nights. One of the musical works performed was Haydn's little lyric comedy, "L'infedeltà delusa." The Empress was so delighted that she is said to have remarked: "If I want to enjoy good opera, I go to Eszterháza." On the same evening there was a superb masked ball, following which, in the Chinese Pavilion, the orchestra, in brilliant uniforms, played a number of pieces under Haydn's leadership, one of them the conductor's new *Maria Theresa* Symphony. The ball continued all night, though the Empress—understandably enough—had retired. Next day she heard another Haydn opera (for marionettes), *Philemon and Baucis,* which Maria Theresa enjoyed so much that she had the whole production sent to Vienna for her entertainment. Haydn received the usual snuff-box filled with gold pieces. He, in return, presented the imperial lady with three grouse he had shot down; the Empress "graciously accepted them" and took them home for dinner!

But all this is anticipating. When Haydn settled at Eszterháza he found at his disposal a competent orchestra, but one much smaller and less capable than it soon became. The newcomer, though the aged and desiccated Gregorius Joseph Werner remained nominally chief Capellmeister and railed at Haydn as "a mere fop" and a "scribbler of songs," lost no time reorganizing his forces, yet very tactfully and without ruffling any feelings. He infused new blood into the personnel, by acquiring a number of young and greatly talented players. One of these was a youthful violinist, Luigi Tomasini, whom Prince Paul Anton had found in Italy and taken to Eszterháza as his valet, and whom

Haydn instantly secured for his orchestra and treated as a brother. Still another was a cellist of uncommon gifts, Joseph Weigl. Haydn obtained the musical results he wanted, but always with the discretion of a born diplomat. Never had he to fight his "superiors," after the manner of such stormy petrels as Bach, Handel, Beethoven. His musicians (he always referred to them as his "children") idolized him and, because they respected him, strove to satisfy his demands, which were by no means light. His duties were staggeringly heavy. Dr. Geiringer recounts that, on one occasion, the exhausted Haydn became so sleepy while writing a horn concerto that he "mixed up the staves for oboe and violin, and noted in the score as an excuse 'written while asleep.'"

* * *

It was not long before the musicians fell into the habit of calling their conductor "Papa Haydn," on account of his solicitude for their well-being and his musical knowledge which they recognized as remarkable. But nothing could be more misleading than the age-old convention of using "Papa Haydn" as a nickname for this master as if to imply that he was an artist of outworn, discredited sympathies and of unprogressive attitude. The antique "Papa Haydn" idea was neatly scuttled on one occasion by Anton Rubinstein—of all people! When someone of his acquaintance alluded contemptuously to "Papa Haydn" the great pianist retorted: "Let me assure you that long after I have become 'great-grandfather Rubinstein' he will still continue to be 'Papa Haydn.'" Yet Haydn at the time of which we speak was still some distance from the master who created the greater symphonies and chamber music, the finest clavier sonatas and certain other memorable keyboard works, let alone the six most inspired masses and the two oratorios (*The Creation* and *The Seasons*), the ripest fruits of his old age. If physically Haydn developed late, the same is true of his creative genius. Musically and otherwise it appeared for some time as if his brother, Michael, would surpass him; and if Joseph had died soon after entering the Eszterházy service it may be seriously questioned if the world would have felt it had been deprived of an irreplaceable master.

* * *

In more ways than one the sumptuous palace of Eszterháza was the best possible home for Haydn's art. Prince Eszterházy, great as were his demands on Haydn, did his art a service by allowing him to experiment and thus "forcing him to become original." He would hardly have become "original" in the way he did had he been obliged to earn his bread wandering about Vienna, for he was differently constituted than, let us say, such an unmistakably Viennese soul as Schubert. Haydn's early masters (let us rather say "models") were not men of imposing creative dimension. Johann Sebastian Bach died while Haydn was still a youth, his work had gone out of fashion and was unobtainable in Vienna for years to come. But the influence of Philipp Emanuel Bach was vastly stronger at the time than that of his father and Haydn, as we have seen, felt its impact. Guido Adler, for one, names as Haydn's early masters minor composers like Georg Reutter, Georg Christoph Wagenseil and Georg Matthias Monn. There is evidence that he knew the music of Ignaz Holzbauer, Johann Stamitz and the Sammartini brothers. Basically more important for Haydn's early style was the changed taste which pervaded the musical world, supplanting the intricate polyphonic style by homophony and the decorative pleasings of the so-called *style galant*.

It was some time before he can be said to have earned the title of "father of the symphony" (or, in the deepest sense, of the sonata or the string quartet). The early symphonies of Haydn seem much closer to the concerto grosso of the baroque period than to the later "Paris" and "London" symphonies. The musical form which occupied Haydn perhaps most of all was the string quartet, of which as many as eighty-three were enumerated in a catalogue of his works Haydn prepared in 1805. "We do not know the exact number of Haydn's string quartets," declares Karl Geiringer, who also adds "the composer was in his early twenties when he wrote his first quartet and he had passed his seventieth birthday before he began to work on his last."

*   *   *

In 1766 Gregorius Werner died and Haydn was officially appointed Capellmeister of the Eszterházy orchestra. He had by now brought the ensemble to a high state of perfection. Besides the cellist Weigl (who later joined the Vienna court orchestra), Haydn could boast, in addition to "brother Luigi" Tomasini, as concertmaster, the fine cellists, Franz Xaver Marteau and Aanton Kraft. Prince Eszterházy, who paid even higher salaries than the imperial court at Vienna, could have his pick and choice of any artist he wanted. The schedule at Eszterháza called for two opera performances a week, two weekly concerts and, in Prince Nicholas's private salon, plenty of chamber music. The prince greatly enjoyed playing the baryton, a now obsolete form of viola da gamba. It was uncommonly difficult and the Prince enjoyed it all the more for that reason. Haydn had his work cut out for him supplying his employer with new music for the instrument. Once he thought he would give Prince Nicholas pleasure by learning to play the baryton himself and declared he was ready to play it for his Serene Highness. This time he had miscalculated—his Highness returned no more than a glacial stare! Nicholas, moreover, insisted he must have *all* the most difficult passages in anything Haydn might write for him. The cellist, Kraft, was once given a particularly easy part in a baryton duet to perform with the prince, who cut short any possible argument with the words: "It is no credit to you to play better than I do; it is your duty."

The normal schedule of the artists was, of course, far heavier and more complicated when distinguished visitors arrived for longer or shorter sojourns. Under the circumstances, neither Haydn nor anyone else had a chance to be bored at Eszterháza. Now and then, however, these birds in a golden cage longed for a little freedom. Haydn himself once wrote in a letter: "I never can obtain leave, even to go to Vienna for twenty-four hours. It is scarcely credible, and yet the refusal is always couched in such polite terms as to render it utterly impossible for me to urge my request." This is the place to speak of the so-called "Farewell Symphony," a piece of music with a definite purpose (if not exclusively an artistic one) in which Haydn got the better of his prince. In 1772 Nicholas ruled that none of the musicians might bring his wife or children to Eszterháza. In only three cases was an exception made. Prince Nicholas, having paid his musicians an extra fifty florins to provide for the families they were not permitted to visit, considered that he had no further obligations. Finally, the players who had to pass the greater part of the year without seeing their wives, rebelled. In Griesinger's words: "The affectionate husbands appealed to Haydn to help them. Haydn decided to write a symphony in which one instrument after the other ceases to play. The work was executed as soon as an occasion presented itself, and each player was instructed to put out his candle when his part was ended, seize his music and leave with his instrument tucked under his arm. The prince instantly understood the meaning of pantomime and the next day he gave the order to leave Eszterháza."

All the same, the advantages of Haydn's life at Eszterháza, even when it threatened to grow dull, were inestimable. He once told Griesinger: "My prince was always satisfied with my works. Not only did I have the encouragement of constant approval, but as conductor of an orchestra I could make experiments, observe what produced an effect and what weakened it, and was thus in a position to improve, to alter, make additions or omissions, and be as bold as I pleased. I was cut off from the world; there was no one to confuse or torment me . . ."

*　　*　　*

Prince Eszterházy, in 1779, engaged an Italian violinist, Antonio Polzelli, and his wife, Luigia, a mezzo-soprano. Polzelli was a sickly man and not particularly competent. Still less was Luigia, who needed much help from Haydn to fit her for minor musical duties. What moved the Prince to pick this misfit pair for his establishment is a problem. They were not a happy couple, scarcely more than were Haydn and his "Infernal Beast"! Luigia was nineteen, lively, graceful —an adorable type of Italian beauty. The Prince soon decided that the imported couple represented a needless expense, though the two were pathetically underpaid. But this time Haydn was resolute. The Polzellis must stay in Eszterháza under *any* conditions! Eszterházy, being a man of the world, realized that in certain things an irreplaceable orchestral conductor must be allowed his way, whatever the conventions.

Luigia was attracted to Haydn as were numerous other women whose path he crossed. He himself often admitted it could not have been for his beauty. Dr. Geiringer says that we know "practically nothing about Luigia." At any rate Haydn never made any secret of his love for her or she for him—not, at any rate, till much later, when new interests entered his life. At Eszterháza the affair was an open secret. Doubtless they would have married. But the invalid Antonio and the venomous Maria Anna Aloysia settled that. There are no letters extant dealing with those first years of their love. But in 1791 he wrote Luigia: "I love you as on the first day, and I am always sad when I cannot do more for you. But be patient, perhaps the day will arrive when I can show you how much I love you." When Antonio Polzelli died, not very long afterwards, Haydn wrote Luigia: "Perhaps the time will come, for which we have so often wished when two pairs of eyes will be closed. One is shut already but what of the other? Well, be it as God wills." Luigia had two sons, the first born in 1777, the second six years later, in Eszterháza. Haydn was devoted to both, and gossip insisted he was the father of the younger. He taught the two boys music and, irrespective of the question of paternity, he made no distinction between them. Singularly enough, the "Infernal Beast" who abominated Luigia, showed herself exceptionally kind to Pietro Polzelli when he visited her in 1792.

*   *   *

About 1781 Haydn established a friendship which was to grow increasingly profound and more influential. He made the acquaintance of Wolfgang Amadeus Mozart, who had come from Salzburg to settle at last in Vienna. The sympathy was mutual, though the two masters were in many ways the absolute reverse of each other. Mozart was from his childhood a genuine virtuoso, such as Haydn had never pretended to be. Neither had Haydn matured artistically with anything like the speed of the sensitive and mercurial genius from Salzburg, nor possessed anything like the universality of the latter's gifts. Be these things as they may, the pair seemed to have come into the world to complement one another. Their friendship is one of the most beautiful and productive the history of music affords. "Haydn was fascinated by Mozart's quicksilver personality, while Mozart enjoyed the sense of security that Haydn's steadfastness and warmth of feeling gave him." And it was as if the two kindled brighter artistic sparks in their respective souls. The two played chamber music together whenever Haydn made a trip to Vienna. When Leopold Mozart visited his son, in 1785, Wolfgang, Haydn and several friends performed some of Mozart's new quartets for father Mozart. It was on this occasion that Haydn made to Leopold the oft-quoted remark: "I tell you before God and as an honest man that your son is the greatest composer known to me either in person or by reputation. He has taste and, what is more, the most profound knowledge of composition." Wolfgang was delighted, but declared at the same time that it was only from Haydn that he had learned how to write string quartets. And the half-dozen he issued in 1785 and dedicated with moving phrases to his "beloved friend Haydn" are doubtless among the finest he composed. On the other hand, Mozart never permitted a derogatory word to be said in his presence about Haydn. And when the Bohemian composer and pianist, Leopold Kozeluch, once said to Mozart on hearing a boldly dissonant passage in a Haydn quartet: "I would never have written that," Mozart instantly retorted: "Nor would I! And do you know why? Because neither you nor I would have had so excellent an idea. . . . Sir, even if they melted us both together, there would still not be stuff enough to make a Haydn." When some years later Haydn was asked his opinion about a debated passage in *Don Giovanni* he answered with finality: "I cannot settle this dispute, but this I know: Mozart is the greatest composer that the world now possesses!" And hearing an argument about the harmony in the beginning of Mozart's C Major Quartet, Haydn put a stop to the controversy then and there by saying: "If Mozart wrote it so he must have had good reason for it." And when someone in Prague invited Haydn to write an opera for that city he declined on the ground—among other things—that he "would be taking a big risk, for scarcely any man could stand comparison with the great Mozart. Oh, if I could only explain to every musical friend . . . the inimitable art of Mozart, its depth, the greatness of its emotion, and its unique musical conception, as I myself feel and understand it, nations would then vie with each other to possess so great a jewel. . . . Prague ought to strive not merely to retain this precious man, but also to remunerate him; for without this support the history of any great genius is sad indeed. It enrages me to think that the unparalleled Mozart has not yet been engaged by some imperial or royal court. Do forgive this outburst—but I love that man too much."

*   *   *

It should not be imagined that the various operas of Haydn have anything like the vitality, the dramatic life or the quality of "theater" we find in the stage works of Mozart. The greater part were com-

posed for the playhouse at Eszterháza and in certain cases for marionettes. Sometimes they were slender comedies, on the "Singspiel" order,
sometimes masques, intermezzi, scenic cantatas. Possibly the two operas
which in modern times have experienced most frequent revival are
the comedy, *Lo Speziale* ("The Apothecary") and *Il Mondo della Luna*
("The World of the Moon").

His life at Eszterháza had the advantage of preserving Haydn from
the intrigues and jealousies that ran riot in Vienna and from which
even a Mozart had to suffer so bitterly. Yet without traveling far from
Eisenstadt Haydn was now rapidly becoming widely famous. One of
the first countries where he gained glory in distinguished circles was
Spain. In 1779 his music was already becoming a subject of high-flown
poetic praise. In 1781 King Charles III sent the composer a gold snuff-
box. The secretary of the Spanish Legation went to Eszterháza in
person to convey his sovereign's esteem to Haydn, whose princely
employer must have swelled with pride at such a lofty distinction so
ceremoniously conferred upon his "servant." The composer, Luigi Boc-
cherini, a protégé of the Spanish king's brother, strove so successfully
to imitate Haydn's style that someone called him "Haydn's wife."
Perhaps the most important Spanish honor of all came from a canon of
Cadiz for a work called *The Seven Last Words of Our Saviour on
the Cross*. Let us cite Haydn's own words which preface the score
published by Breitkopf and Härtel in 1801:

"About 1786 I was requested to compose instrumental music in *The
Seven Last Words*. It was customary at the Cathedral of Cadiz to
produce an oratorio every year during Lent, the effect of the performance being not a little enhanced by the following circumstances. The
walls, windows, and pillars of the church were hung with black cloth,
and only one large lamp hanging from the center of the roof broke
the solemn obscurity. At midday the doors were closed and the ceremony began. After a short service the bishop ascended the pulpit,
pronounced the first of the seven words and delivered a discourse
thereon. This ended, he left the pulpit and prostrated himself before
the altar. The pause was filled by music. The bishop then in like
manner pronounced the second word, then the third, and so on, the
orchestra following on the conclusion of each discourse. My composition was subject to these conditions, and it was no easy matter to

compose seven adagios to last ten minutes each, and succeed one another without fatiguing the listeners; indeed, I found it quite impossible to confine myself within the appointed limits."

Haydn looked upon the composition as one of his most important and, as a matter of fact, it widely exercised a profound impression. It was even performed in the United States in 1793. When it came to paying Haydn for his work the Spanish ecclesiast presented the composer with a large sum of money concealed in an enormous chocolate cake! *The Seven Last Words* was, in the course of years, done by a string quartet, by an orchestra, as an oratorio. Today the work is hard to listen to with patience, impressive as it once seemed. A series of adagios, one much like the other, it has precisely the effect that the composer at first feared: the various movements as they succeed one another end by sorely "fatiguing the hearers."

France and England, in their turn, presently developed unmistakable signs of Haydn worship, which progressed increasingly. In Italy the composer steadily won favor. The Philharmonic Society of Modena made him a member as early as 1780. Ferdinand IV, of Naples, a few years later ordered concertos for an instrument called the lira organizzata. The king wanted Haydn to visit Italy; the composer would have loved to do so, but could not leave Eszterháza. Frederick William II, of Prussia, who played the cello, sent Haydn a superb and costly diamond ring. We are told that he put on the ring whenever he began an important work because "when he forget to do so no ideas occurred to him." He also received a costly ring from his pupil, the Russian Grand Duchess Maria Feodorovna, whom he taught in 1782 in Vienna and for whom he composed numerous songs more than twenty years later. Then, in 1781, Haydn informed the Viennese publisher, Artaria, that "Monsieur Le Gros, director of the Concerts Spirituels in Paris, wrote me a great many nice things about my *Stabat Mater* which had been given there four times with great applause. . . . They made me an offer to engrave all my future works on very advantageous terms." In 1784 a Paris society, the Concerts de la Loge Olympique (patronized by French royalty, and where audiences were required to pass a kind of examination before they were admitted to its functions) commissioned Haydn to write six symphonies for them, to which solicitation we owe the composer's great series of "Paris" Symphonies. Not only did French publishers now make profitable proposals to Haydn; in Luigi Cherubini, meanwhile, he had one of his most impassioned advocates in Paris.

Haydn could probably have gone to England and become associated with the musical life of that country much sooner than he did. When in 1783 the Professional Concerts were founded in London an attempt was made to secure him to take over their direction. The composer, not feeling that Prince Eszterházy would have given his consent, had to refuse and the English public contented itself with listening to a Haydn symphony as the opening offering of the series. By that time Haydn's music was so well known and stood so high in British favor that his works had gained a preponderant place in the musical life of the country. The Prince of Wales, an excellent cellist, caused Haydn's quartets to be performed continually at the palace musicales. And invitations to come to England poured upon Haydn from every corner of the Island Kingdom. For all that, he remained as simple and unspoiled as ever. He never forgot his humble origin. To Griesinger he once said: "I have had intercourse with emperors, kings and many a great personage, and have been told by them quite a few flattering things. For all that, I do not care to be on intimate terms with such persons and prefer to keep to people of my own station."

In Vienna the number of Haydn's intimates steadily increased. As the years of his sojourn at Eszterháza passed pleasantly, but monotonously, the composer strove increasingly to widen his Viennese circle of friends. He was able to accomplish this without unusual effort. The publisher, Artaria, who had close business connections with Haydn, was only one of the master's cronies. Then, of course, there were Mozart and his friends Michael Kelly, Stephen and Nancy Storace, the merchant Michael Puchberg (who immortalized himself by lending Mozart money). And Haydn, following the suggestion of Mozart and Puchberg, became a Freemason and joined the lodge *Zur wahren Eintracht*. But in some ways the closest friends of Haydn's in Vienna were Peter L. von Genzinger and his wife, Marianne. Von Genzinger had long been Prince Eszterházy's doctor. Both he and his wife were to the highest degree cultured and musical—Frau von Genzinger, for that matter, was an uncommonly gifted pianist and singer. Haydn was so welcome a guest in that hospitable dwelling that, among other things, his hostess never tired of preparing for him his favorite dishes.

The only drop of bitterness the lovely Genzinger home brought him was the poignant contrast it sometimes furnished to the growing monotony of Eszterháza, to which place he returned with a pang. "Well here I sit in my wilderness, like some poor orphan, almost without human society, melancholy, dwelling on the memory of past glorious days," he wrote to Marianne von Genzinger, in 1790, after he had mournfully returned to Eszterháza. His letters to Marianne have a freedom and a spontaneity not to be found in Haydn's usually stilted correspondence. As time passed it became fairly evident that Haydn deeply, if hopelessly, loved her. To be sure, he wrote that "she need be under no uneasiness . . . for my friendship and esteem for you (warm as they are) can never become reprehensible since I have always in my mind my respect for your elevated virtues, which not only I, but all who know you must reverence. . . . Oh, that I could be with you, dear lady, even for a quarter of an hour, to pour forth all my sorrows, and to receive comfort from you! Well, as God pleases! This time will also pass away and the day return when I shall again have the inexpressible pleasure of being seated beside you at the pianoforte, hearing Mozart's masterpieces, and kissing your hands from gratitude for so much pleasure."

Between the lines it is possible to read that for all his honors and distinctions Haydn was not growing happier at Eszterháza as the years elapsed. By 1790 we find him writing: "I am doomed to stay at home. It is indeed sad always to be a slave." He was growing restive amid all this Eszterházy luxury. He had his orchestra, his palatial little theater, the unending festivities at Eszterháza; he had Luigia Polzelli and he had little occasion to bother about the "Infernal Beast," who, though she still walked the earth, scarcely existed for him. But it irked him that he could not accept those invitations to visit foreign countries which were piling in upon him. The truth, as Dr. Geiringer keenly observes, was that "Haydn had outgrown Eszterháza. . . . Even his attachment to his beloved prince had somewhat diminished. Haydn, now a man of nearly sixty, like a person of half his age, craved for a change, new tasks, new experiences. With the sure instinct of genius he felt that the immense creative forces still slumbering in him could be released only by a cleancut break with the way of life that for nearly thirty years had been dear to him."

* * *

At the psychological moment destiny came to Haydn's aid somewhat as, decades later, it invariably came to Wagner's. In the fall of 1790, Prince Nicholas the Magnificent died suddenly. His successor, Prince Anton Eszterházy, who was unmusical and otherwise unlike his father, instantly dismissed the orchestra, retaining only Haydn, Tomasini and a few others to take care of the church music. He did not, indeed, discharge Haydn and even paid him well to keep him nominally in his employ. But he gave the master leave to travel wherever he wanted. Instantly, Haydn dashed to Vienna, where fate took charge of his interests once more. A relative of the Eszterházys wanted him for another princely post at Pressburg; the King of Naples repeated his earlier invitation to Italy. Then, while the composer deliberated, a stranger burst into his room with the words: "My name is Salomon. I have come from London to fetch you; we shall conclude our accord tomorrow." Haydn was bowled over and almost before he realized the truth, Johann Peter Salomon, of Bonn, superintended everything. Haydn was to be paid three hundred pounds for an opera, three hundred more for six new symphonies, two hundred for the copyrights, two hundred for twenty smaller pieces, two hundred more for a benefit concert in London. He had, then and there, to consider whether it was to be Pressburg, Italy or England. One reason he decided against Italy was because he appreciated that he was not a born opera composer like Mozart. But though Haydn spoke Italian and knew not a word of English (besides which the Channel crossing worried him), he decided—most fortunately as it proved—on England. For one thing, he realized that England was at that time a leader in the orchestral field; in the second place Haydn was surfeited with nobility and the courts of princes. And he longed for the personal freedom which England assured him. So London it should be! His friends—among them Mozart—were frightened. "Oh, Papa, you have had no education for the wide world, and you speak so few languages," protested Wolfgang. "But my language is understood all over the world," gently replied Haydn. Just the same, he found parting from Mozart harder than from any of his other friends. And when they took leave of one another, the younger man exclaimed prophetically: "I am afraid, Papa, this will be our last farewell." Mozart's death was one of the sorest blows Haydn ever suffered, and the pain of it actually sharpened with the passing of time.

94

Ten days before Christmas, 1790, Haydn set out on his journey with Salomon. They took ship at Calais, January 1, 1791, at seven-thirty A.M. ("after attending early Mass"). As he wrote Marianne von Genzinger, he was "very well, although somewhat thinner, owing to fatigue, irregular sleep, and eating and drinking so many things." In spite of a choppy sea he stood the crossing admirably, probably because "I remained on deck during the whole passage, in order to gaze my fill at that huge monster, the ocean." Only once or twice was he "seized with slight alarm and a little indisposition likewise." Yet he arrived at Dover "without being actually sick," even if most of the passengers did "look like ghosts." Doubtless he recalled with amusement his boyish attempts to portray a storm at sea on the harpsichord in the days of Kurz-Bernardon!

Haydn's first impressions of London were overwhelming. He was as struck and delighted with the size and grandeur of the British metropolis, its crowds, its teeming traffic and the "strangeness" of English life as was even the worldlier Mendelssohn, several decades later. Nevertheless, he was not a little frightened and found the street noise "unbearable." He had not a little trouble with the language and was much confused about the right thing to do when people drank his health. He wrote to Frau von Genzinger that he was trying to learn English by taking morning walks alone in the woods "with his English grammar." Salomon did not spare him any of the customary social engagements and amenities. Before he had been in London three weeks he was invited to a court ball and welcomed by the Prince of Wales, who, so Haydn decided, was "the handsomest man on God's earth." The Prince (the future George IV) "wore diamonds worth eighty-thousand pounds." Haydn eventually managed to secure a recipe for the Prince's brand of punch; it called for "one bottle of champagne, one of burgundy, one of rum, ten lemons, two oranges and a pound and a half of sugar."

On March 11, 1791, occurred Haydn's first concert in the Hanover Square Rooms. The function in every respect exceeded the composer's fondest hopes. Its outstanding feature was the D major Symphony (No. 93). The orchestra surpassed both numerically and otherwise the one Haydn had commanded at Eszterháza. The master conducted from a harpsichord, as had always been his custom. The concertmaster was the worthy Salomon, who played on a superb Stradivarius. Dr.

Burney spoke of "a degree of enthusiasm such as almost amounted to frenzy." The Adagio of the symphony had to be repeated. The *Morning Chronicle* wrote: "We cannot suppress our very anxious hope that the first musical genius of the age may be induced by our liberal welcome to take up his residence in England." It was a wish which speedily spread. Even the King pressed the composer to make his home there and when, with the best grace in the world, Haydn assured him his Continental obligations would not permit him to do so, the monarch was more or less offended. One reason the master gave for his refusal was that "he could not leave his wife"—though the "Infernal Beast" was probably furthest from his thoughts! What really stood in the way of a permanent English residence was the fear of the tremendous drain on his creative powers his popularity might entail. He was, indeed, on the threshold of his greatest achievements and he was strong and healthy. All the same he was not growing younger. And he knew what the strain of being incessantly lionized would do in the long run.

For the time being, however, British adulation only had the effect of making Haydn more splendidly productive than ever. The twelve Salomon symphonies (six composed for Haydn's first visit to London, the remaining set written for his second a few years later) are indisputably Haydn's greatest symphonic creations. Let us mention a few of them. There is the so-called "Military" Symphony (Haydn's symphonies are more easily distinguished by their sometimes fanciful titles, than by keys or opus numbers); the "Clock," with its Andante, marked by a persistent tick-tock rhythm; the symphony "With the Kettledrum Roll"; the "Surprise," with its folk-like melody and its title derived from a wholly unexpected fortissimo (which Haydn believed would "wake up the old ladies") following a placid folk-like phase—yet actually more of a "surprise" from the astonishing harmonies heard just before the close of the variation movement.

The London Symphonies, together with *The Creation* and *The Seasons* as well as certain of the great string quartets, parts of which so astoundingly foreshadow the idiom of the Romantic period, are, in reality, the summits of Haydn's inspiration. It is a question if his genius would have unfolded itself so magnificently without the stimulus which came to the master from his two visits to England. In July, 1791, he was invited to the Oxford Commemoration to receive from the University the honorary degree of Doctor of Music. The occasion proved to be a love feast. Three concerts were given in Haydn's honor, at one of which he conducted his G major Symphony (No. 92), written several years earlier, but henceforth called the "Oxford" Symphony. As his "exercise" he wrote for the University a three part crab canon, "Thy Voive, O Harmony is Divine." For three days he went about in "cherry and cream-colored silk." "I wish my friends in Vienna could have seen me," he wrote, remarking in his diary "I had to pay one and a half guineas for the bell peals at Oxford when I received the Doctor's degree, and half a guinea for hiring the gown. The journey cost six guineas." By no means a cheap honor! At the same time it is worthwhile mentioning a statement of his to Dies, his biographer: "I owe much, I might say everything in England to the Doctor's degree; for thanks to it I met the first men and was admitted to the most important houses."

One of Haydn's greatest and most fruitful experiences in London was his attendance in 1791 at a huge Handel Commemoration in Westminster Abbey. It was a prodigious affair with more than a thousand participants. Handel's masterpieces may not have been intimately familiar to Haydn, though the Baron Van Swieten in Vienna made a cult both of Handel and Johann Sebastian Bach. In Westminster Abbey, however, with such a gigantic array of performers and a public brought up in the reverence of Handel's masterpieces the effect of a creation like *Messiah* was no less than shattering on Haydn. When he heard the *Hallelujah* chorus he burst into tears with the exclamation "Handel is the master of us all!" And it seems to have been the impact of Handel which moved him to contemplate an oratorio of his own. The outcome of this Handelian experience and of the great British tradition of massive choruses became, in due time, *The Creation* and *The Seasons*.

Haydn was immensely busy in England but he was thoroughly enjoying himself. He was entertained for five entire weeks at the home of a rich banker who lived in the country and who asked Haydn to give music lessons to his daughters, yet tactfully left the composer as much alone as he wished to be. So he was able to rest a little from the noise of London. Another time he went by boat from Westminster Bridge to Richmond and had dinner on a lovely island in the Thames; or he went to a dance at the home of the Lord Mayor of London, leaving when he found the room too hot and the music too bad; then he remained for three days at a castle where the Duke of York and his bride were spending their honeymoon. "Oh. my dear good lady," he exclaimed in a letter to Marianne von Genzinger, "how sweet is some degree of liberty! I had a kind prince, but was obliged at times to be dependent on base souls. I often sighed for release and now I have it in some measure. I am quite sensible of this benefit, though my mind is burdened with more work. The consciousness of being no longer a servant sweetens all my toil."

At a concert given in York House, where Haydn played, Salomon led an orchestra and the King and Queen were present, the composer was formally presented by the Prince of Wales to George III. The monarch talked for some time to the former "servant" of the Eszterházys and said, among other things, "Dr. Haydn, you have written a good deal." Whereupon Haydn answered: "Yes, Sire, a great deal more than is good." The King had the last word, however, and replied: "Oh, no; the world contradicts you." There can be no question, however, that on both his visits to England Haydn was called upon to subject his creative powers to a terrific strain. The strangest part of it was that the artist, whose years were now accumulating, seemed actually to be making up for the slow development of his genius in his young manhood. Not only were the works he produced greater and greater, but his assimilation of great and new musical influences was progressing steadily.

Apart from his other English activities there was no end of sightseeing to be done, complicated with a considerable amount of teaching. At the end of the music season the "worn out" master, went to Vauxhall Gardens, was delighted with the place where, among other things, the music was "fairly good" and where "coffee and milk cost nothing." However, he did have a few twinges of the "English rheumatism" and almost submitted to an operation for his nose polypus— though when they tied him to a chair and prepared to operate he "kicked and screamed so vigorously," that the surgeon and his assistants had to give it up.

Not even a Haydn escaped intrigues and baseless slander. A rival concert organization, unable to win him away from Salomon, launched rumors that the composer was showing signs of exhaustion and then sought to play off against Haydn the aging master's devoted pupil, Ignaz Pleyel. Another thing he seems not to have managed avoiding was a love affair. "There were certainly quite a few innocent friendships with beautiful women," relates Dr. Geiringer, "but they did not prevent the inflammable master from enjoying a more significant romance as well." Strangely enough, we know about it only from the letters of the lady in question, which Haydn carefully copied because, presumably, she wanted her correspondence back! So far as we have this interchange it is quite one-sided and none of Haydn's letters to her remain. The lady in the case was a widow, a Mrs. Schroeter. Dr. Burney referred to her as "a young lady of considerable fortune." Later, Haydn spoke of her to Dies, as "an English widow in London who loved me. Though sixty years old, she was still lovely and amiable, and in all likelihood I should have married her if I had been single." Like Marianne von Genzinger, Mrs. Schroeter was musical and did copyist work for the composer. Actually, she seems to have been much younger than Haydn's estimate.

Here are a few extracts from the letters he received from her in London: ". . . Pray inform me how you do, and let me know my Dear Love: When will you dine with me? I shall be truly happy to see you to dinner, either tomorrow or Tuesday . . . I am truly anxious and impatient to see you and I wish to have as much of your company as possible; indeed my dear Haydn I feel for you the fondest and tenderest affection the human heart is capable of, and I ever am with the firmest attachment my Dear Love, most Sincerely, Faithfully and most affectionately Yours. . . ." Another time, the devoted Mrs. Schroeter is concerned about his health: "I am told you was (sic!) at your Study's yesterday; indeed, my D.L., I am afraid it will hurt you . . . I almost tremble for your health. Let me prevail on you my much loved Haydn not to keep to your study's so long at one time. My dear love if you could know how precious your welfare is to me, I flatter myself you wou'd endeavor to preserve it, for my sake as well as your own." Another time: ". . . I hope to hear you are quite well, shall be happy to see you at dinner and if you can come at three o'clock it would give me great pleasure, as I should be particularly glad to see you my Dear before the rest of our friends come."

All the same, Haydn amid his numberless duties, found time to write to Luigia Polzelli, who was now in Italy. She was not a little jealous and the composer found it wise to placate her with extravagantly ardent letters and money. He would have been happy to see her son, Pietro, in London but he was much less anxious to have Luigia. Meantime, the "Infernal Beast" again stirred up trouble by sending notes to her detested rival hinting at Haydn's infidelities!

Let us herewith end the story of Luigia. Haydn had once promised to marry her when he should be free. When at long last Maria Anna Apollonia died in 1800, the Polzelli chose to remind him of his promise. But he solved the difficulty by giving her black on white, his solemn word to marry "no one else" and he also promised her a substantial pension for the rest of her life. Having pocketed that "promise" Luigia promptly married an Italian singer! Her son, Pietro, died in 1796. Haydn sincerely mourned him but turned his attention to another pupil of his, Sigismund Neukomm.

The wanderer came back to Vienna in midsummer, 1792. After the exhilaration of the first English trip the return to Vienna, for all his honors and distinctions, was chilling. No one seemed to care greatly. Moreover, there was one irreplaceable loss; Mozart was no more; and early in 1793 another blow struck Haydn—Marianne von Genzinger died at thirty-eight. Here was a calamity in its way rivaling the tragedy of Mozart. Haydn's resilient nature recovered even from the death of Marianne. But a certain sweetness departed with her and never returned. Singularly enough, there entered into his musical life about this time a force one might assume would have fortified him to bear the burden of his poignant losses. Beethoven arrived in Vienna from Bonn bearing the following message from Count Waldstein: "Dear Beethoven, you are traveling to Vienna in fulfillment of your long-cherished wish. The tutelary genius of Mozart is still weeping and bewailing the death of her favorite. With the inexhaustible Haydn she has found refuge, but no occupation, and now she is waiting to leave him and associate herself with someone else. Labor assiduously and receive Mozart's spirit from the hands of Haydn."

* * *

Haydn was the wrong teacher for Beethoven and Beethoven the wrong pupil for Haydn. The young man's relations with the old master were kind and friendly (Beethoven, according to his diaries, treated Haydn to "chocolate twenty-two times" and to "coffee six times"). But there was a spiritual gulf between them of which they both became aware. Haydn, indeed, foreshadowed musical romanticism, yet he did not, like his new pupil, arrogantly identify himself with it. Beethoven had none of that soul of a servitor which Haydn had acquired through his long career; so it was not without reason that the teacher used to allude to the hot-headed pupil as "the Grand Mogul." Moreover, Beethoven wanted to be instructed in counterpoint the hard way; and he was greatly irritated when Hayden did not carefully correct his technical exercises. Therefore, though the relationship remained outwardly amicable and the lessons went on, Beethoven changed teachers. He placed himself in the hands of the composer, Johann Schenk, and of the contrapuntist, Johann Albrechtsberger. As Schenk had told Beethoven in looking over some of his technical work, Haydn was now too busy composing great masterworks to be occupied by the needs of a particularly obstreperous student.

In 1794 Haydn started out a second time for London, but this time not in Salomon's company. Yet as he did not wish to make the journey unattended he decided on one of his young friends for an escort— Polzelli, Beethoven or some other. His usual luck attended him when he picked Johann Elssler, whose father had copied music at Eszterháza. Johann was Haydn's godson and in the fullness of time he became the father of the famous dancer, Fanny Elssler. He idolized Haydn, served him hand and foot, was secretary, copyist and the first to assist Haydn in cataloguing his works. On this English visit Haydn traveled rather more extensively than the first time. He went to the Isle of Wight, to Southampton, to Waverly Abbey, to Winchester. He went to Hampton Court, which reminded him of Eszterháza. He heard "miserable trash" at the Haymarket Theatre and even worse at Sadler's Wells. In Bath he met a Miss Brown, "an amiable discreet person," who had the additional advantage of "a beautiful mother"; he saw the grave of "Turk, a faithful dog and not a man"; and he composed music to a poem by the conductor of the Bath Harmonic Society, "What Art Expresses."

In August, 1795, Haydn was back in Vienna, and although the heart-breaks of the previous return were spared him he found plenty of new organizational labor awaiting him at Eszterháza, where a new prince, Nicholas II, a grandson of "The Magnificent" now held sway. His artistic tastes, though pronounced, did not run primarily in the directions of music. He gave Cherubini a gorgeous and costly ring, he liked the music of Reutter and Michael Haydn more than that of the great Eszterházy Capellmeister, and then insulted Beethoven with a stupid remark about the latter's C major Mass. He even criticized Haydn's management of some detail at an orchestral rehearsal, whereupon the now thoroughly irascible master turned on his patron with a wrathy: "Your Highness, it is my job to decide this!" He felt now that a Doctor of Music at Oxford should be addressed more respectfully than simply as "Haydn."

* * *

In London the composer once said: "I want to write a work which will give permanent fame to my name in the world." After his numberless symphonies, his masses, his clavier works, his vast store of chamber music, his concertos, his operatic miscellany, his songs and arias—after all these what could remain? England had given him one unrivaled experience from which he could nourish his genius—the mighty Handel Commemoration in Westminster Abbey. Haydn had experimented in countless forms, but not one. That was the oratorio and in this he could undertake new flights.

Where should he find a subject? Some say that a musical friend of Haydn's answered the master by opening a Bible standing handy and exclaiming: "There! Take that and begin at the beginning!" Others maintain that Salomon gave him a libretto which one Lidley had pieced together from Milton's "Paradise Lost" for Handel. Dr. Geiringer believes that both accounts may be true. At all events, Haydn returned to Vienna with the text. It was, however, in English, which Haydn understood imperfectly. It was necessary, consequently, to find an accomplished translator. As usual, good fortune attended him. Gottfried van Swieten, a litterateur, prefect of the Vienna Royal Library, friend of Mozart, worshipper of Handel and Bach, who thought highly of Haydn, was wealthy even if despotic, yet still after a fashion musical—this man was able to furnish Haydn what he required. Nay, more, "he got together a group of twelve music-loving noblemen and each guaranteed a contribution to defray the expenses of performance and pay an honorarium to the composer." And Haydn set jubilantly and, withal, reverently to work. He "spent much time over it, because he intended it to last a long time."

The labor gave him extraordinary happiness. It answered his inmost wants. Here he could give the freest possible rein to all that inborn optimism of his nature. Always profoundly religious, as free from doubt and skepticism as a child, his reverence was as sincere as it was sunny. Here he walked, literally, "hand in hand with his God." There came to the surface, moreover, all those springs of folk-song influence which were either remembered or subconsciously wrought into the fabric of his being. And he was now working on a newer and larger scale than hitherto. "Never was I so devout as when composing *The Creation*," he later said. "I knelt down every day and prayed to God to strengthen me in my work." If his inspiration ever threatened to grow sluggish "I rose from the pianoforte and began to say my rosary." This cure, he insisted, never failed.

The curious aspect of *The Creation* is that, though composed to a German translation of the English text, it is one of those rare masterpieces which actually sound better in a translation than in the original. The answer to this springs probably from the circumstances that *The Creation* is, in point of fact, an Anglo-Saxon heritage. An examination of numerous details of its setting and declamation make it clear that, almost subconsciously, Haydn has set and accompanied the English words in more subtly revealing fashion than the German. Similarly, Haydn achieved in the whole work that effect at which he was aiming. Writing to her daughter, the Princess Eleanore Liechtenstein said of the oratorio, "One has to shed tears about the greatness, the majesty, the goodness of God. The soul is uplifted. One cannot but love and admire."

The first performance of *The Creation* was given at the palace of Prince Schwarzenberg in Vienna on April 29, 1798. Only invited guests attended this and the second performance, though the mobs outside were so great that extra detachments of police had to be summoned. Haydn conducted, not from a keyboard, but in the modern way, with a baton. The rendering was superb, the audience enraptured. Haydn himself said later: "One moment I was as cold as ice, the next I seemed on fire. More than once I was afraid I should have a stroke." *The Creation* promptly spread over the world. In England it "was to prove so unfailing an attraction that proceeds from it, mostly given to charitable institutions, by far surpassed even the receipts from the London benefit concerts that once had seemed so extraordinary to Haydn." In Paris Bonaparte was on his way to hear a performance of it when a bomb exploded in the street through which he was passing, narrowly missing his carriage. In America it took root in short order.

The score deserves, in reality, a much more detailed scrutiny than can be given here. The introduction, the "Representation of Chaos," does not receive the attention it actually merits. There is a warmth of color to the writing, particularly to the woodwind, which is something new in Haydn. And the closing bars of the amazing page are the more startling because they provide a foretaste of one of the most striking passages in Wagner's *Tristan und Isolde*. It may be mentioned, in passing, that this is by no means the only time when Haydn affords an amazing Wagnerian presage.

The great and even more celebrated moment in the opening choral number of the oratorio is the passage "Let there be Light and there was Light." From a thin, gray C minor we are suddenly overwhelmed with a sudden and mighty C major chord—an unmistakable sunburst in tone. In all music this tremendous moment has not its like unless it be a similar episode—also a sunrise and by curiously related means—at the opening of Richard Strauss's *Thus Spake Zarathustra*. From the very first this moment in *The Creation* overpowered the listeners and after a century and a half it has lost not a vestige of its glory. At his last appearance in a concert hall, Haydn, only a few weeks from his end, was taken to a performance of his work. At this episode the old master pointed upwards with the words "Not from me—from there, above, comes everything!"

The strain of unending toil was beginning to tell on Haydn, though the amazing aspect of it is that these latest works of his do not betray the slightest diminution of freshness or inventive powers. Yet on June 12, 1799, he wrote to Breitkopf and Härtel a letter which deserves attention: "My business unhappily expands with my advancing years, and it almost seems as if, with the decrease of my mental powers, my inclination and impulse to work increase. Oh God! how much yet remains to be done in this splendid art, even by a man like myself! The world, indeed, daily pays me many compliments, even on the fervor of my latest works; but no one can believe the strain and effort it costs me to produce them, inasmuch as time after time my feeble memory and the unstrung state of my nerves so completely crush me to earth, that I fall into the most melancholy condition. For days afterwards I am incapable of formulating one single idea, till at length my heart is revived by providence, and I seat myself at the piano and begin once more to hammer away at it. Then all goes well again, God be praised. I only wish and hope that the critics may not handle my 'Creation' with too great severity and be too hard on it. They may possibly find the musical orthography faulty in various passages, and perhaps other things also, which for so many years I have been accustomed to consider as minor points, but the genuine connoisseur will see the real cause as readily as I do, and willingly ignore such stumbling blocks. This, however, is entirely *entre nous;* or I might be accused of conceit and arrogance, from which, however, my Heavenly Father has preserved me all my life long."

Haydn had still a prodigious amount of work before him. Chief of all was another full length oratorio, *The Seasons,* based on James Thomson's didactic poem. Here again the Baron van Swieten edited and translated, though he made use of several German poems in addition to Thomson's (of which he altered the "unhappy" ending). The composer worked for three years on *The Seasons,* not completing it till 1801. It seems to have tested his powers sorely. It was no less optimistic a document than *The Creation,* but by and large an outspoken Nature piece (conceived in Rousseau's "Back to Nature" philosophy), yet with only transient religious undertones and without the genuinely Biblical quality of *The Creation.* Still, the truly amazing part of *The Seasons* is its incessant vitality, the charm of its pictorial aspect and the unending freshness of its inspiration. All the same, the magnificent work made unmistakable inroads on Haydn's vitality. He paid for its success with his health and was in the habit of saying, from now on, " 'The Seasons' has given me the death blow!" Actually, he had suffered a physical breakdown of a sort shortly after one of the productions of *The Creation.* He had to take to his bed and, intermittently, the flow of his inspiration threatened to halt. But invariably he would recover, both physically and mentally. He revised his earlier "Seven Last Words" as an oratorio; he arranged two hundred and fifty Scotch folksongs for the Edinburgh publisher, George Thomson; the number of his string quartets increased. Performances of *The Creation* multiplied everywhere. Honors poured in upon him from all quarters. He was warmly invited to come to Paris and his old pupil, Pleyel, was dispatched to fetch him. Fortunately, Haydn spared himself the exertions of such a trip. Still, France struck a medal in his honor, which gave the master no end of pleasure; and he received the warmest expressions of affection from the inhabitants of the little Baltic island of Rügen, where a performance of *The Creation* was given. He even strove to be his own publisher and sought subscriptions for the score of the oratorio. His friends rallied magnificently to his aid— the English royal family, the Empress of Austria, the innumerable friends from his native country and from Britain (England as much as Austria now claimed him as one of her very own!). Lord Nelson and Lady Hamilton visited Eszterháza and it is said that for two days the Lady "would not budge from Haydn's side," while Nelson gave him a gold watch in exchange for the master's pen!

The great composition of this later period of Haydn's life is beyond dispute his patriotic anthem, "Gott erhalte Franz den Kaiser"—the Austrian hymn, as, through thick and thin, it has remained. That, too, was indirectly a product of his English experiences! He had always been stirred in London by "God Save the King" and it became his ambition to provide something similar for his own nation. The great melody that resulted bears a distinct resemblance to a Croatian folk-song of the Eisenstadt region, "Zalostna zarucnica," which certain musicologists maintain served as the inspiration for Haydn's melody, though the derivation has not been definitely established. But others than Austrians have made the song their own. The Germans, for instance, added it to a poem by Hoffmann von Fallersleben and thereby it became "Deutschland über alles"; the English speaking nations put it to churchly uses and made of it the hymn "Glorious Things of Thee are Spoken."

While he was still engaged in exacting creative work he set a schedule for himself which he appears to have followed rigorously. A daily plan of activities (written by Elssler, Dr. Geiringer surmises) furnishes a picture of "Herr von Haydn's" routine. He was living in a house he had bought in the "Gumpendorfer" district of Vienna. We read that "in the summertime he rose at six-thirty A.M. First he shaved, which he did for himself up to his seventy-third year, and then he completed dressing. If a pupil were present, he had to play his lesson on the piano to Herr von Haydn, while the master dressed. All mistakes were promptly corrected and a new task was then set. This occupied an hour and a half. At eight o'clock sharp, breakfast had to be on the table, and immediately after breakfast Haydn sat down at the piano improvising and drafting sketches of some composition. From eight o'clock to eleven-thirty his time was taken up in this way. At eleven-thirty calls were received or made, or he went for a walk until one-thirty. The hour from two to three was reserved for dinner, after which Haydn immediately did some little work in the house or resumed his musical occupations. He scored the morning's sketches, devoting three to four hours to this.. At eight P.M. Haydn usually went out and at nine he came home and sat down to write a score or he took a book and read until ten P.M. At that time he had supper, which consisted of bread and wine. Haydn made a rule of eating nothing but bread and wine at night and infringed it only on sundry occasions when he was invited to supper. He liked gay conversation and some merry entertainment at the table. At eleven-thirty he went to bed, in his old age even later. Wintertime made no difference to the schedule, except that Haydn got up half an hour later."

* * *

But despite this pleasant and comfortable routine Haydn was now beginning to age rapidly. On December 26, 1803, he conducted for the last time and, characteristically, for a hospital fund, the work he directed being the *Seven Last Words.* He wrote two movements of a string quartet, but by 1806, he had given up all idea of finishing it and, as a conclusion, added a few bars of a song he had written in the past few years, "Der Greis," which begins "Hin ist alle meine Kraft, alt und schwach bin ich" ("Gone is all my strength, old and weak am I"). Friends and admirers in ever increasing numbers sought him out to pay their respects. There came Cherubini, the Abbé Vogler, the violinist Baillot, Pleyel, members of the Weber family, Mme. Bigot—a friend of Beethoven and afterwards one of the piano teachers of Felix and Fanny Mendelssohn; Hummel, the widow of Mozart, the Princess Eszterházy, the actor, Iffland.

In 1805 a rumor gained currency that Haydn had died. The world was shocked. Cherubini even composed a cantata on Haydn's passing; Kreutzer a violin concerto based on themes from Haydn's works, while in Paris a special memorial concert was arranged and Mozart's Requiem was to be given. Suddenly there came a letter from the master saying that "he was still of this base world." And he thanked his French admirers for their well-meant gestures adding "had I only known of it in time, I would have traveled to Paris to conduct the Requiem myself!" Johann Wenzel Tomaschek told how Haydn greeted any visitor who might drop in: "He sat in an armchair, very much dressed up. A powdered wig with sidelocks, a white neckband with a bold buckle, a white richly embroidered waistcoat of heavy silk, in the midst of which shone a splendid jabot, a dress of fine coffee-colored cloth with embroidered cuffs, black silk breeches, white silk hose, shoes with large silver buckles curved over the instep, and on a little table next to him a pair of white kid gloves made up his attire."

He made one last public appearance. It was at a performance of *The Creation* given at the Vienna University in celebration of the master's seventy-sixth birthday. About the only person of prominence not present was Prince Eszterházy; but he at least sent his carriage to bring the master to the concert! At the hall were assembled not alone the high nobility but all the most distinguished musicians of the capital, among them Beethoven, Salieri, Hummel, Gyrowetz. Salieri conducted. The concertmaster was Franz Clement, for whom Beethoven wrote his violin concerto. The French ambassador, seeing Haydn wearing the gold medal of the Parisian Concerts des Amateurs, exclaimed: "This medal is not enough; you should receive all the medals that France can distribute!" The Princess Eszterházy not only sat next to the master but wrapped her own shawl about him. It was on this occasion that Haydn made his historic remark when the audience burst into applause at the sublime passage "And there was Light." As the concert progressed he became visibly excited and it was thought advisable to take him home. As Haydn left the auditorium Beethoven knelt down before him and reverently kissed his hand and brow. Before the old man finally vanished from view he turned one last time and lifted his hand in blessing on the assemblage.

*   *   *

By the spring of 1809 the Napoleonic wars were again devastating Austria. The bombardment of the western suburbs of Vienna brought the battle uncomfortably close to Haydn's home. Nevertheless, the master refused to leave and when a bomb fell close to the Gumpendorfer house the old man reassured his frightened servants with the words: "Children, don't be frightened; where Haydn is, nothing can happen to you!" But the continuous noise and excitement shook the invalid's nerves so severely that he took to his bed and left it only once. This was to be carried to his piano, there to play three times in succession and with the deepest possible feeling his own Austrian hymn, as if to defy those hostile powers unwilling to let him die in peace. On the same day, however, he was visited by a French officer, Clément Sulémy, who called to pay his respects to the composer of *The Creation* and who, before he left, sat down at the piano and sang the aria *In Native Worth* "in so manly and so sublime a style, with so much truth of expression and musical sentiment" that Haydn embraced him and said he had never heard the air delivered in so masterly a fashion. Sulémy fell in battle the same day, a fact which the composer, fortunately, never learned.

But his strength was now quite gone. He could only whisper to those about him: "Children, be comforted, I am well." Then he lapsed into unconsciousness and shortly after midnight, May 31, 1809, he passed. Napoleon saw to it that a military guard of honor was stationed at his door. At his obsequies not only the cultural world of Vienna but also the highest French military officials were present. And Mozart's Requiem was sung.

*　　*　　*

The story cannot be ended without an allusion to its macabre epilogue. Haydn was laid to rest in the Hundsturm Cemetery. But soon afterwards Prince Eszterházy received permission to re-inter the master in Eisenstadt. There were lengthy delays, however, and in 1814 Sigismund Neukomm was shocked to find the tomb in a state of dilapidation. He placed on it a marble slab with Haydn's favorite quotation from Horace, "Non omnis moriar" ("I shall not wholly die"), set as a five part canon. Six years later the Duke of Cambridge remarked to Prince Eszterházy, "How fortunate was the man who employed this Haydn in his lifetime and now possesses his mortal remains!" The Prince said nothing, but experienced a sharp twinge of conscience. So he gave orders for the exhumation and the reburial in the Eisenstadt Bergkirche, where Haydn had conducted a number of his masses. When the coffin was opened the officials were appalled to find a body without a head! It developed that a certain Carl Rosenbaum, once a secretary to Prince Eszterházy, and a penitentiary official, one Johann Peter, had bribed the Viennese gravedigger to steal the skull which they wanted for phrenological experiments. Peter had made an elaborately decorated box (with windows and a satin cushion) for the gruesome relic. The outraged Prince sent the police to Peter, who meantime had given the skull to Rosenbaum. The police were quite as unsuccessful at the Rosenbaum house, for the singer, Therese Gassmann Rosenbaum, promptly hid the skull in her mattress and went to bed, pretending illness. The hideous farce went a step further, when Rosenbaum, expecting a bribe, substituted the head of some unidentified old man. When Rosenbaum died he left Haydn's skull to Peter, obligating him to bequeath it to the museum of the Society of the Friends of Music, in Vienna, where it was preserved since 1895.

It was reported that the Nazis, after the Austrian Anschluss in 1938, proposed to bury the head in Haydn's coffin at Eisenstadt. Whether they carried out this plan is not known to the present writer.

H. F. P.

Wolfgang Amadeus Mozart

BORN: SALZBURG, JAN. 27, 1756. DIED: VIENNA, DEC. 5, 1791.

*I declare to you before God, and as an honest man, that
your son is the greatest composer I know, either personally
or by name.—*JOSEPH HAYDN *to Leopold Mozart.*

MOZART'S EARTHLY CAREER was so poignantly short yet so filled
with incalculable achievement that the author finds himself confronted
with an impossible task. He has, consequently, preferred to outline as
best he could in the space at his disposal a few successive details of
a life that was amazingly crowded with incident, early triumphs, and
subsequent crushing tragedies, rather than to consider (let alone eval-
uate) the staggering creative abundances the master bequeathed mankind.

It is scarcely necessary to disclaim for this thumbnail sketch any
new slant or original illumination. If it moves any reader to renew his
acquaintance with the standard biographies of the composer or, better still, to deepen his artistic enrichment by a study of modern inter-
pretations of contemporary Mozart scholars like Alfred Einstein, and
Bernhard Paumgartner, its object will be more than achieved.

*　　*　　*

If the Mozartean family tree was nothing like the prodigious trunk
of the Bachs it was still not without striking features. There were
Mozarts in South Germany as far back as the end of the sixteenth
century; and as remotely as the thirteenth the name stood on a document in Cologne. To be sure, various spellings of Mozart existed in
those distant times. It appeared as "Mosshard," "Motzhart," "Mozert,"

and in still other variants. Bernhard Paumgartner, Director of the Salzburg Mozarteum, thinks it derived from the old German root *mod,* or *muot,* from which came the word *Mut* (courage). Be this as it may, German "Mozarts" were anything but exceptional a couple of hundred years before Leopold Mozart or his son, Wolfgang, came into the picture. In Augsburg there was an Anton Mozart who painted landscapes "in the manner of Breughel." Another Mozart from the same town, one Johann Michael, was a sculptor, who in 1687 moved to Vienna and became an Austrian citizen.

But of all these "Mossherts," "Motards," and the rest, only one, the mason apprentice David Motzert, born in the village of Pfersee, close to Augsburg, really belongs to our story. The *Augsburger Bürgerbuch* of 1643 mentions him and sets his fortune at one hundred florins. By his marriage with the *Jungfer* Maria Negeler he was to become the great-great-grandfather of the creator of *Don Giovanni.* In the fullness of time David's grandson, Johann Georg, abandoned the occupation of his forebears for that of a bookbinder. His second wife blessed him with two daughters and six sons. One of these sons, Franz Aloys, gained a kind of immortality as the father of Maria Anna Thekla, Wolfgang's cousin, the "Bäsle," to whom he wrote that series of notoriously smutty letters with which this lively young lady's name is eternally linked.

Johann Georg's first-born, Johann Georg Leopold, became for posterity simply Leopold Mozart, composer of arid music, author of a celebrated violin method, and father of Wolfgang and of Maria Anna Walburga Ignatia, whom the world remembers almost solely as "Nannerl." It is to Nannerl, incidentally, that we have to look for a sort of continuation of the Mozart line down almost to our own time. On January 9, 1919, there died in the Feldhof Insane Asylum, near Graz, the seventy-seven-year-old Bertha Forschter, a great-grand-daughter of Nannerl, who had lived on in Salzburg till 1829, highly revered because of her exalted kinship.

EARLY LIFE IN SALZBURG

What brought Leopold Mozart to Salzburg in the first place? A choir singer in the Augsburg Church of St. Ulrich and a graduate of the Augsburger Jesuit Lyceum, he seemed to be shaping for a priestly career. He did not, at all events, follow the bookbinder's trade like his brothers. Alfred Einstein finds it difficult to grasp why he should have preferred Salzburg to Munich or Ingolstadt for an orthodox theological education. Possibly a suggestion of the canons of St. Ulrich had something to do with it. Whatever the reason, he enrolled at the University in the town on the Salzach, July 22, 1738. There he studied philosophy, logic, and music, understood Latin, composed Passion cantatas and instrumental works, acquired some proficiency on the violin, and obtained a smattering of legal knowledge. Five years later he became fourth violinist in the court orchestra of the archbishop, but he maintained his close family connections with Augsburg and later encouraged his son not to relax these ties.

It is not quite certain exactly when he met Anna Maria Pertl, whose father was superintendent of a clerical institution at St. Gilgen on the nearby Wolfgang See. In the fall of 1772 he wrote her from Milan: "It was twenty-five years ago, I think, that we had the sensible idea of getting married, one which we had cherished for many years. All good things take time!" Anna Maria was her husband's junior by a year. Jahn questions if she rose in any way above the average woman of her type. A good provincial, she had not the suspicious, mistrustful qualities of Leopold. She lacked intellectual depth, but she was a good wife and affectionate mother, a genuinely lovable creature, a receptacle of all the community gossip and local tittle-tattle. "She judged with an eye just as friendly as her husband's was critical and sarcastic." And from his mother Wolfgang inherited his gaiety and some of his more incorrigible *Hanswurst* characteristics.

Though the Mozart couple had seven children, only two of these survived infancy—Nannerl, the fourth, and her great brother, who came last. Wolfgang was born on January 27, 1756, at eight o'clock in the evening in the house belonging to Lorenz Hagenauer, on the narrow Getreide Gasse, Salzburg. The very next morning the newcomer (whose birth came near costing the mother's life) was carried to church and baptized with the name Johannes Chrysostomus Wolfgangus Theophilus, the last in honor of his godfather, Johann Theophilus Pergmayr. Subsequently the Greek Theophilus was changed to its more euphonious Latin equivalent Amadeus. Wolfgang, like the other Mozart children, was at first nourished with water instead of milk, according to a preposterous superstition of the time. We have to thank the good health of the infant that he did not succumb, as did most of the other Mozart offspring, and even withstood later illnesses.

A sensitive and affectionate lad, Wolfgang was extraordinarily devoted to his parents, especially to his father, despite Leopold's humorless and obstinate nature. "Next to God comes papa!" was a childhood expression of the boy. To be sure, the inflexible martinet commanded a certain respect by reason of his very genuine love for his family and his determination to rear his children according to what he considered their best interests. But he seemed unable to rise above his middle-class prejudices and, when all is said, his attitude toward his son was like that of a conventional Victorian father, who guided the footsteps of his son according to his lights, yet refused to permit him any freedom whatever for explorations of his own. All the same, Leopold could be self-sacrificing in the interest of his children and therein lay one of the saving features of an unlovable character.

It was one of his merits to have perceived at once the musical predispositions of his children, to have cultivated them, even to have grasped early the most advantageous ways of exploiting them. Nannerl was by no means slow in showing uncommon aptitude for music, and Leopold lost no time in embarking upon her training. Wolfgang in his cradle listened to his sister's lessons in the adjoining room and we can only surmise what mystical instincts vibrated in the childish consciousness. He was hardly more than three when these impelled him to the keyboard, there to search for consonant intervals and to shout with delight when he discovered and sounded thirds. He had an abnormally refined and sensitive hearing, was distressed by impurities of pitch, and perturbed by any violence of sound (who does not remember the story of the child Mozart fainting on hearing the tone of a trumpet?). We are told that he was very soon able to play light piano pieces without any signs of effort and to memorize and perform them without notes, "cleanly and in perfect time," in less than half an hour. Nor was the violin unfamiliar to him and, though he is not supposed to have started his studies on that instrument till his sixth year, Nissen tells that a certain Herr von Murr heard Wolfgang play the violin at four!

Leopold Mozart's chief trouble lay not in making his son practice but in getting him away from the piano. Music occupied his waking hours almost exclusively, and for the customary games and amusements of childhood the boy showed little interest; or, if it was a question of fun, it had to be in some way associated with music. Before putting him to bed in the evening his father would stand him on a chair to give him a good-night kiss, whereupon the child would declaim Italian nonsense syllables, like "oragnia figatafa" and such, to some scrap of folk tune, as if imitating an opera singer. Then he would return his father's caresses, kissing him on the tip of his nose and promising when he grew up "to enclose him in a capsule and carry him about at all times!" In after years Leopold reminisced in a letter to his son: "When you sat at the piano or otherwise occupied yourself with music nobody was allowed to joke with you in any way. Indeed, the expression on your face would become so serious that many, struck by what they considered your prematurely ripened talent, feared that your life might be short"—fears that were to be only too well founded. And, when barely six, he stubbornly refused to play before any audience that did not include at least one musically cultured listener.

Abraham Mendelssohn used to say that, whereas he had once been famous as the son of his father, he was now celebrated as the father of his son. Leopold Mozart was most indisputably the father of his son. His juiceless compositions, his violin method, and the rest of his dreary talents and moral virtues have a kind of museum value only as they contributed to Wolfgang's artistic upbringing and guidance. Alfred Einstein observes that "the first signs of musical talent in Wolfgang completely changed the direction of Leopold's life and thought." Unquestionably it was better so, and in the long run he was far more richly rewarded for cultivating the fruitful soil committed to his tillage.

Systematic piano instruction was the first thing on which he seems to have concentrated. Composition was a by-product. Wolfgang improvised unceasingly, which meant that numberless minuets and simple pieces of various types took shape under his fingers, the father writing down industriously what his son's fancy dictated. Nannerl extemporized no less actively. Leopold spurred his children by acquainting them with short works by himself and recognized musicians to divert them after dry technical exercises. Each had a little study book of pieces. The one that Wolfgang received from his father on October 31, 1762, has come down to us complete and contains one hundred and thirty-five examples for study. Among them Wolfgang tried his hand at brief works of his own. In the father's writing we can read the following: "Di Wolfgango Mozart, May 11, 1762 und

July 16, 1762." Some of the masters given the boy to study were Wagenseil, Telemann, Hasse, and Philipp Emanuel Bach. Wolfgang's compositions include an innocent minuet and trio with very simple basses and a little Allegro in three-part song form. In these and other childish efforts the improving hand of Leopold can be repeatedly detected. It was to be so for some time to come and when the father did not have a correcting finger in the pie we become aware of it. It is evident in a sketch book Wolfgang was given in London a year or two later when Leopold fell ill and, in order not to be disturbed by the sounds of practicing, asked the boy to write something and refrain from noise. The book is filled with a great variety of minuets, contradances, rondos, gigues, sicilianos, preludes, and even an unfinished sketch for a fugue. Here one sees indisputable genius in conflict with technical lapses and other evidences of inexperience that somewhat modify the notion that Wolfgang had acquired all his skill by instinct rather than by carefully disciplined study.

First Visit to Vienna

The five-year-older Nannerl being a remarkable clavier performer and Wolfgang absorbing his father's instructions with the utmost facility, Leopold was not long in deciding that he might profitably bring his pair of prodigies before the public and make them known in aristocratic circles, where he had a good chance of capitalizing on their talents. Besides, there were new artistic currents astir in the world to which the boy, in particular, might be exposed to his advantage. "If ever I knew how priceless time is for youth I know it now and you know that my children are used to work," he wrote to H. Hagenauer, insisting he had no idea of permitting the youngsters to fall into habits of idleness. He seems to have given little thought to the strain of travel, especially since the children were healthy and Wolfgang, though small, appears to have been of wiry physique. So in January 1762, he took them on a three-weeks' excursion to Munich, where they appeared before the Elector Maximilian of Bavaria with success.

The following September, however, the family began their travels in earnest. With a small clavier strapped to their vehicle the little band of wanderers set out along the Danube by way of Linz and several smaller localities to Vienna. By October 6 they had reached the capital and they drank in its wonders with the astonished eyes of small-town folk. A week later they stood in the presence of the music-loving empress, Maria Theresa, and her family and court at the Palace of Schönbrunn. The children played and were admired and duly rewarded. There have come down to us a quantity of pretty anecdotes about the pair—how Wolfgang climbed up in the lap of the Empress and was kissed by her; how he insisted on having the composer Georg Christian Wagenseil in the room when he was to play ("because he understands such things"); how, when he slipped on the polished floor and was helped to his feet by the princess, Marie Antoinette, he thanked her and then added, "I shall marry you for this when I grow up!" Unquestionably the motherly tenderness of Maria Theresa went out to the child from Salzburg. Yet it is a question whether she actually saw in Wolfgang and his sister more than a pair of precocious little people in spite of Leopold's extravagant claims. Certainly she was less agreeable several years later when she wrote her son, the Archduke Ferdinand, governor-general of Lombardy, who contemplated taking Wolfgang into his service: "I do not know why you need saddle yourself with a composer or useless people . . . It discredits your service when such individuals run about the world like beggars."

At all events Leopold was voluble in the letters he wrote to his Salzburg landlord, Hagenauer, about the wonders of the Vienna visit and the impression exercised everywhere by Wolfgang's talents and his lively intelligence and unaffected manner. Leopold built towering air castles. Two weeks later Wolfgang came down with what was said to be scarlet fever but which was actually (according to Bernhard Paumgartner) diagnosed by a German doctor, Felix Huch, as "erythema nodosum," which could have had serious consequences and may have planted the seeds of Mozart's last illness. Before returning to Salzburg, Leopold accepted the invitation of a Hungarian magnate to make a flying trip to neighboring Pressburg after Wolfgang had recovered. Finally, on January 5, 1763, the Mozarts came home to Salzburg. It is uncertain how much musical stimulation Wolfgang obtained from this first Viennese visit. The one important event in Vienna at this period—the première of Gluck's *Orfeo*—went unmentioned by either Wolfgang or his father.

However, the success of the trip whetted Leopold's appetite for more of the same thing. After a brief period for recuperation, plans were laid for a much more elaborate odyssey to include nothing less than

Paris and London. On June 9, 1763, consequently, the family carriage set out for the Bavarian frontier—"the same road by which Leopold Mozart, then a hopeful student, had wandered into Salzburg." This trip was to keep the Mozarts away from home for three years.

SUCCESS IN PARIS AND LONDON

The "celebrity tour" began, strictly speaking, in Munich where the pair of prodigies performed with sensational success before the Bavarian Elector Maximilian III, who wished to hear the young people "soon and often." But Leopold was out for bigger game and wanted, incidentally, to exhibit his wonder children to his relatives in Augsburg before proceeding to world conquests. Besides old acquaintances the "Herr Kapellmeister" had the good luck to present his "gifts of God" to the noted Italian violinist, Pietro Nardini, then concertmaster of the court orchestra of Stuttgart, and to the Italian composer, worthy Niccolo Jommelli, who was struck by Wolfgang's abilities but against whom the mistrustful Leopold harbored various unjust suspicions. In Schwetzingen the Mozarts had the first opportunity to hear the then unrivaled Mannheim orchestra, which was to play a significant part in Wolfgang's development. He and his sister were put through all their paces as the weeks went by; besides playing and improvising they were made to perform all manner of showy stunts. Wolfgang had to name tones and chords sounded on keyboards covered with a cloth, as well as guess the exact pitch of bells, glasses, and clocks.

The travelers went on to Bonn, Cologne, and Aachen, where lived the Princess Amalia, sister of Frederick the Great, whose pressing invitations to Berlin left Leopold cold as soon as he realized she had no money; he reflected that the kisses without number which she gave the children would have pleased him better if they had had cash value! Finally, after further progress through the Low Countries the little band reached Paris, where the father discovered that most of his letters of recommendation and introduction amounted to little. Only when they were taken in charge by the Bavarian-born Baron Melchior Grimm, a literary figure of some distinction, did results begin to shape themselves. A first-rate publicity man, Grimm launched a campaign for the youngsters in his *Correspondance littéraire,* with the result that doors promptly opened and invitations began to pour in. On New Year's Eve, 1764, the Mozarts were asked to a *grand couvert* at the court in Versailles. Wolfgang stood next to the Queen who fed him dainties and translated for the King—Louis XV—what the boy said to her in German.

The great Madame Pompadour was on hand and the elder Mozart noted that she must once have been a great beauty for all her present stoutness. Later, when Wolfgang offered to give her a kiss, she drew back; whereupon the boy indignantly asked, "Who does she think she is, anyhow? Our Empress herself did not refuse to kiss me!" Leopold was careful to note the countless features of the Parisian scene. For one thing, the abundance of make-up on the faces of the French-women was something to revolt "an honest German." He saw eye to eye with Baron Grimm in his preference for Italian over French music, declaring that the latter was "not worth a farthing." Wolfgang was eventually to share his distaste for French customs, French art, even the French language. Leopold brought his son to the attention of several prominent German musicians who happened to be in Paris, such as Johann Schobert, Gottfried Eckhart, and Leontzi Honnauer, all of whom registered appropriate astonishment and presented the children with some of their own compositions, suitably inscribed. Four sonatas for clavier with *ad libitum* violin parts by Wolfgang were printed, and on the title page it was duly noted that their author was "only seven years old." For all their charm and freshness these works clearly betray the improving touch of Leopold.

On April 23, 1764, after an easy Channel crossing, the Mozarts arrived in London, where the children were announced as "Miss Mozart of Eleven and Master Mozart of Seven years of age, Prodigies of Nature." The Hon. Daines Barrington subjected the boy to "scientific tests," which demonstrated that his talents were, indeed, "out of the ordinary." The musical George III and Queen Charlotte received them at St. James's Palace on April 27. A few weeks later there was another concert before the royal couple, when the King asked Wolfgang to play at sight pieces by Wagenseil, Johann Christian Bach, Handel, and Carl Friedrich Abel. The monarch praised the lad's performances on the organ even more than on the clavier, and had him accompany the Queen in a song and improvise a melody on a figured bass of Handel's. Leopold wrote home that what his son knew now completely overshadowed his earlier abilities. At a charity concert in Ranelagh Gardens they made over a hundred guineas. Yet these successes did not last: several concerts had to be postponed because of Leopold's sudden indisposition; a mental illness of George III increased alarmingly; the political situation was unfavorable; and the public began to lose interest in the wonder children.

But apart from the sympathy Wolfgang was always to feel with the English people, one experience of his London sojourn really outweighed all others. This was the friendship he and Johann Christian Bach, the son of Johann Sebastian, formed for each other and the influence the older musician exercised on the creative genius beginning to blossom in the child. As Hermann Abert has written, "Christian Bach signified for Mozart a blithe, elegant counterpart to Schobert by virtue of the modernized Italianism that came to pervade his style." The "gallant" manner, the fresh, playful rhythms of his finales, and the relaxation modifying the dry composition technique of Leopold's are elements for which Mozart is deeply indebted to the "London Bach." Wolfgang's early symphonies and piano music make it plain how much he looked upon Johann Christian as his model and how fully this master was the chief inspiration of that "singing allegro" that became a hallmark of the mature Mozart.

Not only for his boyhood symphonies and sonatas but for his piano concertos was Wolfgang obliged to his great London friend. His earliest clavier concertos are largely copies or rearrangements of the concertos and sonatas of Johann Christian, as of Schobert, Honnauer, and similar masters. From these seeds came those glorious fruits of concerto literature that stand among his grandest and most original achievements.

Leopold had overstayed his leave from his Salzburg post but he seemed in no hurry about returning to it. He had originally planned to go home by way of Italy, since an Italian trip was regarded as an indispensable finishing touch to an artistic education. At the beginning of August 1765, the Mozarts landed once more on the Continent. Both father and son fell ill, and then Nannerl came down with pneumonia and was actually given the last rites. Wolfgang, scarcely convalescent from a siege of fever, composed a medley for piano and orchestra—a *quodlibet* of popular tunes—the *galimathias musicum,* a thing of rough humors revealing in its contrapuntal workmanship the tastes and teachings of his father. Variations on a Dutch patriotic song, six sonatas for violin and piano, a mellifluous symphony in B flat, and various other "trifles" indicate that sickness was not regarded as a valid excuse for idling.

Paris, to which they returned in May 1776, seemed less stirred by the prodigies than it had been on the earlier visit, though Prince Karl Wilhelm of Brunswick, on hearing Wolfgang, exclaimed in amazement, "Many a kapellmeister dies without ever having learned anything like what this child knows!" In July they left the French capital and arrived in Salzburg the last day of November 1766, laden with gifts and rich in glowing memories. A considerable quantity of new music from Wolfgang's pen filled their luggage. The artist was supplanting the prodigy. Wolfgang had seen something of the world and had made many valuable contacts. The Archbishop, Sigismund von Schrattenbach, skeptical of the brilliant reports he had heard, asked him to compose a contata—*Die Schuldigkeit des ersten Gebotes*—and isolated him for a week to see how much truth there was in all the talk.

VIENNA AND *La Finta semplice*

Not quite a year later the Mozarts were off again, this time to Vienna, for the betrothal festivities of the Archduchess Maria Josepha and King Ferdinand of Naples. But their great expectations were hardly realized. A smallpox epidemic in the capital carried off the royal bride, and Leopold fled with his family to Olmütz, where both the children contracted the disease. Wolfgang lay blind for nine days and for some time had to be careful of his eyes. Only on Christmas Eve were they well enough to set out again. On their return to Vienna, Maria Theresa received them kindly, but things had changed. Economy was the order of the day: the aristocracy followed the example set by the imperial household, musical activities were reduced, and the Mozarts felt the pinch. Interest in the prodigies diminished.

Joseph II, who had succeeded his mother on the throne, expressed a desire to hear in Vienna an opera of the twelve-year-old boy's composition and suggested such a work to the lessee of the court theater, Giuseppe Afflisio. The result was *La Finta semplice,* its libretto based on a Goldoni farce, and it was arranged that the composer should lead it from the harpsichord. Nothing came of the scheme, however, presumably because of intrigues.

The youth was partly consoled for this check by a noted physician, the celebrated Dr. Anton Mesmer (an early practitioner of mesmer-ism), at whose suburban home the one-act German *Singspiel, Bastien und Bastienne,* based on a parody of Jean-Jacques Rousseau's famous pastoral *Le Devin du village,* was performed. The little piece for all its simplicity lives on. Perhaps the most striking thing about the score is the fact that the prelude, or *intrada,* begins with the theme that was to be the main subject of Beethoven's *Eroica.*

The travelers came back to Salzburg early in 1769. The trip had not been a financial profit, but Wolfgang was undoubtedly richer in experience and had added to his creative store. The Archbishop de-lighted them by ordering a performance of *La Finta semplice,* though he had no genuine *opera buffa* personnel at his disposal. The leading soprano part of Rosina was sung by Maria Anna Haydn, Michael Haydn's wife. The year was largely devoted to further study and com-position—chiefly of masses and other church music written at the com-mand of the friendly Archbishop and, in addition, of symphonies and other forms of "entertainment" music for garden parties, festivities, and social functions of the high-placed and well-to-do. And Wolfgang was appointed concertmaster in the archiepiscopal orchestra.

ITALY AND MOZART'S EARLY OPERAS

Leopold realized that the hour had now struck for that long-projected trip to Italy which he wished to take "before Wolfgangerl reached the age and stature which would deprive his accomplishments of all that was marvelous." Plainly, it would not do to let the boy out-grow his precocity. And so on December 13, 1769, father and son set out on an adventure that was to resolve itself into three separate jour-neys to what was, rightly or wrongly, esteemed as the home of music and of art in general.

The youth was now ripe for Italy. The language he absorbed by second nature, as it were. Everywhere he made valuable new friend-ships and came across old acquaintances. In Milan he was commis-sioned to write an *opera seria* and the following October he composed *Mitridate Re di Ponto,* which, produced on December 26, 1770, amid cries of "Viva il Maestrino," had twenty performances. In Bologna he greatly impressed the aged *castrato* Farinelli and the great Padre Mar-tini, dean of Italian musicians. At Naples he had to remove a ring from his finger upon playing to convince the superstitious that it was not the real explanation of his "magic" skill. In Rome, after a single hearing of the Papal choir singing Allegri's celebrated *Miserere,* which nobody was allowed to copy under penalty of excommunication, he wrote it down from memory and then listened to it a second time to make a few minor corrections. The Pope bestowed on Wolfgang the Order of the Golden Spur, which enabled him to sign his letters with the whimsical "Chevalier de Mozart." He was invited to undergo a difficult examination for membership in the Philharmonic Academy of Bologna and passed it by working out in an hour a problem that consisted of producing in the "strict" church style an antiphone *Quaerite primum.* The real truth, however, is that the authorities accepted him only *after* they had charitably "corrected" what he submitted. It was not long before the Philharmonic Society of Verona likewise conferred membership upon him—this time presumably without the preliminary of a test. Now "Maestro di Cappella," he was ordered to provide a serenata—*Ascanio in Alba* (Wolfgang completed its fairly voluminous score in twelve days)—for the impending marriage of Archduke Rudolf and the Princess Maria of Modena.

Leopold imagined his son "made" for life. But the boy's music, for all its charm and fluency, still wanted the unmistakably creative touch. The tireless traveler, Dr. Burney, wrote a little later: "If I may judge of the music which I have heard of his composition, in the orchestra, he is one further instance of the early fruit being more extraordinary than excellent." And the composer Hasse believed that "young Mozart is certainly a prodigy for his age. The father adores his son overmuch and does all he can to spoil him; but I have so good an opinion of the innate goodness of the boy that I hope that, despite his father's adulation, he will not allow himself to be spoiled."

The pair went briefly to Salzburg in 1771 and started south again for Milan, where *Ascanio in Alba* was to be given in October. The work was duly presented for the princely nuptials along with Hasse's opera *Ruggiero,* likewise commissioned for the festivities. According to the father's report, the youth's *festa teatrale* completely eclipsed the work of the venerable master who, far from being jealous, is said to have remarked, "This boy will throw us all into the shade."

Scarcely were the travelers home once more than the kindly Archbishop died. His successor was the former Bishop of Gurk, Hieronymus, Count of Colloredo. Like many others, the Mozarts scented trouble, for Colloredo was a hard-boiled bigot and in every respect the reverse of his predecessor. He lives on in history principally as Mozart's evil genius and as the man who, in the end, was to fan Wolfgang's detestation of Salzburg to white heat and to drive him to open mutiny. Hieronymus knew by a kind of intuition that his new subjects were not well disposed to him so, in the words of a contemporary chronicler, "he despised them and held himself aloof." His rule, says Paumgartner, was something other than the "ancient regime" of his forerunner, the musical highlights of which had been Leopold Mozart, Ernst Eberlin, and Cajetan Adlgasser. Colloredo was a revolutionary and a deadly foe of routine and sought to put his ideas into force by sharpest disciplinary measures. His taste, however, ran to the easy grace of Italian music; yet he did in his chilly way at first look upon Wolfgang as a talent he might use for the greater glory of his court. For his new master's festive installation in 1772 the composer wrote a one-act serenata along the lines of his *Ascanio,* entitled *Il Sogno di Scipione,* to a text by Metastasio, adapted from Cicero. The score was a typical "occasional work" of allegorical character. Far more important in the creative sense are at least eight symphonies and four *divertimenti,* in all of which are traces of the ripening genius shortly to emerge.

The third Italian visit differed in some ways from the earlier ones. *Lucio Silla,* produced in Milan on December 26, 1772, was not acclaimed as *Mitridate* had been. Outwardly it was successful and enjoyed more than twenty performances but did not hold the stage. To begin with, the opera had an inferior libretto and Wolfgang, absorbing other musical influences, was less concerned about catering meticulously to Italian tastes. Moreover, he was no longer the child prodigy whose every action was to be considered phenomenal. But the real reasons lay deeper. A prophetic ear might have detected the vibrations of a "storm and stress" period beginning to ferment in the spirit of the artist. Leopold made a vain effort to secure his son a post at the Grand Ducal Court of Tuscany, but Wolfgang received no more operatic commissions for Italy. So early in March 1773, taking a last leave of that land, they returned to Salzburg, where Leopold was angered to see Colloredo appoint an Italian rather than a German to the position of conductor.

The elder Mozart now determined to try his luck in Vienna. After

the death in 1774 of Florian Gassmann, the court composer Leopold
hoped to secure the appointment for Wolfgang and the two obtained
an audience with Maria Theresa, who, for all her graciousness, merely
replaced Gassmann by one Giuseppe Bonno. At the moment there was
no opportunity to earn anything in the capital; but the young man
became acquainted with something that, in the long run, was to prove
even more rewarding. This was the music of Joseph Haydn, whom he
was not to meet personally until later. The influence of Haydn on
Mozart as of Mozart on Haydn was to be incalculable from every
standpoint.

On December 9, 1774, father and son were on a journey once more,
this time to Munich where the Bavarian Elector, Maximilian III, had
commissioned Wolfgang to write an opera for the following Carnival.
It was a *buffa, La Finta giardiniera,* and on January 14, 1775, the
composer wrote to his mother: "My opera went so well yesterday that
I find it impossible to describe the applause. In the first place the
theater was so packed that many had to be turned away; after every
aria there was a wild tumult, with handclappings and shouts of 'Viva
Maestro,' which began again as soon as it ended!" And Christian
Daniel Schubart wrote in the *Teutsche Chronik:* "I heard an opera
buffa by the marvelous Mozart. The fires of genius lurk and dart in it.
Yet this is still not the sacred fire which rises to the gods in clouds of
incense. If Mozart does not become a hot-house plant he should be
the greatest composer who ever lived."

Il Re pastore

However, Archbishop Colloredo was growing irritable over these
continual absences of his servants. He had not been able to refuse
the request of the Elector to permit the Mozarts to go to Munich but
he at last wanted his Vice-Kapellmeister and son back. Henceforth it
was not going to be so easy to obtain the great cleric's leave to go
wandering, whatever the reason. So for the immediate future the impatient young genius settled down to compose and to perform. A stream
of works were put on paper in 1775 and 1776. Five violin concertos
were written the first year. They are the best known of Mozart's concertos for that instrument and were conceived, in the main, for the
violinist Brunetti of the court orchestra. With all their charm they still
stand below the great clavier concertos in grandeur and epoch-making

qualities. Wolfgang did not particularly enjoy the violin although his father exhorted him to practice and told him that he could be the greatest violinist in Europe.

Another work in 1775 was *Il Re pastore,* a cross between opera and cantata, to a poem by Metastasio composed for a visit to the Archbishop of Archduke Maximilian. A score of sensitive loveliness, it is known today chiefly for its tender soprano aria with violin solo, "L'amero, saro costante." Of the many other creations of this period we can only mention in passing the six clavier sonatas for the Baron Dürnitz, the innumerable variations, the serenades, *notturni, divertimenti,* masses, offertories, organ sonatas, litanies, *graduales;* the stunning clavier concertos for his own use, for the French pianist Mlle. Jeunehomme, the Countess Lützow, and other high-placed local amateurs. Last, but far from least, he composed the *Serenade* (later transformed into a symphony by the elimination of a movement or two) for the wealthy Haffner family, of whom Sigmund Haffner, a merchant prince, was Burgomaster of Salzburg.

MANNHEIM AND PARIS

Despite all this work, the young man chafed at the narrow provincialism of his native town, at the absence of true artistic interest, at the company he was obliged to keep at the Archbishop's table, and, most of all, at that cleric's attitude. Leopold, seeing the dangerous way in which the situation was shaping itself between the young man and his master, made an effort to stave off a catastrophe by planning another trip. Wolfgang applied to the Archbishop for his discharge, whereupon Colloredo, who was not really anxious to lose the composer's services, told the pair to "seek their fortunes where they pleased" —but at the same time would not permit Leopold to leave. The father thereupon decided that his son should go to Paris, perhaps to find some lucrative position at the French court, unless he should be lucky enough to discover one somewhere else. But since he was forbidden to go along he deputed his wife to go in his place and keep a careful eye on the impulsive young man.

THE WEBERS AND PARIS

Early on September 23, 1777, Wolfgang and his mother (who would much rather have remained in Salzburg) drove off in a newly purchased carriage. The departure was a bitter event for Leopold, whose trouble was such that he forgot to give his son his blessing before the vehicle was out of sight! Nannerl, equally distraught, was sick and had to take to her bed. To add to the melancholy of the occasion father Mozart darkened the house and fell asleep till roused hours later by Bimperl, the dog. The woeful day finally dragged itself to an end; it would have been far more terrible had they known that poor Maria Anna was never to return!

They went first to Munich, where Wolfgang made an ineffectual appeal to the Elector and received that answer with which he was in the course of his life to become so tragically familiar: "Yes, my dear child, but there is no position free! Now if only there were . . . ," etc., etc. At Augsburg, the next stop, he divided his time between Andreas Stein, the pianomaker whose instruments stirred his interest, and his cousin, the "Bäsle," with whom he freely indulged in those ribaldries that so shocked the puritanical generations of the next century. From that ancestral seat they turned to Mannheim, which was a very different story. For here Mozart found all manner of musical interests and important personalities. And here he fell devastatingly in love!

He had made the acquaintance of the family of Fridolin and Maria Cäcilie Weber. A streak of bohemianism ran through the lot of them. The father, in straitened circumstances, eked out an existence in Mannheim as singer, musician, copyist, prompter—in short, a kind of man-of-all-work in the theater and orchestra. The mother was a sinister creature—an out-and-out adventuress. The couple had four daughters, Josefa, Aloysia, Constanze, and Sophie. Constanze was, in the fullness of time, to become Mozart's wife. But his feelings were at first kindled by Aloysia, who was then only fifteen and with whom Maria Cäcilie at this stage set about to tempt the young man, who was quickly bowled over by the girl's feminine charms, her lovely voice, and her musicianship. In the years to come each of these women was to play some part in the composer's life. (A few years later there was born in a closely related branch of the Weber family that figure who made the name immortal—Carl Maria von Weber; so that through marriage the creators of *Der Freischütz* and of *Die Zauberflöte* became cousins!)

Love caused Wolfgang to build castles in the air and to concoct extravagant schemes. He composed abundantly in Mannheim, planned operas and what-not for his idolized Aloysia, and before long was writing to his father proposing to give up the Paris venture altogether and set out on a trip to Italy with the Webers. Leopold was horrified, the more so as his wife wrote telling him exactly how things stood. Father Mozart sternly laid down the law to his son and ended with the words: "Off with you to Paris! And that soon! Find your place among great people. *Aut Caesar aut nihil*. The mere thought of seeing Paris ought to have preserved you from all these flighty ideas!" Wolfgang did not, it is true, rebel and in the end he went to Paris. But he answered his father with some heat. He declared that he was no longer a child and had no intention of tolerating aspersions on his conduct with Aloysia. "There are some people," he added, "who think it impossible to love a girl without evil designs and this pretty word mistress is indeed a fine one!"

But Leopold had, for the moment, won his point and in March 1778, Wolfgang and his mother were off. The Paris adventure turned out a dismal fiasco. Even Melchior Grimm, once so helpful, was not interested this time. He was willing to promote a sensation who gave promise of being a moneymaker. But, as Alfred Einstein has noted—

"It was Wolfgang's character that made Leopold wrong in his estimate of Paris and the Parisian nobility. For Wolfgang was no conqueror and he could not have conquered Paris even if he had wanted to . . . How carefully Gluck's conquest of Paris had been prepared! Not only ambassadors and queens but the entire public took part in these preparations . . . Mozart slipped into Paris quietly and unobserved, accompanied by his mother, who had come along to keep an eye on him."

He detested Paris, thought continually of Aloysia, had no use for the now-surly Grimm, turned down the offer of an organist post in Versailles (feeling that the place was no more than a suburb), had some unsatisfactory dealings with Le Gros, director of the Concert Spirituel, composed for the Parisian stage no more than the ballet *Les Petits Riens,* easily succumbed to some of Le Gros' intrigues, and was demoralized generally. Only one work of his—the *D major Symphony* (K. 297)—was outspokenly successful. To climax his woes his mother fell ill and died on July 3, 1778. He had to ask the old Salzburg family friend, Abbé Bullinger, to break the news to his father and sister. And he wrote, "You have no idea what a dreadful time I have been having here . . . until one is well known nothing can be done in the matter of composition . . . From my description of the music here you may have gathered that I am not very happy and that I am trying to get away as quickly as possible."

"As quickly as possible" was not till September 1778. He decided reluctantly to return to Salzburg, to the Archbishop's service, where he would conduct and accompany, but not play violin. Even so, he was momentarily tempted to stay on in Paris and might even have done so if Grimm had not been obviously eager to be rid of him. He did not hurry back to the hated Salzburg but stopped off in Strassburg, Mannheim, and Munich, where he found the flighty Aloysia already the wife of Joseph Lange (the itinerant actor to whom posterity owes the familiar unfinished portrait of Mozart). When he finally did submit to the inevitable trip home he lacked the courage to meet his bereaved father alone and so took his "dear little Bäsle" with him.

IDOMENEO

At the Archbishop's table he sat between the *castrato* Ceccarelli and the violinist Brunetti. If he felt revolted by his present circumstances he seems, however, to have taken refuge in the inner sanctuary of his spirit. He created quantities of priceless works and, in so doing, could forget situations in themselves repugnant. There were church compositions, serenades, *divertimenti;* the gorgeous *Symphonie Concertante* for violin and viola (K. 364); a triple concerto for violin, viola, and cello; the adorable E flat concerto for two pianos (K. 365); three symphonies in G, B flat, and C; some music for Gebler's drama, *Thamos, König in Aegypten,* which he had begun five years earlier and was a foretaste of *The Magic Flute;* and lastly, an operatic fragment, entitled *Zaide* after Mozart's death and destined to remain a torso.

By 1780, however, Wolfgang was to some degree compensated for his disillusionments. While laboring on *Zaide* he was commissioned by the Bavarian Elector, Carl Theodor, to write an *opera seria* for the Munich Carnival of 1781. The Munich authorities picked a libretto *Idomeneo, re di Creta; ossia Ilia ed Idamante,* which was based on a book by Antoine Danchet and which, as composed by André Campra as far back as 1712, had enjoyed a day of fame in Paris. It dealt with the tale of the Cretan king who had made a rash Jephtha vow to Neptune on returning from the Trojan war and was saved from sacrificing his son only by a *deus ex machina*. The libretto was put in shape by the Salzburg cleric, Giambattista Varesco, and called for, in accordance with French models, massive crowd scenes, ballets, choruses, and all the effects of a large-scale spectacle as well as vocal virtuosity and elaborate instrumental tone painting.

For a change Mozart had things more or less his own way. The Weber family had moved to Vienna, much to Leopold's relief, and for the moment the composer had no time to worry about Aloysia but went ahead putting his new opera into shape and helping to prepare the production. On the whole he met with sympathetic cooperation. The Elector, Carl Theodor, welcomed him cordially. The Intendant, Count Seeau, was helpful, and the women singers declared themselves pleased with their arias. The chief difficulties were caused by the aging tenor, Raaff, who had the title rôle, and the sixteen-year-old artificial soprano cast for the part of Idamantes. Mozart, who used to call him "mio molto amato castrato Del Prato," deplored the poor boy's lack of stage experience, musicianship, and vocal method. Nevertheless, *Idomeneo,* when brought out late in January 1781, was warmly acclaimed, and the Elector, who had followed the rehearsals from the first, marveled that "so small a head should contain such great things," insisting he had never been so stirred by any music.

He had reason for his enthusiasm. The score of *Idomeneo* is one of its composer's most superb achievements and, if it lives on today chiefly as a museum piece, it does so because, like *Mitridate, Lucio Silla,* and *Il Re pastore* before it and *La Clemenza di Tito* after it, the work is a specimen of *opera seria*—a form that had lost every trace of vitality and dramatic punch. Yet to the end of his days its creator valued it highly and made some unavailing efforts to reanimate it.

Mozart's Break with Salzburg

Mozart had reason to suppose that the work might gain him a permanent and rewarding position. Once more he was disappointed; and a short time after the production he received a summons from Salzburg to join the Archbishop in Vienna, whither Colloredo had gone with a part of his musical staff. Leopold, it should be added, was left at home. Wolfgang boiled inwardly at the prospect of "having the honor once more of sitting above the cooks at table." His father begged him to be patient, but to no avail. In a way he welcomed the present call to Vienna and seemed to sense his impending liberation, if without knowing exactly how it was to come. "It seems as if good fortune is about to welcome me here," he wrote his parent not long afterwards from the capital, "and now I feel that I must stay. Indeed, I felt when I left Munich, that, without knowing why, I looked forward most eagerly to Vienna." He was seeking an opportunity to break forever with his detested chief, to whom he alluded as an "Erzlümmel" ("Archbooby").

He soon found his chance. The Archbishop at first refused Mozart permission to appear at the Tonkünstler-Societät, about which he wrathfully wrote to his father (yet a postscript added that, in the end, he got it). That his place at table was between the valets and the cooks is, Alfred Einstein says, rightly shocking both to the composer and to us. But Mozart's rank as court organist was actually that of personal servant, and according to eighteenth century etiquette, which knew nothing of special treatment for genius, this seating at table was formally correct. In the end the threatened explosion did occur. Colloredo ordered him back to Salzburg on a certain day. Alleging some "important engagement" in Vienna, he refused and, when the Archbishop told him he could "go to the devil," he applied for his dismissal from the cleric's service. Three times he presented applications. Finally, when he made an effort to enter Colloredo's apartment to hand him the paper personally, Count Arco, son of the court chamberlain, kicked him out of the room. But Mozart *did* get the discharge he had demanded.

The tale of the kick is familiar even to people who have not the vaguest familiarity with eighteenth-century codes. We might be well advised, however, to suspend our judgment till we know both sides of the celebrated story.

"No more Salzburg for me!" Wolfgang gaily wrote his father. Barring repeated journeys to different cities, Vienna was to be his home for the rest of his days. He was not to find the material rewards and the secure position he had sought for so long, but he had that freedom his spirit craved. And in Vienna he was to absorb those creative impulses that Haydn had known before him and Beethoven was to know after him. In a mood of elation he begged his father to leave Salzburg and join him in Vienna. But Leopold was no longer young and, besides, he was made of other clay.

MARRIAGE

Mozart renewed his ties with the Webers once more. Aloysia, indeed, was now out of his reach, but there were three other daughters, the youngest still a child, to be sure. The oldest, Josepha, had a good voice but she left Wolfgang cold. He was more attracted to Aloysia's sister, Constanze, a fact that was not lost on the scheming Mother Weber, now a widow, content to rent rooms and take in boarders. In May 1781, he settled in the Weber house, *Zum Auge Gottes,* just off the Graben. Needless to say, Leopold was greatly upset, for he had as low an opinion of the Webers as ever. But Wolfgang was no longer disposed to let his father's tastes sway him and, when he felt that he really loved Constanze, he determined to make her his wife regardless of parental wishes. The unscrupulous Madame Weber, pleased at the turn of affairs, took care that gossip should spread, and people began to talk about the probability of the marriage. Mozart, yielding to Mother Weber's "advice," left the *Auge Gottes* in September 1781, though returning for daily visits. Constanze's mother played her cards cleverly so as to compromise her daughter and enjoyed the satisfaction of having Mozart ask his father for his "approval." A Weber for a daughter-in-law was the last thing Leopold wanted. Finally on August 4, 1782, the couple married, the elder Mozart's reluctant consent not arriving in Vienna until August 5. He never forgave his son, however, for this step. No more did Nannerl, who had quite as little use for her brother's wife.

Later, after the composer's death, Schlichtegroll's necrology said of Constanze: "Mozart found in her a good mother for the two children she bore him, who sought to restrain him from many follies and dissipations . . ."—the rest of which passage Constanze was subsequently moved to make illegible. Be all of which as it may, there is no use pretending that Mozart was, earlier or later, in the least indifferent to feminine allurements. Sometimes it was the women who plagued him with attentions, a capital instance of which was his pupil, the pianist Josephine Aurnhammer, a talented but exceedingly repulsive person, of whom he left us a gruesome picture in a letter dated August 22,

1781: "She is as fat as a farm wench, perspires so that you feel inclined to vomit, and goes about so scantily clad that you really can read as plain as print: 'Pray, do look here.'" It was for this same Aurnhammer, nonetheless, that he wrote the clavier concerto, K. 453.

Alfred Einstein maintains that Constanze owes her fame "to the fact that Wolfgang Amadeus Mozart loved her, and in so doing preserved her name for eternity, as a fly is preserved in amber. But this does not mean that she deserved either his love or the fame it brought her." Certainly, she could not follow his flights of genius; neither was she always above reproach in her private conduct. Before their marriage her "honest and devoted" lover was writing to point out her thoughtless behavior in allowing some man "to measure her leg" in a game of forfeits; and nearly a decade later he was begging her "to consider appearances," to be "careful of her honor," and to keep away from the Baden casino because "the company is . . . you understand what I mean!" Einstein believed that the only woman of whom Constanze had a right to be jealous "was Nancy Storace, his first Susanna . . . Between Mozart and her there must have been a deep and sympathetic understanding. She was beautiful, an artist and a finished singer . . ."

Die Entführung aus dem Serail

The composer was probably delighted to have the chance to place on the stage a character named Constanze; and in the summer and autumn of 1781 he began the music of his next major opera, *Belmonte und Constanze* or *Die Entführung aus dem Serail* ("The Abduction from the Seraglio"). This *Singspiel,* the book of which was originally the work of Christian Friedrich Bretzner, had been presented a year earlier in Germany with a score by Johann André. Under Wolfgang's careful supervision the three-act piece underwent dramatic and textual modifications by Christian Gottlob Stephanie the Younger. Mozart had written his father: "The book is good; the subject is Turkish and is called 'The Abduction from the Seraglio.'" Rehearsals did not start till June 1782, and on July 16 of that year the work was produced in Vienna with extraordinary success. The stimulus back of Stephanie's revisions was unquestionably the penetrating theater sense of the composer himself. Into the love songs of the tenor, Belmonte, Mozart poured all his tender feelings for Constanze Weber, whom he was shortly to lead to the altar. The characterizations throughout have a life, a diversity, and a psychological truth that had not been met with in any previous Mozartean operatic effort.

The Emperor, though he recognized the genius in the work, thought it necessary to warn Mozart that the music seemed to him "too good for the Viennese" and contained "a powerful quantity of notes"—whereupon the ready-witted Mozart retorted, "Just as many as are necessary, Your Majesty!" His older contemporary, Gluck, was himself stirred to enthusiasm by the work (in which he unquestionably detected the influence of his own exotic *Les Pèlerins de la Mecque*) and invited the composer to dinner. *Die Entführung*—which Carl Maria von Weber was to say was such a work as Mozart could have written only once in his lifetime—quickly spread through most other theaters of Central Europe, where, after close to two hundred years, it still leads a lusty existence. The more amusing, therefore, is a notice the disgruntled Bretzner inserted in a Leipzig newspaper: "A certain person in Vienna named Mozart has had the effrontery to misuse my drama 'Belmonte und Constanze' for an opera libretto. I herewith protest most solemnly that I reserve the right to take further steps against this outrage."

On the surface the newly married couple were happy. Yet it might be inquiring too closely to ask whether Wolfgang did not, as time passed, suffer from that deep-seated loneliness and lack of understanding that are sooner or later the lot of a genius of this caliber. Under today's conditions we have reason to assume that a triumph like *Die Entführung,* and the numberless other treasures he was giving the world, would lift him above material cares. Instead, financial troubles began to thicken about him and grew continually more burdensome. They were, indeed, to beset him to his end.

For all the stir it created, the opera did not bring its composer the appointment he expected. And money was becoming a pressing necessity. Constanze's pregnancies were frequent during her married life and, though only two children survived infancy (to become, it is ironic to reflect, wretched but fairly long-lived mediocrities), her various confinements and her slow recovery from them did not help to further her housewifely qualities. It is not wholly surprising that Mozart's religious conviction, which had earlier been a sort of childlike faith, weakened little by little—the more so because he was brought into growing contact with men who were profound thinkers and of whom many belonged to the secret society of Freemasons. Freemasonry had political implications and was frowned upon by the Church. Frederick the Great had been a Freemason, Goethe was one, likewise Joseph II, Gluck, and Joseph Haydn. Eventually Mozart persuaded his father to join the society. Who shall say that its principles and philosophies did not serve Wolfgang as a protective armor, enabling him the more bravely to endure his social and material tribulations?

Pupils and Friends—Haydn

Mozart took his wife to Salzburg in the summer of 1783. He had made a vow the previous year that when he married Constanze and presented her to his father he would bring along a newly composed mass for presentation in his native town. The superb one in C minor was the outcome, but for some reason it remained unfinished. We cannot speculate here on the reasons for its incompleteness. The torso (or shall we say patchwork?) was rehearsed in St. Peter's Church in Salzburg, and Constanze sang some of the soprano solos. Despite its incompleteness the C minor Mass is a soaring masterwork, the music of which Mozart later put to use in the oratorio *Davidde Penitente*.

The relentless dislike for the Webers that both Leopold and Nannerl continued to harbor was not mollified by this visit, which proved uncomfortable as long as it lasted. Wolfgang and his wife were relieved when the troublesome "duty call" came to its chilly end and they were back in Vienna once more. There was no end of professional business for Mozart to transact—composition in flooding abundance, lessons to give, concerts ("academies") to organize, musical personages to cultivate. Just now, at least, there were no interminable travels such as had filled Mozart's boyhood years. His pupils were sometimes talented, sometimes the reverse. A few striking names stand out among them— Johann Nepomuck Hummel, Xaver Süssmayer, Thomas Attwood. Of the composers and executants with whom he came in contact we must mention Clementi, Salieri, Paisiello, Righini, Haydn. With Clementi he appeared as a pianist in a contest before Joseph II and some visiting Russian bluebloods. So evenly were the two players matched that the competition was declared a draw. Paisiello, composer of *The Barber of Seville,* was a lovable character for whom Wolfgang developed a great liking. Salieri, a disciple of Gluck and a teacher of Schubert, appears to have criticized some of Mozart's works, and Viennese gossip did what it could to make the matter worse. The result was that Salieri lives on in history largely because of a wild slander that he had given Mozart a poison causing the latter's untimely death!

The meeting with Joseph Haydn resulted in one of the noblest and most rewarding friendships the records of music afford. Artistically their creations benefited inestimably from the mutual influence of their works and personalities. Haydn, says Dr. Karl Geiringer, "was fascinated by Mozart's quicksilver personality, while Mozart enjoyed the sense of security that Haydn's steadfastness and warmth of feeling gave him." It was as if the two men kindled brighter sparks in each other's souls. They played chamber music together whenever Haydn made a trip to Vienna, and the younger man was quick to acknowledge that it was from his older colleague he first really learned to write string quartets. The six that he composed between 1782 and 1785 and dedicated with moving words to his "beloved friend Haydn" are doubtless among the finest he wrote. It was on a visit of Leopold Mozart's to Vienna that Haydn made to him the oft-quoted remark: "I tell you before God and as an honest man that your son is the greatest composer known to me either in person or by reputation!" And later, when someone questioned a detail in *Don Giovanni* and asked Haydn's opinion, he replied: "I cannot settle this dispute, but this I know: Mozart is the greatest composer that the world now possesses . . . It enrages me to think that the unparalleled Mozart has not yet been engaged by some imperial or royal court! Do forgive this outburst; but I love the man too much!" It is heartbreaking that Haydn was not able, as he would have loved to be, to secure a post for Mozart in England.

Mozart had another encounter of a different sort at this period in Vienna—acquaintance with the music of Johann Sebastian Bach. Through the Baron van Swieten he had an opportunity to know the scores of Bach and Handel and later even to write for certain Handel oratorios "additional accompaniments" for use in performances Van Swieten was in the habit of giving on Sundays at the Imperial Library and in some private homes. And the depth, the grandeur, and the polyphony of these masters he assimilated to the added greatness of his own most mature works.

"HAFFNER" SYMPHONY

With his concerts, teaching, clavier playing, and miscellaneous composing Mozart may well have felt, as he remarked on one occasion, that "people sometimes expected impossibilities of me." The Haffner family in Salzburg, for instance, asked Leopold to write a symphony for some family festivity, to be ready in something like a fortnight! Wolfgang, at that time up to his ears in a quantity of other schemes, found the labor shifted to his own shoulders by his father, who was otherwise busied. Somehow or other he contrived to turn out (in a trifle over the appointed time, it is true) the work we now know as the *"Haffner" Symphony.* The excellent Salzburg burgomaster, Sigmund Haffner, appears to have been well pleased. The composer himself instantly forgot the work and was astonished and delighted when, a considerable time afterwards, his father sent him the score. He worked at several operatic projects but nothing lasting came of them —not even of *The Goose of Cairo,* which contains charming passages and which, now and then, people have attempted to revive. There was, indeed, an amateur performance in Vienna of *Idomeneo.* But these and several other schemes must all be dismissed as transient compared with the masterpiece we now approach—*Le Nozze di Figaro* (The Marriage of Figaro).

LE NOZZE DI FIGARO

Mozart had longed for years to write a German opera. He boasted of himself as a thoroughly patriotic German and longed for the day when "we should dare to 'feel as Germans and even, if I may say so, to sing in German.'" The nearest he had come to composing a German *Singspiel* was when as a child he had produced his little songplay *Bastien und Bastienne* and again when, in 1782, he turned out the inimitable *Die Entführung aus dem Serail.* But his ambitions soared even higher and he consumed no end of time and energy perusing the countless opera books sent to him without finding anything that suited his true artistic and dramatic purposes. For a while he had dreamed of accomplishing something in his Mannheim days, even listening with interest, but nothing more, to stuff like Holzbauer's *Gunther von Schwarzburg.* Though he briefly thought of a *Rudolf von Habsburg,* he had no choice, in the end, but to return to Italian models—now, however, with a difference!

Soon after the amateur presentation of *Idomeneo* in Vienna he had the good fortune to be brought together with Lorenzo da Ponte, whose real name was Emmanuele Conegliano and who belonged to a Jewish family in Ceneda, near Venice. The youth entered a theological seminary and became an industrious student with a poetic bent, which resulted in quantities of Italian and Latin verse. An outspoken adventurer, with countless amorous escapades *à la* Casanova to his credit, he began his theatrical career in Dresden, went to Vienna where he was to enjoy the favor of Joseph II, and in the process of time went to London and finally to America, where he became a teacher of languages, a liquor merchant, a theater enthusiast, and what-not. He died in New York many years after Mozart but, like him, was buried in a grave of which all traces have been lost.

Mozart suggested to his picturesque collaborator (who cheerfully wrote opera books for Salieri, Martin, Righini, and others) a libretto to be adapted from Pierre Augustin Caron de Beaumarchais' *Les Noces de Figaro*. Paisiello had recently used Beaumarchais' earlier work, *Le Barbier de Seville*. But *Figaro* had been prohibited in France because it reflected on the morals of the aristocracy and the same ban had been in effect in Vienna. Da Ponte, altering it for Mozart's purposes, adroitly eliminated its barbed satire and then, tactfully explaining his alterations to the Emperor, secured his permission for the performance. The composer, who limited his teaching to the afternoon in order to complete the score, had been "as touchy as gunpowder and threatened to burn the opera" if it were not produced by a certain time. To Joseph II's credit it must be said that the music delighted him as soon as Mozart played him a few samples.

Figaro was produced at the Burgtheater on May 1, 1786. A lucky star shone on its birth in spite of intrigues set in motion against it. Its success was tremendous and was abundantly foreshadowed during the rehearsals. The Irish tenor, Michael Kelly (Italianized as "Occhelly"), left us in his memoirs a striking account of the delight with which the singers and orchestra joined the listeners at the end of the first act in acclaiming the composer. "I shall never forget," he says, "his little animated countenance when lighted up with the glowing

138

rays of genius; it is as impossible to describe as it would be to paint sunbeams." Father Mozart wrote to Nannerl that, not only had almost every number to be repeated, but that, at the following performance, five were encored, the "Letter Duet" having to be sung three times. In the end the Emperor forbade repetitions. That season *Figaro* received nine hearings—and for the two following years not a single one! Mozart's opponents, after a momentary check, had conspired successfully once more.

PRAGUE

Luckily, the incorrigibly musical Czechs championed Mozart to the limit! With *Die Entführung* he had won them heart and soul, and by the time *Figaro* reached Prague, that city was on the way to becoming the true Mozart capital of Europe. From that moment nothing seemed greatly to matter but that opera. In the composer's own words, people would listen to nothing else and talk of nothing else. Its melodies were worked up into dance arrangements. Players in beer gardens and even the wandering street musicians who begged for pennies on corners had to sing or strum their *Non piu andrai* and the rest of the tunes if they wanted any passer-by to pay attention to them. "Truly a great honor for me," mused the composer. Prague, now a high altar of Mozart worship, was for some time to remain so.

The creator of *Figaro* had valued friends in Prague. Among the dearest of these were the Duscheks, whom he had known in Salzburg —Franz, a gifted pianist and composer, and his wife, Josefa, both older than Mozart. Josefa, an excellent musician, became an exceptional singer, and for her Wolfgang was to compose some superb though difficult concert arias. She was well-to-do and, with the money an admirer lavished on her, she bought herself an estate known as the *Bertramka*—still one of the show places of Prague, despite the vicissitudes of more than a century and a half. Here Mozart was often an honored guest, and to this day the villa and the hilly gardens surrounding it seem to breathe his spirit.

The permanent Italian company that supplied opera to the people of Prague, though not large, was exceedingly capable. At this time it was managed by a certain Pasquale Bondini. Its two efficient conductors (both of them Bohemians), Josef Strobach and J. B. Kucharz, were heart and soul devoted to Mozart. The intensely music-loving Czechs jammed Mozart's academies and could not hear enough of his symphonies and clavier works. Small wonder, therefore, that Bondini resolved to take advantage of the heaven-sent opportunity of Mozart's presence to commission him to write a new opera for the company next season. The fee was the usual sum of one hundred ducats (no more!), the opera—*Don Giovanni.*

Actually, much more could be said of this Prague visit of Mozart's. At one of his concerts he presented for the first time the *D major Symphony* which sent its hearers into such raptures that the world has forever named it the *"Prague" Symphony.* When he arrived from Vienna it had been arranged that he was to stay with the Duscheks, but, Josefa being away, Mozart accepted the hospitality of the aristocrat, Count Thun, and sat as an honored guest among the great of the land. He doubtless remembered how at Colloredo's court his table companions had been cooks and grooms! He was taken to the sumptuous dwelling of still another local patrician, the Count Canal. And so it continued from day to day. Yet he found time to write a piece for a wandering harpist, which the latter played everywhere, boasting that Mozart had specially composed it for him.

DEATH OF LEOPOLD MOZART

In February 1787, Mozart was back in Vienna in a joyous frame of mind. One may question that this jubilant mood was of long duration. That the new opera was to be ready as early as the following October was hardly the greatest of his worries, for Mozart, like Haydn, Bach, and other masters of that century, was accustomed to a speed of creative production that puts our machine age to shame. The welcome the Viennese accorded the returning traveler, flushed by the recollection of his recent triumphs, was frosty. Also, there came the news that his father's health was failing. "Naturally," reflected Leopold, "old people do not grow younger!" Wolfgang wrote his parent in words that nobly convey the essence of his own mature philosophy:

"I need not tell you with what anxiety I await better news from you . . . although I am wont in all things to anticipate the worst. Since death is the true goal of our lives, I have made myself so well acquainted during the past two years with this true and best friend

of mankind that the idea of it no longer holds any terror for me, but rather much that is tranquil and comforting. And I thank God that He has granted me the good fortune to obtain this opportunity of regarding death as the key to our true happiness. I never lie down in bed without considering that, young as I am, perhaps I may on the morrow be no more. Yet not one of those who know me say that I am morose or melancholy, and for this I thank my Creator and wish heartily that the same happiness may be given to my fellow men."

One is moved to think of Schubert's words to his father a few years later when, looking upon the lakes and peaks of the Austrian Alps, he wrote:

"As if death were the worst thing that could befall one . . . could one but look on these divine lakes and mountains . . . he would deem it a great happiness to be restored for a new life to the inscrutable forces of the earth!"

All the same, Mozart was profoundly shaken when, on May 28, his father passed away without the opportunity of seeing his son once more. "You can realize my feelings," he wrote his friend Gottfried von Jacquin. We shall not go far wrong when we surmise that these deep and solemn emotions colored to a considerable degree some of the more tragic pages of the nascent *Don Giovanni,* the book of which Da Ponte was now writing for him while working at the same time on librettos for Salieri and Martin!

In the spring of 1787 the composer had a brief but memorable encounter; for at this time there came briefly to Vienna from Bonn a sixteen-year-old youth—Ludwig van Beethoven, a protégé of the Count Waldstein—presumably to study with Mozart. The latter heard his visitor improvise and was at first unimpressed because he believed the extemporization had been "memorized," but was converted as soon as he gave the young Rhinelander a complicated theme to treat on the spot. The originality and seriousness of what he heard stirred the older musician to the prophecy: "This young man is going to make the world talk about him!" But Mozart had, at the moment, no leisure for this prospective pupil, who returned shortly to Bonn and on his later trip after Mozart's death placed himself under the direction of Haydn.

141

DON GIOVANNI

In mid-September Mozart and Constanze went to Prague, bringing the partly finished *Don Giovanni* score. Bondini had found the composer lodgings at the house on the Kohlmarkt called the "Three Lion Cubs." Across the way, at the inn *Zum Platteis,* rooms were engaged for Da Ponte and, as the windows faced each other, composer and librettist had long discussions across the narrow street about details of the book, in the preparation of which Mozart, with his keen dramatic instincts, played a dominating role. He and Constanze appeared, however, to have spent quite as much time with the Duscheks at the *Bertramka* as at the "Three Lion Cubs." Rehearsals consumed a great amount of energy, there were numerous modifications to be made in the music (the young baritone, Luigi Bassi, who had the title rôle, demanded *five* recastings of the duet *La ci darem* before he was satisfied with the music), and Mozart had all manner of trouble with Catarina Micelli, the Elvira. In addition, the singer of Zerlina, Caterina Bondini, could not utter the peasant girl's shriek in the first finale to the composer's satisfaction until he terrified her by grasping her roughly and thus causing her to scream exactly as he wanted. After one of the last rehearsals the conductor, Kucharz, being asked by the master for his candid opinion of the opera, replied encouragingly: "Whatever comes from Mozart will always delight in Bohemia." "I assure you, dear friend, I have spared myself no pains to produce something worthy for the people of Prague!" declared the composer, who had already boasted that "my Praguers understand me."

Here is the place, no doubt, to tell once more the oft-repeated tale of the overture, put on paper, according to a hoary legend, the night before the première while Constanze kept the master awake by plying him with punch and telling him stories. As a matter of fact, the overture was written the night before the dress rehearsal—and it was nothing unusual for Mozart to write down at the last moment a work mentally finished in every detail.

A few days after the first performance the Prague *Oberpostamtszeitung* published a review that probably excels anything ever written about the opera. It read simply: "Connoisseurs and musicians say that nothing like it has ever been produced in Prague." The opinion is probably as true today as in 1787. For there is literally nothing like

Don Giovanni, either among its composer's creations or elsewhere. One can only share the emotion of Rossini when, being shown the manuscript score, he said to its owner, the singer Pauline Viardot-Garcia: "I want to bow the knee before this sacred relic!" And echo the words of Richard Wagner: "What is more perfect than *every* number in *Don Giovanni?* Where else has music won so infinitely rich an individuality, been able to characterize so surely, so definitely and in such exuberant plenitude as here?"

Figaro is, if you will, the more perfect artistic entity of the two; *Don Giovanni* is looser, less consistent, on the surface even grossly illogical. But so, too, is human nature. And if all the world's a stage, what more than a *dramma giocoso* is the experience of life? Whatever the narrow intent of Lorenzo da Ponte, when he carpentered the book out of well-worn odds and ends, it was with a profound knowledge of the sorrows and absurdites of humankind that Mozart breathed into it an abiding soul.

"Long live da Ponte, long live Mozart!" had written the stage director, Domenico Guardasoni. "All impresarios, all artists must exalt them to the skies; for as long as such men live there can be no more question of theatre miseries!" The Duscheks outdid themselves to make life pleasant for their guests. Mozart found time to compose several songs and even a superb concert air, *Bella mia fiamma, addio,* for Josefa after that lady had locked him up in the garden house till he had finished the promised music.

On November 15, 1787, which virtually coincided with the composer's return to Vienna, Gluck died. Less than a month later Joseph II appointed Mozart to the older master's post of Kammerkompositeur, with an annual salary of eight hundred gulden. Gluck had received two thousand; and before long Mozart was complaining that his pay was "too much for what he did, too little for what he could do." What he did was principally to supply minuets, contradances, and *Teutsche* for court balls and similar occasions.

The year 1788 dawned in gloomy fashion for Mozart. To be sure, *Don Giovanni* had its first Viennese hearing on May 7, with a cast including his sister-in-law, Aloysia Lange, as Donna Anna, Catarina Cavalieri (the original Constanze in *Die Entführung*) as Elvira, and Francesco Benucci, the first Figaro, as Leporello. Mozart had cut out some numbers, replacing them with new ones, eliminated the platitudinous epilogue, and ended the work with the prodigious hell music of Don Giovanni's disappearance. The Emperor remarked: "The opera is divine, perhaps even finer than *Figaro*. But it is a rather tough morsel for the teeth of my Viennese"—to which Mozart replied, "Let us give them time to chew it!"

SYMPHONIES IN E FLAT, G MINOR, AND C MAJOR

Yet from now on he was to pay for his Prague triumphs. With a kind of fateful persistence things seemed to go wrong. That an infant daughter died was a rather familiar affliction (of the children of the Mozart couple only the sons, Karl and Raymund Leopold, survived infancy). Money troubles plagued him unremittingly. Again and again he had to appeal for loans to Michael Puchberg, a merchant and brother Mason, and later to Franz Hofdemel, a jurist of his acquaintance whose wife was one of his pupils. But, by and large, these pupils were becoming scarcer and there seemed steadily less patronage for the academies he planned. To complicate matters Constanze's management of the household appeared to go from bad to worse. The arrangements of works like Handel's *Acis and Galatea* and *Messiah,* which he was making about this time for the parsimonious Baron van Swieten, brought in as good as nothing. Mozart's affairs were falling into a sordid, not to say a tragic, state.

Small wonder, therefore, that he grasped at the opportunity to settle outside of Vienna proper in a house in the Waehring district, where the air was purer than in the heart of the city and where he had the added advantages of quiet and a garden. A change of residence had never been a particular hardship for the Mozarts. In the space of nine years they moved eleven times in Vienna alone.

"Their life," says Alfred Einstein, "was like a perpetual tour, changing from one hotel room to another. . . . In one of the handsomer dwellings, Schulergasse 8, the ceiling of Mozart's workroom had fine plaster ornamentation with sprites and cherubs. I am convinced that Mozart never wasted a glance on it. He was ready at any instant to exchange Vienna for another city, Austria for another country. . . . He was thinking of a trip to Russia, as a result of conversations with the Russian ambassador in Dresden in 1789. But he had to be satisfied with smaller journeys, and with 'journeys' within Vienna."

In his Waehring surroundings, however, he boasted of being able to accomplish more work in a few days than elsewhere in a month. The finest fruit of this suburban sojourn is the glorious symphonic trilogy, the masterpieces in E flat, G minor, and C major, composed in June, July, and August, respectively—the third, the sublime *"Jupiter,"* the last of Mozart's forty-one symphonies and given its deathless name no one knows exactly by whom or why. The three, which have a profound psychological connection, were written, in all probability, for a series of academies that never took place. However this may be, they are the crown of Mozart's symphonic compositions and rank indisputably as the greatest symphonies before Beethoven.

Così fan tutte

In April 1789, a ray of hope suddenly appeared to illuminate his depression horizon. A friend and pupil, the young prince Carl Lichnowsky, who had estates in Silesia and an important rank in the Prussian army, invited Mozart to accompany him on a trip to Berlin. Lichnowsky enjoyed influence at the court of the music-loving Prussian king, Frederick William II, and seemed ready to recommend his teacher to the good graces of the monarch. At last Mozart had reason to anticipate a well-paying post! The pleasure-loving Constanze resigned herself with the best grace possible to remain behind. The travelers stopped off in Prague, in Dresden, in Leipzig (where Mozart played the organ in St. Thomas's Church in so masterly a fashion that Bach's erstwhile pupil, the aged cantor, Johann Friedrich Doles, believed for a moment that his old master had come back to life and hastened to show his delighted guest one of the Bach motets the church possessed). On April 25 Mozart arrived at the court in Potsdam, where the King gave him one hundred Friedrichsdor, ordered six string quartets and some easy clavier sonatas for his daughter, but did nothing about a Kapellmeister position or a commission for an opera! Mozart did go to the theater in Berlin where he heard his own *Entführung,* was applauded by the audience, and audibly scolded a blundering violinist in the orchestra!

But his fortunes had not materially changed and in May he was writing to Constanze: "My dear little wife, you will have to get more satisfaction from my return than from any money I am bringing." When he reached home and found her suffering from a foot trouble he sent her, regardless of his depleted purse, to near-by Baden for a cure—at the same time admonishing her to beware of flirtations! Then he set to work on the quartets for the Prussian king, of which he finished three (the last he was to write), and a single "easy" sonata, instead of the promised six, for the Princess Friederike. In September 1789, he was to compose for his friend, the clarinet virtuoso Anton Stadler, the celestial *Clarinet Quintet* (K. 581), which for sheer euphony is almost without parallel in its composer's writings.

The success of a revival of *Figaro* in August 1789 appears to have moved the Emperor to approach Mozart with a commission for a new opera. The outcome was *Così fan tutte,* the incentive to the plot being an incident said to have taken place in Viennese society. Once again Lorenzo da Ponte was called upon to put the piece into shape. The fundamentals of the story are to be found in Boccaccio and it may well have been in the *Decameron* that Da Ponte discovered the real basis of his dexterous and amusing, though highly artificial, comedy. We know little about the circumstances surrounding the composition of the piece.

On January 21, 1790, *Così fan tutte* was performed at the Burgtheater. The reviews, if middling, were not outright unfavorable. "The music of Mozart is charming, the plot amusing enough," wrote Count Zinzendorf in his diary; and the *Journal des Luxus und der Moden* remarked: "It is sufficient to say of the music that it was composed by Mozart!" Until the following autumn the work achieved only ten performances. It is not unreasonable to explain this by the fact that in 1790 Joseph II, who for some time had been ailing, died and was succeeded by a ruler of very different tendencies—his brother, Leopold II.

LATER WORKS

With the accession of the new emperor, Mozart briefly imagined the "gates of his good luck were about to open." He was quickly disillusioned. Leopold II was hard, cold, unmusical. He instantly dismissed some of his predecessor's most faithful artistic servitors. Da Ponte, for one, was dropped. Mozart's opponent, Salieri, cautiously withdrew into obscurity and waited behind the scenes for a new opportunity. Van Swieten tried to obtain for Mozart a position as teacher of the Archduke Franz, but nothing came of the well-meant effort, and presently the composer found his pupils reduced to two. His health began to trouble him alarmingly, with headaches and tooth troubles. He had the mortification of being ignored when the King of Naples visited Vienna, while Salieri and Haydn enjoyed special honors.

He was not even asked to participate in the musical festivities in connection with the Emperor's coronation in October 1790, or to travel to Frankfurt, where the ceremony was to take place. So he decided to make the journey at his own expense, hoping against hope for some distinction or reward. Though he did not obtain either, he at least had the satisfaction of knowing that his *Don Giovanni, Figaro, Entführung,* and even the early *Finta giardiniera,* were relished in neighboring Mainz. The opera chosen for the actual coronation was Wranitzky's *Oberon.* However, the Frankfurt town council "graciously" allowed Mozart to give a concert "on his own responsibility" at a local theater, October 13 at eleven in the morning! "Plenty of honor, but little money," he wrote. He played two concertos (probably the F major, K. 459, and the D major, K. 537) and a rondo. As ever, his improvisation impressed deeply—only a royal luncheon party and a maneuver of Hessian troops were counter attractions that cut down the attendance. On the way home he stopped off in Mannheim and Munich, saw his old friends Cannabich and Ramm, played at an academy the Elector Carl Theodor gave for the returning King of Naples, and went home to Vienna, where Constanze had moved their effects into a new apartment in the Rauhensteingasse—destined to be his last home on earth!

In his new dwelling the composer completed by December two superb works—the *String Quintet* in D (K. 593) and the stunning *Adagio* and *Allegro in F minor* (K. 594) "for an organ cylinder in a clock." About that same time the director of the Italian Opera in London, one O'Reilly, suggested that he come for half a year to England, to write two operas for that theater and give concerts, and promised him three hundred pounds sterling. Nothing stood in the way of O'Reilly's suggestion, except operas that the master was soon to provide for Vienna and Prague. Soon afterwards, Haydn on his way to London took leave of his younger friend who bade him farewell with the heart-shaking words: "I fear, Papa, this is the last time we shall see each other!" Salomon, Haydn's manager, had planned to bring Mozart to England on the older composer's return to the Continent.

To be sure, there was other work to be done, if in large part trifling. But early in January 1791, Mozart completed his last clavier concerto, the singularly affecting one in B flat (K. 595), which harks back to earlier models and lacks some of the more original and dramatic elements of the incomparable ones in D minor, E flat, A major, C major, and C minor. And in June 1791, on a visit to Constanze in Baden (where she had gone for another cure!), he wrote for a local choirmaster, Anton Stoll, that short *Ave Verum* motet, than which nothing of Mozart's is more unutterably seraphic.

The Magic Flute

He was ill and despondent but his activity was untiring. It is an infinite pity that he did not take the hint of Da Ponte and others who were urging him to come to England, where he might easily have made a fortune and become a British idol like Handel before him and Haydn and Mendelssohn after him. He went on writing because, as he was soon to say, "composition tires me less than resting." In the spring of 1791 he was commissioned to compose another opera, which was to be his last and, in a number of respects, his most epoch-making —*The Magic Flute* (*Die Zauberflöte*). And with it he was to write one of the most extraordinary works of operatic history, to create German opera in accordance with a long-cherished ambition of his but, like Moses, never to do more than cross the frontier of the promised land he had beheld in vision.

Emanuel Schikaneder, who had known Wolfgang and Leopold Mozart in Salzburg, was a wandering actor and a playwright of sorts. The head of a traveling company, which gave Shakespeare, Goethe, Schiller, Lessing, and, for better or worse, operas by Gluck and *Singspiele* by Haydn and Mozart, he had like numberless barnstormers a keen knowledge of the tastes of audiences, particularly of the plebeian ones to which his players catered. In his own way as adventurous a person as Da Ponte, Schikaneder took over in 1789 the direction of a playhouse on the Starhemberg estates, the Freihaus-Theater, in the Wieden district. There he produced comic shows, *Singspiele,* and operettas. With his grasp of suburban tastes he combined a thorough understanding of what could be done with his brother Mason and old acquaintance, Mozart. A business rival of the impresario Marinelli, who ran a theater in the Leopoldstadt quarter and made a specialty of "magic plays," he now approached the composer with his own *Singspiel*.

We cannot here examine the courses from which he assembled his libretto. There ran through it a powerful strain of Masonic influence, love interest, low comedy in abundance (Schikaneder took care to tailor to his own measure the rôle of the wandering bird-catcher Papageno), and other sure fire theatrical ingredients. He asked Mozart to supply the music, and the latter, after warning him that since he had never yet written a "magic opera" he hesitated to court failure in this sphere, at length complied. Between March and the end of September 1791, *The Magic Flute* was written. Schikaneder, aware of the glorious bargain he had struck, strove to be the soul of complaisance. He supplied the composer with every comfort at his disposal—a charming summerhouse on the grounds of the theater where he could work at the score, with food, wine, and pretty actresses to divert him—in short, whatever promised to humor the musician and promote the flow of inspiration. He even hummed or sang the sort of tunes he considered appropriate to the rôle he designed for himself.

Let us at this stage dispose of a few legends that, in the course of one hundred and sixty years, have accumulated about the work. One is that the play is a farrago of childish nonsense, made tolerable only by the variety and grandeur of Mozart's music; another, that the plot was altered at a late hour because another manager was about to produce a work similar in its story; a third, that the piece was a failure. As a matter of fact, the book of *The Magic Flute* happens to be one of the best librettos in existence from the point of view of good theater. The imagined "revision" never took place, for considerations of "parallels," let alone plagiarisms, never bothered theater directors at this epoch. On the contrary, if a play or opera had one feature that pleased its public, a rival manager was quick to copy this very point on an even broader scale. Although at the first performance *The Magic Flute* did not achieve such an overwhelming triumph as its composer had hoped, before many months had passed it was attracting throngs; and not many years later Schikaneder was able to build out of the wealth it brought him that famous Theater an der Wien which still stands and was to become the cradle of various storied masterworks. As for the much-maligned book, it appealed so powerfully to none other than Goethe that he set out to write a sequel!

While the sick and harried Mozart worked with still inexhaustible fertility at the score of his magic opera he was interrupted by a sufficiently distasteful order from Prague for an opera to be produced there at the coronation of Leopold II as "King of Bohemia." With no more than eighteen days to compose the music and assist in the production of this "occasional piece," he was ordered to set an old text of Metastasio's (retouched, it is true, by one Caterino Mazzolà)—*La Clemenza di Tito,* an antiquated specimen of *opera seria,* such as the composer had not bothered with since the period of *Idomeneo.* The available time being so short, Mozart took along with him his pupil Süssmayr, who was asked to perform the almost secretarial job of writing the *secco* recitatives, leaving the more important parts of the music to the master. His good friend, the impresario Guardasoni, mounted the opera in sumptuous fashion. But good will did not supplant genuine inspiration and, for all its craftsmanship, *La Clemenza di Tito* did not strike fire. The Empress dismissed it as *porcheria tedesca* (German rubbish). A correspondent of *Studien für Tonkünstler und Musikfreunde* reported that the "beloved Kapellmeister Mozart" did not obtain this time the applause he had a right to expect. For once, clearly, "his Praguers did not understand him." Doubtless, *Tito* is not a *Figaro* or a *Don Giovanni,* but those unfamiliar with the work may well ask themselves if it is as bad as history paints it. Anyway its reception did not raise the master's spirit. And he took leave of his friends with tears.

He was now seriously ill. He had fainting fits and accesses of exhaustion. On September 28, 1791, he finished *The Magic Flute*—the March of the Priests and the overture being the last numbers set down. The Masonic symbols and meanings with which the opera is filled (comprehensible, however, only to initiates) are heard in the thrice-reiterated three chords at the opening of the superb tone piece. This overture is a fully developed sonata movement built on a fugal plan, the mercurial subject having been borrowed from a clavier sonata of his old friend and rival, Clementi. At the first performance the composer Johann Schenk (later, one of Beethoven's teachers) crept through the orchestra to Mozart, who was conducting, and reverently kissed his hand, while the composer, continuing to conduct with his right hand, affectionately patted Schenk's head with his left. He took pleasure in playing the glockenspiel during Papageno's air "Ein Mädchen oder Weibchen" and once, in fun, introduced an unexpected arpeggio which threw Schikaneder completely out for a few minutes.

The Requiem

As he was boarding his coach on the trip to Prague, Mozart was startled on being accosted by a gaunt, gray-clad stranger of mysterious mien who asked him if he were willing to undertake, for a certain sum, the composition of a requiem mass to be delivered at a specified time. He agreed but from this moment the weird visitor, whose identity he was admonished not to try to discover, gave him no rest. He became convinced that a messenger from the Beyond had sought him out, that the incident had a supernatural aspect, that he was, indeed, ordered by a higher power to compose a death mass for *himself!* And the certainty that his time was at hand grew steadily upon him.

The incident, in reality, had nothing macabre or mysterious about it. The "gray messenger" was a certain Leutgeb, steward of the Count Walsegg zu Stuppach who had lately lost his wife and who, aspiring to be known as a composer, planned to perform the requiem as his own work. But Mozart knew nothing of this. He had a letter from his old friend, Da Ponte, entreating him to join him in England. But it was too late and Mozart's tragedy had to be played out to the bitter close that was now swiftly approaching. To Da Ponte he dispatched this pathetic missive:

"I wish I could follow your advice, but how can I do so? I feel stunned, I reason with difficulty, and cannot rid myself of the vision of this unknown man. I see him perpetually; he entreats me, he presses me, impatiently demands the work. I go on writing . . . Otherwise I have nothing more to fear. I know from what I suffer that the hour is come; I am at the point of death; I have come to the end before having had the enjoyment of my talent. Life was so beautiful, my career stood at first under so auspicious a star! But one cannot change one's destiny!"

What tortured him more than anything was the thought that, as furiously as he worked, the *Requiem* might remain unfinished at the death he knew was imminent. He had numberless discussions with his pupil, Xaver Süssmayr, but it was daily becoming clearer to him that he had small chance of completing the mass himself. On a walk in the

Prater with Constanze in the early autumn he exclaimed: "It cannot last much longer . . . Certainly, I have been given poison; that is a feeling I cannot shake off!" And this, presumably, is the basis of the age-old slander that Salieri had been his murderer! At all events growing weakness forced him to take to his bed on November 20. He was never to leave it. "I know," he had said shortly before, "that my music-making is about at an end. I feel a constant chill which I cannot explain. I now have no more to do save with doctors and apothecaries!"

His hands and feet were beginning to swell. Yet he struggled desperately to get on with the composition of the mass. The visits of a few friends seemed to comfort the sick man, and he asked them to try over in his presence certain completed pages of the score. At the beginning of December he himself struggled to sing some of the alto part of the work. When the *Lacrymosa* was reached he gave up the attempt after a few measures and, overcome by the certainty that he was doomed never to finish the music, he broke down in a fit of weeping. And in these days, with tragic irony, there dawned a promise of better things! The rapidly growing popularity of *The Magic Flute* augured a carefree future; a group of Hungarian nobles began to raise a subscription that would have assured Mozart an annual income of one thousand gulden; and from Holland there came, almost at the twelfth hour, news of an even more gratifying project.

Mozart's Death

In the last hours his sister-in-law, Sophie Haibl, lent what assistance she could. Constanze, grief-stricken and stupefied, was helpless. The sick man, tortured to the last by the thought of his unfinished *Requiem,* was shaken by the chills and fires of fever. It was found necessary to take a canary out of the sickroom because the singing of the bird seemed to cause the sufferer physical pain. He appealed to Sophie to remain with him, to comfort Constanze, and to "see me die. I have the taste of death on my tongue already and who is to care for my Constanze when I am gone?" A doctor who attended him was at the theater when summoned and, realizing the hopelessness of the case, promised to come "when the play was over." Sophie was dispatched to call a priest. When she returned she found the dying man bending over some sketches of the *Requiem* and giving Süssmayr some final directions about the work. At last he lapsed into unconsciousness, a few moments before the end puffing out his cheeks and making what the tearful bystanders imagined to be an effort to imitate the sound of the drums in his unfinished score. And five minutes before one on the morning of December 5, 1791, he died.

Of what illness did Mozart die? Typhus say some; a result of childhood illness, say others, complicated by the strain of overwork, traveling, disappointments, and deprivations. The most plausible medical explanation would appear to have been supplied by a modern Salzburg physician, Dr. H. Kasseroller, who diagnosed the cause of the master's early demise as uremia resulting from Bright's disease. And this may explain the composer's persistent idea in his last weeks that he had been administered poison.

The rest of the pitiful story need not detain us. The parsimonious Baron van Swieten advised Constanze to observe economy in making the funeral arrangements; and so Mozart was buried in a pauper's grave. On December 6, the body was taken to the cemetery of St. Marx. A handful of mourners who followed the hearse dispersed when a heavy snowstorm made progress difficult. The stricken Constanze found it impossible to accompany the pathetic little cortege; and when some time later she attempted to discover her husband's resting place, a new gravedigger who replaced the earlier one had no idea whatever where he lay.

What matter that posterity has never discovered the whereabouts of his sepulcher? Mozart, the incessant wanderer, the infinitely lonely, now lives more fully and gloriously than ever in the hearts and souls of all true worshipers of the divinest in music. And if his earthly tragedy has never seemed so poignant as it does today, we can take consolation from the circumstance that our generation has learned to prize the greatness, elevation, and beauty of his art more, perhaps, than did any of our predecessors.

H. F. P.

Ludwig van Beethoven

BORN: BONN, DEC. 16, 1770. DIED: VIENNA, MAR. 26, 1827.

𝆑𝆑𝆏⌒𝆑𝆑𝆑

Keep your eye on him; he will make the world talk about him some day.—MOZART, *in a letter to his father, 1787.*

(The late Pitts Sanborn wrote this essay under the title *Beethoven and His Nine Symphonies* and stated in a short preface that it made "no claim to originality and no secret of its indebtedness to the masterly treatises on the same subject." I have left Mr. Sanborn's pages on the symphonies virtually intact and have only expanded the work a little by incorporating here and there matter about other major works of Beethoven's, especially some of the concertos, overtures, piano and vocal works, besides certain of the greater specimens of his chamber music. Even if this procedure probably lends the essay a patchy character, I have followed it in order to supply a rather fuller picture of the composer's creative achievements. No more than my predecessor do I make the slightest claim to originality of matter or treatment, or deny my indebtedness to Thayer and Paul Bekker.   H. F. P.)

*   *   *

LUDWIG VAN BEETHOVEN was born on December 16, 1770, at Bonn, then one of the most important cities on the lower Rhine. Though Bonn was German and Beethoven's mother and his father's mother were both Germans, he was of Flemish descent through his father's father, a native of the country that eventually became Belgium, whence the "van" in the name. Louis van Beethoven, a tenor singer, went to Bonn in his youth and promptly became a court musician to the resident archbishop-elector. His son Johann, Beethoven's father, was also a singer in the elector's employ, but he was a worthless fellow, who was fortunate, however, in having as wife a woman of character. Realizing that his son Ludwig had been born with uncommon musical talent, he had the child begin to study violin and piano very early with the idea of putting him forward as a prodigy, as Mozart's father had done. But the young Ludwig was less precocious than Mozart and rebelled strenuously against the enforced training. However, he did appear at a concert on March 26, 1778.

So strong was the boy's musical gift that it triumphed over every obstacle, including his own childish reluctance, and the elector thought it worth while to send him to Vienna, then the musical capital of Europe. He had now been composing for several years, and Haydn accepted him as a pupil in counterpoint, an arrangement that did not turn out altogether to Beethoven's satisfaction. He studied with other teachers in Vienna and in March 1795, made his first public appearance in that city, playing his own piano concerto in B flat major. This date marks the beginning of a kind of recognition that could only spur the young composer on to the activity that in a nature so vigorous and energetic meant enthusiastic creation. Of course he wanted to write a symphony. Mozart, dead in 1791, had left a legacy of forty-nine symphonies. Haydn, the author of many more, was in full career at sixty-three. They were the world's foremost symphonists.

Symphony No. 1, in C Major, Op. 21

Beethoven's First Symphony was brought out at a concert which he gave in Vienna on April 2, 1800. It was immediately successful and within a few months carried its composer's fame all over Germany. In the musical city of Leipzig it was described as "intellectual, powerful, original, and difficult." That was in 1802. Today it is no longer difficult for our accomplished orchestras, but, as in the case of other works that have come to seem simple through the passage of time and changes in fashions, it is no easy matter now for a conductor to catch and express the frank joyousness of its youthful speech.

The symphony is in the customary four sections or movements. The key is C major. Yet it does not begin in that key, but with a discord in F major which shocked some pedants at the time. The slow introduction of twelve measures leads to the first movement proper ("Allegro con brio"). Its pages have spirit, gaiety, elegance, for this symphony has well been termed a symphony of comedy, though here and there a cloud may for the moment obscure its sunny brightness. The eighteenth century was not over when Beethoven composed it, and he was still looking at music through the eyes of Haydn and Mozart, in spite of the fact that the student may readily discover Beethovenish characteristics that are not derived from either Haydn or Mozart and distinct intimations of the moods and manners of the nineteenth century to come. However, comedy itself is not all compact of sunshine and, as the German proverb has it, laughter and weeping dwell in the same bag.

This brisk Allegro is followed in the then-prevailing order by the slow movement ("Andante cantabile con moto," in F major and consequently not too slow). It is mainly built up on a tricky tune that no less an authority than Professor Tovey described as "kittenish." The attentive listener should observe in this movement the recurrent passage of dotted notes for drums on G and then on C, the drums being tuned not in the tonic, but in the dominant. Yet bold though this device might have seemed, it was not wholly original. Mozart had anticipated Beethoven in his "Linz" Symphony.

The third movement in name is the minuet usual in symphonies of the eighteenth century ("Menuetto: Allegro molto e vivace," in C major), but in reality Beethoven was already looking forward to the scherzo (Italian, joke) with which he was presently to replace the minuet. This movement, then, is much less the stately dance in triple rhythm than a scherzo of generous proportions, rich in modulations and glowing color. The scherzo, like the minuet, always includes a trio section. Listen in this trio to the delicious dialogue between wind instruments and strings and to the rousing crescendo that ends it just before the repetition of the minuet.

The Finale, in C major, opens with seven measures of Adagio devoted to the gradual release of a scale passage. So much accomplished, the music plunges into an "Allegro molto e vivace," beginning with this sprightly theme which races along to the conclusion in a whirl of merriment and humorous sallies.

First Three Piano Concertos

Beethoven had settled permanently in Vienna in the autumn of 1792 and the body of his work originated, of course, in the Austrian capital. We cannot, however, dismiss the compositions preceding the First Symphony as wholly negligible. The creations of this period are to a large extent relatively small in scale. There is a quantity of piano music largely in the form of variations, a number of songs and several arias, odds and ends of chamber music, dances, marches, and such. Some of the variations for piano and strings are based on melodies of Handel, Mozart, and a number of lesser lights. During his Bonn days Beethoven had composed a score for a "knightly ballet" (*Ritterballet*), performed by members of the Bonn aristocracy and ascribed at first to Count Waldstein. It was Beethoven's first ballet score and preceded by some years his far more pretentious *Creatures of Prometheus,* written in Vienna to a scenario by the noted dancer, Salvatore Vigano.

The vocal compositions of this early period are not, perhaps, of conspicuous quality. Beethoven's best-known song and, indeed, his most famous (though not the best) is the setting of Mathisson *Adelaide*—more a *cantate* than what we have come to classify as a genuine *Lied*. Considerably later he was to write the cycle *An die ferne Geliebte,* which together with some of his settings of Goethe poems and the stark but majestic *Die Ehre Gottes aus der Natur,* may pass as Beethoven's most memorable achievements in the province of the solo song. To his Bonn days, however, belongs a genuine cantata, the one composed in 1790 on the death of the Emperor Joseph II. This work survives chiefly because one of its finest pages was later utilized in the last scene of *Fidelio,* into which it fits admirably.

Three years before the First Symphony Beethoven began the first orchestral score he decided to publish. This was the B-flat Piano Concerto, which though we know it as No. 2, opus 19, actually preceded the one in C major, opus 15. It was performed for the first time by the composer March 29, 1795, on the occasion of his first appearance "as virtuoso and composer" before the Viennese public. It had been announced that he would play "an entirely new concerto" on this occasion of the first two annual concerts given for the benefit of the widows of the Tonkünstler Society. Thayer, following the lead of Nottebohm, felt certain that this "new" concerto was the one in B flat. Beethoven was tardy in completing it, and we are told that two days before the concert the Rondo was not yet on paper. In spite of illness he wrote it out at the eleventh hour, while four copyists sat in the next room and were handed the piece, sheet by sheet, as soon as the music was set down.

We know practically nothing of the public reaction to the work. We do know, however, that the composer was far from satisfied with it and revised the score before playing it in Prague in 1798. At that, he confided to the publisher, Franz Hoffmeister, that he "did not consider it one of his best." The first movement has a vigorous and arresting first theme, followed by a tranquil, songful one. Some of the cantabile phrases that follow have a rather Mozartean character. The Adagio begins with a devout, rather hymnlike melody, on which the piano subsequently embroiders. The Finale, a Rondo with a playful recurrent theme suggestive of Haydn, contains a second lilting melody and another, partly syncopated, which, though in minor, does not lessen at all the high spirits of the movement.

Just as the composer considered the B-flat Concerto "not one of his best works," so he also questioned the value of the subsequent C major Concerto, written in 1797 and not published (like the First Symphony) until 1801. Yet this concerto is a great advance over its predecessor; it contains a beautifully expressive Largo and a deliciously brisk and zestful "Allegro scherzando" Rondo, marked by jocose *sforzandi* on weak beats and various striking rhythmic displacements. Taken as a whole, there is far more of what we recognize as a true Beethoven quality in this misnamed First Concerto than there is in the so-called Second.

The Third Piano Concerto (C minor, opus 37), composed in 1800 but not played publicly till about three years later, is a great advance on its two predecessors from every standpoint. The proximity of the more "heroic" Beethoven is immediately evident. Indeed, it probably possessed more of the unmistakably heroic quality than any other concerto written before its time. The solo part is different and more striking in originality than anything in the concertos in B-flat and C major; and a symphonic breadth pervades the work, notably the opening movement. The second movement—a Largo in E—begins in the piano and is then sung by muted strings. There is a passage that, strangely enough, sounds like a prophecy of the melody of the tenor air *Salut demeure* in Gounod's opera *Faust* and may easily have suggested it to the French composer. Before the close of the Largo there is a cadenza "con gran espressione." The Rondo brings back the key of

C minor and is, in a variety of ways, a most remarkable movement. Curiously enough, the coda appears to have been inspired by the closing page of Mozart's C minor Concerto which, some time earlier, had so struck Beethoven that he remarked to another musician: "None of us will ever write anything like that!" And the composer was not to occupy himself further with piano concertos for several years till in 1806 he created his most deeply poetic (the Fourth, in G major, opus 56), and again till 1809, when he wrote his most spacious and lavish, the E-flat ("Emperor"), by which time he had behind him several of his monumental productions.

SYMPHONY No. 2, IN D MAJOR, OPUS 36

Beethoven composed the Second Symphony in very different circumstances from the first. The deafness that had first manifested itself several years previously and was in time to become complete had reached such a point that on the advice of his doctor he decided to spend the summer of 1802 in the village of Heiligenstadt, which, though near Vienna, was then deep in the country. It was a tragic summer for Beethoven, as he himself has testified in that infinitely pathetic document known as the "Heiligenstadt Will." He would probably have taken his own life but for his determination to consecrate himself with new courage to his art. His life was further complicated by a love affair with the youthful Countess Giulietta Guicciardi. Whether or not this love affair was as serious as some have maintained, the Countess preferred Count Gallenberg to the turbulent composer and accordingly married him.

In such a setting Beethoven undertook his Second Symphony. This work, however, reflects his tragedy only here and there and in a richer romanticism than his music had previously expressed—a romanticism of the nineteenth century. As in the case of the First Symphony, the Second, in D major, has a slow introduction ("Adagio molto"), but this introduction is much longer and, though based in style on Haydn's symphonic introductions, is instilled with the new romantic freedom and contains a surprising prediction of the Ninth Symphony in a descending octave passage.

The "Allegro con brio" that follows starts off with a buoyant theme which sets the pace for an energetic and generally cheerful movement. It is in the ensuing Larghetto in A major that we hear in full proclamation the individual voice of Beethoven as we have not heard it before. This has been aptly called one of the most luxurious slow movements in the world, and its richness in melodies has been set down as "reckless."

The next movement, again in D major, is this time called frankly a "Scherzo," not a "Menuetto." This concise Allegro is particularly noteworthy for the prophecy in its Trio of the Trio of the Scherzo of the Ninth Symphony.

The Finale, "Allegro molto" in D, is a forthright, humorous Rondo. In view of the tragedy of that summer, this symphony, at once romantic and exuberant, might perhaps best be looked upon as an escape. Brought out on April 5, 1803, at a concert of Beethoven's works given by the composer at the Theater an der Wien, Vienna, it was coolly received, being regarded by many listeners as extravagant or enigmatic.

SYMPHONY NO. 3, IN E-FLAT MAJOR ("Eroica"), OPUS 55

Beethoven's next symphony, though begun in the summer of 1803, was not completed till the following year. As long before as 1802 Beethoven had declared his dissatisfaction with his works up to that time: "From today I mean to take a new road." This symphony boldly takes that road. The Second Symphony still belongs largely to the eighteenth century. The Third embodies the developments with which Beethoven revolutionized the symphony. In amplitude and opulence no previous symphonic movement had ever equaled or even approached the initial "Allegro con brio," and it may be doubted whether any has subsequently surpassed it. Sensitive listeners hearing it for the first time may well have cried out with Miranda: "O brave new world!"

There ensues a Funeral March that is one of the most tremendous lamentations conceived in any art. The Scherzo is not only the first but one of Beethoven's symphonic Scherzos, it is also among the greatest. For the Finale Beethoven provides a theme and variations of astonishing diversity and splendor.

The first and dominating theme of the "Allegro con brio" Beethoven very likely remembered from Mozart's little *Bastien und Bastienne* overture, but he uses it here in the grand manner. The Funeral March begins with a striking phrase in C minor. A tender lyric passage in C major introduces an elegiac element into the sternness of the dirge. The Scherzo ("Allegro vivace" in E-flat major) is an enormously energetic movement and is interrupted by a Trio, prophetic in its turn of the Ninth Symphony and including a particularly brilliant and difficult passage for the horns.

The theme of the concluding variations ("Allegro molto" in E-flat major) Beethoven had previously employed in his ballet, *The Creatures of Prometheus*. This theme, simple as it appears, contains the germ of one of the most remarkable sets of variations ever put down on paper.

The Third Symphony is universally known today less by its number and its key than by the title "Eroica" ("Heroic"). Everybody is familiar with the story of the relation of this symphony to Napoleon Bonaparte. Beethoven, sympathetic toward the republican ideals of the French Revolution, originally hailed General Bonaparte as the Great Liberator, but when in May 1804 he accepted the imperial crown of France, Beethoven saw him in an entirely different light. Such was his rage that he was on the point of destroying this symphony, which he had intended to dedicate to Bonaparte as a tribute to his services to mankind. Fortunately he desisted, tore Bonaparte's name from the inscription, and entitled the work "Eroica." It should not be forgotten, though, that when seventeen years later he heard of the death of Napoleon at St. Helena, he remarked, "I have already composed the proper music for that catastrophe," which was an allusion to the Funeral March.

The meaning of the symphony as a heroic work is clear enough to anyone who hears the first movement and the Funeral March. Perhaps only Anton Rubinstein has ever questioned the heroic quality of the first movement and nobody has or could doubt the heroism of the mighty threnody that follows. But to fit the brilliant Scherzo and the dazzling set of variations into the picture has occasioned any amount of controversy. To go at length into the various theories is impossible here, but one might point out that the Scherzo has been interpreted as a scene in the hero's camp, as an excited crowd waiting for the hero's return and his triumphant address in the Trio, and as a picture of funeral games at the grave of the hero, such as one finds in the epic poems of Homer and Virgil, this last theory being that of Berlioz. The variations of the Finale have been plausibly explained as the nations of the earth bringing each its tribute of flowers to deck the hero's monument. The first performance of this transcendent symphony took place in Vienna on April 7, 1805.

SYMPHONY NO. 4, IN B-FLAT MAJOR, OPUS 60

Three years elapsed between the completion of the "Eroica" Symphony and the emergence of the Fourth Symphony. The latter was brought out in Vienna at a special subscription concert organized for Beethoven's benefit some time toward the latter part of March 1807. Little is known about the origin and composition of this work and its relation to the other circumstances of Beethoven's life. Apparently he had been busy with his C minor Symphony (the Fifth) when in 1805 he laid that aside to write a symphony in B flat. This act of his is in line with his general procedure in regard to his symphonies, a lighter work following one of deep import. Robert Schumann, a distinguished critic as well as a great composer, described the Fourth Symphony as related to the "Eroica" and the Fifth to "a slender Greek maiden between two Norse giants." This comparison, however, lays too much emphasis on youthful ingenuousness, for humor and the joy of living have their place here, and romance as well, with touches of passion and of mystery. One of its admirers has called it a "symphony of love."

Mystery and romance are evoked in the elaborate introduction (Adagio), which this symphony like the Second possesses, but the mood turns to merriment when the "Allegro vivace" enters with a skipping tune. The second movement (Adagio in E-flat major) is related in its luxuriance and melodic richness to the Larghetto of the Second Symphony, establishing another bond between the two works. A hint of the beauty of this movement may be gathered from the very first theme. The fervor that breathes through its measures has been attributed to Beethoven's contemporaneous engagement to the Countess Therese von Brunswick, to whom many believe he addressed the famous "Immortal Beloved" letter. Berlioz, like Schumann eminent not only as composer but as critic, accounts for this Adagio in a still loftier vein: "The being who wrote such a marvel of inspiration as this movement was not a man. Such must be the song of the Archangel Michael as he contemplates the world's uprising to the threshold of the empyrean."

For the third movement Beethoven returns to the name "menuetto"

162

("Allegro vivace" in B-flat major; Trio, "un poco meno Allegro," in B-flat major), though "Scherzo" would do quite as well. This minuet is planned on a particularly large scale and is further remarkable for the fact that, as in the Scherzo of the Seventh Symphony, the Trio is played twice and the Minuet proper repeated each time. The attentive listener should also heed the striking change of key to B-flat minor at the fifth bar. The exuberant Finale ("Allegro ma non troppo" in B-flat major) is perpetual motion in music, flashing and glittering with tunefulness and fun.

SONATAS

"Beethoven's work," says Paul Bekker, "is based on the pianoforte; therein lie its roots and there it first bore perfect fruit." Yet it is a curious paradox that he abandoned this phase of composition relatively early, producing the majority of his works for the keyboard before he was forty. A number of reasons might be cited for this—his growing deafness, the consequent impossibility of his public appearances as performing virtuoso, the circumstance that his intellect outgrew the expressive capacity of the piano, and the immense broadening and deepening of his creative faculties which demanded subtler and more ramified channels of expression. "The pianoforte is and always will be a disappointing instrument," he said at one stage of his career. And he was distressed that his compositions for the piano exclusively always produced on him the most regrettable impression. "Oh! Beethoven, what an ass you were!" he exclaimed on one occasion when someone played him his own Variations in C minor.

Nevertheless, the tremendous series of thirty-two sonatas, which began, roughly speaking, in 1795 and continued more or less intermittently till 1822, are among his most moving, gracious, original, adventurous and completely extraordinary achievements. They range all the way from the so-called "Pathétique," "Pastoral," and "Moonlight" to the "Waldstein," the "Appassionata," and the programmatic "Les Adieux, l'Absence et le Retour," to the mighty series beginning in 1816 with the A major, opus 101, and culminating in the gigantic B flat, opus 106 (universally known as "for the Hammerklavier"), the extraordinarily imaginative ones in E major and A flat, opera 109 and 110, and the transcendent, Promethean C minor, opus 111. Within the cosmic limits of this stupendous succession there stretches a whole world of emotional experience and an incalculable diversity of invention. And we may as well mention here (though it was not composed till 1823) that prodigious set of Thirty-three Variations on a Waltz by the publisher Diabelli, which has not its like in the whole range of Beethoven's output. Looking back over the immense panorama of the composer's piano works (including variations, bagatelles, and solo sonatas) stretching, let us say, from the awesome summits of the "Hammerklavier," the C minor, and the "Diabelli" Variations backward to the comparative simplicities of the sonatas Opera 2, 22, 26, and 27 leaves one with the dizzy impression of surveying a whole Alpine panorama.

SYMPHONY No. 5, IN C MINOR, OPUS 67

As we have seen, Beethoven interrupted work on a symphony in C minor to write his Fourth Symphony. That done, he returned to the C minor Symphony, finishing it late in 1807 or early in 1808. Both this Fifth Symphony and its successor, the Sixth, were brought out in Vienna at the same concert on December 22, 1808. The Fifth Symphony has turned out to be the most unreservedly admired, the most generally beloved, and the most frequently performed of all Beethoven's nine, in fact, of all symphonies. It is the drama in tone of man's victorious struggle with destiny and it was largely composed at Heiligenstadt, Beethoven's own spiritual battlefield. In 1801 Beethoven had made himself this promise: "I will take Fate by the throat; it shall not wholly overcome me." The C minor Symphony opens with an intensely dramatic figure of four notes which Beethoven explains as "Fate knocking at the door." This rhythmic group not only dominates the concise first movement, but appears in every succeeding movement. The second movement ("Andante con moto" in A-flat major) consists of a graceful, flowing set of variations on a brave and lovely theme.

The uncanny Scherzo (Allegro in C minor), introduced merely by the common chord of C minor in arpeggio, is the musical embodiment of the terror that walketh by night. Berlioz said of the opening, "It is as fascinating as the gaze of a mesmerizer." An extraordinary bridge passage, a supreme example of musical suspense, leads from the nightmare of the Scherzo finally in a breathtaking crescendo to the triumphant proclamation of the C major Finale. The effect produced by this symphony on a contemporary composer is indicated in the frantic outburst of the veteran composer Lesueur to the youthful Berlioz: "Ouf! Let me get out; I must have air. It is unbelievable! Marvelous! It has so upset and bewildered me that when I wanted to put on my hat, *I could not find my head!*"

SYMPHONY No. 6, IN F MAJOR, "PASTORAL," OPUS 68

In the three symphonies that successively precede the Sixth, Beethoven, as we have seen, is concerned with man as lover or as hero, for the spiritual conflict of the Fifth Symphony is no less heroic than are the exploits and lamentations of the Third. The Sixth Symphony, however, though quite as personal, treats of man from a totally different angle. This symphony, which the composer himself called "Pastoral," is Beethoven's monument to Nature. It expresses his personal devotion to the country and to what life in the country meant to him. He spent a great deal of time in the lovely Viennese countryside, especially at Heiligenstadt, but here the country is no battlefield as it had been in the summer of 1802, the summer of the "Heiligenstadt Will"; it is rather the cheerful, sunlit province of Nature's healing power.

Copious and quaint is the verbal testimony to Beethoven's pleasure in Nature. A lodging had once been bespoken for him at the coppersmith's at Baden (near Vienna). When he saw there were no trees around the house, he exclaimed, "This house won't do for me. I love a tree more than a man." According to the Countess Therese von Brunswick, his one-time betrothed, "he loved to be alone with Nature, to make her his only *confidante.* When his brain was seething with confused ideas, Nature at all times comforted him. Often when his friends visited him in the country in summer, he would rush away from them." Charles Neate, one of the founders of the London Philharmonic Society, who was on intimate terms with Beethoven in Vienna in 1815, assures us that he had "never met anyone who so delighted in Nature, or so thoroughly enjoyed flowers or clouds or other natural objects. Nature was almost meat and drink to him; he seemed positively to exist upon it." Michael Krenn, Beethoven's body-servant during the last summer of his life when he was staying at his brother's house at Gneixendorf, relates that Beethoven spent most of his time in the open air from six in the morning till ten at night, ranging over the fields, often hatless, shouting (he had long been completely deaf), gesticulating, and in general quite beside himself from the torrent of ideas in his mind.

The character of the Sixth Symphony Beethoven immediately makes plain on the dedicatory page. "Pastoral Symphony" he calls it, "or a recollection of country life. More an expression of feeling than a painting." The word "more" is important, for actually the symphony is in part a painting in tone, even if not for the greater part. Instead of keeping to the traditional four movements, this symphony rejoices in five, each carrying an identifying title. The first, "Allegro ma non troppo" in F major, explains itself thus: "The cheerful impressions excited on arriving in the country." It begins immediately with a theme which really holds the germ of the entire movement and, as Beethoven develops it, becomes as the whole countryside in Maytime bloom.

The second movement, "Andante molto moto" in B-flat major, is more definite in its treatment of Nature. Beethoven calls it "Scene by the brookside," and from the very first note you hear the purling of the water in the lower strings.

Against this murmurous background lovely melodies bud and flower and the whole orchestra seems filled with the tiny, numberless noises of summer. Near the end occurs a specific imitation of the call of birds, nightingale, cuckoo, and quail. Beethoven himself said that he meant these measures as a joke, and others have termed them parody or caricature. But joke or parody, the unconquerable artist in Beethoven has made them of one substance with the heavenly summer light and shade that pervade this interlude of leisure by the brook.

Though not entitled Scherzo, the third movement, Allegro in F major, is one in fact. Here the human beings that people this countryside possess the picture. Beethoven labels the movement "Jolly gathering of country folk." Its downright gaiety brings in its train an amusing takeoff on a village band, especially the befuddled bassoon. The middle part of the movement, "In tempo d'allegro," corresponding to the usual trio has been construed by some as a quarrel among the dancers, by others as just a rude episode in the dance. The jolly character of the movement is evident in the consecutive tunes, in the contrasting keys of F and D, that start it off.

The last three movements of the symphony are continuous. A dominant seventh of F ends the "Jolly Gathering," but, instead of its resolving, an ominous drum roll in D flat immediately ushers in the fourth movement, "Thunderstorm; Tempest" (Allegro in D minor), the storm without which no country scene is perfect. In spite of the formidable title, this is by no means a devastating outburst, though quite sufficient to postpone festivities. Memorable is the feeling of tension in the opening measures, the distant grumbling of the thunder, the first staccato raindrops. The disappearing tempest is followed directly by the last movement: "Shepherd's Song; joyous and thankful feelings after the storm." Happiness settles on the landscape once more, as an endearing and light-hearted tune abundantly proves.

Some of the melodies in this symphony are said to be derived from Carinthian or Styrian folk songs. As we have observed, the work was originally brought out at the same concert in Vienna (December 22, 1808) with the Fifth Symphony. Since it had an earlier place on the program, it was known for a while as the Fifth and the Fifth as the Sixth, but the mistake was soon rectified.

Fidelio AND THE Leonore OVERTURES

The period of Beethoven's Second, Third, and Fourth Symphonies covers, roughly speaking, a number of other compositions, some of them relatively trifling, others of greater moment, still others of altogether sovereign importance. Among the first type we can mention the Romances in G and F for violin and orchestra, composed in 1802; the oratorio "Christ on the Mount of Olives," from the same year; and the Triple Concerto for piano, violin, and cello, which dates from 1805. The two Romances are fluent, lyrical movements, but without special depth or originality. The "Mount of Olives," a sort of dramatic cantata which at first enjoyed an almost incredible popularity, for which it has paid with speedy and wholesale neglect, is a score of extremely uneven value, which handles a religious subject in a superficial, operatic fashion scarcely in keeping. Here and there it is possible to find in it interesting details but the chances for a revival of this work (which Beethoven's intelligent contemporary, Rochlitz, criticized in spots as "comic") are remote. The Triple Concerto, though not a masterwork of the first order, has been somewhat too harshly dismissed by many and therefore seldom visits our concert halls.

Otherwise the principal productions of these years include a quantity of the brightest jewels in Beethoven's crown. Leaving aside the chamber music, which we prefer to consider by itself, they comprise the opera *Fidelio* and the three *Leonore* Overtures written in connection with it; the Violin Concerto (which the composer also arranged as a sort of piano concerto); and the *Coriolanus* Overture.

Fidelio, which Beethoven originally called *Leonore*, was begun in 1804. A child of sorrow to its composer, it was not to achieve the form in which we now know it till 1814. In the odd century and a half of its existence it has been attacked for countless reasons in spite of which it lives on with an incredible tenacity and obstinately refuses to die. It has been reproached for being poor theater, undramatic, unvocal, patchy, and countless other things. The book, originally adapted from *Leonore ou l'amour conjugale,* by the Frenchman, Bouilly, and translated into German by Joseph Sonnleithner, was cast into its definitive form by Friedrich Treitschke. For a variety of reasons the work failed when it was first performed at the Theater an der Wien in November 1805. A bold attempt at revision the following season did not manage to keep it afloat and it was not till eight years later that the composer, with the clever dramatic surgery of Treitschke, made a final attempt to salvage it. Just how drastic were the alterations that the composer and librettist made in the piece can best be appreciated by those who have had the opportunity to examine the reconstruction of the original version which Erich Prieger published in 1905 on the occasion of the centenary of the work. From this it can be seen that not only have entirely new musical numbers supplanted the old but the opera (or rather *Singspiel*) has been reduced from its original three acts to two and that the dramaturgy betrays a vastly more experienced hand. The musical changes and condensations of Beethoven have, in their way, been no less thorough.

Far from being bad theater or unoperatic as sometimes charged, *Fidelio* is basically one of the most dramatic and profoundly moving masterpieces the lyric theater can show. The 1805 version lacked a number of its most striking musical features. The original, for example, shows no trace of the great outburst, *Abscheulicher,* which introduces Leonore's tremendous *scena* in the first act; and in the second, Florestan's dungeon air lacks its present "Und spür ich nicht holde, sanft säuselnde Duft," which took the place of the long-winded bravura phrases the composer originally gave the presumably starving prisoner to sing. Even the present touching close of the dungeon episode was originally quite different.

It has often been claimed that the previous "failure" of the work so discouraged the composer that his operatic achievements ended then and there. As a matter of fact, Beethoven to the end of his days never gave up his search for another libretto. That he never found it was due to the very special slant of his requirements. As for the "unvocal" character of his writing for voices, it is necessary to remember that, for all the opera's undeniable exactions, generations of great dramatic singers have repeatedly triumphed in the chief rôles of *Fidelio*.

Beethoven composed four overtures to his opera—the three so-called *Leonore* Overtures in C and the one in E major, known as the *Fidelio* Overture. The last-named was written in 1814 for Treitschke's new version of the piece. It is the slightest of them all and is the one that invariably prefaces performances of the opera. For years controversies have raged as to the order in which the *Leonore* Overtures were written and for what reason one supplanted the other. The Second Leonore was the first used to preface the drama at its 1805 hearing; the Third introduced the 1806 revision. Theories have been bandied about for generations to account for the First Overture, which was issued as Opus 138 only some years after the composer's death. The researches of Dr. Joseph Braunstein in his exhaustive study *Beethovens Leonore-Ouvertüren, eine historischstilkritische Untersuchung* have settled the problem for us. The overtures were composed in the order of their numbering. *Leonore* No. 1 was found too light for its purpose and, after a private tryout, was discarded before being publicly performed. Leonore No. 2, less polished and formally perfect than the more structural and popular No. 3, ranks if anything as more dramatic, modern, and powerful, even if it does lack the brilliantly jubilant coda that is the particular glory of No. 3. Neither of these two, however, is a wholly well-conceived introduction to *Fidelio*, for the reason that both overpower the opera as a whole and might almost be said to render the drama superfluous. Actually, a *Fidelio* representation profits by the omission of all the *Leonore* Overtures, though practically every audience these days expects the *Leonore* No. 3 quite as a matter of course and ordinarily gets it as a sort of interlude between the dungeon and the concluding scenes.

A word as to the *Fidelio* Overture of 1814, which has none of the features of the *Leonore* tone poems, either thematically or otherwise. It is more in the character of a *Singspiel* overture and has practically no dramatic connection with the opera itself—no reference to Florestan's dungeon song nor to the off-stage fanfare of the rescue scene; yet it leads quite properly into the light moods of the opening episodes of the chattering Marzelline and Jacquino in the first scene and does not, like the Second and Third *Leonore,* completely overweight the remainder of the score. At that, it is structurally and otherwise fully worthy of its composer and is a more logical adjunct to *Fidelio* than any one of the *Leonore* Overtures. Actually, it is a good deal more interesting in its own right than the average person imagines and merits far closer study than it ordinarily receives.

The *Coriolanus* Overture virtually coincides, in point of time, with the Fourth, Fifth, and Sixth Symphonies. One of its creator's most striking yet economically fashioned works, it is in no way related to Shakespeare's *Coriolanus* as has frequently been imagined, but was derived from a Coriolanus tragedy by Heinrich von Collin. Yet many (including Richard Wagner) have interpreted it in terms of Shakespeare's drama, the basic emotional pattern of which it can suggest.

SYMPHONY NO. 7, IN A MAJOR, OPUS 92

After the Fifth and Sixth Symphonies, Beethoven let several years pass without giving the world another, though he continued to compose diligently in spite of uncertain health and ever-increasing deafness. At length, in 1812, he finished two symphonies, which were probably played in private for the first time at the house of the Archduke Rudolph in Vienna on April 20, 1813. He was unable, however, to obtain a public performance for either of them till the Seventh Symphony was given in the great hall of the University of Vienna on December 8 of the same year.

Beethoven himself spoke of this work as his "most excellent" symphony, an opinion that not a few have echoed. He composed it in all the exuberance of his creative maturity, and each of its four movements brims over with the fiery essence of his inspiration. The listener is overpowered by the very lavishness of its beauty. In this symphony you feel Beethoven's genius as something inexhaustible, glorying in its own titanic power, as of a high god ignoring lesser breeds, proud in the knowledge of invincible strength, unfettered, carefree, save where the Allegretto acknowledges a divine melancholy.

Coming after the "Pastoral" with its avowed meaning, does this symphony "mean" anything in the sense in which that work and the "Eroica" do? Beethoven has not helped us with the clue of a title. However, there are students of the Seventh to whom it has yielded a quite definite meaning. Two of the most eminent are Richard Wagner and the French composer Vincent d'Indy. To Wagner the Seventh Symphony is the "apotheosis of the dance." To d'Indy it is a second "Pastoral" Symphony, full of bird-calls and other country sounds. Of course Wagner's definition recognizes the great part played in it by rhythm.

The Seventh Symphony begins in its title key of A major with a long introduction ("Poco sostenuto"), which almost has the importance of a separate movement. The second theme of this introduction —a capricious, tripping melody, first given out by a solo oboe—is not only one of the most captivating that Beethoven ever invented, but might very well be taken for an invitation to the dance or, perhaps equally well, for the caroling of a bird. The principal theme of the main body of the movement (Vivace in A major) first announced by the flute, dominates the whole movement with its dotted dactylic rhythm. This theme, in its turn, might be a further invitation to the dance or again the piping of a bird.

The second movement, an Allegretto opening in A minor on a long-held, mysterious 6-4 chord of the tonic, is one of the most remarkable pages in all Beethoven. Here, if the dance simile is to be preserved, it must be a solemn, ritual dance. Thus the movement has been likened to a procession in the catacombs. But it has been likened as well to the love dream of an odalisque!

The third movement is a brilliant Scherzo, though marked only "Presto" (in F major). Twice it is interrupted by the fascinating strains of the somewhat less rapid Trio ("Assai meno presto" in D major), enshrining a melody that is said to be taken from a pilgrims' hymn of Lower Austria.

The Finale is an Allegro of enormous energy and rhythmic incisiveness, whose tumultuous measures have been specifically compared to widely diverse dances. Some have heard here the rough jollity of dancing peasants, a "Bauerntanz" or "Dance of Peasants," while to others it is nothing less than the ceremonial dance of those priests of Cybele, the Corybantes, around the cradle of the infant Zeus.

OVERTURES

In 1809-10—or only two or three years before the Seventh and Eighth Symphonies—Beethoven was commissioned to write incidental music for Goethe's tragedy of the Netherlands under Spanish oppression, *Egmont*. The F minor Overture ranks indisputably as one of his finest, if it is less spare and less dour than the one to *Coriolanus*. It is a dramatic tone poem, but not a theatrical compendium in the manner of the *Leonore* Overtures. Yet it has an exultant coda not wholly dissimilar to the tremendous close of *Leonore* No. 3. This coda is identical with the so-called "Triumph" Symphony which concludes the play and was actually composed before the overture proper.

The greater Beethoven overtures might be termed off-shoots or by-products of the symphonies. Let us consider them briefly at this stage irrespective of their precise dates of composition. Not all the rest, to be sure, rise to the heights of the *Leonore* Overtures, the *Egmont,* or the *Coriolanus*. But it is only proper to allude to such symphonic prefaces as the early overture to the *Creatures of Prometheus* ballet (from the period of the First Symphony), the tenuous ones for the Kotzebue plays *The Ruins of Athens* and *King Stephen,* the "Namensfeier" Overture (an "occasional" piece, written in 1814), and the magnificent, if slightly known and largely undervalued, "Consecration of the House," composed as late as 1822 for the opening of the Josefstädter Theater in Vienna. The influence of Handel is powerfully manifest in this late creation, which is strongly contrapuntal in its texture but at the same time strangely suggestive from a dramatic, even a pictorial, standpoint.

Having paid something of a compliment to Handel in the "Consecration of the House" Beethoven was on the point of composing an overture on the letters of Bach's name a couple of years later. The formula B-A-C-H represents in German notation B flat, A, C, and B as employed contrapuntally not only by Bach himself but by countless other masters since Bach's epoch. Unfortunately, though he worked on studies for such an overture till 1825, Beethoven was too occupied with other schemes and never lived to complete it.

LUDWIG VAN BEETHOVEN

SYMPHONY No. 8, IN F MAJOR, OPUS 93

Although played privately in Vienna at the Archduke Rudolph's on April 20, 1813, the Eighth Symphony had no public performance till it was brought out at the Redoutensaal (Vienna) on February 27, 1814. The Seventh Symphony was on the same program and its Allegretto was encored, as it had been at its world première of the previous December. But the new work was received with less favor. A reviewer generously remarked that it was a mistake to place it after the manifold beauties of the Seventh. He had no doubt that it would be well received in future if given alone. Nevertheless this symphony was long neglected, in spite of attempts to make it succeed with the public by interpolating the popular Allegretto of the Seventh!

Beethoven himself called the Eighth his "little symphony in F" in contrast to the "great" symphony in A (Seventh). Yet the indifference of the audience at the Redoutensaal annoyed him and he testily remarked that the Eighth was "much better" than the Seventh, perhaps saying more than he really meant. There have been attempts to interpret this symphony, to provide it with a specific program. One such would make of it a "military trilogy" and d'Indy, still under the spell of the "Pastoral," detects in it the impression made by Nature on Beethoven's soul. He also hears a peasant band burlesqued in the Trio of the Menuetto, and the Hungarian theme employed in the Finale suggests to him the presence of gypsy musicians amid the festivities.

Be all that as it may, this is the symphony of laughter—not the laughter of childlike glee or of a reckless or despairing levity. Rather it is the "vast and inextinguishable laughter" that Shelley speaks of in *Prometheus Unbound*. It is the laughter of a man who has lived and suffered and, scaling the heights, has achieved the summit. So he has fashioned his own humor and dares survey the very stars in their appointed courses as integrals of a cosmic comedy. Only here and there does a note of rebellion momentarily obtrude itself, and here and there, in brief lyrical repose, we have, remembering Sir Thomas Browne, an intimation of Divinity more than the ear discovers.

The first movement ("Allegro vivace e con brio" in F major) begins at once with a sprightly tune which tells right away the nature of the work. The second subject of the rollicking movement is one of Beethoven's most delicious inspirations.

The second movement ("Allegretto scherzando" in B-flat major) is unique in symphonic literature. The persistent staccato ticking that runs through it has lent credibility to the story that the movement is based on a canon or round, "Ta, ta, ta, lieber Maelzel" sung as a tribute to Maelzel—the inventor of that invaluable mechanical timebeater, the metronome—at a dinner given for Beethoven before he left Vienna for the country in July 1812. Thayer, who investigated the story carefully, says: "That Maelzel's 'ta, ta, ta' suggested the Allegretto to Beethoven, and that at a parting meal the canon on this theme was sung, is doubtless true; but it is by no means sure that the canon preceded the symphony." There is a story that Beethoven himself set the date of the dinner late in December 1817. In any event, the irrepressible sixteenth notes tick away metronomically, led on by an airy theme.

Berlioz says of this movement: "It is one of those productions for which neither model nor pendant can be found. This sort of thing falls entire from heaven into the composer's brain. He writes it at a single sitting, and we are amazed at hearing it." This would be all very well but for the fact that Beethoven's sketches show how mightily he labored over the wholly spontaneous-seeming movement. When that eminent pessimist, the philosopher Schopenhauer, heard it, he declared it could make one forget that the world is filled with nothing but misery!

Instead of a Scherzo Beethoven proceeds with a stately minuet ("Tempo di Menuetto" in F major), which is not the symphonic minuet of the First and the Fourth symphonies, but a minuet in the noble manner of the eighteenth-century dance and perhaps not untinged with irony.

In the Finale ("Allegro vivace" in F major) the joy is truly unconfined and the music roars and billows with the impact of Olympian laughter.

Mass in C Major and the Missa Solemnis

Aside from the above-mentioned oratorio *Christ on the Mount of Olives,* Beethoven's major religious compositions consist of the *Mass in C major,* written in 1807, and the stupendous one in D—the overpowering *Missa Solemnis*—begun in 1817 but not completed till 1825. The C major Mass must not be thought of as an early creation or a thing in the manner of the *Mount of Olives*. Actually, it is a work of the composer's maturity, virtually contemporaneous with the great *Leonore* Overture and the Fifth Symphony. It was written at the instance of one of the Eszterházy princes who, when he heard the Mass, infuriated Beethoven by asking: "Well, my dear Beethoven, what is it you have gone and done now?" Strangely enough, the C major Mass for all its unquestionable beauties is treated rather as a stepchild. No greater mistake could be made than to compare it with the *Missa Solemnis* of a much later date and of basically different premises. "It expresses in the region of sacred music the joyful and victorious mood of the overture and the Symphony," says Paul Bekker. "An atmosphere of simple piety pervades the Mass; no inner disunion, no brooding doubt, no unsatisfied thirst for knowledge finds expression here. The Mass in C is a confession of the composer's faith and is at the same time liturgically practicable; it expresses a great artist's confident belief, at a time when he was one in thought and feeling with the 'spiritual powers that be' of his period."

The great Mass in D is a totally different proposition. It was the slow and gradual outgrowth of one of the periods of Beethoven's life where soul-shaking problems crowded ceaselessly upon him. He began to work upon it with the idea of producing it at the enthronement of his friend and pupil, the Archduke Rudolph, as Archbishop of Olmütz. But as it slowly expanded the composer forgot more and more why he had originally conceived it. It became in the grandest and deepest sense an expression of its creator's profoundest philosophies. Barring three movements of the work, none of the *Missa Solemnis* was ever performed during the composer's lifetime. And, singularly enough, those three movements were presented at the concert on May 7, 1824, at which the Ninth Symphony was heard for the first time. They had one other performance before Beethoven died—in St. Petersburg at the instigation of the Prince Galitzin.

The Mass in D, stupendous creation that it is, is far from a practical church work. It lacks all pretense of ritualistic use. For one thing, its vast proportions, the length of the individual sections, and the duration of the score as a whole would completely unfit it for ecclesiastical ceremony. The Mass is "unchurchly" in the highest degree. According to Bekker, Beethoven "breaks through the walls which divide the church from the world; his church extends to the limits of his vision; his altar is the heart of the universe, and he will suffer no dogmatic limitations." Above the Kyrie the composer inscribed the words: "From the heart—may it go to the heart." He intended the work "for the democratic concert hall rather than for polite social circles."

The peak of the *Missa Solemnis* is undoubtedly the great fugue "Et vitam venturi" of the Credo. And here, incidentally, the demands on the singing voices are perhaps more cruel than anywhere in the last movement of the Ninth Symphony or in the most arduous pages of *Fidelio*. Only now and then is there a wholly satisfying performance of the Mass in D. Be this as it may, there are two pages so extraordinary that no listener can ever fail to be stirred to the depths by them. One is the "Benedictus," with its transfigured violin solo and a prefatory orchestral movement so spiritualized that it takes rank by the side of the loftiest slow movements the composer ever wrote; the other is the "Agnus Dei" and its "Prayer for inner and outer peace," in which Beethoven causes the drum and trumpet calls of war to alternate with agonized supplications for peace.

All the same, despite the sublimities of the work and the vaunted "morality" of the composer, Beethoven did not hesitate to offer the score to at least three different publishing houses at practically the same time! Small wonder that, before long, a London concert agent was writing: "For heaven's sake, don't have any dealings with Beethoven!" If the master was not above attempting a little business skulduggery now and then he did not go about it cleverly!

Symphony No. 9, in D Minor, with Final Chorus on Schiller's "Ode to Joy," Opus 125

More than ten years passed after the initial performance of the Eighth Symphony before Beethoven brought out its successor, his ninth and last, on May 7, 1824. The earlier part of this period was comparatively unproductive. Beethoven was profoundly disturbed by quarrels over his guardianship of his nephew Karl, which eventually were taken to court. His health and spirits suffered and, meantime, his deafness became complete. Nevertheless his creative impulse found expression in two works of the grandest dimensions, the Mass in D and the Ninth Symphony. Sketches for the symphony were made as early as 1815—perhaps even earlier—and he went to work on it in earnest in 1817.

The première took place at the Kaerthnerthor Theater, Vienna, on May 7, 1824. The problems of performance were complicated by the composer's using in the final movement a chorus and a quartet of soloists. Michael Umlauf conducted and the solo singers were Henriette Sontag (one of the most famous sopranos of her day), Karolina Unger, Anton Haitzinger, and J. Seipelt. The difficulty of Beethoven's voice parts gave trouble at rehearsals. Mmes. Sontag and Unger begged him to alter their music, but in vain. Mme. Unger declared in his presence that he was a "tyrant over all the vocal organs." Still, at the first performance it was she who led the composer from where he had been sitting in the midst of the orchestra to the edge of the stage to see the excited waving of the audience and to bow.

These solo parts have lost none of their difficulty for singers, and from the sopranos of the chorus Beethoven well-nigh demands the superhuman. With a view to helping matters some conductors have transposed the Finale down a whole tone, thus dimming its brilliance and upsetting Beethoven's scheme of keys. Wagner believed that Beethoven by having words and singers in the Finale had closed the cycle of purely orchestral music. Others, however, regard the singers as a mistake and maintain that Beethoven recognized his error.

So devout and searching a student of Beethoven as Professor Tovey, while dismissing as absurd the theory of Beethoven's discontent with instrumental music, holds that every part of the Ninth Symphony becomes clearer when we assume that the choral Finale is right, and that hardly a point in the work but becomes difficult and obscure when we assume that the choral Finale is wrong. Though he admits that Beethoven, long after the production of the symphony, told some friends that the choral inclusion was a mistake and that perhaps some day he might write an instrumental Finale, he sets this down to a fit of depression. At any rate, the Finale stands as written and there is no choice but to grapple with its problems.

For three movements the symphony is of course, purely instrumental. Of the first movement ("Allegro, ma non troppo, un poco maestoso," in D minor) Ricciotto Canudo has written: "In the beginning was space; and all possibilities were in space; and life was space." It begins pianissimo in empty fifths. A descending figure of two notes, from the heights to the depths, is reiterated while a tremendous crescendo leads to the theme that dominates the movement, given out fortissimo in unison and octaves. The entire movement, which is well stocked with other themes, has the majesty and impetus of a titanic tragedy, and its propulsive drama ends with a defiant proclamation of the chief theme.

Now Beethoven reverses his usual procedure by postponing the slow movement and introducing a "Molto vivace" (in F minor), which has been called at once the greatest and the longest of his Scherzos. A phrase of three notes, repeated on each interval of the chord of D minor, begins it, followed immediately by a fugal subject. The enormous vitality and rhythmic drive of the Scherzo have deafened some hearers to the bitter strain in the jest. Joy unalloyed has not yet burst upon the scene.

And meanwhile Beethoven gives us the slow movement, a combination of an "Adagio molto e cantabile" (in B-flat major) and an "Andante moderato" (in D major), which as a whole has been described conveniently and with reasonable accuracy as a set of variations on two alternating themes. Language has been ransacked for words to express the beauty and elevation of this Adagio-Andante. Its seraphic song is dying away when the initial D minor of the Finale, presto and fortissimo, roughly smites our ears.

A series of orchestral sections, in contrast and conflict, occupy the battleground of the earlier pages before the baritone soloist, first using words by Beethoven himself, introduces the human voices and Schiller's "Ode to Joy." Two of the themes brought in here the listener should keep carefully in mind: the first is employed later by the baritone in demanding sounds of gladness, and the second is the so-called theme of joy. Now chorus and soloists join valiantly in the good fight for "mirth and rapture blended" till the symphony ends in the victorious D major paeans, vocal and at the very last instrumental, of universal rejoicing. The burden of Schiller's praise of Joy is held in these two lines:

> "All mankind are brothers plighted
> Where thy gentle wings abide."

And universal brotherhood is thus voiced by the tenors and the basses in unison.

LUDWIG VAN BEETHOVEN

CHAMBER MUSIC

If Beethoven's best-known and most widely performed works are the nine symphonies, his chamber music represents the most far-reaching, diversified, profound, original, spiritualized, and at the same time the most problematic manifestations of his genius. It is through his quartets, when all is said, that his influence has been most felt. In these dwell the germs of more or less everything out of which subsequent music has, in one way or another, developed. If Beethoven may be called a "musician of the future" it is by reason of his sixteen string quartets more than by anything else. More than all else he composed they continue, in great measure, to be in advance not only of the master's own time but even of our own.

It may be said that his chamber music spanned his life. The earliest specimens of it date from his Bonn days, from around his fifteenth year. From then on they continued (intermittently, it is true) almost up to the time of his death. Indeed, the last composition he completed was a new finale for the B-flat Quartet, opus 130, to replace the original one, the Great Fugue, now opus 133, which early audiences could not grasp—and which, to this very day, is a stumbling block for most hearers although one of the most extraordinary and transcendent pages Beethoven ever produced. And though at his demise he left a quantity of sketches (including studies for a tenth symphony) there is every reason to assume that an even more copious quantity of chamber music might have come from his pen had he lived five or ten years longer.

The mass of such chamber music as he did bequeath us includes sonatas for piano and violin as well as for piano and cello; a Quintet in C major, opus 29, for two violins, two violas, and cello, dating from 1801; a quintet fugue in D, written in 1817 but published as opus 137; a number of trios for a variety of instrumental combinations, several duets and serenades, and other miscellany for more or less intimate performance. Lastly, the famous Septet in E flat, for clarinet, horn, bassoon, violin, viola, cello, and double-bass, opus 20. This septet was composed about 1800 and was at one time so immeasurably popular that Beethoven himself wearied of it. Despite the vogue it long enjoyed, it is far from one of its creator's most inspired flights.

179

The series of trios for piano and strings constitute something of a counterpart to the great string quartets. Opus 1 consists of three such trios, and the composer's friend Ries wrote that "when the three were first heard by the musical world at one of Prince Lichnowsky's soirées nearly all the foremost artists and amateurs of Vienna were invited, among them Haydn, whose opinion was awaited with intense interest." The trios caused a sensation. Haydn, who was enthusiastic about them on the whole, had reservations to make about the third, in C minor, and advised the composer not to publish it. Beethoven took this advice in bad part, the more so because he regarded this trio as the best, and imagined that his famous contemporary was actuated by envy. The truth of the matter was that Haydn, struck by the bold originality of the score, was honestly afraid that the public might not understand it. But it is precisely this quality that has lifted the C minor Trio far above the other two of opus 1.

The other trios for piano and strings are the pair in D major and E flat, opus 70, and the supremely great one in B flat, opus 97, called the "Archduke" Trio because it was dedicated to the composer's friend and pupil, the Archduke Rudolph. The opus 70 creations are remarkable for the somewhat restless, indeed forbidding, quality that fills some of their pages. The first has been named the "Ghost" Trio on account of an eerie figure that pervades the slow movement and lends it a strangely weird and hollow sound. The "Archduke" Trio has a spaciousness and elevation, particularly in its Largo, which is a series of five variations on a theme in the character of a hymn. Wisely enough, Beethoven placed the Scherzo before the profound slow movement, as he was again to do in the "Hammerklavier" Sonata and the Ninth Symphony. But this Scherzo utilizes in its middle part a curious, winding chromatic figure which ranks with the master's most striking ideas at this stage of his progress.

Between 1799 and 1802 Beethoven wrote eight of his ten sonatas for violin and piano. The most famous of these eight are the fifth—the so-called "Spring" Sonata in F, opus 24, which opens with a theme of lovely grace and has a beautiful serenity throughout its four movements—and the set in A major, C minor, and G major, opus 30, which was published with a dedication to Czar Alexander I of Russia. The C minor Sonata reveals a heroic quality which lends it something of the spirit of the "Eroica" Symphony, and the closing Presto of the finale has about it an element of dramatic grandeur. However, none of these sonatas quite reaches the level of the "Kreutzer" or the much later Sonata in G major, opus 96. The A major, opus 47, derived its name from the fact that it was dedicated to Rudolph Kreutzer. It was first played by a mulatto violinist named Bridgetower, while the composer performed the piano part. Despite the haste with which the work was composed (Czerny spoke of "four days"), the sonata, "written in a very concertante style," has remained probably the best-known and most widely popular of all Beethoven's sonatas for violin and piano. The music has an expansiveness and plenitude that surpass any other work Beethoven designed for this instrumental combination. The finale, a whirlwind Presto originally conceived for the first sonata of the opus 30 set, influenced Schubert when he composed the last movement of his D minor Quartet. Undoubtedly it is the most original, not to say the most exciting, part of the work—more so, indeed, than the Andante, with its series of variations so arranged that each artist is given his adroitly balanced share.

The G major Sonata, composed in 1812 and first performed by the French violinist Pierre Rode and the Archduke Rudolph, is unquestionably the most intellectual and the subtlest of Beethoven's violin sonatas. In any case it has some of the unmistakable traits of the master's later style about it.

The sonatas for cello and piano, in F major and G minor, were composed as early as 1796 and performed in Berlin before the King of Prussia by Beethoven and the Court cellist, Duport. But the memorable cello sonatas of Beethoven's are the one in A major, opus 69, one of his most lavish and magnificent works; and the C major and D major, opus 102. The first named, like the "Kreutzer" Sonata or the "Appassionata" of the piano series, is a creation that needs no defense and no far-fetched explanations. On the other hand, the opus 102 pair, despite their indisputable profundities, are among Beethoven's more unapproachable and recondite works. Indeed, they have about them a certain hard-shelled quality which scarcely lends them an especially intimate or endearing effect.

STRING QUARTETS

The great series of string quartets begins with the six of opus 18, published in 1801, and concludes, officially speaking, with the masterpiece in F major, opus 135, completed only in 1826, but not printed till something like half a year after his death. The half-dozen works constituting the earlier opus had been ripening in the form of sketches and experiments of one sort or another for several years. They were finally issued in two numbers, each consisting of three scores. It is not possible to determine precisely the order in which they were written, but that fact is unimportant because the lot do not exhibit any definite line of development. It seems that one version of the first quartet, in F, was completed in 1799. Beethoven gave it to his friend, the young ecclesiastical student Carl Amenda, but asked him to show it to nobody because "I have altered it considerably, having just learned to compose quartets aright." Bekker finds that the revision "tends to a freer, more soloistic treatment of the accompanying parts, a clearer individualization of the cello part and a greater tonal delicacy in the ensemble effects . . . The main idea of the composition, however, remained unchanged. This is no disadvantage, for the fresh naiveté of the content and the unassuming clarity of structure are great charms, and more would have been lost than gained by overmeticulous revision. As the work stands it is gratifying to the performer and offers pleasant, not over difficult problems to the listener."

The finest part of the work is undoubtedly the second movement, an "Adagio affetuoso ed appassionato." It is the richest in texture and certainly the most poetic and emotional of the four. When the composer played it to Amenda he is said to have inquired what the music suggested to him. "It suggests a lover's parting," replied Amenda; whereupon Beethoven replied, "Well, the tomb scene from *Romeo and Juliet* was in my mind." And Bekker insists that this Adagio is "a most moving song of sorrow such as only Beethoven could accomplish when he turned to the grave D minor key."

The second quartet, in G major, has been christened in some German countries the "Compliment Quartet." It is graceful and rather courtly but it reaches none of the depths of the more moving pages of the preceding work. The Finale, however, is an instance of that "unbuttoned humor" that Beethoven was to exhibit on later occasions and of which he gave us supreme instances in the last movement of the Seventh Symphony, the Eighth Symphony, and moments in the last quartets, the "Diabelli Variations," and several of the final piano sonatas. Opus 18, No. 3, in D, is likewise marked by a quality of gaiety, though hardly of the "unbuttoned" kind.

The fourth work of the opus 18 set, in C minor, is more or less a work distinct from its companions. "A mood of deep seriousness is common to it and the C major Quintet, opus 29," believes Bekker, "but the Quartet is full of passionate excitement," and he alludes to its "mournful earnestness . . . and restless dissatisfaction, the very opposite of the cheerful sense of concord with the world and mankind expressed in the other five." The Quartet in A major has been termed Mozartean by some, operatic by others. Certainly it is fluent and lilting music, of which the Minuet is in some respects the most winning portion even if the final Allegro excels it in expressiveness.

The B-flat Quartet, sixth of the series, is particularly significant for the somber adagio beginning of its otherwise jubilant allegretto Finale. Beethoven has headed this introduction (which is recalled dramatically during the movement) "La Malinconia: Questo pezzo si deve trattare colla più gran delicatezza" ("Melancholy: this piece must be played with the greatest delicacy"). This eerie and wholly romantic movement is a true glimpse of the Beethoven into whose newer world we shall presently penetrate.

With the three monumental quartets of opus 59 we have entered this new sphere. They belong to the year 1806, which means that they are of the epoch of the Fourth and Fifth Symphonies, the third *Leonore* Overture, and the Violin Concerto and the G major Concerto for piano. Beethoven dedicated them to the Russian Count Rasoumovsky, whose name is thus imperishably linked with these masterpieces; and it was perhaps as a compliment to this nobleman that he introduced into the first and second of these works authentic Russian themes. Indeed, the Scherzo of the E minor Quartet utilizes that great melody around which, more than half a century later, Moussorgsky was to build the coronation scene in his opera *Boris Godunov*.

The "Rasoumovsky" trilogy exhibits Beethoven's inventive and technical faculties at the ideal symmetry they had achieved at the flood tide of his so-called "Second" period. The F major, C major, and E minor Quartets are in some ways the most ideally "balanced" ones he ever wrote; and, with all their splendor of form and substance, they are still replete with the most astonishing originalities and departures. Indeed, the amazing "Allegretto, scherzando" movement of the F major Quartet so astounded the players who first undertook to perform it that they imagined Beethoven's rhythmic motto theme was intended as a joke at their expense and almost refused to go through with it. The Adagio, on the other hand, develops, with the utmost richness of sonority and color possible to four stringed instruments, two gorgeously songlike themes till it seems as if they had become expanded to orchestral dimensions. The E minor Quartet, less a display piece than its companion works, is in a totally different and quite as unprecedented manner, while its slow movement ("Molto Adagio") sounds a deep, spiritual note which seems to have been inspired in the composer by a nocturnal contemplation of a starry sky in the country around Baden, near Vienna. As for the C major Quartet, the third of the "Rasoumovsky" set, it closes in a jubilant, sweeping fugue, which is like a paean of triumph.

There are two E-flat quartets in Beethoven's output: the first, opus 74, is known as the "Harp" Quartet by reason of the numerous passages of plucked strings in the first movement; the second is the tremendous opus 127. The former is the dreamier, less challenging of the two; it is rich not only in a sort of romanticism that looks forward to the age of Schumann, but also in unexpected effects bearing the unmistakable stamp of the Beethoven of the "Emperor" Concerto period, though in its way it is rather less venturesome than the "Rasoumovsky" trilogy. But the quartet that was written down in 1810—the F minor, opus 95—is in another category. It is the product of a new period of emotional ferment and a disquiet pervades the score with the irascible pertinacity of a gadfly. There is, indeed, a new quality of storm and stress in this *Quartetto Serioso,* as the composer himself designated it. Here he is in no mood for trifling. "At the moment when Beethoven had fought out his battle, when he could look back on all stages of the contest and taste the fruits of victory, he became most intensely aware of what it had cost him," writes Paul Bekker, adding that "the autographed title shows that the composer sought no happy solution of his problem"—in spite of which the F minor Quartet does, surprisingly enough, end on a note of laughter.

Beethoven did not busy himself with the composition of string quartets for another fourteen years. This stretch of time is longer than any other interval in the various series of his compositions. It must be recalled, however, that in this space he wrote the last three symphonies, the last half-dozen piano sonatas, the *Missa Solemnis,* the definitive revision of *Fidelio* together with its new E major overture, the *Ferne Geliebte* song cycle, the "Consecration of the House" Overture, and a quantity of other works only less significant. Spiritually, of course, he had traversed cycles of experience and had become, in an intellectual and artistic sense, another being.

It is almost inevitable, therefore, that the next great masterpiece of chamber music should lift the curtain on a new creative realm. The E-flat Quartet, opus 127, has been properly likened to a majestic portal opening on the grand landscape of the last four quartets—the B-flat, opus 130; C-sharped minor, opus 131; A minor, opus 132; and the relatively short F major, opus 135, which may be described as a sort of epilogue to the series.

There is nothing quite like these "last quartets" in Beethoven's myriad-faceted output. In its way the series may be said to transcend even the Ninth Symphony, the "Hammerklavier" Sonata, and the "Diabelli" Variations. The novelty, the explosive qualities, the far-darting influence of these works (which span the nineteenth century and might even be said to help leaven the musical art of our own time) cannot be fully evaluated, let alone described, in this book.

It must suffice here to point out that the E-flat Quartet places the listener at once in a world of unimagined wonders. The very opening measures of the first movement with their powerful chords sound like a heraldic annunciation. The second movement ("Adagio ma non troppo e molto cantabile") is a series of variations of deepest earnestness. It is as if the composer endeavored to bring to his hearers revelations newly unfolded to his searching vision. The "Scherzando vivace" that follows is wildly and even uncannily humorous—and, incidentally, the longest of Beethoven's Scherzos. The Finale is a sort of triumphal march in which "some adventurer from the heavens seems to visit the earth . . . with tidings of gladness, to return to his home in the heavens once more."

The B-flat Quartet is, if anything, more unusual and amazing, and it is in reality bound by a kind of mystical thematic kinship with the A minor and the C-sharp minor Quartets which come next. This kinship can be traced through the Great Fugue and is carried through the following quartets with a variety of profound philosophical modifications. The seven relatively brief movements of the B-flat masterpiece culminate in the hyper-emotional Cavatina (of which Beethoven said that remembrance of the feelings that inspired him to compose it always stirred him to tears); and to this sentimental outburst the harsh if stupendous fugue provided a truly beneficent purgation. The later-written closing Allegro, if lively and effervescent, is much less truly "in the picture."

While it is risky, if not really impossible, to speak of the "greatest" of the last quartets, more than one musician would vote for the fourteenth —the tremendous one in C-sharp minor. The composition has seven movements, extraordinarily diversified. Beethoven tried out one of his little pleasantries on Schott, the publisher, and declared at first the quartet was "pieced together out of sundry stolen odds and ends." A little later he reassured the frightened, unimaginative man of business telling him that it was really "brand new." And subsequently he said impulsively that he considered the C-sharp minor "my best." The introductory "Adagio non troppo" was called by Wagner "the most sorrowful thing ever said in music." All the same, the mighty creation, after passing through unbelievable emotional transformations, closes in a triumphal frenzy which Wagner likened to "the dance of the whole world."

The A minor Quartet, opus 132, doubtless begun somewhat earlier than the two preceding, is scarcely less amazing. Its heart is the "Molto Adagio" movement which Beethoven called "Song of Thanksgiving in the Lydian mode offered to the Deity by a convalescent." It is filled with a mystical quality, a religious mood explained by the circumstance that the composer wrote the movement (one of his longest) when recovering from an illness. But the still more amazing fact about this quartet is that some pages of it were conceived for other works. It is a strange phenomenon that Beethoven on several occasions designed a quantity of pages not wholly sure where they would best fit, though in the end his artistic intuitions invariably led him to discover the right place. Just as he once intended the last movement of the "Kreutzer" Sonata for one of the sonatas of the opus 30 set, so he at one time intended the "Alla Marcia" that begins the finale of the A minor Quartet for the Ninth Symphony. And the last quartets furnish other instances of the same kind of thing.

The sixteenth quartet, last of the series, is rather different from the philosophical quartets that immediately preceded it. It is, on the whole, of lighter weight, though its brief "Lento assai" movement touches hands with the ineffable Cavatina of the B-flat Quartet. It is the shortest, though one of the most moving, of Beethoven's slow movements. The last movement opens with a three-note motto under which the composer wrote the words "Must it be?" and followed it with another three-note theme (Allegro) inscribed with the words "It must be!" Explanations have been numerous and often far-fetched. There is reason to believe that this formula and the musical embodiments of this interrogation and answer must be construed in the light of the master's philosophy, with its cheerful acceptance of the inevitable. It looks almost like a purposeful reversion to the mood of "La malinconia" episode in the B-flat Quartet of opus 18.

P. S. (with additions by H. F. P.)

Franz Schubert

BORN: LICHTENTHAL, SUBURB OF VIENNA, JAN. 31, 1797. DIED: VIENNA, NOV. 19, 1828.

My music is the production of my genius and my misery.—SCHUBERT.

THE MOST LOVABLE and the shortest-lived of the great composers, Franz Seraph Peter Schubert was doubly a paradox. He was the only one of the outstanding Viennese masters (unless one chooses to include in this category the Strauss waltz kings) actually born in Vienna; and, though there has never been a composer more spiritually Viennese, Schubert inherited not a drop of Viennese blood. His ancestry had its roots in the Moravian and Austrian-Silesian soil. His grandfather, Karl Schubert, a peasant and a local magistrate, lived in one of the thirty-five towns called Neudorf in Moravian-Silesian territory and married the daughter of a well-to-do farmer, acquiring by the match a large tract of land and ten children of whom the fifth, Franz Theodor Florian, was destined to beget an immortal.

At eighteen Franz Theodor, who was born in 1763, determined to follow the example of his older brother, Karl, and become a schoolmaster. He went to Vienna and secured a post as assistant instructor in a school where Karl had already been teaching for several years. In spite of starvation wages he married (1785) Maria Elisabeth Vietz, from Zuckmantel, in Silesia, the very town whence the Schuberts had originally emigrated to Neudorf. She was a cook, the daughter of a "master locksmith," and she was seven years older than her husband. The couple had fourteen children, nine of whom died in infancy. The

188

survivors were Ignaz, Ferdinand, Karl, Therese and our Franz Peter, who came twelfth in order.

A year after his marriage father Schubert was appointed schoolmaster of the parish of the Fourteen Holy Helpers, in Lichtental, one of the thirty-four Viennese suburbs (or *Vorstädte*), located at greater or lesser distances from the "Inner Town," which in those days represented Vienna proper. The schoolhouse (unless it has been demolished in the late war) still stands. Franz Theodor took lodgings for himself and his family a few steps away at the House of the Red Crab (*Zum rothen Krebse*), Himmelpfortgrund 72, now Nussdorfer Strasse 54 and since 1912 a Schubert museum, owned by the municipality of Vienna. Here Franz Seraph Peter was born on January 31, 1797, at half past one in the afternoon.

Father Schubert's position was far from lucrative; in fact, it offered no salary at all, nothing but a tax of one gulden a month per child levied on the parents. And yet this inflexible, God-fearing pedagogue, imposed such merciless economies and Spartan discipline on himself, his family and his pupils that he not only managed to make both ends meet but, when Franz Peter was four, to buy the schoolhouse where he taught and to take up his quarters there. In modern times the little house had become a garage, though a memorial tablet placed on it in 1928 reminded the passerby that Schubert lived and taught there for several years besides composing under its roof a number of his works, among them *Der Erlkönig*.

Not the least remarkable thing about father Schubert was the fact that, despite the endless grind of making a living, teaching and raising a family, he should have found time to cultivate music. Yet he was a tolerable amateur cellist and his great son's first music teacher. After giving the boy "elementary instruction" in his fifth year and sending him to school in his sixth he taught Franz Peter at the age of eight the rudiments of violin playing and had him practice so thoroughly that the boy was "soon able to play easy duets fairly well."

The youngster was next handed over to his elder brother, Ignaz, who gave him some piano instruction. But here an uncanny thing happened! The child showed such an instinctive grasp of everything his brother tried to teach him that Ignaz, nonplussed, confessed himself hopelessly outstripped. Franz, for his part, declared he had no need of help but would go his own way in musical matters. Thereupon his parents entrusted him to the choirmaster of the nearby Lichtental parish church, one Michael Holzer, who knew something about counterpoint and consumed more alcohol than was good for him. It was not long before poor Holzer was experiencing with his pupil the same difficulties as Ignaz. He had the little fellow sing and was delighted by his bright voice and his musical accuracy. He let him accompany hymns on the organ, had him improvise and modulate back and forth, taught him a little piano and violin, familiarized him with the viola clef and a few principles of thorough bass. But in the end his labors were largely superfluous. Holzer admitted that "the lad has harmony in his little finger." A nearby shop of a piano maker offered a more fertile field for experiments in harmony. Released from the organ loft Franz Peter hurried to this shop and spent hours there forming chords on the keyboard.

He Joins the "Sängerknaben"

It is not impossible that Schubert may have made a few attempts at composition at this stage, though there is no actual proof. But a real turning point came on May 28, 1808. On that date there appeared in the official journal, the *Wiener Zeitung,* an announcement that two places among the choristers of the Imperial Chapel (the so-called Sängerknaben) had to be filled. Father Schubert saw his chance. A chorister who showed the necessary qualifications could enjoy free tuition, board and lodging at the Imperial Konvikt (or Seminary); and if the boy distinguished himself "in morals and studies" he might remain even after his voice had changed. The Konvikt was a former Jesuit school reopened in 1802 by the Emperor Franz and supervised by a branch of the Jesuits called the Piarists. In addition to ten choristers there were pupils of middle and high school standing. The Konvikt occupied a long, cheerless building which in modern times looked quite as bleak as it did in Schubert's day.

The tests took place on September 30, 1808, and the examiners consisted of Antonio Salieri, a prolific opera composer, an intimate of Gluck and Haydn, a teacher of Beethoven and an implacable enemy of Mozart; the Court Kapellmeister Eybler; and a singing teacher at the school, Philip Korner. Schubert presented himself for the examination wearing a grayish smock, which caused the other boys to jeer and call him a miller. But as millers were popularly supposed to be musical the young mockers agreed that he could not fail. They were right. Not only did he meet all the requirements but his voice and musicianship aroused the surprise and enthusiasm of the committee. Schubert was promptly accepted. In other required subjects as well as in music, he easily surpassed the other competitors. Not in vain was he his father's son!

So the boy shed his "miller's" vesture and put on the fancy, gold-braided togs of the Sängerknaben. In a few days he was settled at the Konvikt. He was amenable to discipline—having learned it plentifully at home—and does not appear to have suffered the tribulations of some other Konvikt scholars who were less conformable and more adventurous. The shyness which clung to him more or less throughout his life made him shun his fellow students as much as he conveniently could. The food was poor and scanty and even four years later we find him appealing pathetically to his brother Ferdinand for a few pennies a month to buy a roll or an apple as a fortifying snack between a "mediocre midday meal and a paltry supper" eight hours later! The music room at the school was left unheated, hence "gruesomely cold" (anyone who has experienced the unheated corridors of a Viennese house in winter can shudder in sympathy!). But there was plenty of music and the school orchestra, in which Schubert occupied the second desk among the violins, delighted him.

Every evening this orchestra played an entire symphony and ended up with "the noisiest possible overture." The windows were left open in summer and crowds used to collect outside, till the police dispersed them because they obstructed traffic. The concerts were conducted by a singularly lovable old Bohemian organist, viola player and teacher, Wenzel Ruziczka, who at an early date defended and explained some of the boldest "modernisms" in Schubert's compositions. The orchestra performed a good deal of trivial music but every now and then there would be works by Haydn, Mozart, Cherubini, Méhul and even some of the less taxing scores of Beethoven. Schubert on these occasions felt himself in heaven! He was "entranced" by the slow movements of Haydn, but his god was Mozart. With a subtlety of perception almost uncanny in a boy of twelve he said that the G minor Symphony "shook him to the depths without his knowing why." He called the overture to the *Marriage of Figaro* the "most beautiful in the whole world," then quickly added "but I had almost forgotten that to the *Magic*

Flute." It is certain that this student orchestra was a most valuable factor in Schubert's musical education. It was with these young players in mind that he composed his First Symphony in October, 1813, at the age of sixteen.

At a first violin desk in front of Schubert there played another youth, some nine years older, a student of law and philosophy from Linz, Josef von Spaun, and thus began one of those Schubertian friendships that was to last for life and play an important part in Schubert's story. Amazed by the beautiful playing he heard behind him, Spaun looked around and saw "a small boy in spectacles." Not long afterwards he surprised the youngster in the freezing music room trying a sonata by Mozart. Franz confided to his sympathetic new friend that, much as he loved the sonata, he found Mozart "extremely difficult to play" (another acute observation!). Then, "shy and blushing," he admitted that he "sometimes put his thoughts into notes." However, he trembled lest his father get wind of the fact, for while Franz Theodor had no objection to music as a pastime and also had every reason to be satisfied that it paid for his son's education and kept a roof over his head, he had other plans for him in mind. The real business of the young man's life was to be schoolmastering. No two ways about it!

So Franz Peter had need to be wary. Besides, there was another obstacle to his composing. Music paper was scarce and costly. He did, it is true, rule staves on paper himself but even ordinary brown paper was not plentiful. So the generous Spaun, though he had a rather restricted budget, bought paper out of his own allowance and did not remonstrate when Schubert used up the precious commodity "by the ream." The only difficulty, now, was that Franz composed in study hours and fell back in his school work, a fact that was not slow in coming to his father's notice. And yet the records of the Konvikt do not show that Schubert was a poor student. At various times certificates signed by the school director, Father Innocenz Lang, pronounce him "good" or "very good" in almost everything, while in Greek he is even described as "eminent." Somewhat later when at normal school, preparing to teach in his father's schoolhouse, his weaker subjects were mathematics, Latin and "practical religion."

However, not all the parental thundering could keep nature from taking its course, even if it temporarily embittered Franz's young life. Father Schubert at one stage went so far as to forbid his son to enter his house. The lad had been in the habit of going home on Sundays and holidays and there taking part in string quartet concerts with his father and his brothers, Ignaz and Ferdinand, Schubert himself occupying the viola desk and being the real director of the ensemble. He roughly scolded his brothers when they blundered, but cautiously corrected Franz Theodor's errors with nothing more scathing than: "Herr Vater, something must be wrong here." Now this diversion was denied him and he suffered. Not until May 28, 1812, was he permitted to return to the Lichtental roof-tree and then only because a tragic event softened the paternal heart. On that Corpus Christi day Franz's mother died of typhus (or, as they called it then, "nerve fever") the same malady which sixteen years later was to carry off Franz himself. In due course the chamber music sessions were resumed and in time they outgrew their humble environment.

THE EARLIEST COMPOSITIONS

Let us look back briefly to consider a few of Schubert's early creative accomplishments. How many experimental efforts preceded his earliest extant compositions we can only surmise. His first surviving one is a four-hand piano Fantasie, 32 pages long, running to more than a dozen movements with frequent changes of time and key. A little later, on March 30, 1811, he began his first vocal composition, an immensely prolix affair called *Hagar's Klage* to a discursive poem about Hagar lamenting her dying child in the desert. With its varying rhythms, its pathetic slow introduction, its elaborate Allegro and its passionate prayer, it shows the influence of the popular German ballad master, Johann Rudolph Zumsteeg, who had himself composed the same text. Not only Zumsteeg but composers like Reichhardt and Goethe's friend, Zelter, exercised moulding influences on Schubert in his formative stage. A setting of Schiller's *Leichenphantasie* is carried out on much the same lines and so is a ballad, *Der Vatermörder,* to a text by Pfeffel. And there were other things besides long, trailing ballads—an orchestral overture in D, a so-called quartet-overture and quintet-overture, an Andante and a set of variations for piano, three string quartets "in changing keys" (Schubert wrote seven quartets in all during his Konvikt days), thirty minuets "with trio" for strings, "German dances," some four part Kyries for the Lichtental church and other matters bearing the dates 1811 and 1812.

The good Ruziczka, finding himself unable to teach his young charge anything he did not know already, handed him over to Salieri, who began to give him lessons in counterpoint on June 18, 1812 (Schubert made a record of the date). He must have profited by Salieri's instruction or he would hardly have remained his pupil all of five years, as he did. One circumstance may astonish us—that he briefly suffered himself to be swayed by the prejudice Salieri harbored against Beethoven. Yet when Salieri celebrated his fiftieth year of musical activities, in 1816, Schubert made a slighting entry in his diary about "certain bizarreries of modern tendencies." That this could have been only a passing aberration is clear from the fact that Beethoven remained his divinity and his despair to his dying day. He once told his friend, Spaun: "There are times when I think something could come of me; but who is capable of anything after Beethoven?" Indeed, Beethoven remained to such a degree an obsession of his that the older Master's name was almost the last word he ever uttered.

Franz Theodor found it inexpedient to remain long a widower. Less than a year after the loss of the quiet woman who had been his "deeply treasured wife" he married the daughter of a silk goods manufacturer, the "wertgeschätzte Jungfrau" Anna Kleyenböck, a woman of thirty, twenty years his junior. The entire Schubert family, including the black sheep from the Konvikt, was present at the wedding on April 25, 1813. Five more children were born and this time only one died. Anna Kleyenböck fitted perfectly into the Schubert *ménage*. Contrary to the tradition of stepmothers she idolized her stepson, Franz, and was no less adored by him in return. Later, when father Schubert's pecuniary position somewhat improved, Anna showed herself a model of economy and thrift, always putting what occasional savings the schoolmaster gave her into a woolen stocking! It was from this stocking that she more than once furnished a helping mite to her stepson in his days of need.

Franz's voice changed in 1812 and logically his days at the Konvikt should have been numbered. But the authorities were by no means anxious to be rid of him and his father would probably have been pleased if he had stayed on. Even the Emperor, to whom representations were made and whose attention the boy's talents seem to have attracted, agreed that he might remain and take advantage of the "Meerfeld scholarship"—provided he made an effort to improve his standing in mathematics. Franz himself must have realized that to return home meant to court renewed trouble with his father, not to mention the risk of actual starvation. Yet he was fed up with the Konvikt and about the end of October, 1813, he left what he called the "prison." His last work written there (it is dated October 28, 1813) was his First Symphony. But he maintained cordial relations with the Seminary for some years, tried out some of his new compositions in the Konvikt music room and preserved his interest in the school orchestra.

THE EARLY SYMPHONIES

This is, perhaps, as good a place as any to consider for a moment the early symphonies of Schubert. One says "early" because Schubert's symphonic output falls sharply into two distinct halves. Six of them —two in D major, two in B flat, one in C minor and one in C major— belong to the years from 1813 through 1817. They are relatively small in scale, melodically charming, in numerous detail of harmony and color unmistakably Schubertian, yet by and large derivative. They naïvely reflect phraseology and other influences the young composer assimilated from the music he was then studying and hearing. Thus, in the Second Symphony may be heard echoes of Beethoven's Fourth and jostling one another through the pages of the others are reminiscences (if not outright citations) of Haydn, Mozart, Beethoven, Rossini, Weber. The Fourth (in C minor) is for some not clearly defined reason entitled *Tragic;* the Sixth, still more inexplicably, the composer characterized as *Grosse* (great) *Symphonie in C.* Perversely enough, it is probably the weakest of the six, the one which least satisfied its creator. Time has paradoxically rechristened this symphony the "little" C major to distinguish it from the great C major of 1828. The Fifth, in B flat, remains with its endearing reminders of Mozart, perhaps the loveliest and most frequently played of all this symphonic juvenilia. Most of these scores, however, are oftener heard today than they were till recent years. For all their (perhaps half-conscious) borrowings they are still palpable Schubert, even if lesser Schubert. Such a master as Dvorak was always ready to break a lance in their behalf and one of his proudest boasts was how often, as Conservatory director in New York, he used to conduct his students' orchestra in the Fifth of the set.

No sooner was Schubert liberated from the Konvikt than he found himself faced with a worse menace—conscription. Service in the Austrian army was in those days no laughing matter. Its duration was fourteen years and the prospect of such a lifetime of soldiering might have appalled an even less sensitive nature than Schubert's. There were loopholes, of course, particularly for those who had wealth and position. For those who did not, the best road of escape lay through the schoolroom. Since there was need of teachers, the government exempted them. It almost looked as if the State were conspiring with father Schubert against his son. Poor Franz Peter had no alternative and so, barely out of the Konvikt, he enrolled in the Normal School of St. Anna for a ten months' preparatory course to teach a primary class at his father's school, a chore which was to occupy him for the next three years.

Hateful as he found his labors he seems to have discharged them conscientiously enough. Yet if the Konvikt, where he had numerous friends, was a "prison" what was this? He was only one of many "assistants" and he had to live under his father's roof, though he *did* earn forty gulden a year. Was he a good disciplinarian? He himself once confessed to his friend, Franz Lachner, that he was a "quick-tempered teacher," who when disturbed by the little imps in his class while he composed, thrashed them soundly "because they always made him lose the thread of his thought." His sister, Therese, later told Kreissle von Hellborn (Schubert's first biographer) that he "kept his finger in practice on the children's ears." Another story has it that he was finally dismissed for a particularly smart box on the ear of a particularly stupid girl. Still, when Schubert later applied for another school position, Superintendent Josef Spendou commended the applicant's "method of handling the young."

While he was at the St. Anna School, Schubert composed among a quantity of other things his first complete mass and his first opera. The former (in F) is the more important of the two. It was written with the limited resources of the Lichtental parish church—which on October 14, 1814, celebrated its centenary—in mind. The work of the seventeen-year-old composer was heard with unconcealed pleasure. He conducted it himself, his former teacher, Holzer, led the choir and the soprano soloist was Therese Grob, a year younger than Schubert and daughter of a Lichtental merchant who lived around the corner from father Schubert's schoolhouse. Ten days later the mass was repeated in the Church of St. Augustine, in the imperial Hofburg. This performance seems to have aroused even more enthusiasm and good will than the first. Salieri proudly pointed to the boyish composer as his own pupil and Franz Theodor, now that he knew his son safely caged in a classroom, made him a present of a five-octave piano. The Mass itself, a tenderly felt, lyrical, simple work, is sensitive and promising rather than something epoch-making, such as the composer was soon to achieve in the less pretentious province of the solo song.

A word about Therese Grob, who more or less properly figures in Schubert's story as his first love. Her family was refined and musical and Franz Peter, who was a visitor at the Grob household, may have found there some of the same sympathy and understanding the young Beethoven did in the home of the von Breunings. Certainly, he composed a number of things for Therese and her brother, Heinrich. His friend, Holzapfel, declares that Therese was "no beauty, but shapely, rather plump, with a fresh round little face of a child." In after years Schubert told Anselm Hüttenbrenner that he had loved her "very deeply." She was not pretty, he said, and was pock-marked but "good to the heart." He had "hoped to marry her" but could find no position which would insure him the means to support a wife. Her mother having decided it was no use to wait for a penniless composer to become a somebody made her take a well-to-do baker instead. Poor Schubert told his friend this had greatly pained him and that he "loved her still," but added philosophically "as a matter of fact, she was not destined for me." Did Schubert, we may ask, really contemplate marriage? If he did, how are we to understand an entry he made in his diary in 1816: "Marriage is a terrifying thought to a free man . . ."? Actually, Schubert's life was devoid of what might be described as urgent affairs of the heart—outwardly, at least. One will seek vainly in his case for the periodic transports of a Beethoven or even the passing dalliances of a Mozart. Friendships rather than passionate ardors were Schubert's specialties—and his friendships with women were quite as sincere as with men and had the same basis of sentimental conviviality. Hüttenbrenner had small reason to chaff his companion (as he once did) for being "so cold and dry in society toward the fair sex." Certainly, the delightful Fröhlich sisters (whom we shall meet shortly) did not find him "dry." It is so easy to mistake shyness for coldness—and if Schubert was anything he was diffident, sometimes tragically so!

Opera had exercised a strong attraction on Franz Peter even while he was a student at the Konvikt. He used to accompany Spaun to the Kärntnertor Theatre whenever holidays or the state of Spaun's purse permitted. The friends sat in the top gallery and heard operas like Weigl's *Schweizerfamilie*, Spontini's *Vestale*, Cherubini's *Medea*, Boieldieu's *Jean de Paris* and Gluck's *Iphigenia in Tauris*. Among the great singers Schubert heard in this way were Pauline Milder and Johann Michael Vogl. Both artists were soon to become his friends—Vogl, indeed, the high priest of his songs.

What wonder, then, that Schubert planned an opera of his own? In May, 1814, while at the St. Anna School, he completed a "natural magic opera" in three acts called *Des Teufels Lustschloss* ("The Devil's Pleasure Palace"). The libretto was by a popular dramatist of the time, August Kotzebue, who could hardly have attached much importance to it or he would never have permitted an unknown beginner to compose it. The piece was the first of a pageant of ugly ducklings, an operatic progeny of sorrow destined to span Schubert's life from his schooldays to his grave. If we add up his works for the stage—completed, fragmentary, partly sketched or lost—in less than a decade and a half we shall arrive at the astonishing total of eighteen. And today there is almost nothing to show for all this heartbreaking industry because an ancient (and largely untested) tradition calls Schubert's operas "undramatic" and otherwise "poor theater." Possibly they are. But how many now living can speak of a Schubert opera from actual experience?

Des Teufels Lustschloss was never performed in Schubert's Vienna, though Prague was once on the point of staging it. The plot has to do with the adventures of an impecunious Count Oswald who, on the way to his tumbled-down castle with his wife, stops at a wayside inn. There the peasantry of the neighborhood entreat the knight to free a nearby ruin from ghosts and other spooky visitants. He consents and, together with his squire (a kind of Sancho Panza), penetrates the infested premises. The spectres take him captive and subject him to grisly tests—the worst of which is a command to marry a "ghostly" but extremely substantial Amazon who suddenly appears on the scene.

In despair Oswald springs into the abyss and lands—in the arms of his wife! Her wealthy uncle, it transpires, being displeased with his niece's marriage to the penniless Count has "arranged" the whole ordeal as a test of Oswald's fidelity, with the help of his gardener's buxom daughter—the "Amazon"—and "machines of all kinds brought at considerable expense from foreign parts."

It should be remembered, however, that such extravagances were habitual ingredients of innumerable "magic" plays and comedies which for generations, indeed for centuries, formed the stock-in-trade of the Viennese suburban theater and the most sublimated outgrowth of which was Mozart's *Magic Flute.* Moreover, not the effect of such a wild tale in the *reading* but in *performance on the stage, in a theater, before an audience* is the proof of the pudding. The same with the text—a specimen of the poetry of *Des Teufels Lustschloss* is the ensuing of Count Oswald's squire:

> *I'm laughing, I'm crying, I'm crying, I'm laughing*
> *I'm laughing, ha, ha, ha,*
> *I'm laughing, hi, hi, hi,*
> *I'm laughing, ho, ho, ho,*
> *I'm laughing, hu, hu, hu . . .*

The test of such a thing is not the verbiage but the composer's treatment of it. There is no question here of a masterpiece any more than there is in the Mass, or indeed, in the various orchestral or chamber works, he had produced thus far. It was different, however, with the songs (*Lieder*) which he was turning out in effortless abundance. He had made settings among other things of poems by Schiller, Fouqué, Mattheson (*Adelaide,* for one, though smoother, more lyrical and less varied in its mood than Beethoven's famous song). Then, on October 19, 1814—"the birthday of the German Lied" it has been called—there comes like a bolt from the blue the epoch-making *Gretchen am Spinnrade,* from Goethe's *Faust.* It is a simple, plaintive melody above a murmuring spinning wheel figure and a pulsing rhythmic throb, but nevertheless a marvel of jointless form and a miracle of psychology, the emotional experience of ages concentrated into one hundred bars of music of such infinite art and uncanny perfection that it almost defies analysis.

As if a gigantic dam had burst, a torrent of immortal mastersongs now begins to pour forth. Not everything, to be sure, either now or later is a deathless creation but the number of those that are will probably remain baffling to the end of time. Schubert frequently made two, three or more settings of one and the same text, differing in greater or lesser degree from the earlier one though not invariably better than the preceding version. Of the more than six hundred Lieder Schubert composed, almost a third are such re-settings. It was nothing unusual for him to turn out four, five, six songs a day. "When I finish one I begin another," was his carefree way of describing the incredible process. Sometimes he even forgot which songs were his own. "I say, that's not a bad one; who wrote it?" he once asked on hearing something he had composed only a few days before. He was careless, too, about what became of some of his manuscripts and there is no telling how much posterity may have lost as a result. Once he came near ruining a page on which he had written his song *Die Forelle* by pouring ink instead of sand over the wet writing; being sleepy, he did not bother to notice which receptacle he had picked up.

DER ERLKÖNIG

In the year following *Gretchen am Spinnrade* there came into being (and once more in his father's school in the Säulengasse) what is, in some ways perhaps, the most famous of Schubert's songs—*Der Erlkönig*. Spaun, who went to visit his friend one afternoon, found him "all aglow," a book in hand, reading Goethe's ballad. Schubert walked up and down the room several times, suddenly seated himself at a table "and in the shortest possible time the splendid ballad was on paper." Franz having no piano, the pair hastened down to the Konvikt where the song was tried out that very evening. Several listeners objected to the sharp dissonances of the accompaniment to the child's cry but it was none other than old Ruziczka who showed himself the best "modernist" of them all, actually championing the "cacophony," explaining its artistic function and praising its beauty. Schubert himself had a pair of sore wrists from the unmerciful triplets of the piano part! Not everywhere, one regrets to say, did *Der Erlkönig* create such a stir. At the insistence of his friends Schubert sent it, along with some other songs, to Goethe with an appropriate dedication. His Excellency in Weimar did not even deign to acknowledge it. Meanwhile the publishing firm of Breitkopf and Härtel, to whom Spaun also dispatched the ballad, thought that someone was playing a practical joke. Before deciding what to do with "wild stuff" they addressed themselves to a Dresden violinist who chanced also to be called Franz Schubert (he composed a trifling piece called *The Bee,* which some fiddlers still play) and asked his opinion. The Saxon Franz (or François) Schubert exploded, insisted he had never composed the "cantata" in question but would see who was misusing his good name for such a patchwork and promptly bring the miscreant to book!

Various piano compositions—Ecossaises, German Dances, variations, sonatas—a number of string quartets and other chamber music swelled the ever-increasing output. The quantity of songs mounted like a tidal wave. And although nothing had come of *Des Teufels Lustschloss* (part of which the composer, moved by purely artistic impulses, even went so far as to rewrite), Schubert continued the woeful job of piling up unwanted operatic scores. He wrote *Der vierjährige Posten* (the story of a sentry who was posted and not relieved on the departure of his regiment and who, when it returned four years later, still stood on duty); *Fernando, a Singspiel; Claudine von Villa Bella; Die Freunde von Salamanka* and *Adrast* (texts by Johann Mayrhofer).

And, while we are on the operatic subject, let us look ahead into the years of Schubert's maturity and list what other operas he wrote (it should be understood, by the way, that certain of these are more on the order of operettas than what we understand by lyric dramas). In 1819 he composed *Die Zwillingsbrüder,* which has a plot along *Comedy of Errors* lines; in 1820 a "magic and machine" comedy called *Die Zauberharfe* ("The Magic Harp"), the overture of which is familiar to us as the *Rosamunde*—though the overture which Schubert used three years later to the musical play of that name was the introduction that prefaced a full-length romantic opera, *Alfonso und Estrella,* dated 1821. An *actual* overture to *Rosamunde* was never written. The piece known universally by that title was not so designated till 1827, when it was published in an arrangement for piano duet. Other operatic works we may cite in passing are *Die Verschworenen,* a treatment of the "Lysistrata" motive; and the large-scale "heroic-romantic" opera, *Fierrabras,* composed in the summer of 1823. After 1823 Schubert let opera alone—at least temporarily. On his deathbed he was still planning another, a *Graf von Gleichen,* for a book by his boon companion, Eduard von Bauernfeld. But the project had never gone beyond some sketches.

Mayrhofer, whom we just mentioned, had made Schubert's acquaintance in 1814, when the composer set to music his poem, *Am See.* A close friendship immediately sprang up between them though Mayrhofer—the older of the two by ten years—was of a moody, brooding nature (he subsequently committed suicide by jumping out of a window). By 1819, Schubert, having grown heartily sick of schoolmastering some time before, went to share for a while the somber, dilapidated quarters of Mayrhofer in the Wipplinger Strasse (the danger of the army draft was now over) and the pair, for all their temperamental differences, hit it off famously. Although Schubert composed pretty much anywhere and everywhere he accomplished a prodigious amount of creative work in Mayrhofer's depressing room. The poet on opening his eyes in the morning used to see Franz, clad only in shirt and trousers, writing vigorously at a rickety table. His favorite working hours were from six in the morning till noon, though he was in the habit of sleeping with his spectacles on in case the lightning of inspiration should strike him the minute he awoke. If any visitor came unannounced Schubert would greet him, without looking up from his work, with the words: "Greetings! How are you? Well?" —whereupon the intruder realized it was an invitation to disappear.

After writing all morning Schubert, like a true Viennese, usually went to enjoy the incomparable relaxation of a coffee house, drinking a *Mélange* (café au lait), eating *Kipferl* (crescents, if you prefer!), smoking and reading the newspapers. In the evening there was the opera and the theater (provided one had money or somebody bought the tickets) or else the gatherings of the clans at the various "Gasthäuser," "Stammbeisel" and taverns. The friends discussed questions of the day, literature, plays, music. They criticized each other's work with unsparing frankness. Schubert's uncommonly keen musical opinions were relished by everybody.

Although Schubert wished to have done with teaching as soon as possible, he attempted (perhaps to placate his father) to obtain a pedagogical post in a normal school at Laibach. He was turned down in favor of some local applicant, which was no doubt just as well. Had it been otherwise the brilliant coterie of "Schubertians" might have been nipped in the bud and the term "Schubertiads," as they called their revels and their discussions had it entered the dictionary at all, might have had another meaning.

Who were these "Schubertians," this group of younger and older intellectuals and Bohemians held together, somehow, by the indefinable attraction of Schubert's personality? They came and went with the years and when one or another vanished a different one would generally take his place. "Kann er was?" ("What's he good at?") was Franz's usual query if a newcomer appeared—a question which earned him the nickname "Kanevas"! Virtually all who stepped into the charmed circle were good at something. Among the most prominent were Spaun, Mayrhofer, Stadler, Senn, and later Moriz von Schwind, the painter; the Kupelwieser brothers, Leopold and Josef, Josef Gahy, Karl Enderes, the poet Matthaeus Collin, the blue-stocking novelist, Karoline Pichler, Eduard von Bauernfeld, Franz von Schober —to cite only a handful that come to mind. Schober, particularly, who wrote, drew, acted and was in every sense a clever man of the world, played a considerable rôle in Schubert's life—some even hint a rather nefarious one. Still, he was well-to-do, his rooms were at Franz's disposal whenever he needed them and he introduced the composer to the great Michael Vogl.

The latter, whom Schubert had long worshiped at the opera, was not only one of the greatest baritones of his time, but a singular and romantic creature, who became a social favorite on the strength of his handsome face and figure, developed some harmless affectations yet remained a mystic at heart. He passed much of his spare time reading the Bible, Plato, Epictetus and other ancient and medieval poets and philosophers. He greeted Schubert in the condescending manner assumed by some popular artists when they first met aspiring beginners. He seemed unimpressed on glancing over the first song or two Schubert put before him, but after reading through *Der Erlkönig* he patted the composer on the back, remarking as one not wholly dissatisfied: "There's something in you, but you're too little of an actor or a charlatan. You squander your fine thoughts without developing them." Yet before long he had become Schubert's chief interpreter and propagandist, and spoke grandly of "these truly god-like inspirations, these revelations of musical clairvoyance."

The chamber music concerts given on Sundays at the Schubert

homestead in Lichtental had outgrown their strictly domestic character quite some time before father Schubert had been transferred (late in 1817) to a new school in the neighboring Rossau district. The string quartet had expanded into a small orchestra and now performed symphonies and such in the homes of several musical acquaintances, lastly in that of a wealthy landowner, Anton Pettenkofer, who lived in the Inner Town, not far from St. Stephen's. It was for this amateur orchestra that Schubert composed at least four of his early symphonies. The occasional absence of drums and trumpets (in the Fifth, for instance) indicates the constitution of the orchestra at different times. Schubert himself occupied a viola desk delighting, like Mozart and Bach before him, to be "in the middle of the harmony."

Up to 1818 there had not been what one might describe as public performances of Schubert's works other than church music. On March 1 there occurred the first of these, at a Musical-Declamatory Academy (that is to say, a miscellaneous concert) organized by a violinist, Eduard Jaell. One of Schubert's pieces heard was a so-called *Italian Overture*. It was surprisingly well received by the critics and in less than three weeks other Schubert overtures were heard in Vienna, at similar entertainments. One aristocratic hearer prophesied in type (and correctly, as it proved) that Schubert's works "would occupy an advantageous place among the productions of the present day." Only a little earlier Franz had the satisfaction of seeing a composition of his appear for the first time in print! It was a setting of Mayrhofer's poem *Am Erlafsee* and it was published in a kind of pictorial guide "For Friends of Interesting Localities in the Austrian Monarchy."

Financially, Schubert reached in the spring of 1818 a rather desperate pass, as he was earning nothing and could not depend everlastingly on his friends. So when the father of the singer, Caroline Unger, recommended him to Count Johann Eszterházy, of Galantha, as piano teacher for his two young daughters, Schubert accepted out of sheer need, much as he detested teaching of any kind. The summer estate of this branch of the Eszterházy family was at Zseliz, in Hungarian-Slovakian frontier land, actually not far from Vienna but for Schubert the farthest away he had ever been. The pay was not generous but at least board and lodging were free, the country was a relief after the summer heat in Vienna, the Eszterházys and their friends were not unmusical. The daughters, Maria and Caroline, were thirteen and eleven, respectively, whom Schubert found "amiable children." He is now and then represented as having been in love with Caroline. If he really was it could only have been on his second visit to Zseliz, in 1824, when she had become a young lady of seventeen. Like Haydn, Schubert was quartered with the servants, which does not seem greatly to have irritated him, despite the boorishness of certain grooms (a pretty chambermaid, he wrote home, "sometimes kept him company"). The chief annoyance came from the cacklings of a nearby flock of geese.

One man whom Schubert met at Zseliz was destined to become as inspired and outstanding an interpreter of his songs as Vogl—Karl Freiherr von Schönstein, whose singing of Schubert later drew tears of emotion from Liszt. He brought to the more lyrical songs an extraordinary artistry, sensitiveness and devotion. The *Schöne Müllerin* cycle in particular was to be his specialty. And Zseliz, both now and a few years afterwards, enriched Schubert still further by fertilizing his inspiration with Slavic and Hungarian folk music. "I compose and live like a god," he wrote his brother, Ferdinand, though to Schober he speaks in a less exuberant strain. However, the Eszterházys and Schönstein sang not a little of Schubert's music and also ventured on more or less of Haydn's *Creation* and *Seasons* as well as upon the whole of Mozart's *Requiem.* Strangely enough, though he had far more time to write songs during these carefree months than he had some years earlier, he wrote appreciably fewer. His maturing genius was about to take other directions.

Schubert returned to Vienna in November in a jubilant mood. This was the period when Josef Hüttenbrenner—brother of the shrewder Anselm and sometimes rather irritating to the composer by the injudiciousness of his enthusiasm ("Everything I write seems to please him," said Schubert querulously)—made it his business to collect from near and far every manuscript of Franz he could lay his hands on. In this manner Josef recovered fully a hundred songs—a fortunate thing for posterity though at the time it buttered no bread and paid no bills. Anselm, for his part, went with Schubert (in a remote gallery seat) to the first performance of the latter's opera *Die Zwillingsbrüder.* The applause warranted the composer's appearance for a curtain call, but he declined to take it because of the shabby coat he wore. Anselm wanted Franz to put on his for a moment, but Schubert declined, glad, perhaps, to escape even a brief lionizing. So he merely sat back and smiled wistfully when Vogl came forward to tell the audience that the author was "not in the house."

One of Schubert's most influential acquaintances about this time was Leopold Sonnleithner, a member of a noted Viennese musical family. It was through Sonnleithner that Schubert came to know the poet Heinrich von Collin and in his circle the composer met men like the so-called "music count" Dietrichstein, the poet and bishop, Ladislaus Pyrker, Patriarch of Venice, court secretary Ignaz von Mosel and others well qualified to be his patrons and helpers had he but exerted himself to gain their assistance and good will. Better still, Sonnleithner introduced him to the four enchanting Fröhlich sisters, whose father had been a merchant of considerable means. Josefine, Käthi, Barbara and Anna Fröhlich, Viennese to the core, were uncommonly musical. All four sang well, three of them taught and Barbara painted miniatures. One prominent guest of this delightful household was the poet, Franz Grillparzer, who long outlived Schubert and wrote his epitaph. Sonnleithner cleverly brought some of Schubert's songs to the Fröhlich home before introducing the composer in person and whetted the curiosity of the sisters to such a degree that the stage was ideally set for his entrance.

Käthi Fröhlich tells of Schubert's joy when music—not necessarily his own—particularly pleased him. "He would place his hands together and against his lips and sit as if spellbound." Once, after hearing the sisters sing, he exclaimed: "Now I know what to do" and shortly afterwards brought them a setting of the Twenty-third Psalm for four women's voices and piano. Another time, Anna Fröhlich appealed to Schubert to set some verses of Grillparzer's as a birthday serenade to one of her pupils, Luise Gosmar. Schubert glanced at the poem a couple of times, murmuring "how beautiful it is" and then announced: "It is done already. I have it." A few days later he returned with the serenade "Zögernd leise" and the charming piece was sung shortly afterwards beneath Luise Gosmar's window. Characteristically, Schubert forgot to come and he almost missed his work on a later occasion when it was sung at a concert devoted wholly to his compositions. When he finally did hear it he seemed like one transfixed. "Truly," he murmured, "I did not think it was so beautiful!"

FRANZ SCHUBERT

The "Sketch Symphony"

The "Schubertiads" were not invariably indoor affairs. In spring and summer they took the shape of longer or shorter excursions, jaunts into the suburbs or even farther out into the country, with picnicking, dancing, ball-playing, charades and what not. If music of one sort or another was needed, Schubert was always ready to provide it. One of the most charming sites of these frolics (which sometimes lasted several days) was the hamlet of Atzenbrugg, an hour or so from Vienna, and it was here that Schubert produced a delightful set of dances, the *Atzenbrugger Deutsche*. It may have been at Atzenbrugg, as well, that Schubert composed in August, 1821, a symphony in four movements, sketched out but never completed. This is not, of course, the two-movement torso which the world calls the *Unfinished*. The *Sketch Symphony* in E major (with a slow introduction in E minor), is unfinished in a different sense. The first one hundred and ten measures are complete in every detail. The rest of the work is carried out only melodically, though with bar lines drawn, tempi and instrumentation indicated, harmonies, accompaniment figures and basses inserted and each subject given in full. The autograph remained at Schubert's death in the keeping of his brother Ferdinand who later gave it to Mendelssohn, whose brother, Paul, presented it to Sir George Grove. He, in turn, permitted his friend, the English composer, John Francis Barnett, to complete the work and in this form it was first produced in London, in 1883. Only a little over ten years ago the late Felix Weingartner finished it according to his own lights but in a style far less Schubertian than Barnett's conscientious piety.

We have no means of knowing why Schubert never bothered to carry out in full so elaborately projected a work. Nor have we of his failure to complete the immortal *Unfinished*. Whatever theories may be advanced are purely speculative. Schubert left large quantities of unfinished work—chamber music, piano sonatas, operas; so why not symphonies? In some cases he may simply have forgotten certain of his creations (as he had a manner of doing), in others he may have lost interest, for others, still, lacked time. Explanations may be plausible yet wholly wide of the mark. Is the *Unfinished Symphony* unfinished because it has only two movements? Are Beethoven's two-movement sonatas in any manner "unfinished"? That a 130-bar fragment of a Scherzo exists does not mean we have a right to decide it would have been "inferior"—we have no way whatever of knowing *what* Schubert would have done with a partial sketch. For that matter, piano sketches of the first and second movements of the *Unfinished Symphony* have actually come down to us. Could we, from an examination of them, tell what the final product would be like if we were not familiar with it?

From what we can judge of the *Sketch Symphony* its style proves it a bridge between the six early symphonies of Schubert and the two later ones. We say two—were there, peradventure, three? Yes, if there was indeed a *Gastein Symphony,* of which nobody has ever found a trace though some serious Schubert students have believed and still believe in it. Many have been confused by the manner that has prevailed for years of numbering the last two of Schubert's symphonies—the *Unfinished* and the great C major of the "heavenly length." Why is the C major sometimes called the Seventh, sometimes the Ninth, the *Unfinished* now the Eighth, now the Seventh?

In reality, the answer is simple. In order of composition the *Sketch Symphony* is the Seventh, the *Unfinished* the Eighth, the C major of 1828, the Ninth. In order of publication the great C major is the Seventh, the *Unfinished* (which was not discovered till 1865), the Eighth, the *Sketch Symphony* (not published till 1883), the Ninth. The consequence of leaving the *Sketch Symphony* out of one's calculations is obvious. However, if we maintain that Schubert *did* write a *Gastein Symphony* in 1825, we find ourselves obliged to number that legendary opus Nine, whereupon the C major becomes Number Ten!

The "Unfinished"

As for the B minor Symphony, the sweet, grief-burdened, nostalgic *Unfinished,* the fable has prevailed for years that it was written as a thanks offering to the Steiermärkischer Musikverein of Graz, which had elected Schubert to membership and of which Anselm Hüttenbrenner was artistic director. As a matter of fact, the date on the title page of the manuscript is October 30, 1822. But not till April 10, 1823, was Schubert proposed for membership in the society and not till September, 1823, was the composer informed of his election. He wrote a letter to Graz promising to send the Musikverein, as a token of his gratitude, the score *of one of his symphonies*. But it was not until a year later that, prodded by his father, who was shocked by the idea that a son of his had waited so long to thank the society "worthily," he gave Josef Hüttenbrenner the score of the B minor Symphony to deliver to Anselm in Graz.

So much for facts! We may as well pursue the epic of the *Unfinished* to its close. We do not know whether Anselm ever showed the symphony to the society and there is no record that he mentioned it to a soul, though he is said to have made a piano arrangement of the symphony for his own use. Not till 1860 did Josef Hüttenbrenner speak of it to Johann Herbeck, conductor of the Vienna Society of the Friends of Music, and five more years were to elapse before Herbeck, on a visit to Graz, obtained the score from Anselm on the plea of wanting to produce some "new" works by Hüttenbrenner, Lachner and Schubert. On December 17, 1865, Vienna heard the *Unfinished* for the first time. The autograph shows no trace of any dedication to the Graz Music Society or to anybody else! But from the start the symphony was acclaimed an undefiled masterpiece.

The "Rosamunde" Overture

In 1823, the same year in which Schubert brought to paper the operas *Die Verschworenen* and *Fierrabras* he wrote for a romantic play called *Rosamunde, Princess of Cyprus,* by the half-mad poetess Helmine von Chezy, a number of vocal and instrumental pieces which are perhaps the best loved samples of theater music he ever composed. The play itself was a sorry failure, had exactly two performances (though Schubert gallantly assured the unfortunate librettist that he considered her work "excellent") and the book was lost. The Overture we call *Rosamunde* today and which had been written originally for *The Magic Harp* was never used to preface the work whose name it has borne for generations—was, in fact, not entitled *Rosamunde* till later. The one with which Schubert had prefaced Helmine von Chezy's drama was the introduction he had used for *Alfonso und Estrella*. There are lovely and striking things in the *Rosamunde* score—a soprano romanza, an ensemble for spirits and two other choruses as well as some ballet music and various entr'actes. The third interlude brings us that deathless melody which seems to have haunted Schubert's imagination and reappears in the slow movement of the A minor Quartet and the B flat Impromptu for piano.

The *Rosamunde* score disappeared from view for more than forty years and the tale of its recovery belongs to the exciting legends of music. Like most legends even this one needs to be qualified. The story usually goes that the Englishmen, George Grove and Arthur Sullivan, in 1867 came upon the manuscript in a dusty cupboard at the Viennese home of Dr. Eduard Schneider, husband of Schubert's sister, Therese. What the two British explorers found in that famous closet were the complete orchestral and vocal parts of the score, which made clear the correct sequence of the pieces and supplied certain accompaniments which had been missing. But Grove himself records that "besides the entr'actes in B minor and B flat and the ballet numbers 2 and 9, *which we had already acquired in 1866,* we had found at Mr. Spina's (the publisher) an entr'acte after the second act and a Shepherd's Melody for clarinets, bassoons and horns. . . . But we still required the total number of pieces and their sequence in the drama. . . ."

For all his difficulties and privations Schubert's health had been, up to 1823, perhaps the least of his worries. But early in that year he had been ailing and soon his illness took a serious turn. Confined to his lodgings at first he was presently taken to the General Hospital. He became darkly despondent and wrote to his friend, Leopold Kupelwieser, a mournful letter in which he alluded to himself as "a man whose health can never be right again . . . whose fairest hopes have come to nothing . . . who wishes when he goes to sleep never more to awaken and who joyless and friendless passes his days." A little later he sets down in his diary the bitter reflection: "There is none who understands the pain of another and none his joy." Nor is this by any means his only pessimistic entry.

The exact nature of Schubert's malady has never been definitely established, even by modern medical authorities who have studied the case. We know that his hair fell out and that till it grew in again he had to wear a wig. Some have hinted at "irregularities" of one sort or another. At different times he complained of "headaches, vertigo and high blood pressure." His condition was to improve greatly in the course of time but he was never again wholly well.

The melancholy of Schubert was surely not lessened by his dealings with publishers, who took the most despicable advantage of his woeful inexperience in business affairs. Diabelli once persuaded him to sign over for a mere eight hundred gulden *all* his rights in a set of works. The publisher (and later his successor) made twenty-seven thousand gulden on the *Wanderer Fantasie* (for piano) alone. Schubert got exactly twenty (about ten dollars)! Another Viennese firm went so far as to ask him to sell them his compositions at the most favorable starvation rate "paid a beginner," while publishers in Germany were, if anything, even worse! Yet when Schubert had a few dollars in his pocket he thought nothing of spending a part of it on tickets for himself and his friend Bauernfeld for a concert by Paganini, whose spectacular violin playing excited Schubert quite as much as it did the rest of Vienna.

In spite of illness and discouragement many of his works at this time rank among his very greatest. There are, first of all, the twenty-three songs of the *Schöne Müllerin* cycle—the unhappy story of the love of a youth for a miller's daughter who jilts him for a green-clad hunter —containing such lyrics as *Wohin* and *Ungeduld,* which have virtually become folksongs; the piano sonata, Op. 143; the fabulous Octet, written for an amateur clarinetist, Count Troyer (and after a few hearings put away and forgotten till 1861); and that sweetest and most tender of Schubert's chamber music works, the A minor Quartet, with its lovely *Rosamunde* melody, the indescribable lilt of its minuet and the Slavic and Hungarian influences in its finale.

He was to experience more of these influences the summer of 1824, for at that time he went once again to the Eszterházys in Zseliz. The country air and the quiet life of the place in addition to regular meals and comfortable quarters exercised a recuperative effect. Moreover, the Countess Caroline was now a sightly young lady of seventeen. Possibly Schubert was not indifferent to her charms. But his letters to his father and his brother Ferdinand made it clear that he was homesick and often decidedly blue. Still, he wrote some admirable music at Zseliz— the *Divertissement à l'Hongroise,* the stunning *Grand Duo* for four hands, the sonata for arpeggione and piano; and thoughts of a great symphony, more imposing than any he had composed so far, began to occupy his mind. He had heard, also, that Beethoven intended to give a concert at which his Ninth Symphony would be produced. And he wrote to Kupelwieser: "If God wills, I am thinking next year of giving a similar concert!"

In May, 1825, Vogl invited Schubert to accompany him on an outing which proved to be the longest trip he was ever to take. Franz brought with him a number of compositions, finished and unfinished, among them settings of songs from Sir Walter Scott's *The Lady of the Lake,* of which the *Ave Maria* is one of the best loved things he ever wrote. The friends revisited the haunts of their previous journey, but this time Vogl took Schubert farther—to Gmunden, on the Traunsee in the Salzkammergut; to Salzburg; then southward as far as Bad Gastein. All along the way there was no end of music making, charming new acquaintances, hospitable folk who threatened to kill the travelers with kindness. Schubert cut up all manner of musical capers on occasion (one of his favorite pranks was to give a performance of *Der Erlkönig* on a comb covered with paper!). He was careful not to forget his parents. In an affectionate letter to his father he asks, chaffingly, if his brother, Ferdinand, "has not been ill seventy-seven times again" and surmises that he has surely imagined at least nine times that he was going to die. "As if death were the worst thing that could befall one!" he suddenly exclaims, growing serious; "could Ferdinand only look on these divine lakes and mountains which threaten to crush and overwhelm us he would no longer love this puny human life but deem it a great happiness to be restored for a new life to the inscrutable forces of the earth!" It is a question how pleased father Schubert was with this pantheistic declaration of his son's; when Franz was in Zseliz, Ferdinand had warned him against discussing religious matters when writing to his parent.

Curiously enough, Schubert passed through Salzburg without any allusion to his idol, Mozart. In Gastein he found time to complete the great piano sonata in D and to write several songs, one of them a setting of Ladislaus Pyrker's *Die Allmacht*—a grandiose musical duplication of that statement of faith he had fearlessly written his father. At this health resort, furthermore, Schubert is supposed to have completed that famous *Gastein Symphony* of which nobody has ever been able to find a trace. All manner of theories have been advanced with respect to this mysterious work. Some of Schubert's intimates have insisted that the composer worked on it in the summer of 1825 and intended it for a benefit concert by the Vienna Society of the Friends of Music. Others charge the Society with negligence resulting in the loss of the score, while still other investigators have imagined that the *Grand Duo,* composed a year earlier, might be an unorchestrated version of the missing score; or else that Schubert had merely contemplated a revision of the early Sixth Symphony, with which he had never been satisfied. Whether the hypothetical *Gastein* or the subsequent C major of 1828 represents the "great symphony" to which Schubert aspired we have no way of knowing.

In 1826 a conductor's post had become free and although Schubert had not long before turned down an organ position offered him (probably because he did not like the idea that his freedom might be curtailed) he did apply for this conductorship, attracted by the moderate salary it promised. It was not Schubert who got it but the popular mediocrity, Josef Weigl. How little Schubert harbored jealousy is clear from his satisfaction that the job had gone to "so worthy a man as Weigl." Then a vacancy occurred at the Kärntnertor Theatre. The candidate for a minor conductor's post had to submit a specially composed dramatic air for the singer, Nanette Schechner, and of course Schubert did so. But the Schechner, we are told, demanded changes in the music and Schubert peremptorily refused to make them. In spite of passionate entreaties and a spectacular fainting fit by the soprano, the composer pocketed his score and walked off coldly announcing: "I will change nothing." So things remained about as they were. True, the Friends of Music in 1825 had permitted him to substitute for a viola player at some of their concerts—after first rejecting his plea to do so on the ground that he "made a living of music" and that professionals were ineligible! Thus when in the summer of 1826 he would have liked to go once more to Linz there was no money for him to go anywhere. He had to content himself with the suburb of Währing and to aggravate matters it rained for a month.

All the same, 1826 was a year of significant works. In June Schubert composed within ten days his last string quartet, the vast and almost orchestrally colored one in G major. During the preceding winter he had written what is undoubtedly the most familiar of his quartets, the D minor, the slow movement of which consists of those variations on his song *Death and the Maiden* which are among the supreme variations of musical literature. Further, there were the melodically blooming B flat Trio for piano, violin and cello, the lovely G major piano sonata, the "Rondo Brilliant," for violin and piano and numerous songs, among them the two Shakespearean settings *Hark, hark, the Lark* and *Who is Sylvia?* Almost everybody who has ever interested himself in Schubert is familiar with the fable about the origin of *Hark, hark, the Lark*—how one day Schubert picked up a volume of Shakespeare in a Währing beer garden and how, after skimming through *Cymbeline,* he suddenly exclaimed: "A lovely melody has come into my head—if only I had some music paper!" Whereupon a friend drew some staves on the back of a bill of fare and the song was instantly written. Unfortunately for legend, the song was written originally *not* on a bill of fare but in a small notebook including a number of other compositions—one of them on the reverse side of the very page containing *Hark, hark, the Lark.* What seems a likelier story is that Schubert wrote it in Schwind's room, while the latter was trying to draw his picture.

March, 1827, was the date of Beethoven's death. Schubert was one of the torchbearers at the funeral. Back from the Währing cemetery he went with some friends to a coffee house in the "Inner Town." The gathering was in a solemn yet exalted mood. Schubert lifted his glass and drank a toast "To him we have just buried," then another "To him who will be next." Did that strange clairvoyance in which Michael Vogl once said he composed his music show him in mystic vision that his own sands had just twenty months more to run?

But before this he still had a little worldly journey to make—and a pleasant one. Karl Pachler, a cultured and musical lawyer, and his wife, Marie Leopoldine Koschak, an accomplished pianist whom Beethoven admired, invited Schubert to visit their home in Graz. The honored guest was to have been Beethoven but shortly after his passing Marie Koschak expressed a desire to know Schubert, whose importance she fully realized. So accompanied by his friend Jenger (who some years earlier had brought him his notice of membership in the Styrian Musical Association) he went in September, 1827, to Graz. In the home of the Pachlers, Schubert passed a happy, carefree, inspiring time. There was no end of sociability, music, picnics, excursions. He was even introduced to a local celebrity named Franz Schubert, who had a reputation as a folksong singer and who rendered Styrian folk melodies for his Viennese namesake. The Music Society gave a concert in honor of its visiting member, who also went to the theater with

Anselm Hüttenbrenner to hear an early opera of Meyerbeer's—though after the first act he protested: "I can't stand it any longer, let's get out into the air." He played his own *Alfonso und Estrella* to an operatic conductor, who made wry faces over its "difficulties" so that Schubert ended by leaving the score with Pachler, who kept it till 1841. Several songs were composed at Graz, also a quantity of waltzes and galops. Franz left Graz promising to come back another year—which was never to dawn.

It is probably unlikely that, at the gathering of the Schubertians on New Year's Eve, Schubert realized as poignantly as some may imagine that he was standing on the threshold of his last year on earth. But the winter was hard, there was little or no money and it seems likely that the good stepmother up in the Rossau schoolhouse had to help out with occasional pennies from the household stocking. To be sure, a little earlier the Friends of Music had elected Schubert a member of the Representative Body of the Society and the composer felt much honored. But such "honor" would not buy a meal. Even when half starved Schubert contrived to work. Between January and November, 1828, he turned out some of the most incomparable songs he ever composed (yes, even though planning to give up such trifling matters as *Lieder!*) issued posthumously under the collective title *Schwanengesang;* the *Great Symphony* in C major "of the heavenly length" (the score is dated March, 1828); a cantata, the three wonderful piano sonatas in A, C minor and B flat; that towering monument of chamber music, the C major String Quintet; the Mass in E flat (he had written a so-called *Missa Solemnis* in A flat as far back as 1820 besides a quantity of smaller masses) and much else. He devoted himself to the E flat Mass with such intensity that Josef Hüttenbrenner described him as "living in his Mass." The supreme Lieder—one is tempted to say the most grandiose and prophetic of all the odd six hundred he wrote —are the settings of six poems from Heinrich Heine's *Buch der Lieder,* which had just come to his notice. They are *Am Meer, Der Doppelgänger, Die Stadt, Der Atlas* and *Ihr Bild,* anticipations of the whole song technique of the nineteenth century!

The C major Symphony is without its like in the whole range of music and by one magical pen stroke Schubert made it even a greater thing than when he first conceived it. The autograph score shows that by the substitution of a D natural for a G in the theme of the first

Allegro the composer transformed what was scarcely more than a rhythm into one of the great symphonic subjects of all time. But he was never to hear the work. It came to a rehearsal by the Friends of Music, was found too difficult and "overloaded" and on the composer's own advice, dropped in favor of the Sixth—the "little" C major. And yet it was the one symphony of its time which could have endured the sunlight of Beethoven undiminished and unashamed.

Exactly a year after Beethoven's death Schubert at last gave the concert of his own works that he meant "if God wills" to give some day. It was the urging of Bauernfeld and other friends which finally caused things to materialize. The idea was that if all went well Schubert might offer his private concert annually and the rascally publishers would at long last be singing a different tune. His friends rallied nobly to his aid. Vogl sang, Josefine Fröhlich's pupils gave Luise Gosmar's birthday serenade, there was chamber music and a male chorus. The Musikverein hall was packed, encores were innumerable, the applause would not end and, best of all, there was a clear profit of more than half a hundred dollars. The only fly in the ointment was that no critics came, though several foreign publications carried flattering accounts.

But the little wealth quickly ebbed away. Again there were futile bickerings with publishers. Schubert would have liked to go to Graz once more but Baden and excursions to nearby Grinzing and Sievering were as much as he could allow himself. Headaches and other symptoms of a year before troubled him alarmingly. His doctor advised him to leave the stuffy center of town for some place where he could have plenty of fresh country air. So in September he moved to a house in the Neue Wieden section, where his brother Ferdinand had taken rooms. The building was new, still damp and unhealthy. Aside from a pilgrimage to Haydn's tomb at Eisenstadt and some annoyances with the publisher, Schott, both September and October were uneventful. Suddenly, while at dinner one day in the Lichtental neighborhood of his birth, he threw down his work, shouted that the food tasted like poison and refused to eat further.

Probably nobody suspected a serious illness, let alone a fatal one. At that Schubert did not immediately take to bed. He dragged himself a few days later to hear a Requiem by his brother, shortly before which he had been fearfully agitated by a first hearing of Beethoven's

C sharp minor Quartet. Yet so little does his condition appear to have worried him that he went to the theorist Simon Sechter to arrange for instruction in counterpoint—his intimates and a study of Handel's oratorios having supposedly persuaded him of his deficiencies in that branch technique. Nothing came of the project. By November 12 he wrote Schober that "he is sick, has eaten nothing in eleven days and can do no more than crawl from his bed to a chair." And he implores his friend to procure him reading matter, preferably Fenimore Cooper. The sickness made rapid inroads, though he continued to toy with the operatic scheme of the *Count of Gleichen,* and carefully corrected the proofs of his *Winterreise cycle.* Soon he became delirious and the doctors held a consultation. The diagnosis was "nerve fever," or typhus, the same sickness which had carried off his mother. Pathetically he begged his brother not to leave him "in this corner under ground"; and when the anguished Ferdinand assured him he was in his own room he insisted: "No, that's not true, Beethoven is not here!" A little later he turned his face to the wall and murmured, we are told, "Here, here is my end!" "The days of affliction," wrote father Schubert to Ferdinand, "lie heavy upon us"; and he presently made in the old list of births and deaths in the Schubert family the entry with the mortuary cross: "Franz Peter, Wednesday, Nov. 19, 1828, at three o'clock in the afternoon, of nerve fever, buried Saturday, Nov. 22, 1828."

It was Ferdinand who decided that his brother should, in death, be brought closer to Beethoven than ever he had been in life. And since "Beethoven was not there," where Schubert would ordinarily have been buried, Ferdinand saw to it that Franz should rest as close to his divinity as an intervening grave or two permitted. They were destined in the process of time to lie closer still. For three score years later the two masters were exhumed and placed side by side in two of those "graves of glory" in Vienna's great Central Cemetery.

"Music has buried here a rich treasure, but fairer hopes," read the epitaph which Grillparzer set on the original tomb in the Währing cemetery. "Fairer hopes," indeed! How could Grillparzer know what even the wisest musical heads of his day did not know? Eleven years after Schubert died "all Paris" was said to be astounded at the "posthumous diligence of a song writer who, while one might think his ashes repose in Vienna, is still making eternal new songs"! It took decades to reveal the incalculable richness of this "treasure" and even now the world is not finally aware of its fullness. Another deathless master, Robert Schumann, gave the world Schubert's C major Symphony, redeeming it from Ferdinand's heaped but silent hoard of unprinted, nay, unsuspected scores. "Who can do anything after Beethoven?" the half-starved Konvikt student had wistfully asked. Here was at least one triumphant answer, made by Schubert himself, at a distance of only eight months from his early tomb!

H. F. P.

Felix Mendelssohn

BORN: HAMBURG, FEB. 3, 1809. DIED: LEIPZIG, NOV. 4, 1847.

To the Noble Artist, who, surrounded by the Baal-like worship of debased art, has been able, by his genius and science, to preserve faithfully, like another Elijah, the worship of true art, and once more accustom our ear, amid the whirl of empty, frivolous sounds, to the pure tones of sympathetic feeling and legitimate harmony: to the Great Master, who makes us conscious of the unity of his conception, through the whole maze of his creation, from the soft whispering to the mighty raging of the elements.—Inscribed in grateful remembrance by ALBERT (*Prince Consort*)

Buckingham Palace, 24th April, 1847.

IN 1729—THE year of Bach's "St. Matthew Passion"—a humble Jew of Dessau on the Elbe, Mendel by name, became the father of a boy whom he called Moses. Mendel was something of a scholar as the times went, but desperately poor. He kept body and soul together by running a small Hebrew day-school and transcribing the Pentateuch. His infant son might know the pangs of hunger but he should have the boon of a sound education. The training was begun almost before the child could walk. Mendel would rout him out of bed at three or four on winter mornings, fortify him with a cup of tea and carry him, wrapped in a shawl, to a public seminary where he was put in charge of the learned Rabbi David Frankel.

Moses showed himself an extraordinarily gifted pupil. For one thing, he was consumed by a restless spirit of inquiry. He set about making an exhaustive study of the Scriptures, read voraciously, acquired languages with uncanny facility and, before he was ten, composed Hebrew verses. Nothing influenced him so deeply as Maimonides' "The Guide of the Perplexed." But the intensity of his intellectual occupation was such that he fell prey to a nervous malady which deformed his spine for life. He bore his ailment with the patience of Job and was never heard to complain. "If Maimonides weakened my body," he had a habit of saying, "has he not made ample atonement by invigorating my soul with his sublime instructions?"

According to a traditional Jewish manner of forming a surname, Moses called himself "Son of Mendel"—in German, "Mendels Sohn" —albeit he long alluded to himself as "Moses Dessauer." When Rabbi Frankel transferred his activities to Berlin, his disciple, though only fourteen, followed him on foot. Hunger, sickness, deprivations, bitter antagonisms, far from breaking the youth's spirit, deepened his perceptions and broadened his vision. He wrote and studied with fanatic zeal and in the fullness of time developed into one of the greatest scholars and philosophers of the age. The poet Lessing was one of his intimates. His work, "Phaedon, or the Immortality of the Soul," gained such currency that it was translated into every language of Europe.

Moses Mendelssohn endured without a murmur the numberless hardships and disabilities to which the German Jews of the period of Frederick the Great and his tyrannical father were subjected. One of the most preposterous of these regulations obliged every Jew when he married to buy a certain amount of chinaware from the royal porcelain factory in Berlin, whether he needed it or not. Not even the choice of articles was left to him, so long as the factory manager decided the place was overstocked. In this way Moses Mendelssohn when in 1762 he took to wife Fromet, daughter of Abraham Gugenheim, of Hamburg, acquired twenty life-sized china apes which had been found unsalable. Much later the apes became valued family heirlooms.

The domestic happiness and tranquility he had never known in his youth were at last to be the philosopher's portion. Moses and Fromet had a considerable family, though only six of the children—three sons and three daughters—survived to maturity. Moses himself died in Berlin at fifty-seven. Longevity, as it proved, was not to be a trait of the Mendelssohns.

Of the three sons the second, Abraham, was destined to play a rôle in musical history. True, he was not himself a trained musician although he had very sensitive artistic instincts; and he labored under a mild sense of inferiority, which used to find expression in his whimsical phrase: "Formerly I was the son of my father, now I am the father of my son." In any case he had not to endure anything like the paternal struggles and poverty. Of his boyhood not much is known. But in his twenties he was sent to Paris and worked for a time as cashier in the bank of M. Fould. When he returned to Germany he entered a banking business founded in Berlin and Hamburg by his brother, Joseph. It was possibly on his trip home that he met his future wife, Leah Salomon. If marriages are made in heaven this match assuredly could boast a celestial origin! Leah Salomon was a wholly unusual woman. She came of a Berlin family of wealth and position, she was exquisitely sensitive and cultured and, although she strictly limited her singing and playing to the home circle, was a musician of gifts quite out of the ordinary. Moreover, she drew, was an accomplished linguist (she even read Homer in Greek, though only in the privacy of her boudoir, lest anyone suspect her of "immodesty"), and dressed with studied simplicity. Among Leah's elaborate virtues was her tireless devotion to her mother. She kept house for her and granted her a substantial income.

Small wonder that such a union was blessed with exceptional offspring. Of the four children of Abraham and Leah Mendelssohn, Fanny Cäcilie, Jakob Ludwig Felix and Rebecka saw the light at Hamburg, in the order named. The youngest, Paul, came not long after the family had removed to Berlin. It may not be inappropriate to call briefly into the picture at this point Leah's brother, Jacob Salomon Bartholdy, if for no other reason than to account for a surname which formed an adjunct to part of the Mendelssohn family, including the composer. Salomon, a distinguished art critic who spent his later years in Rome as Prussian consul-general, had embraced Protestantism (despite a traditional curse launched by his mother) and adopted the name "Bartholdy" after "the former proprietor of a garden belonging to the family"—a garden which subsequently passed into the hands of Abraham Mendelssohn. It was Salomon Bartholdy who at length persuaded his brother-in-law to procure for his children what Heinrich Heine had called "a ticket of admission to European culture"—in short, conversion to the Christian faith. To distinguish between the converted members of the family and those who clung to their old belief, "Bartholdy" was henceforth affixed to "Mendelssohn." In time, Abraham and Leah followed their children into the Lutheran faith, Leah adding to her own name those of Felicia and Paulina, in allusion to her sons.

Felix was born on Friday, Feb. 3, 1809, at 14 Grosse Michaelisstrasse, Hamburg. Long afterwards the place was marked by a commemorative tablet above the entrance, a tribute from Jenny Lind and her husband. Curiously enough, the violinist Ferdinand David, Felix's friend and associate of later days, was born under the same roof scarcely a year after. Hamburg became an unpleasant place during the occupation by Napoleon's troops and in 1811, soon after the birth of Rebecka, the family escaped in disguise to Berlin where Abraham, at his own expense, outfitted a company of volunteers. The Mendelssohns took up residence in a house belonging to the widow Fromet. It was situated in what was then an attractive quarter of north-eastern Berlin, on a street called the Neue Promenade that had houses on one side and a tree-bordered canal on the other. It offered a spacious playground for the children and the singer, Eduard Devrient, recalled seeing Felix play marbles or touch-and-run with his comrades.

Abraham Mendelssohn, having severed the partnership with his brother, started a banking business of his own which soon prospered famously. Somehow even the myriad cares of running a bank did not prevent the father from scrupulously overseeing the education of his sons and daughters. If the young people were virtually bedded on roses, Abraham was of too strong a character and, indeed, too much of a martinet not to subject them to the discipline of a carefully ordered routine. Wealth and ease did not cause him to forget the privations and the conflicts which helped to forge the greatness of his own father's soul. His children need not hunger, they need not be denied opportunities to develop what talents nature had bestowed on them. But given such opportunities they must labor unremittingly to make the most of them. They had to be up and about at five in the morning and, shortly after, repair to their lessons. Felix always looked forward to Sundays when he could sleep late! In some ways one is reminded of the manner Leopold Mozart supervised the training of Wolfgang and Nannerl. If Abraham Mendelssohn was not, like father Mozart, a practising musician, he had an artistic insight which nobody valued higher than Felix himself. "I am often unable to understand," he wrote his father when he was already a world celebrity, "how it is possible to have so accurate a judgment about music without being a technical musician and if I could only say what I feel in the same clear and intelligent manner that you always do, I should certainly never make another confused speech as long as I live." It is easy to believe that some of the adoration Felix felt for his father above all others grew out of his unbounded respect for the older man's intellectual superiority.

Business connected with war indemnities associated with the Napoleonic conflicts obliged Abraham in 1816 to go to Paris and on this journey he took his family with him. Felix and Fanny were placed for piano instruction under a Madame Marie Bigot de Morogues and both appear to have profited. Their first piano lessons had been given them at home by their mother who, in the beginning restricted them to five minute periods so that they ran no risk of growing weary or restive. Fanny no less than her brother disclosed an unusual feeling for the keyboard at an early age, and even when she was born Leah noted that the infant seemed to have "Bach fugue fingers."

When the Mendelssohns returned to Berlin the young people's education was begun systematically. General tuition was administered by Karl Heyse, father of the novelist; the painter, Rösel, taught drawing, for which Felix exhibited a natural aptitude from the first; Ludwig Berger, a pupil of Clementi's, developed the boy's piano talents, Carl Wilhelm Henning gave him violin lessons, and Goethe's friend, Carl Zelter, taught thorough bass and composition. Nor were the social graces neglected. Felix learned to swim, to ride, to fence, to dance. Dancing, indeed, was one of his passions all his life. Father Mendelssohn always found time to supervise his children's studies and to guide their accomplishments. For that matter he never considered his sons and daughters—even when they grew up—too old for his discipline; and, certainly, Felix welcomed rather than resented it.

On Oct. 28, 1818, the boy made his first public appearance as pianist. The occasion was a concert given by a horn virtuoso, Joseph Gugel. Felix collaborated in a trio for piano and two horns, by Joseph Wölffl. He earned, we are told, "much applause." But Abraham, though pleased, was not the man to have his head turned by displays of precocity, shallow compliments or noisy acclamations. Neither did Zelter flatter his pupil on his never-failing facility. No problem seemed excessive for the boy, who could read orchestral scores, transpose, improvise—what you will. "Come, come," Zelter would grumble contemptuously, as if these feats were the most natural thing in the world, "genius ought to be able to dress the hair of a sow and make curls of it!" Yet to Goethe he made no effort to conceal his satisfaction. "Felix is a good and handsome boy, merry and obedient," he confided in a letter; "his father has brought him up the proper way . . . He plays piano like a real devil and is not in the least backward on string instruments. . . ." And the crusty contrapuntist saw to it that the ten-year-old genius entered the Singakademie and sang among the altos where he could learn to know, inside and out, works by Palestrina, Bach, Handel and lesser masters, distinguish between styles and observe the minutest technicalities of fugal construction.

It was only natural that Felix should, at this stage, have tried his own hand at composition. He wrote to his father, in Paris, asking for music paper. Abraham took the request as the text for a mild sermon: "You, my dear Felix," he admonished his son, "must state exactly what kind of music paper you wish to have—ruled or not ruled; and if the former you must say distinctly *how* it is to be ruled. When I went into the shop the other day to buy some, I found that I did not know myself what I wanted to have. Read over your letter before you send it off and ascertain whether, if addressed to yourself, you could execute the commission contained in it." Sooner or later he must have received his music paper for in 1820, when Felix began to compose, it is figured that he wrote fifty or sixty movements of one sort or another, solo and part songs, a cantata and a comedy. In every instance his methodical training caused him to inscribe the work with the exact date and place of its composition—a practice which saved no end of doubt and conjecture in later years, the more so as Felix remained quite as systematic his life long. These scores (of which he kept a painstaking catalogue) are headed in many cases with the mysterious formula "L.v.g.G." or "H.d.m.," which though never satisfactorily deciphered, reappears again and again in his output.

Some of these compositions, together with several by Fanny, were dispatched to Abraham in Paris. The father was particularly pleased with a fugue and wrote home: "I like it well; it is a great thing. I should not have expected him to set to work in such good earnest so soon, for such a fugue requires reflection and perseverance." He was perturbed over his daughter's composing, though he appreciated her talent. It was well enough, he declared, for Felix to take up music as a profession but Fanny must bear in mind that a woman's place is in the home. As a warning example he points to the sad end of Madame Bigot, who busied herself professionally with music and now is dead of consumption!

In 1821 there took place in Berlin an event which stirred the musical world of Germany to its depths—the first performance of Weber's "Der Freischütz." The composer, who supervised the rehearsals, was generally accompanied by his young friend and pupil, Julius Benedict. One day while escorting his master to the theater, Benedict noticed a boy of about eleven or twelve running toward them with gestures of hearty greeting. " 'Tis Felix Mendelssohn!" exclaimed Weber delightedly, and he at once introduced the lad to Benedict, who had heard of the remarkable talents of the little musician even before coming to Berlin. "I shall never forget the impression of that day on beholding that beautiful youth, with the auburn hair clustering in ringlets round his shoulders, the look of his brilliant, clear eyes and the smile of innocence and candour on his lips," wrote Benedict much later in his "Sketch of the Life and Works of the late Felix Mendelssohn Bartholdy." Felix wanted the pair to visit the Mendelssohn home at once, but as Weber was expected at the opera house he asked Benedict to go in his stead. "Felix took me by the hand and made me run a race till we reached his house. Up he went briskly to the drawing-room where, finding his mother, he exclaimed: 'Here is a pupil of Weber's, who knows a great deal of his music of the new opera. Pray, mamma, ask him to play it for us'; and so, with an irresistible impetuosity, he pushed me to the pianoforte and made me remain there until I had exhausted all the store of my recollections."

A more spectacular event in Felix's young life was his first visit to Goethe, in Weimar, the same year. It was Zelter who, anxious to acquaint the poet with his prodigious young pupil, had engineered the meeting. Felix had never gone anywhere without his parents and the family was not a little concerned about this expedition. He was plied with no end of advice before setting out, told how to behave at table, how to eat, how to talk, how to listen. "When you are with Goethe, I advise you to open your eyes and ears wide," admonished Fanny;

"and after you come home, if you can't repeat every word that fell from his mouth, I will have nothing more to do with you!" His mother, for her part, wrote to Aunt Henrietta (the celebrated family spinster, "Tante Jette"): "Just fancy that the little wretch is to have the good luck of going to Weimar with Zelter for a short time. You can imagine what it costs me to part from the dear child even for a few weeks. But I consider it such an advantage for him to be introduced to Goethe, to live under the same roof with him and receive the blessing of so great a man! I am also glad of this little journey as a change for him; for his impulsiveness sometimes makes him work harder than he ought to at his age."

The Mendelssohns need not have worried. The old poet took the boy to his heart from the first. Nor was Felix remiss about communicating his impressions. "Now, stop and listen, all of you," he writes home in an early missive which forms part of one of the finest series of letters any of the great composers has left posterity. "Today is Tuesday. On Saturday the Sun of Weimar, Goethe, arrived. We went to church in the morning and heard half of Handel's 100th Psalm. After this I went to the 'Elephant,' where I sketched the house of Lucas Cranach. Two hours afterwards, Professor Zelter came and said: 'Goethe has come—the old gentleman's come!' and in a minute we were down the steps and in Goethe's house. He was in the garden and was just coming around a corner. Isn't it strange, dear father, that was exactly how you met him? He is very kind, but I don't think any of the pictures are like him . . .

"Every morning I get a kiss from the author of 'Faust' and 'Werther' and every afternoon two kisses from my friend and father Goethe. Think of that! It does not strike me that his figure is imposing; he is not much taller than father; but his look, his language, his name— they are imposing. The amount of sound in his voice is wonderful and he can shout like ten thousand warriors. His hair is not yet white, his step is firm, his way of speaking mild. . . ."

Felix made much music for the poet's enjoyment. Every day he played him something of Bach, Mozart, Beethoven or compositions of his own (he had even brought some of Fanny's songs for Goethe's daughter-in-law, who had a pretty voice).

"Every afternoon," wrote Felix, "Goethe opens the Streicher piano with the words: 'I haven't heard you at all today; make a little noise for me'; then he sits beside me and when I am finished (I usually improvise), I beg him for a kiss or else I just take it!" Once Felix played a Bach fugue and suffered a slip of memory. Nothing daunted, he went on improvising at considerable length. The poet noticed nothing! At other times he would sit by the window listening, the image of a Jupiter Tonans, his old eyes flashing. And when the boy finally left Weimar Goethe missed him sorely. "Since your departure," he lamented, "my piano is silent. A solitary attempt to waken it to life was a failure. I hear, indeed, much talk about music but that is only a sorry diversion." A certain classical symmetry and a halcyon beauty in the boy's music and in his performances seem to have appealed to a deep-seated element of the poet's nature. When some time afterwards Felix dedicated a quartet to him, Goethe accepted it with a letter of fulsome praise. Yet when poor Schubert about the same period sent him a number of his finest Goethe settings the Olympian did not even deign to acknowledge them!

Leah Mendelssohn, delighted with the letters Felix was writing from Weimar, proudly forwarded them to Aunt Jette, in Paris. "If God spare him," replied that worthy person, "his letters will in long years to come create the deepest interest. Take care of them as of a holy relic; indeed, they are already sacred as the effusion of so pure and child-like a mind. You are a happy mother and you must thank Providence for giving you such a son. He is an artist in the highest sense, rare talents combined with the noblest, tenderest heart. . . ." The good woman spoke prophetically! Not all of Mendelssohn's letters have been preserved and some of them were withheld out of scruples which today are rather difficult to appreciate. Whether the anti-Semitic excesses of the Nazi regime spared those portions of the correspondence not previously given to the world is still unknown. Perhaps we shall never read it in all its inundating fullness. There were times in his short life when he wrote as many as thirty-five letters in one day! At any rate, those we have are precious.

It must not be imagined that Felix's numerous boyhood compositions served student ends primarily. This early spate of symphonies, concertos, songs, piano and organ pieces, chamber music and what not furnished matter for regular family musicales. The Mendelssohns had for some time been in the habit of holding miscellaneous concerts on alternate Sunday mornings in the big dining room of the house on the

Neue Promenade. In these the young people participated and invariably some work or other by Felix made up a part of the program. Felix and Fanny usually played piano, Rebecka sang, Paul played cello. Felix also conducted and had at first to be placed on a stool so that his small figure could be seen. Little operas and operettas varied the programs, the boy being the author of four of them. These "operas" were not given in costume or with any attempt at dramatic action. The characters were duly assigned and sung, but the dialogue was read and the chorus sat grouped around a table. The listeners offered their opinions freely, Zelter (who never missed one of these events) commending or criticizing, as the case might be.

On Felix's fifteenth birthday, Zelter suddenly rose and, "in masonic phraseology," promoted his pupil from the grade of "apprentice" to that of "assistant," adding that he welcomed him to this new rank "in the name of Mozart, of Haydn and of old Bach." This last name was significant. For a little earlier the boy had received as a Christmas present a score of the "St. Matthew Passion" transcribed by Zelter's express permission from a manuscript preserved in the Singakademie. Henceforth the "assistant" was to immerse himself in this music and it was the exhaustive study of the treasured score which resulted a few years later in the historic revival of the work an exact century after its first production under Bach's own direction.

The summer of 1824 Felix for the first time saw the sea. His father took him and Rebecka to Dobberan, on the Baltic, a bathing resort in the neighborhood of Rostock. Here he received those first marine impressions which in due course were to shape themselves musically in the "Calm Sea and Prosperous Voyage" and "Fingal's Cave" Overtures. For the moment, the scope of this inspiration was less ambitious. He wrote for the military band at the local casino an overture for wind instruments ("Harmoniemusik"), which stands in his output as Op. 24. It is sweetly romantic music, with a dulcet *andante con moto* introduction that has a kind of family resemblance to the softer phraseology of Weber, a spirited, vivacious *allegro* forming the main body of the piece.

But the "Harmoniemusik" Overture was only an incident of the creative activity marking the year 1824. The chief composition of the time was the Symphony in C minor, which ranks as Mendelssohn's First. Actually, it is his thirteenth in order of writing, though for conventional purposes the preceding twelve (for strings) may pass for juvenile efforts. We may as well record here that, irrespective of the dates of the composition, the official order of Mendelssohn's symphonies is as follows: The Symphony-Cantata in B flat (the so-called "Hymn of Praise," dated 1840) stands as No. 2, the A minor ("Scotch"), written between 1830 and 1842, as No. 3, the A major ("Italian"), composed in 1833, as No. 4, and the "occasional" one in D minor, known as the "Reformation Symphony" (1830-32), as No. 5.

The Mendelssohn family was outgrowing the old home on the Neue Promenade and late in the summer of 1825 Abraham bought that house on Leipziger Strasse which was henceforth to be inalienably associated with the composer. If it had its drawbacks in winter, the spacious edifice with its superb garden (once a part of the Tiergarten) was ideal at all other seasons. The so-called "Garden House" was one of its most attractive features and became the scene of those unforgettable Sunday concerts where a number of new-minted masterpieces were first brought to a hearing. The young people published a household newspaper, in summer called the "Garden Times," in winter the "Tea and Snow Times." Pen, ink and paper were conveniently placed and every guest was encouraged to write whatever occurred to him and deposit it in a box, the contributions being duly printed in the little sheet. These guests included the cream of the intellectual, social and artistic life of Europe who chanced to be in Berlin. It was a point of honor to be invited to the Mendelssohn residence.

To this period belongs Felix's operatic effort *"Die Hochzeit des Camacho"* ("Camacho's Wedding"). The text, by Karl Klingemann, a Hanoverian diplomat who played a not inconsiderable rôle in Mendelssohn's life, was based on an episode from "Don Quixote." The story has to do with the mock suicide of the student, Basilio, to rescue his beloved from the wealthy Camacho. Possibly the little work would never have been written but for the ambitions of Leah Mendelssohn to see her son take his place among the successful opera composers of the day. Having embarked upon the scheme Felix went about it with his usual zeal. But the piece was played exactly once, and in a small playhouse, not at the big opera. Although there were many calls for the composer he seems to have sensed a defeat and left the theater early. It was not long before he lost interest in the work altogether.

However, better things were at hand to obliterate the memory of the check suffered by "Camacho's Wedding." For we are now on the threshold of the composer's first mature masterworks. It must be understood that there was really no relation between Mendelssohn's years and the extraordinary creations of his adolescence. In point of fact, his creative mastery at the age of sixteen and seventeen is maturity arrived at before its time. That preternatural development, as remarkable in its way as Mozart's, is the true answer to the problem why the later creations of Mendelssohn show relatively so little advance over the early ones. We can hardly believe, for instance, that the F sharp minor Capriccio for piano or the Octet could have been finer if written twenty years after they were. How many not familiar with the respective dates of composition could gather from the music itself that the incidental pieces fashioned for the *"Midsummer Night's Dream"* by royal command came fully seventeen years after the immortal Overture? The whole might have been created at one sitting, so undiscoverable is any sign of cleavage.

The Octet for strings, finished in the autumn of 1825 represents, perhaps, the finest thing Mendelssohn had written up to that point. It is a masterpiece of glistening tone painting, exquisite in its mercurial grace and color, imaginative delicacy and elfin lightness. The unity of the whole is a marvel. But the pearl of the work is the Scherzo in G minor, a page as airy and fine-spun as Mendelssohn—whose Scherzos are, perhaps, his most matchless achievements—was ever to write. Not even the most fairylike passages in the *"Midsummer Night's Dream"* excel it.

Before passing on to the last-named, however, we must not fail to signalize the "Trumpet" Overture, composed about the same time (which Abraham Mendelssohn liked so much that he said he should like to hear it on his deathbed); the Quintet, Op. 18, the Sonata, Op. 6, the songs of Op. 8 and 9, the unfailingly popular Prelude and Fugue in E minor, of Op. 35. Let us not be confused, incidentally, by opus numbers in Mendelssohn which have as little to do with priority of composition as they have in the case of Schubert.

Felix and Fanny read Shakespeare in translations of Schlegel and Tieck. Their particular favorite was the "Midsummer Night's Dream." In August 1826, in the delightful garden of the Leipziger Strasse home the youth of seventeen signed the score of an Overture to the fantastic comedy which, as much as anything he was to write, immortalized his name. The famous friend of the family, Adolph Bernhard Marx, claimed to have given Felix certain musical suggestions. Be this as it may, the Overture was something new under the sun and not a measure of it has tarnished in the course of an odd one hundred and thirty years. It was first performed as a piano duet and shortly afterwards played by an orchestra at one of the Sunday concerts in the garden house.

Felix entered the University of Berlin in 1826 and offered as his matriculation essay a translation in verse of Terence's "Andria." Nevertheless, he seems to have had no time to bother about a degree. Music was absorbing him completely, especially his weekly rehearsals of Bach's "St. Matthew Passion" with a small choir. The more intimately he penetrated into this mighty work the keener became his desire to produce it at the Singakademie. Together with his friends, Eduard Devrient, he divulged his scheme to Zelter, only to be rebuffed. Spurred by the energetic Devrient he returned again and again to the attack, till Zelter finally weakened. Having carried the day Mendelssohn left the Singakademie jubilantly exclaiming to the elated Devrient: "To think that it should be an actor and a Jew to give this great Christian work back to the world!" It was the only recorded occasion on which Mendelssohn alluded to his Hebraic origin.

Three performances were given of the "St. Matthew Passion" at the Singakademie—the first on March 11, 1829—a century almost to a day since the original production in the Leipzig Thomaskirche. Mendelssohn conducted the first two. It was the real awakening of the world to the grandeur of Bach, the true beginning of a movement which has continued undiminished right up to the present. Fanny spoke more truly than perhaps she realized when she declared that "the year 1829 is likely to form an epoch in the annals of music."

Scarcely had Mendelssohn restored the "St. Matthew Passion" to the world than he left Berlin for the first of those ten trips he was to take to the country that was to become his true spiritual home. Abraham Mendelssohn having finally decided his son might safely adopt music as a means of livelihood, resolved to let him travel for three years in order to gain experience, extend his artistic reputation and settle on the scene of his activities. Felix was not averse to the idea. Already he was feeling some of those pin-pricks of hostility which Berlin, for reasons of jealousy or latent anti-Semitism was to direct against him in years to come. It was Moscheles who counseled a visit to London, where another friend, Klingemann, filled a diplomatic post.

Mendelssohn's first Channel crossing was not calculated to put him in a pleasant frame of mind. He was seasick, he had fainting fits, he quarreled with the steward and solemnly cursed that "Calm Sea and Prosperous Voyage" Overture he had composed scarcely a year earlier. The boat trip lasted almost three days! Luckily his friends had found him comfortable quarters in London, at 103 Great Portland Street. At once it developed that he and London were predestined for each other. The metropolis both appalled and enchanted him. "It is fearful! It is maddening!" he wrote home; "I am quite giddy and confused. London is the grandest and most complicated monster on the face of the earth. How can I compress into a letter what I have been three days seeing? I hardly remember the chief events and yet I must not keep a diary, for then I should see less of life . . . Things roll and whirl round me and carry me along as in a vortex."

He had arrived at the height of the season. The wife of Moscheles took him about in a carriage ("me in my new suit, of course!"). He went to the opera and to the theater, saw Kemble in "Hamlet" and was incensed at the way Shakespeare was cut. Still "the people here like me for the sake of my music and respect me for it and this delights me immensely." He made his first London appearance with the Philharmonic on May 25, 1829, and even at the rehearsal found two hundred listeners on hand, "chiefly ladies." The program contained his C minor Symphony, though later an orchestrated version of the Scherzo from the Octet was substituted for the original minuet. J. B. Cramer led Mendelssohn to the stage "as if I were a young lady." "Immense applause" greeted him. This was soon to be an old story. When people spied him in the audience at a concert someone was sure to shout: "There is Mendelssohn!" whereupon others would applaud and exclaim: "Welcome to him!" In the end Felix found no other way to restore quiet than to mount the stage and bow.

He played piano for the first time in London at the Argyll Rooms on May 30. His offering was Weber's "Concertstück" and he caused a stir by performing it without notes. One might say he was heard *before* the concert—for he had gone to the hall to try a new instrument several hours earlier but, finding it locked, seated himself at an old one and improvised for a long time to be suddenly roused from his reverie by the noise of the arriving audience. Whereupon he dashed off to dress for the matinee in "very long white trousers, brown silk waistcoat, black necktie and blue dress coat." Not long afterwards he gave concerts with Moscheles and with the singer, Henrietta Sontag. The Argyll Rooms were so crowded that "ladies might be seen among the double basses, between bassoons and horns and even seated on a kettledrum."

London life, for that matter, seemed made to order for Felix, the more so as he was received with open arms by those influential personages to whom he brought letters of introduction. For the whole spirit of London was vastly to his taste. Writing later from Italy he confided to his sister that, for all the luminous atmosphere of Naples, "London, that smoky nest, is fated to be now and ever my favorite residence. My heart swells when I even think of it!"

The admiration was mutual! England of that age (and for years to come) adored Mendelssohn quite as it had Handel a century earlier and peradventure even more than it did Haydn and Weber. Musically, the nation made itself over in his image. And Felix loved the rest of the country as he loved its metropolis. The London season ended, he went on a vacation in July, 1829, to Scotland, accompanied by Klingemann. The travelers stopped first at Edinburgh, where they heard the Highland Pipers and visited Holyrood Palace. Like any conventional tourist Felix saw the apartments where Mary Stuart lived and Rizzio was murdered, inspected the chapel in which Mary was crowned but now "open to the sky and . . . everything ruined and decayed; I think I found there the beginning of my 'Scotch' Symphony." And he set down sixteen bars of what became the slow introduction in A minor. It was to be some time, however, before the symphony took its conclusive shape. If Holyrood quickened his fancy "one of the Hebrides" (which he saw a few days later) struck even brighter sparks from his imagination. A rowboat trip to Fingal's Cave inspired him to twenty bars of music "to show how extraordinarily the place affected me," as he wrote to his family. He elaborated the overture—than which he did nothing greater—in his own good time and recast it before it satisfied him. For in the first form of this marine mood picture, he missed "train oil, salt fish and seagulls." Yet the twenty bars he set down on the spot form its main subject.

Back in London his mind was occupied with numerous compositions, among them the first stirrings of the "Scotch" and "Reformation" Symphonies and the "Hebrides" Overture. But before developing these he wanted to write an organ piece for Fanny's marriage to the painter, Wilhelm Hensel (whom Leah Mendelssohn had put on a five years' "probation" before she consented to give him her daughter's hand!); and a household operetta for the approaching silver wedding of his parents. Klingemann wrote the libretto of this piece ("Heimkehr aus der Fremde," which the critic Chorley in 1851 Englished as "Son and Stranger"). It contained special rôles for Fanny, Rebecka, Devrient and Hensel—the last-named limited to one incessantly repeated note, because he was so desperately unmusical.

Felix returned to Berlin for the parental festivities. But Fanny's wedding he missed, having injured his leg in a carriage accident and being laid up for two months. He might, had he chosen, have accepted a chair of music at the Berlin University in 1830, but he preferred to continue his travels. It seemed almost a matter of routine that he should stop off at Weimar to greet Goethe once more. He may or may not have suspected that he was never to see the poet again. Another friend he visited was Julius Schubring, rector of St. George's Church in Dessau. Nürnberg, Munich, Salzburg, the Salzkammergut and Linz were stations on the way to Vienna, where his enjoyment was poisoned by the depressing level of musical life and the shocking popular neglect of masters like Mozart, Beethoven and Schubert. He made a side trip to nearby Pressburg to witness the coronation of the Austrian crown prince as King of Hungary. The most exciting incident of the day was the smashing of Mendelssohn's high hat by a spectator whose view it obstructed!

Italy was another story. "The whole country had such a festive air," he wrote in one of the first of those Italian letters which are among the gems of his correspondence, "that I seemed to feel as if I were myself a prince making his grand entry." To be sure, there was not much music worth listening to and he was horrified by some of the things he heard in the churches. But there were the great masters of painting, there was the beauty of the countryside, the unnumbered attractions of Venice, Bologna, Florence, Rome, Naples, the fascination of Italian life and the charm of the Italian people. He heard the Holy Week musical services in the Sistine Chapel with works of Palestrina, Allegri and lesser men; wrote long and detailed letters to Zelter about the technical aspects of church singing in Rome, composed industriously, saw his boyhood playmate Julius Benedict and became acquainted with a wildly eccentric young French musician named Berlioz. On his way northward, in Milan, Felix met Beethoven's friend, Dorothea von Ertmann; also, Karl Mozart, whom he delighted by playing some of his father's music.

With his incredible dispatch he had managed to accomplish a great amount of creative work in Italy, despite his social and sight-seeing activities. He had finished a version of the "Hebrides" Overture, had made progress with his "Scotch" and "Italian" Symphonies, written a Psalm, several motets, the "First Walpurgis Night" (later recast), piano pieces, songs. Returning to Germany via Switzerland he stopped off in Munich and gave a benefit concert on Oct. 17, 1831. It was for this event that he composed his G minor Piano Concerto. In a letter to his father Felix referred to it, somewhat contemptuously, as "a thing rapidly thrown off." It has been assumed that Mendelssohn may have had Paris in mind when composing this work. At any rate, the first three months of 1832 found him once more in the French capital, where he made new musical acquaintances. One of these was the conductor, Habeneck; others, Chopin, Liszt, Ole Bull, Franchomme. Yet Mendelssohn found it difficult, even as he had earlier, to adjust himself to some musical insensibilities of Paris. He was appalled on one occasion to learn that his own Octet was given in a church at a funeral mass commemorating Beethoven. "I can scarcely imagine anything more absurd than a priest at the altar and my Scherzo going on," he wrote his parents. Habeneck, who had him play at one of the Conservatoire concerts, wanted to produce at one of them the "Reformation" Symphony, which Felix had composed in 1830 for the tercentenary of the Augsburg Confession. The performance never took place; the orchestra disliked the work, finding it "too learned, too much fugato, too little melody."

Were these objections wholly unfounded? Irrespective of what passed in those days for excessive "learning" the "Reformation Symphony" is, in good truth, a stodgy work, far more willed than inspired. The most engaging thing in it is the citation in the first movement of that "Dresden Amen" formula, which half a century later Wagner was to employ in "Parsifal." Strangely enough, some pages of the symphony sound like Schumann without the latter's melodic invention. It is only just to point out that the composer himself came to detest it, declared it was the one work of his he would gladly burn and refused to permit its publication.

Zelter died not long after Goethe and the Singakademie found itself without a head. Mendelssohn seemed his old teacher's logical successor and he would gladly have accepted the post. But many of the old ladies of the chorus did not take kindly to the idea of "singing under a Jewish boy." When it came to a vote Felix was defeated by a large majority and one Karl Rungenhagen installed as Zelter's successor. Rather tactlessly the Mendelssohns resigned their membership in a body. Felix's popularity in Berlin was not improved by the situation, despite the family's wealth and influence. He said little but the wound rankled, somewhat as happened earlier over Berlin's rejection of "Camacho's Wedding."

The Cäcilienverein, of Frankfurt, asked the composer to write an oratorio based on St. Paul. But if Mendelssohn was unable to oblige at once, the seed was planted and, in proper season, was to take root. Late in 1832 a different kind of offer came from another quarter. The Lower Rhine Festival was to be given in Düsseldorf the spring of 1833. Would Felix conduct it?

The Düsseldorf commission was accepted and as soon as preliminaries were arranged Felix was off to his "smoky nest" once more. He had now completed his "Italian" Symphony and placed it, along with his "Calm Sea and Prosperous Voyage" and "Trumpet" Overtures at the disposal of the London Philharmonic. The Symphony was produced on May 13, 1833. To this day it remains one of the most translucent, gracious and limpid creations imaginable—"kid glove music," as some have called it, but no less inspired for its gentility. Is it really Italian, despite the Neapolitan frenzy of its "Saltarello" finale? Is it not rather Grecian, like so much else in Mendelssohn's art, with its incorruptible symmetry and its Mediterranean *limpidezza?* Where has Mendelssohn instrumented with more luminous clarity than in the first three movements? The second one, a kind of Pilgrims' March, has none of the sentimentality which wearies the listener in some of the composer's *adagios.* The third, in its weaving grace is, one might say, Mendelssohnian in the loveliest sense.

"Mr. Felix," as he was freely called, returned to Germany for the Düsseldorf festival, which began on May 26 (Whitsuntide), 1833.

Abraham Mendelssohn came from Berlin to witness his son's triumph. The Düsseldorf directorate was so pleased with everything that Mendelssohn was asked to take charge "of all the public and private musical establishments of the town" for a period of three years. He was to have a three months' leave of absence each summer. "One thing I especially like about Felix's position is that, while so many have titles without an office he will have a real office without a title," declared the father.

Meanwhile, the projected "St. Paul" oratorio was more and more filling its composer's mind and probably a large part of it had already taken shape. As a matter of fact, he looked upon his appointment at Düsseldorf less as a lucrative engagement than as furnishing him an opportunity "for securing quiet and leisure for composition." Still, he gave much attention to his duties, particularly those in connection with church music "for which no appropriate epithet exists for that hitherto given here." In an evil hour he had lightly agreed to take charge of the activities at the theater. It was not long before he regretted it. Felix was never made to cope with the intrigues and irritations of an opera house. On the opening night, at a performance of "Don Giovanni," there was a riot in the theater and the curtain had to be lowered four times before the middle of the first act. Associated with him was Karl Immermann, with whom he had previously negotiated about an opera book based on Shakespeare's "Tempest." In Düsseldorf their relations became strained and eventually Felix, in disgust, gave up his theatrical labors and the salary that went with them.

"St. Paul" was not so swiftly completed as the composer may have hoped from his Düsseldorf "leisure" (actually, it was finished only in 1836). But he could not, from a creative standpoint, have been called an idler. To the Düsseldorf period of 1833-34 belong the Overture "The Beautiful Melusine," the "Rondo Brillant" in E flat, for piano and orchestra, the A minor Capriccio for piano, the concert aria, "Infelice," a revision of the "Calm Sea and Prosperous Voyage" Overture and not a little else. The "Melusine" is one of his most poetic and mellifluous inspirations, with its lovely "wave figure" based on the arpeggiated form of the F major chord and so intimately related to one of the Rhine motives in Wagner's "Ring." How Mendelssohn managed to accomplish so much without slighting in any way his social obligations, his watercolor painting, his excursions here and there is hard to grasp.

In good truth, the enormous productivity which his unremitting facility encouraged, his piano playing and conducting, his incessant travels were subtly undermining his system. The effects did not make themselves felt at once but they contributed, bit by bit, to a nervous irritation that grew on him. Whether or not he appreciated that he came from a stock which, though healthy, bore in itself the seeds of an early death he made no effort to spare himself and never hesitated to burn the candle at both ends. The Mendelssohns had delicate blood vessels, they were predisposed to apoplexy. Abraham may or may not have been forewarned when, on returning to Berlin from Düsseldorf with his wife and Felix, he fell ill at Cassel. For a time his sight had been failing and he was becoming an outright hypochondriac. The more difficult he grew, the more intense was the filial devotion Felix lavished on him.

Early in 1835 the composer received from Dr. Conrad Schleinitz a communication which showed that his good fortunes were to remain constant. It was nothing less than an invitation to accept the post of conductor of the Gewandhaus concerts in Leipzig. Mendelssohn was flattered but experience had made him canny. Before giving his reply he demanded categorical answers to a number of questions touching artistic and business matters. Everything was settled to his satisfaction and, with his parents, his sisters and their husbands, he returned to the Rhineland to conduct another Lower Rhine Festival, this time to be held in Cologne.

If there was one place which promised to provide as happy a home for Felix as London did, it was Leipzig. The atmosphere of the town was a spiritual balm after the hectic life of Düsseldorf. Who shall say that it was not with symbolic intent that the newcomer led off his activities with his own "Calm Sea" Overture and Beethoven's serene Fourth Symphony? And although Felix's circle of musical friendships sometimes appeared boundless, he now came into intimate contact with certain choice and master spirits of the age whom he might otherwise have known only casually. An early visitor at Mendelssohn's new home was Chopin and in a letter to his parents in Berlin he writes of his pleasure in being able to associate once more with a thorough musician. One of those to whom Felix introduced Chopin was Clara Wieck, then only sixteen. On October 3—a historic date, as it proved —another stepped into the charmed circle, Robert Schumann, to whom

Mendelssohn was to become a god. "Felix Meritis entered," wrote Schumann describing in his best Florestan vein the first Gewandhaus concert. "In a moment a hundred hearts flew to him!"

Light-heartedly Felix accompanied his sister, Rebecka, and her husband on a trip to the family homestead in Berlin. There seemed to be even more gaiety than usual and a greater amount of extempore music-making for the entertainment of the father. A short time after he had returned to Leipzig in great good humor, he was shocked by the entrance of his brother-in-law, Hensel, with the news that Abraham Mendelssohn had died in his sleep on Nov. 19, 1835. The blow was heavy but Felix, once he regained control of himself, endured it with fortitude. Yet the loss of the father whom, to the last, he idolized marked the first great sorrow of his life. To Pastor Schubring he wrote: "The only thing now is to do one's duty." It sounds like a copy-book maxim but it was undoubtedly sincere. His specific "duty" in this case was to complete the still unfinished "St. Paul," about which Abraham had been ceaselessly inquiring.

Logically the oratorio should have been given by the Cäcilienverein, in Frankfurt, which had originally commissioned it. But Schelble, the director of the Society, was ill. So the premiere took place at the Düsseldorf Festival of 1836. Klingemann, who sent an account of it to the London "Musical News," said that the performance was "glorious," that he "had never heard such choral singing." The composer himself was more restrained. "Many things gave me great pleasure, but on the whole I learned a great deal." He had come to the conclusion that the work, like so many of his others, would benefit by a careful over-hauling. And in due course he set about recasting and improving. He had grounds for satisfaction. If "St. Paul" does not reach some of the prouder dramatic heights of the later "Elijah" it is a woeful error to underrate it.

Mendelssohn felt he owed it to his old friend, Schelble, to take over the direction of the Cäcilienverein; so he canceled a Swiss vacation he had planned and went to Frankfurt. He hobnobbed with the Hiller family and with Rossini, who happened to be in Germany for a few days. But more important, he made the acquaintance of Cécile Charlotte Sophie Jeanrenaud, daughter of a clergyman of the French Reformed Church. Cécile's widowed mother was herself still so young and attractive that for a time people thought that she, rather than the seventeen-year-old girl, was the cause of Felix's frequent visits. Fanny Hensel had latterly been urging her brother to marry, alarmed by his somewhat morbid state of mind. Cécile Jeanrenaud, according to Wilhelm Hensel, complemented Felix most harmoniously; still, "she was not conspicuously clever, witty, learned, profound or talented, though restful and refreshing." Mendelssohn was not the man to let his affections stampede him into marriage. So before an engagement might be announced, he accompanied his friend, the painter Schadow, on a month's journey to the Dutch seaside resort, Scheveningen, there to take long walks on the beach, think things over and come to an understanding with himself. Only then did he settle definitely upon the step.

The marriage took place in Frankfurt on March 28, 1837, and the couple went for a honeymoon to Freiburg and the Black Forest. The wedding trip was followed by a seemingly unending round of social obligations. Nevertheless, Mendelssohn found time for considerable work. Then a summons to England, to produce "St. Paul" at the Birmingham Festival (the oratorio had already been given in Liverpool and by the Sacred Harmonic Society in London). If only "St. Paul" had been the whole story! But Mendelssohn had enormous miscellaneous programs to conduct, he played the organ, he was soloist in his own D minor Piano Concerto. Back in Leipzig he settled with his wife in a house in Lurgenstein's Garden, welcomed Fanny, who saw for the first time those "beautiful eyes" of Cécile, about which she had heard so much, and greeted the arrival of a son, named Carl Wolfgang Paul. The Gewandhaus concerts flourished as never before. Felix produced much Bach, Handel and Beethoven; also he had many of those typical German "prize-crowned" scores of sickening mediocrity to perform. Musical friends came and went—Schumann, Clara Wieck, Liszt, Berlioz, and a young Englishman, Sterndale Bennet, whom both Mendelssohn and Schumann praised to a degree which we, today, can scarcely grasp. Small wonder that, amidst all this unmerciful and never-ending ferment Felix occasionally became worried about his health. "I am again suffering from deafness in one ear, pains in my throat, headaches and so on," he wrote to Hiller. Occasionally his friends made fun of his intense love of sleep. One can only regret that he did not yield to it more often!

We must pass over Mendelssohn's unending labors in Leipzig, at a number of German festivals and in England (where his new "symphony-cantata," the "Hymn of Praise," was featured) to follow him once more to Berlin. In 1840 Frederick William IV had become King of Prussia. One of the pet cultural schemes of the monarch was an Academy of Arts, to be divided into classes of painting, sculpture, architecture and music. For the direction of the last department the king wanted none but Mendelssohn. Hence much correspondence passed between Mendelssohn and the bureaucrats concerning the royal scheme. Time had not softened his hostility toward officialdom, particularly of the Berlin brand. However, he bound himself for a year, took up residence on the Leipziger Strasse once more, submitted his scheme for the Musical Academy and received the title "Kapellmeister to the King of Prussia" along with a very tolerable salary. Frederick William wished, among other things, to revive certain antique Greek tragedies, beginning with Sophocles' "Antigone." The scheme led to exhaustive discussions between Mendelssohn and the poet, Tieck, touching the nature of the music to be written. In due course there followed *"Oedipus at Colonos."* The kind of music needed was, as it will probably remain forever, a problem defying solution. What Mendelssohn finally wrote turned out, by and large, to be adequate Mendelssohnian commonplace.

Greek tragedy was not the only sort of dramatic entertainment projected by the King of Prussia. Racine's "Athalie," Shakespeare's "Tempest" and "Midsummer Night's Dream" likewise took their place on the royal schedule. Nothing came of "The Tempest" so far as Mendelssohn was concerned. But he fashioned some excellent music for Racine's play and enriched the "Midsummer Night's Dream" with an incidental score which may well be inseparably associated with the immortal fantasy to the end of time. There was, to be sure, no need for a new overture, Felix having written the most perfect conceivable one in his boyhood. But a dozen other numbers, long or short, were called for and, with the most consummate ease and soaring inspiration, Mendelssohn produced them. They are exquisitely delicate settings of Shakespeare's elfin songs and choruses, a "funeral march" of extravagant grotesqueness, clownish dance music, a flashing Intermezzo, depicting the pursuit of the lovers through the wood, and other "background" pieces. The memorable concert numbers, however, are the incomparable Scherzo—perhaps the most priceless of all the famous scerzi the composer wrote; the romantic Nocturne, with its rapturous horn reverie, and the triumphant Wedding March, a ringing processional which, in reality, belongs to all mankind rather than to Shakespeare's stage lovers.

The royal scheme for the Academy was not advancing and presently the plans began to gather dust in official pigeon holes. Frederick William, seeing the turn things were taking, appointed his Kapellmeister the head of the music performed in the Dom. The Singakademie, conscience-stricken over its earlier treatment of the composer, now made him an honorary member. For all that, Mendelssohn was not fundamentally happier in Berlin than he had been previously. Fortunately he had not resigned his Gewandhaus post when he left Leipzig and it had again become more desirable to him than all the royal distinctions Berlin could confer. He had added greatly to his creative output during this period (for one thing he had rewritten the "Walpurgisnacht" and finished the "Scotch" Symphony) and now he was occupied with plans for a new music school in Leipzig—the famous Conservatory, first domiciled in the Gewandhaus. In January, 1843, its prospectus was issued. The faculty was to include men like the theorist Moritz Hauptmann, the violinist, Ferdinand David, the organist, Carl Becker and finally, as professors of composition and piano, Schumann and Mendelssohn. Felix was not really overjoyed at the prospect of pedagogical drudgery; yet to Hiller he wrote "I shall have to go . . . three or four times a week and talk about 6-4 chords . . . I am quite willing to do this for the love of the cause, because I believe it to be a good cause."

Quite as peacefully as her husband, Leah Mendelssohn died shortly before Christmas, 1842. Felix grieved, though he was perhaps less stricken than by the passing of his father. Doubtless he felt once more that nothing remained but "to do his duty"—and these duties were unsparing and seemed to grow more numerous and complex as the years went by. One sometimes questions if, truly, the labors of a Bach, a Haydn and a Mozart were more ramified and unending than Mendelssohn's—even if he had no need to toil in order to keep the wolf from the door!

As time passed the Mendelssohn craze in England grew steadily by what it fed on and it was only natural that Felix should find himself repeatedly in London. He alluded to his successes and to the intensity of his welcome by his British friends as "scandalous," and declared himself completely stunned by it all. "I think I must have been applauded for ten minutes and, after the first concert, almost trampled upon!" The young Queen Victoria was quite as effusive as her subjects. She invited the composer to Buckingham Palace and was graciousness itself. He played her seven of his "Songs Without Words," then the "Serenade," then Fantasies on "Rule Britannia," "Lützow's Wilde Jagd" and "Gaudeamus Igitur." It was by no means the only time British royalty was to show him favor. Up to the year of his death Victoria and Albert were to shower distinctions upon him, to treat him, as it were, like one of the family.

Doubtless this is as good an opportunity as another to particularize. On one memorable occasion the Queen sang to his accompaniment and both she and her Consort scrambled to pick up sheets of music that had fallen off the piano. On another, the sovereign asked if there were "anything she could do to please Dr. Mendelssohn!" There was, indeed! Could Her Majesty let him for a few moments visit the royal nursery? Nothing Dr. Mendelssohn could have wished would have delighted Victoria more! Unceremoniously leading the way, she showed him all the mysteries of the place, opened closets, wardrobes and cupboards and in a few minutes the two were deep in a discussion of infants' underwear, illnesses and diets. Mendelssohn and Cécile's own family was growing by this time and might easily profit by the example of Buckingham Palace.

The Queen found so much delight in the "Scotch" Symphony that the composer promptly dedicated it to her. But for that matter, England could scarcely hear enough of it. Whether or not one ranks it as high as the "Italian," the A minor unquestionably represents the other half of Mendelssohn's chief symphonic accomplishment. The question to what degree it embodies Scottish elements or any appreciable degree of local color is less important than the fact that it is strong, impassioned music, informed with a ruggedness and conflict unlike the sunnier A major. There is a mood of tumult and drama in the first movement, whose closing subject is a definite prefiguration of the songful theme in the opening *allegro* of Brahms' Second Symphony. The Scherzo begins with a sort of jubilant extension of the Irish folksong "The Minstrel Boy" and the buoyant movement, as a whole, is full of tingling life. On the other hand, the *Adagio* undoubtedly displays a weakness characterizing so many of Mendelssohn's slow movements—it is sentimental rather than searching or personal, since with Mendelssohn grief is "only a recollection of former joys." Yet the *finale* is superbly vital and the sonorous coda with which it concludes has a regal stateliness and a bardic ring.

Whatever honors, labors, irritations and unending travels and fatigues were his portion on the Continent (and they seemed steadily to increase) it was to England that Mendelssohn continually turned to refresh his spirit. Not that his toil there was lighter or his welcome less hectic! But there was something about it all that filled his soul. People presented him with medals, commemorative addresses, they organized torchlight processions, sang serenades—and almost killed him with kindness. Yet we are told that "he never enjoyed himself more than when in the midst of society, music, fun and excitement." "A mad, most extraordinary mad time . . . never in bed till half-past one . . . for three weeks together not a single hour to myself in any one day . . . I have made more music in these two months than elsewhere in two years." He ordered a huge "Baum Kuchen" from Berlin (though usually, Grove informs us, he made no great ado over "the products of the kitchen," his chief enjoyments being milk rice and cherry pie). His power of recovery after fatigue was said to be "as great as his powers of enjoyment." With it all "he was never dissipated"; the only stimulants he indulged in were "music, society and boundless good spirits." Seemingly it never occurred to him that even a strong constitution can have too much of these.

When Mendelssohn became conductor of the Gewandhaus Orchestra he appointed as his concertmaster his old friend, the violinist Ferdinand David, who it will be recalled was born in the same house at Hamburg. As early as 1838 Felix had written to David: "I should like to write a violin concerto for you next winter. One in E minor runs through my head the beginning of which gives me no peace." Actually, he had tried his hand at a violin concerto accompanied by a string orchestra during his boyhood though this was only a kind of student effort. But David took the promise seriously and when nothing came of it for a time, determined not to let Mendelssohn forget it.

Fully five years elapsed before the composer finished in its first form the concerto which to this day stands with the violin concertos of Beethoven, Brahms and Tschaikowsky as the most enduring of the repertoire. For the various technical problems of the solo part and even of the orchestration David was constantly at the disposal of his friend. He offered numberless hints of the utmost value and is even believed to have shaped the cadenza in the first movement as we know it. Even after the score was presumably complete, David advised further changes and improvements, so that the work did not acquire its conclusive aspect till February, 1845. On the following March 13 it was performed by David at a Gewandhaus concert. Not under the composer's direction, however. The latter was in Frankfurt, in poor health and greatly worn out, and had no stomach for the excitements of another première. The conductor was his Danish friend, Niels W. Gade. It was not till two weeks later that David apologized by letter for his delay in describing the triumph of the concerto. "The work pleased extraordinarily well and was unanimously declared to be one of the most beautiful compositions of its kind." In more than a century there has been no reason to alter this verdict.

Mendelssohn's constitution may have been resilient and his recuperative powers as remarkable as his friends imagined, but it should have been clear to the more far-sighted among them that sooner or later these incessant journeys, this interminable business of composing, conducting, playing, teaching, organizing must exact a stern penalty. It is not surprising that, at the time the violin concerto was given in Leipzig, he preferred to remain in Frankfurt with his wife and the children (who had gone through quite a siege of juvenile illnesses) and make a serious effort to rest. But truly efficacious rest is a habit that must be systematically cultivated. Felix did not possess it in his earlier years, nor could he acquire it now when overwork promised to consume the sensitive fiber of his being.

Yet in the summer of 1845 he was approached once more with a scheme of major dimensions. The Birmingham Festival Committee offered him the direction of a festival planned for August, 1846, and asked him to "compose a performance"—in this case, a new oratorio. He was sensible enough to refuse to conduct the whole festival but he was willing to produce such an oratorio, even if only ten months remained to compose most of the score and rehearse the performance.

The prophet Elijah had engrossed his imagination as an oratorio subject ever since he had completed "St. Paul" and discussed the new work with his friend Klingemann. In 1839 he had corresponded with

Pastor Schubring about a text and he had even made rudimentary sketches for the music. Other obligations crowded it out of his mind. Now, six years later, he returned to it. He realized that the time was short but his heart was set on "Elijah," although he was prudent enough to suggest some other work if the oratorio should by any chance strike a snag.

Mendelssohn could write fast—too fast, perhaps, for his artistic good. Still, *"Elijah"* was a heart-breaking assignment. It is only just to say that he realized certain inadequacies of the first version and revised not a little of the score after hearing it. His labors were complicated by the lengthy correspondence he was obliged to carry on with William Bartholomew, the translator. Mendelssohn insisted on a close adherence to the King James version of the Bible, with the result that the English words often conform neither to the accent nor the sense of the German originals. The choice of a soprano offered another problem. The composer wanted Jenny Lind, whom he admired extravagantly (he loved her F sharp and the note seems to have haunted his mind when he wrote the air, "Hear Ye, Israel"). But Jenny Lind was unavailable and he had to be satisfied with a Maria Caradori-Allan, whom he disliked and whose singing he afterwards described as "so pretty, so pleasing, so elegant and at the same time so flat, so unintelligent, so soulless that the music acquired a sort of amiable expression about which I could go mad." Be all of which as it may, Caradori-Allan was paid as much for singing in the first "Elijah" as Mendelssohn was for composing it! The precious creature actually told him at a rehearsal that "Hear Ye, Israel" was "not a lady's song," and asked him to have it transposed and otherwise altered.

However, the first performance in Birmingham, Aug. 26, 1846, was a triumph for the composer though, to be candid, the uncritical adulation of the audience had settled the verdict in advance. The report of Mendelssohn's boyhood friend, Julius Benedict, is typical: "The noble Town Hall was crowded at an early hour of that forenoon with a brilliant and eagerly expectant audience . . . Every eye had long been directed toward the conductor's desk, when, at half-past eleven o'clock, a deafening shout from the band and chorus announced the approach of the great composer. The reception he met from the assembled thousands . . . was absolutely overwhelming; whilst the sun, emerging at that moment, seemed to illumine the vast edifice in honour of the bright and pure being who stood there, the idol of all beholders!"

It enhances one's respect for the artistic probity of Mendelssohn that he preserved his balance. He evaluated his work critically, carefully modified or enlarged it and obliged Bartholomew to make a quantity of changes in the English text. On April 16, 1847, he conducted the revised version in the first of four performances by the Sacred Harmonic Society in Exeter Hall, London. On April 23 the Queen and the Prince Consort heard the work. Albert wrote in the book of words and sent to Mendelssohn a dedication: "To the Noble Artist who, surrounded by the Baal-worship of debased art, has been able by his genius and science to preserve faithfully, like another Elijah, the Worship of True Art, and once more to accustom our ears, amid the whirl of empty frivolous sounds, to the pure tones of sympathetic feeling and legitimate harmony: to the Great Master, who makes us conscious of the unity of his conception, through the whole maze of his creation, from the soft whispering to the mighty raging of the elements. Inscribed in grateful remembrance by

Albert"

It was a fitting climax to Mendelssohn's tenth visit to England—in some ways his most memorable, in any case his last.

Before Mendelssohn left London he paid a farewell visit to Buckingham Palace. He had a mysterious presentiment that he must leave hurriedly. Friends pressed him to remain in England a little longer. "Ah! I wish I may not already have stayed too long here! One more week of this unremitting fatigue and I should be killed outright." He was manifestly ill. Fate caught up with him at Frankfurt. Scarcely had he arrived in a state of prostration when he abruptly learned that his sister, Fanny Hensel, had died while at the piano conducting a choir rehearsal. With a shriek, Felix collapsed. The shock of the news and the violence of his fall on hearing it, brought about a rupture of one of those delicate cerebral blood vessels which had caused so many deaths in the Mendelssohn family.

In a measure he recovered. He went to Baden-Baden and later to Switzerland. He wrote letters, sketched and still composed. He greeted friends from England, he learned that London and Liverpool wanted new symphonies and cantatas. This time he did nothing about it. When he, finally, returned in September to Leipzig, he seemed to feel better, though Moscheles, meeting him, was frightened to see how he had aged and changed. On October 9, while visiting a friend, the singer Livia Frege, in connection with some Lieder he planned to publish, he was seized with a chill. He hurried home and was put to bed, tortured by violent headaches. He had planned to go to Vienna late in the month to conduct "Elijah" with Jenny Lind as the soprano. Of this there could now be no question. On November 3, he suffered another stroke and lay, it is claimed, unconscious, though Ferdinand David says that, till ten in the evening, "he screamed frightfully, then made noises as if he heard the sounds of drums and trumpets . . . During the following day the pains seemed to cease, but his face was that of a dying man." Some time between nine-fifteen and nine-thirty in the evening he ceased to breathe. He was exactly three months short of thirty-nine years old. Grouped about the bed were his wife, his brother Paul, David, Schleinitz and Moscheles. "Through Fanny's death our family was destroyed," wrote Paul Mendelssohn to Klingemann; "through Felix's, it is annihilated!" Leipzig was stunned by the news. "It is lovely weather here," wrote a young English music student, "but an awful stillness prevails; we feel as if the king were dead . . ."

Posthumously, Mendelssohn's fate seemed like a strange reversal of his supreme idol's, Bach. Bach passed into long eclipse, then, largely through Mendelssohn's heroic efforts, underwent a miracle of resurrection which has grown more overpowering clear down to our own time. Mendelssohn, almost preposterously famous at his death, was before very long pronounced outmoded, overrated, virtually negligible. The whole history of music scarcely shows a more violent backswing of the pendulum. To take pleasure in any but a handful of Mendelssohn's works was for decades to lose caste, if not to invite ignominy. By 1910—just about the centenary of his birth—the low water-mark of derogation had been reached.

Now, a hundred years after his death, a most definite reaction is in progress. Is it not, rather, a salutary readjustment than a mere reaction? If Mendelssohn's poorer works have not endured is it not better so? Struggle and suffering might, indeed, have lent a deeper undertone to his songs or enabled his adagios, in old Sir George Grove's words, "to draw tears where now they only give a saddened pleasure. But let

248

us take a man as we have him. Surely there is enough conflict and violence in life and in art. When we want to be made unhappy we can turn to others. It is well in these agitated modern days to be able to point to one perfectly balanced nature in whose life, whose letters and whose music alike all is at once manly and refined, clever and pure, brilliant and solid. For the enjoyment of such shining heights of goodness we may well forego for once the depths of misery and sorrow."

And Grove's words have taken on an added poignancy precisely because they were *not* spoken of an epoch as grievous as our own!

H. F. P.

Robert Schumann

BORN: ZWICKAU, SAXONY, JUNE 8, 1810.
DIED: ENDENICH, NEAR BONN, JULY 29, 1856.

More than to the intelligence, it is to the heart that this soul unveils itself. Those of others, it is true, are grander, and more loftily dominate the centuries. None, not even that of Beethoven, is more winged with love, more human, more rare, and more like Tancred's enchanted forest where, from every tree, there escape sighs, laughs, or groans.—
ROBERT DE LAUNAY.

TOGETHER WITH HAYDN and Schubert, Schumann was, perhaps, the most completely lovable of the great masters. It is hard, moreover, to think of a composer more strategically placed in his epoch or more perfectly timed in his coming. Tone poet, fantast, critic, visionary, prophet—he was all of these! And he passed through every phase, it seemed, of romantic experience. The great and even the semi-great of a fabulous period of music were his intimates—personages like Mendelssohn, Chopin, Liszt, Moscheles, Ferdinand David, Hiller, Joachim, Brahms. He won the woman he loved after a bitter struggle against a tyrannical father-in-law. He created much of the world's greatest piano music, many of its loveliest songs, four great symphonies, superb chamber compositions and a good deal else which, even today, is insufficiently known or valued. A poetic critic, if ever there was one, he proclaimed to a world, still indifferent or uncertain, the greatness of a Chopin and a Brahms. His physical and mental decline was a tragedy even more poignant than Beethoven's deafness or the madness of Hugo Wolf. His life story is, in point of fact, vastly more complex

250

and many-sided than the following handful of unpretentious and un-original pages suggest. These will have served their purpose if they induce the reader to familiarize himself more fully with the colorful and endlessly romantic pattern of Schumann's vivid life and grand accomplishment.

*   *   *

At 9:30 on the evening of June 8, 1810 (the same being Saint Medard's Day), the book publisher August Schumann and his wife Johanne Christiane, living in the Haus am Markt No. 5, Zwickau, Saxony, became the parents of a boy whom they determined to call Medardus, in honor of the saint of the occasion. Reasonably well to do if not precisely affluent they were pleased at the idea of another addition to their little brood of three boys and a girl—Eduard, Karl, Julius and Emilie, respectively. Overnight they seem to have thought better of saddling the newcomer with such a name as Medardus and six days later the infant was carried to the local Church of Saint Mary's there to be christened Robert Alexander. In proper season the "Alexander" seems for all practical purposes to have vanished.

August Schumann had not always dwelt on easy street. Born in 1773 in the village of Entschütz, near Gera, he was the son of an impecunious country pastor who, despite his poverty, became a cleric of some eminence. Unwilling to see the youngster grow up as an object of charity the preacher gave him four years of high school education, then apprenticed him to a merchant. But the lad was not cut out for business; books were his world and in them he sought refuge from the misery of shopkeeping. Moreover, he soon developed literary aspirations of his own and, even though a well-meaning bookseller tried to discourage him, wrote a novel entitled "Scenes of Knighthood and Monkish Legends." The unremitting labor of study, writing and business chores told on his health and for the rest of his life he was never wholly a well man. Yet nothing could diminish his energies or dampen his ambitions to achieve the glories of authorship. When he eventually fell in love with a daughter of one Schnabel, official surgeon of the town of Zeitz, and met with a downright refusal from that hard-shelled individual to give his daughter to anyone but a merchant of independent means, August Schumann was equal to the challenge. For a year and a half he wrote day and night, saved up about seven hundred and fifty dollars (a respectable sum at the time), opened a shop in partnership with a friend in the town of Ronneberg, married Schnabel's daughter and was happy. A circulating library formed an adjunct to the store and the new Mrs. Schumann divided her time between handling books and selling goods. Her husband for his part combined the satisfactions of an extremely prolific authorship with the management of a bookshop, not to mention the direction of a prosperous business. In 1808 he moved to Zwickau where he founded the publishing house of Schumann Brothers, which lasted till 1840. The firm brought out among other things translations of the works of Sir Walter Scott and Lord Byron. One of its showpieces was a so-called "Picture Gallery of the Most Famous Men of all Nations and Ages." At fourteen Robert busily puttered around the place, reading proofs and performing many of the other odd jobs common to printing establishments.

For all his zeal and strength of character August Schumann paid the price of his unsparing toil in the shape of a nervous malady complicated by other ailments and attended by accesses of profound melancholy. He died on Aug. 10, 1826. His children without exception inherited the diseased strain. Curiously enough, about the only quality Robert could not regard as an outright heritage was his musical talent. His father had none of it and his mother only the most superficial trace. She was an excellent housewife and a tender soul but of wholly provincial mentality (which explains, perhaps, why her restlessly active husband chose her as his mate). Robert looked like his mother and loved her devotedly. But his features were about the sole birthright he owed her. From his father, on the other hand, he acquired virtually all of those qualities which were to fertilize his greatest inspirations—ambition, high principle, productive activity, imagination, poetic fantasy, whimsicality, the gift of literary expression and even to a certain degree that shrewd practical sense which marked some of his business dealings. Yet to none of his immediate forebears does he seem to have been indebted for his musical instincts as such.

Robert's early upbringing was chiefly the business of his mother. His father, swamped by literary and mercantile pursuits, had no time for nursery duties. Possibly the child would have been less spoiled if a paternal hand had more actively guided him. As it was, Robert became not only his mother's darling but the pet of every woman of her large acquaintance. He had his way in everything and in later years this error of his early training was reflected in the irritation he sometimes showed when crossed in his wishes. All the same, this female adulation did not soften the lad who, at the age of six, was sent to the private school run by an Archdeacon Döhner. In the games and sports of his comrades he was as wild and turbulent as the roughest of them. Nevertheless, he did not neglect his school work and exhibited a lively intelligence. Music fascinated him early. A pupil from a Latin school, one August Vollert, who obtained free board at the Schumann home in exchange for a bit of teaching, gave Robert a little elementary instruction in the art, though hardly systematic guidance. The spark was kindled, however. At seven the boy composed a few little dances. We need not say "wrote," for these trifles were chiefly improvised on the piano. One aspect of his gift manifested itself early—a knack for "characterizing" people in tone with a kind of delineative justness that both moved and amused listeners. The child was obviously father to the man who composed the "Carnival"!

In Zwickau at the time there was no better musician than Johann Gottfried Kuntzsch, who long before Robert was born, had gained a certain distinction by conducting a performance of Haydn's "Creation." August Schumann, who secretly hoped that his youngest boy might become such a poet as he himself had always aspired to be, resolved to cultivate that musical talent which was beginning to flower. It was to the care of Kuntzsch, therefore, that he confided him. We know little of the kind of teaching Robert enjoyed at this stage. Frederick Niecks surmises that it may have consisted "in little more than telling the pupil what to practise and the first elementary rules of fingering . . . in short, prescription without exemplification, happy-go-lucky chance without purposeful system." Niecks adds that Kuntzsch's pupils could never be sure of escaping a box on the ear and that "on one occasion Robert's bad timekeeping was even corrected by a stout blackthorn." Yet Robert preserved a good opinion of Kuntzsch all his life and as late as 1832 wrote asking permission to dedicate a composition to "the only one who recognized the predominating musical talent in me and indicated betimes the path along which, sooner or later, my good genius was to guide me."

In 1820 Robert entered the Zwickau Lyceum ("Gymnasium") to emerge, eight years later, with a certificate inscribed with a flattering *eximie dignus*. He was a personable youngster, blond, bright-eyed, sensitive, temperamental, prankish. The two subjects particularly dear to his heart were music and literature. His teachers thought kindly of his talent for languages. An uncommonly developed instinct for rhythm and meter expressed itself in effusions of poetry. At home he spent much time concocting "robber comedies" and producing them with the assistance of his schoolmates. Meanwhile, he was carrying on his musical studies with the son of a local bandmaster. The two became fast friends, played overtures and symphonies in four hand arrangements and even tackled compositions by Hummel and Czerny. Kuntzsch was anything but pleased by his pupil's displays of independence. Not having been consulted about the latter's music-making he suddenly declared that Robert could now shift for himself. Yet when Kuntzsch produced an oratorio by F. Schneider at Saint Mary's Church, young Schumann played the piano accompaniments while his father, though unmusical, beamed approvingly. Indeed, August Schumann did everything to further his son's musical inclinations. The paternal publishing firm obtained gratis quantities of music from which Robert was free to take his pick and choice. Father Schumann provided plenty of music stands for household concerts and bought a Streicher piano. With some of his musical comrades Robert produced at home a setting of the 150th Psalm he had composed. A little earlier he had heard a concert by the celebrated Ignaz Moscheles on a trip to Karlsbad in his father's company. For a long time he was fired with the ambition to study with this virtuoso. Nothing came of it but the youth preserved the program of that recital like a sacred relic.

Zwickau duly woke up to the accomplishments of the wonderchild in its midst. The more prominent citizens invited him to play at their homes. At the evening musicales of the "Gymnasium" he performed things like Moscheles' Variations on the Alexander March and showpieces by Herz, much in vogue at the time. August, who had no use for half-baked artists, thought of placing his boy under Carl Maria von Weber. But just about this time Weber embarked on the journey to London from which he was never to return alive. One person who was more pleased than grieved by the mischance was Mother Schumann, who harbored an insurmountable dread of the "breadless profession" for her idolized boy. Never did she tire of describing its miseries, the better to scare him off. Why not adopt a lucrative profession? The law, for instance. And so, for the time being, Robert remained in

Zwickau, obtaining, as he used to say later, "an ordinary high school training, studying music on the side and out of the fulness of his devotion"—but alone! In the broadest sense he was to grow up like his father—self-taught.

Adolescence subdued the wildness which had so often characterized the schoolboy. More and more Robert became a dreamer. He grew selective, too, in his choice of friends, of whom he had relatively few. One who stood closest to him was his sister-in-law, Therese, the wife of his brother Eduard. August Schumann, who had always hoped that this youngest son might inherit his own literary and poetic tastes, lived long enough to see the boy's talents developing along these lines. Robert kept diaries, notebooks, memoranda for verses and similar jottings. He was scrupulously honest with himself; in one scrapbook, for instance, he made this entry after some rhymed lines: "It was my dear mother who composed this lovely and simple poem." In another case he wrote: "By my father," and elsewhere: "Not by me." Once he made a timid effort to break into print and sent some of his effusions to Theodor Hell (otherwise Karl Winkler), of the Dresden *Abendzeitung*. He got them back.

At seventeen he became acquainted with the writings of Jean Paul Richter, then at the peak of his romantic fame. Perhaps none of Robert's youthful encounters influenced him so profoundly. Jean Paul colored in one fashion or another everything he was to write or compose for years to come. They were kindred souls—both the poet of lyric sentimentalisms, fantastic humors, moonlight raptures, dawns, twilights, tender ecstasies and other stage settings and properties of romanticism, and his ardent and sensitive young worshipper. But if more than any other Jean Paul fired Robert's literary impulses, it was Franz Schubert who lent wings to his musical fancy. His experience of Schubert began at the home of Dr. Ernst August Carus and his wife, Agnes, exceptionally cultured musical amateurs. Schubert was one of their particular enthusiasms and Robert, whom the couple quickly took to their hearts (they nicknamed him "Fridolin," after a gentle page boy in one of Schiller's ballads), played four hand compositions with Mrs. Carus, heard her sing Schubert songs and became familiar with a good deal of other music, including that of Spohr. Robert would not have been himself had he not come to look upon the worthy lady with a kind of exalted devotion. Soon we find him expressing the state of his feelings in his best (or worst!) Jean Paul manner: "I feel now for the first time the pure, the highest love, which does not for ever sip from the intoxicating cup of sensual pleasures, but finds its happiness only in tender contemplation and in reverence. . . . Were I a smile, I would hover round her eyes; were I joy, I would skip softly through her pulses; were I a tear I would weep with her; and if she then smiled again, I would gladly die on her eyelash and gladly—yes, gladly—be no more."

* * *

Shortly after his father's death he had suffered two cases of calf love —one for a person called Liddy, the other for a certain Nanni. First he found them "glorious maidens," whom he longed to adore like the madonnas he felt sure they were. In the next moment they became "narrow-hearted souls," ignorant of the Utopia in which he lived.

This Utopia, by the way, was bathed in champagne. All his life champagne was his favorite beverage, even as it was of his great contemporary, Richard Wagner, though like Wagner he would modulate now and then to beer or a glass of wine. Both masters craved their champagne whether they had the price of it or not. And Robert in his student days only too often "had not." His biographer, Niecks, notes disapprovingly that Schumann's "worst failing" was: "He had no sense of the value of money and found it impossible to square his allowance with his expenditures." When his funds ran out he had a remedy for replenishing them. Again like Wagner, he seems to have been a virtuoso in the art of writing begging letters that generally brought results. If his mother, his brothers, his sisters-in-law, his crusty old guardian, Rudel, ever hesitated a threat of the pawnshop or the moneylender was always efficacious. No wonder Christiane Schumann was frightened by the idea that her Robert might, for all her efforts, land in the "breadless profession." Successful barristers might easily indulge their champagne tastes but certainly not musicians lacking even "beer pocketbooks"!

In Schneeberg, a town near Zwickau, Robert played publicly and with immense success a concerto movement by Kalkbrenner. Alone among his enthusiastic listeners his mother remained cool. Soon her wishes prevailed and, though both she and Rudel were aware of the youth's "eternal soul struggle" between music and the law, Robert

256

made a promise of a sort to embrace jurisprudence. And so, at Easter, 1828, we find him enrolled at the University of Leipzig as a "studiosus juris." Scarcely arrived in Leipzig he struck up a warm friendship with another law student, Gisbert Rosen, who shared Robert's poetic enthusiasms, particularly his devotion to Jean Paul. Rosen was on the point of removing to Heidelberg to continue his legal studies and Schumann quickly formed a plan to accompany his friend on his journey, with a few stopovers on the way. After a short visit to Zwickau the two made a pilgrimage to Bayreuth, where Jean Paul's widow still lived and where the young men visited every spot which had been sanctified by the presence of their idol. They continued to Munich by way of Nürnberg and Augsburg, where Robert obtained from a friend of his father a letter of introduction to Heinrich Heine, then in Munich. He had a lively conversation with the poet. Possibly if the latter had been able to foresee that the youth before him would become, some years later, one of the greatest musical interpreters of his lyrics he might have treated him with more warmth than he did.

The law was quite as chilling and distasteful as he had foreseen. In a few weeks he wrote to his mother telling, among other things, that "cold jurisprudence, which crushes one with its icy-cold definitions at the very beginning, cannot please me. Medicine I will not and theology I cannot study. . . . Yet there is no other way. I must tackle jurisprudence, however cold, however dry it may be. . . . All will go well and I won't look with anxious eyes into the future which can still be so happy if I do not falter." Actually, Robert's mind was made up from the start. He would continue with the law only as long as he had to. Before renouncing it altogether he would try the University of Heidelberg, where his friend Rosen was studying and the sympathetic and extremely musical jurist, Anton Friedrich Justus Thibaut, was lecturing.

* * *

The unromantic and featureless environment of Leipzig at first repelled the youth, who keenly missed the amiable surroundings of his native Zwickau. Neither was he happy among the rowdy, swashbuckling students, ever penniless, ever drunk, ever ridiculous in their notions of "patriotism." For a while Robert was a member of some of the "Burschenschaften," the student clubs, though he shunned his rough associates as much as he could. In one respect, however, he resembled them—he was continually poor and everlastingly driven to borrowing.

Unquestionably the circle of acquaintances Robert made during his first days in Leipzig was not large, though he was very happy to find his old friends from Zwickau, Dr. and Mrs. Carus. At their home he met some musicians of prominence—Heinrich Marschner, then conductor of the Leipzig Stadttheater; Gottlob Wiedebein, a song composer of some distinction at the time; and two people who, almost more than any others, were destined to play crucial rôles in his life —the piano teacher, Friedrich Wieck, and his nine-year-old daughter, Clara, whom her father was assiduously grooming for a great artistic career.

*   *   *

Wieck, in particular, was a rather extraordinary if unsympathetic person. He had had a difficult and impecunious youth, kept body and soul together by giving music lessons for a few pennies a week and subsisted largely on the bounty of friendly families who invited him, now and then, to a dinner of roast mutton and string beans. He aspired to become a minister, studied theology but preached no more than a trial sermon. He was something of a traveler and had been to Vienna, where he met Beethoven. The privations and troubles of his youth hardened his character. His first wife stood his spectacular tantrums for eight years, then obtained a divorce and married a Berlin musician named Bargiel. By this second marriage the mother of Clara Wieck had a son, Woldemar, who later made a name for himself as a composer.

Though a hard-boiled martinet and, as time went on, a tyrant of the first order, Wieck was not wholly without good qualities. His unscrupulous treatment of Schumann and his own daughter has made him the object of much historical obloquy, in the main abundantly justified. Yet he was a good teacher, for all his irascible, disputatious ways and his devotion to the artistic causes he believed in could be very genuine. From the first he appreciated Schumann's creative talent and never concealed the fact, outrageously as he came to demean himself to the composer and Clara alike. Clara was, of course, her father's most famous pupil. Yet he had others, notably his daughter by his second marriage, Marie, and Hans von Bülow. The qualities he aimed to cultivate in his pupils were, according to Clara, "the finest taste, the profoundest feeling and the most delicate hearing." To this end he demanded that his students listen to great singers as much as possible and even learn to sing themselves.

Exactly a year after he had come to Leipzig Robert was off to Heidelberg there, ostensibly, to carry on his legal studies with Thibaut and another famous jurist, Mittermeier. Yet what chiefly busied him at Heidelberg was not jurisprudence but music. Under the teaching which, in Leipzig, he had begun to enjoy with Wieck he was developing into a first rate virtuoso and stirred all who heard him, especially by his fantastic skill in improvisation. Before long he was turning down invitations to concertize in places like Mannheim and Mainz. He practiced tirelessly, played, composed, read, "poetized" and became one of the social lions of the neighborhood as well. Out of his old guardian, back in Zwickau, he wheedled money enough to defray the expenses of a summer jaunt to Italy. Shortly after his return he heard Paganini in Frankfurt and reacted to the overwhelming impression in much the same manner as his contemporary, Liszt, and in an earlier day, Schubert. It was out of this revelation of diabolical virtuosity that his piano transcriptions of certain Paganini violin Caprices—overshadowed subsequently by those of Liszt—were to grow.

To his mother Robert confided little about his creative achievements in his Heidelberg days, the better to prepare her for the more remunerative plan he was forming of a virtuoso career. Yet in this period he conceived several works which were to become part of the foundations of his fame—things like the "Abegg" Variations, the "Papillons," the superb, vertiginous Toccata. To be sure, the "Papillons" were only begun in Heidelberg and the Toccata revised several years later. A word, however, about the "Abegg" Variations, the composer's Op. 1. The theme is one of those "alphabetical" inspirations he was to utilize even more imaginatively later on. That is to say it is based on the note succession A, B flat, E, G, G, and its inversion. Schumann had, indeed, known a flirtatious Meta Abegg in nearby Mannheim and had developed a tender feeling for her. Yet when he published the work he found it wiser to resort to mystification and so he dedicated it to an imaginary Countess Pauline von Abegg, who served the purpose just as well. The "Abegg" Variations, though unmistakable Schumann, have rather less than their creator's subsequent technical ingenuity and seem more like outgrowths of the virtuoso principles of Hummel and Weber.

But the elaborate dreamings and light-hearted pleasures of Heidelberg could not go on forever. On July 30, 1830, Robert took the bull by the horns and confided to his mother that music, not law, was for weal or woe to be his destiny. Wieck was invited to settle the question. That awesome pedagogue wrote to the widow Schumann a long and circumstantial letter, larded with many an "if" and "but." Having considered the problem from every angle he urged the good woman to yield to her son's wish. Robert, so Wieck assured her, could under his training become one of the foremost pianists of the time. If the plan misfired he could always return to his legal studies.

To every intent the youth's course was now clear and, for all time, he was freed from his nightmare. Back in Leipzig Robert took up his residence in the Wieck home, the quicker to pursue his pianistic studies. But in one thing he was less moderate than his teacher could have wished; he obstinately declined to make haste slowly. He would become a great pianist, yet he wanted a short cut to that goal. The idea of practicing dull finger exercises for hours on end every day revolted him. Already in Heidelberg he had discussed with his friend, Töpken, a project for overcoming the weakness of the fourth finger. He found an excuse for breaking off his lessons with Wieck a little while and, with his fourth finger held up by some home-made contrivance, he practised furiously in solitude. Precisely what happened we do not know. The first intimation that something was amiss emanated from a letter written to his brother, Eduard, on June 14, 1832. Eduard is instructed to show this passage to his mother: "Eduard will inform you of the strange misfortune that has befallen me. This is the reason of a journey to Dresden which I am going to take with Wieck. Although I undertake it on the advice of my doctor and also for distraction I must do a good deal of work as well there." Soon afterwards he wrote that his room "looked like an apothecary's shop." For years to come letters to one person or another speak of treatments and cures, prospects of improvement or stubborn developments which promise to futilize all his virtuoso ambitions. The long and the short of it was that Robert had so incurably lamed his right hand that for purposes of a public career it was as good as useless. After a fashion he could still play piano; but the particular glory to which he aspired was nipped in the bud.

*   *   *

Who shall say that the accident was an unmitigated misfortune? Would Schumann have bequeathed us the treasures he did had he wandered incessantly over the map of Europe to gain the transient rewards of an itinerant pianist? Would his characteristic style of piano writing have been what it is? It has been surmised that certain distinctive traits of it are, directly or indirectly, the products of his self-made physical disability. And can we be sure that the nervous instability associated with the inherited illness of the entire Schumann line might not have struck him down even earlier, precipitated by the worries and strains to which an executant is forever subject? If Robert still wished to be a musician it had to be in a creative sense.

Under the circumstances he would require a fuller training than he had yet had in the technique of composition. Wieck had recommended for a master in theory none other than Cantor Weinlig, the teacher of his own daughter, Clara, and of a certain irresponsible young firebrand named Richard Wagner. Robert did not accept the suggestion. Instead he became a pupil of Heinrich Dorn, recently come to Leipzig, who promised to be a more progressive person. Schumann esteemed Dorn personally and long remained his friend. But soon he was writing to Wieck and his daughter, then off on a concert tour: "I shall never be able to amalgamate with Dorn; he wishes to get me to believe that music is fugue—heavens! how different men are . . ." Nevertheless he slaved away at his exercises in double counterpoint and when the study became too intolerably dry he moistened it with draughts of champagne! His best lessons in counterpoint he obtained from Bach, who was to remain his supreme divinity all his life. The fugues of the Well Tempered Clavier he analyzed "down to the smallest detail." When in his melancholy late days he received a visit from the young Czech, Bedrich Smetana, with a plea to advise him about musical studies, the taciturn master said no more than: "Study Bach." "But I have studied Bach," protested Smetana. "Study him again," replied the declining composer and relapsed into moody silence.

It was at Dorn's home, incidentally, that Schumann made his first acquaintance with Wagner, to whom he played the "Abegg" Variations. Wagner did not care for them on account of their "excess of figuration." Nevertheless, they soon found a publisher. When the firm of Probst brought out the work the composer was in the highest measure elated, promised each of his Heidelberg acquaintances a free copy and wrote that "his first marriage with the wide world" made him feel as proud as the Doge of Venice at his ceremonial wedding with the Adriatic! The critics were, on the whole, encouraging, though the notorious Rellstab in his review "Iris" deplored the lack in it of any canon or fugue and made fun of "a name one can compose."

*   *   *

With the children in the Wieck home Robert was a great favorite. What the youngsters especially enjoyed were the charades he was in the habit of devising for their pleasure, the frightening ghost stories he improvised for them day after day and his shivery enactment of the various spooks. Riddles, fairy tales—there was seemingly no end of the parlor tricks he knew how to provide on the spur of the moment for the tots. This deep understanding of children and their psychology was bound, sooner or later, to find artistic expression and lovely embodiment in music like the "Kinderscenen" and the "Album for the Young," the one with its "Träumerei," the other with its "Happy Farmer."

His grown-up friends he endeavored to choose only among people who genuinely interested him and who shared his tastes. Persons who could not partake his high-flown enthusiasm for Jean Paul or for Bach amounted almost to mortal enemies! As for Clara, his early feelings toward the talented daughter of Wieck were scarcely more than a brother-and-sister affection, even though some of his more extravagant biographers have written nonsense about his worshipping her "like a pilgrim from afar some holy altar-piece." In his diaries one can find such entries as: "Clara was silly and scared," "With Clara arm in arm," "Clara was stubborn and wild," "Clara plays gloriously," "She plays like a cavalry rider," "The 'Papillons' she plays uncertainly and without understanding!" And so it goes in continual contradiction. We must bear in mind, however, that Clara was then only about twelve and, however artistically precocious, hardly more than a child. Her father had seen to it that she studied violin and singing and had stiff courses in theory and composition. But it was only after she had been in Paris in Wieck's company and known Chopin, Mendelssohn, Kalkbrenner, Herz and other great personages of the day that she matured into a young woman who, as Robert said, "could give orders like a Leonore."

For his part Schumann was composing industriously. It is necessary to bear in mind that his early work, which comprises some of his greatest, is almost exclusively for the piano. Songs form his second creative stage, then chamber, then orchestral music. To be sure, choral works, an opera and miscellaneous creations sometimes cut athwart the other categories. But his works can be easily arranged in their respective classifications. The "Papillons" is probably the first masterpiece which achieved what might be called universality. Doubtless Schumann would have been grieved that anyone should think of the fantastic little dance movements and mood pictures which constitute the set without appreciating their relationship to Jean Paul and his "Flegeljahre." But the whirligig of time has quite reversed the position of Schumann's enamoring miniatures and the faded romantic work which inspired them. Today we remember the "Flegeljahre" chiefly because the "Papillons," after a fashion, recalls it to our attention. But it would be erroneous to imagine that Jean Paul, exclusively, accounts for those captivating musical fancies that we meet in this Op. 2—the clock which strikes six at the close, indicating that the imaginary throng of revelers is dispersing; the chord which dissolves, bit by bit, till only a single note remains; the "Grandfathers' March," typifying the old fogies and Philistines generally (an ancient tune of folk character, which Bach had introduced into his "Peasant Cantata" many years earlier). Not without reason could Schumann claim "that Bach and Jean Paul exercised the greatest influence on me in my early days."

*   *   *

Let us at this point enumerate a few of the men and women who were gradually coming into Schumann's orbit, who became, more or less, fixtures in his circle, or else grazed its circumference and went their different ways. Among one of the first names we encounter are those of Henriette Voigt, a lady whom Robert was presently to call "his A flat soul," and Ernestine von Fricken, from the town of Asch, just across the Czech border. Ernestine was a lively and coquettish young person, an adopted illegitimate child, who fascinated Robert, to whom she briefly became engaged, and who passed out of his life as breezily as she had come into it. But if Ernestine was hardly more than a butterfly Robert nevertheless immortalized her. She is the Estrella of the "Carnival" for one thing; and, for another, it was on her account that he utilized in a diversity of ways the musical motto embodied in the letters of her home town, Asch. These "Sphinxes" as the composer called the series of long-held notes (A flat, C, B, natural, E flat, C, B, and A, E flat, C and B) are combinations which constitute the basis of numerous pieces in the "Carnival." They are not only letters which form the name of "Asch" but are also common to that of "Schumann." Robert was plainly indulging in some more of his little romantic whimsies, mystifications or epigrams!

Other names we must mention—irrespective of chronology—include Ludwig Schunke, an uncommonly sympathetic young pianist, who succumbed early to consumption; Carl Banck, Julius Knorr, A. W. F. Zuccalmaglio, Felix Mendelssohn, Frédéric François Chopin, Hector Berlioz, Franz Liszt, Richard Wagner, Ferdinand Hiller, Robert Franz. The list might run on indefinitely!

* * *

These individuals were, for the most part, Davidsbündler. Let us briefly explain: The "League of the Davidites" was an imaginary company, a creation of Schumann's fancy, composed of many of his friends who appeared to think as he did and were moved by fresh musical and poetic impulses. Their sworn duty was to war on those stodgy traditionalists who harbored principles which impeded artistic progress. Imaginary apostles of the biblical David, the giant killer, they were sworn to smite the Philistines of music, defend and uphold novel, adventurous and worthy trends, publicize or advance indubitable merit and, each after his own fashion, promote the vital and the soundly revolutionary. Schumann enhanced the play-acting spirit of the movement by investing various members of the fraternity with fanciful names. He himself, in true Jean Paul spirit, gave distinctive labels to the opposing aspects of his own creative soul. Thus his fiery, soaring, active personality he called "Florestan"; the tender, dreamy, passive part of his nature he identified as "Eusebius." When, as sometimes happened, these two irrepressible Davidites threatened to get out of hand, there was called in a moderator to re-establish sanity and balance —one Master Raro, whose model in real life seems to have been Friedrich Wieck. The cast of characters further included "Chiara," "Chiarina" and "Zilia"—otherwise Clara Wieck; "Felix Meritis," a thin disguise for Felix Mendelssohn; "Julius," in actuality Knorr; "Serpentinus," Carl Banck; "Eleanore," Henriette Voigt; "St. Diamond," Zuccalmaglio, and so on for quantity!

As a mouthpiece for his idealistic band Schumann founded, in April 1834, the *Neue Zeitschrift für Musik*—a periodical which endured for over a century. Part of the time he was its acting editor and in any case certain of its most penetrating and prophetic criticisms were his own contributions. Possibly the most famous of these was the jubilant salutation of Chopin's early Variations on Mozart's "La ci darem." This is the article entitled "An Opus 2," which begins with the excited entrance of "Florestan" shouting to his fellow Davidites those words that have become something like a household expression: "Hats off, gentlemen, a genius!" The other is that greeting to the youthful Brahms, a kind of visionary glorification entitled "New Paths," written for the *Neue Zeitschrift* almost on the threshold of Schumann's last illness and including that pathetic cry: "How I should like to be at the side of the young eagle in his flight over the world!"

A stronghold of conservatism such as Leipzig was not the most fertile ground for a journal like the *Zeitschrift*. More than once Schumann thought very seriously of transferring it to Vienna, which had had such resplendent musical associations and promised much. But when he went there and considered the prospects his heart sank. What chance had such a paper in a city where the iron hand of Metternich unmercifully crushed the life out of every vestige of liberalism and progress? Still, Schumann's various trips to Vienna were not wholly unproductive. The city provided the inspiration for one of his most treasurable piano works, the buoyant "Faschingschwank aus Wien." In the first movement of this Robert gave his sly humor and spirit of mockery momentary play by incorporating into the texture of the exuberant music a phrase from the "Marseillaise," which Metternich's henchmen had sternly forbidden in the Austrian Empire. Then, too, in Vienna he made the acquaintance of Schubert's brother, Ferdinand, in whose home countless musical treasures were gathering dust. One of those which he was able to rescue from oblivion was Schubert's great C major Symphony, which he dispatched to Mendelssohn in Leipzig, who in turn conducted it at a concert of the Gewandhaus.

* * *

But we are anticipating! What should concern us now is the courtship of Clara by Robert which, though it ended happily, was actually a long martyrdom for both and in the best traditions of romantic melodrama. To be sure it left a deep imprint on Schumann's creative fancy and for this, if for no other reason, the soul struggle was a cloud lined with shining silver. Almost all the piano works of the composer's early period—in some ways the most yeasty and influential music he gave the world—are in one way or another the fruits of his love.

Clara was nine years younger than her future husband. Their first relationship was, as he had remarked, a thoroughgoing brother and sister one. Robert always admired the pianistic talents of Wieck's daughter though he never hesitated to criticize defects that came to his attention. But there was hardly a serious love angle to the familiarity. It had been different with the shallow but provocative Ernestine von Fricken, who for some time made her home at the Wieck residence as a piano pupil, and applied her coquetries so successfully to Robert's susceptible heart that before a year was out he had bought her an engagement ring.

Clara, though she made no complaints, doubtless suspected with her feminine intuition how matters were shaping themselves. At one time Schumann's mother had said to her: "Some day you must marry my Robert." Clara never forgot the remark which seemed to be dictated by a kind of presentiment. Somewhat later he told Clara that she was "his oldest love"; and he added: "Ernestine had to come on the scene the better to unite us." But at this stage Clara's father gave her little time for brooding even if she had been disposed to indulge in any. He worked her hard, took her on concert tours, culminating in the one to Paris. When she returned home from one of the longest of these absences, Robert was the first caller at the Wiecks. What impressed her most was what she considered Robert's coolness; he gave her "hardly so much as a passing greeting," she later complained to a woman friend. Actually, it was shyness at his sudden realization that Clara was no longer a child but a lovely girl that struck him dumb.

Not till she had gone off on another tour was he a little more explicit. In a letter he wrote her from Zwickau he said: "Through all the joys and heavenly glories of autumn there gazes out an angel's face, a perfect likeness of a certain Clara whom I well know"; and he ended with "you know how dear you are to me." Even at that there was no question on either side of outspoken love. There was much music-making to absorb the pair, and musical friends were thronging Leipzig. Mendelssohn arrived and the Davidsbündler jubilated at his coming. Chopin, whom Clara had already met in Paris, was steered by Mendelssohn directly to the Wieck home, where Clara was made to play something of Schumann's—in this case the F sharp minor Sonata—and then some Chopin Etudes and a concerto movement. Chopin in his turn performed some of his Nocturnes. The fanciful Robert wrote: "Chopin has been here. Florestan rushed upon him. I saw them arm in arm, floating rather than walking—Eusebius!"

Then, one November night, on the eve of another of Clara's concert trips with her father, Robert called to say farewell for some weeks. At the foot of the stairs down which she lighted him he turned and impulsively took her in his arms. The lightning had struck. "When you gave me the first kiss," Clara wrote later, "a faintness came over me; everything went black before my eyes; I could scarcely hold the light which was to show you the way." He went over to Zwickau to hear her. She kissed him again and during the recital he sat in the audience thinking: "There she sits, dainty and lovable in her blue dress, loved and applauded by all, and yet she is mine alone. She knows I am here but must pretend to be unaware of me. You cannot give me so much as one look, you, Clara, in your blue dress!"

For a short time they kept their secret, but Wieck was not long in ferreting out the truth. And now began a conflict which might easily have wrecked the happiness, not to say the lives, of any two sensitive young people less determined and fundamentally hard-headed than this pair. For Robert things were complicated at the outset by the death of his mother, following shortly that of his brother, Julius, and his sister-in-law, Rosalie. The sadistic hate and the almost psychopathic villainy with which Wieck now over a space of years persecuted his daughter and her beloved have been variously explained. It has been claimed—perhaps not wholly without reason—that he was fully aware of the malady which lurked in the Schumann family. Instability and morbid depression had assailed Robert's sensitive spirit as early as 1833 and he became afflicted with a fear of insanity which was to grow on him and, in the end, to destroy him. Moreover, Wieck, though he prized Schumann's creative gift highly, questioned the solidity of his material position and the brightness of his prospects. But not even these considerations could really justify such elaborate meanness and robustious fury. There was literally nothing at which he would stop. He threatened at one stage to shoot Robert if ever he crossed the Wieck threshold. He forbade all correspondence between the two lovers. He intrigued against the pair ceaselessly, intercepted letters, lied, conspired. More than once Schumann was driven to desperation by Clara's long periods of apparent silence. Wieck encouraged Carl Banck to visit his house, then circulated rumors that his daughter had fallen in love with that friend of Robert's. On one of her visits to Vienna with her father poor Clara, wishing to write to Robert but fearing that the removal of an inkstand for a few minutes might arouse Wieck's suspicions, found it necessary to tiptoe endlessly from one room to another in order to dip her pen. Her faithful maid, Nanny, abetted her in all her ruses and when, in Leipzig, Clara exchanged a few hurried words with Robert on a dark street corner, Nanny stood guard to make sure the coast was clear.

Clara, planning another concert trip to Paris where a smashing artistic success might bring her independence, was horrified to learn that her father washed his hands of the whole scheme and bade her go alone, taking care of all the complicated arrangements of concertizing as best she could. It was a harrowing experience, for the first thing she did was almost to succumb to the wiles of an impostor in Stuttgart. Then, when she reached Paris (her French, incidentally, was very imperfect), she learned to her dismay that all of her more influential friends and colleagues—Mendelssohn, Chopin, Liszt, Paganini among them—were not there as she had expected. Having inherited not a little of her father's obstinacy Clara stuck it out and, without conquering the French capital, broadened her experience in many ways, even to the extent of learning to cook, and cementing new and valuable friendships, such as one with the singer, Pauline Garcia, which was to endure for a lifetime.

Despite the machinations of Wieck, Clara, back in Germany, found a means of making her feelings known to Robert. A devoted friend,

Ernst Adolf Becker, suggested that she perform at a Leipzig concert one of Robert's works. She chose the "Symphonic Studies" (the theme of which the composer had obtained from the Baron von Fricken, the adoptive father of Ernestine). Wieck approved. Tyrant as he was he still kept a soft spot in his heart for Schumann's music. The composer came to the hall, sat inconspicuously at the rear, listened and—knew! In a flash he understood that when she had lately returned him a package of his letters unopened, she had been acting under duress.

They still had much to bear, but greatly as it revolted them they realized that the only solution of their difficulties lay in a legal decision. To law, accordingly, they went. Bit by bit Wieck's case disintegrated. With the help of a friendly advocate Robert was able to show that his means were ample to support a family. Then Wieck played what he believed would be his trump card. He maintained that Schumann was a drunkard! Instantly Robert's friends rallied to his support, Mendelssohn even declaring himself ready to testify in court that the accusation was outrageously false. On August 12, 1840, the decision was handed down in favor of the sorely tried couple and their marriage received judicial sanction.

On Sept. 5, she gave a concert in Weimar, "my last as Clara Wieck." One week later (and a day before Clara's twenty-first birthday) they were married at Schönefeld, a tiny suburb of Leipzig. On the previous evening Robert had brought her a bridal offering richer than fine gold —the song cycle, "Myrthen," inclosing such deathless blooms as "Die Lotosblume," "Der Nussbaum," "Du bist wie eine Blume," "Widmung." And when they returned from church next morning Clara wrote in her diary: "A period of my life is now closed . . . Now a new life is beginning, a beautiful life, a life in him whom I love above all, above myself. But grave duties rest with me, too. . . ."

*　　*　　*

The period through which we have passed witnessed the birth of many of Schumann's greatest piano compositions—the "Davidsbündler Tänze," the "Carnival," the F sharp minor Sonata, the "Kinderscenen," the "Symphonic Studies," the "Kreisleriana," the C major Fantasie, the "Fantasiestücke"—things which along with others scarcely less great, were to become what might be called daily bread of pianists. His circle of musical friends was steadily widening. Those he esteemed most

269

highly, perhaps, were Mendelssohn and Chopin. Mendelssohn was to both Robert and Clara nothing less than a god. The strange thing about this friendship is that, much as the Schumanns worshipped Mendelssohn's music, Mendelssohn, to the end of his days, had virtually nothing to say on the subject of Schumann's. No doubt its novelty, its bold fantasy, its unprecedented imaginative qualities were in a measure alien to Mendelssohn's ideals of formal logic, clarity, order. It was not in his artistic nature to enjoy the work of a composer who, like Schumann, "dreamed with the pedal down." By the same token it was the fluency, technical ease and polished workmanship in Mendelssohn's scores which Robert held in such envious admiration. Yet with all his skill it is certain that Mendelssohn could never, for one thing, have painted so unapproachable a portrait in tones of his friend Chopin as Schumann achieved in one of the most extraordinary pages of the "Carnival."

Liszt was another master with whom Schumann's relations were, to put it mildly, singular and paradoxical. For a long time both Robert and Clara were captivated by Liszt's phenomenal virtuosity and amazing musicianship. Liszt preached Schumann's greatness both in word and deed. He played his works inimitably and with an originality that brought to light beauties which Schumann, by his own admission, did not even suspect in his own creations. When Liszt first heard Clara play the "Carnival" he exclaimed that it was one of the greatest pieces of music he knew, vastly to Clara's delight. Robert impulsively dedicated to Liszt the C major Fantasy (in later years Clara removed the dedication) but as time went on a coolness developed between the two masters, which led to at least one highly embarrassing scene when, on a certain occasion, Liszt, possibly in a spirit of irony, praised the archvulgarian, Meyerbeer, at the expense of the recently deceased Mendelssohn. Schumann left the room, fiercely slamming the door behind him. The breach was eventually healed and Liszt championed Schumann quite as he had done earlier. But the friendship had been troubled and, as Schumann's mental condition worsened, the old relation was never quite restored. Clara, who developed into a good hater in the years of her widowhood, came to harbor an implacable enmity for Robert's one time friend.

Yet in the early days of their married life things were on the whole ideal. Robert aspired to deepen Clara's musical understanding and the pair undertook a systematic study of Bach's Well Tempered Clavier, he "pointing out the places where the fugue subject reappears" and giving her an insight into technical mysteries which she had hitherto lacked. He himself was inspired by his new found happiness to a perfect deluge of songs—master lyrics which rank with those of Schubert as among the greatest treasures of song literature. The year 1840 was Schumann's "song year." Even before they were married Robert delighted his prospective bride with the information: "Since yesterday morning I have written nearly twenty-seven pages of music, of which I can tell you no more than that I laughed and cried for joy of it. . . . All this music nearly kills me now, it could drown me completely. Oh, Clara, what bliss to write songs! Too long have I been a stranger to it." And a little later: "I have again composed so much that it sometimes seems quite uncanny. Oh, I can't help it, I should like to sing myself to death like a nightingale. Twelve Eichendorff songs! But I have already forgotten them and begun something new!" So it runs on, more extravagantly in letter after letter, as he enriches the world quite effortlessly with the "Lieder und Gesänge," Op. 27, the Chamisso songs, Op. 31, the "Liederreihe," Op. 35, the Eichendorff "Liederkreis," Op. 39, the wonderfully psychological "Frauenliebe und Leben" cycle, the incomparable "Dichterliebe," the Eichendorff and Heine "Romanzen und Balladen," and so on—a lyric inundation, seemingly without end. And just because Schumann had developed in his piano works such an individuality of style, and such new phases of keyboard technique, the accompaniments for many of these Lieder made the songs artistic creations of an entirely unprecedented order.

*　　*　　*

Robert and Clara found out before long, no doubt, that married people sometimes get in one another's way. For instance, Robert needed hours and sometimes days and weeks of quiet for his creative work. On such occasions Clara had to put a stop to her practicing. The two realized that they were rather more hampered than was agreeable and Robert felt keenly how needful it is for an artist appearing in public to keep up his technical practice. Nevertheless she did manage somehow to get in her necessary hours of practice. Her husband found that "as she lives in nothing but good music her playing is now certainly the wholesomer and also more delicate and intelligent than it was before. But sometimes she has not the necessary time to bring mechanical sureness to the point of infallibility and that is my fault and cannot be helped. . . . Well, that is the way of artist marriages —one cannot have everything at once."

The Schumanns would have been glad to see Robert occupied with some regular work outside his compositions and his writings for the *Neue Zeitschrift*. Clara felt that her husband ought to be occupying an important conductor position. She would like to have seen him in such a post at the Leipzig Gewandhaus concerts, which his friend Mendelssohn had raised to such a level of distinction. "Don't be too ambitious for me," gently chided Robert, who realized that he was not cut out for a conductor. Yet this ambition was one of Clara's tragic failings. We have to thank it for Schumann's later misfortunes when he let himself be stampeded into accepting a batonist's post at Düsseldorf which probably accelerated his final breakdown. "I wish no better place for myself than a pianoforte and you near me," he had said not long after they were married. But Clara was to be incorrigible. She was one of those typical ambitious wives who drive their husbands into careers for which they know themselves to be totally unfitted. Yet the greater the inroads made by Robert's deep-seated malady on his nervous system, the more incapable he seemed of resisting Clara's urging.

What promised to be a solid and permanent position for Schumann materialized in the spring of 1843 when Mendelssohn founded the Leipzig Conservatory. Robert was given charge of the classes in piano playing; and he taught private composition. His colleagues were men like the theorist Hauptmann, the violinist, Ferdinand David, Moscheles, Plaidy, Richter, Klengel and others of distinguished standing. But it does not appear that Schumann's actual teaching can have amounted to much. For he was growing more and more uncommunicative and the fitness as a pedagogue of such a silent teacher may be doubted. In 1844 his duties at the Conservatory were interrupted for four months when he accompanied Clara on a concert tour to Russia and finally ceased in the autumn when he suffered a severe nervous breakdown which led to his removal to Dresden. Some months earlier he had renounced the editorship of the *Zeitschrift*. To his friend, Verhulst, he wrote in June, 1844: "I have given up the paper for this year and hardly think I shall ever resume it. I should like to live

entirely for composition." Shortly afterwards the *Zeitschrift* passed
into the hands of Liszt's friend, Franz Brendel.

Schumann was now definitely a sick man. Clara wrote in her diary
that she feared he would not survive the journey to the Harz mountains and to Dresden which they had planned in the hope of restoring
him; "Robert did not sleep a single night, his imagination painted the
most terrible pictures, in the early morning I generally found him
bathed in tears, he gave himself up completely." The change of scene
and society helped him, however, and they resolved to settle permanently in Dresden, whither they moved in the last days of 1844.

*   *   *

A period of fertile productivity lay behind him. If 1840 was Robert's
"song year," 1841 was his "symphony year" and 1842 his "chamber
music year," though this should not be taken as meaning that his creations at this time were limited to a few works in these genres exclusively. First of all came the B flat Symphony—the "Spring" Symphony
—which Schumann wrote down with a steel pen he had found
in Vienna in the Währinger Cemetery, on Beethoven's grave. The
"Spring Symphony," though it had its detractors, put Schumann on
the map, so to speak, more almost than anything else he had written
heretofore. Immediately after the symphony came two other large-scale
works—the so-called "Overture, Scherzo and Finale" (which modern
conductors have singularly neglected) and a Phantasie in A minor, for
orchestra and piano, which was to become the first movement of the
glorious Piano Concerto—for not a few musicians the greatest of its
kind in existence!

On the heels of this soaring masterpiece Schumann embarked on
another symphony. "As yet I have heard nothing about it," wrote Clara
in her diary, "but from Robert's way of going on and the D minor
sounding wildly in the distance, I know that another work is being
created in the depth of his soul." Less than four months later Robert
handed his wife as a birthday gift the score of the D minor Symphony.
It was not to see the light of publicity for some time, however. Before
Schumann had put the finishing touches on it his thoughts began to
be occupied with the subject of "Paradise and the Peri," from Thomas
Moore's "Lalla Rookh," and he opined that "perhaps something fine
can be made out of it for music." He was right, though the beautiful

oratorio—one of the finest yet (in America) least familiar of Schumann's major works—was not completed for nearly two years more. When it finally appeared the composer described it as "an oratorio for cheerful people, not for the place of prayer."

In the spring of 1842 Robert and Clara had been occupied with the study of the string quartets of Haydn and Mozart. The following October he wrote to the publisher, Haertel: "During the summer months I worked with great zeal at three quartets. . . . We played them several times at David's and they seemed to please players and listeners alike, in particular, Mendelssohn. . . ." They are the Quartets in A minor, F major and A major, Op. 41. For one thing, they contain some of the most unusual effects of syncopated rhythm to be found in the entire range of Schumann's compositions. On the heels of the quartets came the most popular sample of Schumann's chamber music, the E flat Piano Quintet, Op. 44, the first movement of which is perhaps as fine a thing as its creator ever achieved. Other chamber works followed—the E flat Piano Quartet, Op. 47, the so-called Phantasiestücke, for piano, violin and cello, Op. 88, none of them, however, rising above the level of the Quintet.

The first of the Schumann children, Marie and Elise, were born in 1841 and 1843, respectively. The succeeding ones were Julie, Emil, Ludwig, Ferdinand, Eugenie and Felix. Alone, Marie and Eugenie lived to what one can call a ripe old age. The hereditary Schumann illness passed on to another generation.

*   *   *

Dresden promised to be a pleasant home for the Schumanns and their growing family. The town was a center of art and literature. Painters, sculptors, architects, writers, musicians assembled there, lured by an art loving Court. Among the prominent musical figures of the town were Ferdinand Hiller, Karl Gottlieb Reissiger and Richard Wagner. Reissiger was, of course, a mediocrity of the sorriest kind. Hiller, on the other hand, was a pupil of Hummel and a friend of Berlioz, Liszt and Mendelssohn and the Schumanns were thoroughly at home in his company. Wagner was a horse of another color! It is everlastingly to be regretted that temperamental differences kept him and Schumann from amalgamating, for their liberal artistic slants and their incorruptible idealism should have made them fellow fighters in the cause of musical progress. Unfortunately the pair seemed almost to bristle at each other's approach. Had Wagner matured in his art as early as Schumann in his, or could they have known one another in the fine frenzy of Schumann's early Davidsbündler days the story might have been of an inspiring artistic relationship.

Wagner had been a contributor to Schumann's *Zeitschrift* and had entertained a flattering idea of some of Robert's earlier music. Rightly enough, he noted in it "much ferment but also much originality." He continued to like "Paradise and the Peri" and the Piano Quintet and, afterwards, during his Swiss exile, he went so far as to entreat Clara to play at one of her Zurich concerts the "Symphonic Studies." But thrown frequently together in Dresden the two repelled rather than attracted each other. Wagner, who talked incessantly, complained that one could get nowhere with a person who refused to open his mouth; Schumann, that he could not possibly exchange ideas with a man who never allowed one the opportunity to say a word. Moreover, Wagner's far-darting and flamboyant ideas were unintelligible to poor Schumann and even frightened him. And so the two seemed everlastingly at cross purposes.

Wagner gave Schumann a score of his "Tannhäuser" as soon as it appeared in a lithographed form. Writing to Mendelssohn Robert repudiated the music as weak, forced, amateurish, deficient in melody and wanting in form. Not long afterwards he went to hear the work and took back much of what he had said, declaring that the impression created by a stage performance was very different and that, though the score did not radiate the "pure sunlight of genius" the opera, nevertheless, exercised on the hearer "a mysterious magic which held one captive." He had been deeply moved by much of it; and he praised the technical effects and above all the instrumentation (a thing for which Schumann himself had always been reproved). Yet in another missive he declared that Wagner could not write four consecutive bars of "correct" music, that he was, all in all, a "bad musician." From the viewpoint of his own art Robert was to a certain degree logical in his claims. But his prophetic vision and artist's conscience refused to let him reject the work outright. Nor should we judge him too severely for his conclusions. After "Tannhäuser" he never heard a note of Wagner's music. However he might have reacted to "Tristan" it is hardly possible that

Schumann could have brought himself to dismiss Wagner as a "bad musician" if he had been spared to hear "Die Meistersinger"!

Schumann was present when Wagner read one evening to an assemblage of acquaintances his "Lohengrin" libretto. Like a number of other listeners he could not grasp just what method Wagner could employ in setting such a text to music. Furthermore he was upset that another had beat him to the subject of the swan knight, which he had half a mind to utilize for an opera himself.

*   *   *

Ill health pursued Schumann more and more implacably during the six odd years of his Dresden sojourn. He had moments when things seemed to brighten. At other times the slightest mental effort produced sleepless nights, auricular delusions, new and terrifying symptoms which came to haunt him as others disappeared. He was morbid, irritable, had visions of "dark demons" and was assailed by "melancholy bats."

Music sometimes helped and sometimes hindered. Nevertheless the Dresden period saw the creation of some of his greatest works—the completion in 1845 of the A minor Piano Concerto, by the addition of the Intermezzo and the Finale to the Phantasie written in 1841; the magnificent C major Symphony, with its melting Adagio, its breathless Scherzo, its resplendent finale; the "Scenes from Faust," the Overture and incidental music to Byron's "Manfred" and the opera, "Genoveva."

Limitations of space forbid us to consider in any detail works like the Piano Concerto, the C major Symphony and the rugged "Manfred" Overture—so different in its somber moody character from the romantic effusions of Schumann's earlier day. But the opera, "Genoveva" though branded a failure contains superb music, beginning with the overture which, in its different fashion, ranks with the one to "Manfred." The prayer of the fated Genoveva in the last act is a long *scena* comparing in its far-flung lyric line with the noblest vocal pieces Schumann ever wrote.

*   *   *

Clara cared tenderly for her ailing husband and left nothing undone to comfort him. She would use all her culinary skill to make it certain that his meals would be bright spots in his often troubled days. A friend who met her returning from market in one instance inquired what she was carrying in a strange-looking package. "Something to tempt my poor husband's appetite—mixed pickles," she answered. They had friends in a certain Major Serre and his wife who had a country estate at a place called Maxen, near Dresden, and she took Robert there from time to time to benefit by the pleasant country surroundings. But his stay in Maxen was spoiled by the view from one of the windows of a lunatic asylum nearby. And as the years passed and his condition deteriorated, the sight of an asylum brought his melancholy to an almost intolerable stage.

It was to Maxen that Clara brought him and her children when, during the revolutionary uprising in May, 1849, they found it necessary to flee from Dresden till order was restored. Pretending to take her husband for a walk she picked her way at sundown through the fields and hills surrounding the city and reached the Serre estate in the small hours of the morning, terrified by the armed mobs they continually met and the sounds of shooting in the distance. Then, without waiting to rest or refresh herself, Clara had to set out for Dresden once more to bring the children to a place of safety. Back in Maxen she restrained her feelings with difficulty when she was met by contemptuous allusions from her aristocratic hosts to "canaille" and "rabble." "How men have to fight for a little freedom!" she confided in her diary. "When will the time come when all men will have equal justice? How is it possible that the belief can so long have been rooted among the nobles that they are of a different species from the bourgeois?"

In the fall of 1849 Schumann received a letter from Ferdinand Hiller, on the point of leaving Düsseldorf, inquiring whether he would be disposed to succeed him as Musical Director in that Rhenish town? The salary was good, the duties heavy but stimulating. Schumann reflected that Dresden had never shown itself in the least inclined to give the illustrious artist couple within its gates the faintest official recognition. Hiller's offer seemed promising. Robert started to look up information about Düsseldorf. In an old geography book he found that the town's attractions included "three convents and a lunatic asylum." Nevertheless, they decided in its favor.

They took a cool farewell from Dresden and arrived in Düsseldorf on Sept. 2, 1850. They were greeted with extreme cordiality, wined and dined, serenaded and threatened with the exhausting honors of dances, picnics and excursions. Until they could find a suitable house and garden they were lodged in the best (and most expensive!) hotel. The Music Committee turned itself inside out to make life pleasant for its new conductor and his illustrious artist-wife. Robert was forty, seemingly in the prime of life but actually past his best creative period, and glad that an apparently desirable opportunity was opening up to him at last.

*   *   *

Tragic deception! Whether or not Schumann realized it from the first, the Düsseldorf period was the beginning of the end. It quickly became obvious that Robert had no ability whatever as a conductor, none of the dominating qualities to impose his wishes on orchestras or choral masses. He could think of no better methods of correcting a defect of execution than to ask his players or singers to repeat a passage over and over, without ever making plain to them what he wanted. The performers became listless, inattentive or downright rebellious. Things grew progressively worse and the decline of musical standards in Düsseldorf became town talk. The worry and physical strain involved told sorely on Schumann's afflicted nervous constitution. He developed an embarrassing habit of dropping his baton at rehearsals, till he hit on the scheme of fastening it to his wrist with a piece of string! "There, now it can't fall again!" he sheepishly told a friend who gazed at his arm in questioning wonder. His mental ailment bit by bit robbed him of alertness, concentration, presence of mind, "even the ability to speak audibly." Clara, unable apparently, to recognize the truth, suspected intrigues on every hand. Her blood "boiled" over the "disrespectful behaviour of some of the choir" at a rehearsal of the "St. Matthew Passion" and she developed a particular enmity against the well-meaning if uninspired conductor, Julius Tausch, who gradually took over some of Schumann's most taxing labors.

Robert's taciturnity had been growing on him for years but it finally took utterly fantastic forms. We are told that in Düsseldorf he could not say: "Ladies and gentlemen, our next rehearsal will be tomorrow at seven," without breaking down once or twice. In another case a certain Carl Witting was commissioned to visit Schumann in order to settle a debated point about the tempi in the "Manfred" Overture. After putting his question to the composer who was smoking a cigar (Robert had been an inveterate smoker from his youth) he received for all answer only the query: "Do you smoke?" Witting said he did and waited respectfully. Schumann neither offered a cigar nor gave a reply. Two more inquiries brought only another "Do you smoke?" The persistent silence finally impelled Witting to take his leave, thinking one knows not what. Still another idiosyncrasy of Robert's later days was to frequent a restaurant, order a glass of wine or beer and leave without attempting to pay. The proprietor was not disturbed, but simply gave Schumann what amounted to a charge account and sent the bills to Clara.

One of the first excursions Robert and Clara took after their arrival in Düsseldorf was to Cologne. Schumann was charmed by the surrounding countryside and deeply impressed by an ecclesiastical ceremony he witnessed in the Cologne Cathedral. The visit provided the inspiration for the Symphony in E flat, the so-called "Rhenish," published as the third, actually the fourth in date of composition (if we except the 1851 revision of the earlier D minor). The resplendent work has a freshness and a youthful ardor which seem to belie the composer's encroaching mental impairment. The climax of the symphony is its monumentally conceived fourth movement in which Schumann strove to picture the solemnity he had witnessed in that stately fane. The other movements abound in those shifted accents and other rhythmic surprises which were always a hallmark of the composer's style.

One marvels at the quantity if not always at the quality of Schumann's Düsseldorf compositions. These include overtures to Shakespeare's "Julius Caesar," Goethe's "Hermann und Dorothea" and Schiller's "Braut von Messina"; the "Pilgrimage of the Rose," the "Peri"; a fine cello concerto in A minor, and a violin concerto in D minor, written for Joseph Joachim, but secreted for years in the Berlin State Library and, though once tried out by Joachim, never played or published till recent years on the plea that it might by its weakness diminish Schumann's reputation. As a matter of fact the concerto, which is typical late Schumann, seems to have been much too severely judged by Joachim and even Clara herself.

*　　*　　*

The impossible situation in Düsseldorf could not continue. At first the Schumanns resolved to leave and settle down in Vienna. But that scheme proved impractical. The sorry conductorship came to its inevitable end. The Schumanns, much relieved, set out on a tour of Holland which had triumphal results for Clara. Back in Düsseldorf, though no longer in an official capacity, Robert on Sept. 30, 1853, was handed a card inscribed "Herr Brahms from Hamburg." Next day he scribbled in a diary: "Visit from Brahms (a genius)." And there began one of the most touching friendships in musical history, one that long survived the mortal Schumann and continued for the duration of Clara's years on earth.

To Joseph Joachim, who had armed the twenty-year-old North German with the introduction he presented, Robert instantly wrote "in prophetic style" the words: "This is he who should come." And only a few days later, another concerning "Johannes the true Apostle —the young eagle that has flown so suddenly and unexpectedly from the hills to Düsseldorf. . . ." Then snatching his long unused editorial pen he began that famous essay, "New Paths," published on Oct. 28, 1853, in the *Neue Zeitschrift für Musik,* and which definitely started Brahms on the path of glory leading to deathlessness.

Brahms, Joachim, Albert Dietrich, J. O. Grimm—these perhaps more than any others were the men whose friendship was the chief solace of Schumann in his now rapid decline. He still took his walks with Clara and the children. With his lips pursed as if whistling and his hands clasped behind him he was a familiar figure as he wandered in a kind of abstraction through the parks of Düsseldorf. New and alarming symptoms steadily manifested themselves. In 1854 he had "marked and painful auditory sensations," including a maddening affliction that took the shape of hearing melodies in two conflicting keys at once. His speech was heavier and his demeanor grew more and more apathetic. With increasing hallucinations he developed a morbid enthusiasm for spiritism and table rappings. He had dreams in which the spirits of Schubert and Mendelssohn dictated musical themes to him; or else he heard angelic voices which presently changed to the howling of demons threatening him with torments. On Feb. 26, 1854, he rose in a state of terrible melancholy, begged to be sent to an asylum and began to pack up the things he wished to take with him. Clara, wishing to speak to their friend and physician, Dr. Hasenclever, left the room for a moment. Suddenly Schumann opened his bedroom door and—vanished! A few minutes later he was brought back, dripping with water. Half clad, he had gone out, thrown himself into the Rhine but was saved from drowning by some fishermen who had seen the suicidal leap. On March 4 he was taken at his own wish to the private asylum of Dr. Richarz at Endenich, near Bonn. He left in a carriage accompanied by two doctors. Clara, from whom he took only a perfunctory leave, stayed behind, crushed. Someone had handed Schumann flowers as he drove away. He gave a few of them to Dr. Hasenclever, who afterwards took them to Clara. For a while his condition seemed to improve. He worked now and then at his music, composed a few variations on the theme he claimed to have received from the spirit of Schubert and wrote a piano accompaniment for some of the Paganini Capriccios. But by 1855 all hope was abandoned and in 1856 Clara, on a concert tour in England, was informed that Robert was "irretrievably lost." Soon a telegram summoned her to Endenich "if she still wanted to see her husband alive." With Brahms, who for nearly two years had watched over Robert and the sorely tried Clara with unexampled devotion, she went to the sanatorium, saw Robert and believed that, though he seemed to converse with spirits, he recognized and welcomed her after the long separation. On July 29, 1856, he was, in Clara's words "to be freed from his troubles; at four in the afternoon he passed gently away. His last hours were peaceful and so he passed in sleep, unnoticed—nobody was with him at the moment. I saw him half an hour later. Joachim had come from Heidelberg on receiving our telegram. . . ."

*   *   *

Two days afterwards Schumann was laid to rest in the lovely Old Cemetery at Bonn. Members of the Düsseldorf "Concordia," which had serenaded the Schumanns on their arrival from Dresden six years earlier, were the pallbearers. Hiller, Joachim and Brahms walked in front, Clara, alone and unobserved, far behind—"certainly as he would have wished." Forty years later, on Whit-Sunday, 1896, she was reunited with him in the same tomb, in the presence of her surviving children and a few friends, chief of these the faithful Brahms, himself barely a year from his end.

H. F. P.

Hector Berlioz

BORN: LA CÔTE SAINT-ANDRÉ, DEC. II, 1803. DIED: PARIS, MAR. 8, 1869.

All modern programmists have built upon him—Liszt, Richard Strauss, and Tschaikowsky. Wagner felt his influence, though he belittled it. His own words, "I have taken up music where Beethoven left it," indicate his position. He is the real beginner of that interpenetration of music and the poetic idea which has transformed modern art.—
ERNEST NEWMAN.

$\mathscr{A}$ THUMBNAIL SKETCH like the present is, of course, the last place in the world to recount even an infinitesimal part of a life so vivid and crowded with bitter conflict and tragic experience as that of Hector Berlioz; and the person who attempts it is beaten in advance. Moreover, such an effort seems almost gratuitous. For Berlioz has told his own story better than anyone else could possibly do it. When Ernest Newman was asked at one time to write a new biography of the epoch-making composer he informed the publisher who suggested it that "no Life by any other hands will ever be able to bear comparison as a piece of literature with Berlioz' Autobiography. All others are for the most part a watering down into the author's inferior style of the sparkling prose of Berlioz himself." How much more futile is it to attempt on the minuscule scale of the following tiny, if rambling, essay to touch upon even a thousandth of those achievements and unremitting conflicts which entered into the texture of this master's agitated and inharmonious life! Actually, it aims to do no more than contribute a mite toward a larger interest in the writings and the great

282

mass of insufficiently discovered compositions of a Romanticist whose labors are still surprisingly unrecognized art works of the future.

*   *   *

The little mountain town, La Côte Saint-André, where Louis-Hector Berlioz was born on December 11, 1803, had briefly been called La Côte Bonne-Eau during the Revolution and the Reign of Terror when "saints," for a while, went out of fashion. It was not far from Grenoble on one side or from Lyon on another. The Berlioz family originated in Savoie and can be traced back to the sixteenth century. Hector's father, Louis Berlioz, a doctor and a property owner, had at one time been mayor of La Côte Saint-André. In 1802 he had married Marie-Antoinette-Joséphine Marmion, a good-looking woman, religious to the point of bigotry. Hector was the oldest of six children, two of whom died at an early age. The surviving daughters, Nanci and Adèle, were followed as late as 1820 by a son, Prosper, a "problem child" in the truest sense of the term, vague and unmanageable up to the time of a belated adolescence, then developing into a mathematical genius and dying in his twentieth year before people had ceased to marvel at his talents.

Hector's father supervised his early education, though it was probably as a concession to his wife that he placed the youngster in the local Catholic Seminary. The boy did not stay there long even if his mother harbored ambitions of making a saint of him. For a time he went uncomplainingly to mass, communion, confession and the rest. In his Memoirs Hector tells us details of his weekly "confessions" when he would say to the "director" of his conscience "My father, I have done nothing" and that worthy would reply "Go on, my child, as you have begun." And so he did—for several years, at least.

Yet his mother's religiosity was to have the effect of turning Hector's thoughts away from the church and toward the great figures of classical mythology. He "felt his heart throb and his voice quiver and break" when he construed the fourth book of Virgil's "Aeneid" to his father; and when the good man tactfully cut the lesson short Hector was "intensely grateful to him for taking no notice of my emotion and rushed away to vent my Virgilian grief in solitude." Mythology was not the only love with which his father filled him; under the

283

paternal guidance he developed an interest in geography and stories of travel helped fire his imagination.

From an early age Hector had shown a sensitiveness to musical impressions and, besides learning to sing at sight, acquired some proficiency in playing the flute and the flageolet—though "I was twelve before the magic of music was revealed to me." Presently he added to his musical accomplishments the playing of the guitar. The piano he never, apparently, undertook to master. But in later years he made a virtue of necessity and insisted he was glad to compose "silently and freely" without having to depend on the keyboard. With harmony it was rather different and after an unsuccessful start with Rameau's treatise on the subject, even in a simplified form, he had recourse to a textbook by Catel in order to pick up some elementary principles. These he presently put to use in a "six part potpourri on a collection of Italian airs" and in the composition of a couple of quintets for flute and strings. The first was played by some local amateurs and aroused the enthusiasm of all the hearers except Hector's father. Dr. Berlioz preferred as much of the later quintet as his son was able to play him on the flute, but the piece being much more difficult, the amateur executants who tried it quickly suffered shipwreck. The composer eventually burned both scores yet salvaged a theme his father had liked and then used it in his overture, "Les Francs-Juges."

Simultaneously with these hit or miss musical studies the boy's emotional life was heightened at about this time by an incipient love affair, if one can call it so. Hector's relatives, the Marmions, had a country house near Grenoble in the village of Meylan, where he spent his vacations. Not far away, in a white cottage, surrounded by vineyards and gardens there lived with her mother and sister a tall and exceedingly pretty girl of eighteen, Estelle Duboeuf. At a family garden party, to which Hector and his relations had been invited, Estelle picked him for her partner in some game. Poor Hector was conquered in the twinkling of an eye. When a few minutes later he caught sight of Estelle dancing with his uncle Marmion—who had been a soldier in Napoleon's armies and cut a superb figure in his gaudy uniform and clanking spurs—the boy flew into a jealous rage, only to have the whole party laugh at him! But Estelle—his "Stella montis," his "Star of the Mountain"—remained enshrined in his memory for life. Their ways were to separate and they lost track of each other for years. A haggard old man, wracked and buffeted by numberless woes and disappointments, he found her again and sought solace (vainly, as it proved) in an attempt to recapture the shadow of a childhood fancy. His reward was a polite note signed Estelle Fornier—her married name—and a conventional "affectionate greetings," into which he chose to read meanings that the old lady never remotely intended!

* * *

Hector's parents determined he should follow in his father's footsteps and become a physician. The idea revolted him and he struggled against it much as Schumann combated his mother's wish to make a jurist of a youth with the soul of a poet. Nevertheless, he made as if to comply with the parental will—though one can guess with how many unspoken reservations! And so in the autumn of 1821, he set off for Paris to study medicine. But what fascinated him there were the theaters, the opera houses, the concert halls—things which up to that time he had never enjoyed the opportunity of visiting—and not the loathsome hospitals, anatomical amphitheaters, dissecting rooms and other nauseating horrors. He had felt all along that he was never intended to spend his life "at the bedside of sick people, in hospitals and dissecting chambers." His father had made the cardinal mistake of "using his love of music as a lever for removing his 'childish aversion' to embark on the study of medicine" and, as a reward for working earnestly at osteology had given his refractory son nothing less to the purpose than "a splendid flute, with all the new keys!"

In Paris Hector lost no time visiting the Opéra, the Théâtre Italien, the Théâtre Feydeau, the Ambigu-Comique. He heard Salieri's "Danaides," Boieldieu's "Voitures Versées," Dalayrac's "Nina." Above all, he heard Gluck's "Iphigénie en Tauride," and this masterpiece definitely settled the question. His life would be dedicated to music and medicine could go hang! Berlioz the scarlet Romanticist was born at the moment he solemnly made this resolve. It was farewell, henceforth, to the "human charnel house, littered with fragments of limbs, ghastly faces and cloven heads . . . where swarms of sparrows fought for scraps and rats in the corners gnawed human vertebrae." He had, to be sure, grown somewhat hardened after his first appalling impression and had even gone so far as to "cast a shoulder blade to a great rat which was staring at me with famished eyes!" But the physical reactions he experienced to the music he loved attracted him in the same degree as the horrid displays of the hospital laboratories revolted him. In the theater listening to Gluck and Spontini "his knees would tremble convulsively, his teeth chatter, he suffered with dizzy spells till he could not stand unsupported, he was bathed in sweat, his scalp contracted, tears choked him, he lost all sensation in fingers and toes, he was seized with chills and hot flashes . . ." If this was not actually a type of celestial intoxication it was certainly a romantic imagination conveyed through the empurpled diction of the hour!

Down at his home in the Dauphiné Dr. Berlioz gradually got wind of what was happening and endeavored to reason with his son. The latter was frequenting the library of the Conservatoire, voraciously devouring the scores of Gluck, and leaving to those who had a taste for that sort of thing the sanguinary details of the anatomical chamber. And not only did he study the music of Gluck, Méhul and others but he addressed himself to the first two symphonies of Beethoven, at that time as good as unknown in Paris. In the Conservatoire library he met a certain Hyacinthe Christophe Gerono, a pupil of Lesueur, who counseled Hector to study with his affable old master, at one time a great favorite. Lesueur received Hector amiably at the first visit, examined a few compositions of the young man, pronounced them faulty but urged him to undertake some preparatory studies under Gerono, a task he willingly accepted.

In a short time Gerono indoctrinated him so thoroughly in Lesueur's harmonic system that the latter cordially took him as a pupil. Not that Hector accepted his mentor's teaching without many unspoken questions, but he quickly decided that the most diplomatic thing to do was to curb whatever impatience he felt and listen in silence. He had already written a choral work, "Le Passage de la Mer Rouge" and a Mass, and though they were youthful attempts and obviously unripe he found it possible to dispense with conventional rules. And now he felt moved to attempt an opera! The obliging Gerono supplied him with a libretto and the fruit of this collaboration was called "Estelle et Némorin," Estelle Duboeuf doubtless floating before his mind's eye. Berlioz admits that the music was "feeble" and called the entire work "wishy-washy." As for the Mass, composed by request for the feast day of the choir children of the Church of Saint Roch, portions of it met the approval of Lesueur. When it came to paying the costs of its performance Hector was in a quandary about raising the necessary 1,200 francs. Finally he borrowed the sum from a friend, Augustin de Pons—a step he was presently to regret though Pons had lent him the money with the best of intentions. The Mass itself was praised and some years later was repeated at the Church of St. Eustache. By this time, however, the composer had become dissatisfied with the work and then burned it together with several juvenile effusions. Meanwhile he had a stormy first meeting with Cherubini, head of the Conservatoire; and he failed to pass a preliminary examination for that august school.

Hearing of this misfortune, Dr. Berlioz, usually slow to wrath, lost his temper and resolved to stop his son's allowance. If anything Lesueur aggravated the situation by attempting to intercede on his pupil's behalf. Hector was summoned home and ordered to renounce his ideas of a musical career and take up some other occupation. In spite of the chilling reception the young black sheep encountered there, he was astonished and delighted to learn a few days later that the good doctor had once more reconsidered. "After several sleepless nights I have made up my mind," he gravely told his son. "You shall go to Paris and study music; but only for a time. If after further trials you fail, you will, I am sure, acknowledge that I have done what was right, and you will choose some other career. You know what I think of second-rate poets; second-rate artists are no better and it would be a deep sorrow and profound humiliation to me to see you numbered among these useless members of society." And he swore the youth to secrecy. But the news leaked out and before Hector could take his place in the stagecoach his mother, blazing with anger, confronted him "with flashing eyes and exciting gestures": "Your father," she exclaimed, "has been weak enough to allow you to return to Paris and to encourage your mad, wicked plans; but I will not have this guilt on my soul and, once and for all, I forbid your departure . . . I beseech you not to persist in your folly! See, I, your mother kneel to you and beg you humbly to renounce it." And when the appalled Hector begged her to rise she defied him, wildly: "No; I will kneel! So, wretched boy, you refuse? You can stand unmoved with your mother kneeling at your feet? Well, then, go! Go and wallow in the filth of Paris, sully your name and kill your father and me with sorrow and shame! I will not reenter this house till you have left it. You are my son no longer! I curse you!" Hector had to leave, as he says, "without bidding her good-bye, without another word or a look, and with her curse on my head!"

*   *   *

Back in Paris his first object was to repay Pons part of the money he owed him for the performance of the Saint Roch Mass. He earned a few francs by giving occasional lessons in singing and by teaching flute and guitar. His monthly allowance amounted only to one hundred and twenty francs, so the repayment was a slow and painful business. Most unhappily Pons, wishing to spare Hector this continuous drain on his purse, resolved to "help" his friend by writing Dr. Berlioz and asking him to settle the remainder of the debt. Pons got his money—but poor Hector lost his allowance!

Somehow he managed to scrape along. He had a tiny room, five flights up, in the Cité, at the corner of the Quai des Orfèvres and the Rue de Harley; he gave up dining in restaurants and confined his diet to dry bread and salt, with now and then raisins or dates. When the weather was favorable he took this meal on the Pont Neuf, beside the statue of Henri IV, watching the passersby or gazing at the muddy waters of the Seine. He worked tirelessly at his music. Cherubini, now apparently mollified, put the youth into Reicha's class for counterpoint and fugue at the Conservatoire, even while he continued with Lesueur. Hector struck up a life-long friendship with young Humbert Ferrand, who wrote him an opera book, "Les Franc-Juges"—"The Judges of the Secret Court"—which he enthusiastically set to music but of which only the overture remains. It is a fine thing of its type, bearing melodically, instrumentally and harmonically, the unmistakable imprint of Berlioz even to the reminders of Gluck. One of its most striking themes survives from the boyish quintet of Hector's and anticipates in a fashion the "idée fixe" of the "Symphonie Fantastique," not very far ahead.

Working on his opera young Berlioz had somewhat neglected his flute and guitar pupils and once more needed money. Even a franc a lesson would not help greatly when it became a question of winter clothes and firewood. Far from capitulating and returning, beaten, to Dauphiné, he first toyed with the idea of seeking a position as first or second flute in some orchestra "in New York, Mexico, Sydney or Calcutta, of becoming a sailor, filibuster, buccaneer or savage in China" or attempting any other wild scheme since "it is futile and dangerous to thwart my will when I am resolved on anything." In the end he tried a safer, less exciting method. Aided by a streak of luck and an exceptionally good musical memory, he obtained an engagement as a chorus singer at the Théâtre des Nouveautés, where basses were wanted but where a passable baritone could also be of use. By singing as a trial piece a recitative from Sacchini's "Oedipe" he prevailed over a weaver, a blacksmith, an actor and a choir member from St. Eustache. The job paid him fifty francs a month. Hector had not only to sing all manner of rubbish but "the colossal manager," a Mr. St. Léger, sometimes obliged him to be "the rear leg of an artificial camel!" Even so, it was luck of a sort. At the same time, two new pupils applied for lessons and he met Antoine Charbonnel, a young man from La Côte Saint-André, whose father had often scandalized Mme. Berlioz because, being a tireless woman chaser, he flew in the face of her family's ancient motto, "respectability above everything." Charbonnel, a budding pharmacist, found it advisable to share economies with Hector and the pair set up bachelor quarters in two little rooms in the Rue de la Harpe. Charbonnel cooked and Hector marketed, grossly violating the hygienic codes of his friend by carrying the day's provisions unwrapped under his arm.

* * *

Hector calls the "Francs-Juges" overture his "first grand instrumental work." It was soon followed by another overture, "Waverly." He was, he tells us, so ignorant of the mechanism of certain instruments at that period, that he had written the trombone solo in the earlier score in the key of D flat, uncertain whether this choice of tonality was a wise one or not. On submitting the passage to a trombone player at the Opéra he was delighted to learn that it was the best possible key for the purpose and that the solo in question could not fail to produce a powerful effect. Greatly elated he walked home as in a dream and was recalled to himself by suddenly spraining his ankle. From that moment he could never hear the piece without experiencing a sharp pain in his foot. "Perhaps," he muses in his Memoirs, "it gives others a pain in their heads!" Curiously enough, neither Reicha nor Lesueur taught him anything about instrumentation. Thanks to a friend at the

Opéra he obtained free tickets and by close listening at such performances and study of such scores as were given he "perceived the subtle
connection . . . between musical expression and the special art of instrumentation, which no one had actually pointed out to me. It was
by studying the methods of . . . Beethoven, Weber and Spontini; by
an impartial examination of the regular forms of instrumentation, and
of unusual forms and combinations; partly by listening to artists
and getting them to make experiments for me on their instruments,
and partly by instinct, that I acquired what knowledge I possess" and
was later to disseminate in his great treatise on instrumentation, subsequently modernized by Richard Strauss.

* * *

Hector was officially admitted to the Conservatoire when, the next
examination period having come around, he succeeded at last in passing the test. He was less fortunate with an orchestral *scena* on the
death of Orpheus which the students were required to compose, though
Berlioz ascribed his failure to the incompetence of a mediocre pianist
obliged to play the reduction of the original score. He had obtained a
brief leave from his duties at the Théâtre des Nouveautés when he
came down with a dangerous attack of quincy sore throat. Alone one
night and on the point of strangling he suddenly sat down before his
shaving mirror, seized a pen knife and, in a paroxysm of agony, lanced
the obstruction which was suffocating him. By some miracle he was
on his feet again in a few days and had the satisfaction of hearing
from his suddenly repentant father that his allowance was to be restored. Having no further need of continuing his chorister chores he
was now free to devote his evenings to opera performances.

These evenings, he declares, were "solemn" occasions. They could be
tumultuous ones, as well; for Hector was violent when matters outraged him and as often as not became an irrepressible claqueur. More
than once he helped precipitate riots in the theater. When at a performance of "Iphigénie en Tauride," for instance, cymbals were introduced into a ballet passage where Gluck has only strings and when
trombones were omitted from a passage in Orestes' third act recitative,
Hector would suddenly shout with all his might: "There are no cymbals there; who has dared to correct Gluck?" Then, in the Orestes passage: "Not a sign of a trombone; it is intolerable!" Again, during a

performance of Dalayrac's "Nina," Berlioz missed a violin solo scheduled to be played by the violinist, Baillot. Just as the cue for the expected solo was reached a furious voice was heard to exclaim: "So far good, but where is the violin solo?" "Very true," cried someone else, "it looks as if they were going to leave it out. Baillot, Baillot, the violin solo." The pit took fire, the entire house rose and loudly demanded that the program should be carried out according to schedule. Before long people dashed into the orchestra, overturning chairs and music desks, smashing the kettledrums. Meanwhile, Hector who had sown the wind tried to control the whirlwind with sarcastic protests: "Gentlemen, don't smash the instruments! What vandalism! Don't you see you are destroying Father Chenie's beautiful double-bass, with its infernal tone?" But the mob was beyond control and broke not only instruments but innumerable seats and music stands as well!

*   *   *

It was 1827 and he was beginning to harbor more far-darting ambitions. In June he planned to try for the Prix de Rome, though he really laid small value on the "honor" the winning of it conferred. How often was it no more than a means to an end!

Three times Berlioz competed (four if we count the preliminary test of 1826, in which he failed), but not till 1830 did he carry off the honor. In 1827 he had written for the purpose "La Mort d'Orphée," in 1828 he gained the second prize, in 1829 (when no prize was finally given) he turned out a "Cléopâtre"—which, had it been less audacious, might have won him the award—while in 1830 his cantata, "Sardanapale," finally achieved the ultimate distinction. But this honor, so highly regarded among the rank and file of Frenchmen, was for Hector soon to turn to something like Dead Sea fruit.

On Sept. 11, 1827, Kemble's company from London inaugurated a Shakespearian season at the Odéon Theatre. "Hamlet" was the first offering, with the famous English actor in the tile role. The Ophelia was Henrietta Smithson, tall, lithe and Irish. All literary and artistic Paris was on hand. From the moment the daughter of Polonius stepped on the stage Hector was lost! No thunderbolt could more completely have devastated him. When the performance ended he rushed home, avoiding all acquaintances to whom he might have had to talk. Then he went out again and walked all night along the Seine, determined to wear himself out to obtain the temporary solace of sleep. It was useless. Next evening the visitors were giving "Romeo and Juliet." Hector dashed to the Odéon early in the day and bought himself a ticket, to be sure no unforeseen hitch might prevent his obtaining his usual admission. As he knew no word of English, he procured a translation and strove for a few hours to re-create in his mind a picture of Henrietta Smithson before again looking upon her in the flesh. If possible the effect of the previous evening was intensified.

He would now wander aimlessly through suburbs and countryside, sometimes even sleeping in open fields; or he would set to music Irish lyrics by Thomas Moore; or steep himself in more Shakespeare, dabble in Byron and Walter Scott, set about discovering Goethe and acquainting himself with "Faust"! He moved from the quarters of his friend Charbonnel and installed himself in a room in the Rue Richelieu directly opposite the house where Henrietta lived. He had never so much as exchanged a word with the actress who, for her part, never yet dreamed that such a person as Hector Berlioz existed—let alone that he loved her wildly. Nonetheless, Hector made a point of avoiding further Shakespeare performances—or so at least, he claims in his Memoirs. "More experiences of the kind would have killed me!" But the inspiration of this Juliet and Ophelia, further enhanced by the romantic literature with which he was suffusing himself and the grandeur of those Beethoven works he was beginning to discover, was stimulating his creative fancy. He wrote overtures based on "Waverly," "King Lear," "The Corsair"; he wrote (in 1829) "Eight Scenes from Faust" and a "Ballade of the King of Thule, in Gothic Style" (things which were later to form the basis of "La Damnation de Faust"); he composed a set of "Nine Irish Songs"; above all, he wrote (and then revised) a work which was to become, in some respects, his most widely known and famous, the "Symphonie Fantastique"—a kind of symphonic phantasmagoria, with Henrietta as its chief motivation and himself as its chief actor.

It was not till December, 1827, that the actress first had a fleeting glimpse of her worshiper. This happened quite by chance at a rehearsal for a benefit performance at the Opéra-Comique where Hector was to offer an overture of his and where some of the English actors were to perform a couple of Shakespearian scenes. By this time he had begun to write her letters, to which she never replied, for they frightened her and she presently ordered her maid not to accept any more from the postman. When Berlioz at a rehearsal caught sight of Henrietta talking to her colleagues backstage he uttered a loud cry and rushed from the theater, wildly wringing his hands. Thinking she had to do with a madman the actress begged her associates to watch him closely, for "she did not like the look of his eyes." The mop of red hair that surmounted his head like an umbrella, his gaunt visage, fiery appearance and generally hysterical demeanor must have given her reason for alarm and she probably breathed more freely when she left Paris for Holland.

* * *

Everyone who has interested himself even slightly in Berlioz is doubtless familiar with the lurid fiction the composer invented to form the "plot" of the "Fantastic Symphony." In this "Episode in the Life of an Artist" a high-strung youth is represented as seeking release from the torments of disappointed love by means of an overdose of opium. Instead of killing him the drug afflicts him with a succession of perturbing, not to say terrifying, grotesque or macabre visions. Through each of them there moves the image of the Beloved, musically represented by a recurrent string of notes—a sort of representative theme, or "idée fixe." The youth is a plaything of passions, reveries, jealousies, frenzies at the outset; then he sees his idol, apparently indifferent to him, the central figure at a brilliant ball; amorous thoughts mingle in his mind with dark presentiments as he wanders over the countryside, rendered more melancholy by the pipings on rustic instruments of two lovesick shepherds till thunderclaps interrupt their mournful dialogue. Then he dreams he has murdered his beloved and is marched to the scaffold; after which his disembodied spirit becomes the sport of a noisome rout of demons, witches, succubi and other infernal things, among whom the cherished one, now a devilish harridan, pursues him, while the Dies Irae resounds blasphemously in his ears.

Doubtless much of the astounding score incorporates musical ideas originally conceived for other projected works. One way or another, the "Fantastique" is a formidable, if overdimensioned monument of its period, and a landmark of history. With all its flamboyant and parodistic monstrosities, this fresco of psychopathic experience remains the first great and influential specimen of program music created in France; and it is no less amazing to reflect that the epochal score came into being when its composer was but twenty-seven and only at the time he was adjudged worthy of the Prix de Rome.

Berlioz subsequently sent tickets for a performance of the symphony to Henrietta Smithson. She appears to have been about the only person in the hall unaware at that time that she was the heroine of the piece. More or less vaguely she had been hearing of the infatuation of her harassed admirer. Her reaction, lightly expressed, had been "There could be nothing more impossible!" It was not in Hector's nature to accept such a rejection as final. Still, she had unwittingly wounded him! For a while he decided that, with all her beauty and her gifts, she was no different from the average run of females. If she could think of repudiating his love the "Fantastique" was *his* derisive answer! This musical caricature of the actress, he intended as a gesture of vengeance.

The new symphony, however, helped gain him a friend and defender, who was to remain one of his most valiant supporters for life—Franz Liszt. Liszt had met Hector shortly before and, transported by the symphony, he made a piano arrangement of it, which propagandized the work as, at the time, nothing else could have done.

*   *   *

Scarcely liberated (as he thought) from Henrietta, Berlioz succumbed to another woman. This young person, decidedly no better than she should have been, was a friend of Ferdinand Hiller and a piano pupil of Kalkbrenner and Herz. Camille Moke set her nets for Hector and captured him without the slightest trouble. She came into his life at the worst possible moment! With the consent of her mother, briefly blinded by the young man's success in winning the Roman Prize, Camille became engaged to her admirer, who was just about to set out for that sojourn in Rome which was the chief reward of a lucky contestant. He seems not to have foreseen trouble, though his sister, Nanci, was beset by premonitions; and Ferdinand Hiller sent to Berlioz, in Rome, the ironic message that his betrothed "was bearing the separation with fortitude." Shocked but still only half convinced, Hector took to bed and waited vainly for Camille's expected letters to Italy. Time passed and nothing came. Whatever interest he might have found in the Eternal City, where he had been warmly received by his fellow students at the Villa Medici and by its director, Horace Vernet, he was unable to pay any attention to his work or his agreeable surroundings. Little really mattered—neither the monuments of Rome, the French Academy, his meeting with the well-graced youth, Felix Mendelssohn, his future prospects. Vernet, noticing Hector's worry, began to entertain serious misgivings. Summoning the newcomer he warned him against any rash step. Finally, on Good Friday the tormented lover impulsively left Rome, resolved to return to Paris and find out for himself what lay behind Camille's silence. In roundabout ways he got as far as Nice. On the journey he bought a pistol and some poison determined to learn the truth and if worst came to worst to shoot Camille and then make an end of himself. He was not obliged to go to these spectacular extremes. For at long last he received a letter —not, indeed, from his presumed fiancée, but from her mother. That lady informed Hector that her daughter was on the point of marrying Mr. Pleyel, the famous piano manufacturer; and she requested her "son-in-law" not to kill himself!

Of course he would kill himself—and the Mokes as well! But as he looked at the lovely Côte d'Azur landscape unrolled before him from the heights of the Grande Corniche he suddenly experienced a revulsion of feeling. For the time being he would go on living! He dispatched a letter to Horace Vernet saying he was returning to Rome and pledging his honor to remain in Italy. Then he settled down for three weeks in Nice and wrote his "King Lear" Overture.

*   *   *

Hector became more or less resigned to Rome, now that the Moke affair was definitely at an end; but was never completely at home there. He enjoyed the company of Mendlessohn, for the two were well matched, intellectually, if not balanced by temperament. However, Felix adored Gluck as much as Hector and the two youths delighted in singing and playing "Armide" together. They agreed wholeheartedly in their worship of Mozart, Beethoven and Weber but disagreed on Bach, whom the German idolized but to whom Berlioz remained cold. When the pair went over Hector's prize-crowned "Sardanapale" and the Frenchman frankly expressed his dislike for a certain number in it, Mendelssohn told his friend he was happy to see that he really displayed such good taste! Hector made the usual excursions, saw the regulation sights, visited the mountains of the Abruzzi, wandered about the Campagna, renewed his Virgilian recollections, sang, strummed his guitar, heard the operas and the generally trivial and ill performed church music and mingled with the painters at the Café Greco. In short, he went more or less through the customary tourist routine.

Also, he composed. He made changes in the score of the "Fantastique" adding, for one thing, a coda to the Ball Scene; he wrote overtures to "The Corsair," based on Byron, and "Rob Roy" based on Scott, not to mention an ambitious pendant to the "Fantastique," "Le Retour à la Vie," to which he subsequently gave the alternative title of "Lélio." But by 1832 he decided he had endured as much of Rome as he could stomach. After a compromise with Horace Vernet he cut short his stay at the Villa Medici by six months promising to spend a year in Germany—an ambition he had always cherished.

In November, 1832, Berlioz was back in Paris, and in that very house where Henrietta Smithson had lodged on her first visit. In fact, she had moved out only a day earlier and settled in an apartment on the Rue de Rivoli. Small wonder that Hector discerned the working of destiny once more!

This time Henrietta had come to Paris with her own theatrical company. Incredible as it may seem, she and Hector had not yet actually met. The Irish actress divined his passion fully when, at a performance under the conductor Habeneck (at which not only the "Fantastique" but also the monodrama, "Lélio," were performed) she heard from the actor who spoke the text the words: "Ah, could I but find this Juliet, this Ophelia, whom my heart is ever seeking. . . . Could I but sleep my last sad sleep in her beloved arms!" Instead of going to Germany at New Year's, 1833, Berlioz determined to remain, for the moment, in Paris. His love for Henrietta had been newly awakened; and she was now willing to be formally introduced to him.

"From that day I had not a moment's rest. Terrible fears were succeeded by delirious hopes. What I went through . . . cannot be described. Her mother and sister formally opposed our union. My own parents would not hear of it. Discontent and anger on the part of both families, and all the scenes to which such opposition gives birth in these cases."

Portents of trouble followed thick and fast. Henrietta Smithson's theatrical venture failed disastrously. Financially she was utterly ruined, the more so as she had contracted immense debts. Next, she fell and broke her leg. She was bed-ridden and she remained an invalid. Hector organized a benefit concert for her. Among the first to offer their services were Liszt and Chopin. Enough was realized to settle "Harriet's" most pressing obligations. And then, despite his parents' objections and the venomous hostility of Henrietta's hunchbacked sister, Hector married her in the autumn of 1833—first, however, staging a spectacular suicide act to frighten her into wedlock. She was, he assured his friend Humbert Ferrand, "aussi vierge qu'il soit possible de l'être."

To keep the domestic pot boiling he found it advisable about this period to take up musical journalism. Although Berlioz had been contributing on and off to certain publications, his present connection with *L'Europe littéraire* is, to all intents, the official beginning of that critical activity of his which was to span almost the remainder of his life. As subsequent music reviewer on the influential *Journal des Débats* he spent no end of time and effort in commenting on compositions and performances, good, bad and indifferent, which he might infinitely better have dedicated to creative work. The labor revolted him but he found himself as helpless as a galley slave. Enforced attendance at innumerable concerts and operas he came to loathe to such an extent that, late in his career when he was finally able to shake off the journalistic fetters, he enjoyed walking up and down in front of a theater or concert hall just for the pleasure of reflecting that he did *not* have to go in! And yet, of all celebrated composers, Berlioz was by all odds the most brilliantly gifted litterateur, whose writings even today preserve most of their individuality, polished style, barbed irony and scintillant humor. Aside from his countless feuilletons and other articles, his Memoirs, Soirées de l'Orchestre, A Travers Chants and much else are literary masterpieces of their kind, which even today retain their freshness and sparkle. Undoubtedly his important journalistic affiliations had the effect of involving him in numberless intrigues and difficulties inseparable from posts of influence, besides sapping his energies that should have been employed otherwise. Yet he knew how to draw profit from the means of publicity and power which his connections placed in his hands and he did not hesitate to promote, as much as possible, his personal interests.

*   *   *

When their marriage was solemnized at the British Embassy (with Liszt as best man) Hector had exactly two hundred francs and Harriet —a mountain of debts! For their honeymoon they could travel no farther than the suburb of Vincennes. The wedding trip, according to the groom, was "a masterpiece of love." All the same, he soon had chances to notice that his bride was not in the least musical; likewise, that she harbored a streak of jealousy. Not even the birth of their son, Louis, on August 15, 1834, at their home on the hill of Montmartre helped smooth this unhappy state of affairs, which was to deepen as time went on. Harriet grew violently opposed to her husband's traveling, though Berlioz claims that "a mad and for some time an absolutely groundless jealousy was at the bottom of it."

Was it "absolutely groundless"? The composer's intimate associate, Ernest Legouvé, has let us into many secrets about the rift in the lute in his book "Soixante Ans de Souvenirs." The blond Irishwoman, some years older than her husband, was gradually losing her looks, her failures as an actress had for some time increasingly embittered her and she presently took to drink. The more the sentiments of the formerly so ardent Hector "changed to a correct and calm good fellow-ship," says Legouvé, "the more his wife became imperious in her exigencies and indulged in violent recriminations that were unfortunately justified. Berlioz, whose position as critic and as composer producing his own works made the theatre his real world, found there occasions for lapses that would have proved too much for stronger heads than his; moreover, his reputation as a misunderstood great artist endowed him with a halo that easily tempted his female interpreters to become his consolers. Madame Berlioz searched his feuilletons for hints of his infidelities. And not only there: fragments of intercepted letters, drawers indiscreetly opened, brought her revelations just sufficient to make her beside herself without more than half-illuminating her. Her jealousy was always outdistanced by the facts. Berlioz's heart went so fast that she could not keep pace with it; when, after so much research, she lighted upon some object of his passion, *that* particular passion was no more; and then, it being easy for him to prove his innocence at the moment, the poor woman was as abashed as a dog which after having followed a track for half an hour, arrives at the lair only to find the quarry already gone." Yet the jealous instincts of the once lovely Ophelia and Juliet were, in fact, only too sound and, if her shrewishness increased by leaps and bounds, she had no little cause for it.

Hector's friends seemed, perhaps, a little less devoted to him since his marriage, and since his miseries were a trifle less spectacular than they had been during his bachelor days. But these comrades included not a few personages illustrious in their respective spheres. Among them were the musical chroniclers Janin and d'Ortigue; the essayists and novelists Legouvé, Eugène Sue, Alexandre Dumas, Sainte-Beuve, Victor Hugo; among the creative and performing musicians, Liszt of course and Chopin, who though personally the antithesis of Berlioz, never wavered in his faithfulness to the man. And further, flashing like a comet across the firmament of Hector, there was the "demon fiddler," Paganini.

In 1834 Berlioz composed the "descriptive" symphony "Harold in Italy," in which Byron's Childe Harold, the central figure of the work was represented by a viola solo. Whether Hector's account of the genesis of the composition is wholly authentic or not, the tale he relates in his Memoirs runs somewhat as follows: Having heard the "Symphonie Fantastique" one day Paganini came to see the composer and told him that he owned a wonderful Stradivari viola which he would love to play in public, though he had no music for it which he considered suitable. Would Hector write him such a work? He had no confidence in anyone else. The only thing the violinist insisted upon was that "he must be playing the whole time." The work should not be an ordinary concerto, but rather something along the lines of the "Fantastique." After many doubts and hesitations the composer produced a series of scenes for orchestra, the pictorial background of which was shaped out of Hector's recollections of his Italian wanderings; while the viola strain, representing Byron's dreamer, was added to the rest of the orchestral texture "with which it contrasts both in movement and character, without hindering the development."

Paganini did not hear the symphony till some time after it had been first performed, for he had been south, vainly seeking relief from that cancer of the larynx which had robbed him of his voice and was shortly to prove fatal. At the close of the work he ordered his son to tell the composer "he had never in his life been so impressed at a concert" and were he to follow his inclination, he would "go down on his knees to thank him." And then, in full view of the audience, the great violinist did just that and kissed Hector's hand! Next day he received a letter in Paganini's writing which ran: "Beethoven is dead and Berlioz alone can revive him. I have heard your divine compositions, so worthy of your genius, and beg you to accept, in token of my homage, twenty thousand francs . . ."

Almost on the heels of this windfall Berlioz had the additional luck of being commissioned by the government to compose a *Requiem,* for an official ceremony. The work is one of his most monumental—one might say apocalyptic—even if the quality of its musical inspiration may be open to question. One thing, however, is certain—nothing he ever wrote is so overwhelming in point of sheer sonority as the appalling Tuba Mirum, with its five orchestras, its sixteen kettle drums and its phalanxes of trombones. At the climax of this fresco of the Last Judgment one of the participating singers succumbed in public to a shrieking frenzy of nervous prostration!

*   *   *

There was talk in governmental circles of "purchasing" the *Requiem,* of a grand decoration, of a professorship at the Conservatoire, of a generous pension from the Beaux Arts ministry. Nothing came of all these plans. As far as the Conservatoire post was concerned, Berlioz was rejected as teacher of harmony at that institution on the ground that he could not play piano—which was as true as it was irrelevant. But a far greater and more fateful disappointment lay ahead. Early in 1838 his mother—who had cursed him—died at La Côte Saint-André. Her curse did not perish with her; in fact, it smote him soon afterwards when his lyric drama, *"Benvenuto Cellini,"* failed grievously at the Opéra, where after long and torturing efforts he at length managed to have it performed. Not even today can it be said to have gained anything like a permanent foothold on the stage.

As time went on Hector tried to master his inhospitable fate in the operatic theater by various compromises and subterfuges. He sought to create a "dramatic symphony," based on "Romeo and Juliet," and neither outright drama nor outright symphony—which accounts for its infrequent performance, despite the extraordinary beauty of some of its music. He wrote a "concert opera" which is, in effect, a cantata masquerading as an opera and vice-versa. *"La Damnation de Faust,"* one of the three most essential capturings in music of Goethe's "Faust" drama, was at its first hearing in 1846 possibly the most distressful defeat he ever suffered at the hands of his countrymen. Not until decades after his death did he enjoy a kind of posthumous revenge when Raoul Gunsbourg, in Monte Carlo, fashioned a stage production which is now one of the mainstays of the Paris Opéra. A destiny in some respects even more deplorable was that of his music drama, *"Les Troyens,"* which he was never to rear in its completeness. The one theater work of Berlioz to enjoy something like an uncontested triumph at its launching was his two-act opera comique, *"Béatrice et Bénédict,"* for which Shakespeare provided the original incentive. As for *"Roméo et Juliette,"* its high points are found in two movements—the rapturous love scene, which includes the most enamoring melodic ideas Berlioz ever conceived, and the unparagoned Queen Mab Scherzo, embodying the composer's instrumental fancy at its most subtle and ravishing— even if Parisian criticism of the time could see no more in it than "a little noise like that of an ill-greased syringe!"

That long scheduled visit to Germany continued to be deferred. Meantime Berlioz had been appointed assistant librarian at the Paris Conservatoire, a small distinction, to be sure, but offering at any rate a few additional francs. A more ponderable achievement was the composition for band of a three movement "Symphonie funèbre et triomphale," planned for performance in the open air in memory of those fallen in the Revolution of 1830. The *"Funeral and Triumphal Symphony"* was one of the first compositions of Berlioz which Wagner heard when he arrived in Paris in 1840. Wagner was struck by the nobility of the work, ranked it among the loftiest achievements of its composer and retained an undissembled admiration for it all his days. Berlioz had reason to believe that, after this official labor, he might be called to step into the shoes of Cherubini at the Conservatoire when that worthy went to his reward in 1842. But the choice fell upon Georges Onslow and Hector, realizing that if he was ever to obtain in Paris the distinction to which he felt himself entitled, he would have to enhance his French reputation by properly publicized successes abroad. So he began by giving several concerts in Brussels, the second of which was destined to be important—less so for musical reasons than because of domestic entanglements it initiated.

Knowing Harriet's jealousy Hector seems to have been strangely incautious about keeping secret the identity of his "traveling companion." It did not take his alternately maudlin and acidulous Irish wife many days to find out from the papers that a certain Marie Recio was the snake in the grass. The Recio was a second rate singer, whose real name was Marie Genevieve Martin. Hector had met her in 1841. We are told that she rekindled in his heart those romantic emotions the now slatternly and alcoholic Harriet could no longer feed. Marie's mother encouraged the liaison because she realized the power Berlioz had come to be in the journalistic field. He had been so imprudent as to impose her on one operatic management and the game had turned out badly. Before long poor Hector found himself as luckless in his second love affair as he had been in his first.

*   *   *

The various tours which Hector undertook in Germany brought him artistic honors and material successes of which in France he never dreamed. Among average audiences he discovered a seriousness and a degree of taste such as were limited to a few circles at home. He refashioned old musical friendships and cultivated new ones. Mendelssohn met him in Leipzig and the pair continued the old artistic discussions and arguments as they had years before in Rome. Felix "was charming, fascinating, ceaselessly obliging and determined to be a guarantee for his French colleague's success." The two exchanged batons to symbolize their professional amity. Felix praised some of Hector's songs but avoided saying a word about his symphonies, overtures or the Requiem (actually, he detested them!). Berlioz saw Robert and Clara Schumann, the former appeared "wholly electrified by the Offertory of my Requiem." The Schumanns were hospitality itself, even if Clara sometimes found the Frenchman "cold, indifferent, morose" and "not the kind of artist I like." Robert, however, "feels a sympathy for him which I cannot explain." Mendelssohn privately confessed that he felt like washing his hands after he had been through a Berlioz score. In Dresden there was Richard Wagner, whose "Rienzi" and "Flying Dutchman" Hector listened to with interest and who turned himself inside out to assist the extraordinary visitor in training orchestra and chorus for his concert in that city. One thing astonished Berlioz and grew to be something of a fly in the German ointment: that worship of Bach with which he was surrounded! "People do not believe that this divinity can ever be subjected to question," he sighed. "Heresy on the subject is forbidden; Bach is Bach, just as God is God!"

*   *   *

On these travels, which went on intermittently for years, Hector visited not only Germany but also Austria, Bohemia, Hungary, Russia. He went to Russia in 1847 and later. There he was greeted like a conqueror and more than any other nation that country proved, materially, a gold mine to him. A pity that the harsh climate of places like St. Petersburg was, in the end, to try him so sorely! For whenever he went there he was literally overwhelmed with honors, decorations, costly gifts. In short, whenever neglect or disappointment became unbearable he could turn to Russia for at least temporary alleviation.

In Vienna (1845) he found much to delight him. To be sure he was often painfully struck by many things, such as the lamentable "ignorance prevailing with respect to the works of Gluck." He was in the habit of asking musicians if they knew "Alceste" or "Iphigenia" and invariably he received the answer: "They are never performed in Vienna; we do not know them." Whereupon his mental reaction would be: "But, you wretched creatures, whether they are performed or not, you ought to know them by heart!" On the other hand, he heard numbers of remarkable artists and admits he "would have to write a book to do justice to each and to catalogue all the musical wealth of Vienna in detail." He received, naturally, the usual silver baton "inscribed with the titles of his works." Also, a little present of a hundred ducats from the Emperor after one of his concerts in the Redouten Saal; and, from the same exalted source, the message, conveyed by the Imperial master of ceremonies: "Tell Berlioz that I was greatly amused!"

Meanwhile the composer had been working by fits and starts on "The Damnation of Faust." He wrote page after page of it at the most unbelievable times of day and night and in the unlikeliest places—on the Boulevard Poissonière, on a stone of the Boulevard du Temple, in the park at Enghien (when in a somnambulistic trance he had boarded a suburban train and it had simply deposited him there); at

303

Lille, at Rouen, in Passau, in Prague, in Silesia; while walking, while eating, while traveling. When he left Vienna for Budapest he prepared to perform at his first Hungarian concert the Rakoczy March of which he had made what, in effect, has long been the standardized and most overpowering orchestration of all. This national melody invariably drove Magyar listeners into frenzies of patriotic enthusiasm (for that matter few audiences even now can hear it unstirred). And on the program piloted by Berlioz it led to such a wild demonstration that, as he directed it, the composer's hair stood on end and he was seized for a few moments with a kind of nightmare terror. He thereupon introduced the march into the score of "The Damnation" and placed the opening scene of the Faust action in Hungary so as to motivate the presence in the score of the volcanic page.

* * *

It is hard to grasp today that the first performance of the "Damnation of Faust" at the Paris Opéra Comique (December 6, 1846) was the most heart-breaking fiasco of Berlioz' life. It was not a question of violent opposition (if only it had been!) but of abysmal, devastating indifference. Only a scattering of friends occupied the first rows of the Salle Favart, with farther back a handful of cynical faces. Otherwise an inhuman emptiness sat enthroned in the gaping theater (the comic journal, *Charivari,* sniggered that if the Song of the Rat went unnoticed it was because there was not so much as a cat in the house!). From the outset Berlioz knew himself ruined, materially and spiritually. It was less the few remaining francs saved on his travels which mattered than the irreparable hurt done the morale of the afflicted man. "Nothing in my artistic career wounded me more deeply than this unexpected indifference," he was to write in his Memoirs—lapsing, for once, into pitiful understatement! Not till 1877 was "The Damnation of Faust" revived in Paris, by which time the composer had been dead eight years.

Although Berlioz recouped some of his financial losses from the "Faust" misadventure when he went to Russia the following year he was the plaything of destiny once again when, late in 1847, he accepted an invitation from Louis Antoine Jullien to go to London and conduct opera at the Drury Lane Theatre, of which Jullien was then the manager. This spectacular French adventurer and charlatan, who speculated ruinously, went to jail for debt and died in a lunatic asylum, failed shortly after Berlioz suffered himself to be inveigled into what he thought would be a six years' engagement; and the composer, after giving a few concerts of his own music, found himself back in Paris by July, 1848. But England saw him again in 1851-52, when the New Philharmonic Society of London secured him as conductor, and in 1855 when he occupied the same post—not to mention a visit two years earlier when he was lured across the Channel to witness a Covent Garden representation of his first opera, "Benvenuto Cellini." This turned out almost as distressingly as "The Damnation of Faust" had done in Paris.

It is one of the real misfortunes of musical history that Hector Berlioz and Richard Wagner never became to each other the kinsmen and spiritual brothers they should have been. Some unhappy flaw in their respective natures always thwarted a consummation which, one feels, fate should have preordained. Or some barrier sprang up between them precisely at the moment they should best have complemented each other. They had, in the larger sense, the same ideals, the same luminous visions, the same majestic aims, the same reluctance to palter and to compromise. They were both tortured by nerves and exacerbated by futile suspicions and jealousies. Yet each had the true measure of the other's importance, whether admitted or not. Prejudices and preconceptions, sometimes artificially fostered, if not fed by envy or rankling disappointment had a way of cropping up to blind them as soon as they gave promise of seeing eye to eye. Wagner was the stronger of the two, not only as to creative power but in toughness of fiber. But if they were not equally matched, the differences and asperities of the one fitted perfectly into the natural flaws and crudities of the other, as Wagner himself once took occasion to point out.

Berlioz appears to have recognized in Wagner, much as he may have resented it, a force of the future which sooner or later must challenge him. All the same, it is wrong to imagine that Wagner underrated his French rival, however much he discerned the weaknesses of his work. His appreciation of the artist Berlioz was broader and more fundamental than the appreciation of Berlioz for him, which was so often soured by jealousy and blinded by bias. Wagner was incontestably sincere when he wrote: "We must honor Berlioz as the true renewer of modern music." Too few people are familiar with that extraordinary episode at Bayreuth, long after the Frenchman's death, when the aging Wagner flew into a towering rage on hearing the still youthful Felix Mottl criticize some detail of a Berlioz work. "When a master like Berlioz writes something you are too shallow to grasp, your duty is to accept it without question or murmur!" he had 'screamed at his astonished disciple.

Only once did the pair draw close enough to justify the belief that they might have developed, under more hospitable circumstances, a lasting friendship. This was in 1855, when the two men, in the depths of discouragement, met in London whither Wagner had come to conduct the Old Philharmonic. The improved relations were only temporary. The creater of "Tristan" appreciated that the jealous Marie Recio stood in the way of any lasting rapprochement. And he confided to Liszt that "a malicious wife can ruin a brilliant man . . . and bring out the worst aspects of his character; indeed, I have sometimes to wonder if God would not have done better to have left women out of the scheme of creation." In 1861, at the "Tannhäuser" fiasco at the Paris Opéra, Berlioz played a part that reflects eternal discredit on his memory, even if the shabby treatment he so often endured at the hands of his countrymen could account for his spitefulness.

* * *

The domestic situation of Berlioz had hopelessly deteriorated. Harriet, lame, coarse, shrewish had lost the last vestiges of her once admired beauty and talent. She was in due course to suffer paralytic strokes and then to become bedridden. Her son, Louis, having grown to young manhood, became an "aspirant-marinier" at Le Havre and decided to follow the sea, inheriting an early but unfulfilled ambition of his father. A true sailor he had a wife in every port and Hector, who was aware of the wanderer's inclinations, sometimes longed to meet those grandchildren of his he knew lived scattered through the hemispheres. Now and then Louis would return briefly to Paris and look in on his wretched mother at her little house on the hill of Montmartre. Occasionally he would seek out his father at his domicile near the Place Pigalle—though only when Mare Recio was out! The moment he heard her footsteps in the hall he would flee. He could not pardon his father and he said so unmistakably. So did others! To all reproaches the unhappy composer had only one helpless answer: "What would you? I love her."

Yet if that far-off adoration of his Ophelia and Juliet had, apparently, long since turned to ashes, something like retribution was to overtake him. For years he had been paying her routine visits, understanding her solitude even as she divined his misery. But early in March, 1854, he was called to her bedside and found her dying. At that, he was not even granted the wretched solace of receiving her last breath! Harriet expired a few moments after he had left the house on some trivial errand. The blow was far more terrible than Hector had thought possible. In a flash he recognized that he really loved the wife more than he did the mistress; and in prodigious rebellion he cursed "that stupid God, atrocious in his infinite indifference." To his son he wrote: "You will never know what your mother and I suffered because of each other and it was these sufferings which brought us so close together. It was as impossible for me to live with her as without her!" He was to see her once again! Ten years later they exhumed her and, in Hector's presence, placed her ghastly remains in a new coffin and reinterred them in the Montmartre Cemetery.

In October, 1854, Berlioz legalized the situation of Marie Recio by marrying her.

*   *   *

More wanderings lay ahead of him. He could have gone to New York, had he so chosen, and conducted concerts there. Rightly or wrongly he declined the offer. But in 1855 he harvested rich honors at a Berlioz Festival which his untiring champion, Liszt, staged in Weimar. A work which greatly stirred the audience at the Weimar Court Theatre was the newly composed "L'Enfance du Christ." This exquisite "legend," as simple, transparent and unpretentious as most of his other works are huge in scale and demanding, is a delicate little trilogy divided into sections respectively called "Herod's Dream," "The Flight to Egypt" and "The Arrival in Sais." It looked, for a while, like a turn in Hector's fortunes. Almost wherever the oratorio was performed it met with a favor to which the composer was quite unaccustomed. In Paris there actually were ovations and the press spoke of a "masterpiece"!

Berlioz was aware that Wagner, slowly but surely, was elaborating his gigantic "Nibelungen" project and he, too, became gradually filled with a scheme for a mythological opera. His old love for Virgil's gods and heroes, dating back to the days of his boyhood and his Latin readings in his father's library, reasserted itself. He dreamed of a vast fresco in which the siege of Troy, Aeneas, Hector, Priam, Cassandra, Dido and the rest of the splendid personages of the Mediterranean world should be combined in the action of a great lyric tragedy carried out "in the Shakespearian manner." But though the idea fired him it also terrified him as he thought of the giant efforts it involved and the disappointments it was sure to entail. He confided his ambitions and his fears to Liszt's friend, the Princess Caroline Sayn-Wittgenstein. It was she who spurred him to the task and overrode his doubts and scruples.

"You must create this opera, this lyric poem or whatever you choose to call it," the Princess insisted, and as he continued to plead the troubles it meant, she silenced him with a pretended severity: "Listen! If you shun the sufferings which this labor may and, indeed, ought to cause you—if you are so weak as to be afraid of it, if you refuse to dare everything for the sake of Dido and Cassandra, then stay away from me, I never want to see you again!"

It was a liberating word and Berlioz returned to Paris for the heart-breaking business of writing poem and music. He had foreseen its pains and obstacles only too clearly, but he wrestled furiously with them and kept the oath he had given. Somber and lonely, he composed, revised, expanded, cut down, suppressed and altered in a thousand different ways. The epic seemed to be taking all sorts of impractical forms and the composer realized that even all the conventional devices of dramaturgy might not avail to fit it for the theater. Two years of intensive work brought the end of the score in 1858. Meanwhile Berlioz had terminated his Memoirs, which he kept at the Conservatoire out of fear that his second wife, in the course of her often indiscreet searchings, might light upon some secrets he preferred to hide. In the end he confided the manuscript to Liszt, to thwart Marie's curiosity if he were to die. For Hector had been much haunted by thoughts of death as the time went by. Years of disappointment were more and more taking toll of his nervous system. He was tortured by what the doctors called "intestinal neuralgia," against which medicine appeared to be unavailing.

"*Les Troyens*" was, in many ways, the supreme blow of his life and more than anything else his child of sorrow. In the year of its completion he tried in vain to have it sung at the Opéra. Three years later that institution accepted it but did not give it. Finally, Léon Carvalho, manager of the Théâtre Lyrique, mounted it on November 4, 1863. The composer had found it necessary to divide his six and a half hour opera into two parts—"La Prise de Troie" and "Les Troyens à Carthage"—to make a performance possible at all. At that there were cuts, changes, revisions without end, and to this day versions and "editions" have been found indispensable if the work is to be made a practical stage piece. The first presentation did not include the "Prise de Troie" half, and this portion of the work, of which Cassandra, the composer's beloved "heroic virgin" is the central figure, Berlioz was never to witness. In spite of innumerable difficulties and the unfinished state of the representation the piece was moderately successful at first, the reviews in the main favorable, the box office fair and Hector himself delighted with as much of his creation as he heard. But the worries and tribulations the opera involved (for any change he wanted Hector had to pay out of his own pocket) brought a nervous breakdown and he managed to attend no more than four performances. As soon as his back was turned the management cut and slashed the score without compunction. By the end of a month audiences had fallen off to such an extent that, before Christmas, "Les Troyens" disappeared from the repertoire. This new blow promised to break the unhappy composer's spirit altogether. "My career is finished," he told someone who hoped for an early resumption of the work. "I have neither hopes, illusions nor great ideas left," he reflected bitterly; "my contempt for the stupidity and dishonesty of people has reached its peak . . ." And when he was told that audiences were beginning to flock to hear some work of his he would reply: "Yes, they are coming; but I am going!"

On June 14, 1862, Marie Recio died suddenly of a heart attack. The blow struck Hector much less violently than did the passing of his first wife. Possibly the circumstance that he was engaged on a new work at the time somewhat blunted the edge of his grief. This latest creation—his last, as it proved—was the two act opera comique, "*Béatrice et Bénédict,"* a lyric version of "Much Ado About Nothing"—given for the first time at the newly built casino in Baden-Baden. "Béatrice et Bénédict" proved to be a repetition of the "Enfance du Christ" surprise—a brilliant success from the first. Berlioz was happy, but also cynical. "People are now discovering that I have melody, that I can be jubilant and even humorous!" he wrote. Another triumph of the new work at Weimar, in 1863, further demonstrated that the piece had been born under a lucky star. Like Verdi, thirty years later, Berlioz was disposed to conclude his creative career with a comedy inspired by his idolized Shakespeare. "I have written the final note with which I shall ever soil a scrap of music paper. No more of that! Othello's occupation's gone; I should like to have nothing more to do—nothing, absolutely nothing!" Actually, he had much more to do—conducting, writing, traveling, suffering. Yet so far as making music was concerned he was finished.

After Marie Recio's death Hector lived with his mother-in-law, whom he esteemed and who, in turn, loved him. Love of a different kind still lured him on. He met a young girl, by name Amélie and felt a fresh upsurge of romantic passion. But in six months she, too, was dead. Meanwhile Berlioz and his son had drawn much closer together, spiritually. Yet Louis was generally far from France and the pair, though they corresponded, saw but little of each other. One evening a number of Hector's closest musical friends, angered by the persistent neglect of the composer by his own countrymen, staged a little private glorification in his honor. They waited for the guest of the occasion and when time passed and he did not come a messenger was sent to fetch him. Berlioz lay on the floor of his room, writhing in an agony of grief. He had just received word that Louis was dead in Havana!

He was inspired by a sudden wish to renew one of the ties of his boyhood. And the thoughts of the eternal adolescent turned to Estelle Duboeuf, his "Stella Montis" of long ago. She was now a widowed old lady, patrician and proper, who had had a number of children, all of whom she had carefully reared and some of whom she had lost. She lived in Lyon and to that city Hector presently turned his steps. Estelle Fornier, amazed by the unexpected visit and the importunities of her aging and weather-beaten guest, received him in kindly fashion, alluded tactfully to his agitated life but, with gentle firmness, discouraged his pleas for a somewhat closer friendship. Nevertheless, Berlioz was carried away by the mere joy of the meeting; and he chose to place an extravagant interpretation on a few commonplace phrases of hers and the words "affectionate sentiments" with which she had concluded a brief message. He continued from afar to worship this mirage and to build it up into elaborate fictions. He corresponded further with the decorous old lady, imagined vain things and confided to the Princess Wittgenstein "this kind of suffering is indispensable to me."

Meanwhile, he was off again on travels. In 1866 he conducted *"La Damnation de Faust"* in Vienna and in 1867 led half a dozen concerts in St. Petersburg where he made the acquaintance of Balakireff, Tschaikowsky and other Russian musicians, till, unable to endure the rigors of that climate, he returned to France, longing passionately for the sunshine and warmth of the Riviera. Walking on the beach at Monaco he suffered a bad fall the consequence, it appears, of a slight stroke, which recurred a few days later. He rallied, however, though once back in Paris he found it necessary to spend long and dreary days in bed. He had made his will, leaving his books and scores to the Conservatoire and distributing his meager "fortune" to his nieces, besides settling a sum of eighteen hundred francs on Estelle Fornier (which she is said to have declined) and providing a tiny income for his mother-in-law. Of his various crowns, laurel wreaths and other "trophies" he made a superb bonfire! "I feel that I am going to die," he wrote his Russian friend, Vladimir Stassoff. "I believe in nothing any more . . . I am exorbitantly bored. Farewell! Writing causes me no end of trouble."

Gradually his faculties refused to function; little by little his brain became clouded, his tongue thickened, he made no attempt to talk and appeared to want nothing. On March 8, 1869, the long-embattled and sore-tried fighter, who had never attained inner or outer harmony, found peace. A final touch of irony was provided by the fact that his graveside valedictory was spoken, in the name of the Conservatoire, by a certain Elwart, to whom Berlioz had once said: "If *you* are to make a speech at my funeral I prefer not to die!"

H. F. P.

Richard Wagner

BORN: LEIPZIG, MAY 22, 1813. DIED: VENICE, FEB. 13, 1883.

He had one mistress to whom he was faithful to the day of his death: Music. Not for a single moment did he ever compromise with what he believed, with what he dreamed. There is not a line of his music that could have been conceived by a little mind. Even when he is dull, or downright bad, he is dull in the grand manner. There is greatness about his worst mistakes.—DEEMS TAYLOR.

No ARTIST HAS KNOWN a fiercer urge to create than Richard Wagner. None has labored more mightily to indoctrinate mankind with his convictions. None has been more scathing in his contempt of reaction, of pretense, of outdated mannerisms. He wanted his works to be sagas of epic spiritual and moral power; and, whether or not he achieved his aims, he wrote music that is voluptuous and emotionally overwhelming.

In a way he glamorized human suffering or, at least, that side of human suffering expressed through the symbol of renunciation, which one encounters frequently in his operas. His librettos are filled with super-noble purpose, with superhuman aspiration. In *Der Ring des Nibelungen* he created a world of divinities who are imperfect and humans who unconsciously strive toward perfection. It is not a new world, nor is it a brave one, except through the promise of humanity's elevation. With *Tristan und Isolde* he rises to metaphysical heights in his argument. The theme generally is again renunciation, the attaining of perfection and solace through it. One comes upon it again in *Die Meistersinger*, in *The Flying Dutchman*, in *Parsifal*, and so on.

Yet for an artist whose works so idealized all that is good and lofty and noble, Wagner did little in his own life that could possibly approach those superior motives. There is a distinction to be made, therefore, between Wagner the man and Wagner the artist.

Richard Wagner was born in Leipzig, on May 22, 1813, the son (allegedly) of Karl Friedrich and Johanna Wagner. The theory has been advanced that the composer's real father was Ludwig Geyer, an intimate friend of the family, who married Frau Wagner about a year after her first husband's death.

Even as a young boy Richard was tremendously fond of the theater. His mother, not particularly interested in it, threatened to hurl a curse on his head if he attempted to make a career of the stage.

In any case, when Geyer died several years later, Richard was sent to Eisleben to become apprenticed to a goldsmith. After a year of puttering around as a tyro goldsmith he returned to Dresden where the family now was. In that city he found many opportunities to express his dramatic urge.

Soon the family moved back to Leipzig and Wagner began to study with Theodor Weinlig, who was one of the authorities on counterpoint.

His early essays in music (composition now being his aim) were nothing to become excited about. But the musical life of Dresden and his intercourse with leading figures of the day worked their influence on him nevertheless. He spent nights copying Beethoven's Fifth and Ninth Symphonies. He wrote an overture which Heinrich Dorn, director of the Leipzig Theater, liked well enough to perform, but it was poorly received. With characteristic suddenness he entered Leipzig University as a *studiosus musicae,* really a student with few privileges. But he plunged with great gusto into all sorts of student activity, which was, apparently, the real reason for his enrollment at the school.

One of his sisters, Rosalie, and his brother both followed the acting profession, and they gave him the benefit of their counsel, though no one knows how much of it he followed.

He wrote a symphony and then began work on an opera, *Die Hochzeit,* which he never completed. That was in 1832. In the same year he tried again, actually finishing a work entitled *Die Feen.* It was rejected, but Wagner, after one or two little pouts, regained his composure. He accepted an engagement as conductor at Magdeburg and in the course of his work he composed another opera, *Das Liebesverbot,* which, however, was given one performance.

At Magdeburg he met Minna Planer, a member of the operatic troupe, who later became his wife. When she left for Königsberg he followed her and obtained a conductor's position at the theater in that city. Then came a succession of changes. The restless Wagner scurried about with the spontaneity of a gypsy. When things lagged in one place he quickly moved to another. So that we find him going to Riga, where he directed both opera and symphony, to London, to Paris. In the last named he thought he might finally awaken a musical public to his genius. But he suffered untold agonies. Poverty possessed him. He and his wife lived in constant economic turmoil. With all that he managed to compose two more operas, *Rienzi* and *The Flying Dutchman.* Both were produced at Dresden under the sponsorship of Meyerbeer, then a dominant figure in German music.

All this time, though, he wrote a host of compositions, besides penning many articles on music for various publications, and his fame spread. His rebellious temperament got him into difficulty often enough, but he managed, most of the time, to slip out of it. However, in Dresden, where he officiated as a conductor of the Royal Opera, he clashed with certain musical authorities who would not brook his bold opposition to standard ideas. Yet still another opera came to the light of performance when *Tannhäuser* was given its first hearing, again at Dresden, on October 19, 1845.

During the previous summer Wagner began work on the libretto of *Die Meistersinger* while vacationing at Marienbad. He soon abandoned it, taking on the libretto for *Lohengrin* instead. The following year saw the completion of the *Lohengrin* score. In 1848 he joined a revolutionary movement that spread through Europe, launched by the French Revolution. When the disturbance was quelled some months later, he fled to Switzerland, but remained there for a short time, heading soon for Paris.

His wife refused to join him there, remembering too well the poverty of the previous stay in the French capital. But he started on *Siegfried's Death,* which was to grow into the gigantic *Ring.* He flitted about again, leaving Paris, returning a little later.

Wagner fell in love with Jessie Taylor Laussot, who proved a benefactress in a financial way. In the meantime, he decided to leave Minna forever. In Zurich, whither he repaired, he labored unceasingly on the libretto for *The Young Siegfried*. Then he created the subject of *The Valkyrie* and finally that of *The Rheingold*.

It is amusing to note that he wrote his *Ring* librettos in reverse order, that is, from what is now *Götterdämmerung* back to *Das Rheingold*. Having hit upon a huge theme, he found it increasingly necessary to broaden its scope, thus accounting for the four operas. Parenthetically, however, he wrote the music in the correct order.

Now in Wagner's life there appears a strange and beautiful influence, Mathilde Wesendonck, wife of a very wealthy silk merchant. It has been pointed out that under the spell of this beguiling woman his composing flourished as never before. At the home of the Wesendoncks he completed the poem for *Tristan und Isolde*. It is not known how friendly Richard and Mathilde were, but this is fact: Wagner left his friends' abode because he would not bring grief upon Otto Wesendonck.

He went once more to Paris where some very ridiculous things happened having to do with a suggested ballet for the opera *Tannhäuser*. Wagner, adamant, would not change the order of his work merely to please influential gentlemen of the Jockey Club.

In 1864, when Wagner was fifty-one, he settled in Munich—he had been forgiven for his revolutionary surge—and in this musically flourishing city he came under the high patronage of King Ludwig of Bavaria. Here he renewed acquaintance with Liszt's daughter Cosima, whom he had met some years before. She was now married to Hans von Bülow, a highly gifted conductor. The composer and Cosima were thrown together a lot and their mutual regard soon ripened into love. Poor little Minna, who had been ill for a long period, died in 1866, a piece of news which saddened Wagner greatly.

That same year, however, he and Cosima took a place at Triebschen on Lake Lucerne in Switzerland. Bülow, at first angered by his wife's deed, soon came to realize the inevitability of it. Besides, he adored Wagner and his music. He acted sanely therefore, sacrificing his personal feelings for the sake of Wagner's art. Cosima and Richard were married in 1870.

At Triebschen he completed *Die Meistersinger, Siegfried,* and the first two acts of *Götterdämmerung,* besides writing any number of treatises, articles, and the like. Here, too, the idea of a great festival theater was born in him, and the originality of the thing soon won many influential supporters to the cause. By 1871 a site was found for it at Bayreuth, Germany. The next year he put the finishing touches to the *Ring* and the Bayreuth project grew in proportion to his frantic efforts to raise money for it. In all, it took some four years to erect this shrine to Wagnerian music. And finally, the première of the Wagnerian Cycle, running from August 13 to 16, was a tremendous success, in spite of the heartaches, the headaches, and the discouragement.

With all that he had already accomplished, Wagner could have retired to the easy life he often so fervently spoke about. But the urge to compose never left him. He set to work on *Parsifal,* the poem he had completed some months before. When the opera was all finished he endeavored with his usual kinetic energy to raise money for its production. It was given its first performance on July 26, 1882. There were sixteen more performances.

Wagner, after all the excitement of Bayreuth, left for a vacation in Venice. In spite of repeated heart attacks, he considered seriously the writing of another symphony. But he had done his work. There was to be no second symphony. Wagner died of his heart illness on February 13, 1883. He was buried at Bayreuth.

Overture to "Rienzi"

Bulwer's *Rienzi* revived an old desire of Wagner's to make an opera out of the story of the last of the Tribunes. He was in Dresden during the summer of 1837 and there he read Barmann's translation of the Bulwer novel. However, he did not begin actual work until the following July. First, of course, came the text. Later that month he started on the music. By May 1839, he had completed two acts. The remainder of the score, with the exception of the Overture, was written and orchestrated in Paris. The Overture was finished on October 23, 1840.

On October 20, 1842, *Rienzi* was given its world première at the Royal Saxon Court Theater, Dresden. Amusingly, the performance began at 6 p.m., and it went on and on until midnight. America was not to become acquainted with the opera until March 4, 1878, when it was given at the Academy of Music, New York.

The thematic material employed in the Overture stems from music in the opera itself, such as the "long-sustained, swelled and diminished

A on the trumpet," which is the signal for the people's uprising against the nobles; Rienzi's Prayer; a theme of the chorus, *Gegrüsst sei hoher Tag;* the theme of the revolutionary forces, *Santo spirito cavaliere;* the stretto of the second Finale, *Rienzi, dir sei Preis;* and a subject similar to the phrase of the nobles set to the words, *Ha, dieser Gnade Schmach erdruckt das stolze Herz!*

The score of the Overture calls for one piccolo, two flutes, two oboes, two clarinets, two bassoons, two valve-horns, two plain horns, one serpent (nowadays replaced by the double-bassoon), two valve trumpets, two plain trumpets, three trombones, one ophicleide (replaced by the bass-tuba), two snare-drums, bass drum, triangle, cymbals, and strings.

Overture to "The Flying Dutchman"

This compact and brilliantly written Overture calls for the following instrumentation: piccolo, two flutes, two oboes, English horn, two clarinets, four horns, two bassoons, two trumpets, three trombones, bass tuba, kettledrums, harp, and strings.

John Runciman once remarked about this music, "It is the atmosphere of the sea that counts; the roar of the billows, the 'hui!' of the wind, the dashing and plunging . . . The sea, indeed, is the background, foreground, the whole environment of the drama . . . The smell and atmosphere of the sea is maintained with extraordinary vividness to the last bar."

In the construction of the Overture Wagner makes important use of the theme of the Dutchman, which appears in the opening measure by horns and bassoons, and of the up-and-down theme of Senta, the Angel of Mercy, softly and tenderly sung by English horn, horns and bassoons. This is the theme which at the conclusion of the piece rises to a triumphant sonority, indicative of redemption attained.

Overture to "Tannhäuser"

The first concert performance of this well-known Overture took place at Leipzig, on February 12, 1846, under the direction of Mendelssohn. The event was a benefit for the Gewandhaus Orchestra Pension Fund.

Wagner himself furnished a "program" for the Overture when the musicians performing it at a Zurich concert requested an explanation of the music. The "program" in a translation by William Ashton Ellis follows:

"To begin with, the orchestra leads before us the Pilgrim's Chorus alone; it draws near, then swells into a mighty outpour, and passes finally away.—Evenfall; last echo of the chant. As night breaks, magic sights and sounds appear, a rosy mist floats up, exultant shouts assail our ears, the whirlings of a fearsomely voluptuous dance are seen. These are the Venusberg's seductive spells, that show themselves at dead of night to those whose breasts are fired by the daring of the senses. Attracted by the tempting show, a shapely human form draws nigh; 'tis Tannhäuser, Love's minstrel . . . Venus herself appears to him . . . As the Pilgrim's Chant draws closer, yet closer, as the day drives farther back the night, that whir and soughing of the air— which had erewhile sounded like the eerie cries of the soul condemned —now rises, too, to ever gladder waves; so that when the sun ascends at last in splendor, and the Pilgrims' Chant proclaims in ecstasy to all the world, to all that lives and moves thereon, Salvation won, this wave itself swells out the tidings of sublimest joy. 'Tis the carol of the Venusberg itself, redeemed from the curse of impiousness, this cry we hear amid the hymn of God. So wells and leaps each pulse of Life in chorus of Redemption; and both dissevered elements, both soul and senses, God and Nature, unite in the astonishing kiss of hallowed Love."

The Overture to Tannhäuser is scored for piccolo, two flutes, two oboes, two clarinets, two bassoons, four horns, three trumpets, three trombones, bass tuba, kettledrums, cymbals, triangle, tambourine, and strings.

Bacchanale from "Tannhäuser"

The opera was first produced at the Royal Opera House, Dresden, on October 19, 1845. Sixteen years later, thanks to the interest and influence of Princess Metternich, wife of the Austrian Ambassador to France, the work was introduced to Paris. For that production Wagner extended his first scene to include a Bacchanale, the reasons for this being as amusing to us as they must have been tragic to Wagner. The Princess revealed, in an article written for the *Pall Mall Magazine* (London, 1894) some of the reasons for the failure of the opera there, and it was a complete failure. The Princess says:

"The day of the performance drew nigh and in most circles little good will was confessed. It was stated generally that a protest should be made against the abominable futurist music, and it was rumored that stormy scenes might be expected at the Opera. In the clubs men were annoyed because Wagner would not have a regular ballet, but only a few poses of the ballerinas in the Venusberg. The club subscribers to the Opera expected a ballet at nine-thirty sharp, no matter what the opera. This, at least, was the custom of the time. No one who knew anything of art could conceive where a ballet could be introduced into the midst of 'Tannhäuser.' Wagner declared that he would not accede to the silly wishes of the subscribers, because he could not. And he was perfectly right, but his refusal was to be paid for dearly."

Wagner had entertained great hopes for this Parisian production of *Tannhäuser*. To produce his work at the justly famed Opera was reason enough, what with that organization's habit of letting expense go hang. He labored industriously at making revisions, which included a complete rewrite of the Bacchanalian scene as well as of the music for Venus and Tannhäuser in Act 1.

When he had completed his revisions he played the music for several friends. Charles Nuitter, one of these, reported on that private hearing as follows:

"When we arrived the composer sat down to the piano. He played with indescribable animation and fury. His hands pounded the keys, and at the same time he strove to acquaint me with the action of the scene, crying out the entrance of the various groups. 'Arrival of the fauns and satyrs; all are put to flight; the confusion mounts to its climax,' he flung at me, and his hands continued to bang the keys, the musical delirium always augmenting. When he was piling on a succession of quivering chords Wagner suddenly cried, 'Now a crash of thunder. We are all dead!' At that moment a wagon of paving stones discharged its load into the street, thus producing a prolonged and terrible noise. Wagner turned round and regarded us with stupefaction, his eyes staring wildly. It took us some moments to recover from this stirring of our feelings. Thus it was that I was initiated into the new music."

The first Paris performance of *Tannhäuser* took place on March 13, 1861. That was the first of three fiascos in the French capital. The second occurred on March 18. Napoleon III and the Empress both attended, but their presence had no effect on the rest of the audience, whose cat-calls, howls, and kindred strange noises were even louder, if not funnier, than the first time.

The work was given for the third time on March 24. This was not a regular subscription performance, and it seemed to all and sundry that finally a Parisian audience would be honest and unprejudiced in its attitude toward the opera. However, the composer's enemies had bought out the house and the result was the same. Whereupon Wagner withdrew his score. *Tannhäuser* was not given again in Paris until thirty-four years later.

PRELUDE TO "LOHENGRIN"

In the summer of 1845, while Wagner was at Marienbad, he worked out the plan for *Lohengrin*. The libretto he wrote during the following winter. Then came a topsy-turvy scheme of creation. In composing the music he began with the hero's Narrative in the last act, "because the monologue contained the most significant musical germs in the whole score." He finished the third act on March 25, 1847, the first act on June 8 of that year, the second act on August 2, and the Prelude on August 28. The orchestration was done during the following winter and spring. Franz Liszt conducted the première of the opera at Weimar on August 28, 1850. The Prelude was played for the first time in concert on January 17, 1853, at the Leipzig Gewandhaus, Julius Rietz conducting.

Discussing the Prelude, William Foster Apthorp wrote:

"Like the hero's career in the opera, it begins, as it were, in the clouds, then gradually descends farther and farther until it embraces all the lower tones of the orchestra, and then returns to the clouds again. Its single theme is developed in free polyphony by various successive groups of instruments, each of which groups proceeds with free counter-thematic work as the next group enters with the theme. First we have the violins *piano* in their higher registers; then come the flutes, oboes, and clarinets; then the violas, 'cellos, horns, bassoons, and double-basses; lastly the trumpets, trombones, and the tuba *fortissimo;* then comes the *decrescendo,* ending *pianissimo* in the high violins and flutes."

The composer, who could descant with the best of them, paraded his rhetorical gifts on the Prelude (the translation is by William Ashton Ellis):

"Love seemed to have vanished from a world of hatred and quarreling; as a lawgiver she was no longer to be found among the communities of men. Emancipating itself from barren care for gain and possession, the sole arbiter of all worldly intercourse, the human heart's unquenchable love-longing, again at length craved to appease a want which, the more warmly and intensely it made itself felt under the pressure of reality, was the less easy to satisfy on account of this very reality. It was beyond the confines of the actual world that man's ecstatic imaginative power fixed the source as well as the output of this incomprehensible impulse of love, and from the desire of a comforting sensuous conception of this supersensuous idea invested it with a wonderful form, which, under the name of the 'Holy Grail,' though conceived as actually existing, yet unapproachably far off, was believed in, longed for, and sought for.

"The Holy Grail was the costly vessel out of which, at the Last Supper, our Saviour drank with His disciples, and in which His blood was received when out of love for His brethren He suffered upon the cross, and which till this day has been preserved with lively zeal as the source of undying love; albeit, at one time this cup of salvation was taken away from unworthy mankind, but at length was brought back again from the heights of heaven by a band of angels, and delivered into the keeping of fervently loving, solitary men who, wondrously strengthened and blessed by its presence, and purified in heart, were consecrated as the earthly champions of eternal love.

"This miraculous delivery of the Holy Grail, escorted by an angelic host, and the handing of it over into the custody of highly favored men, was selected by the author of 'Lohengrin' for the introduction of his drama, as the subject to be musically portrayed; just as here, for the sake of explanation, he may be allowed to bring it forward as an object for the mental receptive power of his hearers.

"To the enraptured look of the highest celestial longing for love, the clearest blue atmosphere of heaven at first seems to condense itself into a wonderful, scarcely perceptible but magically pleasing vision; with gradually increasing precision the wonder-working angelic host is delineated in infinitely delicate lines as, conveying the holy vessel (the

Grail) in its midst, it insensibly descends from the blazing heights of heaven. As the vision grows more and more distinct, as it hovers over the surface of the earth, a narcotic fragrant odor issues from its midst; entrancing vapors well up from it like golden clouds, and overpower the sense of the astonished gazer, who, from the lowest depths of his palpitating heart, feels himself wonderfully urged to holy emotions.

"Now throbs the heart with the pain of ecstasy, now with the heavenly joy which agitates the breast of the beholder; with irresistible might all the repressed germs of love rise up in it, stimulated to a wondrous growth by the vivifying magic of the vision; however much it can expand, it will break at last with vehement longing, impelled to self-sacrifice and toward an ultimate dissolving again in the supremest bliss as, imparting comfort the nearer it approaches, the divine vision reveals itself to our entranced senses. And when at last the holy vessel shows itself in the marvel of undraped reality, and clearly revealed to him to whom it is vouchsafed to behold it, as the Holy Grail, which from out of its divine contents spreads broadcast the sunbeams of highest love, like the lights of a heavenly fire that stirs all hearts with the heat of the flame of its everlasting glow, the beholder's brain reels —he falls down in a state of adoring annihilation. Yet upon him who is thus lost in love's rapture the Grail pours down its blessing, with which it designates him as its chosen knight; the blazing flame subsides into an ever-decreasing brightness, which now, like a gasp of breath of the most unspeakable joy and emotion, spreads itself over the surface of the earth and fills the breast of him who adores with a blessedness of which he had no foreboding. With chaste rejoicing, and smilingly looking down, the angelic host mounts again to heaven's heights; the source of love, which had dried up the earth, has been brought by them to the world again—the Grail they have left in the custody of the pure-minded men, in whose hands its contents overflow as a source of blessing—and the angelic host vanishes in the glorious light of heaven's blue sky, as, before, it thence came down."

"Der Ring des Nibelungen"

A colossal work in four parts, the *Ring's* central theme is one of redemption. The Norse God Wotan, addicted to the amassing of power, may not achieve it through deceit or treachery. By trickery he obtains from the Nibelung Alberich a ring possessing untold powers, made of the gold of the Rhine. Alberich hisses a curse, in losing it, which only a pure hero acting as a free agent may remove.

Wotan's attempts to get the ring, his often devious reasoning, and the panoplied purpose of the whole, make of the tetralogy an epic study in the emotions, the humanities, the loyalties, the shortcomings, in short, in the whole moral and spiritual concept of the individual and society.

THE RIDE OF THE VALKYRIES FROM "DIE WALKÜRE"

In the time intervening between *Das Rheingold* and *Die Walküre* Wotan has worked out a plan to save the gods from destruction. The ring must not fall into the wrong hands, those of Alberich, for instance, for the wily and greedy creature knows full well its powers. The thing to do, then, is to regain possession of it without "craft or violence." He must employ some means above such devices. Consequently his plan is to bring into being a hero who shall not be his servitor, but rather the agency for the accomplishment through a free, totally unguided will. Thus we come to the saga of the Walsungs, human descendants of Wotan, and one of them, Siegmund, is the hero chosen.

The Valkyries are the nine daughters of Wotan by the earth goddess of wisdom, Erda. And of these Brünhilde is Wotan's favorite. She interferes with her father's wishes in order to aid Siegmund, however, and she is given the penalty of mortality by her father. The duet in the last act of the opera between Wotan and Brünhilde is one of the most moving sequences in all Wagner.

The Ride of the Valkyries is an excerpt from the music which leads into Act III, made into a concert piece by Wagner himself. A great rock dominates the scene in the opera. It is the Valkyr Rock where now the maidens are gathering. Fully equipped in shining mail, carrying spears and shields, they ride swiftly through the storm. At the curtain's rise only four of the maidens are discernible on the stage. The others may be heard announcing their entrance with the exultant Valkyr call. The music surges to great heights of sound, wild, untrammeled, passionate, driven relentlessly by powerful rhythms.

A SIEGFRIED IDYL

In a letter dated June 25, 1870, Wagner wrote of his wife Cosima, "She has defied every disapprobation and taken upon herself every condemnation. She has borne to me a wonderfully beautiful boy, whom I call boldly Siegfried; he is now growing, together with my work [he was working then on the opera *Siegfried;* hence the name]; he gives me a new long life, which at last has attained a meaning. Thus we get along without the world, from which we have wholly withdrawn."

The composer wrote the music of the *Idyl*—originally called the *Triebschen Idyl*—as a birthday gift for his wife. On Christmas morning, 1870, Wagner and a group of musicians assembled on the stairs of his home at Triebschen and performed the lovely music, which, cramped though the musicians were because of tight quarters, obtained a fine rendering, according to ear-witnesses.

When the *Idyl* was first played in Berlin, in 1878, a music critic gave it as gospel that the music was taken from the second act of the opera *Siegfried*. The truth of the matter is that the *Idyl,* while based on several themes from the opera besides that of a folk song, is a complete entity in itself, for the themes were developed in a manner entirely different from their treatment in the opera. In addition to which, it must be remembered that the folk song, *Schlaf', mein Kind, schlaf'ein,* does not appear in the opera at all.

Forest Murmurs from "Siegfried"

The music for this sequence is taken from the scene before the dragon's cave in the second act of *Siegfried*. In arranging it for concert use, Wagner gave it the name *Waldweben (Forest Weavings* or *Forest Murmurs)*. The young hero Siegfried is left to his own thoughts by the dwarf Mime. The rustling of the leaves is first heard in D minor, then in B major. Siegfried is daydreaming. He ponders on the question of his origin. He knows that he is not of Mime's blood, and the clarinet, paralleling, and explaining the idea, intones the theme of the Volsungs.

As his thoughts turn to his mother the Love-Life motive emerges through the 'cellos and violas and double basses, next in all the strings, and finally horns and bassoons take it over. A solo violin plays a subject associated with Freia, goddess of youth and love. The rustling of the leaves is again heard and the theme of the Forest Bird comes in by way of the oboe, flute, clarinet and other wood winds. The music ends in a Vivace which incorporates the Fire, the Siegfried, and the Slumber motives, besides the twittering of the Forest Bird.

EXCERPTS FROM "GÖTTERDÄMMERUNG"—SIEGFRIED'S RHINE JOURNEY

This music comes between the Prologue and the first act. It is frequently referred to as a "Scherzo." Siegfried has taken leave of his wife Brünhilde and, exhorted by her, sallies forth on new adventures. The music brings up the hero's past achievements, whose themes are presented in new guises. They are cleverly interwoven, the pattern being rich in colors and effects as well as in sonorities. Through the orchestral web may be detected threads akin to such thematic ideas as Siegfried's horn call, the Rhine motive, the motive of Renunciation, the motive of the Rhine Daughters, the motive of the Rheingold and, last, that of the Nibelungs' servitude. Climactic and exultant, the music yet gives forth many implications of impending tragedy.

FUNERAL MUSIC

Through the trickery of Hagen, villainous half-brother of Gunther, Siegfried is slain. His body is lifted tenderly by Gunther's followers and carried back to the hall of the Gibichungs. As that happens on the stage, the orchestra sings out with a giant dirge, lamenting the fall of the Volsungs while reviewing previous moments in the history of the tragic race. There is the reference to the love of Siegmund and Sieglinde from *Die Walküre*. Toward its conclusion the horns and bass trumpet announce sonorously the motive of Siegfried the hero. There is a rhythmic variant of the horn call and with the dying away of the music Brünhilde is momentarily mentioned.

BRÜNHILDE'S IMMOLATION

The end of the gigantic *Ring,* specifically Brünhilde's scene of immolation, is frequently performed in concert with a soprano soloist. The heroine's great monologue, delivered in the hall of the Gibichungs, writes finis to a drama that takes four separate operas to tell. In her grief over the death of her hero-husband she stills the "loud, unworthy" lamentations of the others who are gathered about the slain Siegfried. She commands them to erect a funeral pyre and to place the hero's body upon it. His ring is taken from his finger and she puts it on her own. After applying a torch to the pyre she leaps on her horse Grane and rushes into the flames.

Prelude and 'Love-Death' from "Tristan und Isolde"

In 1854, when Wagner was in the midst of composing the *Ring,* the idea for an opera on the Tristan theme came to him. Not till three years later, however, did he begin actual work on it, and the music-drama was finished in August 1859. Complications of various kinds interfered with the production of the opera, but it finally obtained its première at the Royal Court Theater in Munich, on June 10, 1865, under the direction of Hans von Bülow.

Wagner's version of the tale combines features from numerous legends. Very likely of Celtic origin, the story, as the German composer utilized it, makes room for myriad delvings into psychology and metaphysics, some of which are not easy to follow. We must assume, as Ernest Newman suggests, that the characters and their motivations were perfectly clear to the composer, if they seem not to be altogether to the listener. Here is the essence of the music-drama's plot, extracted from Wagner's own description:

We are told of Tristan and Isolde in an ancient love poem, which is "constantly fashioning itself anew, and has been adopted by every European language of the Middle Ages." Tristan, a faithful vassal of King Mark, woos Isolde for his king, yet not daring to reveal to her his own love. "Isolde, powerless to do otherwise, follows him as a bride to his lord." In the meantime the Goddess of Love, balked by all this, plans revenge. The Love Potion, which had been intended for the king in order to insure the marriage, is given to Tristan and Isolde to drink, a circumstance which ". . . opens their eyes to the truth and leads to the avowal that for the future they belong only to each other . . . The world, power, fame, splendor, honor, knighthood, fidelity, friendship, all are dissipated like an empty dream. One thing only remains: longing, longing, insatiable longing, forever springing up anew, pining and thirsting. Death, which means passing away, perishing, never awakening, their only deliverance . . . Shall we call it death? Or is it the hidden wonder-world out of which an ivy and vine, entwined with each other, grew upon Tristan's and Isolde's grave, as the legend tells us?"

The Prelude, A minor, 6-8, makes a very gradual and long *crescendo* to a mighty *fortissimo,* followed by a briefer *decrescendo,* which leads to a whispered *pianissimo.* Free as to form and ever widening in scope of development, it offers two chief themes: a phrase, uttered by the 'cellos, is united to another, given to the oboes, to form a subject called the "Love Potion" theme, or the theme of "Longing." Another theme, again announced by the 'cellos, "Tristan's Love Glance," is sensuous, even voluptuous in character.

After the Prelude, the orchestra enters into the "Liebestod" or "Love-Death," that passionate flow of phrases, taken mostly from the material in the second act Love-Duet. Isolde (in the opera) sings her song of sublimated desire. Franz Liszt is responsible for the application of the term "Liebestod" to that part of the music which originally had been named "Verklärung" by Wagner himself.

PRELUDE TO "DIE MEISTERSINGER VON NÜRNBERG"

"The completion of *Die Meistersinger,* Triebschen, Thursday, October 24, 1867, 8 o'clock in the evening, R. W." These words were inscribed on the last sheet of the manuscript of Wagner's only operatic comedy. This was some twenty-two years after the very first drafts were drawn at Marienbad. The doctor had ordered a complete rest. But rest to Wagner meant ennui. Perhaps, he thought, he might be able to rest while composing a lighter work. The idea took hold. He gave it considerable thought. He could just about see this airy piece's "rapid circulation through the European opera houses." Indeed, he judged that "something thoroughly light and popular" might be the thing to make his everlasting fame.

Hans Sachs, of course, is the hero of this masterpiece. A historic character, Sachs was built by the composer into something of an ideal of homespun charm and wit and philosophy. But Wagner also evened a score with an old enemy in his composition of this work. The music critic Eduard Hanslick appears as the crotchety, pedantic and unprincipled Beckmesser, thus earning for himself a ridiculous immortality.

How Wagner could have written this opera with all the troubles besetting him is hard to comprehend. Yet no financial snarls, domestic tribulations, romantic attachments or what-not could stay it even though it took years to come forth.

As for the Prelude, Wagner himself has written an interesting analysis, which is here appended:

"The opening theme for the 'cellos has already been heard in the third strophe of Sachs' cobbler-song in Act II. There is expressed the bitter cry of the man who has determined to renounce his personal happiness, yet who shows the world a cheerful, resolute exterior. That smothered cry was understood by Eva, and so deeply did it pierce her heart that she fain would fly away, if only to hear this cheerful-seeming song no longer. Now, in the Introduction to Act III, this motive is played alone by the 'cellos, and developed in the other strings till it dies away in resignation; but forthwith, and as if from out the distance, the horns intone the solemn song wherewith Hans Sachs greeted Luther and the Reformation, which had won the poet such incomparable popularity. After the first strophe the strings again take single phrases of the cobbler's song, very softly and much slower, as though the man were turning his gaze from his handiwork heavenwards, and was lost in tender musings. Then, with increased sonority, the horns pursue the master's hymn, with which Hans Sachs, at the end of the act, is greeted by the populace of Nuremberg. Next reappears the strings' first motive, with grandiose expression of the anguish of a deeply-stirred soul; calmed and allayed, it attains the utmost serenity of a blest and peaceful resignation."

The plot of *Die Meistersinger* deals with a song contest which is to be held in Nuremberg on St. John's Day. Naturally, there is to be a handsome prize for the winner and in this case it is the hand of Eva, daughter of the goldsmith Veit Pogner. A young knight, Walther von Stolzing, has seen Eva meanwhile, and he has fallen in love with her. Because he is a likable young man, he is given permission to enter the contest. Another contestant is Beckmesser, the town clerk, who attempts to bring Walther to ruin.

However, Walther and Eva have confessed their love for each other to Hans Sachs, a cobbler, who happens also to be in love with Eva. But he makes the supreme sacrifice, rejoicing at the same time in the knowledge that the maid will be deliriously happy with her young knight. He helps their cause along, writing down the notes of a song Walther has heard in a dream. At the contest Beckmesser tries to sing that same song, offering it as his own, but his raucous efforts make him the laughing stock of the affair. Of course, Walther's song is adjudged the best and he wins his Eva.

EXCERPTS FROM "DIE MEISTERSINGER"

Often heard in the concert hall are several other excerpts from *Die Meistersinger*. These include the Procession of the Guilds, the Dance of the Apprentices, the Procession of the Masters, the Homage to Sachs, and the Finale.

PRELUDE, TRANSFORMATION SCENE AND GRAIL SCENE FROM ACT I OF "PARSIFAL"

Most of the *Ring*, all of *Tristan*, and a considerable portion of *Die Meistersinger* had been written by Wagner before he started actual work on the "consecrational festival stage play," *Parsifal*, in 1865. He made a first outline of the libretto in August of that year, some two decades after he had become acquainted with the Parsifal poem of Wolfram von Eschenbach, the Minnesinger. Not till 1877, however, did the text attain its final shape, and it was published in December. Sometime previously Wagner had turned to the task of composing the music and completed it in 1879. The orchestration was finished in January 1882. The opera was given for the first time at Bayreuth on July 26, 1882. The Prelude, written in December 1878, had been given its première performance at Wagner's house, Wahnfried, on Christmas Day, with the composer conducting for the occasion, his wife Cosima's birthday.

The ethical essence of *Parsifal* has thus been expressed: "Enlightenment coming through conscious pity brings salvation." Wagner, whose earlier music-dramas each revolved about some *idée fixe* of philosophical or moral implication, brought to *Parsifal*, besides, religious elements derived from the twin sources of Christian doctrine and Buddhism. Some years before he had done the sketch for a play on the subject of Jesus of Nazareth, and, parenthetically, it is quite likely that he had no intention to write music for it. Nevertheless, here is shown the composer's religious urge, mingled with other aspects of his creative bent. He says, "I was burning to write something that should take the message of my tortured brain, and speak in a fashion to be understood by present life. Just as with my Siegfried, the force of my desire had borne me to the fount of the Eternal Human: so now, when I found this desire cut off by modern life from all appease-ment, and saw afresh that the sole redemption lay in flight from out this life, casting off its claims on me by self-destruction, did I come to the fount of every modern rendering of such a situation—Jesus of Nazareth, the Man."

During that period Wagner drafted another play, which he titled *Die Seger* (*The Victors*), one of Buddhistic import, whose story centers on the dictum that Prakriti, the hero, may not become one with Amanda, the heroine, unless he "shares the latter's vow of chastity." In these two works may be found qualities and tones of thought also incorporated in *Parsifal*.

The locale of *Parsifal* is Montsalvat in the Spanish Pyrenees. The castle of the Holy Grail is tenanted by a company of Knights, guard-ians of the Spear which pierced Jesus' side as He hung on the Cross, and of the Cup He drank from the Last Supper and which received His precious blood from the Spear-wound. This brotherhood of Knights of the Grail refuses membership to all, save the pure in heart, and the Knights go about the world doing good through the high powers given them by the Grail.

A certain other knight, Klingsor, sinful and scheming, enraged against the Knights for having been denied admission to the Brother-hood, has built a magic garden, whose many charms have proved strong enough to tempt several of the weaker-willed Knights. Am-fortas, king of the Grail, is one of these. He has fallen victim to the wiles of Kundry, a creature of Klingsor. The latter has seized the Spear from Amfortas and has humiliated him further by wounding him with it. The wound may be cured only by being touched with the point of the Spear held by a Guileless Fool, a youth who can with-stand all temptation. This youth, of course, is Parsifal, a forest lad who enters into the picture through having killed a swan sacred to the Grail. Parsifal is made to go through the rituals prescribed by the libretto; namely, he is present at the ceremony of the Eucharist or the Lord's Supper without grasping anything of its meaning; he resists the lures thriving in Klingsor's garden; then he seizes the Spear, flung at him by Klingsor and, as he makes the sign of the cross, the garden is destroyed. He wanders about the world and returns to Montsalvat. Kundry, now a repentant woman dedicated to the Grail's service, washes his feet and dries them with her hair. Next he goes with Gurnemanz to the temple where he restores Amfortas to health, and, as the latter bends before him in homage, Kundry dies. Having thus attained "enlightenment . . . through conscious pity," Parsifal has become the savior of Montsalvat.

The Prelude is an abbreviated exposition of the purposes, musical and dramatic, of the opera. It opens with the phrase which dominates the religious scene of the first act during the feast of the Lord's Supper. The phrase, sung first in unison by violins, 'cellos, English horn, clarinet and bassoons, is marked *sehr langsam* (Lento assai), A-flat major, 4-4. It is taken up by trumpet, oboes, and half the first and second violins to the accompaniment of arpeggios in the violas and the other violins, and chords for flutes, clarinets, and English horn with the bassoons and horns sustaining harmony notes. After a series of broken chords, the trombones and trumpets announce a second theme, the Grail motive, which is a phrase long known as the *Dresden Amen* of the Saxon liturgy. There is a change of tempo to 6-4 with the entrance of a third theme, that of Faith. Its first figure is frequently repeated against changing harmonies. A fourth theme appears, suggestive of the suffering of Christ and Amfortas, which originates in the Lord's Supper motive; its first two measures are also employed to characterize the Spear. In the words of Maurice Kufferath, "Like the Prelude to 'Lohengrin,' the introduction to 'Parsifal' is developed by successive degrees until it reaches a maximum of expression, thereafter to diminish imperceptibly to a pianissimo. Thus the synthesis of the whole drama is clearly exposed. That which remains is merely a peroration, a logical, necessary conclusion brought about by the ideas associated with the different themes."

The music of the Transformation Scene in this act is that which is played during the walk of the venerable Gurnemanz and Parsifal through the wood to the Hall of the Grail. The music is of a march-like quality for a spell, subsequently gradually expanding in color and richness to the climactic theme representative of the Penitence of Amfortas, which is given out three times in succession.

The Grail Scene follows. There is the tolling of bells, the Grail Knights march into the hall in stately fashion. One hears the chanting of boys in the lofty dome. The ritual is interrupted by the impassioned song of Amfortas, who, suffering great torment, begs his father,

Titurel, in words of self-abasement, to celebrate the Communion in his place. Titurel answers, however, "Serve thou, and so thy guilt atone! Uncover the Grail!" Presently the ceremony is ended, the knights have departed, and only Gurnemanz and Parsifal remain. The former inquires of the latter how much of the proceedings he has understood. The youth's only answer is to clutch at his heart and shake his head. Gurnemanz, who by this time is convinced that Parsifal is truly a fool, sends him away angrily and then follows the Knights out the door. From somewhere above an unseen singer delivers the motive of the Pure Fool. The theme of the Grail is sung by still other voices. Bells peal once again. The act ends.

It is interesting to note that these excerpts from *Parsifal* represent the only ones authorized by Wagner for concert performance.

Good Friday Spell from "Parsifal"

The Good Friday Spell is placed at the end of the first scene in Act III of the opera. Gurnemanz is now an old hermit who lives in a humble abode at the edge of a forest. He comes out of the hut when he hears a groaning sound in the distance. Presently Parsifal arrives. He is a knight clad in black armor, carrying the sacred spear and a buckler. He is weary. The old Gurnemanz plies him with questions, but Parsifal will not answer until he is apprised of the fact that it is Good Friday. Whereupon he drives the spear into the ground, removes his helmet, and kneels in prayer.

Subsequently Kundry fetches water and washes his feet and anoints him with holy oil. And Gurnemanz, recognizing in him the Guileless Fool now worthy of the title King of the Grail, blesses him and greets him as the king. They soon set out for Montsalvat.

The music of the Good Friday Spell comprises thematically a hymn of thanksgiving, the music of Kundry's Sigh, of the Holy Supper, of the Spear, of the Grail, of the Complaint, of the Flower Girls. All of these are finally fused into a pastoral poem ending with the Good Friday melody, which is suddenly interrupted by the doleful sound of bells. During Gurnemanz's blessing of Parsifal, horns, trumpets and trombones play the Parsifal motive. This is given out in an impressive manner, and it leads into the Grail theme. There follows a series of chords which usher in the motives of Baptism and Faith.

R. B.

Johannes Brahms

BORN: HAMBURG, MAY 7, 1833. DIED: VIENNA, APR. 3, 1897.

*Many new and remarkable talents have made their appear-
ance, and a fresh musical power seemed about to reveal
itself among the many aspiring artists of the day, even
though their compositions were known only to the few. I
thought to follow with interest the pathway of these elect;
there would, there must, after such promise, suddenly appear one who should utter the highest ideal expression of
his time, who should claim the Mastership by no gradual
development, but burst upon us fully equipped, as Minerva
sprang from the brain of Jupiter. And he has come, this
chosen youth, over whose cradle the Graces and Heroes
seem to have kept watch. His name is Johannes Brahms.*
—SCHUMANN, *in the* Neue Zeitschrift für Musik, *Oct. 28,
1853.*

BRAHMS'S FATHER WAS an amiable, humorous man of the lower middle class, of limited intellect, a capable double-bass player, having a
knowledge of the horn and the violoncello, who began by playing in
the lowest taverns for sailors at Hamburg, and finally held a position
as double-bass at the Stadt Theatre and in the Philharmonic orchestra.
Once when a conductor told him to play a little louder, he answered:
"Herr Kapellmeister, this is my double-bass; so I can play on it as
loud as I like."

The mother was upright, of no education, with more mother-wit
than her husband, a good housekeeper, a clever needlewoman. There
were three children. The parents lived apart in later years. Young

Johannes was a stocky, tough, healthy boy. He studied faithfully what the schools had to offer, he even learned a little French. The Bible made a deep impression on him. It was during the early years that his "austerely North German and Protestant view of life and art were firmly laid together with his deep-rooted love for the true Protestant chorale and Protestant church music." He had a long hard struggle to obtain a good education. What he acquired later in life was due to his own efforts and self-discipline.

When he was fifteen he had finished his musical studies with his father and could play the violin, violoncello and horn well enough to act as a stop-gap when necessary. His father made him play his first attempt at a composition to friends, but the father found composition of secondary importance; there was no money to be earned by it. Johannes told Widman that he was always composing. "My finest songs would come to me early in the morning when I was cleaning the boots." He composed only in great secrecy and in the earliest hours. "All day long I was arranging marches for brass bands, and at night I would be seated at the piano in taverns." The father obliged him to help him earn money. He would play second violin in private orchestras and at dances. Late one night there was a knock at the door. Johannes was dragged from bed to play at a ball for two thalers and drink unlimited. He would take walks with a young piano teacher; "as a rule he did not speak a word, but walked along humming to himself, usually carrying his hat in his hand, as he loved to do throughout his whole life." He bid fair to end his days as a ballroom player "in the same narrow, middle-class surroundings, both material and artistic, as his parents." To them and to many talented musicians of Germany art was a business, a practical matter, a means of earning money to ensure good living.

But the father was quick to realize that his Johannes had more than ordinary talent, and impelled by the pressure of other musicians he did what he could to develop the boy musically. So he entrusted the seven-year-old to a pianist, Cossel, who was bound to make him a pianist. "It's a pity," he once said. "He might be such a good pianist, but he will not leave this everlasting composition alone." The boy studied Czerny, Clementi, Cramer, Kalkbrenner, Hummel, but Cossel now and then let him try his hand at a piece by J. S. Bach. He wisely protected him from being exploited as a child prodigy. When Johannes was ten he played at a subscription concert where an agent heard him and wanted the boy with his father to make a concert tour in America. The parents were tempted, but Cossel put his foot down, for which Johannes was grateful all his life.

Johannes during childhood and adolescence had a deep love of nature as "the fount of all sound human and artistic endeavor"; and he had an overmastering bent towards knowledge and culture. There were times when he could not be torn from the harbor. He read "Robinson Crusoe," but while the harbor drove his brother Fritz westward across the ocean, Johannes was drawn more towards the south. He was proud of the city's history; he became acquainted with the writings of Mattheson and C. P. E. Bach; with the plays of Lessing; he haunted the shops of second-hand book dealers. Thus he laid the foundations of wide reading in music, literature and art, betraying what a passionate collector he was to become—"at that time quite a rare thing for a German musician." Books were his favorite presents to his friends of both sexes.

When Johannes was ten years old, Edward Marxen, an excellent man, admirable musician, a man of erudition, a composer in the greater forms, became his teacher. Marxen was pleased with the boy's acuteness of mind. Though the first compositions were insignificant Marxen saw that an exceptional, great, profound talent was dormant in his pupil. "I therefore shrank from no effort or work in order to awaken and form it, that I might one day rear a priest of art, who should preach in new accents what was sublime, true, and eternally incorruptible in art, and that by acts as well as words." This idealistic attitude toward life and art had a great influence on Brahms. It won him over to the "moral in music, and the classical in art." He was initiated into Bach, Beethoven, Weber, though that was a Philistine period in Hamburg of uninspired virtuosity. But Marxen thought more of form than color, more of the contrapuntal and polyphonic than of the homophonic. Thus it was he who gave Brahms the firm foundations of this conception of art, though his own outlook on life was "quite as gentle, sentimental and sleek as that of any Philistine of his day."

Even while he was studying with Marxen, Brahms was anxious about earning a livelihood. He had given lessons, he said in after life, ever since he was twelve years old. Naturally his own pupils gave him little pleasure. He acted as conductor of a male voice chorus; gave his first concert arranged by himself when he was fourteen, including his own variations on a folk-theme in the program. At his first concerts he followed the taste of the period which "tended toward superficial 'tunyness,' sentimental gush, 'pluies de perles' and the fireworks of virtuosi," and so he rarely gave concerts of his own; he taught the piano for a mark a lesson, played at dances, played entr'actes behind the scenes at the Stadt Theatre, accompanied virtuosi on the platform; made transcriptions and arrangements signed "G. W. Marks"—for publishers, signing his own free compositions "Karl Wuerth." He composed some one hundred and fifty fantasias on waltz airs and some serious works.

When Brahms was fifty years old, he said to Gustave Jenner, "Few can have had so hard a time as I."

In 1849 some political refugees from Hungary appeared in Hamburg. Among them was Eduard Rémenyi, the violinist, who long afterwards gave concerts in the United States and died in San Francisco in 1898. He said on his arrival in Hamburg that he was then on his way to America, but giving a "farewell" concert he met with so great a pecuniary success by his playing of national dances that he decided to remain. Brahms was so dazzled by Rémenyi's brilliant playing, his wandering, gypsy-like romantic life, that he offered to be his accompanist. Rémenyi engaged him for a short concert tour, intending to take him to Joachim. There was the meeting that led to the friendship and artistic bond that lasted through life. The meeting was at Joachim's house in Hanover.

Rémenyi was of importance to Brahms as a composer by directing his attention to Hungarian folk music, which led to the composition of the Hungarian dances for piano; for the finales of many of his chamber works; an influence that is seen in the finale of the second piano concerto.

The brilliant, erratic Rémenyi, who would now play like a god even in his later years, sometimes like a pig, to use his own words when he once talked with us, accused Brahms of making free with Rémenyi's own compositions, unpublished, rhapsodies for concert use. He was a singular, fascinating man, this Hungarian virtuoso, entertaining in conversation by his reminiscences, his original views on life and art, his sudden changes from devotion—he had his superstitions—to scepticism, his wit not free from malice. When we knew him he reminded one of a snuff-taking French abbé of the eighteenth century as described in books of anecdotes and gossip. He would grow enthusiastic over the classic works for the violin; and show the same enthusiasm for his own "Hymn to Mount Shasta." Edward MacDowell once said that there was the suggestion of a rope-dancer in every great virtuoso; this was true of Rémenyi—whose name was Hoffmann —but when he was wholly in the vein he played like an inspired musician reverencing his art, as well as a brilliant virtuoso.

Behold our Johannes fairly launched on his career.

P. H.*

Concerto for Piano and Orchestra in D Minor, No. 1, Op. 15

Although Brahms's earlier works included not only compositions for the piano, songs, and chamber music, but also the Serenade for Full Orchestra in D, it was not till the spring and summer of 1854 that we find him engaged on a symphony. This made such progress that in January, 1855, he could write to Robert Schumann: "I have been trying my hand at a symphony during the past summer, have even orchestrated the first movement and composed the second and third."

The symphony was never completed as such, however, but turned into a sonata for two pianos. Still, this was not the end of the matter. Advised that the musical contents of the sonata deserved a more imposing form, Brahms was persuaded to mould the material into a concerto. Accordingly the first two movements took up a corresponding position in the D minor Piano Concerto, the third becoming the chorus "Behold All Flesh" in "A German Requiem."

The first public performance of the concerto took place in Hanover on January 22, 1859, at one of the Court subscription concerts in the Royal Theatre, Brahms being the pianist, Joachim the conductor. Though the cognoscenti admired the new work, the public in general found it a hard nut to crack. And as a matter of notorious fact the concerto was to make its way slowly. Only in the present century, for instance, has it won full recognition in this country.

The first movement (Maestoso, D minor, 6-8) has a long orchestral

* Philip Hale.

introduction before the piano enters. Over a roll on the kettledrums the chief subject is announced in the strings. The second subject is given out by the piano in F major. The movement ends with an extended and brilliant coda. The second movement (Adagio, D major, 6-4) bears in the manuscript score the motto: "Benedictus qui venit in nomine Domini." Max Kalbeck, Brahms's biographer, says that this inscription refers to Robert Schumann, whose death had affected Brahms deeply and whom he had sometimes addressed as "Mynheer Domine." The first theme, to which the fanciful may fit the Latin words, appears in the strings and bassoons, to be taken up later by the solo instrument. The movement has a contrasting middle section. The finale is a long and elaborate Rondo (Allegro non troppo, D minor, 2-4), ending in a majestic and triumphant coda.

This concerto, owing to the exceeding prominence given to the orchestra, really ranks as an orchestral composition, and it was years before Brahms attempted another on a like scale. In 1873 he brought out the "Variations on a Theme by Haydn." Though meanwhile he had written copiously, only the two modest Serenades had been composed for orchestra.

VARIATIONS FOR ORCHESTRA ON A THEME BY HAYDN, OP. 56a

Now a permanent resident of Vienna, Brahms spent his summer holiday in 1873 at Tutzing on the Starnbergersee in southern Bavaria. A version of the Variations for two pianos, Brahms marked "Tutzing, July, 1873." Whether it was the first of the two versions we do not know. On November 2 the orchestral version was brought out in Vienna at a Philharmonic Concert, Otto Dessoff conducting.

The theme by Haydn comes from an unpublished divertimento for wind instruments, preserved at the State Library in Berlin, which is inscribed "Divertimento mit dem Chorale St. Antoni." Though the melody of the chorale is usually supposed to be Haydn's own, we cannot be sure that he had not taken it from a chorale that has now disappeared.

In Haydn's key of B-flat major the theme is given out andante in 2-4 time and repeated. Eight variations follow:

I. (Poco piu animato, major mode.) Throughout the initial variation the concluding notes of the introduction ring like a tolling of bells.

II. (Più vivace, minor mode.) The clarinets and bassoons take the lead. The violins supply an arpeggio figure.

III. (Con moto, major mode.) The theme in this tranquil section is given first to the oboes and bassoons.

IV. (Andante con moto, minor mode.) New melodic material enters. Oboe and horn announce the theme.

V. (Vivace, major mode.) Flutes, oboes, and bassoons have the melody.

VI. (Vivace, minor mode.) Brilliant like its predecessor, this variation introduces a new figure.

VII. (Grazioso, major mode.) In Siciliano rhythm (6-8), the seventh variation is generally regarded as the crowning glory of the set. Against a descending scale for first violins and clarinets, violas and piccolo play the melody. Then the first violins give out a theme whose first four notes provide the movement with its rhythmic basis. There is a wealth of fascinating detail.

VIII. (Presto non troppo, minor mode.) In a mysterious whisper of muted strings the last variation leads darkly to the Finale. (Andante, major mode.) A ground bass, five measures long and repeated twelve times below a variety of harmonies, occupies much of this summing up. At a signal from the triangle an outburst of vernal life sweeps through the orchestra, ending with the theme in fortissimo proclamation.

SYMPHONY IN C MINOR, No. 1, OP. 68

Owing, no doubt, to the experience with the symphony that at last became a piano concerto, Brahms was cautious about trying his hand again at a symphony. In 1862 he had made, however, a version of the Symphony in C minor, without the introduction, of which he wrote to his friend Albert Dietrich, the composer. According to his biographer Walter Niemann, he once remarked it was "no laughing matter" to write a symphony after Beethoven, and the same authority points out that when he had finished the first movement of the C minor symphony he declared to another friend, Hermann Levi, the noted conductor: "I shall never compose a symphony! You have no conception of how the likes of us feel when we hear the tramp of a giant like him (Beethoven) behind us."

This extreme modesty persisted, for Niemann assures us that ten years after the completion of the Fourth Symphony Brahms alluded to that majestic work as "halbschürig" ("mediocre").

Opening Brahms's series of four, the Symphony in C minor was given for the first time on November 4, 1876, at the Grand Ducal Theatre, Karlsruhe. It seems that immediately before the orchestral parts were copied for the first rehearsal Brahms abridged the Andante and the Allegretto, saying that he had the Finale to think of. Otto Dessoff, who had left Vienna for Karlsruhe, conducted the performance, as he had done in the case of the "Haydn" variations at Vienna. Brahms had a low opinion of him. He had even written while Dessoff was still in Vienna:

"Now Dessoff is absolutely not the right man for this, the only enviable post in Vienna. There are special reasons why he continues to beat time, but not a soul approves. Under him the orchestra has positively deteriorated." Three days after the première at Karlsruhe the symphony was repeated at Mannheim, this time with the composer as conductor.

At first the C minor Symphony won little more than a success of esteem. Even Hanslick, Brahms's Viennese prophet, was not wholly enthusiastic. Typical is the judgment expressed by the revered John S. Dwight in his *Journal of Music* after the symphony had been made known to Boston, when it was scarcely fourteen months old. He felt it as something "depressing and unedifying, a work coldly elaborated, artificial; earnest, to be sure, in some sense great, and far more satisfactory than any symphony by Raff or any others of the day which we have heard, but not to be mentioned in the same day with any symphony by Schumann, Mendelssohn, or the great one by Schubert, not to speak of Beethoven's. . . . Our interest in it will increase, but we foresee the limit; and certainly it cannot be popular; it will not be loved like the dear masterpieces of genius."

In spite of this dark prophecy, the symphony has long been one of the most popular, and it is now the established fashion to find in it not only magnitude and ruggedness, but pathos, tenderness, and a profound humanity.

A portentous introduction (Un poco sostenuto, C minor, 6-8) prefaces the first movement (Allegro, C minor, 6-8). The first theme is given out by the violins in the fifth measure. The second theme

(E-flat major) appears in the woodwind. The character of the movement is austere and epic.

The second movement (Andante sostenuto, E major, 3-4) is imbued with a profound lyricism, which flowers into some of the loveliest pages in all Brahms.

Instead of a scherzo there follows a movement marked "Un poco allegretto e grazioso" (A-flat major, 2-4), which Grove aptly characterizes as "a sort of national tune or Volkslied of simple sweetness and grace." The opening subject is sung first by the clarinet. The place of a trio is delightfully filled by a contrasting middle section (B major, 6-8).

The stupendous finale begins with an introductory section (Adagio, C minor, 4-4) that touches briefly on thematic material to be developed later, and here that distinguished American critic, the late William Foster Apthorp, must have our attention:

"With the thirtieth measure the tempo changes to più andante, and we come upon one of the most poetic episodes in all Brahms. Amid hushed, tremulous harmonies in the strings, the horn and afterward the flute pour forth an utterly original melody, the character of which ranges from passionate pleading to a sort of wild exultation according to the instrument that plays it. The coloring is enriched by the solemn tones of the trombones, which appear for the first time in this movement.

"It is ticklish work trying to dive down into a composer's brain and surmise what special outside source his inspiration may have had; but one cannot help feeling that this whole wonderful episode may have been suggested to Brahms by the tones of the Alpine horn as it awakens the echoes from mountain after mountain on some of the high passes in the Bernese Oberland. This is certainly what the episode recalls to anyone who has ever heard those poetic tones and their echoes. A short, solemn, even ecclesiastical interruption by the trombones and bassoons is of more thematic importance. As the horn tones gradually die away and the cloudlike harmonies in the string sink lower and lower—like mist veiling the landscape—an impressive pause ushers in the Allegro non troppo, ma con brio (in C major, 4-4 time)."

Concerning the rest of the movement Apthorp adds: "The introductory Adagio has already given us mysterious hints at what is to come; and now there bursts forth in the strings the most joyous, exuberant

Volkslied melody, a very Hymn to Joy, which in some of its phrases, as it were unconsciously and by sheer affinity of nature, flows into strains from the similar melody in the Finale of Beethoven's Ninth Symphony. One cannot call it plagiarism: it is two men saying the same thing."

With regard to this symphony, Hans von Bülow has often been misquoted. As Philip Hale puts it: "Ask a music-lover, at random, what von Bülow said about Brahms's Symphony in C minor and he will answer: 'He called it the Tenth Symphony.' If you inquire into the precise meaning of this characterization, he will answer: 'It is the symphony that comes worthily after Beethoven's Ninth'; or, 'It is worthy of Beethoven's ripest years,' or in his admiration he will go so far as to say: 'Only Brahms or Beethoven could have written it.'"

What Bülow actually set down in words was this: "First after my acquaintance with the Tenth Symphony, alias Symphony No. 1, by Johannes Brahms, that is since six weeks ago, have I become so intractable and so hard against Bruch pieces and the like. I call Brahms's first symphony the Tenth, not as though it should be put after the Ninth; I should put it between the Second and the 'Eroica,' just as I think by the First Symphony should be understood not the First of Beethoven but the one composed by Mozart which is known as the 'Jupiter.'"

SYMPHONY IN D MAJOR, NO. 2, OP. 73

Having launched a first symphony, Brahms composed a second within a year. However, he kept the writing of it so secret that nobody, we are told, knew anything about it till it was completed. Then, when he did divulge the secret, he was very demure. In September, 1877, he wrote to Dr. Billroth of Vienna, who was a patron of music as well as an eminent surgeon: "I do not know whether I have a pretty symphony; I must inquire of skilled persons." He meant Clara Schumann, Otto Dessoff, and Ernest Frank. Mme. Schumann recorded on September 19 that he had written out the first movement. Early in the following month he played it to her, as well as part of the finale.

Meanwhile he had delighted in mystifying his friends before letting them hear any of the work by describing it as gloomy and awesome and referring to its key as F minor instead of D major. To Elisabeth von Herzogenberg he wrote in November, 1877: "The new symphony

342

is merely a *Sinfonie,* and I shall not need to play it to you beforehand. You have only to sit down at the piano, put your small feet on the two pedals in turn, and strike the chord of F minor several times in succession, first in the treble, then in the bass, fortissimo and pianissimo, and you will gradually gain a vivid impression of my 'latest.' " The day before the first performance he again wrote to Frau von Herzogenberg: "The orchestra here play my new symphony with crepe bands on their sleeves because of its dirge-like effect. It is to be printed with a black edge, too." Such were Brahms's little jokes.

When the symphony was actually performed in public, at a concert of the Vienna Philharmonic, under the direction of Hans Richter, Brahms's friends found it anything but a lugubrious and forbidding composition. The date of that first performance, by the way, is variously given as December 20, 24, and 30, 1877, and January 10, 1878, of which December 30 is favored. The success with the audience at the première was progressive. If at first the response was lukewarm, when the Allegretto grazioso was reached there came an insistent demand that it be repeated, an encore which Richter granted.

Today the Second Symphony is usually regarded as lyrical, suave, even Mendelssohnian, a work of serenity and sweet peacefulness, bearing much the same relation to the austere, dramatic, and often tempestuous First Symphony that Beethoven's "Pastoral" bears to the preceding Fifth, with its conflict between Man and Fate.

Still, not everybody views the D major symphony in quite this gentle light. Walter Niemann in his life of Brahms maintains that the D major is by no means a blameless, agreeable, cheerfully sunlit idyl. Nothing, he declares, could be further from the truth! He describes the period between the 1860's and 1880's as having a heart-rending pathos and a monumental grandeur as its artistic ideal. "Nowadays," he goes on, "regarding things from a freer and less prejudiced point of view, we are fortunately able to detect far more clearly the often oppressive spiritual limitations, moodiness, and atmosphere of resignation in such pleasant, apparently cheerful, and anacreontic [!] works as Brahms's Second Symphony."

He points out that the Second, though nominally in the major, has a veiled, indetermined, Brahmsian major-minor character, hovering between the two modes. "Indeed," he adds, "this undercurrent of tragedy in the Second Symphony, quiet and slight though it may be, is perceptible to a fine ear in every movement." And he sums up the whole matter by putting down the Second Symphony as really a "great, wonderful, tragic idyl, as rich in somber and subdued color as it is in brightness." He even sees mysterious visions of Wagner, who was by no means a friend of Brahms, in the mystic woodland atmosphere of the work, recalling "Das Rheingold" and "Siegfried," and in many somber and even ghostly passages.

The opening movement (Allegro non troppo, D major, 3-4) is remarkable for the lyricism of its themes. After the so-called fundamental motive of the first measure ('cellos and double-basses), the melodious chief theme is given out by horns and woodwind. A graceful subsidiary theme is heard in the violins. The second subject, nostalgic in its wistfulness, appears in the violas and 'cellos. A horn solo in the coda evokes the mystery of forest deeps from an old and bardic time.

The second movement (Adagio non troppo, B major, 4-4) is of a profoundly romantic and yet somewhat elusive character. Not a scherzo, but rather the old-time minuet, is hinted at in the third movement (Allegretto grazioso—*Quasi Andantino*—G major, 3-4). The engaging melody is sung immediately by the oboes over chords in the clarinets and bassoons and pizzicato arpeggios in the 'cellos. Each of the two trios that the movement boasts is a variation on this theme. An acute critic has said of the Allegretto: "Like many well-known things, it is not always remembered in its full variety and range, or we should hear less of its being too small for its place in a big symphony."

The finale (Allegro con spirito, D major, 2-2) is in sonata form. Thematically it is both rich in invention and reminiscent of passages in the earlier movements. A kinship to the finale of Haydn's last "London" symphony has also been remarked. Of the four movements this Allegretto con spirito is the most vigorous and vivacious, concluding, after pages of Olympian struggle, in a victorious coda of overwhelming brilliance.

CONCERTO FOR VIOLIN AND ORCHESTRA IN D MAJOR, OP. 77

Pörtschach-am-See, a picturesque place in Lower Austria, on the Wörthersee, near the Italian frontier, appealed to Brahms as ideal for a summer holiday. To Hanslick he once wrote that the air at Pörtschach was so charged with melodies that he must "be careful not to tread on them." There he began the D major symphony and composed (in 1878) the violin concerto (also in D major).

And even now, with his characteristic modesty and still uncertain about the value of his own work, he could say in a letter to Elisabeth von Herzogenberg, the day announced for the first performance of the violin concerto being only a fortnight away: "Joachim is coming here and I shall have a chance to try the concerto through with him and so to decide for or against a public performance."

Hanslick once quite justly called this concerto "the ripe fruit of the friendship between Joachim and Brahms." For Joachim it was written and to him it stands dedicated. He, furthermore, was the soloist when at a Gewandhaus Concert in Leipzig, on January 1, 1879, it was given to the world. A local reviewer, on good terms with both the composer and the violinist, remarked after the first performance that only too evidently Joachim found the solo part extremely difficult.

The influence of Joachim on the concerto must have been considerable, for Brahms often consulted him with regard to the practicability of this or that passage, and he supplied not only a cadenza but the fingering and the indications for bowing as well. Subsequently Joachim went still further. After he had played the concerto a number of times in public, he advised Brahms to make alterations in the score that he thought were required, and Brahms consented to the alterations before the concerto was published in October, 1879. To Brahms Joachim wrote from London, where he had performed the work twice with the Philharmonic Society:

"With these exceptions the piece, especially the first movement, pleases me more and more. The last two times I played without notes. That a solo composition has been performed at two London Philharmonic Concerts in succession has happened in the history of the society only once, when Mendelssohn played his G minor piano concerto (manuscript)."

It has been pointed out that Brahms's biographers disagree about the reception accorded the violin concerto at the première. Florence May quotes Dörffel, critic of the *Leipziger Nachrichten,* as follows: "Joachim played with a love and devotion which brought home to us in every measure the direct or indirect share he has had in the work.

As to the reception, the first movement was too new to be distinctly appreciated by the audience, the second made considerable way, the last aroused great enthusiasm."

Max Kalbeck, a devotee of Brahms, declares: "The work was heard respectfully, but it did not awaken a particle of enthusiasm. It seemed that Joachim had not sufficiently studied the concerto or he was severely indisposed. Brahms conducted with visible excitement."

J. A. Fuller-Maitland emphasizes Brahms's going back to the tradition of the older concerto form in giving a long exposition of the material of the first movement before the entry of the solo instrument. "When the violin does come in, it is with a kind of breathless passage, on which there was some discussion between the composer and Joachim.

"We cannot fail to trace in the passages for solo the special points in which Joachim was without a rival, such as the handling of several parts and other things. The absence of the slightest trace of passages written for mere effect is as characteristic of the player as of the composer; and, like the other concertos, the work for violin is to be judged first and foremost as a composition, not as a means of display.

"Occasionally it may have happened that in the desire to avoid the meretricious, Brahms allowed himself to make the violin part so harsh as almost to repel the general public at first; even in the short time since the death of Joachim, who was, of course, unrivalled in it, the work has come increasingly into favor with violinists, and nowadays even the prodigies are bold enough to attempt it."

The first movement of the concerto (Allegro non troppo, D major, 3-4) has a chief subject of idyllic nature, announced by violas, 'cellos, bassoons, and horns. The peak of the movement comes with the merging of the cadenza into the return of the first subject.

The second movement (Adagio, F major, 2-4) has been compared to a serenade or a romanza. The principal melody is sung first by an oboe, then in altered form by the solo violin, which also introduces an emotional and highly ornamented second theme. After extended development the original melody comes back in the solo instrument.

The finale (Allegro giocoso, ma non troppo vivace, D major, 2-4) is a rondo on three themes, demanding brilliant execution from the soloist. Compact in its formal body, the movement ends in an elaborate coda. Fuller-Maitland points out the Hungarian flavor of this finale, "as if a dedication to the great Hungarian violinist were conveyed in it."

"Academic Festival Overture," Op. 80

According to a plaque on the outer wall of a house at Ischl in Upper Austria, "the great tone poet Dr. Johannes Brahms" occupied the house for twelve summers. Indeed, Brahms had a marked fondness for Ischl. In spite of the fact that it was one of the most fashionable of spas and that he disliked fashionable life, his attachment to the town persisted, and in the aforesaid house, in the summer of 1880, he composed two overtures, the "Tragic" and the "Academic Festival." Notwithstanding the opus numbers, the "Tragic" was composed first and also performed first.

The origin of the "Academic Festival Overture" is explained by its name. The University of Breslau, on May 11, 1879, conferred on Brahms an honorary doctor's degree. Though not a university man, Brahms had had a taste of university life in 1853 when, with Rémenyi, he had paid a visit to Joachim, who was then at Göttingen, the university bitingly satirized by Heine. There, during his stay of several weeks, he became familiar with the songs best liked by the students. Nearly three decades later the songs were present in his memory ready for use in an overture intended as the composer's tribute to the university honoring him.

Brahms himself conducted the first performance of the "Academic Festival Overture" on January 4, 1881, at Breslau, before an audience that included in the front seats the Rector and Senate of the University and members of the Philosophical Faculty. The honorary Doctor of Philosophy, so often mystifying and coy about a new composition, described the overture to Max Kalbeck, in the autumn of 1880, as a "very jolly potpourri on students' songs à la Suppé." When Kalbeck, a bit sarcastic, inquired whether he had used the "Fox Song" (a freshman song), he replied eagerly, "Yes, indeed!" Kalbeck, taken aback, declared that he could not think of such academic homage to the "leathery Herr Rektor." "That is also wholly unnecessary," answered Brahms.

Minus an introduction, the overture (Allegro, C minor, 2-2) begins immediately with the principal subject given out softly by the first violins. A quieter section follows, the melody in the violas. The first of the students' songs, "Wir hatten gebauet ein stättliches Haus" ("We had built a stately house, and trusted in God therein through bad weather, storm, and horror"), is impressively intoned by the three trumpets (C major, 4-4).

The second students' song, "Der Landesvater" ("The Father of the Country"), appears in E major in the second violins. The mood changes now to one of frank jollity with the ragging of the freshman. The "Fox Song," "Was kommt dort von der Höh" ("What Comes There From On High"), is introduced in G major by the two bassoons to an accompaniment of violas and 'cellos. The fourth and last students' song, "Gaudeamus Igitur," famous wherever there are students the world over (Maestoso, C major, 3-4), is proclaimed by all the wind instruments against rushing scales in the upper strings, ending the overture brilliantly.

"Tragic Overture," Op. 81

Although the "Tragic Overture" had a place on the program of the concert in Breslau at which Brahms, conducting, brought out the "Academic Festival Overture," the "Tragic" had already been played in Vienna at a Philharmonic Concert on December 20, 1880, under the direction of Hans Richter.

There has long been discussion as to what tragedy this overture sets forth. It has been called "a tragedy not of actual happenings but of soul life. No hero, no event, suggested program music or any specific musical portrayal, although Hanslick says that if it be necessary to associate the overture with a particular tragedy, that tragedy is "Hamlet." The Hamletians identify the second theme, in F, with Ophelia and the episode in B-flat with Fortinbras.

It has also been said that though the composer denied that in writing this work he had any specific tragedy in mind, he may have received the impulse from a production of Goethe's "Faust" given by Franz von Dingelstedt in 1876 at the Burgtheater in Vienna, especially since Dingelstedt had asked Brahms to consider supplying incidental music and Brahms, it is said, had consented. To some, then, this is a Faust overture.

Perhaps it is best to allow the overture to stand by itself untroubled by the hazards of literary identification. Heinrich Reimann finds in it the grandeur, the loftiness, the deep earnestness of tragic character,

JOHANNES BRAHMS

"Calamities, which an inexorable fate had imposed on him, leave the hero guilty; the tragic downfall atones for the guilt; this downfall, which by purifying the passions and awakening fear and pity works on the race at large, brings expiation and redemption to the hero himself."

Another biographer of Brahms, Dr. Hermann Deiters, sums up the essence as follows: "In this work we see a strong hero battling with an iron and relentless fate; passing hopes of victory cannot alter an impending destiny. We do not care to inquire whether the composer has a special tragedy in his mind, or if so, which one; those who remain musically unconvinced by the unsurpassably powerful theme would not be assisted by a particular suggestion."

The overture opens (Allegro ma non troppo, D minor, 2-2) with two fortissimo chords, after which the strings give out the first theme. The quieter second theme is uttered by the violins. A more moderate section, in part new and in part derived from earlier material, suggested to Grove a funeral march.

CONCERTO FOR PIANO AND ORCHESTRA IN B-FLAT MAJOR, No. 2, OP. 83

It took Brahms some time to complete his second piano concerto. The first sketches were made on May 6, 1878, at Pörtschach on the Wörthersee in southern Austria, but the work was not finished till the summer of 1881, when he gave it the finishing touches at Pressbaum, near Vienna.

On the day of completion he wrote to his friends the Herzogenbergs with his customary misleading humor: "I don't mind telling you that I have written a tiny, tiny piano concerto with a tiny, tiny wisp of a scherzo." A few days later he sent the four movements of the work to another friend, Dr. Theodor Billroth, telling him, "I am sending you some small piano pieces."

In October Hans von Bülow, then director of the Meiningen Orchestra, conducted at Brahms's request a rehearsal of the concerto with Brahms as pianist. The first public performance took place in Budapest at the Redoutensaal on November 9, 1881. Alexander Erkel was the conductor.

This "tiny, tiny piano concerto" or group of "some small piano pieces," as you prefer, is really a concerto of exceptional dimensions.

MASTERS OF THE ORCHESTRA

Not only has it the three usual movements of the classical concerto, each large in plan, but a highly developed scherzo (though it does not bear that name).

The first movement (Allegro non troppo, B-flat major, 4-4) begins with the initial statement of the first subject in dialogue for horn, piano, and woodwind. A cadenza for the piano leads to a tutti, in which both the first and the second subjects are given full play. The development section is long and elaborate.

The fiery scherzo (Allegro appassionato, F major, 3-4) Max Kalbeck believed had been written for the violin concerto and then discarded. The piano gives out the first theme fortissimo. The strings sing the second theme tranquillo e dolce. After a trio in D major, the first part is repeated, but much altered.

The third movement (Andante, B-flat major, 6-4) opens with an expressive melody, given first to a solo 'cello (an instrument that has a particularly important part in this movement), which resembles Brahms's song "Immer leiser wird mein Schlummer," not written, however, till 1886. A second melody, introduced by piano and clarinet in F sharp, recalls another song by Brahms, "Todessehnen," written in 1878. The first melody comes back in the 'cello and dominates the coda, against trills and arpeggios in the piano.

The finale (Allegretto grazioso, B-flat major, 2-4) is a rondo on a grand scale.

In the words of Philip Hale, "the choice of this concerto shows the high purpose and the pure aim; for the Second Concerto of Brahms is not one to tickle the ear, stun the judgment, and provoke cheap and boisterous applause. And as the Second Symphony of Brahms is to the First, so is the Second Concerto of Brahms to the First. In each case, while the passion is less stormy, the thoughts are less crabbed and gnarled.

Only in the first movement of the B-flat major concerto does Brahms "keep up a terrible thinking." The second fascinates by its sturdiness and rhythmic capriciousness; the third is Brahms at his noblest, when his thought is as lofty and serenely beautiful as a summer sky at noon. And who can describe in words the enchanting, haunting delight of the finale—music like unto the perfect verse of a supreme poet whose imagination is kindled by wild or melancholy tales told him in youth by gypsy lips.

JOHANNES BRAHMS

Symphony in F Major, No. 3, Op. 90

Brahms finished the third of his symphonies at Wiesbaden in the summer of 1883. In October he returned to Vienna with the completed score, which he immediately took to Hans Richter, by that time the conductor of nearly everything in Vienna. Richter brought it out at a Philharmonic Concert on December 2. The reception was mixed. Though Brahms's adherents applauded fervently, groups of Wagnerian followers of Anton Bruckner and Hugo Wolf were there to hiss, and hiss they did! It remained for Berlin, where Joachim conducted the second performance of it at an Academy Concert on January 4, 1884, to bestow the "unqualified approval" that Brahms had written Hans von Bülow he desired.

Such was the enthusiasm in Berlin that Brahms himself conducted two more performances of the symphony there later in the month, and he also conducted it successfully at Wiesbaden on January 18. The triumph of triumphs, however, came at Meiningen on February 4, when Bülow actually led the work twice through at the same concert, and the repetition won an even greater ovation than the first performance. Before the year 1884 was out the Third Symphony had been performed in many places on the Continent, in England, and in the United States, and always with acclaim. Yet it annoyed Brahms that many critics should pronounce this symphony by far the best of his compositions. Expectations that he feared would not be fulfilled were thus aroused, for Brahms, with all his background of achievement, had in his nature a streak of incorrigible modesty.

The adjective "heroic" has often been associated with the Third Symphony of Brahms, as in its Italian form "eroica," it is attached to the Third Symphony of Beethoven. Indeed, Richter, in a toast, christened this symphony, while it was still in manuscript, Brahms's "Eroica." Hanslick, though concurring with Richter, points out that the heroic quality is limited to the first and the last movements. This "heroic" element, however, "is without any warlike flavor; it leads to no tragic action, such as the Funeral March in Beethoven's 'Eroica.' It recalls in its musical character the healthy and full vigor of Beethoven's second period, and nowhere the singularities of his last period; and every now and then in passages quivers the romantic twilight of Schumann and Mendelssohn."

So much for Richter and Hanslick. Joachim discovered a different heroism in the finale—nothing less than the valiant fable of those antique lovers, Hero and Leander! The second subject, in C major, with its rhythmic conflict between four quarter notes to the measure and two groups of triplets, he identified with the ardent swimmer battling victoriously against the waves of the Hellespont.

Another view of the work is taken by Clara Schumann. She called it a "forest idyl," saying specifically of the second movement: "I feel as though I were watching the worshippers round a little woodland chapel, the rippling of the brooklet, the play of beetles and gnats—there is such a swarming and whispering round about that one feels all surrounded with the joys of nature."

The first movement (Allegro con brio, F major, 6-4) begins with a motto theme which at once suggests its heroic character and recurs frequently. It consists of three great ascending chords for horns, trumpets, and woodwind, the top voice of which, F, A-flat, F, is said to be emblematic of the "Frei aber froh" ("Free but happy") that Brahms had chosen as his personal motto. These three notes are then used immediately as the bass against which the real first subject comes streaming downwards in the violins. The second subject, in A major, is of a gracefully lyric quality. Just before it enters there is an apparent allusion to the Venusberg scene in "Tannhäuser"—"Naht euch dem Strande, naht euch dem Lande"—which Hugo Reimann insists is an intentional tribute to Wagner, who died while the symphony was taking shape in Brahms's mind.

The second movement (Andante, C major, 4-4) opens with a hymnlike theme, given out by clarinets and bassoons, which hints at a prayer heard in the overture and again in the finale of Herold's opera "Zampa." A second theme, in G major, with its typical Brahmsian octaves and its air of hushed mystery, sustains Mme. Schumann's woodland comparison.

The third movement (Poco allegretto, C minor, 3-8) is not a scherzo, but a romanza touched with melancholy. The first section is followed by a trio of similar mood, after which the first section is repeated with changed orchestration.

The finale (Allegro, F minor, 4-4) starts softly but menacingly in the strings and bassoons. Subsidiary material is employed before we hear the subject that caused Joachim to think of Leander conquering the Grecian waters. Whether or not Brahms had such an idea in mind, this finale is a colossal struggle between titanic powers, culminating in a tremendous climax. Then peace and the major mode. With respect to this tranquil coda Hanslick remarks: "The raging ocean waves calm down to a mysterious whisper. In an enigmatic strangeness, in marvellous beauty, the whole thing dies away. . . ."

Symphony in E Minor, No. 4, Op. 98

When this symphony was brought out at Meiningen, under the direction of Hans von Bülow, on October 25, 1885, there was a great deal of discussion about the choice of key and actually some dismay. E minor as the key for a symphony was looked at askance, even though Haydn and Raff had both used it. The suggestion has been made that Brahms picked out E minor because of its "pale, wan character, to express the deepest melancholy." This key has also been described as "dull in color, shadowy, suggestive of solitude and desolation."

Haydn perhaps felt strongly the key's doleful implications, for his E minor symphony is the "Symphony of Mourning." Raff's E minor symphony, on the other hand, is by no means the autumnal affair that Brahms's has been called. Its title, "In Summer," tells us that!

Whatever the motives may have been that determined Brahms's choice, it fell on E minor, and he proceeded to compose. The work was written at Mürz-zu-Schlag in Styria in the summers of 1884 and 1885. And at Mürz-zu-Schlag in the latter year the manuscript was endangered by fire. Brahms had gone out for a walk. On his return he found that the house where he lodged was burning. Fortunately he had devoted friends there who were rushing his papers out of the building. Brahms pitched in with the rest and helped get the fire under control. The precious manuscript was saved.

Brahms, in spite of his mature years and all the important work that he had put to his credit, was again somewhat timid about a new symphony. In a letter to Hans von Bülow he described it, oddly enough, as "a couple of entr'actes"; he also termed it "a choral work without text." Yet he was eager for opinions from such valued friends as Elisabeth von Herzogenberg and Clara Schumann. He felt that the symphony had failed to please a group of men, including Hanslick, Billroth, Richter, Kalbeck, to whom he had played a four-hand piano version with Ignaz Brüll. To Kalbeck he said: "If persons like Billroth, Hanslick, and you do not like my music, whom *will* it please?" Had he forgotten Elisabeth and Clara?

The audience that heard the Meiningen première liked the symphony. Indeed, a vain effort was made to have the scherzo repeated. Nevertheless, the symphony was slow in winning general favor. In Vienna, where Brahms resided, it disappointed his friends and delighted his enemies. Hugo Wolf, an arch-enemy, was then writing musical criticism. He devoted a bitter article to the work, in particular poking fun at the key—at last a symphony in E minor! Brahms's friends, on the contrary, celebrated the key, in order, it is said, to help cover up their disappointment in the music. It was usual to hear the symphony called grim, austere, forbidding, granitic. However, eventually it made its way, and now there are those who would rank it first among its author's four.

The initial theme of the first movement (Allegro non troppo, E minor, 4-4), given out by the violins answered by flutes, clarinets, and bassoons, is of a thoughtful and somewhat mournful character, but it could hardly be termed forbidding. Rather it invites to meditation. The second theme, introduced by the wind instruments, is harmonically and rhythmically one of Brahms's most fascinating inspirations. Some undiscourageable seekers after resemblances have discovered a likeness in the thirteenth and fourteenth measures to a passage in the second act of Puccini's opera "Tosca," which followed the symphony after fifteen years. Such resemblances are often mere coincidences.

The second movement (Andante moderato, E major, 6-8), with its unearthly melody announced in the Phrygian mode by the horns, to be taken up immediately by oboes, bassoons, and flutes, has been called the most hauntingly beautiful page in all of Brahms. Of this section Elisabeth von Herzogenberg wrote to the composer: "The Andante has the freshness and distinction of character with which only you could endow it, and even you have had recourse for the first time to certain locked chambers of your soul."

Kalbeck, who finds that the whole symphony pictures the tragedy of human life, compares the Andante to a waste and ruined field, like the Campagna (as it then was) near Rome. But in the ensuing scherzo (Allegro giocosco, C major, 4-4) he sees the Carnival at Milan. The finale reminds him of a passage in *Oedipus at Colonus* of Sophocles: "Not to have been born at all is superior to every other view

354

of the question." Yet there are those who deny the pessimistic interpretation; who find a rugged, full-blooded vigor in the finale as well
as in the scherzo, and who attribute the more specifically thoughtful
portions of the work to the reactions inevitable to any sensitive and
meditative spirit.

Be all that as it may, the finale (Allegro energico e passionato, E
minor, 3-4) is of special interest because it is cast in the classic form of
the passacaglia or chaconne. It is built up on a majestic theme eight
measures long, a noble progression of chords, which recurs thirty-one
times, appearing in the high, middle, and low voices alternately. As to
the distinction between those old, patrician dance forms, passacaglia
and chaconne, the doctors remain in absolute contradiction, some
maintaining a chaconne to be what the others define as a passacaglia,
and vice versa.

The curious may be interested to know that Simrock, the music publisher, is said to have paid Brahms forty thousand marks for the symphony—the equivalent in 1885 of ten thousand dollars.

Incidentally the E minor symphony was the last of Brahms's compositions that their author heard performed in public. It was played
at a Philharmonic Concert in Vienna on March 7, 1897, less than a
month before his death. This was the last concert that Brahms, already
fatally ill, ever attended. Miss Florence May in her "Life of Brahms"
gives an affecting account of the occasion:

"The fourth symphony had never become a favorite work in Vienna.
Received with reserve on its first performance, it had not since gained
much more from the general public of the city than the respect sure
to be accorded there to an important work by Brahms. Today, however,
a storm of applause broke out at the end of the first movement, not
to be quieted until the composer, coming to the front of the artists'
box in which he was seated, showed himself to the audience. The
demonstration was renewed after the second and third movements,
and an extraordinary scene followed the conclusion of the work.

"The applauding, shouting house, its gaze riveted on the figure
standing in the balcony, so familiar and yet in present aspect so
strange, seemed unable to let him go. Tears ran down his cheeks as
he stood there, shrunken in form, with lined countenance, strained
expression, white hair hanging lank; and through the audience there
was a feeling as of a stifled sob, for each knew that they were saying

farewell. Another outburst of applause and yet another; one more acknowledgment from the master; and Brahms and his Vienna had parted forever." He died on April 3, 1897.

CONCERTO FOR VIOLIN, VIOLONCELLO, AND ORCHESTRA IN A MINOR, OP. 102

After the Fourth Symphony Brahms wrote only one more work in which he employed the orchestra, the double concerto for violin and 'cello. Thenceforth until his death his creative activity was devoted to chamber music, piano compositions, and songs for chorus or for solo voice.

This concerto he composed at Thun in Switzerland during the summer of 1887. To Elisabeth von Herzogenberg he referred to it in a letter of July 20: "I can give you nothing worth calling information about the undersigned musician. True, he is now writing down something that does not figure in his catalogue—but neither does it figure in other persons'! I leave you to guess the particular form of idiocy."

The "particular form" Walter Niemann calls an experiment in the revival of the old Italian orchestral concerto, the "concerto grosso" of the seventeenth and eighteenth centuries, so signally illustrated by Handel and Bach, in which the orchestral tutti of the concerto grosso is contrasted with a cencertino for a group of soloists.

But here Brahms was experimenting also with a curious concertino consisting of a violin and a 'cello and with unaccustomed combinations of instrumental timbres. In effect his concerto grosso is distinctly late Brahms and a far cry from the concerto grosso of musical antiquity.

Hardly was the double concerto completed before it was performed privately at the Baden-Baden Kurhaus, Brahms conducting and Joachim and Robert Hausmann, a distinguished 'cellist, playing the solo instruments. The same artistic confraternity took part in the first public performance, on October 18, 1887, at Cologne. On a copy of the work that Brahms presented to Joachim he wrote: "To him for whom it was written."

The first movement (Allegro, A minor, 4-4) opens with an introductory passage in which the orchestra alludes to the chief subject and the 'cello follows with a rhapsodic recitative. The woodwind gives out in

A major the initial phrase of the second subject. Both subjects are heard in the first tutti. A rising syncopated theme in F major is also to be carefully noted.

The slow movement (Andante, D major, 3-4) is described by Niemann as "most lovely . . . a great ballade, steeped in the rich, mysterious tone of a northern evening atmosphere." Four notes for the horns and woodwind bring on the flowing chief melody, broadly sung by the solo instruments in octaves.

The finale (Vivace non troppo, A minor, 4-4), which has been called the "clearest of rondo types," abounds in thematic material. The first subject, announced by the 'cello and repeated by the violin, has the gypsy flavor so dear to Brahms. It can be detected in another melody assigned to the clarinets and bassoons against rising arpeggios by the solo instruments, which is prominent in the development. The coda, tender at first and then exuberantly joyous, concludes the double concerto, and at the same time the composer's employment of the orchestra, in a triumphant A major.

P. S.

* * *

Music lovers like to know something about the composer as a human being. They rejoice in the knowledge that Beethoven was irascible, the despair of his landladies, given to rough joking; that Haydn was nagged by his shrew of a wife and fell in love in London with a widow;* that Mozart was fond of punch and billiards; that César Franck's trousers were too short. There are many anecdotes about the great, some of them no doubt apochryphal.

In the excellent biography of Brahms by Walter Niemann there is an entertaining chapter entitled "Brahms as a Man."

He was not fussy in his dress. At home he went about in a flannel shirt, trousers, a detachable white collar, no cravat, slippers. In the country he was happy in a flannel shirt and alpaca jacket, carrying a

* She was Mistress Schroeter, the widow of the excellent musician Johann Samuel Schroeter. She wrote to Haydn who treasured her letters. He said to Dies who asked him about them, long after Haydn returned to Vienna: "They are letters from an English widow in London. Though sixty years old, she was still lovely and amiable, and I should in all likelihood have married her if I had been single." For some of the letters see the chapter "His English Love" in "Music and Manners" by Henry Edward Krehbiel (New York, 1898).

soft felt hat in his hand, and in bad weather wearing on his shoulders an old-fashioned bluish-green shawl, fastened in front by a huge pin. (In the sixties many New Englanders on their perilous journeys to Boston or New York wore a shawl.) He preferred a modest restaurant to a hotel table d'hôte. In his music room were pictures of a few composers, engravings—the Sistine Madonna among them—the portrait of Cherubini, by Ingres, with a veiled Muse crowning the composer ("I cannot stand that female," Brahms said to his landlady.), a bronze relief of Bismarck, always crowned with laurel. There was a square piano supposed to have been Haydn's, also a grand piano, on which a volume of Bach was usually standing open. On the cover lay notebooks, writing tablets, calendars, cigar cases, spectacles, purses, watches, keys, portfolios, recently published books and music, also souvenirs of his travels. He was passionately patriotic, interested in politics, a firm believer in German unity. He deeply regretted that he had not done military service as a young man. Prussia should be the North German predominant power.

His library occupied the whole of a long wall of the room. The shelves held rare old books on music, autographs, engravings, etchings, etc. Among his favorite writers were Freytag, Heyse, Keller (the Swiss poet), Grillparzer, Kleist, Hebbel, E. T. A. Hoffmann, Arnim, Auerbach, Luther (the translation of the Bible and the "Table Talk"). Folk poetry, fairy tales, sagas, delighted him. Books of travel were dear to him, as was Grimm's German dictionary. As a man, he kept his boyish love for "Robinson Crusoe." "Gil Blas" was on the shelf, as were historical works on Germany's wars. For twenty-four years he subscribed to the satirical *Kladderadatsch*—the numbers were piled in a wardrobe. Well acquainted with modern literature, he was a zealous first-nighter at the Burgtheatre. He had little patience with the hysteria and unrest of the contemporary literary tendencies. "Passions," he wrote to Clara Schumann, "do not pertain to man as a natural thing. They are always exceptions or excrescences."

His traveling trunk and valise were always packed ready for instant use. The windows of the music room and library were always shut; those of his bedroom open day and night.

As a young man he was shy, awkward; this awkwardness had its origin "chiefly in his oppressive consciousness of his lack of ease in the forms of polite society, which he tried, as a rule, to conceal behind an apparently rough manner." He was then slender, walking with an uncertain gait, body bowed a little forward. His voice was then as gentle as his hair was long. He was a good athlete. As a boy he had a pure soprano voice, which he ruined by singing when it was breaking. Forty years later this voice was gruff; he was portly; the once clean shaven face gave way to a great full beard. At the age of thirty his figure was short and squat, his under lip protruded, but "his whole appearance was steeped in force . . . there was something confidently triumphant in his face, the radiant serenity of a mind happy in the exercise of his art," wrote Widmann, observing him playing the piano.

He could take a nap at any time in the day, in the open as in a room; he could sleep at a friend's house on a sofa or under a grand piano. Breakfast was his favorite meal. Coffee and cigars could not be too strong for him. No matter how heavy his supper, he drank coffee for which his recipe was as many coffee beans as would ordinarily make ten cups. He seldom composed at Vienna; when he did, it was standing, never at the piano. Out of bed very early—in summer holiday, at five—he worked without stopping till noon. At twelve-thirty he would lunch at the "Roter Igel"; take his coffee, then a long walk. At night after a concert or an opera he would take his drink at the same restaurant, where he would meet carefully chosen friends. Though he carried his liquor well, he was moderate and simple in what he ate and drank, demanding no delicacies, preferring a solid, middle-class meal. At midday he drank a half-pint of red wine or a small glass of Pilsener beer.

As a young man he had a rough exterior. This roughness grew on him, was noticeable even in his jesting, his physical behavior. Yet his friends said his nature was gentle; that he would weep before certain pictures, or at a performance—especially of his own works. His eyes would brim with tears as he said farewell to intimate friends. As soon as there was talk about music he would become silent. Interested in a subject, he would speak vivaciously but with few words and little gesturing. With close friends he was lively and witty. He would often be curt, abrupt in speech. He could be jovial with men, gallant to beautiful women. The curiosity of professional journalists, reporters, autograph hunters, he detested; also dedications, painters and sculptors after a commission. He made innumerable enemies among critics and journalists by his rudeness. "These petty scribblers are nothing but skirmishers; they delay matters a bit. Only a creative genius can be convincing in art." (What would he have said to Oscar Wilde's theory that the critic is the true creative artist; that the excuse for a work or a performance is the critical article about it?) He let himself be photographed fairly often. Amateur photographs and snap-shots amused him greatly.

"All these are but small things and characteristic trifles. But they spring from the very depths of Brahms's native Low German character, which hated nothing so much as false solemnity, spurious pathos and stilted theatrical pomposity, and show us his simple, modest side." This quality caused him to be grossly misunderstood. Niemann, in a diatribe against some of Brahms's contemporaries, admits that his hero in his relations with his fellow-artists was often "far too prone to follow the impulse of the moment and say hasty, spiteful, disagreeable and stinging things; indeed, he felt he simply must say them, though nobody had less desire to be nasty, and nobody repented of them more sincerely."

Here are a couple of the many illustrative anecdotes that might be told here:

When Bruch, sweating, had played him the whole of his "Odysseus," all that Brahms said at the end was: "Tell me, where do you get your beautiful manuscript paper?"

Seeing some compositions by Reinecke on a friend's piano, he said to the old composer's wife, who was standing by: "What, does your husband compose, too?"

No wonder that Brahms, growing more reserved, harsher, ruder, suffered from his incapacity for "getting outside himself." He told Clara Schumann he longed for affection. He loved his parents, step-family, brothers and sisters, children and animals. Loyal to his friends, he was genuinely religious. He was generous, in secret, to those in need. "Brahms was a convinced and believing member of the Lutheran Protestant church; not as regards dogma, not in the letter, but in the spirit." "We North Germans," he once said, "long for the Bible every day and do not let a day go by without it. In my study I can lay my hand on my Bible even in the dark."

Niemann asks whether Brahms's celibacy was voluntary or not. He bases his answer, in the negative, on occasional remarks of Brahms.

As a young man he was secretly in love with Clara Schumann. He was devoted to her till her death. Though he had a youthful passion for Agathe von Siebold, he let it cool, for his future was not assured. A girl at Oldenburg pleased him when he was in his thirties. He told Widmann years later he had waited too long. He made an unsuccessful attempt to marry Clara Schumann's daughter Julie. When a young woman asked him why he had not married, he answered, "None of them would have me; and if there had been one who would, I could not have stood her on account of her bad taste."

Not that, to use Sir Thomas Browne's phrase, he was "averse from that sweet sex." Dwellers in Vienna who knew Brahms have told us that like Sainte-Beuve, like Hazlitt, he looked with a favoring eye on *bonnes*.

There is a short chapter in Niemann's indispensable book on Brahms as a composer as well as a man—a book as remarkable for the sanity of his criticism as for the orderly information—a chapter about Brahms as a pianist, conductor and teacher, in which Niemann says that as a pianist and conductor Johannes must above all be judged as the interpreter of Brahms the composer. We heard him play in the season of 1883-84 at Berlin his D-minor concerto, and found his performance rough and uninspiring. In that season he conducted the first performance in Berlin of his Symphony No. 3. The orchestra was respectfully obedient to his baton. The testimony of three piano pupils is singularly contradictory. He thought a pupil should never be encouraged with words of praise. He said to Richard Strauss after Strauss's F-minor symphony: "Young man, look at Schubert's dances and practice inventing simple, eight bar melodies." Niemann ends this chapter by saying: "Even during his lifetime Brahms's achievements as a composer by far overshadowed his activity as pianist, conductor and teacher."

P. H.

Peter Ilyitch Tschaikowsky

BORN: VOTKINSK, MAY 7, 1840. DIED: ST. PETERSBURG, NOV. 6, 1893.

Because of its opportunities for soul expansion, music has ever attracted the strong, free sons of earth. The most profound truths, the most blasphemous things, the most terrible ideas, may be incorporated within the walls of a symphony, and the police be none the wiser. Supposing that some Russian professional supervisor of artistic anarchy really knew what arrant doctrines Tschaikowsky preached! It is its freedom from the meddlesome hand of the censor that makes of music a playground for great brave souls.—
JAMES GIBBONS HUNEKER.

INCLUDED IN THIS brief essay are analyses and backgrounds of most of Tschaikowsky's standard concert music. A short sketch of Tschaikowsky's life precedes the section devoted to the orchestral music. Yet, the personal outlook and moods of Russia's great composer are so inextricably bound up with his music, that actually the whole essay is an account of his strangely tormented life. In the story of Tschaikowsky, life and art weave into one closely knit fabric. It is hoped that this simple narrative will aid music lovers to glimpse the great pathos and struggle behind the music of this sad and lonely man.

* * *

Few names in music exert such an immediate spell over the average concert-goer as that of Peter Ilyitch Tschaikowsky. In almost every musical form will be found a work of his ranking high in popularity.

362

And quite deservedly so. Tschaikowsky's music brims with a warm humanity and restless drama. The themes and feelings are easy to grasp. The personal, intimate note is so strong in this music that we find it natural, while listening to the *Pathetic* symphony or the *Nutcracker* ballet suite, for example, to share Tschaikowsky's joys and sorrows. His music seems to take us into his confidence and show us the secret places of his heart. Although Tschaikowsky's range of moods is wide—from the whimsical play of light fantasy to stormy outcries of anguish—essentially he was a melancholy man, in his music as in his life. Perhaps it is the genuineness of his music in conveying great pathos and suffering that has drawn millions to his symphonies and concertos. A frank sincerity and warmheartedness well from his music. The best of his melodies linger hauntingly in the mind and heart. So long as sincere feeling expressed in sincere artistic form can move the hearts of men, Tschaikowsky's music will continue to hold a high place in the concert hall and opera house.

Only Beethoven and Mozart can rival Tschaikowsky in the number of compositions in various musical forms that stand out as repertory favorites. Tschaikowsky's violin concerto is as much a "request" item as Beethoven's. The *Pathetic* symphony ranks with the three or four enduring favorites of the repertory. Tschaikowsky's *Nutcracker* ballet is probably the most popular suite of its kind in music. The opera, *Eugene Onegin,* a masterpiece worthy to stand beside some of the best Italian and German operas, is widely loved even outside Russia. Tschaikowsky's Piano Concerto, or, at any rate, the expansive opening theme, is doubtless known to more people than all other piano concertos put together. The overture-fantasies, *Romeo and Juliet* and *Francesca da Rimini,* rank with the most popular in that form, and the *Overture 1812* is an international "hit" with music-lovers of all ages and stages. Tschaikowsky's song, *None But the Lonely Heart,* is better known to many music-lovers than most of the songs of Brahms and Schubert, and the great String Quartet contains a melody familiar to every follower of popular song trends. For, of all the classical composers, Tschaikowsky has been a veritable gold-mine as a source of themes for popular arrangement.

Yet, this sad and sensitive musical genius who knew so well how to reach the human soul began his career not in music, but as a clerk

363

in the St. Petersburg Ministry of Justice. Like other great Russian composers, Tschaikowsky arrived at music by a circuitous route; indeed, almost by accident. Moussorgsky, one recalls, was long an officer in the Czar's Army before he switched to music. And Borodin always regarded music as a secondary pursuit to his medical practice and his laboratory experiments in chemistry. Tschaikowsky was first a lawyer. But soon he found court action and the preparation of briefs tiresome and unsavory toil, so at twenty-one he returned to his first love, which was music.

Born on May 7, 1840, Tschaikowsky had begun to study piano at the age of seven. When he was ten, his father, a director of a foundry at Votkinsk with next to no interest in music, took the family to St. Petersburg. There young Peter continued his musical studies, never, however, with any thought of preparing for a career in music. Yet, later, even while studying law, he went on playing the piano and taking part in the performances of a choral society. Although he amused friends by improvising on the piano, few detected any signs of creative genius. At twenty-one Tschaikowsky made his crucial break. He abandoned law, began earnestly to master musical theory, and resolved to risk poverty and starvation by devoting himself to music professionally. Today we can only applaud his decision. The repertory would be the poorer without his music. Nor is it at all likely that the law lost a great practitioner when the shy and retiring Tschaikowsky bade it farewell.

His first important step was to enroll in the Russian Musical Society, later to become the St. Petersburg Conservatory. There Anton Rubinstein, the renowned pianist and composer, then teaching composition and orchestration, exerted a lasting influence on him. At that time Anton's brother Nicholas was founding the Moscow Conservatory. Impressed by Tschaikowsky's brilliant showing at the St. Petersburg school, he engaged him as instructor in harmony for the new Moscow organization. Tschaikowsky held the post for eleven years. The pay was scant, but there were weightier compensations. Nicholas Rubinstein gave the young man a room in his Moscow house, encouraged him to compose, introduced him around, and gave him sound advice on sundry matters. Best of all, he produced many of Tschaikowsky's early compositions. Tschaikowsky, loyal and devoted in all his ties, never forgot his friend. After Rubinstein's death, he dedicated his Trio,

In Memory of a Great Artist, to the great man who had given him his real start in music and a creative life.

During his second year in the Moscow Conservatory Tschaikowsky fell madly in love with the French soprano Désirée Artôt, then touring Russia. While the indecisive Russian wasted time weighing the advantages and disadvantages of marriage, a Spanish baritone named Padilla came along, made violent love to Mlle. Artôt, and hurried her off to the altar before she could catch her breath and notify her Russian suitor. We nevertheless owe the fickle French lady a debt of gratitude. Without the emotional disturbance Tschaikowsky might not have been moved to write the *Romeo and Juliet* overture-fantasy. His first serious rebuff in love had at any rate paid dividends in artistic production.

From then on Tschaikowsky wrote at a feverish pace. Whenever his duties at the Conservatory could spare him, he retired to his study and wrote symphonies, overtures, operas, chamber music, songs, and religious choruses. Sometimes a gnawing doubt in his own talents assailed him. To his friends he wrote voluminous letters complaining of the strong sense of inferiority bedeviling his work. There were attacks of bleak gloom and diffidence lasting weeks. Trips to the country or to Italy and Switzerland were often needed to restore his damaged nervous system and jarred self-confidence to normalcy. Unfavorable reviews stung him like wasps. And while Moscow often evidenced great enthusiasm for his music, St. Petersburg was harder to please. The press there was often virulent with abuse.

Then Tschaikowsky pinned great hopes on his operas *Eugene Onegin* and *Pique Dame* ("The Queen of Spades"). Both proved fiascos at their premières, though the public and press later revised their opinions drastically. Moreover, reports reached him of the cold reception accorded his *Romeo and Juliet* in Paris and the catcalls greeting his music in Vienna. And there was a music critic named Eduard Hanslick in Vienna who kept Tschaikowsky awake at night wondering what new critical blast was awaiting his latest Viennese première.

Ironically, America and England were the only two countries instantly attracted to Tschaikowsky's music. There his prestige rose with each new symphony or overture. Cambridge University conferred an honorary doctor's degree on him in 1893. Europe was soon to be won over, however. Despite an often hostile press, the music publics of

France, Germany, and Austria began clamoring for more and more of his music, and conductors were forced to acquiesce. But to the end he remained a sorrowing and morose man, hypersensitive, even morbidly so, but almost always the soul of kindliness and punctilio. When, on the invitation of Walter Damrosch, Tschaikowsky came to America in 1891, he was widely acclaimed by public and press. While here he gave six concerts in all, four in New York, one in Baltimore and one in Philadelphia. In New York he was guest of honor on the programs of the New York Symphony Society celebrating the opening of the Music Hall, now Carnegie Hall. The festival lasted from May 5 to May 9, and Tschaikowsky was widely fêted socially and professionally. He conducted several of his own works in the hall constructed largely from funds provided by the steel magnate, Andrew Carnegie.

The year 1877 is an important one in the chronicle of Tschaikowsky's life. He made his one disastrous experiment in marriage with a romantic-minded young conservatory student named Antonina Miliukov. The girl had aroused his pity and alarm by her passionate avowals of love and equally passionate threats of suicide. The story is discussed below in my account of the Fourth Symphony, which grew partly out of that distressing episode. Suffice it here to note that the experience was so shattering to Tschaikowsky that he attempted to end his life by standing up to his neck at night in the freezing waters of the Neva River. Antonina eventually died in an insane asylum. Tschaikowsky formed another alliance that year, one far more profitable and far less nerve-wracking than his short tie with Mlle. Miliukov. This was his famous friendship with Nadezhda von Meck, a wealthy and cultivated widow. Out of profound admiration for his music and a probable romantic hope to become Mrs. Tschaikowsky, Mme. von Meck settled an annuity amounting to three thousand dollars on the destitute and ailing composer. The gift continued for thirteen years. Many letters about life, music, and people were exchanged between Tschaikowsky and his Lady Bountiful. The two refrained from any closer encounter, however. Tschaikowsky's Fourth Symphony is dedicated to this remarkable woman, who was the most famous Fairy Godmother in music.

Although Tschaikowsky himself thought of the *Pathetic* symphony as his crowning masterpiece, the première on October 28, 1893, in St. Petersburg proved a disappointment. Tschaikowsky took it bitterly.

Two weeks later, however, the tables were turned. Everybody acclaimed it warmly. But Tschaikowsky was not there to bow his
acknowledgment. He had fallen victim to the cholera epidemic then
raging in St. Petersburg. Though warned by the authorities, Tschaikowsky drank some unboiled water on November 2. Four days later
he was dead. No symphony was more appropriately named than this
melancholy masterpiece, the *Pathetic* symphony, the brooding phrases
of which sound truly like the "swan song" of a tired and abysmally
disillusioned man of genius.

MARCHES, OVERTURES, FANTASIAS, ETC.
Marche Slave, OPUS 31

The *Marche Slave* stands foremost among Tschaikowsky's marches,
of which he wrote numerous ones, including several incorporated in
his operas and suites. Most of them were composed for special purposes
or occasions. There is the *Marche Solenelle,* written "for the Law
Students," which figured on the housewarming program at the opening of Carnegie Hall in May, 1891, besides a *Marche Militaire,* which
he wrote for the band of the Czar's 98th Infantry Regiment. In 1883
the city of Moscow requisitioned a *Coronation March* from him. Earlier, Tschaikowsky had written a march in honor of the famous General Skobelev. But he held it in such low esteem that he allowed it to
circulate as the work of a non-existent composer named Sinopov.

The *Marche Slave* was written in 1876 for a benefit concert to raise
funds for soldiers wounded in the Turko-Serbian war, which presently
merged into a greater war between Turkey and Russia. It is based
largely on the old Russian anthem, "God Save the Emperor," and
some South Slavonic and Serbian tunes. The main theme has been
traced to the Serbian folk song, *Sunce varko ne fijas jednako* ("Come,
my dearest, why so sad this morning?"). Divided into three sections,
the march features fragments of the old Czarist hymn in the middle
portion. How the hymn itself came to be written is told by its author,
Alexis Feodorovich Lvov:

"In 1833, I accompanied the Emperor Nicholas during his travels in
Prussia and Austria. When we had returned to Russia I was informed
by Count von Benkendorf that the sovereign regretted that we Russians had no national anthem of our own, and that, as he was tired of

the English tune which had filled the gap for many years, he wished me to see whether I could not compose a Russian hymn.

"The problem appeared to me to be an extremely difficult and serious one. When I recalled the imposing British national anthem, 'God Save the King,' the very original French one and the really touching Austrian hymn, I felt and appreciated the necessity of writing something big, strong and moving; something national that should resound through a church as well as through the ranks of an army; something that could be taken up by a huge multitude and be within the reach of every man, from the dunce to the scholar. The idea absorbed me, but I was worried by the conditions thus imposed on the work with which I had been commissioned.

"One evening as I was returning home very late, I thought out and wrote down in a few minutes the tune of the hymn. The next day I called on Shoukovsky to ask him to write the words; but he was no musician and had much trouble to adapt them to the phrases of the first section of the melody.

"At last I was able to announce the completion of the hymn to Count von Benkendorf. The Emperor wished to hear it, and came on November 23 to the chapel of the Imperial Choir, accompanied by the Empress and the Grand Duke Michael. I had collected the whole body of choristers and re-enforced them by two orchestras. The sovereign asked for the hymn to be repeated several times, expressed a wish to hear it sung without accompaniment, and then had it played first of all by each orchestra separately and then finally by all the executants together. His Majesty turned to me and said in French: 'Why, it's superb!' and then and there gave orders to Count von Benkendorf to inform the Minister of War that the hymn was to be adopted for the army. The order to this effect was issued December 4, 1883. The first public performance of the hymn was on December 11, 1883, at the Grand Theater in Moscow. The Emperor seemed to want to submit my work to the judgment of the Moscow public. On December 25 the hymn resounded through the rooms of the Winter Palace on the occasion of the blessing of the colors.

"As proof of his satisfaction the Emperor graciously presented me with a gold snuff-box studded with diamonds, and in addition gave orders that the words 'God Save the Tsar' should be placed on the armorial bearings of the Lvov family."

PETER ILYITCH TSCHAIKOWSKY

VARIATIONS ON A ROCOCO THEME FOR VIOLONCELLO AND ORCHESTRA, OPUS 33

Tschaikowsky composed two works for 'cello and orchestra—the "Variations on a Rococo Theme," which date from December, 1876, and the "Pezzo capriccioso," written thirteen years later. The earlier composition far surpasses the later in technical ingenuity and expressive content, and Tschaikowsky's symphonic gifts, especially in the vein of sprightly daintiness at which he could be so adept, are better displayed.

Tschaikowsky dedicated the variations to his friend Wilhelm Karl Friedrich Fitzenhagen, who taught 'cello at the Moscow Conservatory and was first 'cellist of the Imperial Musical Society. Some years earlier Fitzenhagen had played 'cello in the world première of Tschaikowsky's second string quartet, in F major, and on March 23, 1882, joined Serge Taneieff and Ivan Hrimaly in the first performance, at the Moscow Conservatory, of Tschaikowsky's Piano Trio, inscribed to the memory of Nicholas Rubinstein who had died one year before.

The earliest recorded performance of the "Rococo" variations would seem to be that of the Allgemeine Deutsche Musikverein, with Fitzenhagen as soloist, at Wiesbaden on June 8, 1879. Since almost three years elapsed between the date of completion of the score and the Wiesbaden première, it is possible that a previous performance, perhaps a private one at the Conservatory, had intervened. In any case, the Wiesbaden audience greeted the variations warmly, one listener reportedly exclaiming: "This is indeed music!" The listener was Franz Liszt.

The "rococo" theme is of Tschaikowsky's own invention. It is announced in A major by the 'cello after some prefatory measures by the orchestra. There follow seven variations, rounded off by a coda. A "ritornello," or refrain, recurs between sections, imparting further charm and unity to the composition. The variations are marked as follows:—

    I. Moderato semplice
    II. Moderato semplice
    III. Andante sostenuto
    IV. Andante grazioso
    V. Allegro moderato
    VI. Andante
    VII. Allegro vivo.

The use of the word "rococo" to describe the theme has often puzzled listeners. It has been suggested that Tschaikowsky so labeled his original theme to prevent anyone from supposing he offered it as a sample of his true style. Strictly speaking, "rococo" belongs to the first half of the eighteenth century, having begun as a bizarre and ornate style of architecture. Later the word was applied to excessive daintiness and preciousness in art, and then somewhat loosely promoted to a term of praise to describe certain traits in the music of Haydn and Mozart. It is doubtless in the sense of eighteenth-century grace and charm that Tschaikowsky employed the word. Thus, in inventing the theme and so labeling it, Tschaikowsky admittedly borrowed a manner out of his "own natural groove."

Overture 1812, Opus 49

Although clearly a *pièce d'occasion* prompted by the commemoration of a crucial page in Russian history, the *Overture 1812* is a minor mystery in the Tschaikowsky catalogue. Supposedly Nicholas Rubinstein commissioned Tschaikowsky in 1880 to write a festival overture for the Moscow Exhibition. At least the composer admits as much in letters to Nadezhda von Meck and the conductor Napravnik.

But his friend Kashkin insisted the piece was requested for the ceremonies consecrating the Moscow Cathedral of the Savior, intended to symbolize Russia's part in the Napoleonic struggle. The overture, accordingly, pictured the great events beginning with the Battle of Borodino (September 7, 1812) and ending with Napoleon's flight from Moscow, after the city was set aflame. To make it more effective, the work was to be performed in the public square before the cathedral. An electric connection on the conductor's desk would set off salvos of real artillery, and all Moscow would thrill with thoughts of its heroic past. In any case Tschaikowsky finished the overture at Kamenka in 1880, and though the cathedral was dedicated in the summer of 1881, there is no record of the planned street scene having come off.

Instead, we find Tschaikowsky offering the overture to Eduard Napravnik, then directing the Imperial Musical Society of St. Petersburg: "Last winter, at Nicholas Rubinstein's request, I composed a Festival Overture for the concerts of the exhibition, entitled '1812.'" Tschaikowsky then makes a statement that possibly suggests an earlier rebuff: "Could you possibly manage to have this played? It is not of great value, and I shall not be at all surprised or hurt if you consider the style of the music unsuitable to a symphony concert." Apparently Napravnik turned down the overture, and its première was postponed to August 20, 1882, when it figured on an all-Tschaikowsky concert in the Art and Industrial Exhibition at Moscow.

Tschaikowsky's attitude to the work is further expressed in the letter to his patroness-saint Mme. von Meck. There he speaks of the overture as "very noisy" and having "no great artistic value" because it was written "without much warmth of enthusiasm." And in a diary entry of the time he refers to it as having "only local and patriotic significance."

The "patriotic significance," of course, is what gives the overture its *raison d'être* as a motion picture of historical events. Tschaikowsky's brushstrokes are bold and obvious. The French and Russians are clearly depicted through the use of the Czarist National Anthem and the *Marseillaise*. Fragments of Cossack and Novgorod folk songs enter the scheme, and the battle and fire scenes are as plain as pictures. As the overture develops, one envisions the clash of arms at Borodino, with the Russians stiffly disputing every step and the *Marseillaise* finally rising dominant. The Russians are hurled back; the French are in Moscow. Finally the city is ablaze and the dismal rout begins, as cathedral bells mingle with the roll of drums and the hymn, *God Preserve Thy People,* surges out in a paean of victory.

Capriccio Italien, OPUS 45

Described by Edwin Evans as a "bundle of Italian folk-tunes," the *Capriccio Italien* draws partly on published collections of such melodies and partly on popular airs heard by Tschaikowsky in 1880 while touring Italy. "I am working on a sketch of an 'Italian Fantasia' based on folk-songs," he notifies his patroness-confidante, Nadezhda von Meck, from Rome on February 17, 1880. "Thanks to the charming themes, some of which I have heard in the streets, the work will be effective."

Tschaikowsky's room at the Hotel Constanzi overlooked the barracks of the Royal Cuirassiers. Apparently the bugle-call sounded nightly in the barracks yards contributed another theme "heard in the streets," for it may be heard in the trumpet passage of the introduction. The *Italian Fantasia* was fully sketched out in Rome and the orchestration begun. With the title now changed to *Capriccio Italien,* the work was completed that summer on Tschaikowsky's return to Russia. Nicholas Rubinstein directed the première at Moscow on December 18, 1880. Six years later Walter Damrosch introduced it to America at a concert in the Metropolitan Opera House, the precise date being November 6, 1886.

After the introductory section, the strings chant a lyric theme of slightly melancholy hue, which the orchestra then develops. Later the oboes announce, in thirds, a simple folk melody of less somber character. This, too, is elaborately worked out, before the tempo changes and violins and flutes bring in another tune. This promptly subsides as a brisk march section sets in, followed by a return of the opening theme. There is a transition to a lively tarantella, then another bright theme in triple rhythm, and finally the Presto section, with a second tarantella motif leading to a brilliant close.

"It is a piece of music which relies entirely on its orchestration for its effects," writes Evans in the Master Musicians Series. "Its musical value is comparatively slight, but the coloring is so vivid and so fascinating, and the movement throughout so animated, that one does not realize this when listening to the work. It is only afterwards that one experiences certain pangs of regret that such a rich garment should bedeck so thin a figure."

SUITE No. 4, "MOZARTIANA," OPUS 61

In the temple of music Tschaikowsky worshiped one god above all others—Mozart. Before this god he knelt in lifelong homage. "It is thanks to Mozart that I have devoted my life to music," he wrote. In later years he confessed to a friend, "Do you know that when I play Mozart I feel brighter and younger, almost a youth." A diary entry of May 17, 1884, gives the first mention of what was eventually to become the Russian composer's graceful little offering at the Salzburg shrine: "Played Mozart with great enjoyment. *Idea for a suite from Mozart.*" But the idea incubated slowly. For it was not till three years later, on August 10, 1887, that Tschaikowsky applied the final touches to the "Mozartiana" suite, at, of all places, Aachen—an odd footnote to the grimmer annals of that historic site. Tschaikowsky had hastened there to be with his friend Kondratiev, who was gravely ill.

When the score was published in Moscow later that year, it carried some words of explanation in Russian, French, and German.

"For some incomprehensible reason, several excellent compositions by Mozart are little known not only to the general public but to many musicians," ran Tschaikowsky's preface, dated October 5. "The arranger of this Suite, which is entitled 'Mozartiana,' hoped to give a fresh impulse to the playing of these little masterpieces. Though simple in form, they are full of inimitable beauties." (Tschaikowsky's adjective is *nyedosyagayetik̲h,* literally "beyond reach," "unattainable.") The basic scoring of the Suite is for two flutes, two oboes, two clarinets, two bassoons, four horns, two trumpets, tympani, and strings. In the *Menuet* the horns are reduced to two and the tympani omitted. The *Preghiera* adds a harp. Glockenspiel and cymbals are added in the *Thème et Variations.*

I. *Gigue* (Allegro, G minor, 6/8). Tschaikowsky found this music in a collection of twelve piano pieces published in Leipzig by Breitkopf & Härtel. It is No. 11 of the set. Alfred Einstein lists it as Opus No. 574 in his edition of Köchel's "Chronological Thematic Catalogue" of Mozart's music, where it is called "Eine kleine Gigue für Klavier." Mozart composed it in Leipzig on May 16, 1789, jotting it down in an album kept by the court organist Engel. This was evidently Mozart's way of paying his respects to Bach, Leipzig's *genius loci,* as Einstein points out. No effort was made to flatter Bach by a strict imitation of style. Divided into two sections, each of which is repeated, the *Gigue* at first follows the patterns of a four-voice fugue, soon loses its strict form and goes its blithe, unhampered way.

II. *Menuet* (Moderato, D major). This is the twelfth in the Breitkopf & Härtel set of piano pieces. Einstein gives it an opus listing of 355, placing its composition in Vienna in 1790. Köchel had dated the minuet ten years earlier. Marked evidence of Mozart's "highest maturity" prompted the later revision of date. The *Menuet* follows the same sequence as the *Gigue:* it is in two parts, each being repeated. Omitting repetitions, the minuet takes up only forty-four measures. The usual Trio is conspicuous by its absence—an omission gallantly repaired in the early nineteenth century by the Abbé Stadler.

III. *Preghiera* (Andante non tanto). Here Tschaikowsky reaches Mozart through an intermediary—Franz Liszt. For the *Preghiera*

("Prayer") is based on Liszt's transcription of Mozart's motet, "Ave, verum corpus" (K. 618). The piano version, in typically rhapsodic vein is entitled, "A la Chapelle Sistine." Mozart's motet, calling for four voices, two violins, viola, bass, and organ, was completed on June 18, 1791, at Baden, where he had gone to visit his wife, who was to bear him his last son, Franz Xaver Wolfgang, the following month. Einstein's conjecture is that the motet was written as a Corpus Christi Day service for Anton Stoll, a school-teacher and choirmaster who had befriended Mozart in time of need and performed many of his church works. The medieval Latin hymn used in the motet is given below with a line-for-line prose translation:—

Ave verum corpus natum	(Hail, true body born
De Maria Virgine;	of the Virgin Mary;
Vere passum, immolatum	truly suffering One, sacrificed
In cruce pro homine;	on the cross for man;
Cujus latus perforatum	whose pierced side
Unda fluxit, sanguine,	ran with water and blood,
Esto nobis adoratum.	be thou worshipped by us
In mortis exanime.	in dread of death.")

IV. *Thème et Variations* (Allegro giusto). In the Mozart piano original these are ten variations on the Kalendar Monk's buffo aria, "Unser dummer Pöbel meint" from Gluck's best opera comique, "Die Pilger von Mecca." The comedy was produced in Vienna in 1764 in its French version, "La Rencontre Imprévue" ("The Unexpected Meeting"), based on a risqué comedy by Lesage and D'Orneval, first staged in Paris in 1726. After a European tour, it came back to Vienna in 1776 as a German *Singspiel*. In the French version, the Kalendar Monk's aria begins with the words, "Les hommes pieusement." Gluck came to hear Mozart play at one of Mme. Lange's concerts on March 11, 1783. Two weeks later he also attended Mozart's own concert. By way of tribute to the older man, Mozart then improvised the variations on the comic monologue. Mozart's own *Singspiel*, "The Abduction from the Seraglio," produced a year earlier, is very similar in plot to "Die Pilger von Mecca." Both revolve around a far-fetched tale of divided and reunited lovers against a mock Oriental background of harem intrigue and Sultanic mercy. In Osmin, Mozart has his own version of Gluck's Kalendar Monk, and he was not above pilfering some ideas from Rézia's music for the first-act aria of his hero Belmonte. For more reasons than one he owed the venerable Gluck the graceful obeisance of a set of variations on a theme from a comic opera so utterly overshadowed by his own. Gluck's aria, if not the opera, lives today largely because Mozart let his nimble fancy and fingers wander over it in 1783 and perhaps because Tschaikowsky, a century later, carried the process a step further.

Suite for Strings, *Souvenir de Florence,* Opus 70

Compared with his output in other forms, Tschaikowsky's chamber music is small, consisting of an early quartet, of which only the first movement survives, three complete string quartets, a trio, and the *Souvenir de Florence,* written for violins, violas, and 'cellos in pairs.

As the title implies, the work grew out of a visit to Italy early in 1890, though as a clew to the mood and manner of the music, *Souvenir de Florence* is a better title for the first two movements than for the others. The remaining *Allegretto moderato* and *Allegro vivace* bear an Italian "memory" only in so far as much other music by Tschaikowsky and other composers may share the same quality. Even a marked Slavic character is evident in places, which is only natural. As is well known, Tschaikowsky's overture-fantasy *Romeo and Juliet* is often dubbed "Romeo and Juliet of the Steppes."

A first mention of the *Souvenir* occurs in a letter to Ippolitoff-Ivanoff dated May 5, 1890, written shortly after Tschaikowsky's return from abroad. It is quoted by his brother Modeste: "My visit brought forth good fruit. I composed an opera, 'Pique Dame,' which seems a success to me. . . . My plans for the future are to finish the orchestration of the opera, sketch out a string sextet [the *Souvenir*], go to my sister at Kamenka for the end of the summer, and spend the whole autumn with you at Tiflis."

On the following June 30 he communicated news of the sextet to his patroness-saint Mme. von Meck, hoping she would be "pleased to hear" about it. "I know your love of chamber music," he writes, "and I hope the work will please you. I wrote it with the greatest enthusiasm and without the least exertion."

In November Tschaikowsky went to St. Petersburg for a rehearsal of *Pique Dame.* While there he arranged for a private hearing of the sextet by friends. The performance left him cold and he resolved to rewrite the Scherzo and Finale. By the following May the work was thoroughly remodeled. It was not till June, 1892, while in Paris, that he actually completed the revision to his satisfaction.

The four movements comprise an *Allegro con spirito* (D minor, 4-4), an *Adagio cantabile e con moto* (D major, 3-4), an *Allegretto moderato* (A minor, 2-4), and an *Allegro vivace* (D minor-D major, 2-4). The form is largely that of the classical string quartet, though characteristically bold and novel devices of color and structure abound. Often the strings are ingeniously treated to suggest wind instruments, and one senses Tschaikowsky's frequent striving for orchestral effects.

Research has failed to unearth the "opprobrious epithets" Tschaikowsky is alleged to have heaped upon this slight but appealing work.

OVERTURE-FANTASY, *Romeo and Juliet*

Shortly before the overture-fantasy on Shakespeare's tragedy took shape in Tschaikowsky's mind, he had been jilted by the French soprano Désirée Artôt, then enjoying a prodigious vogue as opera singer in St. Petersburg. The twenty-eight-year-old composer and Mlle. Artôt had become engaged in 1868, but the lady promptly left him and married the Spanish baritone Padilla y Ramos. The theory is that Tschaikowsky's composition grew out of the resulting emotional upset, or at least that his frame of mind conduced to tragic expression on a romantic theme.

The Artôt episode acted as stimulus, but the concrete suggestion for using Shakespeare's tragedy in a symphonic work came from Balakireff during a walk with Tschaikowsky and their friend Kashkin "on a lovely day in May." Balakireff, head of the group of five young Russian composers (Tschaikowsky was not one of them) bent on achieving a pure national idiom, went so far as to outline the scheme to Tschaikowsky, unfolding the possibilities of dramatic and musical coordination so vividly that the young composer took eagerly to the project. Balakireff even furnished the keys and hints for themes and development.

However, four months went by before Tschaikowsky plunged into the actual composition of the overture-fantasy. Balakireff kept in close touch with him and virtually supervised the process. His dogmatism and narrowness often bored and irritated the young composer. Balakireff accepted this and rejected that, was pitilessly graphic in his comments, and yet somehow egged on the hypersensitive Tschaikowsky to completion of a taxing assignment. Finally, in January of the following year, Balakireff and Rimsky-Korsakoff came to visit him and he could write: "My overture pleased them very much and it also pleases me." Still, the Moscow public responded coolly, and Tschaikowsky felt obliged to revise much of the score that summer. Further rewriting was done for the definitive edition brought out in 1881.

The thematic scheme is easy to follow. Friar Laurence takes his bow in a solemn andante introduction for clarinets and bassoons in F-sharp minor. The feud of the Montagues and Capulets rages in a B minor allegro. Romeo and Juliet enter via muted violins and English horn in a famous theme in D-flat major suggesting Tschaikowsky's song *Wer nur die Sehnsucht kennt* ("None But the Lonely Heart"). The strife-torn Montagues and Capulets return for another bout. Chords of muted violins and violas hinting at mystery and secrecy bring back the love music. The themes of Romeo and Juliet, the embattled families, and Friar Laurence are heard in succession, followed by a fierce orchestral crash, and the storm subsides to a roll of kettledrums.

Francesca da Rimini, FANTASIA FOR ORCHESTRA (AFTER DANTE), OPUS 32

Written in 1876, Tschaikowsky's symphonic treatment of the celebrated love story of Paolo and Francesca grew out of an original project for an opera on the same subject. He abandoned the idea of an opera when the libretto submitted to him proved impossible. Later Tschaikowsky again read through the fifth canto of Dante's *Inferno,* in which the tragedy is related. Stirred by the verses and also by Gustave Doré's illustrations, he resolved to write an orchestral fantasy on the subject.

Prefacing the score are the following lines from Dante's great poem: "Dante arrives in the second circle of hell. He sees that here the incontinent are punished, and their punishment is to be continually tormented by the cruelest winds under a dark and gloomy air. Among these tortured ones he recognizes Francesca da Rimini, who tells her story.

" '. . . There is no greater pain than to recall a happy time in wretchedness; and this thy teacher knows. But if thou hast such desire to learn the first root of our love, I will do like one who weeps and tells.

" 'One day, for pastime, we read of Lancelot, how love constrained him. We were alone, and without all suspicion. Several times reading urged our eyes to meet, and changed the color of our faces. But one moment alone it was that overcame us. When we read of how the fond smile was kissed by such a lover, he, who shall never be divided from me, kissed my mouth all trembling. The book, and he who wrote it, was a Galeotto. That day we read in it no farther.'

"While the one spirit thus spake, the other wept so that I fainted with pity, as if I had been dying; and fell, as a dead body falls."

Tschaikowsky used to insist that the following titles be given in the program-book at performances of his fantasia:

   I. Introduction: The gateway to the Inferno
       ("Leave all hope behind, all ye who enter here")
       Tortures and agonies of the condemned.
   II. Francesca tells the story of her tragic love for Paolo.
  III. The turmoil of Hades. Conclusion.

The composition starts with a descriptive setting, in which a sinister, gruesome picture is painted of the second circle of Dante's *Inferno*. The awesome scene, with its haunting, driving winds, desolate moans, and dread terror, is repeated at the end. In the middle occurs a section featuring a clarinet in a plaintive and tender melody heard against string pizzicati. This instantly evokes the image of Francesca telling her tragic tale, which mounts in fervor and reaches its shattering crisis, before the wailing winds of Dante's netherworld close in again.

BALLET SUITES

Suite from the Ballet, *Swan Lake*
(*Le Lac des Cygnes*)

All told, Tschaikowsky wrote three ballets, plus a scattering of incidental dances for operas, beginning with the surviving "Voyevode" fragments. The composition of *Swan Lake,* first of the trio—the others being *The Sleeping Beauty* and *The Nutcracker*—originated in a two-fold impulse, the need for ready cash and a fondness for French ballet music, especially the works of Delibes and the *Giselle* of Adolphe Adam, which Tschaikowsky regarded as archetype.

He evidently thought little of his initial effort, for shortly after the

Moscow production of *Swan Lake* he recorded in his diary: "Lately I have heard Delibes' very clever music. 'Swan Lake' is poor stuff compared to it. Nothing during the last few years has charmed me so greatly as this ballet of Delibes and 'Carmen.'" Per contra, the same entry bemoans the "deterioration" of German music, the immediate offender being the "cold, obscure and pretentious" C minor symphony of Brahms!

Tschaikowsky was probably sincere when he described his own ballet as "poor stuff" compared with Delibes'. That was in 1877. Performances of *Swan Lake* at the Bolshoi Theater had been flat, shabby, and badly costumed. A conductor inexperienced with elaborate ballet scores had directed. Modeste Tschaikowsky, in the biography of his brother, testifies to this. Numbers were omitted as "undanceable," and pieces from other ballets substituted. At length only a third of the original remained, and not the best. The ballet dropped out of the Moscow repertory, and it was not until 1894 that the enterprising Marius Petipa wrote to Moscow for the full score and produced *Swan Lake* with brilliant success at the Maryinsky Theater in St. Petersburg, on January 15, 1895. It has since remained a repertory staple. Pavlova, Karsavina, and Markova, among others, have interpreted the heroine Odette, and Prince Siegfried has been embodied by Nijinsky, Lifar, Mordkin, and Dolin. *Swan Lake* was one of the first ballets witnessed in his youth by Serge Diaghileff, founder of the famous Ballets Russes.

Tschaikowsky first refers to *Swan Lake* in a letter to Rimsky-Korsakoff, dated September 10, 1875: "I accepted the work partly because I need the money and because I have long cherished a desire to try my hand at this type of music." V. P. Begitche, stage manager of the Bolshoi, offered eight hundred roubles (less than five hundred dollars) and in turn granted Tschaikowsky's request for a story from the Age of Chivalry, making the sketch himself. Tschaikowsky set to work in August, 1875, and had the first two acts planned out in a fortnight, but the score was not completed till the following March and for some reason held up for performance until February, 1877.

The story, possibly of Rhenish origin, tells how Prince Siegfried woos and wins Odette, the Swan Queen. At a celebration the prince is told he must soon choose a bride. A flight of swans overhead distracts him and a hunt is proposed. Siegfried and the hunters are at the lake-side. It is evening. Odette appears surrounded by a bevy of swan-maidens. She begs the hunters to spare the swans. They are maidens under the spell of the enchanter, Rotbart. Swans by day, they return briefly to human form at midnight. The prince and Odette fall in love. Siegfried swears she will be his wife. Odette cautions him about Rotbart's evil power. Breach of promise will mean her death. Rotbart brings his own daughter to the court ball, disguised as Odette. Siegfried makes the false choice of a bride, and the pledge is broken. Discovering Rotbart's ruse, he hastens to Odette, who at first rebuffs him. Siegfried blames Rotbart and Odette relents. At length Rotbart whips up a storm which floods the forest. When Siegfried vows he will die with Odette, Rotbart's spell is shattered and all ends happily.

Tschaikowsky's close friend and collaborator, Kashkin, is authority for the statement that an adagio section in *Swan Lake* was a love-duet in the opera *Undine* before it found new lodgings. Conversely, a Danse Russe in the group of piano pieces, Op. 40, was written for *Swan Lake,* thus balancing matters. Like *The Sleeping Beauty* and *The Nutcracker, Swan Lake* is famed for its waltz. The score brims with typical Tschaikowskyan melody, and probably for the first time in ballet music a scheme of leitmotifs is used, two of the principal subjects being the tremulous theme of the swans in flight and the hauntingly wistful theme of Odette herself, assigned to the oboe against soft strings and harp arpeggios. The music adjusts itself snugly to the technique of pure classical ballet and solos and ensembles are contrasted adroitly.

SUITE FROM THE BALLET, *The Sleeping Beauty*, OPUS 66

Based on Perrault's famous fairy tale, Tschaikowsky's *Sleeping Beauty* ballet dates from the summer of 1889. Its music is generally regarded as superior to that of the *Swan Lake* ballet and inferior to that of the *Nutcracker* suite. Few ballet scores are so suitable in mood and style for the action they accompany. The music is truly melodious in Tschaikowsky's lighter vein. The fantasy is conveyed in bright, glittering colors, and, as Mrs. Newmarch pointed out, the music "never descends to the commonplace level of the ordinary ballet music." There are thirty numbers in all, many of them, especially the waltz, endearing in their lilting and haunting grace. The work was first produced in St. Petersburg on January 2, 1890. In the early twenties, Diaghileff, the great ballet producer, revived the work in London and elsewhere with immense artistic *éclat*. Fragments of the ballet have been gathered in the Monte Carlo Ballet Russe's production of *Aurora's Wedding*. A brilliant and spectacular revival of the complete ballet has been that of the Sadler's Wells company of London.

SUITE FROM THE BALLET, *The Nutcracker*, OPUS 71-A

The usual fit of depression assailed Tschaikowsky while composing the music for his *Nutcracker* ballet, based on E. T. A. Hoffmann's story *Nussknacker und Mausekönig* ("Nutcracker and Mouse King"). Commissioned by the St. Petersburg Opera early in 1891, the work was slow in taking shape. At length, on June 25, Tschaikowsky completed the sketches for the projected ballet. What had taken him weeks should have been finished in five days, he lamented. "No, the old man is breaking up," he wrote. "Not only does his hair drop out, or turn as white as snow; not only does he lose his teeth, which refuse their service; not only do his eyes weaken and tire easily; not only do his feet walk badly, or drag themselves along, but, bit by bit, he loses the capacity to do anything at all. The ballet is infinitely worse than 'The Sleeping Beauty'—so much is certain."

Apparently the first night audience agreed with him, for at the première in the Imperial Opera House, the response was chilling. Yet an earlier concert performance of the music had drawn plaudits from both public and press. The ballet's failure, however, was easy to explain. The producer, Marius Petipa, fell ill, and the work of staging the new ballet was entrusted to a man of inadequate skill and experience. Then, the audience found it hard to thrill to the spectacle of children dashing coyly about in the first act. And balletomanes, accustomed to beauty and glamor in their favorite ballerinas, found the girl dancing the part of the Sugarplum Fairy anything but appetizing to look at.

Act I of the ballet is concerned with a Christmas Tree party. The scene is overrun with children and mechanical dolls. Little Marie is drawn to a German Nutcracker, which is made to resemble an old man with huge jaws. During a game, some boys accidentally break the Nutcracker. Marie is saddened by the tragedy. That night she lies awake in bed, sleepless with grief over the broken utensil. Finally, she jumps out of bed and goes to take one more look at the beloved Nutcracker. Suddenly strange sounds reach her ears. Mice! The Tree now seems to come to life and grow massive. Toys begin to stir into action, followed by cakes and candies. Even the Nutcracker creaks into life. Presently a battle arises between the mice and the toys. The Nutcracker challenges the Mouse King to a duel. Just as the Nutcracker is about to be felled, Marie hurls a shoe and kills the royal rodent. And of course, the Nutcracker promptly is transformed into a handsome prince. Arm in arm, they leave for his magic kingdom.

The scene now changes to a mountain of jam for the second act. This is the land ruled by the Sugarplum Fairy, who is awaiting the arrival of Marie and her princely escort. The court cheers jubilantly when the happy pair appears on the scene. What follows is the series of dances usually heard in the concert hall. The sequence runs as follows:

Miniature Overture (*Allegro giusto,* B-flat, 4-4), featuring two sharply differentiated themes, scored largely for the higher instruments.

March (*Tempo di marcia vivo,* G major, 4-4), in which the main theme is chanted by clarinets, horns and trumpets, as the children make their measured entrance.

Dance of the Sugarplum Fairy (*Andante con moto,* E minor, 2-4). Here the celesta gives out the entrancing melody, with pizzicato strings accompanying.

Russian Dance: Trepak (*Tempo di trepak, molto vivace,* G major, 2-4), which grows out of a brisk rhythmic figure heard at the beginning.

Arabian Dance (*Allegretto,* G minor, 3-8). Intended to convey the idea of "Coffee." A melody in Oriental mood is announced by the clarinet, later picked up by the violins.

Chinese Dance (*Allegretto moderato,* B-flat major, 4-4). Intended to convey the idea of "Tea." The melody is given to the flute against a pizzicato figure sustained by bassoons and double basses.

Dance of the Mirlitons (*Moderato assai,* D major, 2-4). For the main theme three flutes join forces. Then comes a different melody given out by the trumpets in F-sharp minor before the chief subject is back.

Waltz of the Flowers (*Tempo di valse,* D major, 3-4). Woodwinds and horns, aided by a harp-cadenza, offer some introductory phrases. Then the horns give out the fetching main melody. Soon the clarinets take it up. Flute, oboe, and strings bring in other themes, and the waltz comes to a brilliant close.

CONCERTOS

CONCERTO FOR VIOLIN AND ORCHESTRA, IN D MAJOR, OPUS 35

Before occupying its permanent niche in the repertory, Tschaikowsky's violin concerto had to run a fierce gantlet of fault-finding. Friend and foe alike took pokes at it. The wonder is that it survived at all. Even Mme. von Meck, Tschaikowsky's patroness-saint, picked serious flaws in the work, and the lady was known for her unwavering faith in Tschaikowsky's genius.

As a matter of fact, Tschaikowsky, often an unsparing critic of his own music, started the trend by finding objection with the Andante and rewriting it wholly. That was in April, 1878. He was spending the spring at Clarens, Switzerland. Joseph Kotek, a Russian violinist and composer, was staying with him. Tschaikowsky and Kotek went over the work several times, and evidently saw eye-to-eye on its merits.

Then came the first outside rebuff. Mme. von Meck was frankly dissatisfied and showed her reasons in detail. Tschaikowsky meekly wrote back pleading guilty on some counts but advancing the hope that in time his Lady Bountiful might come to like the concerto. He stood pat on the first movement, which Mme. von Meck particularly assailed.

"Your frank judgment on my violin concerto pleased me very much," he writes. "It would have been very disagreeable to me if you, from any fear of wounding the petty pride of a composer, had kept back your opinion. However, I must defend a little the first movement of the concerto.

"Of course, it houses, as does every piece that serves virtuoso purposes, much that appeals chiefly to the mind; nevertheless, the themes are not painfully evolved: the plan of this movement sprang suddenly in my head and quickly ran into its mould. I shall not give up the hope that in time the piece will give you greater pleasure."

Next came a more serious setback from Leopold Auer, the widely respected Petersburg virtuoso. Auer was then professor of violin at the Imperial Conservatory and the Czar's court violinist. Tschaikowsky, hoping to induce Auer to launch the concerto on its career, originally dedicated the work to him. But Auer glanced through the score and promptly decided against it. It was "impossible to play."

Tschaikowsky later made a quaintly worded entry in his diary to the effect that Auer's pronouncement cast "this unfortunate child of my imagination for many years to come into the limbo of hopelessly forgotten things." Justly or unjustly, he even suspected Auer of having prevailed on the violinist Emile Sauret to abstain from playing it in St. Petersburg.

The ice finally broke when Adolf Brodsky, after two years of admitted laziness and indecision, took it up and succeeded in performing it with the Vienna Philharmonic on December 4, 1881. Yet, even Brodsky, despite his wholehearted espousal of the work, complained to Tschaikowsky that he had "crammed too many difficulties into it." Previously, in Paris, Brodsky had experimented with the concerto by playing it to Laroche, who, whether because of Brodsky's rendering or the concerto's inherent character, confessed "he could gain no true idea of the work."

Even the première went against the new concerto. In the first place Brodsky had to do some strong propagandizing to get Hans Richter to include the work on a Philharmonic program. Then, only one rehearsal was granted. The orchestral parts, according to Brodsky, "swarmed with errors." At the rehearsal nobody liked the new work. Besides, Richter wanted to make cuts, but Brodsky promptly scotched the idea. Finally, during the performance, the musicians, still far from having mastered the music, accompanied everything pianissimo, "not to go smash."

Of course, Brodsky outlines the chain of contretemps in a letter to Tschaikowsky partly to assuage the composer's pained feelings on receiving news of the Vienna fiasco. For the première ended with a broadside of hisses, completely obliterating the polite applause coming from some friendly quarters. As the *coup de grâce,* Eduard Hanslick, Europe's uncrowned ruler of musical destinies, wrote a scathing notice, which Philip Hale rendered as follows:

"For a while the concerto has proportion, is musical, and is not without genius, but soon savagery gains the upper hand and lords it to the end of the first movement.

"The violin is no longer played. It is yanked about. It is torn asunder. It is beaten black and blue. I do not know whether it is possible for any one to conquer these hair-raising difficulties, but I do know that Mr. Brodsky martyrized his hearers as well as himself.

"The Adagio, with its tender national melody, almost conciliates, almost wins us. But it breaks off abruptly to make way for a finale that puts us in the midst of the brutal and wretched jollity of a Russian kermess. We see wild and vulgar faces, we hear curses, we smell bad brandy.

"Friedrich Vischer once asserted in reference to lascivious paintings, that there are pictures which 'stink in the eye.' Tschaikowsky's violin concerto brings to us for the first time the horrid idea that there may be music that stinks in the ear."

The pestiferous odors of the Hanslick blast further embittered Tschaikowsky's already gloomy disposition, and it is not surprising to learn that the review haunted him till the day he died. But Brodsky's unflagging devotion to the concerto, together with his practical missionary zeal in acquainting the European public with it, finally started the concerto on its path of glory.

"Nor was that the end of time's revenges," wrote Pitts Sanborn. "Hanslick was to write glowingly of the 'Pathetique' symphony, and in due course Leopold Auer not only played the unplayable concerto himself, but made a specialty of teaching it to his pupils, who have carried its gospel the world over. But while the belated triumphs were accruing Tschaikowsky died."

The dedication is to Brodsky, who certainly earned it.

The first movement (*Allegro moderato,* D major, 4-4), opens with a melody for strings and woodwind. Then the solo violin is heard in a cadenza-like sequence followed by the first theme (*Moderato assai*). A second theme, *Molto espressive,* is next discoursed by the violin in A major. Instead of the usual development there is an intricate cadenza without accompaniment. A long and brilliant coda concludes the movement.

The second movement (*Canzonetta: Andante,* 3-4) starts with the muted solo violin chanting, after a brief preface, a nostalgic theme in G minor. The flute and clarinet then offer the first phrase of this theme, and later the solo violin unreels a Chopinesque second subject, in E-flat major, *con anima.* The clarinet offers an obbligato of arpeggios when the first theme returns. The rousing finale is an *Allegro vivacissimo* in D major, 2-4.

The Rondo-like last movement, typically Russian in theme and rhythm, develops from two folk-like melodies. Listeners will be reminded of the well-known Russian dance, the Trepak, in this movement. The music builds up at a brisk pace to a crashing climax.

CONCERTO FOR PIANO AND ORCHESTRA, IN B-FLAT MINOR, No. 1, OPUS 23

Like the violin concerto, Tschaikowsky's great piano concerto in B-flat minor went through a gruelling ordeal of abusive rebuffs and setbacks before becoming established as one of the world's most beloved symphonic scores. In the case of the violin work, it was Leopold Auer who first flouted it as unplayable, and then made it a popular repertory standby. Nicholas Rubinstein is the name linked with the early stages of the piano concerto. After excoriating the concerto in its first state, Rubinstein grew to like it, humbly apologized for his blunder, and made practical amends by playing it in public with huge success.

Early in its composition we find Tschaikowsky writing to his brother Anatol: "I am so completely absorbed in the composition of a piano concerto. I am anxious that Rubinstein should play it at his concert. The work proceeds very slowly and does not turn out well. However, I stick to my intentions and hammer piano passages out of my brain; the result is nervous irritability." Begun in November, 1874, the concerto was completed the following month. Rubinstein was then invited to hear the work. Rubinstein and one or two musical colleagues gathered in one of the classrooms of the Moscow Conservatory. Unluckily, the great man was in a sombre mood that day. Tschaikowsky sat down and played the first movement. No comment from Rubinstein. Then he played the Andantino. Still no comment. Finally, Tschaikowsky ran through the last movement. He turned around expectantly. Rubinstein said nothing. Uneasily, Tschaikowsky asked him pointblank: "What do you think of it?" And the storm broke. It was vulgar, cheap, pianistic, completely valueless, retorted Rubinstein, who then stepped up to the piano and began to burlesque the music.

"I left the room without saying a word and went upstairs," writes the distraught Tschaikowsky. "I could not have spoken for anger and agitation. Presently Rubinstein came to me and, seeing how upset I

386

was, called me into another room. There he repeated that my concerto was impossible, pointed out many places where it needed to be completely revised, and said that if I would suit the concerto to his requirements, he would bring it out at his concert.

" 'I shall not alter a single note,' I replied. 'I shall publish the work precisely as it stands.' This intention I actually carried out." Tschaikowsky did make some alterations in the score, however.

Tschaikowsky changed his mind about dedicating the score to Rubinstein, conferring the honor on Hans von Bülow, instead. Von Bülow played the world première in Boston on October 25, 1875, and in a letter to the Russian composer conveyed his enthusiasm for the work: "The ideas are so original, so noble, so powerful; the details are so interesting, and though there are many of them they do not impair the clearness and the unity of the work. The form is so mature, ripe, distinguished for style, for intention and labor are everywhere concealed. I should weary you if I were to enumerate all the characteristics of your work—characteristics which compel me to congratulate equally the composer as well as all those who shall enjoy the work actively or passively, respectively." Later Tschaikowsky, reading reports of how Americans were acclaiming his concerto, wrote: "Think what healthy appetites these Americans must have! Each time Bülow was obliged to repeat the whole finale of my concerto! Nothing like this happens in our own country."

The concerto opens with a striking theme, *Allegro non troppo e molto maestoso,* in D-flat major, 3-4, familiar to music-lovers of all tastes the world over. The strings take it up after some brief preluding, and it is then repeated, with rhythmic modification, by the solo piano. There is a piano cadenza, and the theme comes back by way of the strings, minus double-basses, against an ascending obbligato from the piano. For reasons best known to himself, Tschaikowsky never allows this imposing theme to return to the scene.

The "blind beggar tune" is the name often applied to the piano theme serving as chief subject of the main section of the first movement (*Allegro con spirito,* B-flat minor). Tschaikowsky heard it sung on a street in Kamenko and he wrote to his patroness-friend, Mme. von Meck: "It is curious that in Russia every blind beggar sings exactly the same tune with the same refrain. I have used part of this refrain in my piano concerto." Horns and woodwind discourse the second subject (*Poco meno mosso,* A-flat major) before the solo instrument turns to it.

The song-like first theme of the second movement (*Andantino semplice,* D-flat major, 6-8) is given out first by the flute, with the oboe and clarinets bringing in the second subject against a bassoon accompaniment. The *Prestissimo* middle section in F major, has the spirit of a Scherzo. A waltz enters the scheme by way of violas and 'cellos. Tschaikowsky's brother, Modeste, insisted the theme of this waltz was derived from a French song the brothers Tschaikowsky used to sing and whistle in their boyhood days.

The Rondo-like finale develops from three themes, the first of which, a lively dance in Cossack style, is given out by the piano. A further folk-like quality is observable in the second theme, and the violins later chant the third of the finale's themes. In the brisk Coda the Cossack-like first theme is given the dominant rôle.

SYMPHONIES

Symphony in C Minor, No. 2, Opus 17

Embedded in Tschaikowsky's Second Symphony is one of the little ironies of Russian music. Though at one time close to it, Tschaikowsky was never identified with the school of Russian nationalism launched by "The Five"—Balakireff, Rimsky-Korsakoff, Cui, Borodin, and Moussorgsky. In fact, critical spokesmen of the group later denounced Tschaikowsky's music as eclectic, Western, non-Russian. They taunted him with being drawn to German and Italian models, rather than to native sources for inspiration. Much of their criticism reads like a patriotic tirade against some dangerous renegade. Yet, Tschaikowsky's Second Symphony is drenched in Russian color. The themes of the first and last movement are based on "Little Russian" (*Malorusski*) folk melodies, whence the term "Little Russian Symphony," often used as a descriptive subtitle for the C minor. For a time "The Five," the self-styled "Koochka" (literally, "little heap or huddle") of Russian nationalism, hailed the symphony as a token of Tschaikowsky's conversion. But not for long. The cleavage widened again, relations became strained, and Tschaikowsky resolved to continue along his own path. How sharp the divergence grew may be gathered from a

passage in a letter to his brother written only one year after the
Moscow première of the Second Symphony. There he speaks of
Moussorgsky's music as "the lowest, commonest parody of music; it
may go to the devil for all I care." In retrospect the controversy between the "Westerns" and the "Nationals" of nineteenth century
Russian music seems futile and regrettable. The concert repertory, indifferent to the claims of "schools," has found room for their best
compositions. And both Russian and non-Russian audiences would
now probably agree in finding Tschaikowsky's music no less "national"
in feeling and content than that of "The Five." As a matter of fact,
for many he is the Russian composer *par excellence,* though others
would insist on Moussorgsky, whose strong, rugged music is said to
reflect best the sturdy, irrepressible spirit of Russia.

As in the case of the poet Homer, several cities might lay claim to
being the birthplace of the Second Symphony. The process of composing and revising the work is a tale of five cities. Even Rome is included. Tschaikowsky began the symphony at Kamenka, in June 1872.
Work on it continued at Ussovo while Tschaikowsky was visiting a
sick friend. Back in Moscow in November, we find him apologizing to
his brother for a long delay in writing: "What can I do when the
symphony, which is nearing completion, occupies me so entirely that
I can think of nothing else? . . . It seems to me to be my best work,
at least as regards correctness of form, a quality for which I have not
so far distinguished myself." Early in January Tschaikowsky showed
the manuscript to Rimsky-Korsakoff in St. Petersburg. Some alterations
followed. On February 7, 1873 Nicholas Rubinstein led the Imperial
Musical Society in the world première of the C minor. "My symphony
met with great success," writes Tschaikowsky to V. Strassov the following day. "So great in fact, that N. Rubinstein is repeating it at the
tenth concert, 'by general request.'" He then confesses he is not quite
satisfied with the first two movements. Yet, the finale, based partly on
"The Crane," a "Little Russian" folk song, "has turned out admirably." On March 9 Napravnik conducted the new score in St. Petersburg. Most of the "Koochka" received it warmly. Not Cesar Cui,
however. The dread paladin of the pen, something of a Hanslick of
Russia, pounced ruthlessly on the new symphony: "The Introduction and first Allegro are very weak; the poverty of Tschaikowsky's
invention displays itself every moment. The March in the second

movement is rough and commonplace. The Scherzo is neither good nor bad; the Trio is so innocent that it would be almost too infantile for a 'Sniegourotchka.' The best movement is the Finale, and even then the opening is as pompously trivial as the introduction to a *pas de deux,* and the end is beneath all criticism." Whether goaded by Cui's strictures or by his own powers of self-criticism, Tschaikowsky revised the symphony. Six years later, he writes to Mme. von Meck, from Rome: "Today I set out to remodel my Second Symphony. How much seven years can mean when a man is striving for progress in his work! Is it possible that seven years hence I shall look upon what I write today as I look now at my music written in 1872? I know it is possible because perfection—the ideal—is boundless."

One of the earliest American appraisals of Tschaikowsky's Second Symphony, first rendered here by the New York Symphony Society in 1883, was that of the noted critic and essayist, James Gibbons Huneker. "In it Tschaikowsky begins to reveal his skill in orchestration," he wrote; "and the themes of the first movement are all strong; at least two of its movements are not symphonic in character. The first *Allegro,* the strongest, is very Russian in thematic quality. The entire movement is characterized by a bizarre freedom, even recklessness. But there can be no doubt about the skill of its maker. The fantastic *Durchführungssatz* and the melancholy beauty of the opening—and very Slavic theme—are intimations of the greater Tschaikowsky who came later. He omits the slow movement and marches us to the lilting rhythms of Raff and Gounod. The harmonies are more piquant, for the Russian wields a marvelous color brush. It is a clever episode, yet hardly weighty enough for symphonic treatment. For that matter neither is the banal march in Raff's *Lenore Symphony.* The *Scherzo* that follows is in the Saint-Saëns style. It reveals plenty of spirit and there is the diabolic, riotous energy that pricks the nerves, yet never strikes fire in our souls. . . . The *Finale* is very charming and the variation-making genius of the composer peeps out. The movement has the whirl and glow of some wild dance-mood and over all Tschaikowsky has cast the spell of his wondrous orchestration. In the work are potentialities that are realized in his later symphonic works. It is our beloved Tschaikowsky, but as yet in precipitation. In style immature, there is much groping after effects—effects which he used with such a sure touch in *Hamlet* and *Francesca.* Those piano staccato chords for the brass choir, a genuine mannerism, are already here, and his fondness for chromatic scales, contrapuntally used, may be noted. An interesting symphony!"

I. A long introduction (Andante sostenuto, C minor, 4/4) built partly on a typical Slavic theme, elegiac in mood, precedes the main section (Allegro vivo) of the first movement. Violins announce the principal subject, with other strings accompanying. The orchestra develops the material before the oboe brings in a second theme, of lyric and mellow character, supported by clarinets and bassoons. Violas and cellos pick up the theme, as the violins counter with one of their own. Fragments of the folk-line melody first used in the Introduction are heard again in the coda, which dwindles back to an Andante sostenuto.

II. The second movement (Andantino marziale, quasi moderato, E-flat major, 4/4) opens and closes to a roll of tympani rhythms. Clarinets and bassoon join in the opening march theme, taken from Tschaikowsky's unpublished opera *Undine,* which the St. Petersburg Opera turned down in 1869. First violins give out the second theme, *espressivo,* repeated by bassoons and cellos. Then the march theme is back. Both subjects are developed fully. The march is stated again brilliantly by the orchestra, and the movement fades out to the returning beat of the kettledrums.

III. Brimming with rollicking rhythms and sharp changes of mood, the Scherzo (Allegro molto vivace, C minor, 3/8) opens with the first theme in the violins. Descending chromatics in the second violins and violas lead to the second subject, also assigned to the first violins. There is a repetition of the first theme and the trio begins (L'istesso tempo, E-flat major, 2/8). This is based on a simple song of Slavic flavor, first chanted by horns and woodwinds. There is some whimsical bandying about of the material, ending in a crisp exchange between woodwinds and strings. The Scherzo section returns, leading to a coda containing echoes of the trio theme.

IV. After an introductory passage (Moderato assai), the Finale gets under way with the first violins announcing the chief theme (Allegro vivo, C major, 2/4). This is the little tune "The Crane," which, more than anything else, prompted Nicholas Kashkin to christen the C minor the "Little Russian Symphony." A plain, eight-bar melody, it undergoes varied, shifting treatment, before the strings introduce a second theme, more expressive and Tschaikowsky's own this time. This, too, is subjected to interesting variation. Both themes are heard again in succession, finally combined. The material is worked up with furious verve in a brilliant Presto, where the first theme has the last word.

SYMPHONY IN F MINOR, NO. 4, OPUS 36

At first sight, this symphony arouses no "cherchez la femme" mystery. Seemingly, the lady is not far to seek. In fact, Tschaikowsky throws off the search in his dedication. The lady is Madame Nadia Filaretovna von Meck. She was his loyal confidante and benefactress. The least Tschaikowsky could do was to dedicate a symphony to her. Comfort and encouragement in the form of checks and adulatory letters from Mme. von Meck saw the sorrowing Slav through many bleak periods.

The association has been called "the most amazing romance in musical history." That the "romance" was purely platonic does not make it any the less "amazing." Whatever Mme. von Meck's secret hopes and longings, Tschaikowsky shrank from carrying the liaison beyond epistolary scope. Mme. von Meck resigned herself to an advisory rôle of patroness-friend, and played it nobly. The world reveres her for it. "*Our* symphony," Tschaikowsky wrote to her, communicating his intention to dedicate the Fourth to her. "I believe you will find in it echoes of your deepest thoughts and feelings."

What Tschaikowsky meant, of course, was "*my* deepest thoughts and feelings." The plural possessive, "*ours,*" is gallant rather than collaborative. Even so, he could with more truth than courtesy have written to another woman, Antonina Ivanovna Miliukov, in similar style. Antonina was Tschaikowsky's wife in a domestic disaster lasting two weeks. The whole episode—spanning a wild sequence of engagement, marriage, flight in the night, attempted suicide, separation— nestles snugly in the period of the symphony's origin. Antonina would have understood the words "*our* symphony." Only fate and brother Anatol saved it from becoming Tschaikowsky's obituary. Not that it was entirely Antonina's fault. But no psychological analysis of the Fourth can be complete without her.

The girl was a conservatory pupil. Tschaikowsky's music had begun to act like a potion upon her, and through it she had come to a slavish, fanatical worship of the composer. Next followed written avowals of passion which at first amused Tschaikowsky, then alarmed him, and finally, as they became frantic, haunted him. The girl was persistent, and as her pleas became more frequent, they grew more piteous and despairing. To make matters worse, the sensitive Tschaikowsky was immersed at the time in his romantic opera, "Eugene Onegin." He had just composed music for Tatiana's impassioned love letter to Onegin. Antonina's own plight was too much like the spurned Tatiana's to be lost on Tschaikowsky's susceptible nature. Onegin's cold disdain had virtually wrecked the girl's life, and it suddenly dawned on the composer that Antonina might even kill herself. In a moment of dramatic self-analysis, he probably saw himself as another and more heartless Onegin. The situation was not unflattering to his vanity.

At length, he made a courteous offer of friendship, but the gesture only stirred up more trouble. After studious delay, Tschaikowsky finally granted the long-sought meeting. Antonina was convinced she had won. Tschaikowsky depicted himself to her as a morose, ill-tempered neurotic who would assuredly drive her mad. But the girl was not to be balked of her prey: there was only one way out—marriage. With a sigh of helplessness, Tschaikowsky gave in, and they were soon engaged. Attempts to break the engagement proved futile, for Antonina was bent on becoming Mrs. Tschaikowsky at all costs. They were married and in a few lurid days Tschaikowsky had already fled for his sanity. Then came a reconciliation, and there followed two dreadful weeks of tragico-farcical life together. One night, in a frantic daze, Tschaikowsky fled again, wandering about wildly till he reached the Neva River. He had made up his mind. He waded in till he stood waist deep in the cold water, hoping to freeze to death. Luckily, he was seen standing there and rescued in time.

Though for long he bordered on insanity, somehow the bewildered composer came through the crisis with his reason intact. His brother Anatol took him to Switzerland, and slowly Tschaikowsky returned to his normal self. He never saw Antonina Ivanovna again. The clinical aspects of this curious mésalliance have been thoroughly aired in recent years. Through the publication of long-withheld letters, fresh light was thrown on Tschaikowsky's temperament. It is obvious, and should have been obvious to all who knew Tschaikowsky well, that

Antonina and he were mentally and physically incompatible. The gentleman to the end, Tschaikowsky never made a harsh reference to his wife. And Antonina, for her part, graciously cleared him in her memoirs. Reviewing the whole episode in temperate tones, she observed, "Peter was in no way to blame."

During this period, which extends from May to September, 1877, Tschaikowsky worked on his Fourth Symphony. Just how much of his private woes were transmuted into symphonic speech cannot be determined, even from Tschaikowsky's own written confidences. Possibly, the symphony was an avenue of escape from his mounting anxieties. Anyway, his completion of the sketch coincides with his engagement to Antonina in May. The orchestration of the first movement took up a month, from August 11 to September 12—the breathing spell between his two flights from Antonina. Then followed the nerve-racking fortnight in Moscow. The other three movements were completed in the Swiss Alps, where, thanks to his brother, he regained his full sanity and working tempo. A passage in a letter to Mme. von Meck, during the Antonina regime, suggests an explanation of Tschaikowsky's abstract talk of Fate in connection with his Fourth: "We cannot escape our fate, and there was something fatalistic about my meeting with this girl." In January, 1878, when the whole dismal affair was safely locked away in the past, he wrote to Mme. von Meck that he could only recall his marriage as a bad dream:

"Something remote, a weird nightmare in which a man bearing my name, my likeness, and my consciousness acted as one acts in dreams: in a meaningless, disconnected, paradoxical way. That was not my sane self, in possession of logical and reasonable will-powers. Everything I then did bore the character of an unhealthy conflict between will and intelligence, which is nothing less than insanity."

Tschaikowsky wrote to the composer Taneieff that there was not a single bar in his Fourth Symphony which he had not truly felt and which was not an echo of his "most intimate self." He frankly avowed the symphony's "programmatic" character, but declared it was "impossible to give the program in words." Yet, to Mme. von Meck, who insisted on knowing the full spiritual and emotional content of the symphony, he wrote out a detailed analysis which has long been familiar to concert audiences. In reading it the listener usually does one of three things: takes it literally; regards it as irrelevant to the music as such; relates it to Tschaikowsky's private life. There is the fourth choice of combining all three. In that choice lies the synthesis of mind, emotion, and external stimuli which is regarded as the very stuff of art.

"Our symphony has a program," he writes. "That is to say, it is possible to express its contents in words, and I will tell you—and you alone—the meaning of the entire work and its separate movements. Naturally I can only do so as regards its general features.

"The Introduction is the kernel, the quintessence, the chief thought of the whole symphony. This is Fate, the fatal power which hinders one in the pursuit of happiness from gaining the goal, which jealously provides that peace and comfort do not prevail, that the sky is not free from clouds—a might that swings, like the sword of Damocles, constantly over the head, that poisons continually the soul. This might is overpowering and invincible. There is nothing to do but to submit and vainly to complain.

"The feeling of despondency and despair grows ever stronger and more passionate. It is better to turn from the realities and to lull oneself in dreams. O joy! What a fine sweet dream! A radiant being, promising happiness, floats before me and beckons me. The importunate first dream of the Allegro is now heard afar off, and now the soul is wholly enwrapped with dreams. There is no thought of gloom and cheerlessness. Happiness! Happiness! Happiness! No, they are only dreams, and Fate dispels them. The whole of life is only a constant alternation between dismal reality and flattering dreams of happiness. There is no port: you will be tossed hither and thither by the waves until the sea swallows you. Such is the program, in substance, of the first movement.

"The second movement shows another phase of sadness. Here is that melancholy feeling which enwraps one when he sits at night alone in the house exhausted by work; the book which he had taken to read has slipped from his hand; a swarm of reminiscences has arisen. How sad it is that so much has already *been* and *gone!* And yet it is a pleasure to think of the early years. One mourns the past and has neither the courage nor the will to begin a new life. One is rather tired of life. One wishes to recruit his strength and to look back, to revive many things in the memory. One thinks on the gladsome hours when the young blood boiled and bubbled and there was satisfaction in life. One thinks also on the sad moments, on irrevocable losses. And all this is now so far away, so far away. And it is also sad and yet so sweet to muse over the past.

"There is no determined feeling, no exact expression in the third movement. Here are capricious arabesques, vague figures which slip into the imagination when one has taken wine and is slightly intoxicated. The mood is now gay, now mournful. One thinks about nothing; one gives the fancy loose rein, and there is pleasure in drawings of marvelous lines. Suddenly there rushes into the imagination the picture of a drunken peasant and a gutter-song. Military music is heard passing by in the distance. These are disconnected pictures which come and go in the brain of the sleeper. They have nothing to do with reality; they are unintelligible, bizarre, out-at-elbows.

"Fourth movement. If you have no pleasure in yourself, look about you. Go to the people. See how they can enjoy life and give themselves up entirely to festivity. The picture of a folk-holiday. Hardly have we had time to forget ourselves in the happiness of others when indefatigable Fate reminds us once more of its presence. The other children of men are not concerned with us. They do not spare us a glance nor stop to observe that we are lonely and sad. How merry and glad they all are. All their feelings are so inconsequent, so simple. And you still say that all the world is immersed in sorrow? There still *is* happiness, simple, native happiness. Rejoice in the happiness of others—and you can still live."

SYMPHONY IN E MINOR, NO. 5, OPUS 64

If surroundings alone determined the mood of a piece of music, Tschaikowsky's Fifth Symphony, composed one summer in a country villa near Klin, would be a sunlit idyl. Of course it is nothing of the sort, for though Tschaikowsky responded keenly to outdoor beauty, he was a prey to gloomy thoughts and visions that constantly found their way into his music. His own inner world crowded out the other. Frolovskoe, where he wrote his symphony in 1888, was a charming spot, fringed by a forest. Between spurts of composing he took long walks in the woods and puttered around the villa garden.

On his return from Italy two years later he found that the forest had been cut down. "All those dear shady spots that were there last year are now a bare wilderness," he grieved to his brother Modeste. Ironically, Tschaikowsky also composed his *Hamlet* overture in the sylvan retreat at Frolovskoe, though from his own and others' descriptions, the place was an ideal setting for an *As You Like It* symphonic fantasy.

The first intimation that Tschaikowsky was considering a new symphony appears in a letter to his brother Modeste dated May 27, 1888. A dread that he had written himself out as composer had been steadily gaining a grip on Tschaikowsky's mind. He had complained about his imagination being "dried up." He felt no urge to write. Finally he resolved to shake off the mood and convince the world and himself there were still a few good tunes in him.

"I am hoping to collect, little by little, material for a symphony," he writes to his brother on May 27. The following month we find him inquiring of his lady bountiful, Nadezhda von Meck: "Have I told you that I intended to write a symphony? The beginning has been difficult; but now inspiration seems to have come. However, we shall see." In the same letter he makes no bones about his intention to prove that he is not "played out as a composer."

On August 6 he reported progress on the new work. "I have orchestrated half the symphony," he writes. "My age, although I am not very old, begins to tell on me. I become very tired, and I can no longer play the piano or read at night as I used to do." Ill health troubled him during the summer months, but by August 26 he was able to announce the completion of the symphony. At first he was dissatisfied with it. Even the favorable verdict of a group of musical friends, among them Taneieff, did no good. Early performances of the symphony only strengthened Tschaikowsky's misgivings. The work was premièred in St. Petersburg on November 17, 1888, with Tschaikowsky conducting. A second performance followed on November 24, at a concert of the Musical Society, with the composer again conducting. Then came a performance in Prague. The public was enthusiastic. The critics, on the other hand, almost unanimously attacked it as unworthy of Tschaikowsky's powers. In a letter to Mme. von Meck in December he expressed frank disgust with the symphony:

"Having played my symphony twice in Petersburg and once in Prague, I have come to the conclusion that it is a failure. There is something repellent in it, some over-exaggerated color, some insincerity of fabrication which the public instinctively recognizes. It was clear to me that the applause and ovations referred not to this but to other works of mine, and that the symphony itself will never please the public. All this causes a deep dissatisfaction with myself.

"It is possible that I have, as people say, written myself out, and that nothing remains but for me to repeat and imitate myself. Yesterday evening I glanced over the Fourth Symphony, *our* symphony. How superior to this one, how much better it is! Yes, this is a very, very sad fact." A composer who was still to write the *Hamlet* overture-fantasy, the *Sleeping Beauty* and *Nutcracker* ballets, the opera *Pique Dame,* and the *Pathetic* symphony, was anything but "written out," as Tschaikowsky feared!

After the symphony triumphed in both Moscow and Hamburg, Tschaikowsky speedily changed his mind and wrote to his publisher Davidoff: "I like it far better now, after having held a bad opinion of it for some time." He speaks of the Hamburg performance as "magnificent," but expresses his old complaint about the Russian press, that it "continues to ignore me," and bemoans the fact that "with the exception of those nearest and dearest to me, no one will ever hear of my successes." Modeste Tschaikowsky attributed the work's early failure in St. Petersburg (that is, with the critics) to his brother's poor conducting.

The assumed programmatic content of the Fifth Symphony has aroused much speculation. Most analysts are convinced Tschaikowsky had a definite, autobiographical plan in mind. Yet he left no descriptive analysis such as we have of the Fourth Symphony. There he had set out to depict the "inexorableness of fate." One Russian writer discerned "some dark spiritual experience" in the Fifth. "Only at the close," he observed, "the clouds lift, the sky clears, and we see the blue stretching pure and clear beyond." Ernest Newman spoke of the sinister motto theme first announced in the opening movement as "the leaden, deliberate tread of fate." Many have agreed with Newman in classing the Fifth with the Fourth as another "fate" symphony.

SYMPHONY IN B MINOR, No. 6, OPUS 74 (*Pathetic*)

First drafts of a sixth symphony—not the *Pathetic*—were made by Tschaikowsky on his return trip from America in the late spring of 1891. Dissatisfied with the way the new score was shaping up, he tore it up and congratulated himself on his "admirable and irrevocable determination" to do so. It is not till February, 1893, that first mention is made of a fresh start on a sixth symphony. "I am now wholly occupied with the new work," he writes excitedly to his brother Anatol. "It is hard for me to tear myself from it. I believe it comes into being as the best of my works. I must finish it as soon as possible, for I have to wind up a lot of affairs. . . ." Subsequent events were to give the last sentence of this letter a sinister note of prophecy. Like Mozart writing the *Requiem Mass* on his deathbed, Tschaikowsky seemed to be defying some unfriendly fate to stop him in the midst of his great symphony.

There was to be a program to this symphony, a mysterious, profoundly personal program. But Tschaikowsky would never tell the world what it was. "Let them guess who can," he challenged. Amid the beautiful natural scenery of Klin, near Moscow, Tschaikowsky worked at his symphony. Curiously enough, his mood was bright and cheerful for a change. Early in October he left for Moscow to attend a funeral. There he met his friend Kashkin and together they talked jovially of life and death. Tschaikowsky was in excellent spirits and Kashkin assured him that he would outlive them all. Tschaikowsky laughed, and talked excitedly about his new symphony, how he was satisfied with the first three movements, how the finale still needed tinkering.

At length he was in St. Petersburg again. The day of the première of his symphony was approaching. Rehearsals were begun and Tschaikowsky soon found reason to grow morose and pessimistic again. He had counted on the musicians reacting warmly to this new music of his, but he began to notice cool faces, indifferent glances, and—horror of horrors—yawns. This was too much for the hypersensitive Tschaikowsky. He felt his hands suddenly become lifeless, his mind lose its alertness. His confidence ebbed from him. To spare the men any further boredom he cut short the rehearsal. Still, he knew he had written his greatest symphony. At the première of October 28th, the audience received the new symphony coolly, and it was not till shortly after Tschaikowsky's death that it began to make a mighty, overpowering impression on listeners wherever it was played.

But the symphony had been baptized without a name. Tschaikowsky felt the term "No. 6" was too bald and lonely a title for it. "Programme Symphony" was also ruled out, for the good reason that he refused to divulge the "program." His brother Modeste suggested "Tragic," but

Tschaikowsky rejected that too. When Modeste left him, he went on casting about for a title. In a flash it came to him. He rushed back to his brother. "Peter," he exclaimed; "I have it! Why not call it the 'Pathetic' symphony." Tschaikowsky pounced on the proposal eagerly: "Splendid, Modi, bravo—*Pathetic!*" he shouted. In his brother's presence Tschaikowsky wrote on the score the name by which the symphony has since been known. Most programs, however, give the title in its French form, *Symphonie Pathétique.*

Shortly after the conversation with his brother, Tschaikowsky attended a performance of Ostrowsky's play, *A Warm Heart.* Later he went backstage to pay his respects to the leading actor, Warlamoff. The talk somehow turned to spiritualism, and again Tschaikowsky showed a lighthearted mood. When Warlamoff laughingly ridiculed "these abominations which remind one of death," Tschaikowsky agreed jovially. "There is plenty of time before we have to reckon with this snub-nosed horror. It will not come to snatch us off just yet! *I feel that I shall live a long time!*" Five days later, Peter Ilyitch Tschaikowsky, generally regarded as Russia's greatest composer, was dead, one of the many victims of the fearful cholera epidemic then raging in St. Petersburg.

If Tschaikowsky followed a definite emotional or philosophical program in the *Pathetic* symphony, the key to it died with him. Had he lived, the chances are he would have divulged it, since he was not by nature a secretive, unconfiding man. However, many have probed the symphony's content and concluded it harbored a message of impending death. Yet Kashkin, Tschaikowsky's close friend, interpreted the fierce energy of the third movement and the abysmal sorrow of the Finale "in the broader light of a national or historical significance." He refused to narrow down the scope of the symphony to a merely personal experience.

"If the last movement is intended to be prophetic, it is surely of things vaster and issues more fatal than are contained in a purely personal apprehension of death," he said. "It speaks, rather, of *une lamentation large et souffrance inconnue*—a large lamentation and unknown suffering. It seems to set the seal of finality on all human hopes. Even if we eliminate the merely subjective interest, this autumnal inspiration of Tschaikowsky's, in which we hear the *whirling of the perished leaves of hope,* still remains the most profoundly stirring of his works."

I think we may safely agree with Kashkin's judgment, at the same time reserving the right to read into this monumental dirge, for such it unmistakably is, our own individual sense of its profoundly moving theme of tragic resignation. That Tschaikowsky left it as a testament of disillusion and futility is likely. Yet no one can miss the fine vein of tenderness and the flashes of defiance recurring through it. Few artist have bequeathed the world such a poignant and tormented self-portrait.

L. B.

Richard Strauss

BORN: MUNICH, JUNE 11, 1864. DIED: GARMISCH, SEPT. 8, 1949.

Thirty years ago I was regarded a rebel. I have lived long enough to find myself a classic.—RICHARD STRAUSS.

THE WRITER OF a thumb-nail biography of Richard Strauss finds himself confronted with a troublesome assignment. Strauss lived well beyond the scriptural age allotted the average man. He would have been eighty-six had he reached his next birthday. There was nothing romantic or sensational about his passing, for he died of a complication of the illnesses of old age. There was not much truly spectacular about the course of his life, which was most happily free from the material troubles which bedeviled the existence of so many great masters; and he was not called upon to starve or to struggle to achieve the material rewards of his gifts. He had not to pass through the conflicts which embittered the lives of Wagner or Berlioz, and he was never compelled to suffer like Mozart or Schubert. There is no record of his ever humiliating himself or performing degrading chores for publishers in return for a wretched pittance. He had wealth enough without compromising his art to keep the pot boiling—and for this one can only feel devoutly thankful. What if he was taxed with sensationalism? Many of the masters of music have had, at one time or another, to endure this reproach. If *Salome* and *Elektra, Ein Heldenleben* and *Till Eulenspiegel* were in their day scandalously "sensational" did not the whirligig of time reveal them as incontestable products of genius, irrespective of inequalities and flaws? However Richard Strauss compares in the last analysis with this or that master, he contributed to the language of music idioms, procedures and technical accomplishments typical of the confused years and conflicting ideals out of which they were born. His works are most decidely of an age, whether or not they are for all time! In a way he was almost as fortunate as Mendelssohn. Need anyone begrudge him this?

*   *   *

The late spring of 1864 brought two events which, though seemingly unrelated, actually had a kind of mystic kinship and were to stir the surfaces of music. Early in May of that year Richard Wagner was summoned to Munich to become the friend and protégé of the young Bavarian sovereign, Ludwig II, whose real mission on earth was to save the composer for the world. Hardly more than a month later there was born in the same city a boy likewise named Richard who was destined in the fullness of time to become in a sense an heir and continuator of the older master, though by no means a vain copy of his artistic and spiritual lineaments. And long before the span of his days reached its end he had taken an undisputed place in history as a seminal force in music, for all the disagreements and conflicts his art was to engender through a large part of his more than fourscore years.

Richard Strauss first saw the light on June 11, 1864, in a house on the Altheimer Eck, Munich, at the center of the town and a stone's throw from the twin steeples of the Frauenkirche. The edifice in which the future composer of *Salome, Elektra* and *Der Rosenkavalier* was born forms part of a complex of buildings in which a number of larger and smaller beer halls and restaurants, separated by cobbled courtyards, house the brewery of Georg Pschorr, senior, whose son, Georg Pschorr, junior, enlarged the establishment. Furthermore, he improved the quality of its products till Pschorrbrau beer became, it seemed to many (including the writer of these pages), the most incomparable refreshment this side of heaven, despite the close proximity of the Hofbrauhaus, the Löwenbrau, the Augustiner Brau and the unnumbered other Munich breweries and affiliated Bierstuben. At this point the writer ought, logically, to confess that he bases his present recollections on what he remembers from his wanderings in the Bavarian capital prior to the Second World War, since which time changes without number may well have changed the picture. But one thing is reasonably certain—if the old house at Altheimer Eck (Number 2) still stands, it continues to have affixed to its wall the decorative inscription:

403

"Am 11 Juni 1864 wurde hier Richard Strauss geboren." ("On June 11, 1864, Richard Strauss was born here.")

* * *

The Pschorrs apart from being excellent brewers were excellent musicians. One of the four daughters, Josephine, later Richard's mother, a fairly accomplished pianist, taught her son piano in his fifth year. A noted harpist, August Tombo, continued the lessons and by the time the boy was seven he was given violin instruction. Franz Strauss, Richard's father, was an individual of a fiber as tough as Josephine Pschorr, who became his wife, was mild-mannered and sensitive. But he was an amazingly fine horn player, for the sake of whose virtuosity and musicianship, greater men than he put up with his ill manners and incredible tantrums. A venomous reactionary, his particular detestation was Wagner, against whom he never hesitated to exhibit the meanest traits of which he was capable. Even when the author of *Tristan* expressed himself as overjoyed with the sound of the orchestra at a first rehearsal of his work in the little Residenz Theatre Franz Strauss retorted: "That's not true! It sounded like an old tin kettle!" He pronounced Wagner's horn parts "unplayable" so that Wagner had to call upon Hans Richter to try out for him some passages in *Die Meistersinger* in order to demonstrate that they were anything but "impossible." With the elder Strauss Hans von Bülow was repeatedly at loggerheads. And when he once attempted to thank Bülow for some favor the latter had shown young Richard Strauss, Bülow exploded with the words: "You have no right to thank me! I did your son a favor not on your account but only because I consider his talent deserves it!" To the end of his days Franz Strauss remained a cantankerous individual.

Young Richard may not have exhibited the precocity of a Mozart or a Mendelssohn but there could be no doubt that musical impulses stirred in the child. He piled up a considerable quantity of juvenilia, beginning as a six-year-old. In 1871 he turned out a "Schneiderpolka"— a "Tailor's Polka." There followed dance pieces for piano, "wedding music" for keyboard and children's instruments, some marches and more miscellany of the sort. It was related by his naturally proud relations that the lad could write notes even before he had learned the alphabet. There would be no particular point in detailing these boyish accomplishments, yet when Richard was twelve an uncle paid for the publication by Breitkopf and Härtel of a "Festival March," which gained the distinction of appearing as "Opus 1." It need hardly be said that he participated in domestic performances of chamber music with regularity. All the same his school work maintained a high level, even if it did not consume a needless amount of time. He also found leisure to jot in the pages of his mathematics copybook whole passages of a violin concerto which appears to have been set down during his classroom lessons. According to his biographer, Willy Brandl, the piece was written so rapidly that the student contrived a three-line staff instead of the usual five-line one.

At this period his musical tastes were colored by those of his father. Thus there is no reason for surprise that the compositions he turned out up to the end of his high school days were the customary platitudes of classical and romantic models. Especially Schumann and Mendelssohn were rather colorlessly reflected in the products the youth fashioned. Even considering his father's poisonous detestation of Wagner, it still remains hard to grasp how weak was the pressure the creator of *Tristan* and *Meistersinger* exercised on the son precisely when the Wagnerian idiom was beginning to permeate the language of music. More than that, it took time for the boy Strauss to rid his system of the ludicrous prejudices he parroted for a while. To his friend the composer, Ludwig Thuille, he confided that *Lohengrin* (which he heard at fifteen) was "sweet and sickly, in all but the action"; and after his first exposure to *Siegfried* he lamented that he was "more cruelly bored than I can tell!" Then he concluded with this burst of prophecy: "You can be assured that in ten years nobody will remember who Richard Wagner was!"

Young Strauss was to outlive such heresies by the sensible process of steeping himself in Wagner's scores rather than by viewing inadequate performances as truths of Holy Writ. It is hardly necessary to emphasize the dismay of Franz Strauss as, little by little, he became aware of the turn things were taking. He who had striven to bring up his son in his own Philistine ways, was gradually brought face to face with the upsetting fact that the young man might be getting out of hand! Richard was no music school or conservatory pupil, and had presumably none too many academic precepts to unlearn. One advantage of this was that nothing tempted him to cut short other phases of his education; and in the autumn of 1882 he began to attend philosophical, literary and other cultural lectures at the University of Munich, so that there were no serious gaps in his schooling. He continued to compose industriously (a chorus in the *Elektra* of Sophocles was one of his creations in this period); but in after years he warned against "rushing before the public with unripe efforts." Subsequently he visited upon the works of his salad days this judgment: "In them I lost much real freshness and force." So much for those who question even today the soundness of this early verdict.

*　　*　　*

One advantage he came early to enjoy—the good will of Hermann Levi, the Munich conductor (or, let us give him his more imposing official title of "Generalmusikdirektor") who first presided in Bayreuth over Wagner's *Parsifal*. In 1881 the outstanding chamber music organization of the Bavarian capital performed a string quartet of young Strauss's and very shortly afterwards Levi sponsored the first public hearing of a rather more ambitious effort, a symphony in D minor. Before a capacity audience the noted conductor went so far as to congratulate the high school student. It should be set down to the credit of the scarcely seventeen-year-old composer that he did not for a moment suffer the tribute to turn his head. Next morning the student was back in his classroom, as unconcerned with his triumphs of the preceding evening as if they had all been no more than an agreeable dream. The usually peppery father appears to have been somewhat less balanced than his son and a little earlier took it upon himself to dispatch Richard's *Serenade for Wind Instruments,* Opus 7, to Hans von Bülow. "Not a genius, but at the most a talent of the kind that grows on every bush," shot back the latter after a glimpse at the score of this adolescent production. But Bülow's irritable mood softened before long and he was considerably more flattering about others of the composer's works which came to his attention. All the same Bülow grew to like the *Serenade* well enough to make room for it on one of his programs. Meantime—on November 27, 1882—Franz Wüllner produced it in Dresden. And it was a strange quirk of fate which made of this piece the unexpected vehicle for Richard's first exploit as a conductor! It so happened that Bülow eventually scheduled it (1884) for one of his concerts. At the eleventh hour the older musician, suffering from an indisposition, appealed to his young friend to direct his own work. Trusting to luck Richard suffered a baton to be thrust into his hands, and almost in a dream state, hardly knowing how things would turn out, piloted the players through the score. "All that I realize," he afterwards said, "is that I did not break down!"

Young Strauss was not idling. The products of his energetic young manhood if they do not bulk large in his exploits, indicate clearly how carefully he was striving to learn his craft without, at the same time, seeking to blaze trails. One finds him turning out in 1881 five piano pieces as well as the string quartet just mentioned; a piano sonata, a sonata for cello and piano, a concerto for violin and orchestra, *Mood Pictures* for piano, a concerto for horn and orchestra, and a symphony in F minor. This symphony, incidentally, was first produced by Theodore Thomas, on December 13, 1884, at a concert of the New York Philharmonic Society. Perhaps more important, however, were the songs Strauss was writing at this stage. For they have preserved a vitality which Strauss's instrumental products of that early period have long since lost. It is not easy to grasp at this date that it was the early Strauss the world has to thank for such masterpieces of song literature as the incorrigibly popular (one might almost say hackneyed), *Lieder* as "Zueignung," "Die Nacht," "Die Georgine," "Geduld," "Allerseelen," "Ständchen," and a number of other such lyric specimens, many of them in the truest tradition of the German art song. Indeed, the boldness, the diversity, declamatory, rhythmic and melodic features of Strauss's achievements in this field might almost be said to have preceded the more sensational aspects of his orchestral works.

* * *

The songs of Strauss, the earliest specimens of which date from 1882, and which span (though in steadily diminishing numbers), the most fruitful years of his life, aggregate something like one hundred and fifty. If the better known ones are with piano accompaniment, not a few are scored for an orchestral one. A large number long ago became musical household words, along with the *Lieder* of Schubert, Schumann and Brahms, though having a physiognomy quite their own. The woman who became his wife, Pauline de Ahna, was an accomplished vocalist and that circumstance goes far to account for the diversity of his efforts in this province. The joint recitals of the pair stimulated for a considerable period the composer's lyric imagination. If his inspiration eventually sought expression in larger frames it must be noted that the slant of his genius habitually ran to larger conceptions. In any event the *Lieder Abende* of Strauss and his betrothed help explain the creative impulses which at this stage found so much of their outlet in songwriting. The composer was later to explain that a new song might be dashed off at any half-way idle moment—might even be scribbled down in the twinkling of an eye between the acts of an opera performance or during a concert intermission. And as spontaneously as Schubert, Richard Strauss busied himself with poems of the most varied character.

* * *

On the young man's twenty-first birthday Hans von Bülow recommended to Duke George of Meiningen "an uncommonly gifted" musician as substitute while he himself went on a journey for his shattered health. Bülow referred to the suggested deputy as "Richard III," since after Richard Wagner, "there could be no Richard II." Strauss arrived in Meiningen in October, 1885. The little ducal capital boasted a high artistic standing. Its theatrical company enjoyed international fame. The town, to be sure, had no opera, but the orchestra, though numbering only forty-eight instrumentalists, had been so trained by the suffering yet exigent Bülow that it was virtually unrivaled in Germany. The newcomer was encouraged to submit under his mentor's eye to an intensive training. Bülow's rehearsals ran from nine in the morning till one in the afternoon and his disciple from Munich was invariably on hand from the first to the last note. The rest of the day was devoted to score reading and every subtlety of conductor's technique. The young man was absolutely overwhelmed by "the exhaustive manner in which Bülow sought out the ultimate poetic content of the scores of Beethoven and Wagner." And a favorite saying of the older musician was never to be forgotten by his disciple from Munich: "First learn to read the score of a Beethoven symphony with absolute correctness, and you will already have its interpretation."

* * *

Strauss made other friends and valuable connections in Meiningen. One of the most important and influential of these was an impassioned devotee of Wagner, Alexander Ritter. Like so many apostles of the creator of *Parsifal* at that period, Ritter was a violent opponent of Brahms. Besides he was the composer of a comic opera, "Der faule Hans," and of a symphonic poem that once enjoyed a vogue in Germany, "Kaiser Rudolfs Ritt zum Grabe." It was Ritter's service to familiarize Strauss with some of the deepest secrets of the scores and writings of Wagner as well as of Liszt, and he understood how to fire his young friend with soaring enthusiasm for his own ideals. He also did much to inspire the budding conductor with a taste for the writings of Schopenhauer, an inclination he himself had inherited from Wagner. Ritter's influence, in short, was one of the luckiest developments at this stage of Strauss's career.

The first concert the youth from Munich conducted in Meiningen took place on October 18, 1885. It afforded him a chance to exploit his talents as pianist and batonist as well as composer, what with a program that included Beethoven's *Coriolanus* Overture and Seventh Symphony, Mozart's C minor Piano Concerto and that F minor Symphony of his own which Theodore Thomas had conducted the previous year in New York. Strauss had every reason to be pleased with the outcome. Bülow speaking of his debut as pianist and conductor had referred to it as "geradezu verblüffend" ("simply stunning"); even the hard-shelled Brahms, who chanced to be on hand, had deigned to encourage him with a cordial "very nice, young man!" When on December 1 of that year Bülow gave up the orchestra's leadership, Strauss inherited the post, conducted all concerts and had to direct, sometimes on the spur of the moment, almost anything this or that high placed personage might suddenly take a fancy to hear. With the courage of despair he repeatedly attempted compositions he hardly knew or had not directed publicly. Yet he never made a botch of the job, inwardly as he may have quaked.

*   *   *

To this period belongs a composition which has survived and at intervals turns up on our symphonic programs—the curious *Burleske* for piano and orchestra. The piece is something of a problem but it is one of the most yeasty and original products of its composer's youth. It possesses a type of wit and bold humor worthy of the subsequent author of *Till Eulenspiegel*. If it still betrays Brahmsian influences some of those dialogues between piano and kettledrums depart sharply from the more flabby romantic effusions of the youth who still clung to the coat tails of Schumann, Mendelssohn and some lesser romantics. Rightly or wrongly the composer always harbored a dislike for the *Burleske* though when he created it his original instinct led him aright, if more or less unconsciously. Not till four years later did the pianist, Eugen d'Albert, give it a public hearing in Eisenach; at that, Strauss himself never brought himself to dignify the *Burleske* with an opus number and insisted he would not have consented to its publication but for his need of funds. Today the saucy little score seems more alive than certain other early efforts which were rather closer to their composer's heart.

Meiningen had been a sort of stepping stone. Strongly against the advice of Hans von Bülow, who detested Munich from the depths of his being, Strauss, nevertheless, accepted a conductor's post in his native city, where he had the advantage of continuing his stimulating contact with Alexander Ritter, who had followed him to the Bavarian capital. Yet he did not look forward to a Munich position with particular joy. Before entering on his duties he permitted himself a vacation in Naples and Sorrento. In Munich he found the Royal Court Theatre bogged down in a morass of routine. The musical direction of that establishment, though in the capable hands of Hermann Levi, was unfired by real enthusiasm, let alone true inspiration. The first of Strauss's official assignments was the direction of Boieldieu's opéra comique, *Jean de Paris,* and a quantity of similar old and harmless pieces. One promised duty which augured well was a production of Wagner's boyhood opera, *Die Feen.* He would probably never have been promised anything so rewarding, had not the conductor for whom it had been intended in the first place, fallen ill. But even this unusual prize was in the end snatched from his grasp after he had presided over the rehearsals. At the last moment the direction of the Wagner curio was assigned to a certain Fischer. There was a managerial conference concerning the matter at which, we are told, "Strauss was like a lioness defending her young"; but the Intendant put a stop to the argument by announcing that "he disliked conducting in the Bülow style" and that, moreover, Strauss was becoming intolerable because of his high pretensions "for one of his youth and lack of experience!"

Meanwhile, the composer made the most of leisure he did not really want, by occupying himself with more or less creative work. One of his editorial feats of this period was a new stage version of Gluck's *Iphigénie en Tauride,* manifestly inspired by Wagner's treatment of the same master's *Iphigénie en Aulide.* More important still was his first really large-scale work, *Aus Italien,* to which he gave the subtitle *Symphonic Fantasy for Large Orchestra.* He had completed the score in 1886 and on March 2, 1887, he conducted it at the Munich Odeon. To his uncle Horburger he wrote an amusing account of the first performance at which, it appears, moderate applause followed the first three movements and violent hissing competed with handclappings. "There has been much ado here over the performance of my *Fantasy,*" Strauss wrote his uncle, "and general amazement and wrath because I, too, have begun to go my own way." And his biographer, Max Steinitzer, told that the composer's father, outraged by the hisses, hurried to the artist's room to see his son and found him, far from disturbed, sitting on a table dangling his legs! One detail the composer of this symphonic Italian excursion failed to notice—namely that in utilizing the tune *Funiculi, Funicula* for the movement depicting the colorful life of Naples he was quoting, not as he fancied a genuine Neapolitan folksong, but an only too familiar tune by Luigi Denza, who lived much of his life in a London suburb!

Be all this as it may, Strauss had more to occupy his thoughts than the fortunes of his Italian impressions to which he had given musical shape. In 1886-87 he composed (besides a sonata in E flat for violin and piano and a number of fine *Lieder*—among them the lovely and uplifting "Breit über mein Haupt"), the tone poem, *Macbeth* (least known of them all). He revised it in 1890 and on October 13 of that year conducted it in Weimar. But *Macbeth* has been completely overshadowed by the next tone poem (of earlier opus number but later composition), the glowing, romantic, vibrant *Don Juan.* This has a spontaneity and an indestructible freshness that give it a kind of electrical vitality none of the orchestral works of their composer's early manhood quite rival, unless we except that masterpiece of humor, *Till Eulenspiegel*—itself a different proposition. The powerful impressions made on the composer by some of the Shakespearian productions of the dramatic company in Meiningen gave the incentive for *Macbeth*. In the case of *Don Juan* the moving impulse was the poem of Nikolaus Lenau (whose real name was Niembsch von Strahlenau), and who described the hero of his work as "one longing to find one who represented incarnate womanhood" in whom he could enjoy "all the women on earth whom he cannot as individuals possess." Unable in the nature of things to achieve this tall order, Lenau's *Don Juan* falls prey to "Disgust, and this Disgust is the devil that fetches him." Strauss gave no definite meanings to specific phases of his music, though he was not to want for interpreters and one of them, Wilhelm Mauke, found it preferable to discard the model supplied by Lenau and to discover in the tone poem the various women who inhabit Mozart's *Don Giovanni*. Be this as it may, the score delighted the first hearers when it was played in Weimar; they tried to have it repeated on the spot. Hans von Bülow wrote that his protégé had with *Don Juan* had an "almost unheard-of success"; and the young composer might well have seen a good augury in the notorious Eduard Hanslick's outcries to the effect that the score was chiefly a "tumult of dazzling color daubs" and in his shrieks that Strauss "had a great talent for false music, for the musically ugly."

It cannot be said that he was truly happy with his Munich experiences and the disappointments which, if the truth were known, seemed for the moment to dog his footsteps. He was, to be sure, adding to his accomplishments as a composer and plans for an opera began to stir in him. Moreover, he had more and more chances to accept guest engagements as a conductor and such opportunities were taking him on more and more tours in Germany. He had striven to do his best in the city of his birth yet few seemed to be grateful for his efforts to clean up drab accumulations of routine. Bülow realized from long and heart-breaking experience what his friend was undergoing. Very few thanked the idealist for his efforts to better the musical standing of his home town.

*   *   *

At what might be described as a truly psychological moment of his career, Strauss was approached by Bülow's old friend, the former Liszt pupil, Hans von Bronsart, with an invitation to transfer his activities to Weimar. He had every reason to look with favor on the project.

Weimar was hallowed in his eyes by its earlier literary and musical associations. It had harbored Goethe and Schiller and been sanctified in the young musician's sight by the labors of Liszt. His Munich friend, the tenor Heinrich Zeller, who had coached Wagner rôles with him, had settled there, and a young soprano, Pauline de Ahna, the daughter of a Bavarian general with strong musical enthusiasms, soon followed him. In proper course she was to become Richard Strauss's wife. A high-spirited, outspoken lady, never disposed to mince words, a source of innumerable yarns and witticisms, and who saw to it that her celebrated husband carefully toed the mark, Pauline Strauss was in every way a chapter by herself. And when, not very long after his death she followed him to the grave, it seemed only a benign provision of fate that she should not too long survive him.

Strauss almost instantly infused a new blood into the artistic life of Weimar, where he settled in 1889 and remained till 1894. The worthy old court Kapellmeister, Eduard Lassen, was sensible enough to allow his energetic new associate complete freedom of action. True, the artistic means at his disposal were relatively modest and at first they might well have given the ambitious newcomer pause. The orchestra then contained only six first violins; there was a painfully superannuated little chorus and most of the leading singers had seen better days. But the conductor from Munich was disturbed by none of these apparent handicaps. In Bayreuth he had already learned the proper way of producing Wagner, and even when the means were limited, he tolerated no concessions; all Wagnerian performances had to be done without cuts or at least with a minimum of curtailments. A wisecrack began to go the rounds: "What is Richard Strauss doing?" to which the reply was: "Strauss is opening cuts!" The mouldy old settings were replaced by new ones and once when there were insufficient funds to buy new stage appointments, Strauss approached the Grand Duke with a plea that he might lay out of his own pocket a thousand marks to freshen the settings. To the credit of the ruler it should be told that he refused the offer and disbursed the sum himself. But Strauss's reforms were far from ending there. He once confessed that in his comprehensive job he was not only conductor but "coach, scene painter, stage manager and tailor"—in short, a thoroughgoing Pooh-Bah. He threw himself heart and soul into the job, so much so that in spite of a small stage and limited means he produced, in the presence of none other than Cosima Wagner, a *Lohengrin* that deeply gripped her.

*　　*　　*

He had symphonic concerts as well as operas to occupy him. At one of the former he transported his hearers with the world première of his *Don Juan*. The date deserves to be noted—November 11, 1889. That same year he had composed another tone poem, *Death and Transfiguration,* and on June 21, 1889, he permitted an audience in nearby Eisenach to hear it. The work is program music, if you will; but the idea that it originally set out to illustrate the poem about the man dying in a "necessitous little room" and, after his death struggles, translated to supernal glories, is wrong. Moreover the long accepted notion, that the music is based on lines by Alexander Ritter, is fallacious. For, in the first place the composer did not aim to illustrate his friend's word picture; and in the second, Ritter wrote the poem only *after* becoming acquainted with the score. This is what explains a certain incongruity between Ritter's verses and the tones which in reality where never conceived in slavish illustration of them. Hanslick, wrong as usual, was to write misleadingly: "Once again a previously printed poem makes it certain that the listener cannot go awry; for the music follows this poetic program step by step, quite as in a ballet scenario." And he spoke of the score as a gruesome combat of dissonances in which the woodwind howls in runs of chromatic thirds while the brass growls and all the strings rage!

By this time accustomed to such critical nonsense the composer did not suffer himself to be troubled. What disturbed him much more was that his old champion, von Bülow, gave indications of no longer seeing eye to eye with him. At Bülow's suggestion Strauss had revised and newly instrumented *Macbeth* but the piece was to continue a stepchild. Soon he was increasing his output of songs and enriching Liedersingers with such treasures as "Ruhe meine Seele," "Cäecilie," "Heimliche Aufforderung" and "Morgen"; while only a few short years ahead lay "Traum durch die Dämmerung," "Nachtgesang" and "Schlagende Herzen," to delight nearly two generations of recitalists.

*　　*　　*

Strauss had always been blessed with robust health. Unlike Wagner, for instance, he never suffered from exacerbated nerves and violent extremes of unbalanced mood. But at the period of which we speak he did experience one of his rare periods of illness. What between his guest engagements, his rehearsals, the strain of composing, attending to details of publication and myriad other obligations of a traveling conductor and virtuoso, he came down in May, 1891, with a menacing grippe which sent him to bed and threatened serious complications. He was resigned to anything, even if he did confess: "Dying would not be in itself so bad, but first I should like to be able to conduct *Tristan!*" He recovered and had his wish in 1892. But in the summer he was sick once more, this time with pneumonia. Now it looked as if one lung were seriously threatened. He was granted the vacation he requested, from November, 1892, to July of the succeeding year. Taking some works and sketches he started, on the advice of his physicians, for the south.

The convalescent with a finished opera libretto in his baggage went to repair his health in Italy, Greece and Egypt. In Egypt he recovered completely. In the Anhalter railway station, Berlin, he was to see for the last time the mortally sick von Bülow, likewise journeying to Egypt in a last effort to repair his shattered constitution. Poor Bülow was not to survive the trip. The wiry frame of Strauss helped him over any threat of tuberculosis and not only defied any peril to his lungs but seemed actually to renew his creative powers. The libretto which occupied his attention was that of his opera, *Guntram,* the first and least known of his productions for the lyric stage.

Guntram is without question a "Stiefkind" among Richard Strauss's operas. The average Strauss enthusiast's acquaintance with its music may be said to be confined to the brief phrase from it cited in the section called *The Hero's Works of Peace* in the tone poem *Ein Heldenleben.* Nevertheless, the opera cost the composer six long years of his time. It received a performance in Weimar, July 12, 1894. On October 29, 1940, it was to be heard again, and once more in Weimar. Strauss tells in his little volume, *Betrachtungen und Erinnerungen,* that it had "no more than a *succès d'estime* and that its failure to gain a foothold anywhere (even with generous cuts) took from him all courage to write operas." Efforts were made late in its creator's life to revive it, all of them as good as futile. As recently as June 13, 1942, the Berlin State Opera tried, with the help of the conductor, Robert Heger, to pump life into it. Strauss found not a little of the opera "still vital" (*"lebensfähig"*) and felt sure it would produce a fine effect given a large orchestra. He liked particularly in his old age the second half of the second act and the whole of the third. The book has been described as revealing the influence of Wagner. Guntram, a member of a religious order in the time of the Minnesingers, esteems the ruling duke, but kills himself, after renouncing the duchess, the object of his affection. Despite the dramatic resemblances to *Tannhäuser* and *Lohengrin,* Alexander Ritter found in the opera departure from Wagnerian influences.

Slowly as Strauss labored over the three acts of *Guntram* he spent no such time on the tone poems which now began to follow in rapid succession. After the ill-fated opera and a quantity of fine new *Lieder,* superbly diversified in expressive scope and lyric moods, there followed the tone poem which along with *Don Juan* continues even in the present age to address itself most warmly to the public heart—*Till Eulenspiegel's Merry Pranks.* Analysts of one sort and another have provided the work with a program, which has long been accepted as standard. The composer himself declined to supply one, maintaining that the listener himself should seek to "crack the hard nut Till, the folk rogue of ancient tradition" had supplied his public. He himself would say nothing to clear up the secrets of the lovable knave, who came to his merited end on the gallows. If Strauss confided to his public the nature of many of Eulenspiegel's various ribaldries and madcap adventures he might, he maintained, easily cause offense. Concertgoers could cudgel their brains all they chose, Richard Strauss would keep his own counsel! Naturally, his work acquired, rightly or wrongly, regiments of "interpreters." "Nasty, noisome, rollicking Till, with the whirligig scale of a yellow clarinet in his brain," as the worthy William J. Henderson eventually described him, the irrepressible "Volksnarr" was ultimately to become visualized as a kind of medieval ballet fable sporting all the benefits of story-book scenery and dramatic action. The result actually was not too remote from what Strauss originally intended. Its popular musical elements, such as the fetching polka tune (or "Gassenhauer"), the use of the folk melody ("Ich hatt' ein Kamaraden") and a good deal else seemed theatrically conceived. The use of the Rondeau form was ideally suited to the idea which the composer strove to formulate. At one period Strauss, conscious of the operatic elements of *Till*, was moved to give the work a thoroughgoing dramatic setting and began to sketch the piece as a sort of lyric drama, or rather a Scherzo with staging and action. But he lost interest in the scheme and did not progress beyond plans for a first act. Franz Wüllner conducted the première of *Till Eulenspiegel* in Cologne, November 5, 1895.

* * *

It has been pointed out that if the masculine element is idealized in Strauss's tone poems it is rather the feminine which he gives precedence in his operas. Something of an exception to this is exemplified in the next purely orchestral work, the tone poem *Thus Spake Zarathustra*, which followed less than a year later and was produced under its composer's direction at one of the Museum concerts in Frankfurt-on-the-Main, November 27, 1896. The score is described as "freely after Nietzsche." At once there arose protests that Strauss had tried to set Nietzschean philosophy to music! Actually he had aimed to do no such preposterous thing, and *Zarathustra* posed no genuine problems. If the score is the weaker for some of its syrupy and sentimental pages it includes another, such as the magnificent sunrise picture at the beginning, which can only be placed for overpowering effect beside the passage "Let there be Light and there was Light" in Haydn's *Creation*. If ever anything could testify to Strauss's incontestable genius it is this grandiose page! Other portions, it may be conceded, lapse into commonplace, but the close in two keys at once (B and C) offered one of the early examples of polytonality that duly outraged the timid. Today this clash of tonalities has quite lost its power to frighten. In 1898 and for quite some time thereafter, it passed for hardly less than an invention of Satan! Strauss intended this juxtaposition to characterize "two conflicting worlds of ideas." Possibly it can be made to sound sharply dissonant on the piano; the magic of Strauss's orchestration, however, eliminates all suggestion of crude cacophony.

On March 18, 1898, Cologne heard under the baton of Franz Wüllner, a work of rather different order, *Don Quixote*, Fantastic Variations on a Theme of Knightly Character. It is a set of orchestral variations on two themes, the one heard in the solo cello and characterizing the Knight of the Rueful Countenance, the second (solo viola) picturing his squire, Sancho Panza. As a feat of individualizing, these variations are a thing apart. The tone painting is unrivaled in its composer's achievements up to that time. A number of special effects, which long invited attention over and above their real musical worth, called forth considerably more astonishment than they really deserved. The pitiful bleatings of a flock of sheep, violently scattered by the lance of the crack-brained Don, his attacks on a company of itinerant monks, his ride through the air (amid the whistlings of a "wind machine")—these and other effects of the sort are actually only minor phases of the score. Its memorable qualities, aside from striking pictorial conceits, are rather to be found in the moving and tender pages portraying the passing of Don Quixote as the mists clear from his poor addled brain. There are episodes of a melting tenderness in these which rank among the most eloquent utterances Strauss has attained.

Still another tone poem was to follow—*A Hero's Life* (*Ein Heldenleben*) performed under the composer's direction in Frankfurt. The work is autobiographical with the composer himself as its hero and his helpmate (obviously Frau Pauline, his "better half" as she was to be called). For a long time *Ein Heldenleben* passed as the prize horror among Strauss's creations especially its fierce and rambunctious battle scene, which some critics considered a kind of bugaboo with which to frighten the wits out of grown-up concertgoers! For its day *A Hero's Life* was unquestionably strong meat. If people were horrified by the racket and cacophony of the battle scene they were no less disposed to irritation at the cackling sounds with which Strauss pilloried his benighted foes who resented his aims and accomplishments. And they were displeased by the immodesty with which he exhibited himself as a real and misprized hero by the citation of fragments from his own works. Some, among them as staunch a Strauss admirer as Romain Rolland, were disturbed not because the composer talked in his works "about himself" but "because of the way in which he talked about himself." All the same Strauss was to boast no truer champion throughout his career than the sympathetic and keenly understanding author of *Jean-Christophe*.

Ein Heldenleben was the last but one of the series of tone poems which were to lead to a new phase of Richard Strauss's career. The last of this series, the *Symphonia Domestic,* was completed in Charlottenburg, Berlin, on December 31, 1903. Its first public hearing took place under the composer's direction in Carnegie Hall, New York, March 21, 1904. The *Domestic Symphony,* "dedicated 'to my dear wife and our boy" is in "one movement and three subdivisions. After an introduction and Scherzo there follow without break an *Adagio,* then a tumultuous double fugue and finale." The reviewers discovered all manner of programmatic connotations in this depiction of a day in Strauss's family life though he was eventually to tell a New York reviewer that he "wanted the work to be taken as music" pure and simple and not as an elaboration of a specific program. He maintained his belief "that the anxious search on the part of the public for the exactly corresponding passages in the music and the program, the guessing as to the significance of this or that, the distraction of following a train of thoughts exterior to the music, are destructive to the musical enjoyment." And he forbade the publication of what he sought to express till after the concert.

He might as well have saved himself the trouble! There is no room here to point out even a small fraction of what the critics heard in the work, encouraged by a casual note or two the conductor found it necessary to set down at certain stages of the score. The youngster's aunts are supposed to remark that the infant is "just like his father," the uncles "just like his mother." A glockenspiel announces that the time at one point is seven in the morning. The child gets his bath and the ablutions are accompanied by shrieks and squeals. Husband and wife discuss the future of the baby and there is a lively domestic argument which ends happily. Ernest Newman, irritated like numerous other reviewers by the torrents of vain talk the piece called forth, was to complain that "Strauss behaved as foolishily over the *Domestica* as he might have been expected to do after his previous exploits in the same line. . . ."

The first organization to perform the work was the orchestra of Hans Hermann Wetzler, in New York, and it took several months longer for the music to reach Germany. Mr. Newman had found the texture of the whole is "less interesting than in any other of Strauss's works; the short and snappy thematic fragments out of which the composer builds, contrasting badly with the great sweeping themes of the earlier symphonic poems . . . the realistic effects in the score are at once so atrociously ugly and so pitiably foolish that one listens to them with regret that a composer of genius should ever have fallen so low."

*　　*　　*

More than a decade was to elapse before Strauss was to concern himself again with problems of symphonic music. Opera and ballet were to be the chief business of those activities which one may look upon as the middle period of his creative life. One may be permitted a short backward glance to account for some of his previous creations. Songs (a number of the best of them), an "Enoch Arden" setting (declamation with piano accompaniment) occupy the late years of the nineteenth century and the early twentieth, also the choral ballad for mixed chorus and orchestra, *Taillefer*. More important, however, is a second operatic venture. This opera in one act, called *Feuersnot,* is a setting of a text by the noted Ernst von Wolzogen, who was associated with the vogue of the so-called "Ueberbrettl," a sort of up-to-date vaudeville, an "arty" movement typical of the period. *Feuersnot* is a picture of a "fire famine" brought about by an irate sorcerer in revenge for the act of a maiden who scorned his love. Thereby all the fires of the town are extinguished! The piece is rather too long for a short opera and too short for a full-length one. But the text is rich in word play, punning satire, double meanings and topical allusions, interlarded with biting reflections on the manner in which Munich had once turned against Wagner and on the trouble the benighted burghers would have in similarly ridding themselves of the troublesome Strauss! There is not a little of the real Strauss in the music, though at that, less than one might expect from the composer of *Till Eulenspiegel* and *Ein Heldenleben* which already lay some distance in the past. *Feuresnot* was first staged at the Dresden Opera on November 21, 1901, under the leadership of Ernst von Schuch. And the consequence was that for years to come Strauss's operatic premières took place in that gracious city.

*　　*　　*

We now come into view of a milestone of modern music drama. In 1902 Strauss attended a performance of Oscar Wilde's play, "Salome," at Max Reinhardt's Kleines Theater in Berlin. Gertrude Eysoldt had the title rôle. The Swiss musicologist, Willi Schuh, relates that the

420

composer after the performance was accosted by his friend, Heinrich Grünfeld, who remarked: "Strauss, this would be an operatic subject for you!" "I am already composing it," was the reply. And the composer went on to tell: "The Viennese writer, Anton Lindner, had already sent me the play and offered to make an opera text of it for me. Upon my agreement he sent me some cleverly versified opening scenes which did not, however, inspire me with an urge to composition; till one day the question shaped itself in my mind: Why do I not compose at once, without further preliminaries: *Wie schön ist die Prinzessin Salome heute Nacht!* From then on it was not difficult to cleanse the piece of 'literature,' so that it has become a thoroughly fine libretto!

"Necessity gave me a really exotic scheme of harmony, which showed itself especially in odd, heterogeneous cadences having the effect of changeable silk. It was the desire for the sharpest kind of individual characterization that led me to bi-tonality. One can look upon this as a solitary experiment as applied in a special case but not recommend it for imitation."

Difficulties began with von Schuch's first piano rehearsals. A number of singers sought to give back their parts till Karl Burrian shamed them by answering, when asked how he was progressing with the rôle of Herod: "I already know it by heart!" A little later the Salome, Frau Wittich, threatened to go on strike because of the taxing part and the massive orchestra. Soon, too, she began to rail against "perversity and impiety of the opera, refused to do this or that 'because I am a decent woman,'" and drove the stage manager almost frantic. Strauss remarked that her figure was "not really suited to the sixteen-year-old Princess with the Isolde voice" and complained that in subsequent performances her dance and her actions with Jochanaan's head "overstepped all bounds of propriety and taste."

In Berlin, according to Strauss, the Kaiser would permit the performance of the work, only after Intendant von Hülsen had the idea of "indicating at the close by a sudden shining of the morning star the coming of the Three Holy Kings." Nevertheless, Wilhelm II remarked to Hülsen: "I am sorry that Strauss composed this *Salome*. I like him, but he is going to do himself terrible harm with it!" At the dress rehearsal the famous high B flat of the double basses so filled Count Seebach with the fear of an outbreak of hilarity, that he prevailed upon the player of the English horn to mitigate the effect, somewhat, "by means of a sustained B flat on that instrument." Strauss's own father, hearing his son play a portion of the opera on the piano, exclaimed a short time before his death: "My God, my God, this nervous music! It is as if beetles were crawling about in one's clothing!" And Cosima Wagner declared after listening to the closing scene: "This is madness!" The clergy, too, was up in arms and the first performance at the Vienna State Opera in October, 1918, took place only after an agitated exchange of letters with Archbishop Piffl. The orchestra of *Salome* in all numbered one hundred and twelve players. Strauss, however, eventually arranged the opera for fewer players and Willy Schuh tells of the composer having conducted it in Innsbruck with an orchestra of only fifty-six players, but with highly efficient solo instrumentalists.

At all events, Strauss has been described as an inimitable conductor of *Salome*. Willy Schuh (whom Strauss designated late in his life as his "official" biographer, when the time came to prepare his "standard" life story) alludes to Strauss as an "allegro composer," whose direction of *Salome* was of altogether remarkable "tranquillity" and finds that the real secret of his direction of this music drama was to be sought in the "restfulness" and creative aspects of his interpretation, "which avoids every excess of whipped up, overheated effects and sensationalism." It is, therefore, illuminating to consider the modifications the years have wrought on the interpretative treatment proper to the work. Little by little the legend of the decadent, hysterical, hyper-sensual work was replaced by the assurance of its almost classical character; and the truth of Oscar Wilde's declaration to Sarah Bernhardt when the play was new: "I aimed only to create something curious and sensual" has at length come to the fore.

*   *   *

There is scarcely any need to recount in any detail the early difficulties of *Salome* in America, when the scandalized cries that arose after the work received a single representation at the Metropolitan Opera House, in New York, only to be shelved as "detrimental to the best interests of the institution," still ranks among the notorious and less creditable legends of the American stage. Strauss soon after this taste of the operations of American puritanism accused Americans of "hypocrisy, the most loathsome of all vices." He was handsomely avenged, however, when on January 28, 1909, Oscar Hammerstein revived the work (with Mary Garden as Salome) at his Manhattan Opera House and started it on a triumphant American career, which confounded all the ludicrous prognostications and horrified shouts with which it had been greeted only a short time earlier.

The work which followed *Salome* was *Elektra*, the text of which was the creation of Hugo von Hofmannsthal. Here began a collaboration between poet and musician which was to last with fruitful results until the latter's death, and to mark some of the high points of Strauss's achievements. The story of their joint labors is detailed in a priceless series of letters, brought out in 1925 under the editorial supervision of the composer's son, Dr. Franz Strauss. These letters afford glimpses into the workshop of librettist and composer which rank with some of the most illuminating exchanges of the sort the history of music supplies. From them we learn that before settling on the tragedy of the house of Agamemnon the collaborators seriously pondered as operatic material Calderon's *Daughter of the Air* and also *Semiramis.* Then, early in 1908, they seem to have agreed on *Elektra.* Hofmannsthal's version of the Greek legend (based on Sophocles) had been acted in Berlin (again with Gertrude Eysoldt in the title rôle); and no sooner had Strauss witnessed the production than he concluded that the tragedy in this form was virtually made to order for his music.

On July 6, 1908, the composer wrote to Hofmannsthal: *"Elektra* progresses and is going well; I hope to hurry up the première for the end of January at the latest." Strauss was as good as his word. The first performance of *Elektra* took place January 25, 1909, at the Dresden opera, Ernst von Schuch conducting, with Anni Krull in the name part, Ernestine Schumann-Heink as Klytemnestra and Carl Perron as Orestes. If Strauss would have preferred to write a comic opera after *Salome,* the pull of the *genre* of "horror opera" was still strong upon him and he was not yet ready to loose himself from its grip. *Elektra* was, if one chooses, gorier than *Salome* and perhaps more genuinely psychopathic but less susceptible to provocations of outraged morality. Its instrumental requirements are rather larger than those of Strauss's previous operas and the whole more nightmarish in its sensational atmosphere. One had the impression, however, that with *Elektra,* the composer had reached the end of a path. He could hardly repeat himself with impunity along similar lines. A turn of the road or something similar must come next unless Strauss's achievements were to run up against a stone wall or lead him into a blind alley.

This was not fated to happen. What the pair were now to achieve was what was to prove their most abiding triumph—*Der Rosenkavalier,* of all the operas of Richard Strauss the most lastingly popular and if not the indisputable best, at all events the most loved and, peradventure, the most viable—and, if you will, the healthiest. If the piece is in some respects sprawling and over-written it does contain a piece of moving character-drawing which stands with the most memorable things the literature of musical drama affords. In her musical and dramatic lineaments the aristocratic Marschallin, whose common sense leads her on the threshold of middle age to renounce the calf love of the seventeen-year-old "Rose Bearer," Octavian, offers one of the finest and most convincing figures to be found in modern opera—a creation not unworthy to stand by the side of Wagner's Hans Sachs. The Baron Ochs, an outright vulgarian, if the music accorded him does not lie, is a figure who might have stepped out of the pages of Rabelais. Sophie, Faninal and all the rest of the characters who enliven this canvas inhabited by vividly drawn types of eighteenth-century Vienna, add up to a truly memorable gallery with which Hofmannsthal and Strauss have brought to life an era and a culture. Strauss's score has indisputable prolixities and commonplaces. But these traits may pass as defects of the opera's qualities and, as such, they can take their place in the vastly colorful pageant of Hofmannsthal's comedy of manners.

It would be a mistake, however, to imagine that a piece as earthy as *Der Rosenkavalier* should pass without provoking dissent. The German Kaiser, who had small use for Strauss's operas, yielded to the urging of the Crown Prince so far as to attend a performance, then left the theater with the words: *"Det is keene Musik für mich!"* ("That's no music for me!") To spare the feelings of the straight-laced Kaiserin it was arranged to place the Marschallin's bed in an adjoining alcove instead of in high visibility on the stage when the curtain rose. Nor were these the only objections. And, of course, there were the usual exclamations about the length of the piece, and no end of suggestions were advanced about the best ways to shorten the work. Strauss, in protest against some of the cuts von Schuch had practiced in Dresden, once insisted he had overlooked one of the most important possible abbreviations! Why not omit the trio in the last act, which only holds up the action? It should be explained that the great trio is the brightest gem of the act, perhaps, indeed, the lyric climax of the whole score! As for the various waltzes which fill so many pages of the third act (and to some degree of the second) it may be admitted that for all the skill of their instrumentation they are by no means the highest melodic flights of Strauss's fancy, some of them being merely successions of rather trifling sequences.

*   *   *

It was assumed after *Der Rosenkavalier* that the success of the opera indicated that the composer, in a mood for concessions, had tried to meet the public half-way and had renounced the violence, the cacophonies and the dissonances and sensational traits supposed to be his stock-in-trade. The comedy was assumed to be a proof of this. The real truth was that Strauss had not changed his ideals and methods in the least. It was, rather, *that the public, converted by force of habit, was itself catching up with Strauss and that the idiom of the composer was quickly becoming the musical language of the hour*. Sometimes it took even a few idiosyncrasies of the musician for granted. One did not always inquire too closely into just what he meant. There is one case when Strauss even went to the length of *writing music* to the words "diskret, vertraulich" ("discreetly, confidentially") when Hofmannsthal had written them as *stage directions* to be followed *not* as part of a text to be sung! All the same Strauss usually kept an eagle eye on the dramatic action he composed. With regard to the libretto of *Der Rosenkavalier* he wrote to the poet "the first act is excellent, the second lacks certain essential contrasts which it is impossible to put off till the third. With only a feeble success for the second act, the opera is doomed." Be this as it may, *Der Rosenkavalier* was anything but "doomed." It was, in point of fact, the work which Strauss had in mind when, at the close of the first *Elektra* performance he remarked to some friends: "Now I intend to write a Mozart opera!" Whether or not *Der Rosenkavalier* really meets the prescriptions of a "Mozart opera" we feel rather more certain that his next work, *Ariadne auf Naxos* comes closer to filling that bill.

*   *   *

The development of this work hangs together with production in Stuttgart, October 25, 1912, of a German adaption by Hofmannsthal of Molière's comedy *Le Bourgeois Gentilhomme*. Molière's Monsieur Jourdain, who has made money, induces a certain charming widow, the Marquise Dormène, to come to a dinner he gives in her honor. A reprobate noble, Count Dorantes, tells the Marquise that the soirée at Jourdain's home is really intended as a gesture of admiration for her. M. Jourdain has engaged two companies of singers who are supposed to perform a serious opera, *Ariadne on Naxos,* and a burlesque, *The Unfaithful Zerbinetta and Her Four Lovers.* Both pieces are supposed to have been composed by a protégé of M. Jourdain. During a dinner scene Strauss has recourse to bits of musical quotation—a fragment of Wagner's *Rheingold* when Rhine salmon is served and several bars of the bleating sheep music from *Don Quixote* when servants bring in roast mutton. The banquet is interrupted and Jourdain finds it necessary to curtail the scheduled program. As a result the young author is commanded by Jourdain to combine his two works as best he can!

Hofmannsthal's Molière adaptation (in which the operatic part takes the place of the French poet's original "Turkish ceremony") was a clumsy, indeed an impractical distortion. But Strauss had no intention of sacrificing his composition without at least an attempt to salvage something from the wreck. The *Ariadne* portion as well as the *Zerbinetta* companion piece were preserved but carefully detached from the Molière comedy. In place of this Strauss and Hofmannsthal supplied a sort of explanatory prologue whereby arrangements are made for better or worse to combine the stylized *opera seria* about Ariadne and her rescue on a desert island by the god Bacchus, with the comic doings of Zerbinetta and her *commedia del arte* companions. In this shape the piece has succeeded in surviving and actually makes an engaging entertainment, with the young composer (a trousered soprano) reminding one of a lesser Octavian.

There is considerable charming music in what is left of the originally involved and over lengthy entertainment. First of all, Strauss was suddenly to renounce the huge, overloaded orchestra of *Salome, Elektra* and *Rosenkavalier* and to supplant it by a much smaller one designed for a transparent texture of chamber music. In any case, the definitive *Ariadne auf Naxos* is a real achievement and stands among Strauss's better and more memorable accomplishments. In the estimation of the present writer the tenderer romantic portions of the piece excel the comic pages associated with Zerbinetta and her merry crew. In writing these the composer aimed to be Mozartean (or, if one prefers, Rossinian) by assigning the colorature soprano a florid rondo of incredible difficulties—so mercilessly exacting, indeed, that it first moved Hofmannsthal to discreet protest. Eventually, the composer took steps to modify some of the cruel problems of Zerbinetta's solo and it is in this amended form that one generally hears this air today, when it is sung as a concert number.

* * *

It would not be altogether excessive to claim that *Ariadne auf Naxos* marks a midpoint in Strauss's career. He still had a long and fruitful life ahead of him and, as it was to prove, he was almost incorrigibly prolific, not hesitating to experiment with one type of composition as well as another. On the eve of the First World War he became interested in Diaghileff's Russian Ballet and the various types of choreographic and scenic art which it was to engender. Hofmannsthal wanted him to occupy his imagination and "to let the vision of one of the grandest episodes of antique tragedy, namely the subject of Orestes and the Furies, inspire you to write a symphonic poem, which might be a synthesis of your symphonies and your two tragic operas!" And the poet adjured him to think of Orestes as represented by Nijinsky, "the greatest mimic genius on the stage today!" But apparently Strauss had had his fill of the *Elektra* tragedy at this stage and had no stomach for more of this sort of thing, whether symphonic or operatic. So he remained unmoved by Hofmannsthal's urgings. Yet the Russian Ballet gave him a new idea. He thought of a pantomimic ballet conceived in the shapes and the colors of the epoch of Paolo Veronese.

From this conception, based on a scenario by a Count Harry Kessler and von Hofmannsthal dealing with the story of Joseph and Potiphar's Wife, there grew the *Legend of Joseph*, first produced in Paris with extraordinary scenic and decorative accouterments on May 14, 1914. The staging was a pictorial triumph which, though the ballet was several times performed elsewhere, appears never to have been anywhere near equaled visually at its later showings. The score seems to have missed fire and has never been reckoned among the composer's major exploits. None the less the effect of the music in its proper frame and context is compelling. What if much of it sounds like discarded leavings from "Salome"? Strauss confessed that from the first the pious Joseph bored him, "and I have difficulty in finding music for whatever bores me" ("was mich mopst"). To "his dear da Ponte," as he came to call Hofmannsthal, he gave hope and said frankly that though the virtuous Biblical youth tried his patience, in the end some "holy" strain might perhaps occur to him. The present writer has always felt that the *Josefslegende* is a far too maligned work and that it would repay a conductor to disentomb the grossly slandered score, which when properly presented is striking "theatre."

On October 28, 1915, there was heard in Berlin, under the composer's direction, the first symphony (in contradiction to "tone poem") Richard Strauss had written since 1886. Like *Aus Italien* it was again outspokenly pictorial. The composer himself wrote titles into the divisions of the score (which he is said to have begun to sketch in 1911, though the music was set down to the final double bar four years later). Some spoke of the *Alpensymphonie* as a work which "a child could understand." And the various scenic divisions of this Alpine panorama, distended as it undoubtedly is, can be described as plainly pictorial. The orchestra depicts successively "Night," "Sunrise," the "Ascent," "Entrance into the Forest," "Wandering beside the Brook," "At the Waterfall," "Apparition," "On Flowery Meadows," "On the Alm," "Lost in the Thicket," "On the Glacier," "Dangerous Moment," "On the Summit," "Mists Rise," "The Sun Is Gradually Hidden," "Elegy," "Calm before the Storm," "Thunderstorm," "The Descent," "Sunset," "Night."

On account of its length the "Alpine Symphony" has never been a favorite among Strauss's achievements of tone painting. Indeed, it may be questioned whether its sunrise scene can be compared for suggestiveness and purely musical thrill to the glorious opening picture of *Also Sprach Zarathustra*.

*　　*　　*

Strauss's symphonic excursion in the Alps was succeeded by a return to opera. Between 1914 and 1917 (which is to say during the most poignant years of the First World War) he worked on an opera which was to become a child of sorrow to him but which to a number of his staunchest worshipers often passes as one of his very finest achievements—*Die Frau ohne Schatten* (*The Woman Without a Shadow*), first performed under Frank Schalk in Vienna, October 10, 1919. For all the enthusiasm it evokes in some of the inner Straussian circles, this opera, which combines length, breadth and thickness, is a real problem. The writer of these lines, who has been exposed to the work fully half a dozen times always with a firm resolve to enjoy it, has never succeeded in his ambition. Though Strauss and Hofmannsthal discussed the plans for the piece in 1912 and once more in 1914 the first act was not finished till that year; and war held up the completion of the opera three years more.

It has been maintained that *Die Frau ohne Schatten* marks "the combination of a recitative style with the forms of the older opera" and that in it Strauss has yielded to a mystical tendency. Willy Brandl claims that Hofmannsthal's libretto attracted the composer and stimulated him "precisely because of its obscurity"; that he saw in it a series of problems to be "clarified, not to say unveiled, in their complexities precisely through the agency of music." The question of motherhood lies at the root of the opera. Hofmannsthal saw in his poem a "kind of continuation of *The Magic Flute*. On one hand we have the superterrestrial worlds, on another the realistic scenes of the human world bound together by the demonic figure of the Nurse." And he notes a new element in the score—"a powerful, hymnlike character overpoweringly disclosed in the music, a new feature in Strauss's compositions."

It may be questioned whether Strauss was truly content with the bloodless symbolism which fills *The Woman Without a Shadow*. In any case at this juncture he began to long for something new. Somehow Hofmannsthal did not at that moment appear to be reacting sympathetically to the dramatic demands which just then seemed to be filling Strauss's mind. He informed Hofmannsthal that he longed for something to compose like Schnitzler's *Liebelei* or Scribe's *Glass of Water*. He asked for "characters inviting composition—characters like the Marschallin, Ochs or Barak (in *Die Frau ohne Schatten*)." And so, when Hofmannsthal did not "respond" promptly he took up the pen to work out his own salvation. The consequence was *Intermezzo,* a domestic comedy in one act with symphonic interludes. It was produced at the Dresden Opera, November 4, 1924, under Fritz Busch.

Two years before that Strauss had presented in Vienna a two act Viennese ballet, *Schlagobers* (*Whipped Cream*) which can be dismissed as one of his outspoken failures. As for *Intermezzo* it had biographical vibrations in that it pictured a domestic episode in Strauss's own experiences. It had to do with a conductor, Robert Storch, and thus Strauss could make amusing stage use of the unmistakable initials "R.S." and make various allusions to the game of skat, which had for years been a favorite diversion of his. The music of *Intermezzo* has never been acclaimed a product of the greater Strauss. And yet Alfred Lorenz, famous for his series of eviscerating studies of the structural problems of Wagner's music dramas, has made it clear that the Wagnerian form problems are likewise the principles which underlie such a relatively tenuous Straussian score as *Intermezzo*.

In spite of the dubious fortunes which were to dog the steps of an opera like *The Woman Without a Shadow* the composer once again allowed himself to be seduced by a work of relatively similar character, *Egyptian Helen,* a somewhat tortured mythical tale, based on a rather far-fetched "magic" fiction by von Hofmannsthal, relating to a phase of the Trojan war, in which Helen is shown as wholly innocent of the ancient struggle. Magic befuddlements, potions capable of changing the characteristics of people, draughts which rob this or that personage of his memory, an "omniscient shell" which launches oracular pronouncements and a good deal more of the sort lend a singular character to the strange fantasy, in which some have chosen to discern a kind of take-off on the various drinks of forgetfulness and such in *Tristan* and *Götterdämmerung*. *Egyptian Helen* is the only sample of this strange stage of the Strauss who was reaching the frontiers of old age, which American music lovers had the opportunity to know. It would be excessive to claim that, either in Europe or in the western hemisphere, the work was a noticeable addition to the enduring accomplishments of the master. More than one began to obtain the impression that, for all the splendors of his technique, Strauss seemed to be going to seed.

* * *

In the summer of 1929 Hofmannsthal suddenly died. Some time before he had written a short novel, *Lucidor,* about an improverished family with two marriageable daughters for whom an attempt is made to secure wealthy husbands. To facilitate the marital stratagem one of the daughters is dressed in boy's clothes. The disguised girl falls in love with a suitor of her sister, Arabella, to whom one Mandryka, a romantic Balkan youth of great wealth, pays court. The period is the year 1860, the scene Vienna.

Inevitably, *Arabella* turned out to be something of a throwback into the scene, if not the glamorous period or milieu, of *Der Rosenkavalier*. Almost inevitably, the lyric comedy—the final product of the Strauss-Hofmannsthal partnership—is filled with scenes, characters and analogies to the more famous work. In truth, *Arabella* is a kind of little sister of *Rosenkavalier*. At the same time the texture of the score and the character of the orchestral treatment has a transparency and a delicate charm which Strauss rarely equaled, even if the melodic invention and the instrumentation suggest a kind of chamber music on a large scale. As in *Ariadne auf Naxos* the composer does not hesitate to make use of a florid soprano to introduce scintillating samples of ornate vocalism. One feels, however, that *Arabella* is a semi-finished product. The second half of the work does not sustain the level of the first. Many things might have been worked out more expertly if the librettist had been spared to supervise work, which as things stand is far from a really satisfactory or unified piece. But the score contains some of the older Strauss's most enamoring lyric pages and it is easy to feel that his heart was in the better portions of the opera. The score of *Arabella* benefits by the introduction of folksong influence—in this instance of a number of South Slavic melodies, which are among its genuine treasures.

Lacking his faithful Hofmannsthal, Strauss turned to Stefan Zweig, who had made for him an operatic adaptation of Ben Jonson's play, "Epicoene, or The Silent Woman." On June 24, 1935, it was produced under Karl Böhm at the Dresden Opera. At once trouble arose. Hitler and the Nazis had come into power and Zweig, as a Jew, was automatically an outcast. After the very first performances the piece was forbidden, not to be revived till after Hitler's end (and then in Munich and in Wiesbaden). It is actually a question whether the temporary loss of *Die Schweigsame Frau* must be accounted a serious deprivation. *The Silent Woman* is a rowdy, cruel farce about the tricks played on a wretched old man, unable to endure noise and subjected to all manner of torments in order that he be compelled to renounce a young woman, who to assure a lover a monetary settlement, plays the shrew so successfully that the old man is only too willing to pay any amount of his wealth to be rid of her. It is much like the story of Donizetti's *Don Pasquale* and the dramatic consequences are to all intents the same. There is, in reality, nothing serious or genuinely based on musical *inspiration* in the opera, the best features of which are certain set pieces (some rather adroitly polyphonic) and a charmingly orchestrated overture described in the score as a "potpourri." A tenderer note is struck only at the point where, as evening falls, the old man drops off to sleep.

As librettist for his next two operas, *Friedenstag* and *Daphne,* Strauss sought the aid of Joseph Gregor. The first named work (in one act) was performed on July 7, 1938, in Munich, under Clemens Krauss. Ironically enough this work that aimed to glorify the coming of peace after conflict, was first performed with the political troubles which heralded the outbreak of the Second World War, visibly shaping themselves. *Daphne,* bucolic tragedy in a single act, also from the pen of Gregor, was heard in Dresden, October 15, 1938. And Gregor, too, supplied the aging composer with the book of *Die Liebe der Danae,* a "merry mythological tale" in three acts. To date its sole production seems to have been in Salzburg, as a "dress rehearsal," August 16, 1944.

Strauss's last opera (produced under Clemens Krauss in Munich on October 28, 1942), was *Capriccio,* "a conversation piece for music," in one act, Krauss and the composer collaborating on the book. The "conversation" is a discussion of certain aesthetic problems underlying the musical treatment of operatic texts. It was the final work of operatic character Strauss was to attempt. This did not mean, however, that he had written his last score. Far from it! At eighty-one he was to complete several, the real value of which may be left to the judgment of posterity. They include some songs, a duet-concertino for clarinet and bassoon with strings, a concerto for oboe and orchestra, a still unperformed concert fragment for orchestra from the *Legend of Joseph.* More important, unquestionably, is *Metamorphoses,* a "study for twenty-three solo strings," first played in Zurich, January 25, 1946 under the direction of Paul Sacher. This work, despite its length, is music of suave, beautiful texture; a certain nobly nostalgic quality of farewell which seems to sum up the composer's life work, with all its ups and downs. We may allow it to go at that and to spare further enumeration of the innumerable odds and ends he was to assemble from his boyhood to the patriarchal age of more than eighty-five years; or even to allude to his gross derangement of Mozart's "Idomeneo," done in 1930 at Munich.

Having lived through a lively young manhood and endured the bitter experience of two world wars Richard Strauss in the end performed the miracle of actually dying of old age! One might almost have looked for convulsions of nature, for signs and portents at his eventual passing. But his going was to be accompanied by no such things. His death in Garmisch, September 8, 1949, was brought about by the illnesses of the flesh at more than four score and five. He died of a complication of heart, liver and kidney troubles—and he died in his bed! A Heldenleben, if you will! And a death and transfiguration played against the loveliest conceivable background—an incomparable stage setting of Alpine lakes and heights, with streams and gleaming summits furnishing a glorious backdrop for his resting place!

H. F. P.

Serge Prokofieff

BORN: EKATERINOSLAV, RUSSIA, APR. 23, 1891.
DIED: MOSCOW, MARCH 4, 1953.

If we wished to establish Prokofieff's genealogy as a composer, we would probably have to betake ourselves to the eighteenth century, to Scarlatti and other composers of the good old times, who have inner simplicity and naïveté of creative art in common with him. Prokofieff is a classicist, not a romantic, and his appearance must be considered as a belated relapse of classicism in Russia.—LEONID SABANEYEFF.

A COMPOSER'S CREED

The principal lines which I followed in my creative work are these:
The first is classical, whose origin lies in my early infancy when I heard my mother play Beethoven sonatas. It assumes a neo-classical aspect in the sonatas and the concertos, or imitates the classical style of the eighteenth century, as in the Gavottes, the Classical Symphony, *and, in some respects, in the* Sinfonietta.

The second is innovation, whose inception I trace to my meeting with Taneieff, when he taunted me for my rather "elementary harmony." At first, this innovation consisted in the search for an individual harmonic language, but later was transformed into a desire to find a medium for the expression of strong emotions, as in Sarcasms, Scythian Suite, *the opera* The Gambler, They are Seven, *the Second Symphony, etc. This innovating strain has affected not only the harmonic idiom, but also the melodic inflection, orchestration, and stage technique.*

The third is the element of the toccata *or motor element, probably*

434

influenced by Schumann's Toccata, which impressed me greatly at one time. In this category are the Etudes Op. 2, Toccata, Op. 11, Scherzo, Op. 12, the Scherzo of the Second Piano Concerto, the Toccata in the Fifth Piano Concerto, the persistent figurations in the Scythian Suite, Le Pas d'acier, *and some passages in the Third Piano Concerto. This element is probably the least important.*

The fourth element is lyrical. It appears at first as lyric meditation, sometimes unconnected with melos, as in Fairy Tale, Op. 3, Réves, Esquisse automnale, Legend, Op. 21, *etc., but sometimes is found in long melodic phrases, as in the opening of the First Violin Concerto, the songs, etc. This lyric strain has for long remained in obscurity, or, if it was noticed at all, then only in retrospection. And since my lyricism has for a long time been denied appreciation, it has grown but slowly. But at later stages I paid more and more attention to lyrical expression.*

I should like to limit myself to these four expressions, and to regard the fifth element, that of the grotesque, with which some critics are trying to label me, as merely a variation of the other characteristics. In application to my music, I should like to replace the word grotesque by "Scherzo-ness," or by the three words giving its gradations: "Jest," "laughter," "mockery."

SERGE PROKOFIEFF

*   *   *

*I*T IS GIVEN to few composers to become classics in their lifetime. Of these few Serge Prokofieff was a notable example. At his death in Moscow on March 4, 1953, he was a recognized international figure of long standing, a favorite of concert-goers the world over, and in almost every musical form, whether opera, symphony, concerto, suite, or sonata, a securely established creator. Only three contemporaries could seriously dispute Prokofieff's dominant position in world music —Dimitri Shostakovich, Igor Stravinsky, and the Finnish Jean Sibelius. There were those who placed him first. His passing was mourned inside and outside Russia by all who respond to fastidious artistry and the strange wizardry of creative genius. Prokofieff had come to belong to the world. While his musical and cultural roots were firmly planted in the land of his birth, he had achieved a breadth and depth of expression that communicated itself to all. In the vast quantity of his output there is something for everyone everywhere—for the child, for the grown-up, for the less musically tutored, and for the most sophisticated taste. Serge Prokofieff is distinctly deserving of the word "universal." His music knows no boundaries.

* * *

Serge Prokofieff was born on April 23, 1891, in an atmosphere of music and culture at Sontsovka in the south of Russia, where his father managed a large estate. He seems to have begun composing almost before he could write his own name, thanks to the influence and coaching of his mother, an accomplished pianist. At the age of five he had already put together a little composition called "Hindu Galop," and there is a photograph of the nine-year-old boy seated at an upright piano with the score of his first opera, "The Giant." Prokofieff himself has given us a picture of the boy and his mother in their first musical adventures together:

"One day when mother was practicing exercises by Hanon, I went up to the piano and asked if I might play my own music on the two highest octaves of the keyboard. To my surprise she agreed, in spite of the resulting cacophony. This lured me to the piano, and soon I began to climb up to the keyboard all by myself and try to pick out some little tune. One such tune I repeated several times, so that mother noticed it and decided to write it down.

"My efforts at that time consisted of either sitting at the piano and making up tunes which I could not write down, or sitting at the table and drawing notes which could not be played. I just drew them like designs, as other children draw trains and people, because I was always seeing notes on the piano stand. One day I brought one of my papers covered with notes and said:

"'Here, I've composed a Liszt Rhapsody!'

"I was under the impression that a Liszt Rhapsody was a double name of a composition, like a sonata-fantasia. Mother had to explain to me that I couldn't have composed a Liszt Rhapsody because a rhapsody was a form of musical composition, and Liszt was the name of the composer who had written it. Furthermore, I learned that it was wrong to write music on a staff of nine lines without any divisions, and that it should be written on a five-line staff with division into measures. I was greatly impressed by the way mother wrote down my 'Hindu Galop' and soon, with her help, I learned something about how to write music. I couldn't always put my thoughts into notes, but I actually began to write down little songs which could be played."

Prokofieff also recalled how much his mother stressed the importance of a love for music and how she tried to keep it unmarred by excessive practicing. There was only a minimum of that hateful chore, but a maximum of listening to the great classics of the keyboard. At first the lessons between mother and son were limited to twenty minutes a day. This was extended to one hour when Prokofieff was nine. "Fearing above all the dullness of sitting and drumming one thing over and over," Prokofieff wrote, "mother hurried to keep me supplied with new pieces so that the amount of music I studied was enormous."

This exposure to music continued when the family moved to Moscow. There Prokofieff attended the opera repeatedly and soon developed a taste for composing for voice himself. One of these early efforts was submitted to the composer Taneieff, who advised the family to send their son to Reinhold Gliere for further study. This early attraction for the theater was later to culminate not only in several operas of marked originality but in numerous scores for ballet and the screen. To the end Prokofieff never quite lost his childhood passion for the stage. One has only to hear his music for the "Romeo and Juliet" ballet and the opera, "The Love of Three Oranges" to realize how enduring a hold the theater had on him.

Emboldened by Taneieff's reaction, the eleven-year-old boy next showed him a symphony. Prokofieff himself told the story to Olin Downes, who interviewed him in New York in 1919 for the Boston *Post*. Taneieff leafed through the manuscript and said: "Pretty well, my boy. You are mastering the form rapidly. Of course, you have to develop more interesting harmony. Most of this is tonic, dominant and subdominant [the simplest and most elementary chords in music], but that will come."

"This," said Prokofieff to Mr. Downes, "distressed me greatly. I did not wish to do only what others had done. I could not endure the thought of producing only what others had produced. And so I started out, very earnestly, not to imitate, but to find a way of my own. It was very hard, and my courage was severely put to the test in the

437

following years, since I destroyed reams of music, most of which sounded very well, whenever I realized that it was only an echo of some one's else. This often wounded me deeply.

"Eleven years later I brought a new score to Taneieff, whom I had not been working with for some seasons. You should have seen his face when he looked at the music. 'But, my dear boy, this is terrible. What do you call this? And why that?' And so forth. Then I said to him, 'Master, please remember what you said to me when I brought my G-major symphony. It was only tonic, dominant and subdominant.'

" 'God in heaven,' he shouted, 'am I responsible for this?' "

Prokofieff was scarcely thirteen when another distinguished Russian composer entered his life—and again by way of an opera score. Alexander Glazounoff was so impressed by a work entitled "Feast During the Plague" that the boy was promptly enrolled at the St. Petersburg Conservatory. That was in 1904. There he remained for ten years, among his teachers being Liadoff, Tcherepnin, and Rimsky-Korsakoff. From them he absorbed much of the prodigious skill as colorist and orchestrator that later went into his compositions, besides a thorough schooling in the nationalist ideals of Russian music.

At the same time he was already feeling the urge to express himself in a bolder and more unorthodox style of writing. This rebelliousness was later to lead to controversial clashes over several of his scores. By the time he left the Conservatory in 1914, Glazounoff knew that Prokofieff had wandered off into paths of his own. Yet he arranged for a trial performance of Prokofieff's First Symphony. This proved crucial, for it attracted the notice of an influential group of vanguard musicians and, perhaps even more important, a publisher. Yet, when he graduated, it was not as composer but as pianist that Prokofieff carried off first prize. Shortly after his graduation, Prokofieff's father died, and when the First World War broke out later that summer, he was granted exemption from military service because of his widowed mother.

During the war years Prokofieff composed two works that would appear to be at opposite extremes of orchestral style—the "Classical Symphony" and the "Scythian Suite." One is an unequivocal declaration of faith in the balanced serenity and suavity of the Mozartean tradition, and the other rocks with an almost savage upheaval of barbaric power. Over both, however, hovers the iron control and superb sureness of idiom of a searching intellect and an unfailing artistic insight. The two works represent two parts rather than two sides of a richly integrated personality.

The revolution of February, 1917, found Prokofieff in the midst of rehearsals of his opera *The Gambler,* founded on Dostoievsky's short novel, to a text of his own. Production was indefinitely suspended because of the hardships and uncertainties of the social and political scene. Actually it was not till 1929 that the opera was finally produced, in Brussels, Prokofieff having revised it from the manuscript recovered from the library of the Maryinsky Theater of Leningrad. When the October Revolution had triumphed, Prokofieff applied for a passport. His intention was to come to America, where he was assured a lucrative prospect of creative and concert work. The request was granted, with this rebuke from a Soviet official:

"You are revolutionary in art as we are revolutionary in politics. You ought not to leave us now, but then, you wish it. We shall not stop you. Here is your passport."

Prokofieff proceeded to make his way to America, following an itinerary that included Siberia (a small matter of twenty-six days), Hawaii, San Francisco, and New York, where he arrived in August, 1918. A series of recitals followed at which he performed several of his own compositions, and the Russian Symphony Orchestra featured some of his larger works.

A picturesque and revealing reaction to both Prokofieff's pianoplaying and music was that of a member of the staff of "Musical America" who was assigned to review the visitor's first concert at Aeolian Hall on November 20, 1918.

"Take one Schoenberg, two Ornsteins, a little Erik Satie," wrote this culinary expert, "mix thoroughly with some Medtner, a drop of Schumann, a liberal quantity of Scriabin and Stravinsky—and you will brew something like a Serge Prokofieff, composer. Listen to the keyboard antics of an unholy organism which is one-third virtuoso, one-third athlete, and one-third wayward poet, armed with gloved finger-fins and you will have an idea of the playing of a Serge Prokofieff, pianist. Repay an impressionist, a neofantast, or whatever you will, in his own coin:—crashing Siberias, volcano hell, Krakatoa, seabottom crawlers! Incomprehensible? So is Prokofieff!"

A commission for an opera from Cleofonte Campanini, conductor of the Chicago Opera Company, was to result in what ultimately proved to be his most popular work composed for America—the humorous fairy-tale opera, *The Love of Three Oranges*. Campanini, however, had died in the interim, and it was Mary Garden, newly appointed director (she styled herself *directa!*) of the Chicago company, who undertook the production of the opera in Chicago in 1921. Its reception in Chicago and later at the Manhattan Opera House was scarcely encouraging. Almost three decades were to pass before a spectacularly successful production, in English, by Laszlo Halasz at the New York City Center gave it a secure and enduring place in the active American repertory.

Prokofieff next went to Paris, where he renewed ties with a group of Russian musicians and intellectuals, among them the two Serges who were to become so helpful in the development of his reputation as a dominant force in modern music. These were Serge Diaghileff and Serge Koussevitzky. For Diaghileff he wrote music for a succession of ballets, among them *Chout* (1921), *Pas d'Acier* (1927), and *The Prodigal Son* (1929). Considerable interest was aroused by *Pas d'Acier,* which was termed both a "labor ballet" and a "Bolshevik Ballet" by various members of the press both in Paris and in London, where the work was given in July, 1927. It was a ballet of factories and firemen, of lathes and drill-presses, of wheels and workers, and it brought Prokofieff the dubious title of composer laureate of the mechanistic age.

Koussevitzky had begun his celebrated series of concerts in Paris in 1921. This proved a perfect setting for the newcomer. Again and again the programs afforded him a double hospitality as composer and pianist. Koussevitzky introduced the Second Symphony and when he later took up the baton of the Boston Symphony, Prokofieff was among the first composers invited to appear on his programs in either or both capacities. In 1929, on the fiftieth anniversary of the Boston Symphony, it was to Serge Prokofieff that Koussevitzky went for a symphonic score to commemorate the occasion. The resulting work was Prokofieff's Fourth Symphony. It was not till 1927 that Prokofieff, absent from his homeland for nine years, decided to return, if only for a visit. Of this period away from home, Nicolas Nabokov, who knew Prokofieff well, had this to say in an article written for "The Atlantic Monthly" in July, 1942:

SERGE PROKOFIEFF

"From 1922 until 1926 Prokofieff lived in France and travelled only for his annual concert tours. In Paris he found himself surrounded by a seething international artistic life in which the Russian element played a great part, thanks mainly to Diaghileff and his Ballet. Most of these people were expatriates, in various degrees opposed to the new regime in their motherland. Prokofieff had too close and too profound a relation with Russia to lose himself in this atmosphere. He kept up his friendships with those who stayed in Russia and those who were abroad by simply putting himself, in a certain sense, outside of the whole problem. It was interesting to watch how cleverly he succeeded in this position. There was nothing strained or unnatural about it. He earned the esteem of both camps and the confidence of everyone. From a production by the Ballet Russe of his latest ballet, Prokofieff would go to the Soviet Embassy, where a party would be given in his honor, and at his home you would find the intellectuals arriving from Russia, among them his great friend, Meyerhold, Soviet writers, and poets.

"In 1927 he dug out his old Soviet passport and returned for a short while to Russia. As a result of this first trip came his ballet *Pas d'Acier*. This was Prokofieff's greatest success in Paris. It coincided with a turn in French public opinion toward Russia, with the beginning of the Five-Year Plan, and the increasing interest in Russian affairs among the intelligentsia of Western Europe. For several years to come Prokofieff kept up the dual life of going to Russia for several months and spending the rest of the time in Paris, until finally the demands of his country inwardly and outwardly became so strong that he decided definitely to return and settle in Moscow."

Prokofieff had again visited America in 1933. In New York, within the space of a few days, he performed his Fifth Concerto with Koussevitzky and the Boston Symphony, and his Third Concerto with Bruno Walter and the Philharmonic-Symphony. So many references have been made in these pages to Prokofieff as his own soloist, that perhaps a few balanced words from Philip Hale on the subject may be appropriate at this point. After having heard him several times in Boston, the late critic and annotator, declared:

"His pianistic gifts are unusually great; there was reason for his being recognized in America primarily as a pianist and only later on as a composer. Though possessed of all these exceptional attainments,

441

Prokofieff uses them within the rigid limits of artistic simplicity, which precludes the possibility of any affectation, any calculating of effect whereby an elevated style of pianism is sullied. In any case I have never heard a pianist who plays Prokofieff's productions more simply and at the same time more powerfully than the composer himself."

Prokofieff's return to Russia opened a new and active chapter of his career. Almost overnight he began to identify himself with the ideals of Soviet musical organizations in so far as they were concerned with education and the fostering of a community feeling of cultural solidarity. The attraction of the theater was stronger than ever, and soon he was composing operas, ballet scores, incidental music for plays, and music for films. Indeed, the composition that virtually reintroduced him to the Russian public was the striking score for the film *Lieutenant Kije*. This delighted one and all with its pungent wit and satiric thrusts at the parading pomp and stiffness of the court of Czar Paul. Less successful was the first performance in Moscow in 1934 of a "Chant Symphonique" for a large orchestra. This drew the reproach that it echoed "the disillusioned mood and weary art of the urban lyricists of contemporary Europe."

Another composition of this period was a suite prepared by Prokofieff from a ballet entitled, *"Sur le Borysthène."* Interest attaches to this ballet because of a significant verdict pronounced by a Paris judge in Prokofieff's favor. The ballet had been commissioned by Serge Lifar and produced at the Paris Opéra in 1933. The contract had stipulated one hundred thousand francs as payment for the work. Only seventy thousand francs were paid, and Prokofieff sued for the remainder. Lifar contended in court that the unfriendly reception accorded the production proved the ballet was "deficient in artistic merit." The court's judgment, rendered on January 9, 1934, read in part: "Any person acquiring a musical work puts faith in the composer's talent. There is no reliable criterion for evaluation of the quality of a work of art which is received according to individual taste. History teaches us that the public is often mistaken in its reaction."

Prokofieff made his last trip to the United States in February, 1938. In several interviews with the press he laid particular stress on how Russia provided "a livelihood and leisure" for composers and musicians of all categories. Later, the League of Composers invited him to be guest of honor at a concert devoted entirely to his music. Prokofieff

442

was to have made still another visit to America late in 1940 on the invitation of the New York Philharmonic-Symphony Society. The invitation was accepted, but Prokofieff never came. The reason given was that he could not secure the required visas. Prokofieff was to have conducted a series of concerts with the Philharmonic-Symphony. The Society accordingly asked another distinguished Russian composer to direct the concerts, a Russian who had not set foot in his native land since the Revolution—Igor Stravinsky.

Prokofieff was again at work on an opera—*"The Duenna"*—when his country once more found itself at war with Germany. Both the opera and a new ballet, *"Cinderella,"* were immediately shelved, and Prokofieff dedicated his energies and talents to expressing in music the determination of the Soviet people to resist the Nazi invasion and join in the world struggle to crush Fascism. Instead of light operas and fairy-tale ballets, he now composed a march, two war songs, and a symphonic suite "1941," a title which explains itself. As the war dragged on with its deadening weight of horror, and its unprecedented drama of resistance, the feelings it gave rise to inspired Prokofieff to compose an opera based on Tolstoy's monumental historical novel, "War and Peace." America learned of its completion on January 1, 1943 in a communication that conveyed New Year's greetings "to our American friends on behalf of all Soviet composers."

The opera caused Prokofieff considerable trouble because of its unparalleled length. Cuts and revisions were made, scenes transposed and replaced, and yet Prokofieff was never quite satisfied with the work. Excerpts were performed in Moscow, and again the music of Prokofieff became a bone of lively contention between those who thought he had captured the spirit of the novel and those who thought he had not. There was general agreement, however, that Prokofieff had written a magnificent and stirring tribute to Russian valor and patriotism. Together with his music for the films "Ivan the Terrible" and "Alexander Nevsky," the new opera offered an impressive panorama of Russian history. There are in "War and Peace" eleven long scenes and sixty characters. The work was much too long for a single evening, and when it was finally produced in Moscow in 1946, only the first part was performed. A stage première had been promised in Moscow as early as 1943, but technical difficulties caused its postponement. Plans for a Metropolitan production for the season of 1944-45 also had to be abandoned.

In 1945 Prokofieff composed his Fifth Symphony, which is considered by many critics the greatest single achievement of his symphonic career. Prokofieff has himself spoken of it as "the culmination of a large part of my creative life." The symphony was warmly received both in Russia and in America. It has generally been assumed that it depicts both the tragic and heroic phases of the world crisis and an unshaken confidence in final victory over Nazi barbarism. Prokofieff himself would provide no clue to its program other than that it was "a symphony about the spirit of man."

When Germany was at last defeated, Prokofieff's pen was again busy celebrating the event. This time it was an "Ode to the End of the War," scored for sixteen double basses, eight harps and four pianos. In 1947 Prokofieff composed his Sixth Symphony, and it was shortly after its first performance that the Central Committee of the Communist Party issued its stinging denunciation of certain tendencies in the music of Prokofieff and six other Soviet composers. The occasion of the official rebuke was a new opera by Vano Muradeli, *"Great Friendship."* This work was found offensive as a distortion of history and a false and imperfect exploitation of national material. Having disposed of Muradeli, the Committee concentrated its attack on the Symphonic Six —Shostakovich, Prokofieff, Khatchaturian, Shebalin, Popoff, and Miaskovsky.

"We are speaking of composers," read the statement, "who confine themselves to the formalist antipublic trend. This trend has found its fullest manifestation in the works of such composers [naming the six] in whose compositions the formalist distortions, the anti-democratic tendencies in music, alien to the Soviet people and to its artistic taste, are especially graphically represented. Characteristics of such music are the negation of the basic principles of classical music; a sermon for atonality, dissonance and disharmony, as if this were an expression of 'progress' and 'innovation' in the growth of musical composition as melody; a passion for confused, neuropathic combinations which transform music into cacophony, into a chaotic piling up of sounds. This music reeks strongly of the spirit of the contemporary modernist bourgeois music of Europe and America, which reflects the marasmus of bourgeois culture, the full denial of musical art, its impasse."

Like the other six composers, Prokofieff accepted the rebuke and made public acknowledgment that he had pursued paths of sterile experimentation in some of his more recent music. He declared that the Resolution of the Central Committee had "separated decayed tissue from healthy tissue in the composers' creative production," and that it had created the prerequisites "for the return to health of the entire organism of Soviet music."

Prokofieff's *mea culpa* was first contained in a letter addressed to Tikhon Khrennikoff, general secretary of the Union of Soviet Composers. It had been Khrennikoff, who, in a semi-official blast at these "tendencies" had first hurled the charge of "formalism" at Prokofieff and his colleagues Khrennikoff evidently had in mind certain patterns and formulas of the more extreme innovations of modern music, like Arnold Schoenberg's twelve-tone row and the many flourishing European schools of atonality, dissonance, and startling instrumental groupings.

"Composers have become infatuated," said Khrennikoff, "with formalistic innovations, artificially inflated and impracticable orchestral combinations, such as the including of twenty-four trumpets in Khatchaturian's 'Symphonic Poem' or the incredible scoring for sixteen double-basses, eight harps, four pianos, and the exclusion of the rest of the string instruments in Prokofieff's 'Ode on the End of War.'"

In pleading guilty to the charge of formalism, Prokofieff attempted to explain how it had found its way into his music:

"The resolution is all the more important because it has demonstrated that the formalist trend is alien to the Soviet people, that it leads to the impoverishment and decline of music, and has pointed out with definitive clarity the aims which we must strive to achieve as the best way to serve the Soviet people. *Speaking of myself, the elements of formalism were peculiar to my music as long as fifteen or twenty years ago. The infection was caught apparently from contact with a number of Western trends.*"

The spectacle of one of the world's most cherished and gifted composers making apologetic obeisance to political officialdom was hardly a comfortable one for observers outside Russia. The non-Communist press pounced righteously on the Central Committee's resolution as an arbitrary invasion of the sacred province of art. Charges of irresponsible government interference with the free workings of creative endeavor were widely made, and even writers who had been at least culturally sympathetic to the accomplishments of Soviet art and education waxed indignant over the episode. Many wondered why Prokofieff, of advanced musical craftsmen of our time perhaps the most classical and even the most melodious, should have been singled out at all. This bewilderment was perhaps best expressed by Robert Sabin, of the "Musical America" staff:

"His music is predominantly melodious, harmonically and contrapuntally clear, formally organic without being pedantic, original but unforced—in short an expression of the basic principles of classical music.

"Many of the phrases in the Central Committee's denunciation are fantastically inappropriate to Prokofieff's art. Prokofieff has never espoused atonality. He is eminently a democratic composer. Peter and the Wolf is loved by children and unspoiled adults the world over. His music for the film Alexander Nevsky and the cantata he later fashioned from it have been enormously popular. His suite Lieutenant Kijé, originally composed for another motion picture, charmed audiences as soon as it was heard, in 1934. On the contrary, among contemporary masters Prokofieff is precisely one whom we can salute as being close to the people, able to write music that is equally appealing to connoisseurs and less demanding listeners, a man who understands the musical character of simple human beings.

"Perhaps the outstanding psychological trait of Prokofieff's music has been its splendid healthiness. His Classical Symphony of 1916-17 bounds along with exhilarating energy and spontaneity; and in his works of the last decade, 1941-51, such as the ballet, 'Cinderella,' the String Quartet No. 2, and the Symphony No. 5, we find the same fullness of creative power, the same acceptance of life and ability to find it good and wholesome. Prokofieff belongs to the company of Bach and Handel in this respect—not to that of Scriabin and other composers whose genius had been tinged with neurotic traits and a tendency to cultism."

Nothing deterred by this unprecedented official spanking, Prokofieff went about his business, which was composing. The demands and necessities of this post-war period of reconstruction in Soviet life drew him deeper and deeper into the orbit of its community culture. A large proportion of his music became markedly topical and "national" in theme and orientation. Yet for all the strictures leveled at his music, and Khrennikoff was to scold him yet once more for "bourgeois formalism," Prokofieff, in most essentials, followed the unhampered bent of his genius. Ballet music, piano and cello sonatas continued to show that preoccupation with living and exciting form that in the best art can be dictated only by the exigencies of the material. It is possible that towards the very end Prokofieff had found a new synthesis that brought to full flower the abiding lyricism of his nature. That he was now determined to achieve an emotional communication through a lyrical simplicity of idiom about which there could be no mystery or confusion is clear. How much of this was owing to any official effort to discipline him and how much to the inevitable direction of his own creative logic it must remain for later and better informed students to assess.

The Seventh Symphony would seem to be a final testament of Prokofieff's return to this serene transparency of style. The new symphony was proof conclusive to the editors of "Pravda" that Prokofieff "had taken to heart the criticism directed at his work and succeeded in overcoming the fatal influence of formalism." Prokofieff was now seeking "to create beautiful, delicate music able to satisfy the artistic tastes of the Soviet people."

Prokofieff's death on March 4, 1953, the announcement of which was delayed several days perhaps because of the overshadowing illness and death of Premier Stalin, came with the shock of an irreparable loss to music-lovers everywhere. A chapter of world music in which a strong and fastidious classical sense had combined with a healthy and sometimes startling freshness of novelty, seemed to have closed. Dead at sixty-two, Serge Prokofieff had now begun that second life in the living memorial of the permanent repertory that is both the reward and the legacy of creative genius. It is safe to predict that so long as the concert hall endures as an institution, a considerable portion of his music will have a secure place within its hospitable walls.

The Music—Symphonies

"Classical Symphony," in D major, Opus 25

"If we wished to establish Prokofieff's genealogy as a composer, we would probably have to betake ourselves to the eighteenth century, to

447

Scarlatti and other composers of the good old times, who have inner simplicity and naïveté of creative art in common with him. Prokofieff is a classicist, not a romantic, and his appearance must be considered a belated relapse of classicism in Russia."

So wrote Leonid Sabaneyeff, and it was the "Classical Symphony" more than any other composition of Prokofieff that inspired his words, as it has the pronouncements of others who have used this early symphony as an index of the composer's predilections. Yet it is dangerous to so classify Prokofieff, except in so far as he remained loyal to a discipline of compression and a tradition of craftsmanship that seemed the very antithesis of the romantic approach to music. Nor was Prokofieff interested in imitating Mozart or Haydn in his "Classical Symphony." Whatever has been written about his implied or assumed intentions, he made his aim quite explicit. What he set out to do was to compose the sort of symphony that Mozart might have written had Mozart been a contemporary of Prokofieff's; not, it is clear, the other way around—that is, to compose the sort of symphony he might have written had he, instead, been a contemporary of Mozart's.

The symphony was begun in 1916, finished the following year, and first performed in Leningrad on April 21, 1918. Prokofieff conducted the work himself when he appeared in Carnegie Hall, New York, at a concert of the Russian Symphony Society on December 11, 1918. The occasion was its American première, and the "Classical Symphony" speedily became a favorite of the concert-going public. And no wonder! It is music that commends itself at once through a limpid style, an endearing precision of stroke, an unfailing wit of melody, and a general salon-like atmosphere of courtly gallantry.

I. *Allegro, D major, 2/2.* The first violins give out the sprightly first theme, the flutes following with a subsidiary theme in a passage that leads to a development section. The first violins now chant a second theme, friskier than the first in its wide leaps and mimicked by a supporting bassoon. Both major themes supply material for the main development section. There is a general review in C major, leading to the return of the second theme in D major, the key of the movement.

II. *Larghetto, A major, 3/4.* The chief melody of this movement is again entrusted to the first violins after a brief preface of four measures. "Only a certain rigidity in the harmonic changes and a slight exaggeration in the melodic line betray a non-'classical' feeling," wrote one

448

annotator. "The middle section is built on a running pizzicato passage. After rising to a climax, the interest shifts to the woodwinds, and a surprise modulation brings back the first subject, which, after a slight interruption by a recall of the middle section, picks up an oboe counterpoint in triplets. At the end the accompaniment keeps marching on until it disappears in the distance."

III. *Gavotte: Non troppo allegro, D major, 4/4.* This replaces the usual minuet in the classical scheme of things. One senses a scherzo without glimpsing its shape. The strings and the woodwinds announce the graceful dance theme in the first part, which is only twelve measures long in a symphony which lasts, in all, as many minutes. In the G major Trio that follows, flutes and clarinets join in sustaining a theme over a pastoral-like organ-point in the cellos and double-basses. A counter-theme is heard in the oboe. The first part returns, and the movement is over in a flash.

The gavotte was a widely used dance form in the music of the eighteenth century. It was said to stem from the Gavots, the people of the Pays de Gap. Originally a "danse grave," it differed from others of its kind in one respect. The dancers neither walked nor shuffled, but raised their feet. The gavotte was supposedly introduced to the French court in the sixteenth century as part of the entertainment enacted by natives in provincial costumes.

IV. *Finale: Molto vivace, D major, 2/2.* A bright little theme, chattered by the strings after an emphatic chord, serves as principal subject of this movement. A bridge-passage leads to a two-part second subject, in A major, the first part taken up by the woodwinds in a twittering melody (later passed to the strings), the second a counter-theme for solo oboe. The material is briefly and lucidly developed, and a recapitulation brings back the first section, with the woodwinds assuming the theme over a web of string pizzicati. A miniature coda follows, and there is a sudden halt to the music, as if at the precise, split-second moment that its logic and breath have run out.

Symphony No. 5, Op. 100

Of Prokofieff's subsequent symphonies it is only the Fifth thus far that has established itself with any promise of endurance in the concert repertory. The First, composed in 1908 and not included in the catalogue of Prokofieff's works, may be dismissed as a student experiment.

The Second, following sixteen years later, proved a stylistic misfit of noisy primitivism and even noisier factory-like mechanism. The Third, an impassioned and dramatic fantasy, dating from 1928, drew on material from an unproduced opera, "The Flaming Angel." Prokofieff also tells us that the stormy scherzo movement derived in part from Chopin's B-flat minor Sonata. The symphony was first performed in Paris on May 17, 1929, and carries a dedication to his life-long friend and colleague, the composer Miaskovsky. "I feel that in this symphony I have succeeded in deepening my musical language," Prokofieff wrote after his return to Russia and when the work had received its initial performances there. "I should not want the Soviet listener to judge me solely by the March from 'The Love of Three Oranges' and the Gavotte from the 'Classical Symphony.'" According to Israel Nestyev, Prokofieff's Soviet biographer, the Third Symphony was "something of an echo of the past, being made up chiefly of materials relating to 1918 and 1919."

With the Fourth Symphony we come to what might be termed Prokofieff's "American" Symphony. This was composed in 1929 for the Fiftieth Anniversary of the Boston Symphony. Much of the music harks back to the suave and courtly style of the "Classical" Symphony, without its uniform elegance of idiom, however. It was certainly a change from an explosion like the "Scythian" Suite, that had fairly rocked the sedate and cultivated subscribers of Symphony Hall out of their seats.

*　　*　　*

It is the Fifth that constitutes Prokofieff's most ambitious contribution to symphonic literature. It is a complex and infinitely variegated score, yet its composition took a solitary month. Another month was given over to orchestrating the work, and somewhere in between Prokofieff managed to begin and complete one of his most enduring film scores, that to Eisenstein's "Ivan the Terrible." The fact is that Prokofieff had been jotting down themes for this symphony in a special notebook for several years. "I always work that way," he explained, "and that is probably why I write so fast."

Composed during the summer of 1944, the Fifth Symphony was performed in America on November 9, 1945, at a concert of the Boston Symphony Orchestra under the direction of Serge Koussevitzky. Five days later, under the same auspices, it was introduced to New York at Carnegie Hall. Prokofieff had himself directed the world première in Moscow in January of that year. At that time Prokofieff, asked about the program or content of the symphony, would only admit that it was a symphony "about the spirit of man." The symphony was composed and performed in Moscow at a time of mounting Soviet victories over the German invaders. It seemed inevitable that a mood of exultation would find its way into this music. To Nestyev the symphony captured the listeners "with its healthy mood of affirmation." Continuing, this Soviet analyst declared that "in the heroic, manly images of the first movement, in the holiday jubilation of the finale, the listeners sensed a living transmutation of that popular emotional surge . . . which we felt in those days of victories over Nazi Germany."

In four movements, the Fifth Symphony is of basic traditional structure, despite its daring lapses from orthodoxy. The predominant mood is heroic and affirmative, at times tragic in its fervid intensity, sombre recurringly, but essentially an assertion of joyous strength, with momentary bursts of sidelong gaiety reserved for the last movement. A terse and searching analysis of the Fifth Symphony was made by John N. Burk for the program-book of the Boston Symphony Orchestra. It reads:

"I. *Andante.* The opening movement is built on two full-voiced melodic themes, the first in triple, the second in duple beat. Contrast is found in the alternate rhythm as both are fully developed. There is an impressive coda.

"II. *Allegro marcato.* The second movement has earmarks of the classical scherzo. Under the theme there is a steady reiteration of a staccato accompaniment, 4/4. The melody, passed by the clarinet to the other woodwinds and by them variously treated, plays over the marked and unremitting beat. A bridge passage for a substantial wind choir ushers in (and is to usher out) the Trio-like middle section, which is in 3/4 time and also rhythmically accented, the clarinet first bearing the burden of the melody. The first section, returning, is freshly treated. At the close the rhythm becomes more incisive and intense.

"III. *Adagio.* 3/4. The slow movement has, like the scherzo, a persistent accompaniment figure. It opens with a melody set forth *espressivo* by the woodwinds, carried by the strings into their high register. The movement is tragic in mood, rich in episodic melody. It carries the symphony to its deepest point of tragic tension, as descending scales give a weird effect of outcries. But this tension suddenly passes, and the reprise is serene.

"IV. *Allegro giocoso.* The finale opens *Allegro giocoso,* and after a brief tranquil passage for the divided cellos and basses, gives its light, rondo-like theme. There is a quasi-gaiety in the development, but, as throughout the symphony, something ominous seems always to lurk around the corner. The awareness of brutal warfare broods over it and comes forth in sharp dissonance—at the end."

The Sixth Symphony, in E-flat minor, Opus 111

In a letter to his American publishers dated September 6, 1946, Prokofieff announced that he was working on two major compositions—a sonata for violin and piano and a Sixth Symphony. "The symphony will be in three movements," he wrote. "Two of them were sketched last summer and at present I am working on the third. I am planning to orchestrate the whole symphony in the autumn."

The various emotional states or moods of the symphony Prokofieff described as follows: "The first movement is agitated in character, lyrical in places, and austere in others. The second movement, *andante,* is lighter and more songful. The finale, lighter and major in its character, would be like the finale of my Fifth Symphony but for the austere reminiscences of the first movement."

How active and productive a worker Prokofieff was may be gathered from other disclosures in the same letter. Besides the Symphony and Sonata, he was applying the finishing touches to a "Symphonic Suite of Waltzes," drawn from his ballet, *Cinderella,* his opera, *War and Peace* (based on Tolstoy's historical novel), and his score for the film biography of the Russian poet Lermontov. Earlier that summer he had completed three separate suites from *Cinderella* and a "big new scene" for *War and Peace.* No idler he!

The first performance of Prokofieff's Sixth Symphony occurred in Moscow on October 10, 1947. Four months later, on February 11, 1948, the Central Committee of the Communist Party of the Soviet Union issued its resolution denouncing Prokofieff and six other Soviet composers for their failure to "permeate themselves with a consciousness of the high demands made of musical creation by the Soviet people." The seven composers were charged with "formalist distortions and anti-democratic tendencies in music" in several of their more recent symphonic and operatic works. It has been assumed that the Sixth Symphony was among the offending scores which the Central Committee had in mind. While it was not placed under the official ban, it did not figure subsequently in the active repertory. To Leopold Stokowsky, who conducted its American première with the New York Philharmonic on November 24, 1949, in Carnegie Hall, we owe the perceptive analysis of the Sixth Symphony that follows:

I. "The first part has two themes—the first in a rather fast dance rhythm, the second a slower song-like melody, a little modal in character, recalling the old Russian and Byzantine scales. Later this music becomes gradually more animated as the themes are developed, and after a climax of the development there is a slower transition to the second part."

II. "I think this second part will need several hearings to be fully understood. The harmonies and texture of the music are extremely complex. Later there is a theme for horns which is simpler and sounds like voices singing. This leads to a warm *cantilena* of the violins and a slower transition to the third part."

III. "This is rhythmic and full of humor, verging on the satirical. The rhythms are clear-cut, and while the thematic lines are simple, they are accompanied by most original harmonic sequences, alert and rapid. Near the end a remembrance sounds like an echo of the pensive melancholy of the first part of the symphony, followed by a rushing, tumultuous end."

Mr. Stokowski has also stated that the Sixth Symphony represents a natural development of Prokofieff's extraordinary gifts as an original creative artist. "I knew Prokofieff well in Paris and in Russia," he writes, "and I feel that this symphony is an eloquent expression of the full range of his personality. It is the creation of a master artist, serene in the use and control of his medium."

The Seventh Symphony, Opus 131

The work was composed in 1952 and performed for the first time in Moscow on October 11, 1952, under the direction of Samuel Samosud. It is a comparatively short symphony as the symphonies of our time go, lasting no more than thirty minutes. For Prokofieff the orchestration is relatively modest and the division of the symphony is in the four traditional movements:

I. Moderato
II. Allegretto
III. Andante espressivo
IV. Vivace

From first note to last it is a transparent score, lyrical, melodic, and easily grasped and assimilated. Recurring themes are readily identified. "The harmonic structure could hardly be called modern in this *anno domini* 1953," writes Donald Engle, "and the scoring is generally open and concise, at times even spare and lean."

The general impression is that the music has two inevitable points of being, its beginning and its end, and that the symphony is the shortest possible distance between them. Such, in a sense, has been the classical ideal, and thus we find Prokofieff completing the symphonic cycle of his career by returning once more, whether by inner compulsion or outer necessity, to a classical symphony.

PIANO CONCERTOS

Concerto No. 1, in D-flat major, Opus 10, for Piano and Orchestra

Prokofieff's first piano concerto was his declaration of maturity, according to Nestyev. It followed the composition in 1911 of a one-act opera, *Magdalene,* that proved little more than an advanced student exercise for the operatic writing that was to come later. That same year Prokofieff completed his concerto and dedicated it to Nicolai Tscherepnine. Its performance in Moscow early the following year, followed by a performance in St. Petersburg, served to establish his name as one to conjure with among Russia's rising new generation of composers. The work suggested the tradition of Franz Liszt in its propulsive energy and strictly pianistic language. But it revealed the compactness of idiom and phrase, the pointed turn of phrase, and lithe rhythmic tension that were to develop and characterize so much of Prokofieff's subsequent music. The Concerto brought a fervid response, but not all of it was on Prokofieff's side. "Harsh, coarse, primitive cacophony" was the verdict of one Moscow critic. Another proposed a straitjacket for its young composer. On the other side of the ledger, critics in both cities welcomed its humor and wit and imaginative quality, not to mention "its freedom from the mildew of decadence." A particularly prophetic voice had this to say: "Prokofieff might even mark a stage in Russian musical development, Glinka and Rubinstein being the first, Tschaikowsky and Rimsky-Korsakoff the second, Glazounoff and Arensky the third, and Scriabin and Prokofieff the fourth." Daringly this prophet asked: "Why not?" *

Prokofieff was his own soloist on these occasions, and it was soon apparent that besides being a composer of emphatic power and originality, he was a pianist of prodigious virtuosity. "Under his fingers," ran one report, "the piano does not so much sing and vibrate as speak in the stern and convincing tone of a percussion instrument, the tone of the old-fashioned harpsichord. Yet it was precisely this convincing freedom of execution and these clear-cut rhythms that won the author such enthusiastic applause from the public." Most confident and discerning of all at this time was Miaskovsky, who, reviewing a set of Four Etudes by Prokofieff, challengingly stated: "What pleasure and surprise it affords one to come across this vivid and wholesome phenomenon amid the morass of effeminacy, spinelessness, and anemia of today!"

The First Piano Concerto was introduced to America at a concert of the Chicago Symphony Orchestra on December 11, 1918. The conductor was Eric De Lamarter, and the soloist was again Prokofieff himself.

The Concerto is in one uninterrupted movement, Prokofieff considering the whole "an allegro movement in sonata form." While the music ventures among many tonalities before its journey is over, it ends the way it began, in the key of D-flat major. One gains the impression, though only in passing, of a three-movement structure because of two sections marked, respectively, *Andante* and *Allegro scherzando,* which follow the opening *Allegro brioso.* Actually the *Andante,* a sustained lyrical discourse, featuring, by turn, strings, solo clarinet, solo piano, and finally piano and orchestra, is a songful pause between the exposition and development of this sonata plan. When the *Andante* has reached its peak, the *Allegro scherzando* begins, developing themes

* I quote from Nestyev's biography, translated by Rose Prokofieva and published in this country by Alfred A. Knopf (1946).

already presented in the earlier section. One is reminded of the cyclical recurrence of theme adopted by Liszt in his piano concertos, both of which are also in one-movement, though subdivided within the unbroken continuity of the music.

Concerto No. 2 in G minor, Opus 16, for Piano and Orchestra

The Second Piano Concerto of Prokofieff belongs to the lost and found department of music. It was written early in 1913, that is, two years after the First Concerto, and performed for the first time, with Prokofieff at the keyboard, on August 23 at Pavlovsk, a town not far from St. Petersburg. A performance, with the same soloist, took place at a concert of the Russian Musical Society on January 24, 1915. Early the following month Prokofieff left for Italy at the invitation of Sergei Diaghileff, who liked the Concerto and for a while even toyed with the possibility of using it for a ballet. On March 7, 1915 Prokofieff, through the intervention of Diaghileff, performed his Second Concerto at the Augusteo, Rome, the conductor being Bernardino Molinari. The reaction of the Italian press was pretty much that of the Russian press—divided. There were again those who decried Prokofieff's bold innovations of color and rhythm and harmony, and there were those who hailed these very things. There was one point of unanimity, however. One and all, in both countries, acclaimed Prokofieff as a pianist of brilliance and distinction.

Now, when Prokofieff left Russia for the United States in 1918, the score of the Second Piano Concerto remained behind in his apartment in the city that became Leningrad. This score, together with the orchestral parts and other manuscripts, were lost when Prokofieff's apartment was confiscated during the revolutionary exigencies of the period. Luckily, sketches of the piano part were salvaged by Prokofieff's mother, and returned to him in 1921. Working from these sketches, Prokofieff partly reconstructed and partly rewrote his Second Piano Concerto. There is considerable difference between the two versions. Both the basic structure and the themes of the original were retained, but the concerto could now boast whatever Prokofieff had gained in imaginative and technical resource in the intervening years. Thus reshaped, the Second Piano Concerto was first performed in Paris with the composer as soloist, and Serge Koussevitzky conducting. The following analysis, used on that occasion, and later translated by Philip

Hale and extensively quoted in this country, was probably the work of Prokofieff, who was generally quite hospitable to requests for technical expositions of his music.

I. *Andantino-Allegretto-Andantino.* The movement begins with the announcement of the first theme, to which is opposed a second episode of a faster pace in A minor. The piano enters solo in a technically complicated cadenza, with a repetition of the first episode in the first part.

II. *Scherzo.* This *Scherzo* is in the nature of a *moto perpetuo* in 16th notes by the two hands in the interval of an octave, while the orchestral accompaniment furnishes the background.

III. *Intermezzo.* This movement, *moderato,* is conceived in a strictly classical form.

IV. *Finale.* After several measures in quick movement the first subject is given to the piano. The second is of a calmer, more cantabile nature—piano solo at first—followed by several canons for piano and orchestra. Later the two themes are joined, the piano playing one, the orchestra the other. There is a short coda based chiefly upon the first subject.

Concerto No. 3, in C major, Opus 26, for Piano and Orchestra

Prokofieff did not begin work on his Third Piano Concerto till four years after he had completed the first version of his Second Concerto. This was in 1917 in the St. Petersburg that was now Petrograd and was soon to be Leningrad. However, a combination of war and revolution, plus a departure for America in 1918, and the busy schedule that followed, delayed completion of the work. It was not until October, 1921, in fact, that the score was ready for performance, and that event took place at a concert of the Chicago Symphony Orchestra on the following December 17. Prokofieff was again the soloist, as he is once more his own annotator in the analysis that follows.

I. The first movement opens quietly with a short introduction, Andante, 4-4. The theme is announced by an unaccompanied clarinet, and is continued by the violins for a few bars. Soon the tempo changes to Allegro, the strings having a passage in semiquavers which leads to the statement of the principal subject by the piano. Discussion of this theme is carried on in a lively manner, both the piano and the orchestra having a good deal to say on the matter. A passage in chords for the piano alone leads to the more expressive second subject, heard in the oboe with a pizzicato accompaniment. This is taken up by the piano and developed at some length, eventually giving way to a bravura passage in triplets. At the climax of this section, the tempo reverts to Andante, and the orchestra gives out the first theme, ff. The piano joins in, and the theme is subjected to an impressively broad treatment. On resuming the Allegro, the chief theme and the second subject are developed with increased brilliance, and the movement ends with an exciting crescendo.

II. The second movement consists of a theme with five variations. The theme is announced by the orchestra alone, *Andantino.*

In the first variation, the piano treats the opening of the theme in quasi-sentimental fashion, and resolves into a chain of trills, as the orchestra repeats the closing phrase. The tempo changes to Allegro for the second and the third variations, and the piano has brilliant figures, while snatches of the theme are introduced here and there in the orchestra. In variation Four the tempo is once again *Andante,* and the piano and orchestra discourse on the theme in a quiet and meditative fashion. Variation Five is energetic (Allegro giusto). It leads without pause into a restatement of the theme by the orchestra, with delicate chordal embroidery in the piano.

III. The Finale begins (Allegro ma non troppo, 3-4) with a staccato theme for bassoons and pizzicato strings, which is interrupted by the blustering entry of the piano. The orchestra holds its own with the opening theme, however, and there is a good deal of argument, with frequent differences of opinion as regards key. Eventually the piano takes up the first theme, and develops it to a climax. With a reduction of tone and slackening of tempo, an alternative theme is introduced in the woodwind. The piano replies with a theme that is more in keeping with the caustic humor of the work. This material is developed and there is a brilliant coda.

* * *

It was Prokofieff's Third Piano Concerto that launched a young Greek musician by the name of Dimitri Mitropoulos on a brilliant international career. Mr. Mitropoulos had been invited to Berlin in 1930 to conduct the Berlin Philharmonic. Egon Petri, the celebrated

Dutch pianist, was scheduled to appear as soloist in the Prokofieff Third. But Mr. Petri was indisposed and no other pianist was available to replace him in time for the concert. To save the situation Mr. Mitropoulos volunteered to play the concerto himself. The result was a spectacular double début in Berlin for the young musician as conductor and pianist. Engaged to conduct in Paris soon after, Mr. Mitropoulos again billed Prokofieff's Third Piano Concerto, with himself once more as soloist. This time he was heard by Prokofieff, who stated publicly that the Greek played it better than he himself could ever hope to. Word of Mr. Mitropoulos's European triumphs reached Serge Koussevitzky, who immediately invited him to come to America as guest conductor of the Boston Symphony Orchestra. It is no wonder that Dimitri Mitropoulos often refers to this concerto as "the lucky Prokofieff Third."

Concerto No. 5, Opus 55, for Piano and Orchestra

Before concerning ourselves with Prokofieff's Fifth Piano Concerto, a few words are needed to explain this leap from No. 3 to No. 5. A fourth piano concerto is listed in the catalogue as Opus 53, dating from 1931, consisting of four movements, and still in manuscript. A significant reference to its being "for the left hand" begins to tell us a story. Prokofieff wrote it for a popular Austrian pianist, Paul Wittgenstein, who had lost his right arm in the First World War. Wittgenstein had already been armed with special scores by such versatile worthies as Richard Strauss, Erich Korngold, and Franz Schmidt. Prokofieff responded with alacrity when Wittgenstein approached him too. The Concerto, bristling with titanic difficulties and a complex stylistic scheme that would have baffled two hands if not two brains, was submitted for inspection to the one-armed virtuoso. Wittgenstein disliked it cordially, refused to perform it, and thus consigned it to the silence of a manuscript.

Maurice Ravel, approached in due course for a similar work, was the only composer to emerge with an enduring work from contact with this gifted casualty of the war. However, he too had trouble. When completed, the Concerto was virtually deeded to the pianist. Wittgenstein now proceeded to object to numerous passages and to insist on alterations. Ravel angrily refused, and was anything but mollified to discover that Wittgenstein was taking "unpardonable liberties" in public performances of the concerto. . . . Perhaps it was just as well that Prokofieff's Fourth Piano Concerto remained in its unperformed innocence—a concerto for no hands.

It was not long before the mood to compose a piano concerto was upon Prokofieff again. This became his Fifth, finished in the summer of 1932 and performed for the first time in Berlin at a Philharmonic Concert conducted by Wilhelm Furtwängler. Prokofieff was the soloist. It is interesting to note that the program contained another soloist —the gentleman playing the viola part in Berlioz's "Childe Harold Symphony," a gentleman by the name of Paul Hindemith. There was a performance of the Concerto in Paris two months later.

When the concerto and the composer reached Boston together the following year, Prokofieff gave an interviewer from the *Transcript* both a description of the way he composed and an analysis of the score. About his method Prokofieff had this to say:

"I am always on the lookout for new melodic themes. These I write in a notebook, as they come to me, for future use. All my work is founded on melodies. When I begin a work of major proportions I usually have accumulated enough themes to make half-a-dozen symphonies. Then the work of selection and arrangement begins. The composition of this Fifth Concerto began with such melodies. I had enough of them to make three concertos."

His analysis follows:

"The emphasis in this concerto is entirely on the melodic. There are five movements, and each movement contains at least four themes or melodies. The development of these themes is exceedingly compact and concise. This will be evident when I tell you that the entire five movements do not take over twenty minutes in performance. Please do not misunderstand me. The themes are not without development. In a work such as Schumann's 'Carnival' there are also many themes, enough to make a considerable number of symphonies or concertos. But they are not developed at all. They are merely stated. In my new Concerto there is actual development of the themes, but this development is as compressed and condensed as possible. Of course there is no program, not a sign or suggestion of a program. But neither is there any movement so expansive as to be a complete sonata-form.

I. *Allegro con brio: meno mosso.* "The first movement is an *Allegro con brio,* with a *meno mosso* as middle section. Though not in a sonata-form, it is the main movement of the Concerto, fulfills the functions of a sonata-form and is in the spirit of the usual sonata-form.

II. *Moderato ben accentuato.* "This movement has a march-like rhythm, but we must be cautious in the use of this term. I would not think of calling it a march because it has none of the vulgarity or commonness which is so often associated with the idea of a march and which actually exists in most popular marches.

III. *Allegro con fuoco.* "The third movement is a Toccata. This is a precipitate, displayful movement of much technical brilliance and requiring a large virtuosity—as difficult for orchestra as for the soloist. It is a Toccata for orchestra as much as for piano.

IV. *Larghetto.* "The fourth movement is the lyrical movement of the Concerto. It starts off with a soft, soothing theme: grows more and more intense in the middle portion, develops breadth and tension, then returns to the music of the beginning. German commentators have mistakenly called it a theme and variations.

V. *Vivo: Piu Mosso: Coda.* "The Finale has a decidedly classical flavor. The Coda is based on a new theme which is joined by the other themes of the Finale."

Summing up his own view of the Concerto, Prokofieff concluded: "The Concerto is not cyclic in the Franckian sense of developing several movements out of the theme or set of themes. Each movement has its own independent themes. But there is reference to some of the material of the First Movement in the Third; and also reference to the material of the Third Movement in the Finale. The piano part is treated in *concertante* fashion. The piano always has the leading part which is closely interwoven with significant music in the orchestra."

After this rather mild and dispassionate self-appraisal, it comes as something of a shock to read the slashing commentary of Prokofieff's Soviet biographer Nestyev:

"The machine-like Toccata, in the athletic style of the earlier Prokofieff, presents his bold jumps, handcrossing, and Scarlatti technic in highly exaggerated form. The tendency to wide skips à la Scarlatti is carried to monstrous extremes. Sheer feats of piano acrobatics completely dominate the principal movements of the Concerto. In the precipitate Toccata this dynamic quality degenerates into mere lifeless mechanical movement, with the result that the orchestra itself seems to be transformed into a huge mechanism with fly-wheels, pistons, and transmission belts."

To Nestyev it was further proof of the "brittle, urbanistic" sterility of Prokofieff's "bourgeois" wanderings.

VIOLIN CONCERTOS

Concerto in D major, No. 1, Opus 19, for Violin and Orchestra

Although composed in Russia between 1913 and 1917, Prokofieff's First Violin Concerto did not see the light of day till October 18, 1923, that is to say, shortly after he had taken up residence in Paris. It was on that date that the work was first performed in the French capital at a concert conducted by Serge Koussevitzky, who entrusted the solo part to his concertmaster Marcel Darrieux. The same violinist was soloist at a subsequent concert in the Colonne concert series, on November 25. It is said that the work was assigned to a concertmaster after Mr. Koussevitzky had been rebuffed by several established artists, among them the celebrated Bronislaw Hubermann, who relished neither its idiom nor its technique. This attitude was shared by Paris critics, who expressed an almost uniform hostility to the concerto. Prokofieff's arrival in Paris had already been prepared by his "Scythian Suite" and Third Piano Concerto. The new work must evidently have struck Parisian ears as rather mild and Mendelssohnian by comparison. In any case, the Violin Concerto did not gain serious recognition till it was performed in Prague on June 1 of the following year at a festival of the International Society for Contemporary Music. The soloist this time was Joseph Szigeti, and it was thanks in large part to his working sponsorship of the Concerto that it began to gather momentum on the international concert circuit. Serge Koussevitzky was again the conductor when the work was given its American première by the Boston Symphony Orchestra on April 24, 1925, and once more the soloist was a concertmaster—Richard Burgin.

The D major Violin Concerto shows the period of its composition in its frequent traces of the national school of Rimsky-Korsakoff and Glazounoff. Despite the bustling intricacies of the second movement, it is not a virtuoso's paradise by any means. Bravura of the rampant kind is absent, and of cadenzas there is no sign. Neither is the orchestra an accompaniment in the traditional sense, but rather part of the same integrated scheme of which the solo-violin is merely a prominent feature.

I. *Andantino.* The solo violin chants a gentle theme against which the strings and clarinet weave in equally gentle background. There is a spirited change of mood as the melody is followed by rhythmic passage-work sustained over a marked bass. The first theme returns as the movement draws to a close, more deliberate now. The flute takes it up as the violin embroiders richly around it.

II. *Vivacissimo.* This is a swiftly moving scherzo, bristling with accented rhythms, long leaps, double-stop slides and harmonics, and down-bow strokes, "none of which," Robert Bagar shrewdly points out, "may be construed as display music."

III. *Moderato.* More lyrical than the preceding movement, the finale allows the violin frolic to continue to some extent. Scale passages are developed and high-flown trills give the violin some heady moments. The bassoon offers a coy theme before the violin introduces the main subject in a sequence of staccato and legato phrases. There are pointed comments from a restless orchestra as the material is developed. Soon the soft melody of the opening movement is heard again, among the massed violins now. Above it the solo instrument soars in trills on a parallel line of notes an octave above, coming to rest on high D.

Concerto in G minor, No. 2, Op. 63, for Violin and Orchestra

Composed during the summer and autumn of 1935, Prokofieff's second violin concerto was premiered in Madrid on December 1 of that year. Enrique Arbos conducted the Madrid Symphony Orchestra, with the Belgian violinist Robert Soetens playing the solo part. Prokofieff himself was present and later directed the same orchestra in his "Classical Symphony." Jascha Heifetz was the soloist when Serge Koussevitzky and the Boston Symphony Orchestra first performed the new concerto in America.

Twenty-two years had elapsed since Prokofieff had composed his first violin concerto in D, so comparisons were promptly made between the styles and idioms manifested by the two scores. Apart from the normal development and change expected over so long a period, another factor was emphasized by many. The G minor concerto marked

Prokofieff's return to his homeland after a long Odyssey abroad. He was now a Soviet citizen and once more a participant in the social and cultural life of his country.

The new concerto revealed a warmth and lyricism, even a romantic spirit, that contrasted with the witty glitter and grotesquerie of the early concerto. The old terseness, rigorous logic, and clear-cut form were still observable, though less pronounced. There were even flashes of the "familiar Prokofieffian naughtiness," as Gerald Abraham pointed out. But the new mood was inescapable. "So far as the violin concerto form is concerned," wrote the English musicologist, "Prokofieff's formula for turning himself into a Soviet composer has been to emphasize the lyrical side of his nature at the expense of the witty and grotesque and brilliant sides."

The daring thrusts, the crisp waggishness, the fiendish cleverness and steely glitter seemed now to be giving way to warmer, deeper preoccupations, at least in the first two movements. "The renascence of lyricism, warm melody, and simple emotionality is the essence of the second violin concerto," writes Abraham Veinus. The earlier spirit of mockery and tart irreverence was almost lost in the new surge of romantic melody.

I. *Allegro moderato, G minor, 4/4.* The solo instrument, unaccompanied, gives out a readily remembered first theme which forms the basis of the subsequent development and the coda. The appealing second theme is also announced by the violin, this time against soft rhythmic figures in the string section. Abraham finds a "distant affinity" between this second theme and the Gavotte of Prokofieff's "Classical Symphony."

II. *Andante assai, E-flat major, 12/8.* The shift to frank melodic appeal is especially noticeable in the slow movement. Here the mood is almost steadily lyrical and romantic from the moment the violin sings the theme which forms the basic material of the movement. There is varied treatment and some shifting in tonality before the chief melody returns to the key of E-flat.

III. *Allegro ben marcato, G minor, 3/4.* In the finale the old Prokofieff is back in a brilliant Rondo of incisive rhythms and flashing melodic fragments. There are bold staccato effects, tricky shifts in rhythm, and brisk repartee between violin and orchestra. If there is any obvious link with the earlier concerto in D it is here in this virtuoso's playground.

"Ala and Lolli," Scythian Suite for Large Orchestra, Opus 20

It has been supposed that, consciously or not, Prokofieff was influenced by Stravinsky's "Sacre du Printemps" in his choice and treatment of material for the "Scythian Suite." Both scores have an earthy, barbaric quality, a stark rhythmic pulsation and an atmosphere of remote pagan ritualism that establish a strong kinship, whether direct or not. In each instance, moreover, the subject matter allowed the composer ample score for exploiting fresh devices of harmony and color. Another point of contact between the two scores was the figure of Serge Diaghileff, that fabulous patron and gadfly of modern art. Stravinsky had already been brought into the camp of Russian ballet by this most persuasive of all ballet impresarios. Soon it was Prokofieff's turn. Daighileff's commission was a ballet "on Russian fairy-tale or prehistoric themes." The "Scythian" music was Prokofieff's answer. The encounter with Diaghileff had occurred in June, 1914. With the outbreak of war later that year, an unavoidable delay set in, and it was evidently not till early the next year that Prokofieff submitted what was ready to Diaghileff, who liked neither the plot nor the music. To compensate him for his pains Diaghileff did two things: The first was to arrange for Prokofieff to play his Second Piano Concerto in Rome, an experience that proved profitable in every sense. The second was to commission another ballet, with the injunction to "write music that will be truly Russian." To which the candid Diaghileff added: "They've forgotten how to write music in that rotten St. Petersburg of yours." The result was *The Buffoon,* a ballet which proved more palatable to Diaghileff and led to a mutually fruitful association of many years.

What was to have been the "Scythian" ballet became instead, an orchestral suite, the première of which took place in St. Petersburg on January 29, 1916, Prokofieff himself conducting. More than any other score of Prokofieff's, the "Scythian Suite" was responsible for the acrimonious note that long remained in the reaction of the press to his music. "Cacophony" became a frequent word in the vocabulary of invective favored by hostile critics. Prokofieff was accused of breaking every musical law and violating every tenet of good taste. His music was "noisy," "rowdy," "barbarous," an expression of irresponsible hooliganism in symphonic form. Glazounoff, friend and teacher and guide, walked out on the first performance of "The Scythian Suite." But there were those among the critics and public who recognized the confident power and proclamative freedom of this music, and so a merry war of words, written and spoken, brewed over a score that Diaghileff, in a moment of singular insensitivity, had dismissed as "dull." Whatever else this music was—and it was almost everything from a signal for angry stampedes from the concert hall to an open declaration of war—it was emphatically not dull! Even the word "Bolshevism" was hurled at the score when it reached these placid shores late in 1918. In Chicago, one critic wrote: "The red flag of anarchy waved tempestuously over old Orchestra Hall yesterday as Bolshevist melodies floated over the waves of a sea of sound in breath-taking cacophony." Dull, indeed!

Of the original Scythians whose strange customs were the subject of Prokofieff's controversial suite, Robert Bagar tells us succinctly:

"First believed to have been mentioned by the poet Hesiod (800 B.C.), the Scythians were a nomadic people dwelling along the north shore of the Black Sea. Probably of Mongol blood, this race vanished about 100 B.C. Herodotus tells us that they were rather an evil lot, given to very primitive customs, fat and flabby in appearance, and living under a despotic rule whose laws, such as they may have been, were enforced through the ever-present threat of assassination.

"There were gods, of course, each in charge of some aspect or other of spiritual or human or moral conduct—a sun god, a health god, a heaven god, an evil god and quite a few others. Veles, the god of the sun, was their supreme deity. His daughter was Ala, and Lolli was one of their great heroes."

Prokofieff's Suite is based on the story of Ala, her suffering in the toils of the Evil God, and her deliverance by Lolli. The suite is divided into four movements, brief outlines of which are furnished in the score.

I. *"Invocation to Veles and Ala."* (*Allegro feroce, 4/4.*) The music describes an invocation to the sun, worshipped by the Scythians as their highest deity, named Veles. This invocation is followed by the sacrifice to the beloved idol, Ala, the daughter of Veles.

II. *"The Evil-God and dance of the pagan monsters."* (*Allegro sostenuto, 4/4.*) The Evil-God summons the seven pagan monsters from their subterranean realms and, surrounded by them, dances a delirious dance.

III. *"Night."* (*Andantino, 4/4.*) The Evil-God comes to Ala in the darkness. Great harm befalls her. The moon rays fall upon Ala, and the moon-maidens descend to bring her consolation.

IV. *"Lolli's pursuit of the Evil-God and the sunrise."* (*Tempestuoso, 4/4.*) Lolli, a Scythian hero, goes forth to save Ala. He fights the Evil-God. In the uneven battle with the latter, Lolli would have perished, but the sun-god rises with the passing of night and smites the evil deity. With the description of the sunrise the Suite comes to an end.

Orchestral Suite from the Film, "Lieutenant Kije," Opus 60

The Soviet film, "Lieutenant Kije," was produced by the Belgoskino Studios of Leningrad in 1933, after a story by Y. Tynyanov that had become a classic of the new literature. The director was A. Feinzimmer. For Prokofieff, who supplied the music, it represented the first important work of his return to Russia. The music belongs with that for "Alexander Nevsky" and "Ivan the Terrible" as the most effective and characteristic Prokofieff composed for the Soviet screen. From that score Prokofieff assembled an orchestral suite which was published early in 1934 and performed later that year in Moscow. Prokofieff himself conducted its Parisian première at a Lamoureux concert on February 20, 1937, when, according to an English correspondent, it "made a stunning impression." Serge Koussevitzky introduced it to America at a concert of the Boston Symphony Orchestra on October 15 of the same year.

The film tells an ironic and amusing story of a Russian officer, who because of a clerical error, existed only on paper. The setting is that of St. Petersburg during the reign of Czar Paul. The Czar misreads the report of one of his military aides, and without meaning to, evolves the name of a non-existent lieutenant. He does this by inadvertently linking the "ki" at the end of another officer's name to the Russian expletive "je." The result is the birth—on paper—of a new officer in the Russian Army, "Lieutenant Kije." Since no one dares to tell the Czar of his absurd blunder, his courtiers are obliged to invent a "Lieutenant Kije" to go with the name. Such being the situation, the film is an enlargement on the expedients and subterfuges arising from it. There are five sections:

I. *Birth of Kije.* (*Allegro.*) A combination of off-stage cornet fanfare, military drum-roll, and squealings from a fife proclaim that Lieutenant Kije is born—in the brain of blundering Czar. The solemn announcement is taken up by other instruments, followed by a short *Andante* section, and presently the military clatter of the opening is back.

II. *Romance.* (*Andante.*) This section contains a song, assigned optionally to baritone voice or tenor saxophone. The text of the song, in translation, reads:

> "Heart be calm, do not flutter;
> Don't keep flying like a butterfly.
> Well, what has my heart decided?
> Where will we in summer rest?
> But my heart could answer nothing,
> Beating fast in my poor breast.
> My grey dove is full of sorrow—
> Moaning is she day and night.
> For her dear companion left her,
> Having vanished out of sight,
> Sad and dull has gotten my grey dove."

III. *Kije's Wedding.* (*Allegro.*) This section reminds us that although our hero is truly a soldier, like so many of his calling he is also susceptible to the claims of the heart. In fact, he is quite a dashing lover, not without a touch of sentimentality.

IV. *Troika.* (*Moderato.*) The Russian word "Troika" means a set of three, then, by extension, a team of three horses abreast, finally, a three-horse sleigh. This section is so named because the orchestra pictures such a vehicle as accompaniment to a second song, in this case a Russian tavern song. Its words, as rendered from the Russian, go:

> "A woman's heart is like an inn:
> All those who wish go in,

SERGE PROKOFIEFF

And they who roam about
Day and night go in and out.
Come here, I say; come here, I say,
And have no fear with me.
Be you bachelor or not,
Be you shy or be you bold,
I call you all to come here.
So all those who are about,
Keep going in and coming out,
Night and day they roam about."

V. *Burial of Kije.* (*Andante assai.*) Thus ends the paper career of our valiant hero. The music recalls his birth to a flourish of military sounds, his romance, his wedding. And now the cornet that had blithely announced his coming in an off-stage fanfare is muted to his going, as Lieutenant Kije dwindles to his final silence.

Music for the Ballet, "Romeo and Juliet," Opus 64-A and 64-B

As a ballet in four acts and nine tableaux, Prokofieff's "Romeo and Juliet" was first produced by the Bolshoi Theatre in Moscow in 1935. Like many standard Russian ballets, the performance took a whole evening. Prokofieff assembled two Suites from the music, the first premiered in Moscow on November 24, 1936, under the direction of Nicolas Semjonowitsch Golowanow. The première of the second Suite followed less than a month later.

Prokofieff himself directed the American premières of both Suites, of Suite No. 1 as guest of the Chicago Symphony Orchestra on January 21, 1937, and of Suite No. 2 as guest of the Boston Symphony Orchestra on March 25, 1938. Serge Koussevitzky and the Boston unit introduced the Suite to New York on March 31 following.

After a trial performance of the ballet in Moscow V. V. Konin reported to the "Musical Courier" that Soviet critics present were "left in dismay at the awkward incongruity between the realistic idiom of the musical language, a language which successfully characterizes the individualism of the Shakespearean images, and the blind submission to the worst traditions of the old form, as revealed in the libretto."

Fault was also found because "the social atmosphere of the period and the natural evolution of its tragic elements had been robbed of their logical culmination and brought to the ridiculously dissonant 'happy end' of the conventional ballet. This inconsistency in the development of the libretto has had an unfortunate effect, not only upon the general structure, but even upon the otherwise excellent musical score."

Critical reaction to both Suites has varied, some reviewers finding the music dry and insipid for such a romantic theme; others hailing its pungency and color. Prokofieff's classicism was compared with his romanticism. If we are prepared to accept the "Classical" Symphony as truly classical, said one critic, then we must accept the "Romeo and Juliet" music as truly romantic. The cold, cheerless, dreary music "is certainly not love music," read one verdict. Prokofieff was taken to task for describing a love story "as if it were an algebraic problem."

Said Olin Downes of the New York *Times* in his review of the Boston Symphony concert of March 31, 1938: "The music is predominantly satirical. . . . There is the partial suggestion of that which is poignant and tragic, but there is little of the sensuous or emotional, and in the main the music could bear almost any title and still serve the ballet evolutions and have nothing to do with Romeo and Juliet."

Others extolled Prokofieff for the "fundamental simplicity and buoyancy" of the music, finding it typically rooted in the "plain, tangible realities of tone, design, and color." Prokofieff himself answered the repeated charge that his score lacked feeling and melody:

"Every now and then somebody or other starts urging me to put more feeling, more emotion, more melody in my music. My own conviction is that there is plenty of all that in it. I have never shunned the expression of feeling and have always been intent on creating melody—but new melody, which perhaps certain listeners do not recognize as such simply because it does not resemble closely enough the kind of melody to which they are accustomed.

"In 'Romeo and Juliet' I have taken special pains to achieve a simplicity which will, I hope, reach the hearts of all listeners. If people find no melody and no emotion in this work, I shall be very sorry. But I feel sure that sooner or later they will."

In the First Suite which Prokofieff prepared for concert purposes, there are seven numbers, outlined as follows: 1) "Folk Dance"; 2) "Scene"; 3) "Madrigal"; 4) "Minuet"; 5) "Masques"; 6) "Romeo and Juliet"; and 7) "The Death of Tybalt." Perhaps the most significant and absorbing of these is "Masques," an *Andante marciale* of majestic sweep and power, which accompanies the action at the Capulet ball, leading to the unobserved entrance into the palace of Romeo and two friends, wearing masks. One senses a brooding, sinister prophecy in the measured stateliness of the music. Seering and incisive in its pitiless evocation is "The Death of Tybalt," marked *Precipitato* in the score. Both street duels are depicted in this section, the first in which Tybalt slays Mercutio, the other in which Romeo, in revenge, slays Tybalt. Capulet's denunciation follows. This First Suite is listed as Opus 64-A in the catalogue of Prokofieff's works.

The Second Suite, Opus 64-B, also consists of seven numbers:

1) *"Montagues and Capulets"* (*Allegro pesante*). This is intended to portray satirically the proud, haughty characters of the noblemen. There is a *Trio* in which Juliet and Paris are pictured as dancing.

2) *"Juliet, the Maiden"* (*Vivace*). The main theme portrays the innocent and lighthearted Juliet, tender and free of suspicion. As the section develops we sense a gradual deepening of her feelings.

3) *"Friar Laurence"* (*Andante espressivo*). Two themes are used to identify the Friar—bassoons, tuba, and harps announce the first; 'cellos, the second.

4) *"Dance"* (*Vivo*).

5) *"The Parting of Romeo and Juliet"* (*Lento. Poco piu animato*). An elaborately worked out fabric woven mainly from the theme of Romeo's love for Juliet.

6) *"Dance of the West Indian Slave Girls"* (*Andante con eleganza*). The section accompanies both the action of Paris presenting pearls to Juliet and slave girls dancing with the pearls.

7) *"Romeo at Juliet's Grave"* (*Adagio funebre*). Prokofieff captures the anguish and pathos of the heartbreaking blunder that is the ultimate in tragedy: Juliet is not really dead, and her tomb is only that in appearance—but for Romeo the illusion is reality and his grief is unbounded.

Prokofieff's original plan was to give "Romeo and Juliet" a happy ending, its first since the time of Shakespeare. Juliet was to be awakened in time to prevent Romeo's suicide, and the ballet would end with a dance of jubilation by the reunited lovers. Criticism was widespread and sharp when this modification of Shakespeare's drama was exhibited at a trial showing. All thought of a happy ending was promptly abandoned, and Prokofieff put the tragic seal of death on the finale of his ballet.

CHILDREN'S CORNER

"Peter and the Wolf,"
An Orchestral Fairy Tale for Children, Opus 67

As early in his career as 1914 Prokofieff made his first venture in the enchanted world of children's entertainment. This was a cycle for voice and piano (or orchestra) grouped under the general title of "The Ugly Duckling," after Andersen's fairy-tale. It was not till twenty-two years later that he returned to this vein and achieved a masterpiece for the young of all ages, all times, and all countries, the so-called "orchestral fairy tale for children"—"Peter and the Wolf."

Completed in Moscow on April 24, 1936, the score was performed for the first time anywhere at a children's concert of the Moscow Philharmonic the following month. Two years later, on March 25, 1938, the Boston Symphony Orchestra gave the music its first performance outside of Russia. On January 13, 1940, the work was produced by the Ballet Theatre at the Center Theatre, New York, with choreography by Adolph Bolm, and Eugene Loring starring in the rôle of Peter. Its success as a ballet was long and emphatic, particularly with the younger matinée element. Prominent in the general effectiveness of Prokofieff's work is the rôle of the Narrator, for whom Prokofieff supplied a simple and deliciously child-like text, with flashes of delicate humor, very much in the animal story tradition of Grimm and Andersen.

By way of introduction, Prokofieff has himself identified the "characters" of his "orchestral fairy tale" on the first page of the score:

"Each character of this Tale is represented by a corresponding instrument in the orchestra: the bird by the flute, the duck by an oboe, the cat by a clarinet in the low register, the grandfather by a bassoon, the wolf by three horns, Peter by the string quartet, the shooting of the hunters by the kettledrums and the bass drum. Before an orchestral performance it is desirable to show these instruments to the children and to play on them the corresponding leitmotives. Thereby the

472

children learn to distinguish the sonorities of the instruments during the performance of this Tale."

The characters having been duly tagged and labeled, the Narrator, in a tone that is by turns casual, confiding and awesome, begins to tell of the adventures of Peter. . . .

"Early one morning Peter opened the gate and went out into the big green meadow. On a branch of a big tree sat a little Bird, Peter's friend. 'All is quiet,' chirped the Bird gaily.

"Just then a Duck came waddling round. She was glad that Peter had not closed the gate, and decided to take a nice swim in the deep pond in the meadow.

"Seeing the Duck, the little Bird flew down upon the grass, settled next to her, and shrugged his shoulders: 'What kind of a bird are you, if you can't fly?' said he. To this the Duck replied: 'What kind of a bird are you, if you can't swim?' and dived into the pond. They argued and argued, the Duck swimming in the pond, the little Bird hopping along the shore.

"Suddenly, something caught Peter's attention. He noticed a Cat crawling through the grass. The Cat thought: 'The Bird is busy arguing, I will just grab him.' Stealthily she crept toward him on her velvet paws. 'Look out!' shouted Peter, and the Bird immediately flew up into the tree while the Duck quacked angrily at the Cat from the middle of the pond. The Cat walked around the tree and thought: 'Is it worth climbing up so high? By the time I get there the Bird will have flown away.'

"Grandfather came out. He was angry because Peter had gone into the meadow. 'It is a dangerous place. If a Wolf should come out of the forest, then what would you do?' Peter paid no attention to Grandfather's words. Boys like him are not afraid of Wolves, but Grandfather took Peter by the hand, locked the gate, and led him home.

"No sooner had Peter gone than a big gray Wolf came out of the forest. In a twinkling the Cat climbed up the tree. The Duck quacked, and in her excitement jumped out of the pond. But no matter how hard the Duck tried to run, she couldn't escape the Wolf. He was getting nearer . . . nearer . . . catching up with her . . . and then he got her and, with one gulp, swallowed her.

"And now, this is how things stand: the Cat was sitting on one

473

branch, the Bird on another—not too close to the Cat—and the Wolf walked round and round the tree looking at them with greedy eyes.

"In the meantime, Peter, without the slighest fear, stood behind the closed gate watching all that was going on. He ran home, got a strong rope, and climbed up the high stone wall. One of the branches of the tree, round which the Wolf was walking, stretched out over the wall. Grabbing hold of the branch, Peter lightly climbed over on to the tree.

"Peter said to the Bird: 'Fly down and circle round the Wolf's head; only take care that he doesn't catch you.' The Bird almost touched the Wolf's head with his wings while the Wolf snapped angrily at him from this side and that. How the Bird did worry the Wolf! How he wanted to catch him! But the Bird was cleverer, and the Wolf simply couldn't do anything about it.

"Meanwhile, Peter made a lasso and, carefully letting it down, caught the Wolf by the tail and pulled with all his might. Feeling himself caught, the Wolf began to jump wildly, trying to get loose. But Peter tied the other end of the rope to the tree, and the Wolf's jumping only made the rope around his tail tighter.

"Just then, the hunters came out of the woods following the Wolf's trail and shooting as they went. But Peter, sitting in the tree, said: 'Don't shoot! Birdie and I have caught the Wolf. Now help us to take him to the zoo.'

"And there . . . imagine the procession: Peter at the head; after him the hunters leading the Wolf; and winding up the procession, Grandfather and the Cat. Grandfather tossed his head discontentedly! 'Well, and if Peter hadn't caught the Wolf? What then?'

"Above them flew Birdie chirping merrily: 'My, what brave fellows we are, Peter and I! Look what we have caught!' And if one would listen very carefully he could hear the Duck quacking inside the Wolf; because the Wolf in his hurry had swallowed her alive."

To Prokofieff's biographer, Nestyev, "Peter and the Wolf" represents a "gallery of clever and amusing animal portraits as vividly depicted as though painted from nature by an animal artist." Certainly, this ingenious assortment of chirping and purring and clucking and howling, translated into terms of a masterly orchestral speech, is the tender and loving work of a story-teller patient and tolerant of the claims of children, and awed by their infinite imaginative capacity.

"Summer Day," Children's Suite for
Little Symphony, Opus 65-B

Five years after completing "Peter and the Wolf" Prokofieff returned once again to the children's corner. This time it was a suite for little symphony called "Summer Day." Actually the suite had begun as a series of piano pieces, entitled "Children's Music," that Prokofieff had written and published shortly before he turned his thoughts to "Peter and the Wolf." The chances are that it was this very "Children's Music" that precipitated him into the child's world of wonder and fantasy from which were to emerge Peter's adventures in the animal kingdom. It was not till 1941, however, that he assembled an assortment of these piano pieces and arranged them for orchestra. Credit for their first performance in America belongs to the New York Philharmonic-Symphony, which included them on its program of October 25, 1945. Artur Rodzinski conducted. At that time Robert Bagar and I were the society's program annotators, and the analysis given below was written by him for our program-book of that date.

I. *"Morning"* (*Andante tranquillo, C major, 4-4*). An odd little phrase is played by the first flute with occasional reinforcement from the second, while the other woodwinds engage in a mild counterpoint and the strings and bass drum supply the rhythmic anchorage. In a middle part the bassoons, horns, 'cellos and (later) the violas and bass sing a rather serious melody, as violins and flutes offer accompanying figures.

II. *"Tag"* (*Vivo, F major, 6-8*). A bright, tripping melody begins in the violins and flutes and is soon shared by bassoons. It is repeated, this time leading to the key of E-flat where the oboes play it in a modified form. There follows a short intermediary passage in the same tripping spirit, although the rhythm is stressed more. After some additional modulations the section ends with the opening strain.

III. *"Waltz"* (*Allegretto, A major, 3-4*). A tart and tangy waltz theme, introduced by the violins, has an unusual "feel" about it because of the unexpected intervals in the melody. In a more subdued manner the violins usher in a second theme, which, however, is given a Prokofieffian touch by the interspersed woodwind chords in octave skips. As before, the opening idea serves as the section's close.

IV. *"Regrets"* (*Moderato, F major, 4-4*). An expressive, straightforward melody starts in the 'cellos. Oboes pick it up in a slightly revised form and they and the first violins conclude it. Next the violins and clarinets give it a simple variation. In the meantime, there are some subsidiary figures in the other instruments. All ends in just the slightest kind of finale.

V. *"March"* (*Tempo di marcia, C major, 4-4*). Clarinets and oboes each take half of the chief melody. The horns then play it and, following a brief middle sequence with unusual leaps, the tune ends in a harmonic combination of flutes, oboes, horns and trumpets.

VI. *"Evening"* (*Adante teneroso, F major, 3-8*). Prokofieff's knack of making unusual melodic intervals sound perfectly natural is here well illustrated. A solo flute intones the opening bars of a pleasant song-like tune, the rest of which is given to the solo clarinet. Still in the same reflective mood, the music continues with a passage of orchestral arpeggios, while the first violins take their turn with the melody. A middle portion in A-flat major presents some measures of syncopation. With a change of key to C major and again to F major, the section ends tranquilly with a snatch of the opening tune.

VII. *"Moonlit Meadows"* (*Adantino, D major, 2-4*). The solo flute opens this section with a smooth-flowing melody which rather makes the rounds, though in more or less altered form. The section ends quite simply with three chords.

This transcription departs but slightly from the piano originals, and when it does so it is because the composer has obviously felt the need of a stronger accent here or some figure there, unimportant in themselves, which might serve to bolster up the Suite.

March from the Opera, "The Love of Three Oranges," Opus 33-A

It was Cleofonte Campanini, leading conductor of the Chicago Opera Company, who approached Prokofieff early in 1919 for an opera. Prokofieff first offered "The Gambler," of which he possessed only the piano part, having left the orchestral score behind in the library of the Maryinsky Theatre of Leningrad. The offer was put aside for a second proposal—a project Prokofieff had already been toying with in Russia. This was an opera inspired in part by a device prominent in the Italian tradition of Commedia dell'Arte and based, as a story, on an Italian classic. The idea excited Campanini, and a contract was speedily signed. The piano score was completed by the following June, and in October the orchestral score was ready for submission. Preparations were made for a production in Chicago, when Campanini suddenly died. An entire season went by before its world première was finally achieved under the directorship of Mary Garden. This occurred on December 30, 1921, at the Chicago Auditorium, with Prokofieff conducting and Nina Koshetz making her American début as the Fata Morgana. A French version was used, prepared by Prokofieff and Vera Janacoupolos from the original Russian text of the composer. Press and public were friendly, if not over-enthusiastic.

Less than two months later, on February 14, 1922, the Chicago Opera Company presented the opera for the first time in New York, at the Manhattan Opera House, with Prokofieff himself again conducting. This time the critics were far from friendly. One of them remarked waspishly: "The cost of the production is one hundred and thirty thousand dollars, which is forty-three thousand dollars for each orange. The opera fell so flat that its repetition would spell financial ruin." There were no further performances that season. Indeed it was not till November 1, 1949, that "The Love of Three Oranges" returned to American currency. It was on that night that Laszlo Halasz introduced the work into the repertory of the New York City Opera Company at the City Center of Music and Drama. The opera was presented in a skillful English version made by Victor Seroff. The production was "an almost startling success," in the words of Olin Downes. "The opera became overnight the talk of the town and took a permanent place in the repertory of the company. This was due in large part to the character of the production itself, which so well became the fantasy and satire of the libretto, and the dynamic power of Prokofieff's score. An additional factor in the success was, without doubt, the development of taste and receptivity to modern music on the part of the public which had taken place in the intervening odd quarter of a century since the opera first saw the light."

Prokofieff based his libretto on Carlo Gossi's "Fiaba dell'amore delle tre melarancie" (The Tale of the Love of the Three Oranges). Gozzi, an eighteenth-century dramatist and story-teller, had a genius for giving fresh form to old tales and legends and for devising new ones.

The tales were called *fiabe,* or fables. Later dramatists found them a fertile source of suggestions for plot, and opera composers have been no less indebted to this gifted teller of tales. Puccini's "Turandot" is only one of at least six operas founded on Gozzi's masterly little *fiaba* of legendary China. The vein of satire running through Gozzi's *fiabe* has also attracted subsequent writers and composers. It is not surprising that Prokofieff, no mean satirist himself, found inspiration for an opera in one of these delicious *fiabe.*

In view of the great popularity which "The Love of Three Oranges" has won in recent seasons in America, it may be of some practical use and interest to the readers of this monograph to provide them with an outline of the plot. I originally wrote the synopsis that follows for "The Victor Book of Operas" in the 1949 issue revised and edited for Simon & Schuster by myself and Robert Bagar. "The Love of Three Oranges" is divided into a Prologue and Four Acts.

PROLOGUE

SCENE: *Stage with Lowered Curtain and Grand Proscenium, on Each Side of Which Are Little Balconies and Balustrades.* An artistic discussion is under way among four sets of personages on which kind of play should be enacted on the present occasion. The Glooms, clad in appropriately somber rôles, argue for tragedy. The Joys, in costumes befitting their temperament, hold out for romantic comedy. The Emptyheads disagree with both and call for frank farce. At last, the Jesters (also called the Cynics) enter, and succeed in silencing the squabbling groups. Presently a Herald enters to announce that the King of Clubs is grieving because his son never smiles. The various personages now take refuge in balconies at the sides of the stage, and from there make comments on the play that is enacted. But for their lack of poise and dignity, they would remind one of the chorus in Greek drama.

ACT I

SCENE: *The King's Palace.* The King of Clubs, in despair over his son's hopeless defection, has summoned physicians to diagnose the ailment. After elaborate consultation, the doctors inform the King that to be cured the Prince must learn to laugh. The Prince, alas, like most hypochondriacs, has no sense of humor. The King resolves to try the prescribed remedy. Truffaldino, one of the comic figures, is now assigned the task of preparing a gay festival and masquerade to bring cheer into the Prince's smileless life. All signify approval of the plan except the Prime Minister Leander, who is plotting with the King's niece Clarisse to seize the throne after slaying the Prince. In a sudden evocation of fire and smoke, the wicked witch, Fata Morgana, appears, followed by a swarm of little devils. As a fiendish game of cards ensues between the witch, who is aiding Leander's plot, and Tchelio, the court magician, attendant demons burst into a wild dance. The Fata Morgana wins and, with a peal of diabolical laughter, vanishes. The jester vainly tries to make the lugubrious Prince laugh, and as festival music comes from afar, the two go off in that direction.

ACT II

SCENE: *The Main Courtroom of the Royal Palace.* In the grand court of the palace, merrymakers are busy trying to make the Prince laugh, but their efforts are unavailing for two reasons: the Prince's nature is adamant to gaiety and the evil Fata Morgana is among them, spoiling the fun. Recognizing her, guards seize the sorceress and attempt to eject her. In the struggle that ensues she turns an awkward somersault, a sight so ridiculous that even the Prince is forced to laugh out loud. All rejoice, for the Prince, at long last, is cured! In revenge, the Fata Morgana now pronounces a dire curse on the recovered Prince: he shall again be miserable until he has won the "love of the three oranges."

ACT III

SCENE: *A Desert.* In the desert the magician Tchelio meets the Prince and pronounces an incantation against the cook who guards the three oranges in the near-by castle. As the Prince and his companion, the jester Truffaldino, head for the castle, the orchestra plays a scherzo, fascinating in its ingeniously woven web of fantasy. Arriving at the castle, the Prince and Truffaldino obtain the coveted oranges after overcoming many hazards. Fatigued, the Prince now goes to sleep. A few moments later Truffaldino is seized by thirst and, as he cuts open one of the oranges, a beautiful Princess steps out, begging for water. Since it is decreed that the oranges must be opened at the water's edge, the helpless Princess promptly dies of thirst. Startled, Truffaldino at length works up courage enough to open a second orange, and, lo! another Princess steps out, only to meet the same fate. Truffaldino rushes out. The spectators in the balconies at the sides of the stage argue excitedly over the fate of the Princess in the third orange. When the Prince awakens, he takes the third orange and cautiously proceeds to open it. The Princess Ninette emerges this time, begs for water, and is about to succumb to a deadly thirst, when the Jesters rush to her rescue with a bucket of water.

ACT IV

SCENE: *The Throne Room of the Royal Palace.* The Prince and the Princess Ninette are forced to endure many more trials through the evil power of the Fata Morgana. At one juncture the Princess is even changed into a mouse. The couple finally overcome all the hardships the witch has devised, and in the end are happily married. Thus foiled in her wicked sorcery, the Fata Morgana is captured and led away, leaving traitorous Leander and Clarisse to face the King's ire without the aid of her magic powers.

*   *   *

Typical in this "burlesque opera" is Prokofieff's penchant for witty, sardonic writing. This cleverly evoked world of satiric sorcery is perhaps far removed from Prokofieff's main areas of operatic interest, which were Russian history and literature. The pungent note of modernism is readily heard in this music, though compared with the more dissonant writing of Prokofieff's piano and violin concertos, it is a kind of modified modernism, diverting in its sophisticated discourse on the child's world of fairyland wonder. If, as Nestyev says, the work is "a subtle parody of the old romantic opera with its false pathos and sham fantasy," it is primarily what it purports to be—a fairy tale, as gay and sparkling and wondrous as any in the whole realm of opera.

The brilliant and bizarre "March" from this opera has become one of the best known and most widely exploited symphonic themes of our time. It comes as an exhilarating orchestral interlude in the first act at the point where the straight-faced Prince and his Jester wander off in the direction of the festival music. The "March" is built around a swaying theme of irresistible appeal that mounts in power as it is repeated and comes to a sudden and forceful halt, as if at the crack of a whip.

L. B.